Child Development and Personality

FOURTH EDITION

Paul Henry Mussen
University of California, Berkeley

John Janeway Conger
University of Colorado School of Medicine

Jerome Kagan
Harvard University

HARPER INTERNATIONAL EDITION

HARPER & ROW, PUBLISHERS
New York Evanston San Francisco London

Cover photograph by Phoebe Dunn, DPI
Frontispiece by W. Eugene Smith
Part-title drawings by John Sovjani

Acknowledgment is made to the following individuals and organizations
for supplying photographs.

Black Star: D. & A. Pellegrino (p. 617); David Conger (pp. 429, 441); Cynthia Day (p. 489);
Peter Dawson (p. 279 top); Douglas Faulkner (p. 181); Ford Foundation: Robin Forbes (p.
351); Rapho Guillumette: Christa Armstrong (p. 579), Bob Combs (pp. 613, 633), Hella
Hammid (pp. 19, 35, 117, 194, 367), Bob Krueger (p. 225), Inger McCabe (p. 345), Lynn
McLaren (pp. 279 bottom, 399), Bruce Roberts (p. 517), Hanna Schreiber (p. 207); Magnum: Hiroji Kubota (p. 639); Monkmeyer: Hugh Rogers (p. 587); Betty Moore (p. 145 top
and bottom); George Roos (pp. 253, 293, 383, 473, 569)

HARPER INTERNATIONAL EDITION
INT-35-05328   EINT-35-63624   AINT-35-33577

Sponsoring Editor: George A. Middendorf
Project Editor: Sandra Turner
Designer: Rita Naughton
Production Supervisor: Robert A. Pirrung

CHILD DEVELOPMENT AND PERSONALITY, Fourth Edition

Library of Congress Cataloging in Publication Data:
Mussen, Paul Henry.
    Child development and personality.

    1. Child study. 2. Personality. I. Conger,
John Janeway, joint author. II. Kagan, Jerome,
joint author. III. Title. [DNLM: 1. Child
development. WS105 M992c 1974]
BF721.M88 1974   155.4'18   73-10681
ISBN 0-06-044691-9

Child Development and Personality

Contents

Preface to the Fourth Edition   ix

Chapter 1 Introduction   1

Some Historical Perspectives   4
The Emergence of Child Psychology as a Scientific Discipline   10
Contemporary Child Psychology: Recent Trends   18
Ethical Issues in Research   24
Summary   27

Chapter 2 Theory in Developmental Psychology   30

The Reasons for Developmental Psychology   31
The Reasons for Behavior—the Goals of Development and the Nature
    of the Child   33
A Cognitive-Adaptive Approach to Development   38
The Theory of Jean Piaget   38
Freud and Psychoanalytic Theory   41
Learning Theory   45
Types of Learning   49
Basic Conditions of Learning   57
Summary   66

PART I THE PRENATAL PERIOD   71

Chapter 3 Genetic and Prenatal Factors in Development   73

Beginnings of Life   75
Hereditary Transmission   75

v

Determining the Extent of Genetic Influences   82
Results of Human Genetic Research   85
Summary   95
Prenatal Development   96
How Conception Occurs   96
The Earliest Period of Development   97
Prenatal Environmental Influences   110
The Birth Process and Its Consequences   118
Prematurity   120
The Relation of Sex and Social Class to Vulnerability in the Newborn   122
Summary   124

PART II THE FIRST TWO YEARS   129

Chapter 4 Biological Changes in Infancy   131

Body Growth in Infancy   132
The Newborn   135
Maturational Stages in Infancy   141
Perceptual Development   146
Response Capabilities   160
Developmental Trends   166
Basic Needs   167
Vocalization   170
Mental Development   173
Individual Differences Among Infants   179
Summary   183

Chapter 5 Social Factors in Infant Development   192

The Necessity for Making Responses   193
The Concept of Attachment   199
Consequences of Interaction with the Caretaker   214
Cultural Differences in Child Rearing   224
Summary   227

PART III LANGUAGE AND COGNITIVE DEVELOPMENT   231

Chapter 6 The Development of Language   233

Major Aspects of Language   235
Theoretical Approaches to Language Development   237
The Beginnings of Speech   241

Language and Cognition   257
Cultural Influences on Language   261
Summary   266

Chapter 7 Cognitive Development   270

The Units in Cognitive Activity   271
Cognitive Activities   277
Piaget's Later Stages of Intelligence   309
The Role of Motives and Expectancy   318
Summary   322

Chapter 8 Intelligence   326

Types of Intelligence Tests   329
Constancy of IQ   339
Effects of Environment and Personality on Intelligence Test Performance   343
Intelligence, Heredity, Environment, and Race   345
Changing Cognitive Functioning   350
Summary   357

PART IV PRESCHOOL YEARS   361

Chapter 9 Preschool Personality Development   363

Socialization   365
Sexual Motives and Curiosity   369
Hostility and Aggression   370
Dependency   379
Fear and Anxiety   387
Mastery Motivation   393
Identification   395
Sex-Typing   398
Conscience Development and Prosocial Behavior   404
Personality and Social Learning in the Home   406

PART V MIDDLE CHILDHOOD   419

Chapter 10 Development in Middle Childhood   421
I. Personality Development and Problems of Adjustment

Influence of the Family in Middle Childhood   422
Development of Conscience and Moral Standards   444

Psychological and Psychophysiological Problems of Middle Childhood   451
Psychological Problems of Minority-Group Membership   464
Summary   472

Chapter 11 Development in Middle Childhood   486
II. Expansion of Social Environment

The Adjustment to School   487
Socioeconomic Status, Educational Aspiration, and School Achievement   502
Parental and Peer Influences on Educational Aspiration   504
The School and the Disadvantaged Student   507
School Dropouts   510
Relations with Peers   514
Summary   524

PART VI ADOLESCENCE   539

Chapter 12 Adolescence   541
I. Physical Change, Sex, and Social Development

Physical Development in Adolescence   544
Psychological Aspects of Adolescent Growth and Development   548
Effects of Adolescent Mental Growth on Psychological Development   552
Developmental Tasks of Adolescence   556
The Development of Adolescent Independence   557
Sexual Attitudes and Behavior in the Adolescent   564
Adolescents and Their Peers   574
Vocational Choice   580

Chapter 13 Adolescence   599
II. Identity, Values, and Alienation

Identity   600
Moral Development and Values   605
Alienation   611
Alternative Life Styles: Activism Versus Dropping Out   615
Adolescents and Drugs   622
Juvenile Delinquency   629
Summary   638

Epilogue   652
Index of Names   657
Index of Subjects   669

Preface to the Fourth Edition

In the five years since the third edition of this book was published, research in the field of child development has expanded at an impressive and accelerating rate. New areas of inquiry have emerged, and knowledge in established areas has broadened and deepened. Comparison of the status of child psychology as a scientific discipline at present with its status only a decade ago clearly demonstrates that there have been enormous strides in the direction of scientific maturity.

This advance is particularly apparent in such areas as perception, memory, language, temperamental characteristics, and attachment. Recent developments in basic knowledge and improved techniques of investigation have also enhanced our ability to contribute substantially to the solution of urgent social problems that inevitably involve children and adolescents. Thus the present edition presents new information about the role that poverty and racial or ethnic discrimination play in development; the effects of programs of cultural enrichment for socio-economically disadvantaged children; the influence of early stimulation on cognitive development and personality; and the consequences of differences in rearing among children from nuclear or extended families, day-care centers, kibbutzim, or Russian nurseries. The text also considers the kinds of parent-child relationships that promote self-realization, independence, and emotional security.

Among the other areas of concern, both basic and applied, that have become increasingly prominent in the past five years are cross-cultural studies that shed light on the variability of cognitive and personality processes; personal and social factors associated with drug use; the effect of sex-role stereotypes on personality development and the aspirations of children; and changing social and cultural conditions in relation to personality development, values, and the social behavior of adolescents.

As a result of these developments the discipline of child psychology has achieved a new level of sophistication and complexity, greater breadth of knowledge, and an increased relevance for personal and social issues. At the same time the richness of the field poses problems for textbook writers, and in this edition the organization of information is changed from that of earlier editions in several ways. To some extent we have preserved the chronological approach to development that characterized the earlier editions because this approach helps the student to view clearly the complex nature of the many forces—physical, psychological and social—that influence children's behaviors at each age period. However, due to the extremely rapid and significant recent increases in our knowledge of cognitive development, it seemed wiser to bring together in one chapter all the material on cognition from the preschool period to adolescence. Similarly, because of the significant growth of interest, research, and theory pertaining to intelligence and language development, we have devoted a chapter to each of these topics. Discussions of genetics and prenatal development have been condensed and brought up to date in a single chapter. The theory section has also been revised so that it is broader and more general, introducing the student to the major concepts of behavioral, psychoanalytic, and Piagetian theory and reflecting both the increasing influence of Piagetian thinking and the importance of new findings bearing on the meaning of reinforcement and its relationship to learning theory.

The preparation of this fourth edition reinforced the authors' convictions that recent progress in the study of child development has been remarkable and that future research will make the field even more stimulating, important, and exciting. After all, in the last analysis what can be more useful than gaining knowledge to help foster the optimal development of society's most precious resource—its children?

The authors gratefully acknowledge the help of Dr. Greta Fein, who read the entire manuscript and made many valuable suggestions. Roger Brown and Paul and Mary Sue Ammons provided many thoughtful suggestions for the chapter on language development.

For secretarial and bibliographical assistance, we wish to thank Vivien March, Doris Simpson, and Dorothy Townsend.

P. H. M.
J. J. C.
J. K.

Child Development and Personality

Chapter 1

Introduction

W e will introduce the field of developmental psychology by asking you to consider two major American social problems. The first involves minority group children from ghettos and other impoverished areas. When these children enter kindergarten at age 5, their scores on tests of intelligence, reasoning ability, and language are, on the average, significantly lower than those of 5-year-old middle-class children. Furthermore, poor children appear to be less highly motivated for schooling than middle-class children.

What accounts for these differences? Do intelligence test scores and school performance depend on training, experience, and familiarity with school tasks? Or are "native abilities," that is, genetically determined capacities, the determining factors? The question of cultural factors must also be considered. Are the contents of intelligence tests and the school's standards of evaluation appropriate for children of all social classes and backgrounds or are they "culturally biased," favoring the white middle class?

We do not yet have complete answers to all these complicated questions. Yet they are of obvious social relevance since, as a society, we are committed to rapid improvements of the social and educational status of groups that suffer socioeconomic deprivation. To accomplish this goal, children of poverty backgrounds must be provided with educational opportunities at least equal to those of children who are more economically favored and, in addition, they must be able to benefit from these opportunities.

Through their research, developmental psychologists contribute to understanding and, ultimately, to solving these problems. For instance, research in developmental psychology shows that many environmental factors are related to poor performance on tests of intellectual functioning. The tests are culturally biased; many items of the tests involve vocabulary and information that is much more familiar to the middle-class than to the lower-class child. Dietary factors may play an important role; inadequate nutrition, especially protein deficiency, during the mother's pregnancy or in the child's early infancy may adversely affect the child's later intellectual ability. Social class value systems also may affect performance; the lower class does not emphasize competition and intellectual achievement to the extent that the middle class does and consequently lower-class children are less likely to acquire strong motivation for school success or for successful performance in intellectual tests.

It has also been hypothesized that young children in impoverished homes get less intellectual stimulation and are less likely to be rewarded for intellectual achievement, curiosity, and exploration. Would comprehensive programs of compensatory education, involving early intellectual stimulation and the encouragement of intellectual achievement and curiosity have significant beneficial effects, and if so, would these be lasting? A number of such programs have been tried experimentally and systematic study of the results permits a qualified affirmative answer to this question; special training and increased stimulation begun early in life and maintained for a prolonged period of time have positive, lasting consequences on children's performance on intellectual tasks (see pp. 350-357).

The second significant social problem that we will consider is juvenile delinquency, a problem that has been of increasing magnitude and concern in recent years. In this case, too, developmental research has provided some facts and insights that may be useful in helping to solve the problem. The major antecedents of juvenile delinquency are both economic and psychological. Most delinquents come from low-income or poverty families and live in poor neighborhoods. However, not all young people growing up in these circumstances become delinquent and not all delinquents come from low-income or deprived backgrounds; clearly, psychological factors are also involved. Investigations show that the following factors are related to delinquency: poor parent-child relationships, rejection by parents, harsh parental punishment and erratic discipline, feelings of insecurity, jealousy of brothers and sisters, frustration of needs for independence and self-expression. Children who have unsatisfactory relationships with their parents may not adopt their parents' standards of social behavior. If the parents' standards are those generally accepted by the larger society, the child's rejection of his parents' standards may be evidenced in more generalized antisocial, or delinquent, behavior. In other cases, parental social behavior and values may be deviant or socially unacceptable, but the parents may be taken as models. In brief, delinquency is a consequence of unfavorable experiences.

This knowledge may be applied in the prevention of delinquency or in dealing therapeutically with delinquents. Like most forms of maladjustment, delinquency is a learned or acquired kind of behavior and therefore potentially modifiable. Accumulated information about factors underlying delinquency may be used in developing more adequate sociological, social welfare, and educational programs to aid parents, particularly those of low socioeconomic status, to establish better relationships with their children. Furthermore, delinquents and potential delinquents may be helped to anticipate some of their problems and to learn more adequate ways of handling them (see pp. 629-638).

Juvenile delinquency and the relatively poor intellectual performance of socioeconomically deprived children are only two examples of the many social problems that will be discussed in this book. As you will see, developmental psychology as a scientific discipline can expand significantly our knowledge of the critical factors underlying such social problems as drug abuse, school dropouts, prejudice, violence and aggression, emotional disturbance, and "youth" problems and the so-called generation gap. These problems cannot be solved without understanding the development of the personality characteristics and motivations of those who manifest "problem" behavior. This means investigating the development of motives such as aggression, dependency, competition, and achievement;

the effects of frustration, anxiety, fear of failure, and discouragement; the role of adult and peer models in fostering acceptable or disapproved behavior; the consequences of early parental treatment on the child's later behavior. All of these topics are of central concern to developmental psychologists, who attempt to acquire systematic, scientific data about all of these variables.

We can understand the contributions and potential social utility of developmental research more fully if we look briefly at the history of the field—how it has changed over the years, often in response to social pressures. Our discussion in this chapter will deal with the goals and purposes of developmental psychology, with the methods and techniques the developmental psychologist uses in his research, and with the ethical problems he encounters. Finally, we will briefly survey the most notable recent trends in the field, trends which in our opinion are of the utmost social significance.

SOME HISTORICAL PERSPECTIVES

Most sophisticated people take it for granted that the events of early childhood affect the individual's later social and psychological adjustment. Moreover, almost everyone seems to be interested in children and their welfare; in their growth and development; and in their acquisition of skills, abilities, personality, and social characteristics. Contemporary western culture is truly "child centered," and this has clearly facilitated progress in child psychology. As the culture has become increasingly child centered, child psychology has become a more substantial and vigorous scientific discipline.

Until the seventeenth century—a relatively recent period in the total span of western history—there was no special emphasis on childhood as a separate phase of the life cycle. Some exceptional scholars and thinkers of ancient days were interested in children's development because they felt intuitively that what happens in childhood has strong impacts on later development. Plato, for example, recognized the importance of early childhood training in the determination of the individual's later vocational aptitudes and adjustments. In his **Republic,** he discussed inherent differences among individuals and recommended that steps be taken to discover each child's outstanding aptitudes, so that specific education and training along the lines of his particular talents might begin early.

By and large, however, until three centuries ago, children in many western European groups were not regarded as a particular class of humans or treated in distinctive ways. Obviously, infants needed special care and attention, but once they had been weaned and had achieved a minimum of ability to take care of themselves, they were generally considered to be "small adults," mingling, working, and playing with mature people. Phillip Aries, a French intellectual historian, argues that

In the middle ages, at the beginning of modern times, and for a long time after
that in the lower classes, children were mixed with adults as soon as they were
considered capable of doing without their mothers or nannies, not long after a tardy
weaning (in other words, at about the age of seven). They immediately went
straight into the great community of men, sharing in the work and play of their
companions, old and young alike (2, 411).

In medieval art, children were usually depicted as immature adults, and even
as late as the fifteenth and sixteenth centuries were shown in nonreligious paintings
gathering with adults for purposes of work, relaxation, or sport. Their clothing was
not distinctive, rather they dressed like the men and women of their own social
class.

Judging from the art and literature of that period, after the age of 3 or 4, children played the same games as adults, either with other children or adults, and
participated fully in community celebrations and festivities. Moreover, in the
medieval school there was no graduated system of education by which subjects
were introduced in order from easiest to most difficult. Students of all ages from
10 years to 20 or over were mixed together in the same classroom. Children were
not thought to be "innocent" and in need of protection from references to sexual
matters. Children shared in the wild, violent, libertine life of the times; even in
school, they were extremely unruly, disobedient, and violent.

The seventeenth century marked a great change in attitudes toward children
and their morals. For reasons not fully understood—but probably linked with the
strong religious currents of the Reformation and Counter-Reformation—clergymen
and humanitarians of this time began to encourage the separation of children
from adults and even adolescents. Gradually these thinkers influenced parents
and a whole new family attitude, oriented around the child and his education, appeared.

With the great change in attitudes and morals, the concept of the innocence
of childhood—a period of "primitivism, irrationalism and prelogicalism"—won
acceptance. From that time on, children were to be spared all references to sexual
matters lest their innocence be corrupted. The child became a "special" person. He
ceased to be dressed like the grownup. From the seventeenth century on, paintings
depict him wearing outfits reserved for his own age group and which set him apart
from adults.

Moral education became one of the principal objects of school life. Those
concerned with the Reformation believed that all children, even those of the lower
classes, should be given the religious instruction that had hitherto been restricted
to the privileged few. Moreover, religious or moral education became closely
linked with instruction in the utilitarian skills of reading and writing, "which were
now regarded as necessary for the exercise of any trade, even a manual job. In
this way it was hoped to make pious, serious workers out of what had been de-
praved adventurers" (2, 303). Education thus became recognized as "the only

possible means of instilling a sense of morality into the down-and-outs, of turning them into servants and workers, and hence of providing the country with a good labor force" (2, 310).

While the elite reformers and moralists who occupied high positions in church and state argued that lower-class children should receive better utilitarian and religious education, they also maintained that the upper-class child should work even harder to cultivate gentle manners. "The well-bred child would be preserved from roughness and immorality which would become the special characteristic of the lower classes" (2, 328).

The insistence of these seventeenth-century authorities on the moral and social importance of systematic education was accompanied by stress on the need for special institutions for educational purposes. During this period, therefore, the structure of school classes also became modified, assuming a form closer to that of the present: grades or forms in separate rooms, yearly promotion, and one class per year, based largely on the pupil's age.

> In the moralists and pedagogues of the 17th century, we see that fondness for childhood and its special nature no longer found expression in amusement and coddling, but in psychological interest and moral solicitude. The child was no longer regarded as amusing or agreeable, but as in need of help and guidance. In order to correct the behavior of children people must first understand them, and the texts of the late 16th and 17th centuries are full of comments on child psychology.
>
> The first concept of childhood—characterized by coddling—had made its appearance in the family circle, in the company of little children. The second, on the contrary, sprang from a source outside the family: churchmen or gentlemen of the robe, few in number before the 16th century, and a far greater number of moralists in the 17th century, eager to insure disciplined, rational manners. They too had become alive to the formerly neglected phenomenon of childhood, but they were unwilling to regard children as charming toys, for they saw them as fragile creatures of God, who needed to be both safeguarded and reformed (2, 133).

Philosophers and Child Psychology

These new concepts of childhood and of education were also the sources of a new, speculative literature of child psychology and development. The earliest writers were primarily philosophers, clergymen, physicians, educators, humanitarians, and reformers, but they dealt with issues that are still critical for the developmental psychologist. For example, they wrote about the inherent characteristics of children (what is congenital or inherited) and the most effective methods of child-rearing and training. Some, conceiving of childhood as "naturally evil," wrote passionately about the child's "native depravity," while others portrayed the child as a "noble savage," biologically endowed with virtues and characteristics that, if allowed expression, would ensure healthy growth and socially responsible behavior.

The British philosopher John Locke, writing at the end of the seventeenth century, viewed the child's experience and education as the fundamental determinants of his development, although he did allow for "native propensities." The infant's mind, he wrote, is a **tabula rasa**—a blank slate—and he is therefore receptive to all kinds of learning.

Locke was committed to the ultimate rationality of man. The object of all education, as he saw it, is self-discipline, self-control, and the "power of denying ourselves the satisfaction of our own desires, where reason does not authorize them" (**14**). To achieve these goals, parents must begin instructing children in self-denial "from their very cradles."

Jean Jacques Rousseau, a French philosopher, writing in the latter half of the eighteenth century, believed that the child is endowed with an innate moral sense. In **Emile** (**19**) he spoke of the child as a "noble savage" with intuitive knowledge of what is right and wrong, but thwarted by restrictions imposed on him by society.

> Rousseau suggests that no great harm to the child or to society will result if the child grows with little adult supervision and direction! The child will become increasingly fit to live in the world, not by virtue of ceaseless vigilance on the part of his governors, but because nature has endowed him with an order of development that ensures his healthy growth. More than that, the typical interventions of parents and teachers mar and distort the natural succession of the changes of childhood; the child that man raises is almost certain to be inferior to the child that nature raises (**13**, 74).

Locke's and Rousseau's views of how children develop contrast sharply. Locke's view was essentially that of associationistic psychology: The child's development is determined by his education, and, more specifically, his behavior is shaped or molded by his experiences, by the rewards and punishments provided by the environment.

> I grant that good and evil, reward and punishment, are the only motives to a rational creature; these are the spur and reins, whereby all mankind is set on work, and guided, and therefore they are to be made use of to children too. For I advise their parents and governors always to carry this in their minds, that children are to be treated as rational creatures (**13**, 61).

In Rousseau's thinking, the child responded actively to the world around him, engaging

> his environment, using it to suit his interests. He fits his abilities to the world in play and in the solving of problems, not as a passive recipient of the tutor's instruction . . . but as a busy, testing, motivated explorer. Knowledge is not an invention of adults poured into willing or unwilling vessels; it is a joint construction of the child in nature and the natural world. . . . The active searching child, setting his own problems, stands in contrast to the receptive one, even the one equipped with curiosity, on whom society fixes its stamp (**13**, 75).

As we shall see later, modern theories of development also differ (as Locke's and Rousseau's did) in their conceptions of the child's relationship to the world. Some modern theorists see the child's development primarily as passive and receptive, responding to the pressures—rewards and punishments—of the environment. For others, the child develops through active, purposeful engagement with his environment, organizing and interpreting his experiences, and attempting to solve problems.

Locke's and Rousseau's writings were important seminal influences in child development, but these philosophers' theories, though penetrating, were speculative and untested. Contemporary theorists and researchers attempt to check their hypotheses by systematic and careful observations and by experiments.

Baby Biographies

Later in the eighteenth century children came to be regarded as proper subjects for study. Philosophers, biologists, and educators began to discover their own children, and some of the most curious and courageous attempted to learn about them by the novel procedure of observation. Thus, in 1774, Johann Heinrich Pestalozzi (15), a Swiss educator, published notes based on the careful observations of the development of his 3½-year-old son. His book reflected his own theories, which, like Rousseau's, stressed the innate goodness of the child and the role of the child's own activity in development. Thirteen years later (1787), Dieterich Tiedemann published a kind of diary of infant behavior (20), tracing the sensory, motor, language, and intellectual growth of a single infant during the first 2½ years of life.

In the nineteenth century, a series of "baby biographies" began to appear. The most eminent writer of such a biography was Charles Darwin, the evolutionist, who published a diary of his observations of his son's early development (7). Darwin saw the child as a rich source of information about the nature of man—"by careful observation of the infant and child, one could see the descent of man" (13, 115). The fact that such a distinguished scientist and theorist would write a baby biography was impressive; it made the baby biography a legitimate scientific document.

In spite of the brilliance of some of the writers, these early baby biographies are generally not good sources of scientific data. Too often they were based on observations that were unsystematic and made at irregular intervals. Furthermore, like Darwin, most observers had their own special theory about development or education and saw the child they were observing as a living expression of this theory. Also, the writers were usually proud parents, or uncles or aunts, undoubtedly biased and selective in their perceptions. Understandably, they were likely to emphasize the intriguing, positive aspects of early development while neglecting some of the negative factors. Finally, because each account is based on only one case, it is almost impossible to make valid generalizations from any of them.

Nevertheless, like the earlier philosophical works, these biographies were valuable. They contained some information and many hypotheses about the nature of development. However, their importance lies in their influence in delineating major problems of child psychology (many of them still unsolved) and exciting widespread interest in the scientific study of children.

Beginnings of Scientific Child Psychology

No one in the nineteenth century influenced the history of child psychology more than Charles Darwin. The publication of **On the Origin of Species** (1859) was probably the single most vital force in the establishment of child psychology as a scientific discipline. The notion of the evolution of the species—and especially Darwin's continued search for "signs of man in animal life," inevitably led to speculation about the development of man and society. "The irreducible contribution of Darwin to the study of children was . . . in his assignment of scientific value to childhood" **(13,** 115).

Stimulated by Darwin's theory,

> the search for phylogenetic and societal shades in the child marked the beginning of a science of child behavior. Man was not to be understood by the analysis of his adult functions, an analysis that was rational in conception and closely linked to logic; rather, man was to be understood by a study of his origins—in nature and in the child. When did consciousness dawn? What were the beginnings of morality? How could we know the world of the infant? Questions like these which, in form of more or less sophistication, were to dominate child psychology for many years, derive their sense from a genetic view of man **(13,** 116).

Systematic study of larger groups of children began toward the end of the nineteenth century. A pioneer in such study in the United States was G. Stanley Hall, president of Clark University and one of the founders of American psychology. He was interested in investigating "the contents of children's minds" **(9)** because, like Darwin, he was convinced that the study of development was crucial to the problem of understanding man. To conduct his studies of larger groups, he devised and refined a new research technique, the questionnaire, which consisted of a series of questions designed to obtain information about children's and adolescents' behavior, attitudes, and interests. Hall collected written responses to questionnaires from both children and parents.

In a sense, Hall's work, which continued into the twentieth century, marks the beginning of systematic child study in the United States. By modern standards, his work would not be considered controlled or highly objective; the problems with which he was concerned have been investigated with much greater scientific sophistication in recent years. Nevertheless, he did employ large numbers of subjects in an effort to obtain representative data, and he attempted to determine the relationships among personality characteristics, adjustment problems, and background experiences. For these reasons, Hall's approach to child psychology certainly represented a distinct methodological advance over the philosophical and biographical approaches discussed above.

THE EMERGENCE OF CHILD PSYCHOLOGY
AS A SCIENTIFIC DISCIPLINE

The systematic study of children burgeoned in the twentieth century. During the early part of this century the subject matter of child psychology was limited primarily to the discovery and description of age trends, that is, the measurement of age changes in physical, psychological, and behavioral characteristics. Research efforts were devoted to detailed tracings of the sequences of steps or stages in children's acquisition of various types of behavior, such as walking, manipulating objects, and talking, for example, the average age at which the child first stands alone without support, picks up a small cube with his thumb and forefinger, or says his first word.

Precise description of events and phenomena is one of the goals of any scientific discipline, but a mature scientific discipline has more complex goals, including the explanation of the phenomena described and the prediction of future events. For the last 40 years researchers in developmental psychology have become increasingly concerned with the processes underlying human growth and development—with a theoretical synthesis of observed phenomena which can provide us with the **how** and **why** of the origins of behavior and changes in behavior.

Thus, the earliest research efforts in the area of language development were focused on the growth of vocabulary, beginning with the infant's first utterances and extending through childhood. Contemporary research in psycholinguistics (the systematic study of psychological aspects of language) is more concerned with the process of language development—the factors that influence the acquisition of grammar and the evolution of meaning.

Analogously, early research in intelligence and thinking focused on accurately measuring age changes in intellectual functioning and on delineating curves of intellectual growth. Current attention is more sharply centered on such problems as the effects of antecedent conditions, including high achievement motivation or environmental stimulation, on later cognitive functioning. More specifically, until 15 or 20 years ago, the bulk of research on the development of intelligence and cognitive functioning dealt with the kinds of verbal, logical, and arithmetic problems that children are capable of solving at different ages. However, at present there is much more interest in investigating the factors that produce high or low levels of performance on these kinds of tasks. Research is centered on problems such as these: Does social class membership affect intellectual performance, and if so, why? To what extent can special training or environmental stimulation influence intellectual achievement? Does the child's performance in thinking and problem-solving tasks vary with the level of his anxiety or the strength of other motivations? Do children who tend to be reflective perform better on tests of cognitive functioning than children who are more impulsive in responding?

As you would expect, the definition of the field of developmental psychology and the major directions of research have changed radically. Some topics that were formerly ignored or thought to be of minor significance, have become critical research areas. Among these are: perception in infants and the factors affecting its development, learning in infancy, the development of attachment to others, the influence of experiences and training on children's thinking and concept formation, individual differences in "styles" or approaches to cognitive tasks, the relation of child-rearing practices to competence and achievement. In presenting a contemporary view of developmental psychology, we will emphasize these and other recent topics of research as well as the most fruitful modern concepts and theories of human development. Our emphasis is on the origins and the processes of development of many significant aspects of human behavior.

Explanation and Theory

Explanation involves the specification of antecedent-consequent relationships: stating the factors or antecedents that determine certain outcomes or consequents. For example, what kinds of environmental stimulation (antecedents) enhance the development of dependency, curiosity, logical thinking, and problem-solving (consequents)? What parental practices (antecedents) promote conformity or aggression in children (consequents)?

In his search for antecedent-consequent relationships or explanations, the scientist formulates theories, hypotheses, or "best guesses" about the determinants of the phenomena under study. Scientific theories and hypotheses stimulate further research and guide all phases of investigation, determining the variables selected for study, the kinds of data to be collected, and the methods of collecting them. To illustrate, suppose a developmental psychologist hypothesizes that a high level of aggression toward peers (the consequent variable) is the outcome of a frustrating home situation, such as living with cold, punitive, highly restrictive, or rejecting parents (antecedent). To test this hypothesis, the researcher must make some meaningful assessments of children's aggressiveness. These might be derived from intensive observations of children's behavior in the classroom or on the playground, and from teachers' ratings. Groups of highly aggressive and unaggressive children could then be selected for further study on the basis of these assessments. Data on the home situation could come from interviews with the children's parents or, if possible, from observation of parent-child interactions at home. Using these interviews and observations, the psychologist could evaluate parental punitiveness, rejection, and restrictiveness. Then he could assess whether, as he hypothesized, highly aggressive children did in fact suffer more frustrations at home than children who are relatively unaggressive.

After the data are collected, they are organized and interpreted to see if they do, in fact, confirm the hypothesis being tested. The data may point to new relationships which modify that hypothesis or lead to new hypotheses that allow for logical explanation and, in many cases, for the prediction of subsequent events.

The ability to predict phenomena is one of the main advantages of scientific theory. Because we have a theory (or set of interrelated principles) explaining planetary motion, we can predict when the next eclipse will occur. If we had a good theory to explain why some children do not learn well in school, we could predict school failures before they occurred and might be able to take more effective steps to reduce or eliminate such failures.

Developmental psychology is not an isolated or independent field. The principles of learning, perception, motivation, and social behavior are as basic to developmental psychology as they are to other branches of psychology. Many aspects of development remain incomprehensible without these generalizations, and advances in developmental psychology depend upon progress in the entire realm of psychology. For example, data and generalizations derived from research in such diverse areas as behavior genetics, physiological psychology, and learning and motivation may, and often do, have direct relevance to fundamental problems of developmental psychology. Contributions from these fields are vital for understanding the genetic determinants of behavior, the physiological bases of development, and the acquisition of behavior and personality characteristics.

A number of outstanding developmental psychologists, such as Piaget (**16, 17**) and Werner (**21**), have formulated theories that deal specifically with the origin and development of basic psychological processes. But, in addition, as will be evident throughout this book, some of the most fruitful theories and research techniques used in the study of developmental psychology are adopted from other fields of psychology. For instance, psychoanalytic theory is concerned primarily with emotional adjustment and maladjustment, but aspects of this theory deal with the origins of psychological disturbance and with hypotheses about normal personality development. Likewise, learning theory, formulated largely on the basis of research in laboratories (often with animals), has helped enormously in understanding the development of large segments of human behavior. Cognitive theory, constructed to explain adult perception, thinking, and problem-solving, has been the inspiration for much theorizing and research on the origins and development on these processes. These theories will be elaborated in Chapter 2.

Research Methods

As in all scientific research, controlled observation and objective measurement are the fundamental features of the developmental psychologist's investigation of antecedent-consequent relationships.

> Scientific observation is deliberate search, carried out with care and forethought, as contrasted with the casual and largely passive perceptions of everyday life. It is this deliberateness and control of the process of observation that is distinctive of science, not merely the use of special instruments (important as they are) (11, 126).

The scientist's observations must be as free as possible from subjective bias. In his evaluation of his observations he must use standard units of measurement or, if this is not possible, units that can be understood and applied by others. Therefore, instruments potentially provide the most desirable methods of recording natural phenomena. The degree to which the observations can be quantified (translated into numbers) is often a good index of the maturity of a science.

In making his observations, the psychologist uses specialized methods and techniques appropriate for his particular research purposes. Suppose the investigator is interested in the relationship between parental training for independence (the antecedent variables) and the nursery school child's achievement motivation (the consequent variables). The antecedent variables could be measured by direct observation (having trained observers actually go to the home to observe parent-child interactions) or by parental interviews or questionnaires about child-rearing techniques. The children's behavior, the consequent variables, could be measured by means of direct observations in the school or in the home, teacher ratings, mothers' reports, or projective techniques. You will become more familiar with a wide range of techniques of investigation as you read about different kinds of research in later chapters of this book.

As a scientific discipline matures and expands, new methods and tools of observation and measurement are invented and old ones are improved or discarded. During the last few years there have been marked advancements in many research techniques, such as improved methods of measuring the infant's visual perception and attention, of recording psychophysiological responses in a wide variety of environmental settings, and for evaluating the attachment between young infants and their mothers; better controlled, "situational" methods of observing parent-child interactions and children's behavior; ingenious tests of conceptual ability; and more objective methods of making naturalistic observations. As would be expected, some old "facts"—generalizations from earlier studies and exploratory data in which inadequate research techniques were used—no longer seem valid or, at best, seem to have only limited value. They are being replaced by conclusions based on better, more systematic investigations with better methods of research.

Experimental and Nonexperimental Methods An experiment is a most desirable kind of observation because the factors affecting the phenomena to be studied can be controlled. "Basically, experimentation is a process of observation to be carried out in a situation especially brought about for that purpose. . . . There is no sharp distinction between observation and experiment, only a series of gradations and intermediates" (**11**, 144). In its simplest form an experiment is designed to confirm or disprove a hypothesis about the effects of changes in one variable (the antecedent or independent variable) on another variable or variables (the dependent or consequent variables). The experiment itself consists of holding constant all but one of the variables presumably related to a given phenomenon and then manipulating this variable in accordance with the experimenter's plans. The purpose of the experiment is to observe whether, and how, the dependent variable changes as the variable being manipulated by the experimenter (the antecedent or independent variable) is changed.

Suppose, for example, that the psychologist wants to investigate the effects of competition on children's performance in arithmetic tests. Do children who compete with each other do better in these tests than children who are not competing? The psychologist might attempt to test this hypothesis by doing an experiment with two groups of children, one called the experimental group, the other the control group. Since he is concerned only with the relationship between competition and test performance he must be certain that the two groups are matched or equated in intelligence, arithmetic ability, health, or other factors that might affect performance.

In the experiment proper, the two groups would be subjected to different treatments. A competitive situation could be set up in the experimental group by informing the children that the student getting the highest grade on an arithmetic test would be given a prize. In the control group, no such competitive situation would be created. Both groups would then be given the same arithmetic test, and the difference between the performances of the two groups would be determined.

Here the independent variable is competition, and it is regulated by the experimenter. Other important variables are controlled by initial random assignment of children to the two groups and by matching the groups on variables considered likely to affect performance in arithmetic. Therefore, we can be fairly certain that the obtained differences between the two groups will be due to the introduction of competition in one group and its absence in the other.

This example makes clear the unique advantage of experimental method, namely, the direct demonstration of antecedent-consequent relationships, the precise and accurate assessment of the effects of the experimental treatment. Without the use of experimental procedures, we cannot be sure which factors may be most important in determining a particular outcome.

As long as we depend on the observation of occurrences not involving our assistance, the observable happenings are usually the product of so many factors that we cannot determine the contribution of each individual factor to the total result. The scientific experiment isolates the factors one from the other; the interference of man [that is, the experimenter] creates conditions in which one factor is shown at work undisturbed by the others (**18,** 97).

Most observations in the physical sciences are experiments, and experimental methods are applied whenever possible and suitable in child psychology.

But there are problems of profound interest to the child psychologist for which the experimental method is simply not appropriate or feasible. For example, suppose he is testing a hypothesis about the relationship between early deprivation of affection and later learning deficits. He could hardly expect parents to reject their children for purposes of his experiment. But the investigator might be able to study a group of children known to have been emotionally deprived and a control group of children who had received emotional support during infancy. He would attempt to control the effects of other possible relevant variables by equating the two groups as closely as possible in factors such as intelligence, age, sex, health, and socioeconomic status. It would then be possible to compare the learning deficits of the two groups and hence to determine whether there is in fact a relationship between early emotional deprivation and later learning difficulties. The study would not be an experiment in the usual sense because the experimenter did not manipulate the independent variable, emotional deprivation. However, the study would be as close to the ideal of an experiment as would be possible under the circumstances.

Longitudinal Approaches and Cross-Sectional Approaches There are two contrasting broad approaches to the study of children, longitudinal and cross-sectional, each with its distinct advantages and disadvantages. In the **longitudinal approach** the same group of children is studied repeatedly over an extended period of time, often a decade or longer. This approach is especially valuable for investigations in which there is an attempt to discover whether characteristics such as intelligence, dependency, and behavior problems are stable over long periods of time or subject to fluctuations. The longitudinal approach must be used to study the latent or delayed influences of some early experience on later behavior. For example, current theory about personality development suggests that maternal rejection during the first few years of life will lead to disturbed interpersonal relations during childhood and adolescence. The only way to test the validity of this hypothesis is to select mothers who are rejecting during the early period and then to make follow-up studies of their children later on, assessing their subsequent social behavior. Obviously, the longitudinal method is expensive, time-consuming, and difficult to use.

In the second and more common method, the **cross-sectional approach,** the investigator selects a group of children at one age period, or different groups of children at different ages, and makes his observations at that time period. For example, the growth of reasoning ability can be studied with the cross-sectional method by selecting a group of ten children at each of six ages—2, 4, 6, 8, 10, and

12 years—and comparing the average performances of the six groups in reasoning tests. An investigator using the longitudinal method to answer the same question would measure the same group of 60 children at two-year intervals from 2 to 12 years of age and assess the average biennial growth in reasoning ability.

The **short-term longitudinal approach,** also called accelerated longitudinal or convergence approach (**3, 4**), combines some of the advantages of both longitudinal and cross-sectional methods. Groups of children of overlapping ages are tested periodically. Thus, one group might be tested annually at ages 5, 6, and 7, while another group would be tested at 7, 8, and 9. The two groups provide longitudinal data about performance at five ages, even though the study takes only three years. Moreover, different groups may be compared at the same ages. The method is particularly appropriate for studying transitions from one stage to the next in such psychological functions as reasoning (**3, 4**).

Contrasting Conceptions of the Nature of Development

Clearly, there are many different approaches to research in child development. And, as is the case in any young, vigorous, scientific discipline, there are divergent points of view about many critical theoretical issues. Here we will briefly present contrasting points of view about two important issues which will be elaborated in Chapter 2.

Some developmental theories view the child as **active** in relation to his environment; others see him as relatively **passive.** In learning theory and psychoanalytic explanations of behavior, environmental events—what happens **to** the child—are usually viewed as the main determinants of the child's behavior and responses. In contrast, Piaget and other cognitive theorists believe that psychological development is, to a large extent, self-generating, that is, it is activated by the child's inherent tendencies toward adaptation. Developmental changes are a product of the child's activity—his curiosity, searching, problem-solving, perceptions of the environment, and the imposition of structure and meaning on the environment.

Another important issue is whether the course of behavioral development is **continuous** or **discontinuous.** Does the child's behavior change and progress toward maturity continuously by gradual increments? If this is the case, the curve of behavioral development would show a smooth, gradual, upward movement like this:

The alternative conceptualization is that the course of development is segmented or divided into stages and that development advances through a series of rather abrupt changes. In each stage, new abilities, ways of thinking and responding appear. Each stage is defined as a complex pattern of interrelated characteristics or responses that occur together and may therefore be conveniently grouped—"an abstracted and highly compressed description of a limited aspect of . . . behavior" (**12**, 68). Later stages evolve from preceding ones, but each stage is characterized by qualitatively distinct ways of functioning. In stage theories, psychological development is viewed as progressing through a fixed and invariant sequence of stages, with every child going through the same stages in the same order. No stage can be skipped; a child cannot achieve a later stage without going through the earlier one. The stage theorist's curve of development could be represented in this way.

Furthermore, the concept of sequential developmental stages suggests

> . . . the operation of organizing,—i.e., theoretical—principles. Being part of a sequence, the proposed stages of development help us to think coherently about the course of development and at the same time suggest the theoretical basis on which behavior is seen as segmented and developing (**12**, 68).

As we shall see in Chapter 2, both psychoanalytic theory and Piaget's theory of cognitive development make use of stage descriptions. In both theoretical systems there are explicit statements about the behavior and characteristics to be accounted for and the relationship between the stages and the overall developmental theory. In both systems, the stages represent complex patterns of behavior that are parts of an orderly sequence of development and the specific characteristics of each stage are fully described. Thus, in Piaget's theory the child's capabilities and his approach to cognitive problems at each stage are specified, particularized, and related to the general theory. "Each stage involves a period of formation (genesis) and a period of attainment" (**10**, 23) which is characterized by progressive organization of cognitive abilities. The order of succession of stages from early, relatively simple thinking to more mature and more complex abilities is constant. Transition from one step to the next one involves a process of integration, in which earlier cognitive abilities become part of later organizations of cognitive activities (**10**). The accomplishments of earlier stages are carried into later ones, but they are also integrated with new elements that appear to arise spontaneously in later stages.

CONTEMPORARY CHILD PSYCHOLOGY: RECENT TRENDS

As we have already indicated, the major research emphases in child development change in the course of time, often in response to social and historical pressures and events. During the first part of this century, researchers were preoccupied with the establishment of age trends in the development of psychomotor skills and intelligence. At the same time, and related to this interest, studies of individual differences and accurate assessment of these differences were the chief concerns of most researchers.

Most of this book deals with developments in the field of child psychology during the last 25 years—the theoretical advances, the research findings, and the newer methods of investigation that have been developed. Although many investigators are still concerned with age trends—particularly in such areas as thinking and problem-solving, creativity, moral reasoning and behavior (conscience), attitudes and opinions—the most exciting research in child development is concentrated increasingly on the processes or mechanisms underlying these changes, that is, on the explanations of why and how these changes occur—the antecedent-consequent relationships.

Emphasis on the determinants of behavioral development has intensified interest in the generation of theory. Early research in child development, particularly investigations of age trends, was largely empirical; it was concerned with the accumulation of facts and usually lacked theoretical bases. Current research is more often derived from theory, that is, it is designed to test some theoretical issue or explanatory hypothesis. The findings of such studies are, therefore, pertinent to the validity or "truth-value" of some theoretical system, and can be integrated with those from other studies, thus gaining in general significance and applicability. A sample of a few of the most prominent recent trends in developmental psychology can serve as a preview of the field and at the same time provide some further recent historical perspective on the field.

Personality Development

The general public became acutely aware of the prevalence of mental illness and emotional breakdown during and after World War II. These maladjustments were generally regarded as rooted in early developmental experiences, a notion supported by psychoanalytic theory, which was widely accepted at that time. Interest in the antecedents of abnormal behavior and maladjustment expanded into a general interest in personality development. As a result, socialization—the acquisition of personal characteristics, motives, and social behavior—and the factors influencing these became the predominant topics of research in child development and remained so until the late 1950s or early 1960s. These continue to be important and exciting areas of investigation, and new, more fruitful techniques are being

used to study such topics as the stability of personality traits and the influence of variables such as social class, ordinal position, and parent-child relationships on the child's personality structure and social behavior.

However, a shift of focus within this broad research area is noteworthy. In the past most research attention was centered on the development and control of negative motives and social behavior, such as aggression and exaggerated dependency. Many developmental psychologists are still concerned with these characteristics, but there has been a marked increase in research on positive motives and social behavior (sometimes called prosocial behavior), such as competence, cooperation, independence, altruism, and development of humane and moral values.

Cognitive Research

Cognitive research is another area which, like personality development, received increased attention as a result of historical events and social pressures. In 1957 the Russians successfully launched Sputnik, the first man-made satellite. Russia's apparent lead in technology alarmed the American public, which, like educators and psychologists, began to feel that American children were not receiving as thorough an education, particularly in mathematics and science, as their Russian peers. Shortly thereafter the civil rights movement gained a great deal of momentum; public and governmental agencies began a long overdue, intensive push to improve the educational and social status of the socioeconomically deprived and disadvantaged.

These events, and the social pressures stemming from them, became major spurs to research in cognition. Educational practices had to be improved; this required a better understanding of the development of perception, learning, thinking, language ability, concept formation, techniques of problem-solving, and creativity. In addition, problems concerning the effects of early stimulation and deprivation on these cognitive processes assumed immense importance. As a result, research in cognitive development has burgeoned in recent years and is currently the most vigorous research area in child psychology. Moreover, recent studies tend to have strong theoretical bases, particularly, although not exclusively, Piaget's theory of the stages of cognitive development.

Compared with cognitive research of 20 years ago, contemporary investigations are much broader in scope, more rigorous, systematic, ingenious, and challenging. To cite one example, earlier studies established the fact that with increasing age during childhood, memory functions improve, that is, more information can be stored and stored information can be held for longer periods of time. A 9-year-old will remember a longer series of numbers or words than a 5-year-old; children under 6 have greater difficulty than older children in recalling events that occurred hours, days, or weeks earlier. Recent systematic investigations and experimentation are concentrated on the factors underlying age differences in memory, that is, how memory and forgetting are influenced by capacity to sustain attention, language and vocabulary (coding events by labeling or describing them), categorizing or grouping events, spontaneous rehearsal (repeating the stimuli or events to oneself), interfering thoughts, and motivation, particularly anxiety. The latest advances in understanding these problems are described in detail in this book (see pp. 257ff; 286ff), but there is still much to be learned.

Increased attention to cognitive development generated a number of other fascinating research problems. For example, observations of children performing cognitive tasks (solving mathematical or logical problems, categorizing objects, deriving concepts) reveal that there are many individual differences in approaches to these problems and that these differences are linked to personality structure. Some children are impulsive in arriving at solutions; others are more reflective. Some seek out new, creative solutions, while others use routine, customary ways of solving problems. A whole new field of investigation relating these kinds of variables, that is, styles of approach, to cognitive functioning has opened up (see pp. 305).

A number of significant and provocative investigations have focused on the problem of the impact of early environmental stimulation on later cognitive functioning and the related practical social issue of overcoming early cognitive deficiences among poor children (see pp. 350-357).

Interest in the origins and early development of cognitive functions also led to more comprehensive and systematic work on the behavior and capabilities of infants and young babies. We now have at least partial answers to the following questions that are still being investigated: What responses can the newborn make? Are these "built-in" or "prewired" capabilities manifested at birth or shortly afterward? What conditions elicit them? What kinds of stimulation engage the newborn's attention? What aspects of infant behavior are readily modified and under what conditions? Does early environmental stimulation have immediate and/or enduring effects on cognitive processes? Are the behavior or temperamental characteristics of the infant stable and predictive of his later personality? These questions are not new ones, of course, but recently they have received increased attention. Novel methods of investigating them have been devised, and research has become much more rigorous and systematic. Some of the data from infancy studies indicate that newborns are much more capable individuals than we had previously suspected. A great many perceptual and cognitive abilities seem to be "prewired" or "programmed" into the organism, that is, biologically given, rather than learned (see pp. 49, 155, 240).

Language development continues to be a most active and fruitful subject of research. Psycholinguists are giving increasing attention to the relationship between linguistic competence and cognitive ability (see pp. 257-261). In addition to their long-standing interest in the acquisition of grammar and syntax, many psycholinguists are now concentrating their attention on the development of semantics, the acquisition and comprehension of meaning. Many agree with Chomsky, the outstanding contemporary linguistic theorist, that the "study of language may very well, as traditionally supposed, provide a remarkably favorable perspective for the study of human mental processes" (5, 84).

Cross-Cultural Studies

Cross-cultural studies have assumed increasing prominence in recent years and have proven to be a fruitful way of testing hypotheses and discovering new facts about development. In this kind of research, a wide variety of factors—social structure, occupational and economic activities, child-rearing techniques, and life styles—can be related to personality characteristics or cognitive abilities by studying cultural variations. Such studies can help determine which relationships and developmental patterns are products of a particular culture and which have broader implications for the establishment of universal characteristics and development. Also studying such relationships in widely varied forms can give us additional insight into the operation of each relationship. For instance, a relationship between the amount of time infants are in direct contact with their mothers and their later tendency to become attached to them, can be tested cross-culturally. The attachment behaviors of infants in cultures where the mother is in contact with the infant almost all the time, carrying him wherever she goes, can be compared with the attachment behavior of infants in cultures where there is much less mother-infant contact. Analogously, the hypothesis that communal child care reduces children's tendencies to compete can be tested by studying competition in children raised on kibbutzim (collective farms in Israel) and in children brought up in nuclear families (living with parents and siblings).

People from one culture differ from those in other cultures in the ways they think, solve problems, perceive, and structure the world. The intellectual demands upon the individual and the cognitive abilities most highly prized vary from culture to culture. Thus children in one African society have a great deal of difficulty with western-style mathematics and are inaccurate and inconsistent in measuring lengths, but they are exceptionally good at estimating amounts of rice.

Such studies may help make us more aware of our cultural biases in evaluating development. The African children are not "deficient" in intellectual ability or "unable to learn"; cultural factors have determined the development of particular abilities different from those of the white middle-class child. (Members of that African society might, in fact, regard children who could not estimate amounts of rice as somewhat retarded, since they lack what is regarded as a fundamental cognitive ability.) The same awareness of cultural bias is crucial now in research concerning subcultures within our own society.

By examining the distinctive cognitive abilities of members of different cultural groups, we can determine the conditions that produce different ways of learning and problem-solving. From the developmental psychologist's point of view, the critical question is: What is it about the culture that acts upon the children to produce these distinctive patterns of cognitive abilities and deficits? In short, investigators wish "to identify the behavior evoked by different kinds of intellectual tasks and to seek in the cultural environment explanations of the fact that different groups manifest different intellectual behavior" (6, xiii).

It is tempting to make broad generalizations, statements about "universal" developmental phenomena, on the basis of findings from studies in one society and with subjects of one cultural group. Comparative cultural studies can serve as enormously valuable antidotes to overgeneralization. Freud, as a result of his work with Viennese patients, postulated that all male children have an Oedipus complex—feelings of love for the mother and envy of, and fear of retaliation from, the father. But Malinowski, a famous anthropologist, showed there is no evidence of this complex among the Trobrianders, who are reared by maternal uncles. On the basis of observations and studies in western culture, many investigators concluded that adolescence is inevitably a period of "storm and stress." Margaret Mead showed, however, that in some other cultures, especially in Samoa, adolescence is usually a relaxed and happy time.

Many authorities maintain that deprivation of stimulation during the first year of life does permanent damage to the intellectual development of children. One of the authors (Jerome Kagan) has recently studied Guatemalan Indians living in an isolated village who keep their infants alone, in poorly lighted huts, with relatively little stimulation or interaction, for the first year of their life. At the end of this period of isolation, these infants are, according to test data, retarded about four months in comparison to middle-class infants in the United States. Yet, by the age of 11, they do as well as American children in tests of perception, memory, problem-solving, and reasoning. Clearly, then, one can make no "universal" statements about the long-time effects of deprivation during the first year.

By the same token, if there are any universals of development, they can be established only through cross-cultural studies. The first primitive sentences spoken by English-speaking American youngsters are very abbreviated (telegraphic) statements and communicate only very limited meanings or intentions such as naming objects ("that doll") or stating a relationship between an action and its object ("hit ball"). Cross-cultural studies of infant speech indicate that these speech characteristics pertain to infants in all cultures studied; consequently, a universal of language development has been established. Are there universal principles of cognitive development? Do all children advance intellectually through the sequence of stages postulated by Piaget? These questions can be answered only by means of extensive cross-cultural research.

ETHICAL ISSUES IN RESEARCH

Research in child development can potentially make enormous contributions to advancing human welfare and accomplishing humanitarian goals. The knowledge derived from scientific research can be used to benefit everyone: helping people to achieve better adaptations and happier lives; overcoming cognitive deficiencies; reducing prejudices, fears, and anxieties; promoting effective learning and greater creativity; facilitating the development of cooperative, altruistic, humanitarian attitudes and actions. But to establish scientific knowledge, the developmental psychologist must study human beings and this entails many worrisome ethical issues and responsibilities.

All psychologists with humanitarian values would agree that the researcher's paramount obligation is to safeguard the welfare, dignity, and rights of all of his subjects, children and adults alike. Each researcher must accept full responsibility for the treatment of subjects in his study. An experiment on the effects of cruelty, neglect, or extreme deprivation in early life on later personality structure might be of great potential value, but no ethical psychologist would subject infants to such treatment.

The ethical dilemmas encountered in most investigations are much more subtle, however. If the investigator asks children questions about their parents' child-rearing practices, is he invading the children's or parents' right to privacy? Is it possible that the questions he asks will themselves have harmful effects on parent-child relationships? Is the use of deception in research (misinforming the child of the purpose of the experiment or giving him a false report of his performance on a test, for example) ever morally justified? Is it ethical to subject children to mild frustration or stress for experimental purposes? Is it permissible to observe people in natural settings without their consent? These and other ethical questions have no objective or absolute answers that are applicable in all situations and acceptable to everyone.

In efforts to formulate some guidelines for making such decisions, committees of the American Psychological Association examined hundreds of ethical problems reported by members of the organization and then formulated a code of "Ethical Standards for Research with Human Subjects" (1). Drawing on these general standards, a special committee of the Society for Research in Child Development subsequently published a set of principles specifically pertinent to research with children. Each ethical principle or rule deals with a frequently encountered problem or dilemma related to such issues as obtaining informed consent from all subjects, assuring freedom from coercion to participate, fairness and freedom from exploitation in research, protection from physical and mental stress, responsibility to research participants following completion of the research, confidentiality of data and anonymity of the subjects. Here is a section of the report by the Committee on Ethics in Research with Children (Society for Research in Child Development), including some of the proposed ethical principles:

Children as research subjects present ethical problems for the investigator different from those presented by adult subjects. Not only are children often viewed as more vulnerable to stress but, having less knowledge and experience, they are less able to evaluate what participation in research may mean. Consent of the parent for the study of his child, moreover, must be obtained in addition to the child's consent. These are some of the major differences between research with children and research with adults.

1. No matter how young the child, he has rights that supersede the rights of the investigator. The investigator should measure each operation he proposes in terms of the child's rights, and before proceeding he should obtain the approval of a committee of peers. Institutional peer review committees should be established in any setting where children are the subjects of the study.

2. The final responsibility to establish and maintain ethical practices in research remains with the individual investigator. He is also responsible for the ethical practices of collaborators, assistants, students, and employees, all of whom, however, incur parallel obligations.

3. Any deviation from the following principles demands that the investigator seek consultation on the ethical issues in order to protect the rights of the research participants.

4. The investigator should inform the child of all features of the research that may affect his willingness to participate and he should answer the child's questions in terms appropriate to the child's comprehension.

5. The investigator should respect the child's freedom to choose to participate in research or not, as well as to discontinue participation at any time. The greater the power of the investigator with respect to the participant, the greater is the obligation to protect the child's freedom.

6. The informed consent of parents or of those who act **in loco parentis** (e.g., teachers, superintendents of institutions) similarly should be obtained, preferably in writing. Informed consent requires that the parent or other responsible adult be told all features of the research that may affect his willingness to allow the child to participate. This information should include the profession and institutional affiliation of the investigator. Not only should the right of the responsible adult to refuse consent be respected, but he should be given the opportunity to refuse without penalty.

7. The informed consent of any person whose interaction with the child is the subject of the study should also be obtained. As with the child and responsible adult, informed consent requires that the person be informed of all features of the research that may affect his willingness to participate; his questions should be answered; and he should be free to choose to participate or not, and to discontinue participation at any time.

8. From the beginning of each research investigation, there should be a clear agreement between the investigator and the research participant that defines the responsibilities of each. The investigator has the obligation to honor all promises and commitments of the agreement.

9. The investigator uses no research operation that may harm the child either physically or psychologically. Psychological harm, to be sure, is difficult to define; nevertheless, its definition remains the responsibility of the investigator. When the investigator is in doubt about the possible harmful effects of the research operations, he

seeks consultation from others. When harm seems possible, he is obligated to find other means of obtaining the information or to abandon the research.

10. Although we accept the ethical ideal of full disclosure of information, a particular study may necessitate concealment or deception. Whenever concealment or deception is thought to be essential to the conduct of the study, the investigator should satisfy a committee of his peers that his judgment is correct. If concealment or deception is practiced, adequate measures should be taken after the study to ensure the participant's understanding of the reasons for the concealment or deception.

11. The investigator should keep in confidence all information obtained about research participants. The participant's identity should be concealed in written and verbal reports of the results, as well as in informal discussions with students and colleagues. When a possibility exists that others may gain access to such information, this possibility, together with the plans for protecting confidentiality, should be explained to the participants as a part of the procedure for obtaining informed consent. . . .

13. Immediately after the data are collected, the investigator should clarify for the research participant any misconceptions that may have arisen. The investigator also recognizes a duty to report general findings to participants in terms appropriate to their understanding. Where scientific or humane values may justify withholding information, every effort should be made so that withholding the information has no damaging consequences for the participant. . . .

16. When research procedures may result in undesirable consequences for the participant that were previously unforeseen, the investigator should employ appropriate measures to correct these consequences, and should consider redesigning the procedures (8, 3–4).

It is, of course, acknowledged that ethical problems encountered in research with children cannot be solved simply by applying a set of "rules." Rather, the situation in which ethical problems arise is usually

one of weighing the advantages and disadvantages of conducting the research as planned. On the one hand, there is the contribution that the research may ultimately make to human welfare; on the other, there is the cost to the individual research participant. Put in these stark terms, the essential conflict is between the values of science to benefit all mankind and the values that dictate concern for the research participant (1, II).

But who is to decide whether the ultimate contribution of research is greater than the cost to the subjects? The authors of the code concede that "these judgments are subjective and lead to unavoidable difficulties in making ethical decisions" (1, III). Can the individual investigator's judgment be trusted? Often it can be, but many feel that any individual's decisions about ethical problems need to be evaluated or monitored by some sort of jury. Therefore, many universities and other research facilities—as well as the United States Public Health Service which supports a great deal of research in child development—require that an ethics advisory committee, consisting of other researchers and instructors representing several disciplines, review every research proposal that involves human subjects and attempt to insure that the investigators act in accordance with the highest ethical standards. This reviewing committee serves as a panel of judges considering the objectives and potential benefits of the study and weighing these against the possible harmful effects on the subjects. The committee might also suggest possible alternative methods that could be used in the study and that might be less harmful to the participants. Most importantly, the panel of judges would see that all possible steps were taken to safeguard the welfare and integrity of all subjects. Such a group would be particularly cautious in evaluating and approving proposals for research in which children are participants.

Of course, neither codes, even if they are clearly formulated, nor reviewing committees, however judicious, can be substitutes for the investigator's moral integrity, maturity, honesty, sensitivity, and profound respect for the rights of others. Ultimately, the investigator himself is responsible for the conduct of the study and for applying the highest ethical standards in his research.

SUMMARY

This chapter deals with the goals and purposes of developmental psychology, the methods and techniques the developmental psychologist uses in his research, and the ethical problems he encounters. The contributions of developmental psychology are both theoretical and practical. Through research, developmental psychologists contribute to understanding, and thus ultimately to solving, many significant social problems—such as improving the intellectual and school performances of children from ghettos and other impoverished areas and reducing juvenile delinquency.

The fundamental problems of developmental psychology have been major subjects of philosophers' and writers' thoughts for many centuries. However, it was not until the nineteenth century that children became subjects for study, particularly for intensive observations, recorded in "baby biographies" by philosophers, educators, and biologists. Darwin's works, published in the middle of the nineteenth century, marked the beginnings of the science of child behavior. Systematic study of groups of children was initiated by G. Stanley Hall at the end of the last century.

During the first third of this century the goals of developmental psychology were primarily the discovery and description of age trends in physical, cognitive, and behavioral characteristics. For the last 40 years, however, researchers in this field have become increasingly concerned with explanation, with the processes and mechanisms underlying human development.

The search for antecedent-consequent relationships and explanations has led to the formulation of many theories about the nature and determinants of growth and change. These theories differ in several important dimensions. Some theories view the child as active in relation to his environment, while other theories regard him as relatively passive. Some theorists conceptualize the course of behavioral development as a continuous and gradual progress toward maturity, while others see the course of development as steplike, divided into stages, advancing through a series of rather abrupt changes.

To test these theories research methods have been devised, improved, and refined. The major methods of investigation in developmental psychology include naturalistic and controlled observation, experimentation, longitudinal and cross-sectional study. In recent years, cross-cultural studies have assumed increasing prominence in testing hypotheses and discovering new facts about human development.

In conducting his research, the developmental psychologist often encounters difficult ethical problems and responsibilities. The researcher's primary obligation is to safeguard the welfare, dignity, and rights of all of his subjects, children and adults alike. Prominent organizations such as the American Psychological Association and the Society for Research in Child Development have attempted to formulate codes of ethical standards of research. In each specific case, however, it is the investigator himself who is responsible for the ethical conduct of his study and for humane treatment of all those involved in it.

References

1. American Psychological Association, Committee on Ethical Standards in Psychological Research. Ethical standards for research with human subjects. **APA Monitor,** 1972 (May), I-XIX.
2. Aries, P. **Centuries of childhood.** New York: Knopf, 1962.
3. Bell, R. Q. Convergence: An accelerated longitudinal approach. **Child Development,** 1953, **24,** 145–152.
4. Bell, R. Q. An experimental test of the accelerated longitudinal approach. **Child Development,** 1954, **25,** 281–286.
5. Chomsky, N. **Language and mind.** New York: Harcourt Brace Jovanovich, 1968.
6. Cole, M., Gay, J., Glick, A. A., & Sharp, D. W. **The cultural context of learning and thinking.** New York: Basic Books, 1971.
7. Darwin, C. A. A biographical sketch of an infant. **Mind,** 1877, **2,** 285–294.
8. Ethical standards for research with children. **SRCD Newsletter,** 1973 (Winter), 3–4.
9. Hall, G. S. The contents of children's minds on entering school. **Pedagogical Seminary,** 1891, **1,** 139–173.
10. Inhelder, B. Some aspects of Piaget's genetic approach to cognition. In W. Kessen & C. Kuhlman (Eds.), Thought in the young child. **Monographs of the Society for Research in Child Development,** 1962, **27**(2), 19–40.
11. Kaplan, A. **The conduct of inquiry: Methodology for behavioral science.** Scranton, Pa.: Chandler, 1964.
12. Kessen, W. Stage and structure in the study of children. In W. Kessen & C. Kuhlman (Eds.), Thought in the young child. **Monographs of the Society for Research in Child Development,** 1962, **27**(2), 65–86.

13. Kessen, W. **The child.** New York: Wiley, 1965.

14. Locke, J. **Some thoughts concerning education;** 1690. London: Cambridge University Press, 1913. Sections 38 and 40.

15. Pestalozzi, J. A father's diary, 1774. Cited by R. De Guimps, **Pestalozzi, his life and work.** New York: Appleton-Century-Crofts, 1906.

16. Piaget, J. **The origins of intelligence in children.** New York: International Universities Press, 1952.

17. Piaget, J. **Logic and psychology.** New York: Basic Books, 1957.

18. Reichenbach, H. **The rise of scientific philosophy.** Berkeley: University of California Press, 1951.

19. Rousseau, J. J. **Emile, or concerning education.** 1762. Book 2. New York: Dutton, 1938.

20. Tiedemann, D. **Beobachtungen ueber die Entwickelung der Seelenfahrigkeiten bei Kindern.** Altenburg: Bonde, 1787.

21. Werner, H. **Comparative psychology of mental development** (Rev. ed.) Chicago: Follet, 1948.

Chapter 2

Theory in Developmental Psychology

The aim of every scientific discipline is to construct a set of principles that will explain certain puzzling events. For example, one such principle in physics is that the momentum of an object is equal to the product of its mass and its velocity. That principle helps us understand what happens when a moving truck hits a standing telephone pole. In mature sciences, such as chemistry and physics, the principles are related to one another and involve the same set of concepts.

Unfortunately, psychology is not as mature a science and has not as yet generated a large set of profound principles. Psychologists have difficulty agreeing on the phenomena that are most important to study and on the best concepts to be used to explain a specific phenomenon. Some believe that the task of psychology is to explain uniformities and differences in overt behaviors like dependency, mastery, suicide, and murder. Others argue that the primary goal of psychology is to understand mental processes like perception, belief, memory, and reasoning.

THE REASONS FOR DEVELOPMENTAL PSYCHOLOGY

A second basis for psychology's difficulty is that the reactions of human beings, unlike atoms or molecules, are influenced by their long history of experiences. This assumption forms one reason for the establishment of the field of developmental psychology. It is unlikely that we will be able to understand the adult unless we appreciate the exact relations between the experiences of infancy and childhood and the skills, desires, and beliefs of the adult. The reasons for interest in the subfield of child development are not unlike those for work in the special discipline within anatomy called embryology. Each of these scientific specialties uncovers facts and devises laws that explain how the adult is formed.

For example, a small minority of adults possess an abnormal genital anatomy in which both a vagina and a penis are present. The anatomist used to wonder how this phenomenon occurred, in as much as there are many possible ways in which it could develop. An answer was provided by careful study of the embryological development of the genital area. All 6-week embryos, both male and female, possess the same small protuberance. Soon a narrow cleft appears in the protuberance, but all the embroys still look exactly alike from an external point of view. After several additional weeks this area stops changing in the female fetus while it continues to be altered in the male. The tissues that we call the labia in a newborn female close over in the male to become the scrotum and the tissue that we call the clitoris in the female continues to grow in the male to become the penis. The anatomical differences between newborn infant males and females are due to the fact that the male genital area continued to differentiate and to grow after the female area stopped changing. Thus when a child is born with both a vagina

31

and a penis it is likely that the cleft did not close completely and the tissue that was the clitoris continued to grow into the larger penis.

The skills, motives, and fears of adults are also better understood if their development is studied from early childhood. For example, American men exceed women in scientific achievement. Many explanations of this sex difference are possible, but we can eliminate certain explanations by studying the young child. The mental development of girls proceeds a bit faster than that of boys during the first few years of life. Compared with boys, infant girls are more sensitive to sounds and sights, comprehend and speak language earlier, and learn to read more quickly during the first years of school. Therefore, the difference in scientific achievement in adulthood cannot be due to early retardation in intellectual development, but must be caused by other factors.

Let us consider one more example of how the understanding of an adult is aided by knowledge of how the adult's personality was formed. Imagine two women who have decided to remain unmarried. One grew up with her biological mother, who was divorced two times. The mother continually reminded her growing daughter that men are exploitative and she persuaded the daughter that marriage was an unsatisfying way of life. When the daughter approached adulthood she had developed a strong resistance to marriage. The second girl grew up in a home that was extremely secure, and she had an affectionate father who wanted her to become a scientist. In order to maintain the father's love she committed herself to college and postgraduate training and decided that marriage would interfere with that career. In her case the decision to remain unmarried was based on affection for her father; the first girl's decision was based on hostility toward her father. These two highly simplified life histories allow us to make some predictions about the future behavior of these two women. The first, a product of two divorces, will be less likely to marry because of her long history of strong hostility toward men. The second woman will be more likely to marry because her decision was based on affection for a man. Although each woman made the same decision during adolescence, these decisions were held with different strength because they were the result of different motives.

Another reason for studying development is to understand the changing organization of wishes, opinions, anxieties, and skills that are present at different phases of the life cycle. Psychological development is not like the growth of a muscle. A strand of muscle merely becomes stronger and larger with age but never changes its basic form. By contrast, children's fears do change their form over time. The typical 3-year-old is most afraid of losing the affection of his parents. However, in the infant and the adolescent this specific anxiety is relatively weak in relation to other fears. The 10-month-old is most afraid of strange situations; the 18-year-old is most afraid of damaging his self-image. In order to understand why a child of a given age behaves as he does, we must know how his motives, fears, and beliefs are organized.

A final reason for studying development is more practical. It is useful to be able to predict adult behavior from knowledge of early experience. For example, a physician treating a depressed patient would like to know whether that patient is a suicide risk. Although many adults become depressed and write suicide notes, the vast majority of these people do not commit suicide. It is of extreme practical importance to be able to predict which adults are most likely to take their own lives, so that one can provide them with some protection from their own impulses. Knowledge of human development suggests that people who are prone to extreme degrees of guilt over violating internal standards are most likely to make a suicide attempt. Hence questioning the patient, as well as his relatives, about his childhood environment and personality helps the psychiatrist make a better prediction of suicide risk.

Prediction of adult behavior from the facts of childhood can sometimes prevent serious adult personality disturbance. Most of the psychological problems that plague man and, in turn, disrupt society are difficult to modify in the adult. Emotional disturbance, homicide, drug addiction, and alcoholism are frequently the result of a history of special experiences with family and friends. If one knew at what age the damaging experiences were most likely to occur, it might be possible to intervene during those periods and alter the course of deviant development. Aggression and violence are serious problems in our society and it would be useful to know the experiences children have during the first decade of their lives that predispose some of them to serious violence as adults. We do not have that knowledge at the present time, but developmental psychologists are trying to obtain it.

There are, therefore, several good reasons why the discipline of developmental psychology has so much vitality. The answers it hopes to provide in the coming decade may illuminate our understanding of man and contribute to the solution of profoundly disturbing social problems.

THE REASONS FOR BEHAVIOR—THE GOALS OF DEVELOPMENT AND THE NATURE OF THE CHILD

As indicated earlier, a theory helps to answer the question, "Why did that happen?" A psychological theory offers an explanation for a particular behavioral reaction, whether it be a motor response, a belief, or a physiological reaction. But whenever we ask about the reasons for a particular behavior, one of four answers is possible. The **immediate reason** refers to the stimulus or the situation that directly preceded or provoked that behavior. For example, we may see a child sobbing and decide that the immediate cause for the distress was his mother's slapping him lightly for telling a lie. The **historical reason** refers to the child's past history of experiences in the home. Since all children do not cry when they are lightly slapped by their mothers, there must be other factors that made this particular child sob. We might decide that he cried because his parents had treated him in a way that made him fear that his mother would withdraw her affection for this misdemeanor. Most psychologists are interested in either the immediate or historical reasons for behavior, or both.

However, neither of these reasons deals with the purpose of the child's behavior. Biologists are more often concerned with the adaptive quality of the behavior. The **adaptive reason** for the child's crying is to communicate to the mother that the child is experiencing distress. The cry acts as a warning to the mother to stop the punishment and to administer some curative affection, as well as to inform her that she has accomplished the goal of indicating to her child that she disapproves of lying.

A final reason, which usually is of little interest to the psychologist but of maximal concern to the evolutionary biologist, is the **evolutionary** basis for the behavior. For example, why do human children cry when they are punished, since young monkeys are likely to cower and assume a submissive posture when punished by their parents. It is assumed that genetic forces operating during the evolution of man are responsible for the fact that the human child cries when slapped by his mother, while the young monkey cowers.

Goals and Direction in Development

When the developmental psychologist addresses himself to the purpose, or the adaptive value, of behavior, he becomes embroiled in one of the two most controversial issues in human development, namely, does the theorist believe **the child is growing toward some ideal goal?** Put another way, should we conceive of psychological development as a sequence of stages that define progress toward a "most mature" level of functioning? Or, alternatively, should we conceive of development merely as a series of lawful changes, without making the extra assumption that there is an optimal endpoint toward which all children move a little each day? American and European psychologists who believe that there is such an ideal goal say that the mission of developmental psychology is to study the details of the child's progress toward maturity. Both Sigmund Freud and Jean Piaget, whose theories we will consider in some detail, made this assumption. Freud's conception of the goal of development emphasized motives and emotions. The mature adult should be relatively free of the anxiety-arousing conflicts acquired during childhood, able to establish a gratifying love relationship with a member of the opposite sex, and capable of effective work relations with others. In simple terms, he should be able to love another and to take deep personal pleasure from relationships with other persons. Piaget's view of the goal of development emphasized intellectual skills. A mature person should be able to deduce conclusions and to think logically about abstract ideas.

Not all developmental psychologists believe in such specific goals for de-

velopment. Learning theorists do not take a strong stand on the issue of whether certain behaviors are more or less mature, for they are primarily concerned with how the child's behavior changes over time. Learning theorists do not assume that the child is necessarily traveling in any special direction, even though his behavior is changing every day. In this sense they resemble the evolutionary biologists. The evolutionary biologists believe that the principal goal of a species is to survive and to reproduce itself successfully. A species accomplishes that goal by becoming optimally adapted to the place in which it nests, feeds, and mates. The specific habits the animal develops will depend upon the specific environment in which it lives. Aside from that demand, there is no ideal goal of development that holds for all species or for members of the same species who live in different environments.

This view has instructive implications for developmental psychologists. Rather than assume that all children in the world should be moving toward the same "best" goal, it is useful to consider the possibility that each child is trying to adapt to the demands of his specific psychological environment. The goal of his development will depend upon the place in which he lives. An Eskimo child, who lives with many other people in a small igloo for nine months of the year, must learn to inhibit all displays of temper and aggression if he is to remain on good terms with his family and friends. Therefore, the ideally mature adult in this setting should be self-controlled and rarely aggressive. By contrast, an urban American child must learn to defend himself against attack from peers and the ideally mature adult should be capable of reacting with appropriate anger and verbal aggression when attacked or threatened. Neither rigid control nor free expression of anger should be regarded as the more mature trait for all people, no matter where they live. Each is appropriate to the setting in which the child and adult must function.

The Nature of the Child—Active or Passive to Enviromental Forces

A second controversial theme in debates about the child centers on whether he is inherently **active** or **passive** with respect to the world of people and objects. Is the child, as John Locke implied, shaped primarily by experience or does he, as Piaget has suggested, actively select the experiences he wishes to understand and exploit? The first view, which has been elaborated in this century by John Watson, Neal Miller, B. F. Skinner, and Albert Bandura, conceives of the child as easily molded into the form its creators intend. The creators are those who have the power to administer rewards and punishments and are the models the child will imitate. Although Freud was not a learning theorist, he, too, thought of the child as passive to biological forces within him. The child was governed by strong instincts and inevitably dragged into conflicts by relationships with parents and siblings.

The conception of the child as basically active places him in greater control of his own development. There are limits to the environment's power to change the child. A 4-year-old cannot reason abstractly, no matter what he has experienced, and a 15-year-old will begin to question the consistency of his beliefs, even if his environment ignores or punishes such curiosity. The active view of the child assumes that the human mind is inherently attracted toward understanding, and maturation will determine when a simple event is regarded as a problem to understand. A 3-year-old will not be provoked to question why lightning storms are more frequent in summer than in winter, while a 10-year-old will be curious about the seasonal pattern. Exploration of the unusual and the mental construction of objects or ideas from some prior blueprint are inherent properties of human beings. The notion that the child carries with him at all times the essential mental ability to understand new experiences and to make a personal contribution to each novel encounter is at the heart of the active view of the child.

Traditional learning theory has viewed the growing child as extremely vulnerable to the words and reactions of the people who block, praise, or punish him and has resisted giving the child any compass of his own. The active view assumes that the mind has a plan for growth and can make sense of an unusually shaped tree, an odd pain, or a stranger's unexpected smile.

Alternative Views of Development

Although Piaget is an idealist as far as developmental goals are concerned, it is possible to assume that the child is active without assuming some universal developmental goal at maturity. Hence most developmental theorists can be placed in one of four categories, depending on their assumptions concerning, first, the goals of development and, second, the active-passive dimension. The following table summarizes these categories.

The differences in assumptions among the major theorists—Freud, Piaget, and Skinner—derive in part from the fact that each is concerned with slightly different aspects of the child and each wants to explain different facets of his development. Moreover, there is at present no major theory or theorist associated with the category that describes the active child who may not necessarily be growing

Table 2.1 **Categories of developmental theories**

	Ideal goal for development for all environmental settings	No ideal goal for development for all settings
Child actively selects experience	Piagetian theory	Newer cognitive theorists
Child reacts passively to experience	Freudian psychoanalytic theory	Learning theory (Skinner, Bandura)

toward a set of goals that are appropriate for all settings. We shall now discuss each of the four theoretical approaches, beginning with a brief description of the cognitive view because it is the least completely worked out. We shall then proceed to more detailed consideration of Piaget, Freud, and the learning theorists.

A COGNITIVE-ADAPTIVE APPROACH TO DEVELOPMENT

A cognitive-adaptive theory views the child as active but not necessarily growing toward any specific, ideal goal. This theory, borrowing heavily from Piaget, conceives of the child as attempting to make sense of his experience; behavior is not completely shaped by environmental rewards and punishments. However, this theory questions the notion that there is an absolute, optimal goal for all children, and is like learning theory in viewing growth as more open ended and relativistic. Each child lives in a specific family and community and tries to adapt to the demands of both contexts. Further, there are biological limitations at each age. The 2-year-old is not able to think about his experience the way a 12-year-old does.

The desire to resolve uncertainty is regarded as an important driving force in development, that is, the child is motivated to behave when he is confronted with situations or tasks that have moderate uncertainty. For example, if there is no uncertainty over attaining a particular goal, a child will have minimal desire to strive toward that goal. If the uncertainty is too great, he may withdraw. Put more specifically, if the child is certain of his inability to learn a new skill, reading for example, this expectancy of failure will lead him to withdraw effort from the task.

There are two major obstacles to the elaboration of a cognitive-adaptive approach. One is its current inability to specify the mechanisms by which the child resolves uncertainty and moves on to the next stage of development. Second, this theory has difficulty stating why a particular event provokes uncertainty at one age but not at an earlier one.

THE THEORY OF JEAN PIAGET

Jean Piaget, the Swiss psychologist, views the child as trying to make sense of his world by dealing actively with objects and people. From encounters with events he moves steadily toward the ideal goal of abstract reasoning. Piaget has had an extraordinary influence on modern developmental psychology. He has stimulated an interest in maturational stages of development and in the importance of cognition for many aspects of psychological functioning, and has acted as a constructive counterforce to the view that the child's beliefs, thoughts, and ways of approaching problems are primarily the result of what he is taught directly.

Piaget believes that the goals of development include the ability (1) to reason abstractly, (2) to think about hypothetical situations in a logical way, and (3) to organize rules, which Piaget calls operations, into complex, higher order structures. The important ideas in Piaget's theory are considered below.

Construction and Invention

The child is actively trying to make sense of his experience, attempting to understand that which is odd and to fit his ideas into a coherent whole. Piaget focuses on the fact that children invent ideas and behaviors that they have never witnessed or had reinforced. For example, in contrast to the 5-year-old, the typical 7-year-old appreciates that a set of sticks of different lengths or a set of cups of different diameters can be arranged in a series according to their length or diameter. The 7-year-old need not have ever witnessed this arrangement nor have been told about it by any adult. It is one of the discoveries of intellectual growth. The learning theorist, by contrast, focuses on behaviors that are imitative copies of what he has seen or extensions of actions that have been rewarded. Piaget says,

> The problem we must solve, in order to explain cognitive development, is that of invention and not of mere copying. And neither stimulus-response generalization nor the introduction of transformational responses can explain novelty or invention. . . . We would like to point out how peculiar it is that so many American and Soviet psychologists, citizens of great nations, which intend to change the world, have produced learning theory that reduces knowledge to a passive copy of external reality, whereas, human thought always transforms or transcends reality. Outstanding sectors of mathematics have no counterpart in physical reality and all mathematical techniques result in new combinations which enrich reality. To present an adequate notion of learning one first must explain how the subject manages to construct and invent not merely how he repeats and copies (**31**, 714).

The Acquisition of Operations

The central concept in Piaget's theory is the **operation** (**30**). An operation is a special kind of mental routine whose chief characteristic is that it is reversible. Every operation has a logical opposite. The rule that we square the number 8 in order to get 64 is part of an operation, for we can perform the reverse operation and extract the square root of 64 to obtain 8. The knowledge that we can break a circular piece of clay into two elliptical pieces and combine the two ellipses into the same circular whole is also an operation.

Appreciation of the fact that the amount of water in a glass does not change when we transfer it to a container of a different shape is also an operation, for we know we can restore the original state of affairs by pouring the water back into its original glass. The operation allows the child to return mentally to where he began. **The acquisition of operations is the heart of intellectual growth.**

Some rules are not operations. The 7-year-old knows that if he tells a lie he will provoke his parent's anger, but this rule is not reversible for he does not know how to restore his mother's good mood. Most factual rules—oceans contain water, cars are noisy, summers are hot—are not operations. Piaget believes that the child passes through stages acquiring different classes of operations until he gradually arrives at the most mature stage during adolescence. The two major mechanisms that allow the child to move from one stage to the next are assimilation and accommodation.

Assimilation

Assimilation is the incorporation of a new object or idea into an idea or scheme the child already has. (Piaget uses the word schema [schemata, pl.] to stand for the infant's perceptual-motor coordinations, for example, searching for objects or pulling a string.) At each age a child has an existing set of actions or operations. New objects or new ideas are assimilated to older ones. A 1-year-old has acquired a schema for small objects that involves shaking and biting them. When he is given a new object, say, a bar magnet, he reacts to it as he does to all small objects and he shakes or bites it. This application of older schemata of action to a new action is assimilation. In simple language, assimilation is applying old ideas and old habits to new objects and viewing new events as part of existing schemata.

Accommodation and Equilibration

Accommodation is the tendency to adjust to a new object, to change one's schemata of action to fit the new object. The 2-year-old child who had never been exposed to a new magnet may initially assimilate it to his prior schemata and act toward the magnet as he does toward a familiar toy. He may bang it, bounce it, throw it, or try to make it produce a noise. But once he discovers the unique quality of the magnet, that it attracts metal, he will now accommodate to that quality and begins to apply the magnet to a variety of objects to see if they will adhere to it.

Mental growth involves resolution of the tension between assimilation and accommodation, the conflict between using old responses for new situations and acquiring new (or changing old) responses to fit new problems. Intellectual growth occurs as the child adapts to new situations. Initially the child assimilates most problems to his existing schemata. If his father plays a game with him in which the child must guess which of the father's hands contains a small toy, the child may adopt a position habit and always choose the father's right hand, even though the father is alternating the toy from right to left. Eventually the child accommodates to the problem and learns the rule that the father is using.

Each time that the child accommodates to a new event or problem his intellectual growth is nudged closer to maturity, for he has changed his ideas about the world and generated a more adaptive scheme. This adaptation is called **equilibra-**

tion. Initially the child attempts to understand a new experience by using old ideas and solutions. When they do not work, he is forced to change his understanding of the world so that eventually the new event is in harmony with his prior beliefs. One day his intellectual functioning will have matured to a point where he will be capable of a new way of thinking about an old problem, assuming his experiences and knowledge have kept pace with his biological growth. At this point, the child will pass from one stage of intelligence to the next.

Sequential Developmental Stages

As we shall see in Chapter 7, Piaget believes that there are four major stages of intellectual development: sensorimotor (0 to 18 months), preoperational (18 months to age 7), concrete operations (age 7 to 12), and finally formal operations (age 12 onward). The stages are continuous and each is built upon and is a derivative of the earlier one. Piaget believes that no child can skip any stage since each new stage borrows from the accomplishments of the earlier ones. Every new experience is grafted onto what exists and there is always a relation between the child's present ability and beliefs and all of his past.

This hypothesis may be true, but not necessarily. Consider the building of a house as an analogy. During the initial weeks of construction each new piece of wood is added to the existing frame and there is a direct relation of each new part to what existed before. But suppose that after three-quarters of the house were built a second set of carpenters started to replace the older walls, pipe, and wire with new parts in a new architectural design. When the house was finally finished there would be a minimal relation between the early components and the later ones. Put in a slightly different context, it is possible to renovate a 100-year-old house so that eventually every part of the new building is new without the house ever falling down or being obliterated. This is a different view of the growth of psychological processes which is, at the moment, as plausible as Piaget's suggestion that each new development is based on what transpired earlier.

Since the essence of Piaget's theory and data is so central to the discussion of Chapter 7 we shall present that information later along with a more detailed critique of Piagetian theory.

FREUD AND PSYCHOANALYTIC THEORY

Like Piaget, Sigmund Freud had a specific conception of the goals of maturity. Freud's goals included the ability to enter into sexually gratifying love relationships with a member of the opposite sex, productive use of one's talents, and relative freedom from the conflicts and anxiety that lead to personal anguish and behavioral symptoms (**9**). In short, Freud emphasized emotional maturity as the desired prize, while Piaget emphasized reasoning. The two theorists also differed in the facets of psychological functioning with which they were concerned. Piaget was primarily concerned with regularities in growth of thought rather than with individual differences in those regularities among children of the same age. Freud was preoccupied with the wishes, feelings, and fears of children and interested in the personality differences among them. Piaget obtained most of his ideas in observing and talking with middle-class children. Freud obtained most of his ideas about development in listening to the childhood experiences of anxious adults who had sought psychiatric help. Each man focused on a different set of phenomena and gathered information in different ways from different sources. The two theorists wanted to understand different aspects of human development.

According to Freud, the infant and young child are helpless in the face of powerful biological and social forces over which they have little control. These forces include instinctual energy, which is biological in origin, and the social experiences that are part of family life. All children, Freud believed, develop sexual and hostile feelings toward their parents which lead to conflict, anxiety, and, in some, to neurosis.

Biological Energy

Freud's most basic concept was the **biological energy** that he postulated as the source of all basic drives. The child is born with a fixed amount of energy which underlies all of his future behaviors, motives, and thoughts. Although Freud never said so explicitly, he seemed to conceive of psychological energy the way a physicist conceives of the physical energy in a nuclear reactor. The amount of energy is fixed, but it can be channeled in different ways. One of the major reasons for the decreased influence in recent years of some aspects of psychoanalytic theory is that scientists have been unable to measure this "psychological energy."

The three sources of energy—or instinct—are sexuality (sometimes called libido), the life-preserving drives of hunger and pain, and aggression. Freud associated the latter with a "death instinct" (**9**). The function of experience is to bind energy to people, actions, thoughts, and objects the way a person might reach into a cauldron of boiling wax, withdraw single strands, and tie them to objects and people in the world. Each strand would reduce the total amount of wax in the cauldron by some fixed amount. Similarly, binding energy to experiences reduces the total amount of energy available to the person. The process by which sources of energy are tied to, or invested in, thoughts, actions, objects, and people is called **cathexis.**

Psychological Structure

Cathexis is as dynamic and central a process in Freudian theory as equilibration is in Piaget's theory. In Piagetian theory, encounter with an event that is not immediately understandable provokes the psychological processes of assimilation, accommodation, and equilibration. For Freud, excitation of energy is the basic force that provokes action. Reduction of that excitation is the goal. Since the newborn infant only possesses energy, he is born with only one psychological structure, the **id.** The id should be viewed as a storehouse for instinctual energy. As the infant grows and attaches energy to things, he gradually develops two additional psychological structures, the **ego** and **superego.** The ego is that part of the child's makeup that contains his skills, learned wishes, fears, language, sense of self, and consciousness. The superego, which is simply translated as conscience, emerges during the preschool years. When id, ego, and superego are all functioning after age 5 or 6, it is necessary that they function harmoniously, despite the fact that the id demands pleasure now and the superego—acting as strict court justice—demands postponement of pleasure and the carrying out of responsibilities. The function of the ego is to act as wise mediator.

The inevitable conflicts among id, ego, and superego lead to the major sources of distress and tension, which Freud called **anxiety** (10). The ego continually tries to reduce the anxiety by realistic measures. When the ego is unsuccessful, either because the anxiety is too intense or the ego's skills are not sophisticated enough, **defenses** will develop. These defenses can grow into thoughts and actions that psychiatrists call **symptoms.** Some major symptoms include phobias, rituals, obsessions, depression, and aggression. One of the most efficient defenses against anxiety is **repression,** which is the ego's attempt to remove anxiety-arousing ideas from consciousness to unconsciousness. The suggestion that wishes and ideas can be unavailable to consciousness, that is, that they can be unconscious, and still influence a child's behavior is one of the most original and useful ideas in psychoanalytic theory. Over three-quarters of a century after Freud wrote the initial outline of his theory, the notion of the unconscious remains as one of psychology's most powerful ideas.

Psychoanalytic Developmental Stages

Like Piaget, Freud also believed that the child passed through stages (11). But the psychoanalytic stages do not refer to quality of reasoning but rather to the bodily zones that are most highly cathected, the places on the body where the primary sources of pleasure are found.

During infancy, the area and activities surrounding the mouth and feeding are cathected with energy and the infant experiences much pleasure from oral activity. Hence the stage is called the **oral stage.**

During the second and third years the anal area and the activities surrounding defecation become cathected. The child now experiences sensory delight from stimulation of the rectal area as the result of his own defecatory activities, as well as touching, bathing, and smelling the anal region and its products, hence the name **anal stage.**

During the preschool years the genitals become cathected as a primary source of pleasure; hence the name **phallic stage.** During the phallic stage the child begins to identify with the parent of the same sex, because of a process called the **Oedipal conflict.** Freud believed that the phallic-age child has fantasy wishes for sexual affection from the parent of the opposite sex. The child is unconsciously afraid that the same-sex parent will learn of these desires and become angry with the child. In order to reduce this anxiety over possible retaliation by the same-sex parent, the child defends himself by identifying with the same-sex parent, a process similar to an adult's joining a group which has power over him. The child's identification leads him to adopt the values of the same-sex parent. Since most of these values are the "do's-and-the-do-not's" of society, the child's superego is born. Because the strength of the child's superego will influence the kinds of symptoms, if any, that he will develop later, the intensity of his Oedipal conflict is an important determinant of adult personality (see p. 396). Finally, in adolescence, love objects become cathected, hence the name **genital stage.**

If the cathexis during any stage is too intense, the child becomes **fixated,** that is, he resists moving on to the next stage. Fixation can occur if the child receives either too much or too little pleasure during a certain stage of development. Note how passive and helpless Freud made the child. Piaget never suggested that a child could not move from the stage of sensorimotor to concrete operations or from concrete to formal operations. There is no notion of fixation in Piagetian theory for Piaget sees the child as always growing. By contrast, Freud felt that adverse environmental experiences could prevent a child from making further progress toward emotional maturity.

If a child becomes fixated at any of the early stages, predictions about his future personality are possible. Fixation at each of the stages is supposed to have different implications for adult personality. It was a bold suggestion that insufficient or excessive pleasure during the oral stage would have a permanent effect on the child and might lead to adult symptoms like alcoholism, depression, or excessive optimism and pessimism. Fixation at the anal stage presumably leads to miserliness, compulsivity, aggression, and passive resistance. Pompousness, narcissism, and boastfulness are derivative of fixation at the phallic stage. At the moment these ideas must be regarded as hypothetical, but they are imaginative.

Validity of Freudian Theory

Freud's ideas have all the major requirements for a theory of personality development. Freud invented a set of fundamental concepts—energy, id, ego, superego, anxiety, and defense; a set of mechanisms that explained changes from one stage to another—cathexis, fixation, repression, and identification; and a set of theoretical predictions that followed from the relations between the concepts and the mechanisms. Psychoanalytic theory is a good model of what a theory should be, even though it contains very loose definitions of a number of basic concepts.

Research and social change in our society over the past half-century have cast some doubt on the validity of some aspects of Freud's theory. Investigations have failed to show that excessive pleasure or frustration during the oral or anal stages produces the particular symptoms that the theory predicted. There is no good evidence, pro or con, that suicidal patients are fixated at the oral stage or that adults who are negativistic or hoard money are fixated at the anal stage. Moreover, Freudian theory predicts that decreases in anxiety surrounding sexuality should inevitably lead to increased happiness and fewer neurotic defenses. Although there has been a marked increase in anxiety-free sexuality in contemporary America during the last 20 years, there is still considerable individual anxiety and conflict surrounding commitment to goals and people and an increased reliance on drugs and violence as ways of resolving conflict. The prevalence of the symptoms of apathy, drug addiction, and violence suggests that sexual conflict is probably not the only —perhaps, not even the primary—basis of anxiety, defense, and neurosis. It is for these reasons that psychoanalytic theory has lost some of its vitality and early popularity.

But modern psychology and psychiatry have retained several of Freud's basic insights. They continue to believe that unconscious motives and ideas can influence action and thought, that early experience influences later personality, that the child has sexual wishes which make him anxious and lead to defenses, and that dreams contain symbolic representations of wishes and fears. These four major insights are of extraordinary importance for understanding man, and Sigmund Freud must be credited for these illuminating ideas.

LEARNING THEORY

Learning theory, unlike Piagetian or Freudian theory, is primarily concerned with the overt behavior of the child, rather than his problem-solving, thinking, wishes, or feelings. It stresses the power of the environment, minimizes the role of biological maturation, and concentrates on changes in the habits and beliefs of the child as a function of his models and the changing patterns of reward and punishment he experiences as he grows. Hence learning theory would explain a young boy's increasing fear of his father during the period 4 through 8 years as the result of actual or threatened punishment by the father, rather than as a result of the boy's fantasy that the father viewed him as a potential rival for the mother's affection.

Although learning theory acknowledges historical reasons for behavior, it gives particular emphasis to the immediate causes of behavior—the stimuli in the present situation that evoke a particular action. Because learning theorists do not emphasize the importance of maturation as a cause of change, they are not concerned with stages of development and do not celebrate any progression toward some particular goal. There is no "ideal" adult in learning theory.

The child is viewed as a relatively malleable creature who wants more pleasure and less pain and will adopt whatever behaviors will maximize attainment of these goals. The learning theorists assume that what is learned will be determined by the environment in which the child grows. If the environment rewards altruism and punishes competition, altruistic 18-year-olds will be rewarded as more "mature" than competitive ones. But if the environment happens to reward competitiveness and punish altruism, the former would be regarded as more "mature." In a sense, the learning theorists are like the evolutionary biologists who see adaptation of a species to its ecological niche as the goal of a successful life.

What Is Learning

Stated most simply, learning is the process by which behavior or the potentiality for behavior, is modified as a result of experience (16, 19). Learning refers to both the acquisition of a totally new response and the change in the frequency of an action that is already in the child's repertoire. That is, we must distinguish between learning to play tennis, which is a totally new set of motor coordinations, and learning "not to cry" when one falls down. Since crying is an innate response the child learns to alter the circumstances in which he displays that behavior.

The learning theorist proposes two basic mechanisms of behavior change—**forming associations through conditioning** and **observation of models.** These mechanisms are the means by which new behaviors are acquired as well as the reasons for changes in the form and frequency with which existing actions are displayed. Learning represents the establishment of new associations—bonds or connections—between units that were not previously associated. There may be associations between (1) external stimuli and overt responses, (2) external stimuli and internal processes, (3) internal processes and overt responses, or (4) a pair or more of internal processes. Consider an illustration of each of these four types of associations: (1) the child learns an association between the sight of a ball (an external event) and bouncing it (an overt response); (2) he learns an association between the sight of his mother going to the refrigerator (an external event) with the idea (internal process) of a glass of milk; (3) he learns an association between the image (internal process) of his mother walking out the front door and the act of whining or crying (overt response); (4) he learns an association between the thought (internal process) of his father coming in the front door and the thought of playing with his father in the living room.

There has been some doubt about how early in life learning can occur. Recent research indicates that learning may occur from the first day of life, although new responses are established more easily as the child matures. A 3-day-old newborn can learn to turn his head in the direction of the sound of a bell through classical conditioning procedures. The infant lies on his back in a crib and a bell is sounded on the right side of his head. If he does not turn his head to the right when the bell sounds, the experimenter lightly touches the corner of his mouth on the right side in order to facilitate the infant's turning in that direction. When he turns, he is allowed to suck on a bottle containing milk. This pairing of the sound of a bell with receipt of milk, if he turns to the right, is repeated 10 times for each feeding session. The 3-day-old requires about 17 or 18 such feeding sessions (about 177 trials) to learn to turn his head to the right every time the bell sounds, without someone's stimulating the corner of his mouth. He has learned an association between the external stimulus of a bell and the response of turning his head to the right. Infants who are 85 days old require only 42 trials to learn the association; infants 20 weeks old require only an average of 27 trials (28). This dramatic difference in ease of learning this conditioned response is due, in large measure, to the lack of alertness and minimal attentiveness of the newborn baby, rather than to differences in the ability to make the response of turning the head.

The stimuli and responses involved in learning are of many different kinds. A person who learns to respond to a stop light by applying his foot to the brake of his car has established an association between a visual stimulus (the light) and a motor response (braking). The sight of a mother's face or the sound of her voice and internal events like thoughts, feelings, and bodily sensations are also stimuli. Each of these stimuli can be associated with responses.

Similarly, responses can be of many kinds. They can be motor acts like talking, walking, or hitting a baseball or physiological responses like sweating or changes in heart rate. Changes in internal processes—images, beliefs, thoughts, and schemata—are believed to be governed by processes slightly different from those that govern motor acts. Mental structures can be more easily altered and incorporated into other internal processes than motor responses. As Piaget suggests, operations are reversible. A child can run off a series of thoughts and then re-run them mentally in reverse order. It is difficult to simulate reversibility with motor acts—try walking backwards or performing a routine motor habit in reverse.

More important, new symbols and concepts can usually be learned following one exposure, for a child can learn what a "thimble" means after only one explanation. It is more difficult to teach a new motor behavior to a child in only one trial. Furthermore, thoughts and beliefs are evaluated for their consistency and logic and many are regarded as true or false. This is not true of overt behavior. The child is bothered by inconsistency in his thoughts and rejects beliefs he thinks are false. As a result, a child's beliefs can be changed if he encounters an event that is inconsistent with his total set of opinions. A 14-year-old broods about the inconsistency among the following three ideas: (1) God loves man; (2) the world contains many unhappy people; (3) if God loved man, he would not make so many people unhappy. The adolescent is immediately troubled by the incompatibility that is sensed when he examines these statements together. He notes the contradiction and has four choices. He can deny the first premise, that God loves man; this is avoided for love of man is one of the definitional qualities of God. He can deny the second premise, that man is unhappy; that is unlikely for its factual basis is overwhelming. He can assume that the unhappiness serves an ultimate purpose that God has for man; this possibility is often chosen. Finally, he can deny the hypothesis that God exists. Many beliefs about important issues are changed as a result of noting inconsistency and this process can be independent of rewards, punishments, or exposure to models. Hence changes in beliefs and thoughts may not conform to the same laws that apply to changes in overt behavior.

What Learning Is Not

Not all behavior is learned. Some response tendencies exist at birth and even during prenatal life. The pupillary reflex (contraction of the pupil in response to light) has been observed even in premature infants. Many other responses of infants—swallowing, opening and closing the eyes, shuddering in response to a bitter taste, grasping when pressure is applied to the palm—are unlearned.

While the unlearned nature of such "basic" responses may seem obvious to the reader, there are other instances of unlearned behavior which are by no means so evident. One might assume that the tendency of baby ducklings—even ugly ones —to follow their mothers results from their having learned the value of this response through experience. But such is not the case, as the work of animal ethologists has demonstrated (15, 21, 38). The actual fact is that young ducklings, and some animals of other species as well, are born with a tendency to accept a certain range of "mother-figures," characterized by general size, patterns of movement, and sounds. Once any particular "mother" has been accepted and followed, only this particular figure will produce the "following response." Of course, under normal conditions of existence, this figure will be the actual mother. But if these conditions are changed for experimental purposes or by accidents of nature, the "following response" may be obtained to other figures: a toy duck, a goose, or even a distinguished, large, and impressive ethologist such as Professor Konrad Lorenz, who has investigated this phenomenon, technically referred to as **imprinting** (15, 21).

Other equally complex and surprising examples of unlearned behavior have been studied by ethologists. For example, it has been determined in the case of the male stickleback fish that a very specific visual stimulus (namely, a red underbelly) in another fish will provoke complex fighting behavior. In contrast, a smaller, nonred underbelly will elicit courting behavior. Even dummies that look very little like another stickleback fish will provoke these responses as long as the essential key stimulus is present (8, 21).

TYPES OF LEARNING

Having discussed briefly what learning is, and what it is not, let us turn our attention to some basic examples of learning in order to consider, first, what the essential components of any learning situation are and, second, what general principles may be derived to help us to understand (and hopefully to control and predict) learning.

Much of our knowledge regarding learning and its principles stems from studies in which an external stimulus has been associated with an overt external response (e.g., learning to press a lever in response to the stimulus of a light). There are, however, other types of learning that have received increased attention recently, and we will discuss some of the more important of them later in this chapter. While in some instances these other types of learning are more complex, many of the basic principles of learning derived from simple stimulus-response experiments are still applicable. Thus, it is desirable to consider simpler forms of learning first, in order to establish some of the basic principles of learning.

Classical and Operant Conditioning

Classical conditioning The most common, and perhaps the most basic, category of learning involves the establishment of an association between an external stimulus and a response, where prior to learning no such connection existed. Classical conditioning is the purest example of such learning. In classical conditioning a **reflex response,** that is, a response innately elicited by a specific stimulus, such as removing one's hand from a fire or blinking in response to a very bright light, is associated with a previously neutral stimulus. The response can be an overt action (an eye blink or the withdrawal of a hand) or a physiological reaction (salivation or a change in heart rate), but, in classical conditioning, it is always a naturally reflexive reaction to a particular stimulus.

Most readers have already heard of one famous example of classical conditioning, although they may not have thought of it in these terms. Pavlov's pioneering experiments with salivation in dogs have been discussed far beyond the frontiers of psychology—often with considerable dramatic license. They may be viewed either as an illustration of man's ability to control his fate in an orderly fashion or, with equal inaccuracy, as a sign of an impending Orwellian world of **1984,** characterized by thought control, loss of individual freedom, and the development of a race of human robots subject only to the whims of an all-powerful state.

What did Pavlov actually demonstrate? In essence, he showed that a dog can be taught to salivate to the stimulus (or **cue**) of a buzzer (see Fig. 2.1). This was accomplished by pairing the presentation of the sound of the buzzer with the presentation of food. Food is a stimulus that innately (i.e., without learning) elicits the salivation response. Salivation does not ordinarily occur to the cue of a buzzer, but

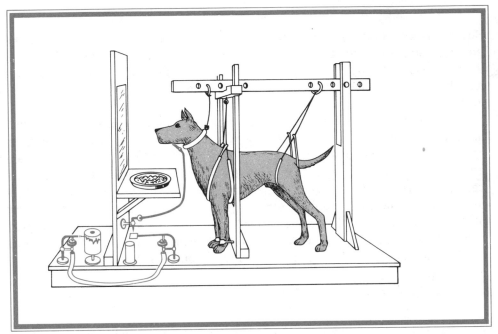

Figure 2.1 Pavlov's dog. The dog is strapped into a harness in which it has grown used to standing. A tube attached to the dog's salivary gland collects any saliva secreted by the gland, and the number of drops from the tube is recorded on a revolving drum outside the chamber. A laboratory attendant can watch the dog through a one-way mirror and can deliver food to the dog's feedpan by remote control. Thus, there is nothing in the chamber to distract the dog's attention except the food, when it is delivered, and any other stimulus that the attendant wishes to present, such as the sound of a metronome. (After R. M. Yerkes & S. Morgulis. The method of Pavlov in animal behavior. **Psychological Bulletin,** 1909, **6** [8], 257–273.)

as a result of repeated pairings of the buzzer with the food, the buzzer sound alone becomes capable of eliciting the salivation response. In other words, a connection or association is learned between the cue of the buzzer and the response of salivation, when prior to learning this connection did not exist.

Let us consider a somewhat more complex case. Dorothy Marquis has studied the infant's very early learning in relation to feeding (**25**). Working with 10 infants between 2 and 9 days of age, she sounded a buzzer in their presence 5 seconds prior to each feeding. Within 5 days after the beginning of this training, 8 of these infants began to exhibit sucking and mouth-opening responses (innate responses to the stimulation of a nipple) as soon as they heard the buzzer. She also noted that the sound of the buzzer tended to reduce crying and general activity. Four control infants heard the sound of the buzzer but were not fed immediately afterward. These infants did not manifest sucking and mouth-opening behaviors in response to the buzzer. In short, the first group of infants learned to suck to the cue of a buzzer as a result of the pairing of the sound of the buzzer with feeding.

It may be noted that in each of the above examples of classical conditioned learning, elicitation of the desired response was automatic. In the case of Pavlov's dog, food is a stimulus that innately produces salivation; similarly, in the case of Marquis' infant, the presence of a bottle in the mouth initiates the inborn sucking reflex.

In classical conditioning a new association is established between an external stimulus and a response that is basically a reflex. Similar associations are continually being established in the young infant. The stimulus of a nipple placed in the infant's mouth elicits sucking movements innately, but the sight of the bottle does not. Yet after several months of bottlefeeding, the infant will begin to make sucking movements when he sees the bottle (20, 25).

Operant conditioning Another example of learning that involves a new relation between a stimulus and an overt response is called **operant** or **instrumental conditioning** or **operant learning.** Here the overt response that is being connected with a new stimulus is not a reflex. An example would be the familiar task of teaching a dog to "shake hands." No known stimulus innately produces such behavior. Instead, the response itself must be gradually and carefully developed, through a technique known as instrumental or operant conditioning. In essence, this technique involves rewarding appropriate responses whenever they happen to occur. In this procedure, the subject's own response is instrumental to the production of the reward—it operates to bring about the reward, hence the term instrumental or operant conditioning.

In some learning situations, the experimenter may simply sit around and wait for the proper response to occur by chance. One of the most common operant learning situations employed by psychologists in recent years involves the use of the Skinner box, named after the innovator and most productive investigator of operant conditioning. Typically, this apparatus consists of a small soundproof box containing a little lever, a food cup, and perhaps a light. The task of an animal placed in the box is to press the lever in order to obtain food. The animal may make many irrelevant responses when first placed in the box, such as running around, attempting to climb a wall, or scratching himself. Eventually, however, he is likely to press the lever, if only by chance. When he does so, he is automatically rewarded by a small pellet of food dropped in the food cup. With continued experience in this situation, the animal becomes increasingly quick and adept in lever-pressing, and irrelevant responses tend to disappear.

In other situations, the experimenter may not wait for chance alone to produce the proper response, but may take steps to increase the likelihood of the proper response's occurring. This, of course, is one of the skills displayed by experienced trainers—and many mothers as well! In the case of the dog being taught to "shake hands," for example, the proper response may be suggested by passive movement of the paw by the trainer, or it may be elicited by a mild shock to the limb, followed by reward. Of course, even in instrumental conditioning, the desired response must be potentially available in the person's or animal's repertoire of possible responses. Even the most ingenious experimenter cannot teach a dog to pronounce the sounds of the alphabet.

Nevertheless, recent investigators, stimulated in large measure by the pioneering work of Skinner and his associates (32, 33, 34), have produced impressive learning in a wide variety of challenging situations by using operant conditioning techniques. By ingenious arrangements of experimental conditions and judicious use of rewards, and sometimes punishments, they have been able to "shape" rather elaborate response patterns under often difficult circumstances, such as teaching pigeons to play ping-pong.

In both classical and operant conditioning, the new association can be between a stimulus and an overt response or between a stimulus and a physiological reaction. The major difference between classical conditioning and operant conditioning is that in classical conditioning the response already exists and only has to be connected to a new stimulus. In operant conditioning the response, particularly one that is complex, must usually be gradually and carefully developed. Initially, a rat placed in a Skinner box does not make the response of pressing the bar. A strong association is gradually established between the sight of the bar and the response of pressing the bar, when prior to this learning the association was nonexistent or very weak. Children acquire many operant associations of this kind. They learn to open doors, to turn on faucets, to hold baseball bats, to write with pencils, and to ring doorbells.

Lovaas and his associates (22, 23, 24) at the University of California at Los Angeles have employed similar techniques of "behavior therapy" in an attempt to increase social responsiveness and to reduce the incidence of self-destructive and self-mutilating behavior in severely withdrawn, psychotic children. Many of these children had been in treatment for extensive periods with no improvement; others had been rejected from treatment because they were poor treatment risks.

> Some of the children were completely unresponsive to social stimuli and evidenced no social or intellectual behavior. They were so oblivious to their surroundings that they behaved as if they were blind and deaf. They were completely engrossed in self-stimulatory behaviors, such as spinning objects, rocking in sitting or standing positions, twirling, flapping their wrists, and gazing at lights and at their cupped hands (22, 8).

In a significant percentage of the children, vocal behaviors were limited to occasional vowel sounds having no discernible communicative intent. Others engaged in **echolalia** (simply repeating whatever sounds they hear).

Using a systematic, carefully controlled program of rewards (for example, food and attention) and punishments (removal of food and withdrawal of affection), these investigators have been able, in successive stages, to increase the incidence of meaningful speech ("I want a cookie") and to reduce the incidence of meaningless, echolalic, or psychotic speech ("spaghetti Irene," "helicopter pillow" (22, 23). They have also been able to reduce self-destructive and self-mutilative behavior and to increase social approaches to adults by using various rewards and punishments, including isolation and electric shock (22). Use of such punishment with children has provoked considerable controversy. However, the authors point out that the alternatives with such severely disturbed children may be much more deleterious. Some children had bitten large chunks of flesh from their own bodies or hit their heads so severely that they broke their nose-bones or detached their retinas. Some had blinded themselves. In this context, the authors view their training procedures, including the use of punishment, as "an act of affection" (22).

In still other studies (5, 17, 37) behavior-modification procedures have been used to promote training in basic social responses among mentally retarded children. In one study (17) toilet training proceeded efficiently when successful elimination was rewarded with candy, and in another study (5) such self-help activities as eating, dressing, and drying hands were facilitated through similar procedures. Similar methods have been used to improve children's reading skills (36, 40) and to reduce overly aggressive behavior among nursery-school children (7).

Observational Learning

Learning many complicated tasks would be extremely difficult if conditioning were the only means by which correct learning could be encouraged. Many human activities are acquired by watching another person or, in other words, by observation. Thus, the teacher may interrupt the student's efforts in order to demonstrate a correct response. If at least the elements of a correct response are already present in the subject's response repertoire, observation can play a significant role in promoting learning.

Observational learning also occurs in animals. Studies have shown that cats will learn to press a lever for food with greater ease if they first watch a well-trained cat perform this response than if they are taught only by traditional operant conditioning procedures in which they receive milk each time they make the response (18).

Bandura and Walters (2, 3, 4) and their associates have demonstrated the usefulness of observational learning in children. They have also provided a great deal of information regarding factors that influence the likelihood of a subject's subsequently imitating responses acquired through observation.

In a typical experiment by these investigators a child is exposed to a real-life or filmed model, either child or adult. The model then performs a series of actions (e.g., pummeling an inflated doll as in Fig. 2.2). Later the child is tested to determine the extent to which he mimics the behavior displayed by the model. His be-

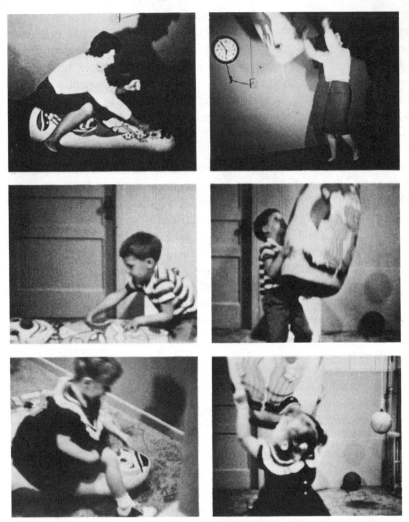

Figure 2.2 Photographs of children reproducing the aggressive behavior of the female model they observed on film. (From A. Bandura, D. Ross, & S. A. Ross. Imitation of film-mediated aggressive models. **Journal of Abnormal and Social Psychology,** 1963, **66,** 8. Published by the American Psychological Association. By permission.)

havior may then be compared with that of control subjects who have not observed the model.

By means of such techniques the effectiveness of observational learning has been demonstrated over a wide range of behaviors, and many variations in the situation can be examined to determine their effects on the subject's tendency to mimic the behavior he has observed. Subjects are more likely to imitate the behavior of prestigeful than nonprestigeful models. Models who are similar to the

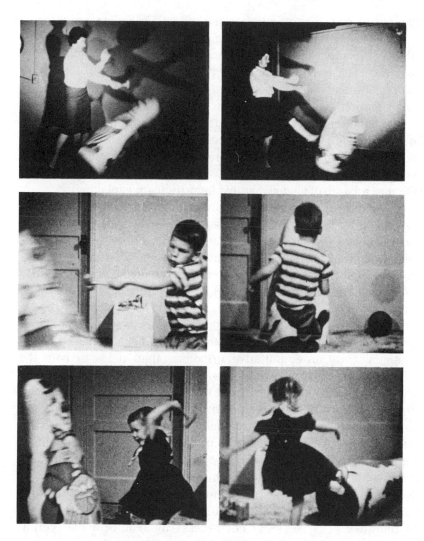

subject themselves have a greater effect on behavior than dissimilar models, for example, the tendency to mimic is greater if the model is another child than if it is a cartoon animal. Children are also more likely to imitate the behavior of models who are rewarded for their actions than those who are punished or not rewarded.

Certain aspects of these investigations are of particular interest. As we have noted earlier, learning of responses and response sequences requires attention to relevant stimuli in the situation. Bandura notes that "motivational factors or the anticipation of positive or negative reinforcement may augment or reduce the probability of occurrence of observing responses" (4, 59)—obviously an essential element in imitative learning. This general readiness may be increased or decreased by a wide variety of factors. These include: the motivational set of given subjects (instructions to pay close attention to the model's behavior, promises of future rewards for subsequent accurate imitation of the model's behavior, and the like); the child's readiness to notice certain elements in the model's behavior on the basis of past experience (Bandura cites one experiment (39) in which advanced police administration students were more attentive to violent aspects of a complex stimulus situation than novice students, presumably because of prior reward for such attention); and the relevance of the model himself or the activity involved to the child's own needs and expectations derived from his past experience. Both children and adults are more likely to be attentive in some situations than others (e.g., a bored husband at a concert with his wife, as compared with that same husband at a baseball game when his favorite team is playing).

Bandura also attempted to differentiate between acquisition of a response capability and actual performance of the response. In one investigation illustrative of those summarized above, Bandura (4) had shown children films of a model displaying aggressive behavior under various conditions: "In one condition of the experiment, the model was severely punished; in a second, the model was generously rewarded with approval and food reinforcers; while the third condition presented no response-consequences to the model" (4, 57). As might be expected, a postexposure test of imitative behavior revealed that these various conditions produced differential amounts of imitative behavior. Children in the model-punished condition performed significantly fewer imitative responses than those in both the model-rewarded and the no-consequences groups.

It was at this point that Bandura introduced his novel extension of the experiment. He offered children in all three groups attractive rewards, contingent on their reproducing the model's behavior. He found that the introduction of these positive rewards completely wiped out the previously observed performance differences, that is, children in all three groups imitated equally, revealing an equivalent amount of learning among children in each of the three groups.

Bandura believes that such experiments demonstrate several important points sometimes neglected by other theorists. In the first place, acquisition of a particular pattern of imitative responses does not necessarily require actual performance of these responses in the immediate situation. In other words, provided the subject is properly attentive (presumably because observing responses have been rewarded in the past), he may learn a particular pattern of responses demonstrated by the model and be able to reproduce them in the future even though he has not, in the past, made these particular responses in this particular sequence or in response to this particular stimulus.

Bandura also draws an important distinction between the factors affecting acquisition and those affecting performance. In this experiment, for example, while the tendency to perform imitative responses (without further instructions) was affected by whether or not the model had been rewarded or punished for his acts, learning to be able to perform the responses was not so affected.

Observational learning and learning by conditioning of overt responses, either classically or instrumentally, often supplement each other. One would not permit an adolescent to learn to drive a car or an army recruit to handle firearms solely through trial-and-error procedures. On the other hand, in these, as in many other instances of complex learning requiring novel responses, actual corrective practice combined with reward for correct responses is necessary. For example, simply telling a youth who is learning to shoot a rifle not to blink his eyes when he fires and not to grab the trigger will not be sufficient. Observational learning is likely to be of less value when it involves responses that are complex and largely new. In contrast, it appears most effective when it involves fairly simple combinations, or responses that have already been acquired, although the new learning situation may require putting these responses together in new or novel sequences or in response to new stimuli. In contrast, behavior "shaping" appears most effective where the response pattern is sufficiently complex or unusual as to constitute, at least in its totality, new and difficult behavior. As already indicated, optimal learning in many situations requires a skillful combination of the two elements. It is the introduction of just such skillful combinations that has produced so many remarkable educational advances in recent years, as, for example, in the newer forms of language training used in our schools.

BASIC CONDITIONS OF LEARNING

As parents and teachers know, learning is not inevitable. It does not always occur even in some situations in which we most expect it. It appears that certain conditions must be satisfied in any given case if learning is to take place. What do we know about the nature of these conditions?

A few basic points seem obvious. In the first place, unless a stimulus is distinctive enough to be discriminable, it will be difficult, if not impossible, to attach a response to it. Further, even a distinctive stimulus may be of little value unless the subject can be induced to attend to or notice it. One of the many problems in teaching appropriate social responses to autistic or schizophrenic children appears to be the difficulty of getting the child to pay attention to relevant stimuli to which we hope to attach responses, even though these stimuli may be both distinctive and simple. One often gains the impression that the child is so preoccupied with his own internal, private world that he pays little attention to the external stimulus to which he is exposed.

The physiological and psychological state of the subject is also important. Learning a response to a stimulus takes place within a living organism, whether animal or man. Obviously, the biological state of a child will effect his capacity for learning. Earlier theories of learning often tended to ignore or to minimize the importance of the state of the organism doing the learning (16).

Learning is thus a function of the nature of the stimulus, the nature of the response, and the state of the learning organism. What other factors may be important? Two which are often cited by most, though not all, theorists are **motivation** and **reinforcement**. The contention of these theorists is that learning is more likely to occur (1) when the organism wants or needs to obtain a certain goal (that is, when he is motivated) and (2) when the response he makes results in acquisition of the goal (that is, the response is rewarded or reinforced). While these concepts may seem reasonable, even perhaps obvious, experimental work in learning indicates that the matter is not actually as simple as it may at first appear.

The Role of Reward or Reinforcement

The reader may have noticed that in some of the examples of learning already referred to the subject was provided with a reward of some sort whenever he made a correct response to a stimulus (for example, giving an autistic child a bit of food when he made an appropriate social response, as in Lovaas' studies). The presumption here was that a reward or **reinforcement**, if given promptly when the subject makes a correct response to a stimulus, strengthens the stimulus-response bond and increases the likelihood that the proper response will again be made the next time the stimulus is presented. How important actually is reinforcement for learning, and, if it is important, what is its nature?

The first of these questions, namely, the importance of reinforcement in learning, has been a topic of dispute among psychologists for many decades, and the matter is still unresolved (**16, 19**). In fact, new experimental evidence derived from learning experiments, rather than settling the issue, has, if anything, made the problem even more complex (**16**). Some psychologists have maintained that reinforcement is not a necessary condition for learning at all, that its apparent importance in some cases is really only incidental in that it helps to insure that the appropriate response will take place in the presence of the stimulus and not under other conditions. Such therapists maintain that **contiguity** alone (i.e., simply the occurrence of the response in the presence of the stimulus) is sufficient to produce learning.

Other psychologists maintain that reinforcement is always necessary for learning and that instances in which conditioning appears to take place without reinforcement are deceptive. In such cases, they argue, it is not that reinforcement was absent; it is merely that the psychologist was not aware of the reinforcement which actually occurred. While these theorists often differ among themselves in their specific views regarding the ways in which reinforcement or reward operates, as a group they are frequently referred to as **reinforcement theorists.**

Still other psychologists, perhaps a majority, argue that while reinforcement may not be a necessary concomitant of all learning, it is important for some forms of learning. Among this group, one cadre maintains that contiguity alone may be sufficient for classical conditioning, particularly when responses of the autonomic nervous system are involved. As a simple example, let us assume that an increase in heart rate is to be conditioned as a response to the sound of a bell. This may be done by first pairing the sound of the bell with a mild electric shock which itself increases heart rate. Subsequently, when the bell stimulus is presented alone, heart rate increases. Was reinforcement present? These theorists would argue that it was not.

In the case of many forms of instrumental or operant conditioning, however, these theorists would insist that reinforcement is necessary or at least helpful. They would point to many examples that appear to support this view. The learning of a complicated maze by a rat is facilitated if he is rewarded by food at the end of the maze. A child who finally makes the correct response in a complicated learning problem is more likely to repeat the correct response the next time it is presented if he is rewarded for this response and not for other (incorrect) responses. The reward itself may consist of a piece of candy, a grade of "A," or simply a congratulatory statement such as "Very good"; the exact nature of the reward is inconsequential, as long as it is rewarding for the particular child.

Reinforcements seem to be helpful in promoting associations that involve overt responses but less important when the association involves acquiring a new cognitive unit (for example, learning that a new fruit is called a kiwi or realizing the logic of multiplication). These new acquisitions seem to require primarily **attention** to the elements of the learning situation.

Perhaps the best example of associations between internal cognitive or mediational units is the phenomenon we call **insight.** Insight in science, art, or poetry involves suddenly perceiving or recognizing an association between two units of thought that have always been separate. When the scientists Watson and Crick had the insight that they could explain the chemical structure of DNA by assuming it was a helix, they connected their knowledge about the behavior of certain organic molecules with an image of a helix. They had learned something; a new connection or association had been established. A person in psychotherapy may suddenly recognize the association or the relation between his anger toward his mother and the fact that he blames his mother for his own shortcomings. This kind of association may be most applicable to human beings, but it does fit our general definition of learning, which involves the establishment of an association between two units that prior to the learning were not associated or connected.

Schedule of Reinforcement The effects of reinforcement on learning of behavior will be influenced by the schedule or pattern of reward. A child may be praised by his teacher every time he does his lessons well or only occasionally. In the latter case, the child is receiving only **partial** or **intermittent reinforcement.** In general, experiments both with animals and with humans indicate that learned behavior that is partially reinforced persists longer than behavior that is constantly reinforced.

In most real-life situations partial reinforcement is the rule rather than the exception. The baby who has learned to say "milk" will not get milk every time, but only on occasions when his mother is present and perhaps not always even then. The boy who swings the baseball bat does not get a home run every time. In adult life the persistence of behavior learned through partial reinforcement helps explain why a man who once won a consolation prize in a slogan contest will keep entering contests for years without further reward and why a woman who once won a daily double at the race track keeps trying despite a long succession of losing days.

The strength of partial reinforcement may account for the persistence of behavior that once served a purpose but no longer does so. Children sometimes manage to get their own way through temper tantrums or through shouting and often continue this kind of behavior in their own adulthoods, when it is unnecessary and inappropriate. Some children succeed at times in avoiding punishment by assuming a very humble and apologetic attitude and, even when they have become adults, continue to behave as if other people were older and stronger than they. Partial reinforcement is one reason old habits, even bad ones, are often so hard to break.

The Nature of Reinforcement What do we actually mean by reinforcement? An operational definition is relatively easy and has already been implied in our previous discussion: a reward is an event that follows a response and increases the likelihood that the response will occur the next time the eliciting stimulus is presented. In a sense, however, such a definition begs the question. It does not tell us ahead of time whether a particular event is likely to promote learning. We have to wait to find out whether it **has** been facilitating in a particular case; if it has, then "the event" can be viewed as rewarding or reinforcing.

Recent experiments have shown that hungry rats will press levers or hungry pigeons peck at discs even when the food is delivered indepedent of the animal's response, that is, learning to press a lever or peck a disc seems to occur even though the response is not followed immediately by a reinforcement (41). Moreover, it seems to be impossible to teach an animal a response that is incompatible with its natural tendencies, regardless of the number of reinforcements it receives. It is impossible to teach a raccoon to carry two coins to a small piggy bank and deposit them; it is impossible to teach a rat to run in a wheel in order to avoid shock because the rat's natural tendency under fear is to freeze rather than to run (6). These results, together with others, have led some psychologists to suggest that those events that have been called reinforcements do not condition a particular response to a particular stimulus. Rather, a reinforcement excites the animal in a specific way and causes him to display those behaviors that he is likely to display when he is excited or aroused by that reinforcement. For example, pigeons normally peck at round objects when they are aroused by hunger. Thus the increase in pecking at a red disc when food is delivered in association with the response of pecking may be the result of the animal's being excited by the food reinforcement. The stimuli of the cage and the disc eventually become conditioned to the state of excitement that accompanies hunger and eating. Hence the next day when the pigeon is put into cage the stimulus of the disc elicits, through association, that state of excitement which, in turn, leads him to peck at the disc. In short, the reinforcement may act to build up an expectancy that the behavior of pecking will lead to food (6).

> In each case, the animal comes into the experimental situation with certain species specific behaviors; food getting responses on the one hand and defensive reactions on the other. In both cases the chief effect of putting the animal in the experimental situation is to produce an expectancy; an expectancy of food in the one instance, and an expectancy of shock in the other. The animal gives us its characteristic behaviors; food getting responses or defensive reactions (6, 399).

This discussion of the role of reinforcement is congruent with the observation that many of the stimuli that are called reinforcements influence the attention of the organism. For example, in Pavlov's classical conditioning experiment, the food that serves as the unconditioned stimulus for the salivary reflex attracts the dog's attention to the situation. It tunes him in to what is also occurring at the time or has just occurred, such as the sound of the metronome. Similarly, in operant conditioning in the Skinner box, the arrival of the food pellet operates to attract the rat's attention as well as excite him. Attention is critical in human learning and social rewards focus the attention of the learner. Thus, contiguity of events plus attention to the relevant stimuli may be the essential ingredients in acquiring a new association and arousal or excitement may be an additional factor necessary to elicit behavior.

Drives and Motivation in Learning Theory The notion of reward implies some prized goal that is attained. The term motivation refers to the forces that provoke a child to seek a particular goal. Learning theory posits a set of biological drives, similar to Freud's instinctual energy, that include hunger, thirst, pain, and sleep. Since adults, primarily parents and other caretakers, gratify these strong drives, the adults acquire an attractiveness; in terms of learning theory, the adults acquire "reward value." As a result of learned associations between the stimulus attributes of these adults and the feelings of pleasure that are associated with gratification of hunger or other needs, specific persons become desired goals in their own right. The child learns to want the presence and the nurturance of these special adults, which presumably, at a later age, results in a general motive for approval and affection from adults. This is the central motive in child development for the social learning theorists who, like the psychoanalytic theorists, assume a small set of biological drives that, through experience, give rise to social motives.

Learning Mechanisms

Generalization and Discrimination When a hungry child has learned to go to the refrigerator for a snack in his own home, it is likely that if he becomes hungry in his grandmother's home he will also go to the refrigerator. Similarly, when a child has been trained to avoid a hot radiator or stove in his home, he will, fortunately, also tend to avoid other radiators or stoves in other homes. How does this happen? Since the cues in the two homes are not identical, why doesn't he have to learn to make the response all over again in this new situation? The answer to this question requires an additional principle, that of **stimulus generalization.** This principle states that when a response has been learned to one cue or stimulus, it is likely to occur to similar stimuli. The greater the degree of similarity between the original stimuli and those in the new situation, the greater the likelihood that the response will occur.

What determines similarity among stimuli? In the case of objects, the importance of color, size, and shape is obvious. Thus, if a child has learned initially to grasp for a blue-tinted nursing bottle, he is more likely to reach for a purple one than for a red one. After language has been acquired, however, the categorical verbal labels applied to things are frequently the primary determinants of similarity. In other words, what we **call** an object constitutes the most important basis for generalization.

For the adult, the word dog refers to everything from a white Afghan to a toy Pekingese. However, in terms of the objective physical quality of the stimulus, a cat is more similar to the toy Pekingese that to the white Afghan. If a response learned to a collie were generalized only to dogs that were physically similar to it, the child would be very limited in the range of animals to which he would respond as he did to the collie. It is quite unlikely that a response learned to a collie would generalize to the toy Pekingese solely on the basis of physical similarity. However, if his parents categorize the collie as a "dog," the word dog becomes as much a part of the total stimulus situation as the physical aspects of the animal. Thus, in the future, the child may come to apply the responses he has learned to his pet collie (patting the animal, expecting him to bark, etc.), not only to other physically similar animals, but also to all animals he labels **dog.** The term **learned** or **mediated generalization** is applied to those cases in which the basis for generalization involves a categorical language label.

Initially, generalization is likely to be extensive. The child who has learned to attach the label dog to the family pet is apt to extend this label to all four-footed animals he meets. Thus, the first cow or horse he encounters is likely to be called a dog. Gradually, however, the extent of the generalization will decrease until finally it is (correctly) limited only to dogs. This learned correction to overgeneralization is called **discrimination** (26) and is based on the elimination, or extinction, of incorrectly generalized responses.

Extinction The fact that a response is learned does not mean that it will always remain strong. If the response is not followed by a reward, the association between the stimulus and the response becomes weak, and eventually the stimulus fails to elicit the response. When this happens, we say that the response has undergone **extinction.** Consider a baby who has learned to cry when he is afraid because the mother always came to him when he cried. In this case, the arrival of the mother was the reinforcement. If the mother suddenly stopped coming to the child when he cried, the response of crying would eventually cease; it would have undergone extinction.

However, lack of reward is not the only condition that can result in a decreased likelihood of the occurrence of a response. This statement introduces us to the notion of what is called a **response hierarchy.**

Response Hierarchy Response hierarchy refers to the fact that in most new situations the child is capable of making a variety of responses. Each of these is of different strength, that is, each has a different probability of occurring. The relative strength of each of these responses determines the response hierarchy. With age, some responses lose in strength and others gain. Thus, response hierarchies change with age. For example, a child learns to reach for a bottle and suck the nipple because these responses are rewarded. These behaviors, therefore, are most likely to occur when the child is hungry. However, when the child is around 2 years of age or earlier, parents usually put pressure on him to give up the infantile habit of nursing from a bottle and encourage him to drink from a glass when he is hungry. The child may begin to anticipate parental displeasure or punishment when he thinks of sucking from the bottle, and a new response, the tendency to drink from a glass, begins to compete with the older one of asking for a bottle. If the motive to avoid parental displeasure becomes strong enough, the child will inhibit the old response and begin drinking from the glass. When alternative responses are available to gratify a need (in this case asking for either a glass or a bottle of milk), the one that actually occurs will be the one with the greatest strength and the least amount of fear or anxiety associated with it.

The concept of hierarchy of response has numerous practical implications. We shall give but one example here. A child of 5 may have learned that the most frequently rewarded method of attracting his parents' attention is to ask questions. This response, therefore, becomes high in his hierarchy of responses in this type of situation. However, let us assume that his parents suddenly become too busy to answer his questions. They may then cease to reward this question-asking response. As a result, this learned response may become weaker and fall to a lower position in the child's response hierarchy. Older responses that have been rewarded earlier in life, such as crying or temper tantrums, may then become the strongest in the response hierarchy and the most likely to occur. A return to earlier forms of responding is called **regression.**

The general principles enunciated above—schedule of reinforcement, generalization and discrimination, extinction, and response hierarchies—are most clearly applicable to instrumental (or operant) conditioning and to classical conditioning, that is, to learning associations between external stimuli and overt responses. As such, they have explanatory and predictive value in our attempts to understand children's learning and development.

Learning Theory and Complex Learning

The learning of complex abilities and knowledge—ideas, concepts, rules, and principles—involves mediated units and associations between internal processes, as well as the principles of generalization or transfer and discrimination.

Gagné, a learning theorist, has proposed a **cumulative learning** theory or model that attempts to account for such learning. He postulates that there are eight types of learning, hierarchically organized; that is, each type of learning is a prerequisite for a successive kind of "higher order" learning. In order of increasing complexity, the eight types are: **signal learning** (learning a response to a signal, as in classical conditioning); **stimulus response learning** (learning a connection between a response and a discriminated stimulus); **chains** (chains of two or more response connections); **verbal associations** (learning of chains that are verbal); **multiple discrimination** (in which the individual "learns to make **n** different identifying responses to as many different stimuli"); **concept learning** (the acquisition of "a capability of making a common response to a class of stimuli that may differ from each other widely in physical appearance"); **principle learning** ("a chain of two or more concepts"); **problem-solving** ("a kind of learning that requires the internal events usually called thinking"). In thinking, two or more previously acquired principles must be combined to produce a new capability (**12, 58–59**).

Learning is regarded as cumulative because each more complex type of learning depends on recall of more primitive types and humans have a "built-in" capacity for generalization "of specific identical (or highly similar) elements. . . . Of course, 'elements' here means rules, concepts, or any other learned capabilities . . . described" (**13**). Moreover," . . . each variety of learning begins with a **different state of the organism** and ends with a **different capability for performance**. It is believed, therefore, that the differences among these varieties of learning far outweigh their similarities" (**12, 60**).

Gagné's formulation of the development of successively more complex levels of learning represents an attempt to bring together, in one theoretical framework, some basic concepts of learning and cognitive theories. Thus, it attempts to bridge the gap between the simple learning phenomena usually investigated by learning theorists (stimulus-response connections) and higher thought processes that generally concern cognitive theorists.

Critique of Learning Theory

The main difficulty with the learning theory approach to human development is that it is inadequate as an explanation of spontaneous changes in the child's beliefs and behaviors that cannot easily be attributed to either conditioning or observation of a model. A 10-year-old child who has been continually rewarded for obedience and has few peer models for rebellion suddenly decides to disobey his parents. Similarly the spontaneous solution of a problem or the emergence of a creative idea is difficult for a learning theorist to explain. Learning theory cannot account for the appearance of novel responses.

Additional problems arise from recent experiments on animals indicating that each species is "wired" by nature in a way that makes it easier for it to learn one set of behaviors rather than another. Rats, who have poor vision but sensitive taste receptors, easily learn to avoid drinking a solution with a distinctive taste if that drinking is followed by a feeling of nausea. But these same rats have great difficulty learning to avoid drinking a solution that is associated with a visual stimulus when that drinking also leads to nausea (14). Moreover, in these experiments on the conditioning of suppression of drinking to taste or to sights, there is often a long delay between the conditioned stimulus (a distinctive taste or a distinctive sight) and the unconditioned response of nausea. The latter can occur several hours after the appearance of the conditioned stimulus.

There is no way for current learning theory to handle these and related phenomena described on page 58, for learning theory has traditionally assumed, first, that any stimulus can be conditioned to any response and, second, that there has to be only a short delay (usually less than a second) between the conditioned stimulus and the unconditioned response. Although learning theory has been helpful in explaining some aspects of the child's behavioral development, for example, the generalization and extinction of crying, it has been far less helpful in explaining the development of language, beliefs, and problem-solving. Recent challenges to the importance of the role of reinforcement are likely to lead to more thorough, critical analyses of the role of learning theory in behavioral development.

It is likely, however, that all three major theoretical views—Piaget, Freud, and learning theory—have something important to contribute to our understanding of development. Since the theories concentrate on different aspects of the child, they are not actually as contradictory as they may appear on the surface.

No single approach is sufficiently complete to explain all that is important about the development of the child. Hence, in the remainder of this book we will borrow from all theories, attempting to integrate their contributions into a more complete picture of the developing child. This book has no single theoretical bias because it is too early to decide which theory will be most useful. The child can be changed as a result of conditioning, exposure to models, and administration of rewards and punishments. At other times he is actively selecting experiences and altering beliefs on the basis of detection of inconsistency. Many of the child's goals will depend on the environment in which he lives, even though freedom from anxiety and pain and the pleasures of sexuality, love relations, mastery, and hostility are universal motives. But that does not mean that all children are progressing toward identical goals in adulthood or that psychological development always means psychological progress toward a better or happier state of functioning.

Finally, it shall be remembered that psychological theorizing in developmental psychology is concerned with three quite different sets of problems. The first concerns the universal sequences that children pass through as they grow and develop the intellectual, emotional, motivational, and attitudinal characteristics of all children and adults. Inquiry into these problems relies heavily on an assumed relation between biological forces that determine when the child will be capable of experiencing certain emotions or displaying certain abilities. Study of the development of language, perception, motor skills, thinking, and reasoning fall into this first class.

A second set of problems concerns the area normally known as personality. The psychologist wants to understand the reasons for the variation within one culture on some particular psychological characteristic. The study of differences in school achievement, dependency on parents, and social aggression toward adults fall into this category.

A third and less frequent set of problems is concerned with the differences among children growing up in different cultures and the forces that produce those differences. It is often the case that the reasons for the cultural differences in independence and autonomy, let us say, are not the same as the reasons for differences in independence and autonomy within any one culture. For example, the rural African child is much more nurturant toward others than the urban American child. This difference seems to be due to the fact that the rural African child lives in a setting that contains many children and a busy mother. The parents assign the child responsibility for taking care of his younger brothers and sisters. This responsibility, which few American children are given, apparently leads this child to be behaviorally more helpful and kind to others. Among American 8-year-olds, differences in nurturant behavior to others are more often the result of specific encouragement and differential identification with parental models.

Since most American psychologists have tried to understand the reasons for variation within our own culture, this book will concentrate on these problems. But the student should not forget the larger issues, namely, what biology contributes to development, what each cultural system contributes, and, finally, what the family, peers, and institutions of any one specific culture contribute.

SUMMARY

Theories in developmental psychology attempt to describe and to explain how the behaviors, beliefs, motives, and cognitive abilities of the adult are gradually formed over the first two decades of life. These theories differ in their basic assumptions about the nature of the child as well as the direction of his growth. Piaget believes that the child is inherently active and that through the combined influences of motivation and experience the adolescent arrives at the stage of formal operational thinking, which Piaget views as characteristic of maturity. Hence Piaget believes in an idealized goal toward which a psychologically active child is traveling. Although Freud also believed that every child passes through stages on his way to the most mature phase of development, the genital stage, he saw the child as psychologically more vulnerable to the environment, believing that particular conflicts were inevitable. The learning theorists see the child as molded by the environment and do not assume any particular direction to development. They believe that the child is continually changing as a function of conditioning and observation of models, but growth is not necessarily headed toward a particular "best" form. A fourth view, which is the least complete, perhaps because it is new, views the child as psychologically active but questions the notion that he is moving toward an ideal goal.

These approaches are less contradictory than they seem, for each has a primary interest in a different aspect of the child. The learning theorists are concerned with overt behavior, the Piagetians with thought, and the Freudians with motives and emotions.

Perhaps the most important change in theoretical views during the last decade has been the realization that nature has awarded every animal, including man, certain biological predispositions which make it easy for him to learn one set of skills or ideas and difficult for him to learn others. It is likely, therefore, that future explanations of development will acknowledge the important role of biological factors in monitoring psychological growth.

References

1. Bandura, A. Social learning of moral judgments. **Journal of Personality and Social Psychology,** 1969, **11,** 275–279.
2. Bandura, A. Social learning through imitation. In M. R. Jones (Ed.), **Nebraska symposium on motivation: 1962.** Lincoln: University of Nebraska Press, 1962. Pp. 211–269.
3. Bandura, A. Vicarious processes: A case of no-trial learning. In L. Berkowitz (Ed.), **Advances in social psychology.** Vol. II. New York: Academic Press, 1965.
4. Bandura, A., & Walters, R. H., **Social learning and personality development.** New York: Holt, Rinehart & Winston, 1963.
5. Bensberg, G. J., Colwell, C. N., & Cassel, R. H. Teaching the profoundly retarded self-help activities by behavior shaping techniques. **American Journal of Mental Defects,** 1965, **69,** 674–679.
6. Bolles, R. C. Reinforcement, expectancy, and learning. **Psychological Review,** 1972, **79,** 394–409.
7. Brown, P., & Elliott, R. Control of aggression in a nursery school class. **Journal of Experimental Child Psychology,** 1965, **2,** 103–107.

8. Dethier, V. G., & Stellar, E. **Animal behavior.** (2nd ed.) Englewood Cliffs, N. J.: Prentice-Hall, 1964.
9. Freud, S. **Introductory lectures on psychoanalysis.** (Standard ed.) Vols. 15, 16. London: Hogarth, 1963.
10. Freud, S. **The problem of anxiety.** New York: Norton, 1936.
11. Freud, S. **Three essays on the theory of sexuality.** (Standard ed.) Vol. 7. London: Hogarth, 1953.
12. Gagné, R. M. **The conditions of learning.** New York: Holt, Rinehart & Winston, 1965.
13. Gagné, R. M. Contributions of learning to human development. **Psychological Review,** 1968, **75,** 177–191.
14. Garcia, J., McGowan, B. K., & Green, K. F. Biological constraints on conditioning. In A. H. Black & W. F. Prokasy (Eds.), **Classical conditioning.** Vol. II. **Current research and theory.** New York: Appleton-Century-Crofts, 1972.
15. Hess, E. H. Ethology. In A. M. Freedman & H. I. Kaplan (Eds.), **Comprehensive textbook of psychiatry.** Baltimore: Williams & Wilkins, 1967. Pp. 180–189.
16. Hilgard, E. R. **Theories of learning.** New York: Harper & Row, 1954.
17. Hundziak, M., Maurer, R. A., & Watson, L. S., Jr. Operant conditioning in toilet training of severely mentally retarded boys. **American Journal of Mental Defects,** 1965, **70,** 120–124.
18. John, E. B., Chessler, P., Bartlett, F., & Victor, I. Observation learning in cats. **Science,** 1968, **159,** 1489–1491.
19. Kimble, G. A. **Hilgard and Marquis' conditioning and learning.** (2nd ed.) New York: Appleton-Century-Crofts, 1961.
20. Lipsitt, L. P. Learning in the first year of life. In L. P. Lipsitt & C. C. Spiker (Eds.), **Advances in child development and behavior.** New York: Academic Press, 1963. Pp. 147–195.
21. Lorenz, K. Z. **King Solomon's ring.** London: Methuen, 1952.
22. Lovaas, O. I. A behavior therapy approach to the treatment of childhood schizophrenia. In J. Hill (Ed.), **Minnesota symposium on child psychology.** Minneapolis: University of Minnesota Press, 1967.
23. Lovaas, O. I., Berberich, J. P., Perloff, B. F., & Schaeffer, B. Acquisition of imitative speech in schizophrenic children. **Science,** 1966, **151,** 705–707.
24. Lovaas, O. I., Freitag, G., Gold, V. J., & Kassorla, I. C. Experimental studies in childhood schizophrenia: Analysis of self-destructive behavior. **Journal of Experimental Psychology,** 1965, **2,** 67–84.
25. Marquis, D. P. Can conditioned responses be established in the newborn infant? **Journal of Genetic Psychology,** 1931, **39,** 479–492.
26. Miller, N. E., & Dollard, J. **Social learning and imitation.** New Haven: Yale University Press, 1941.
27. Olds, J., & Milner, P. Positive reinforcement produced by electrical stimulation of septal area and other regions of the rat brain. **Journal of Comparative and Physiological Psychology,** 1954, **47,** 419–427.
28. Papousek, H. Experimental studies of appetitional behavior in human newborns and infants. In H. W. Stevenson, E. H. Hess, & H. L. Rheingold (Eds.), **Early behavior.** New York: Wiley, 1967. Pp. 249–277.
29. Patterson, G. R., Littman, R. A., & Hinsey, W. C. Parental effectiveness as reinforcers in the laboratory and its relation to child rearing practices and child adjustment in the classroom. **Journal of Personality,** 1964, **32,** 180–199.
30. Piaget, J. **The origins of intelligence in children.** New York: International Universities Press, 1952.

31. Piaget, J. Piaget's theory. In P. H. Mussen (Ed.), **Carmichael's manual of child psychology,** (3rd ed.) New York: Wiley, 1970. Pp. 703–732.
32. Skinner, B. F. **The behavior of organisms.** New York: Appleton-Century-Crofts, 1938.
33. Skinner, B. F. How to teach animals. **Scientific American,** 1951, **185,** 26–29.
34. Skinner, B. F. **Science and human behavior.** New York: Macmillan, 1953.
35. Spelt, D. K. The conditioning of the human fetus in utero. **Journal of Experimental Psychology,** 1948, **38,** 338–346.
36. Staats, A. W., & Butterfield, W. H. Treatment of nonreading in a culturally deprived juvenile delinquent: An application of reinforcement principles. **Child Development,** 1965, **36,** 925–942.
37. Staats, A. W. **Learning, language, and cognition.** New York: Holt, Rinehart & Winston, 1968.
38. Tinbergen, N. Social releasers and the experimental method required for their study. **Wilson, Bulletin,** 1948, **60,** 6–51.
39. Toch, H. H., & Schulte, R. Readiness to perceive violence as a result of police training. **British Journal of Psychology,** 1961, **52,** 389–394.
40. Whitlock, C. Note on reading acquisition: An extension of laboratory principles. **Journal of Experimental Child Psychology,** 1966, **3,** 83–85.
41. Williams, D. R., & Williams, H. Auto-maintenance and the pigeon: Sustaining pecking despite contingent non-reinforcement. **Journal of Experimental Analysis of Behavior,** 1969, **12,** 511–520.

Part I
The Prenatal Period

Chapter 3

Genetic and Prenatal Factors in Development

In our attempt to understand the behavior of the developing child, many factors must be considered. The simplest behavior is often the result of many different influences. Basically, these influences fall into five major categories: (1) genetically determined biological variables, (2) nongenetic biological variables (for example, lack of oxygen during the birth process, malfunctioning of the pituitary gland), (3) the child's past learning, (4) his immediate social psychological environment (his parents, siblings, peers, and teachers), and (5) the general social and cultural milieu in which he develops.

The first two influences have been called the **nature** forces; the latter three, the **nurture** or environmental forces. The child's behavior and personality are, at any one time, a product of the continuing interaction of nature and nurture. In this chapter we will consider two major nature forces—heredity and the biological influence that operate during pregnancy and delivery.

Although we normally speak of biological determinants as separate from environmental determinants, it is important to appreciate that one cannot easily evaluate how much each force contributes to a particular psychological event. Both sets of forces interact continually to produce a given effect. Consider the analogy of a snowfall. Cold temperature and a high proportion of moisture in the air are both required to produce snow; it is not possible to say that the cold temperature was 60 percent responsible and the moisture 40 percent responsible for the snowflakes. Although we speak of genetic and environmental determinants of behavior, we always acknowledge that they act in unison; this is as true of the individual cell as it is of the whole person. The chemical action of the genetic material in a particular cell is a function of the material outside the nucleus as well as the chromosomes themselves. Indeed, the effect of a single gene will depend on the specific collection of other genes in that cell. Scientists try to discover the specific genetic and environmental forces that are controlling a specific behavior; scientists do not ask which influence is more important, just as they would not ask about the relative importance of moisture or cold in the snowfall analogy. This realization of the intimate interaction of genes and environment is relatively recent. Scientists of this century, as well as those of the past, have debated the nature-nurture issue, as the following two statements reveal. Compare these two statements.

Heredity and not environment is the chief maker of man. . . . Nearly all the misery and nearly all the happiness in the world are due not to environment. . . . The differences among men are due to differences in the germ cells with which they were born (1, 102–103).

Give me a dozen healthy infants, well formed, and my own specified world to bring them up in and I'll guarantee to take any one at random and train him to become any type of specialist I might select—doctor, lawyer, merchant, chief, and yes, even beggar-man and thief, regardless of his talents, peculiarities, tendencies, abilities, vocations, and race of his ancestors. There is no such thing as an inheritance of capacity, talent, temperament, mental constitution, and characteristics (1, 103).

The advances in biology and psychology make both statements naive and lead us to search for the way the combined action of our inherited potentialities and the events we experience make us the way we are.

The science of genetics has experienced dramatic advances during the last 25 years and we are beginning to accumulate a great deal of information about the influence of heredity on mental retardation and on aspects of seriously abnormal behavior. This chapter will deal with our knowledge of genetic functions and genetic factors and with prenatal development and the nonhereditary biological factors that operate during pregnancy and delivery.

BEGINNINGS OF LIFE

The life of each individual begins when a sperm cell from the father penetrates the wall of an ovum, or egg, from the mother. As we shall see in some detail later, the fertilization of an ovum by a sperm sets in motion an intricate process called mitosis. In this process the original fertilized ovum divides and subdivides until thousands of cells have been produced. Gradually, as the process continues, the resulting cells begin to assume special functions, as parts of the nervous, skeletal, muscular, or circulatory systems. The embryo, which at first resembles a gradually expanding ball, begins to take shape, and the beginnings of head, eyes, trunk, arms, and legs appear. Approximately 9 months after fertilization, the fetus is ready for birth.

HEREDITARY TRANSMISSION

Life begins at conception. But what of the forces that, throughout the individual's existence, will influence his development? When do they begin? The answer, again, is at conception. For at the moment that the tiny tadpole sperm penetrates the wall of the ovum, it releases 23 minute particles called **chromosomes.** At approximately the same time, the nucleus, the inner core of the ovum, breaks up, releasing 23 chromosomes of its own.

This process is of great interest to us because it has been established through painstaking research that these chromosomes, which are further subdivided into even smaller particles called **genes,** are the carriers of the child's heredity. All the child's physical heritage from his father and his mother is contained in these 46 chromosomes (see Fig. 3.1).

What Is Transmitted?

Long before the geneticists established the existence of chromosomes and genes, scientists were convinced that many characteristics of a child's parents were

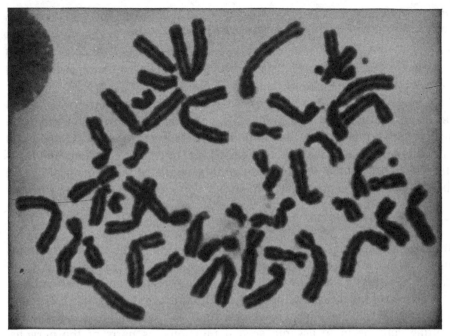

Figure 3.1 Metaphase spread from normal male cells showing the human chromosomes. (Courtesy of Dr. P. S. Moorhead.)

transmitted to the child at conception. People have, however, differed about what was transmitted and how. For example, one school of thought, dating back to Lamarck, a French zoologist who published a book called **Philosophie zooligique** in 1773, long maintained a doctrine that preached the inheritance of acquired characteristics. Lamarck felt that individuals improved or weakened their own physical capacities through experience or training and that the effects of such changes could be transmitted to their offspring. Thus, by developing a diseased lung or poor digestion, a prospective parent would be hurting his child's chances of being healthy. People began to postulate such notions as that the giraffe acquired his long neck because his ancestors had spent a great deal of time reaching into trees for food or that the snake lost his legs as a result of his forebears' propensity for creeping through crevices (51).

Nor were such speculations confined only to obvious physical characteristics. Many people believed that a mother could influence her child's chances of being born with a talent for singing, if she had, in her youth, carefully cultivated her own voice, or that if a father had previously developed an interest in mathematics, this interest was likely to be inherited by his son.

However, such early theories as these, and the inferences based upon them, were dealt a hard blow by Weismann in 1889 (85). He presented evidence suggesting that while the rest of the body may change with increasing age or through exercise, illness, or injury, the germ cells (chromosomes and genes), which an individual harbors and which are passed on to his children at their conception, do not ordinarily change.

Under exceptional circumstances, genes may change or be inactivated, as for example, through direct radiation from X rays or from atomic blasts. Nevertheless, genes are not subject to any of the usual influences that either build up or break down our bodies or improve our minds. Thus the genes that a sick, but well-educated, man of 50 possesses are no different from those that he possessed as a healthy, but untutored, youth of 17. In short, changes in the rest of the body do not affect the genetic characteristics of the germ cells which are passed on to our children. Hence there is no reason for believing that we can affect our children's genetic constitutions by engaging in physical education or self-improvement campaigns.

What Is a Gene? Until recently the existence of a gene was hypothetical. It was assumed to be a complex chemical, the actions of which controlled the development of organs and physiological processes. In 1953 Doctors Watson and Crick suggested a possible structure for the gene and this suggested structure helped us to understand a lot about heredity (83). A gene is composed of a chemical called deoxyribonucleic acid or DNA for short. DNA is the molecule of heredity; it contains the genetic code that determines what is transmitted from one generation to the next. A gene is a segment of DNA, and chromosomes are structures in which the genes are arranged in a linear order together with protein and other chemicals. There are about 1,000,000 genes in a human cell or, on the average, about 20,000 genes per chromosome. The molecule of DNA itself consists of two chains coiled around each other in the shape of a double helix with pairs of structures connecting the chains like rungs in a ladder. The best way to imagine what a molecule of DNA is like is to think of a long rubber ladder twisted around its long axis (see Fig. 3.2). Each lengthwise strip comprising the vertical sides of the ladder is made up of molecules of sugar and phosphate. Each cross step in the ladder represents a pair of chemicals that are called **bases.** The bases are paired in a special way so that the base called **adenine** always appears with the base called **thymine,** and the base **guanine** always appears with the base **cytosine.**

This structure helps us to understand the fundamentals of cell division and heredity transmission. It is necessary that the chromosomes duplicate themselves in the growth of new cells. This ladderlike structure permits the duplication, for the molecule of DNA can unzip itself, split apart, and produce a complement or duplication of itself.

The Mechanisms of Hereditary Transmission

One of the things that must have puzzled parents in prescientific days was why two children of the same parents should be so different physically. The answer lies in the mechanics of hereditary transmission.

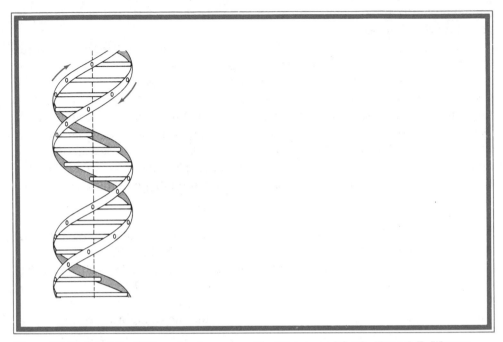

Figure 3.2 Model of the DNA molecule proposed by Watson and Crick. (From J. D. Watson & F. H. Crick. Molecular structure of nucleic acids: a structure for deoxyribose nucleic acids. **Nature,** 1953, **171** [4356], 737. By permission.)

If each child received all of both parents' genes, we could not explain individual genetic differences between siblings, as all brothers and sisters would then have identical heredities. The fact, however, is that each child inherits only half of each parent's genes. Moreover, different children in a family inherit different combinations of their mother's and father's genes. Thus individual differences between them become not only possible but inevitable.

The way in which this happens will become clear as we proceed. It will be recalled that the original fertilized ovum contains 46 chromosomes. As this cell divides to form two new cells, each of its 46 chromosomes first doubles, then each doubled chromosome divides in half by separating lengthwise down its center (see Fig. 3.3). Through a process known as **mitosis,** the chromosomes then go to opposite sides of the cell. Thus, when the cell itself divides down the center, the new cells will each contain 46 chromosomes, as did the original cell.

This process is repeated again and again as development proceeds. Even in the completed human being, when the myriad cells of the body have by this time taken on their special functions as tissue, bone, blood, and muscle, each cell still contains a replica of the original 46 chromosomes of the fertilized ovum.

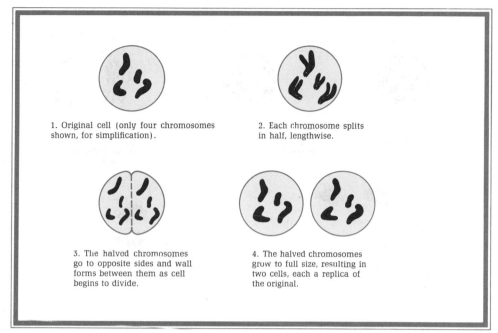

1. Original cell (only four chromosomes shown, for simplification).

2. Each chromosome splits in half, lengthwise.

3. The halved chromosomes go to opposite sides and wall forms between them as cell begins to divide.

4. The halved chromosomes grow to full size, resulting in two cells, each a replica of the original.

Figure 3.3 How a fertilized egg cell multiplies. (From **The New You and Heredity,** by Amram Scheinfeld. P. 12. Copyright 1950 by Amram Scheinfeld. Published by J. B. Lippincott Company. Also reprinted by permission of Paul R. Reynolds, Inc.)

Germ Cells

But if this is true, why don't the sperm and ovum which go to make up a new individual also contain 46 chromosomes each, since certainly they too are cells? It will be recalled that the new individual receives only 23 chromosomes from each parent.

The answer, stripped of genetic complexities, is actually simple. The adult organism contains not one, but two kinds of cells—body cells, which go to make up bones, nerves, muscles, and organs, and germ cells, from which the sperm and ova are derived. While the process of chromosome and cell division described above applies to the somatoplasm (the body cells), it does not apply completely to the germ cells. Throughout most of their history, the latter develop just as the body cells do. But at the time of their final division into recognizable sperm or ova, the pattern changes. At this point, the germ cells split, but the chromosomes do not. Instead, the 46 chromosomes, which in reality are 23 pairs of similar chromosomes —one pair-member from each parent—simply divide into two groups. One member of each pair goes to one of the resulting sperm or egg cells, and one to the other (see Fig 3.4). Thus the ova and sperm have only 23 chromosomes each and the new individual obtains a total of only 46.

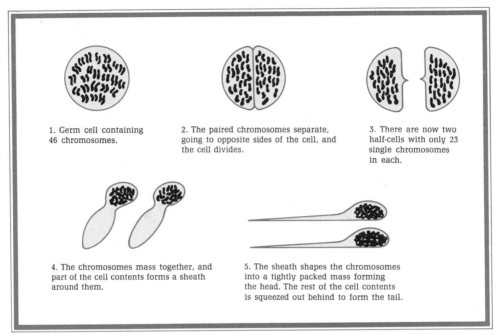

1. Germ cell containing 46 chromosomes.

2. The paired chromosomes separate, going to opposite sides of the cell, and the cell divides.

3. There are now two half-cells with only 23 single chromosomes in each.

4. The chromosomes mass together, and part of the cell contents forms a sheath around them.

5. The sheath shapes the chromosomes into a tightly packed mass forming the head. The rest of the cell contents is squeezed out behind to form the tail.

Figure 3.4 How sperms are produced. (From **The New You and Heredity,** by Amram Scheinfeld. P. 14. Copyright 1950 by Amram Scheinfeld. Published by J. B. Lippincott Company. Also reprinted by permission of Paul R. Reynolds, Inc.)

We can see, too, why it is that the children of the same parents do not all have to be alike. As may be seen from Fig. 3.5, if Sperm A unites with Ovum D, the new individual will possess a different set of chromosomes than if Sperm B unites with it. (Ovum C is indicated in dotted lines because ordinarily at any one conception only one ovum from the mother is ready for fertilization. The same, of course, is not true of sperm. At any one mating millions of sperm are released, as many as a hundred million in one drop of seminal fluid, any one of which might potentially fertilize the receptive ovum.)

Is Identity Possible?

We have seen how it is possible for individuals in the same family to be different in their genetic makeups. But is identity between siblings possible? The answer is no, except in the case of identical twins who develop from the same fertilized ovum which only later splits into two individuals. (For an interesting and simple discussion of the way in which identical and fraternal twins are produced, the reader is referred to Scheinfeld [64]. Somewhat more technical discussions will be found in general texts by Stern [77] and Gates [23].) If the 46 chromosomes in the germ cells always divided the same way, with one combination going to one

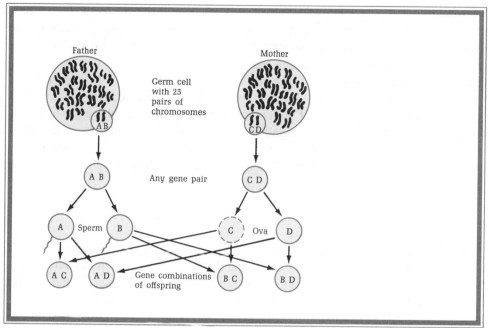

Figure 3.5 Schematic diagram showing possible gene combinations of offspring resulting from gene pairs of parents.

sperm or ovum and the rest to the other, identity would be possible. In fact, it could be anticipated frequently. But these 46 chromosomes do not divide in this way. Except that one member of each of the 23 pairs goes to one sperm or ovum and the other member to the other, the pattern is pretty much random. In other words, the way one pair of chromosomes separates does not influence the way another pair will split.

Moreover, in the formation of the germ cells (the sperm or ova) there is a process called crossing over which further increases the likelihood that each sperm or ovum will be unique and, therefore, that each individual will be unique. When the 23 pairs of chromosomes line up in pairs during the first phases of germ-cell formation (called **meiosis**), they exchange genetic material as if human beings facing each other might exchange parts of their fingers. One part of one member of the pair exchanges some DNA with the other.

If crossing over did not occur, the total number of different combinations of sperm and ovum is estimated at 64,000,000,000,000 different kinds of children—many times the total number of people on the earth today. But **with** crossing over, the number of possible different offspring is many, many times that number. Thus, except for identical twins, each human being is genetically unique and biologically different from every other person on earth. Let us reflect a minute on what this means for the science of psychology. The physicist or chemist, who is concerned with nonliving things, usually does not work with or theorize about unique substances. A chemist assumes that every molecule of oxygen or silver is exactly like every other molecule. A physicist assumes that every electron is exactly like every other electron. But the biologist and psychologist cannot assume that every monkey, rat, or child is exactly like every other one. More seriously, he cannot assume that a nerve cell in one child's brain is exactly like a nerve cell in his brother's brain, for the genetic makeup of the two cells is different. Thus the psychologist is faced with dramatically more variability of the basic forms he is trying to understand. This is one reason why psychology is much less mature as a science than chemistry or physics, and why prediction and understanding of behavior is much more difficult.

Sex Determination

Of the 23 pairs of chromosomes, one pair is called the sex chromosomes and is responsible for determining the sex of the child. In the normal female, both members of this pair are large in size and are called the X chromosomes. In the normal male, one member of the pair is an X chromosome; the second member is smaller in size and is called the Y chromosome. Thus, the body cells of males (except for sperm cells) contain one X and one Y chromosome. One-half of the sperm cells of the male contain an X chromosome; the remaining half contain a Y chromosome. When a female ovum, containing an X chromosome, unites, in conception, with a sperm containing a Y chromosome, a male child is produced. When an ovum unites with a sperm carrying an X chromosome, a female child develops. Since one-half of the sperm cells contain X and one-half Y chromosomes, theoretically the odds are 50-50 that a boy or girl will be conceived. There is actually a slight excess of male over female births (106 boys to 100 girls among whites in the United States) and this may mean that Y sperm are more likely than X sperm to penetrate the ovum (77).

DETERMINING THE EXTENT OF GENETIC INFLUENCES

Although, as we shall see, there is no doubt that many human characteristics are strongly influenced by heredity, it is difficult to determine the nature of this influence. By and large, we cannot directly observe the tiny genes in action. Instead, we are forced to infer their presence from their effects.

Moreover, some genetic effects are not seen until late adulthood. Consider the case of a degenerative disease of the nervous system, Huntington's chorea. This disorder, caused by a dominant gene, strikes in generation after generation of the same family and its frequency can be predicted by genetic principles. Yet it usually does not affect the person until he is about 35 years old.

In most cases, however, the situation is less clear. Some newborn babies are more active than others, and these variations may be caused by genetic factors. (For purposes of this illustration, let us ignore the possibility that prenatal influences also play a part.) However, it has also been found that when people are anxious and under psychological stress, they may become active and restless. Certain drugs have the same effect. Thus it is extremely difficult to sort out the separate contribution of drugs, genetic factors, or psychological influences on the activity level of babies.

Actually, as we must infer the importance of both genetic and environmental factors from their effects on the individual, the only sure way of determining whether either set of factors plays an important role in a specific condition is to find some way of holding one constant while varying the other. If the condition then also varies, we know that the factor we have varied plays an important role.

Identical twins have been used in a number of studies to control as much as possible for genetic factors. As they have identical hereditary backgrounds, any differences between them may be attributed to environmental influences. Newman, Freeman, and Holzinger (56) have used this method to study the effects upon personality of rearing children (of the same genetic makeup) in different home environments. Some of this work will be discussed shortly.

In other studies, particularly those with animals (in which by controlled mating it is possible to experiment on genetic factors), the physical and psychological environments are held as constant as possible, and the effects of varying heredity are noted (57). In cases where we are unable to hold most of the factors constant, we can only make, at best, intelligent guesses concerning the relative importance of genetic or environmental influences.

Putting Genetic Determinants into Perspective

The general question of genetic influence must be asked with respect to specific characteristics. Is it eye color, baldness, intelligence? The relative influences of heredity and environment differ markedly from one characteristic to another. Moreover, we must also ask under what conditions the characteristic is being manifested. This is particularly important in the case of behavioral characteristics. Take, for example, the task of determining the hereditary and environmental antecedents of diabetes. If a thin diabetic woman tells us that she never eats candy, while an obese diabetic woman reports eating a pound of chocolates every day, we would suspect hereditary factors as more likely in the former than in the latter case.

Or take another example, closer to the concerns of this book. Suppose that a child fails a reading-readiness test of the type given children prior to admission to the first grade in school. If the child is suffering from cerebral sclerosis, a form of mental deficiency which is dependent on the coexistence of two specific recessive genes, heredity could reasonably be called an important contributor to his failure.

On the other hand, if the child shows no evidence of specific biological deficiency, but has lived an isolated mountain life with illiterate parents, and later with proper training passes the test, environment would seem to be the sole determinant of his original failure.

The specific effect of the interaction of hereditary and environmental forces will differ for different behaviors and different structural characteristics. Moreover, the important question is not **what** behaviors are influenced by heredity, but **how** the genes are able to exert this influence.

> The traditional questions about heredity and environment may be intrinsically unanswerable. Psychologists keep asking **which** type of factor, heredity or environment, is responsible for individual differences in a given trait. Later, they tried to discover **how much** of the variance was attributable to heredity and how much to environment. . . . A more fruitful approach is to be found in the question, "How?" (2, 197).

It is not sufficient to know that a small body frame or high intelligence are inherited; we must determine the many complicated biological processes that are triggered into action as a result of possessing the genes associated with body size. Do genes affect growth through influencing hormonal action, through direct action on bone or muscle, or through a combination of these actions? When we have the answers to specific questions such as these, we will have a more complete understanding of what it means to say that a trait is inherited. Unfortunately, there are not many clues to help us in understanding the ways in which a gene or combination of genes produces specific behaviors.

One inherited basis for mental retardation provides a good example of the kind of knowledge that is needed. Many of the foods we eat contain a chemical called phenylalanine. Most people possess an enzyme that converts phenylalanine to a harmless by-product. However, a small group of children have a specific hereditary defect in that they do not possess the enzyme that converts the phenylalanine; they lack a gene that produces this critical enzyme. As a result, the concentration of phenylalanine rises above that which is normal and becomes converted to phenylpyruvic acid. The nerve cells of the central nervous system become damaged and mental retardation results. This disease is called phenylketonuria, or PKU for short. Once scientists learned the nature of the specific metabolic disorder in PKU, they began to think about ways of helping these children. They invented a diet that contained very low levels of phenylalanine, yet maintained the children's health. As a result, the toxic acid did not accumulate and the children's mental development was almost normal, and certainly far superior to what it would have been had they not taken the special diet. Knowledge of the exact biological mechanism that mediates a genetic defect can occasionally lead to effective cures.

Unfortunately, we do not have many other examples like PKU. In most instances, the specific influence of hereditary factors is unknown and very indirect. No motive, behavior, or emotion is ever inherited as such. The inheritance of a physical deformity may eventually lead to feelings of inferiority, but it would be nonsense to say that such feelings are inherited. In actuality, the basic characteristics which we know to be inherited are the ability to produce enzymes and proteins (which help form the structure of cells, tissues, and organs) and the ability to produce products which regulate the amounts of each of these materials which are synthesized by cells under a variety of different conditions. All of these phenomena influence psychological variables in many subtle ways.

To cite a few simple examples, genetic forces determine whether an individual is a man or a woman; they help to determine whether he is tall or short, fat or thin, handsome or ugly, sluggish or high-strung. They may influence his resistance to various diseases and, perhaps, the power of his memory.

Because heredity acts directly only upon the individual's biological characteristics, it cannot itself produce a child's jealousy of its mother or an enthusiasm for space guns and rocket ships. These attributes, necessarily depending in part upon learning through interaction with particular objects in the environment, cannot be entirely and simply determined by heredity. Heredity may play a role, however, since it helps to produce the kind of individual who is doing the learning. For example, it may help to influence whether an individual becomes a heavyweight boxer or a jockey, through its influence on the biological mechanisms determining the person's height and weight.

RESULTS OF HUMAN GENETIC RESEARCH

As a result of the difficulties inherent in much genetic research with humans, there are large gaps in our knowledge of the role of heredity in human development. Nevertheless, progress is being made. A brief summary of the findings from some of the more pertinent studies in this area will be presented here.

Some of this research has employed the so-called twin-study method. In this type of approach, an attempt is made to control environmental influences, thus making it possible to note whether genetic factors alone will produce variations in the phenomenon under study. In the case of intelligence, for example, the performances of identical twins on intelligence tests may be compared with those of fraternal (nonidentical) twins. The working assumption is that the environments of fraternal twins are as similar as those of identical twins. In this way, the possible effects of environmental factors on IQ are considered to be controlled. Consequently, if identical twins are found to resemble each other more closely in IQ than fraternal twins, it is concluded that genetic factors affect intelligence. The greater similarity in the IQ scores of the identical twins is considered to be due to the fact that these twins have exactly the same heredity, whereas fraternal twins do not.

However, a word of caution about such reasoning is necessary. It should be readily evident to the reader that the environmental influences to which two children are exposed do differ, even though they are both raised in the same family. Furthermore, it appears that these environmental influences may differ, at least in some respects, more for fraternal twins or other siblings than for identical twins.

Several studies have shown that identical twins spend more time together, enjoy more similar reputations, are more likely to be in the same classrooms, have more similar health records, and in many other respects share a more common physical and social environment than that ordinarily experienced by fraternal twins (39).

Thus, the assumption in twin studies, like the one described above, that the possible effects of environment have been adequately controlled for may not always be justified. In a few studies an attempt has been made to avoid this problem by comparing identical twins reared apart with fraternal twins or other siblings reared together. If, in this instance, identical twins still resemble each other more closely than fraternal twins or other siblings, it may be concluded that genetic factors are playing a role. However, the main reason for separating identical twin infants is that their parents are unable to care for them and put the babies up for adoption. If adoption agencies must place two twins in different homes they try to place them in homes of similar social class and religious backgrounds. Hence, studies of identical twins reared in different homes are not totally free of the effect of similar experience. Nonetheless, if identical twins reared apart are more similar than fraternal twins living in the same home, it is usually assumed that heredity was primarily responsible for that similarity. Scientists can thus attempt to assess the heritability of a trait by comparing the similarity of identical and nonidentical twins.

A typical way of assessing heritability, that is, the degree to which a specific trait is inherited in a given population, is to compare the correlation between the scores or measures of identical twins with the corresponding measures for nonidentical twins for that trait. The mathematical formula for this index of heritability is

$$H^2 = \frac{R \text{ identical twins} - R \text{ nonidentical twins}}{1 - R \text{ nonidentical twins}}$$

The greater the similarity between the identical twins (as indexed by the size of the correlation), the larger the index of heritability and, by inference, the stronger the effect of genes. However, this formula assumes that the environments and experiences of identical twins are no more similar that those of nonidentical twins. Since we have some reason to doubt that assumption, the index of heritability may be spuriously high.

Physical Features

An individual's physical features depend heavily upon his heredity. Birth injury may alter the shape of his face, disease may whiten his hair, but the color of a person's eyes, the shape of his nose, the pigmentation of his skin, the color, curliness of his hair are typically a function of the genes he has inherited. Some features, such as eye color, depend upon quite simple combinations of genes. Others, such as skin color, are more complex and involve many sets of genes acting together.

For the most part, variations in physical features within the American population bear little relation to an individual's biological ability to adapt to the demands of living. An individual with brown eyes can see as well as one with blue. An individual with fair skin may have greater difficulty with sunburn than an individual whose skin has more pigment to protect it, but the difference is of minimal importance in terms of physical survival. The principal effects of variation in physical features upon the individual's adjustment are not biological in the sense of physical adaptation to the environment, but social and psychological. As indicated by America's racial strife, people do not always treat a person with black skin the way they treat one with white skin nor do they always respond similarly to people with hooked noses and straight noses. Knowledge of the ways in which people with different features are often treated in our society is essential to a proper understanding of personality development, as we shall see later.

Infants born with anatomical abnormalities, for example six fingers, are more likely than others to have abnormal chromosome patterns. However, the vast majority of these afflicted infants (over 90 percent) have normal chromosome patterns (78).

Mental Defect and Retardation

There are several genetically determined disorders that lead to gross defects or deterioration in intelligence. One of these, called **infantile amaurotic family idiocy,** results from a peculiar hereditary defect in the nerve cells of the brain and spinal cord. The cells swell and fill with fat, and blindness, paralysis, and mental deficiency result. In most cases, death occurs several years after the onset of the disease. This disorder appears to be caused by the inheritance of a specific recessive gene from both the mother and father and occurs most often when the parents themselves are close relatives (77).

Another inherited syndrome for which the physiological processes have been worked out in more detail is called phenylketonuria or PKU (34). As we indicated earlier, children with this disease lack an enzyme which is necessary for normal metabolic functioning. In the absence of this enzyme, a toxic chemical accumulates in the body and leads to damage to the nervous system and mental deterioration (34, 35). There is a small group of similar diseases in which the child lacks an enzyme that allows him to metabolize a particular chemical in his body. This metabolic failure often results in mental retardation (60).

Genetic Control of Enzymes The mechanisms for PKU or similar disorders may represent a model for many forms of mental retardation, each of which has a different cause. That is, each gene produces a specific protein, some of which are enzymes, the specific enzyme for phenylalanine being only one of many necessary for healthy biological functioning. It is likely that, in the years ahead, scientists will discover a series of inherited diseases in which the child lacks a specific enzyme necessary to metabolize particular sugars, proteins, or amino acids. Lack of the enzymes will lead to nervous system defects and mental retardation. However, it must be remembered that the vast majority of children classified as mentally retarded are probably **not** the victims of any genetic disorder.

Chromosomal Aberration Abnormalities in the structure of the chromosomes may be another basis for mental defects. The best example of this is **mongolism,** which is also called Down's syndrome. These children are born with an Oriental cast to the facial appearance, thus the term mongolism. Most of them function at a very low level of intelligence and, although friendly, are usually not capable of complicated mental performance. These children are mentally retarded, apparently as the result of the presence of an extra member of the Number 21 chromosome pair. These children have 47 instead of the normal 46 chromosomes.

Again, extra chromosomes can occur in any one of the 23 pairs of human chromosomes and some of these abnormalities could lead to defects in development and eventual mental retardation, but the specific cause would be different in each of these cases. Fortunately, the frequency of occurrence of chromosome abnormality is rare, typically less than ½ of 1 percent (**81**).

Mental Disorder

The role of genetic factors in the development of mental disorder has been, and continues to be, a source of controversy in the field of psychiatry. There is general agreement that certain forms of mental disorder such as general paresis (syphilis of the central nervous system) are caused by infection or similar agents attacking the body from without. Some other rather rare forms of mental illness (such as Huntington's chorea) result from definite genetic causes, although the specific underlying genetic structures are not known.

There is less agreement when it comes to the majority of cases of mental disorder, those falling into the categories of (1) the "functional" psychoses (severe mental disorders without known organic cause) and (2) the psychoneuroses (the milder forms of mental disorder and maladjustment). Some experts (**41, 42, 43, 47**) tend to view these disorders as primarily genetic in origin. Others tend to view them as almost entirely dependent on environmental factors, usually early life experiences.

Why is there so little agreement? In order to provide a concrete basis for discussion, let us consider one of the commonest forms of functional psychosis, namely, **schizophrenia.** This illness, manifested by severe defects in logical thinking and in emotional responsiveness, probably comes closest to the average person's idea of what it means to be "crazy." It accounts for the occupancy of more hospital beds in the United States than any other form of illness, mental or physical.

Schizophrenia has been attributed exclusively to hereditary defects by some authors and exclusively to disturbances in early parent-child relationships by others (**61**). Although a generation ago most psychiatrists believed that traumatic experiences in childhood were the major determinants of schizophrenia, recent research suggests that biological and hereditary factors are also important. The probability that a second member of a pair of identical twins will become schizophrenic, if the first has this disease, is between 50 and 70 percent (**30, 60**). Moreover, children of schizophrenic parents who were adopted during infancy and sent to homes with normal adoptive parents are more likely to become schizophrenic than most adopted children. Children born to schizophrenic mothers also have a higher probability of becoming criminals and neurotics (**31**). This finding suggests that there is a specific gene or set of genes that make a person vulnerable to mental disorder. Depending on the environment in which that person is raised, he may develop the hallucinations and disturbed thinking of a schizophrenic or a seriously disturbed adult personality without the thinking disorder or perhaps no serious disorder at all. One psychiatrist (**17**) has suggested that schizophrenia may be similar in origin to the disease pellagra. Pellagra can be caused by either an improper diet or heredity, but the disease will not develop if the environment is optimal. If one applies this logic to schizophrenia, different genetic constitutions in combination with different environments will yield the outcomes given in the following table.

Table 3.1 **Genetic and environmental factors in schizophrenia**

GENETIC CONSTITUTION	QUALITY OF THE ENVIRONMENT		
	GOOD	AVERAGE	POOR
Prone to schizophrenia	Slight possibility of schizophrenia	Moderate possibility of schizophrenia	Strong possibility of schizophrenia
Not prone to schizophrenia	No possibility	No possibility	Slight possibility

Thus, in a good environment it is possible for a child who is genetically prone to schizophrenia not to develop the disorder. In a poor environment, it is possible for both genetically prone and nonprone adults to develop schizophrenia (**17**).

Personality

The role of genetic factors on aspects of human behavior other than serious mental disease is not clear. One reason for the ambiguity is the lack of a specific set of behaviors to study. In Down's syndrome or in the hallucinations of a schizophrenic one has a specific phenomenon to study. The scientist can compare twins on their facial features, low IQ, and abnormality in chromosome numbers, but there are very few personality dimensions that are that specific. Repeated acts of violent aggression toward others is one moderately specific trait, and recent studies suggest that there may be a higher proportion of chromosomal anomalies among criminals than among the normal population (79). Although most psychologists agree that the tendency to display repeated acts of violence is a personality trait, they do not agree on other personality dimensions to study. This lack of agreement leads to slow progress in solving this problem. Another reason for the ambiguity in the study of the genetics of personality is that the behaviors included under the study of personality are less discrete than those in retardation or psychosis. An hallucination is not on a continuum with a nonhallucination; it is a yes or no event. Similarly, an IQ of 25 does not seem to be on a continuum with an IQ of 100; it is a qualitatively different phenomenon. But personality variables such as friendliness, activity, anger, apathy, or shyness are not all-or-none phenomena. Each is present in degrees and blends into a continuum. Therefore, if they are genetically controlled, they are probably controlled by a large set of interacting genes. The popular approach in such research is to compare identical and fraternal twins on a variety of personality traits and then determine traits on which the identical twins are more alike than the fraternal twins.

Careful study of all the research on the genetics of personality suggests that at least one dimension may be partially under genetic control. This can be best described as a tendency toward inhibition and social introversion as contrasted with a tendency toward activity and social extraversion. At a more concrete level, this dimension describes a person who is timid, shy, and withdrawn in contrast to one who is active, friendly, and outgoing.

Sets of adolescent twins in Boston and Minneapolis took a standard personality test and results revealed that the identical twins were more alike on social introversion than the fraternals. The national background of the Minneapolis test population was predominantly Scandinavian, while the Boston population was predominantly Italian, Irish, and Jewish. Thus both the gene pool and the environmental experiences of the two populations were different. The fact that degree of social introversion was more similar for identical than for fraternal twins in both cities suggests that this personality trait may be genetically controlled (27).

Other studies (8, 62) also suggest that on a large set of personality traits (such as aggressiveness, moodiness, dependency, sexual behavior, shyness) identical twins are usually more similar than fraternal twins, primarily on traits such as soberness versus enthusiasm, avoidance of people versus enjoying social contact, and inhibition versus spontaneity (63). These traits are part of the more general personality dimension we call introversion-extraversion. Moreover, this trait appears to be stable over a long period of time—more stable than most personality characteristics. A longitudinal study of typical Ohio children followed from birth to adulthood revealed that the tendency to be inhibited with others was remarkably stable from age 10 to adulthood and, surprisingly, showed some stability from age 3 to adulthood (40). Other longitudinal studies report similar results.

Studies of infants reveal that identical twins are more alike than fraternal twins on the tendency to smile and show fear of strangers (19). Marked similarity in the disposition of newborns from the same national background might also suggest partial genetic control of personality traits, and in one study it was found that Chinese-American newborns are less irritable, less changeable, and easier to console when upset than Caucasian-American newborns (20). These sources of evidence suggest that tendencies to be inhibited (in contrast to having a more impulsive and spontaneous disposition) may be under partial genetic control.

This conclusion fits well with findings from genetic studies of animal behavior. In a classic study of the behaviors of dogs Scott and Fuller studied five breeds over a 13-year period at the Jackson Laboratories in Bar Harbor, Maine (65). The five breeds were African basenjis, beagles, American cocker spaniels, Shetland sheep dogs (shelties), and wire-haired fox terriers. The researchers controlled non-genetic factors such as diet, environment, and physical conditions, and the animals experienced carefully prescribed interactions with humans as well as with other dogs. Some of the major behavioral differences among the five species were related to fear and inhibition. Cocker spaniels were easiest to train, while the beagles and terriers were the most difficult to train. Moreover, the cocker spaniels were less emotional and less likely to try to escape from a threatening situation than the wire-haired terriers (65).

Genetic influences on preferred reactions to a new situation are seen clearly in the different reactions of terriers and beagles to the same traumatic experience. Members of the two species were raised alone (in isolation). The puppies were taken from their mother at 21 days and placed alone in cages which allowed feeding and watering, but no physical or visual contact with a human being. When these animals were placed in an arena at 16–20 weeks of age, the terriers were much more active than the beagles and more active than normally reared terriers; the isolated beagles were less active than normally reared beagles. The two species that were exposed to the same isolated, caged environment for 13 weeks showed different activity levels in a new situation (21).

Similarly, imposing the same prenatal stress on different strains of pregnant mice resulted in different levels of activity in the offspring (13, 84). There is an important principle contained in these results. The genetic makeup of the animal—or person—determines his preferred behavior to a given stimulus. In order to understand human personality we must discover those classes of preferred behaviors that might be under genetic control. The data suggest that degree of inhibition may be one such behavior.

In addition to the psychological characteristics mentioned here, there are other aspects of animal and human functioning that appear to have a genetic component, and the interested student is referred to Fuller and Thompson (22), Stern (77), and Hirsch (32) for a detailed summary of them.

Intelligence

The inheritance of intelligence has been an intensively studied problem that has generated considerable controversy. The major support for the popular view that intelligence is inherited comes from the finding that the more closely related genetically two people are the more similar their IQ scores. If the IQ score accurately reflects the level or quality of a person's intellectual competence, and this is not yet proven, then there is reason to believe that differences in intelligence are partially controlled by heredity (see Fig. 3.6).

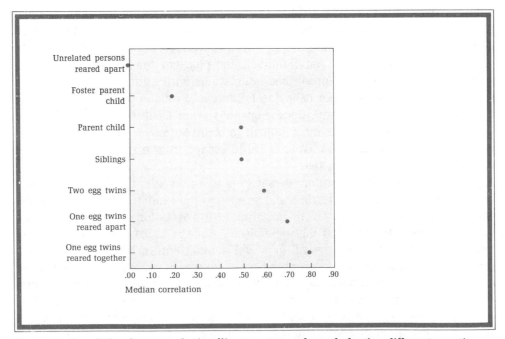

Figure 3.6 Correlation between the intelligence scores of people having different genetic relationships to each other. (From L. Erlenmeyer-Kimling & L. F. Jarvik. Genetics and intelligence. **Science,** 1963, **142,** 1478. Copyright 1963 by the American Association for the Advancement of Science. By permission.)

When the IQs of parents and children or brothers and sisters are correlated, the values hover near the expected value of .50. The correlations between the IQs of pairs of genetically unrelated people, chosen at random, is approximately .00. Although the difference between .50 and .00 may seem sufficient to implicate genetics, one must not forget that in most of these studies the parents and children or brothers and sisters live in the same home, neighborhood, and community and share similar values, motives, and knowledge. On these bases alone, we would expect mothers, fathers, brothers, and sisters to be more similar in IQ than people chosen at random.

A more critical test of the extent of genetic influence comes from comparisons of the IQ scores of identical and nonidentical twins reared in the same environment and the scores of identical twins reared in different environments. Comparison of 90 pairs of identical and 74 pairs of nonidentical twins revealed that the IQs of identical twins, who have the same genes, are more similar than those of nonidentical twins, who are of different genetic structure (69). It should be noted that the identicals were also more similar in behaviors that are likely to be the result of similar experience, not heredity. Identicals reared together were likely to share many experiences, for example, they were likely to study and do their homework together, to have the same set of very close friends, and to have similar food preferences. However, since the IQs of identical twins reared in different homes are also more similar than those of unrelated children as well as brothers and sisters, the role of heredity seems strongly indicated.

Assessing the certainty of this conclusion requires a condition that is rarely met, namely, that the twins be reared in markedly different home environments and encounter markedly different values and treatments. Since, as we have mentioned, officials responsible for the placing of children in foster homes try to place them in similar families, many of the twin pairs separated early in life went to families of similar religious, linguistic, racial, and social class backgrounds and in some cases, to two branches of the same family. Therefore, the separated twins were exposed to similar experiences. In one study of identical twins reared in different homes, 41 percent of the twin pairs grew up with families that were of similar socioeconomic status. Only 26 percent (12 twin pairs) were sent to families markedly different in social class and in 9 of these 12 pairs the twin who lived in the home of higher social class had a higher IQ than the twin living in the home of lower class (6). These comparisons suggest that the similarity in IQ scores between identical twins reared apart cannot be solely, or even primarily, the result of common heredity.

A related source of support for the genetic argument is based on the fact that there is a greater similarity in IQ between a child and his biological mother than between that child and his adopted mother. The average correlation between children's IQs and those of their natural parents ranges between .50 and .60. This degree of relationship may then be compared with the correlation between foster children's intelligence and that of their foster parents. If we find that the latter correlation is significantly lower than .50 (i.e., that foster children resemble their foster parents much less than natural children resemble their parents), we may infer that hereditary factors may account for the greater similarity between true parents and their children.

In one such study Burks (5) obtained the IQs of 204 school-age foster children, all of whom had been placed in foster homes before 12 months of age. In addition she obtained the IQs of the children's foster parents. A control group of 105 children who were living with their true parents was then also set up, and the IQs of these "true" children and their parents were also obtained. Thus Burks was able to compare the correlations in IQ between foster parents and their children with those between true parents and their children. A similar approach was used by Leahy (39). Fig. 3.7 shows the results of both these studies, demonstrating that the relationships between children and their biological parents were higher than those between children and their foster parents.

Another investigator (33) compared the relationships between adopted children's IQs and the estimated intelligence of the children's true and foster parents. The estimate of parental intelligence was based on amount of formal education. Up to age 4, education of either true or foster parent was not significantly related to the IQ of the child. From age 6 on, however, the correlation between the adopted

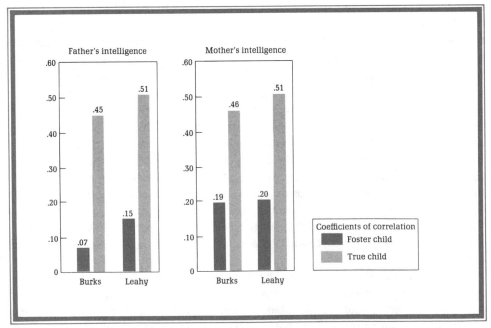

Figure 3.7 A comparison of foster and true parent-child correlations. (After H. E. Jones, Environmental influences on mental development. In L. Carmichael [Ed.], **Manual of child psychology.** New York: Wiley, 1946. P. 622. By permission.)

child's IQ and the education of his true mother and father was about .35, while the corresponding correlation between foster parents' education and the child's IQ was approximately .00. However, both the child and his adopted parents had much higher IQ scores, typically over 100, than the natural parent, suggesting that the foster parents had influenced the child's IQ score.

In most of these studies the similarity between twins, siblings, or parents and children was based on scores on standard IQ tests. If the IQ scores are not a sensitive index of a person's basic intellectual ability then it would be fallacious to assume that intelligence is inherited. (High correlations in IQ scores can confirm only the heritability of IQ scores.) As we shall see in Chapter 8, there is good reason to assume that most of the questions on IQ tests are biased to favor white middle-class children, for the correlation between IQ score and social class (as indexed by income or education) is always between .40 and .60, regardless of whether the sample is black, white, Mexican-American, or Puerto Rican. This fact suggests that exposure to similar language and ideas produces similar IQ scores. Since a person's social class can be changed by acquisition of wealth and education, it is difficult to believe that 80 percent of the variation in IQ scores in American children is due to genetic factors, as Professor Arthur Jensen claims (38). Some scientists find it hard to believe that heredity could exert so much influence on the amount of factual knowledge or the number of words a child knows. Following a thorough examination of the serious methodological flaws in existing studies of IQ similarities between twins, Professor Leon Kamin of Princeton University said, "Upon detailed analysis, there will remain no evidence sufficiently strong to convince a reasonably prudent man to abandon the null hypothesis that intelligence test scores are simply not heritable." (Presented at an address at Harvard University in April, 1973.)

Leading geneticists have also claimed that current genetic knowledge is simply not adequate enough to allow anyone to state the degree to which intelligence is inherited. Although a conservative estimate of the heritability of IQ is about 45 percent (37), suggesting that intelligence is subject to genetic control, the unknown relation between IQ score and a person's basic, or native, intelligence, and our inability to control similarity of experience for twins and siblings reared apart, suggests that even this figure may be in error. We will have to wait for future research to decide the extent of heredity's contribution to obvious differences among children in their intellectual ability.

SUMMARY

As the reader must now appreciate, we know little about the exact influences of genetics for most human psychological attributes, especially those that fall on broad continuums such as intelligence or personality. Behavioral correlates of genetic differences in animals lead to some important conclusions that are likely to apply to man. First, genetic differences are likely to lead to differences in preferred reactions to the same situation. One strain of mice "freezes" in a particular situation, another strain runs around frantically. One strain of dogs becomes excited when a bell rings, another remains placid. The same environmental experience seems to have different behavioral effects on populations that have different genetic makeups. Since males and females have different genetic makeups we might expect accompanying sex differences—and we are beginning to find them. Girls seem to show less variability in their physical growth than boys, and they also seem more predictable. Girls seem to be more precocious in their psychological development, and prediction of rate of cognitive development over a long period of time is easier for girls than for boys. Each of these sex differences may be under genetic control.

The task is to continue to search for those psychological dimensions that may have major genetic control. But the final proof of hereditary control awaits the discovery of the biological processes that link the actions of the genes with specific psychological characteristics, so that we can understand how the genes helped to produce a particular behavioral consequence.

PRENATAL DEVELOPMENT

It is a rather curious fact that while we recognize that the new individual's life begins at conception, we reckon his age from the moment of birth. It would almost seem that we were implicitly saying that the events in a person's life prior to birth are of little importance in determining the future course of his development. This attitude is especially likely to apply to our conceptions of psychological development. And yet the environment in which the unborn child grows can be of tremendous importance in influencing later patterns of growth, not only physically, but psychologically as well.

The Chinese have traditionally been somewhat more realistic in their age computations.

> Each of their babies is given at birth a full year's credit on the reckoning of its age. They know, of course, that the span of our prefatory existence is actually only nine months long, but fractions are a bother, and in China every man claims one more year of age than does the European born of the same day and the same year (10, 1).

In view of the magnitude of the growth processes occurring during the prenatal period, the Chinese approach to age reckoning appears somewhat more appropriate than ours.

HOW CONCEPTION OCCURS

Conception occurs when a sperm from the male pierces the cell wall of an ovum or egg from the female. The occasions on which such mating is possible are strictly limited physiologically and are quite independent of the vagaries of human impulse. Fig. 3.8 shows a schematic diagram of the female reproductive system.

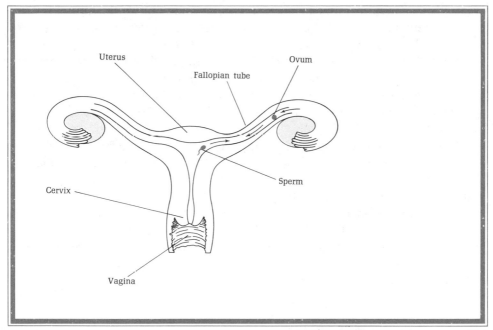

Figure 3.8 Schematic diagram of female reproductive system showing how conception occurs.

Once every 28 days (usually around the middle of the menstrual cycle) an ovum ripens in one of the two ovaries, is discharged into the corresponding Fallopian tube, or oviduct, and begins its slow journey toward the uterus, propelled by small hairlike cilia which line the tube. In most cases, it takes from three to seven days for the ovum to reach the uterus (**36**). If the ovum has not been fertilized in the course of this journey, it disintegrates in the uterus after a few days, "and its remains, which are less than a grain of dust, disperse unnoticed" (**10**).

If, on the other hand, a mating has taken place, one of the many millions of tiny sperm released by the male may find its way up into the oviduct during the time the ovum is making its descent. There if it unites with the ovum, the conception of a new individual will result.

As indicated earlier, each sperm is a tadpolelike cell. The oval head of the sperm is packed with the 23 chromosomes. Behind the head are special structures that supply the energy the sperm cell needs to travel the distance to reach the ovum. It is estimated that the sperm travel at a velocity of about $\frac{1}{10}$ inch per minute.

THE EARLIEST PERIOD OF DEVELOPMENT

At the moment of conception the ovum, the largest cell in the human body, is still very small, only about 1/175 inch in diameter (**10**). The fertilized ovum, called a

zygote, begins to grow immediately. Let us briefly summarize this process. When the sperm enters the ovum a process is initiated which results in the fusing of the nucleus of the sperm with the nucleus of the ovum. It will be recalled that each of the nuclei contains 23 chromosomes. The 23 chromosomes from the sperm and the 23 chromosomes from the ovum then line up and split, yielding 46 pairs of chromosomes. The process of development has now begun. The time from the sperm's penetration of the ovum to the development of the first two cells usually is between 24 and 36 hours.

The process of development from conception to birth is usually divided into three phases. The first phase, called the period of the ovum, lasts from fertilization until the time that the zygote is firmly implanted in the wall of the uterus. This process typically takes about 10 to 14 days.

The second phase, from 2 to 8 weeks, is called the period of the embryo. This period is characterized by a differentiation of all the major organs that will be present in the newborn baby. The last phase, from 8 weeks until delivery (normally 40 weeks), is called the period of the fetus and is characterized by growth of the organism.

The Period of the Ovum

The fertilized ovum continues to double its cells during its journey from the oviduct, where it was fertilized, to the uterus, where it will become implanted.

By the time the fertilized ovum reaches the uterus, it is about the size of a pinhead and has several dozen cells. A small cavity is formed within the mass of cells, resulting in an outer and a separated inner cluster of cells (see Fig. 3.9). The outer layer, called the **trophoblast,** will ultimately develop into accessory tissues which protect and nourish the embryo. The inner cluster of cells will become the embryo itself.

While these developments are taking place, small burrlike tendrils have begun to grow around the outside of the trophoblast. It is by means of these tendrils that in a few more days (around 10 to 14 days after fertilization) the ovum will attach itself to the uterine wall.

In the meantime, however, the uterus itself has begun to undergo changes in preparation for receiving the fertilized ovum (called a **blastocyte** at this stage). At the time of implantation (attachment of the ovum to the uterine wall), the tendrils from the trophoblast burrow into the receptive mucous membrane of the uterus. Extensions of the tendrils reach into the blood spaces which have formed within the maternal tissue. At this time, the period of the ovum comes to an end, and the second phase of prenatal development, the period of the embryo, begins. The new individual has ceased to be an independent, free-floating organism and has established a dependent relationship with the mother.

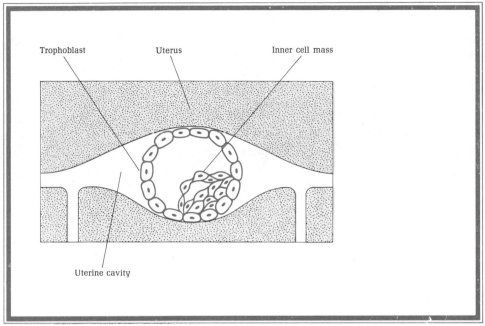

Figure 3.9 Schematic representation of ovum at early stage of implantation in uterine wall.

The Period of the Embryo

Once the growing egg has been successfully lodged in its new home, development is rapid. Its inner cell mass, which will become a recognizable embryo, begins to differentiate itself into three distinct layers: (1) the **ectoderm** (outer layer), from which will develop the epidermis or outer layer of the skin, the hair, the nails, parts of the teeth, skin glands, sensory cells, and the nervous system; (2) the **mesoderm** (middle layer), from which will develop the dermis or inner skin layer, the muscles, skeleton, and the circulatory and excretory organs; (3) the **endoderm** (inner layer), from which will develop the lining of the entire gastrointestinal tract, the Eustachian tubes, trachea, bronchia, lungs, liver, pancreas, salivary glands, thyroid glands, and thymus **(25, 36)**.

While the inner cell mass is being differentiated into a recognizable embryo, the outer layers of cells are giving rise to the fetal membranes—the **chorion** and **amnion.** These two membranes, together with a third membrane derived from the uterine wall of the mother (the **decidua capsularis**), extend from the wall of the uterus and enclose the developing embryo (see Fig. 3.10). They form a sac which is filled with a watery fluid (**liquor amnii** or amniotic fluid) and acts as a buffer to protect the embryo from shocks experienced by the mother. It also helps to provide an even temperature for the embryo and serves to prevent adhesions between the embryo and the amniotic membrane **(60)**.

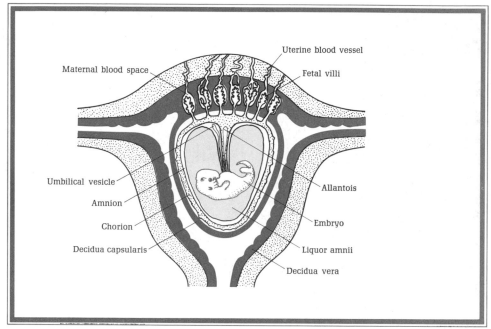

Figure 3.10 Diagram representing the relationship between the uterus, the membrane, and the embyro during early pregnancy. (From L. Carmichael. Origins and prenatal growth of behavior. In C. Murchison [Ed.], **A handbook of child psychology.** (2nd ed.) Worchester: Clark University Press, 1933. P. 50. By permission.)

Simultaneously, other fetal sacs are formed, the most important of which becomes the umbilical cord. It extends from the embryo, and is attached at its opposite end to the section of the uterine wall where the uterus and the chorion are joined. This area is called the **placenta.**

The umbilical cord might well be referred to as the lifeline of the embryo. Through it, two arteries carry blood from the embryo to the placenta, and one vein carries blood to the infant from the placenta. However, the relationship between the child's bloodstream and the mother's is not a direct one. Both the child's and the mother's bloodstreams open into the placenta. But the two systems are always separated by cell walls within the placenta. These cell walls consist of semipermeable membranes which function as extremely fine mesh screens, large enough to permit the passage of gases, salts, and other substances of small molecular size, but too small to allow blood cells to get through.

Although a precise knowledge of all the substances which pass through a normal placenta is lacking, it is known that various nutrient substances from the mother's blood—sugars, fats, and some protein elements—permeate it. Waste products from the infant, primarily carbon dioxide and other metabolites, can also pass through the placenta. In addition, some vitamins, drugs (including nicotine and alcohol), vaccines, and some disease germs (notably those of diphtheria, typhoid, influenza, and syphilis) may also get through and affect the embryo's development (10, 14). Hence, the health of the mother can directly affect the health of the fetus.

It should be noted that there are no direct neural connections between the maternal and embryonic nervous systems; only chemicals can cross the placental barrier.

Despite the fact that there are no nerve fibers joining mother and fetus, a mother's emotional state may indirectly influence the physiological functioning of her child. When the mother is emotionally aroused, a variety of physiological reactions occur, and specific hormones such as adrenalin, as well as other chemical agents, are released into the mother's bloodstream. Some of these substances may pass through the placenta and affect the ongoing physiological processes in the unborn child (10, 14).

Development of the Embryo Much of our knowledge of prenatal development has been derived from the intensive study of embryos and fetuses which, for medical reasons, had to be surgically removed from the uterus.

During the period of the embryo, development is extremely rapid. By 18 days, the embryo has already begun to take some shape. It has established a longitudinal axis and its front, back, left, and right sides, and a head and tail are discernible. By the end of the third week a primitive heart has developed and has begun to beat (26; see Fig. 3.11).

By 4 weeks the embryo is about 1/5 inch long. It has the beginnings of a mouth region, gastrointestinal tract, and liver. The heart is becoming well developed, and the head and brain regions are becoming more clearly differentiated. At this stage, the embryo is still a very primitive organism. It has as yet no arms or legs, no developed features, and only the most elementary of body systems.

By 8 to 9 weeks, however, the picture has changed markedly (see Fig. 3.12). The embryo is now about 1 inch long. Face, mouth, eyes, and ears have begun to take on fairly well-defined form. Arms and legs and even hands and feet with stubby fingers and toes have appeared (25). At this stage the sex organs are just beginning to form. The development of muscle and cartilage also begins, but well-defined neuromotor activity (activation of the muscles by impulses from the nerves) is still absent at this stage (25). The internal organs—intestines, liver, pancreas, lungs, kidneys—take on a definite shape and assume some degree of function. The liver, for example, begins to manufacture red blood cells.

The period of the embryo is characterized by an extremely rapid development of the nervous system. Figs. 3.11 and 3.12 show that, during this period, the head is large in relation to other body areas. This suggests that the first eight weeks constitute a sensitive period with respect to the integrity of the nervous system. Mechanical or chemical interference with development at this time (such

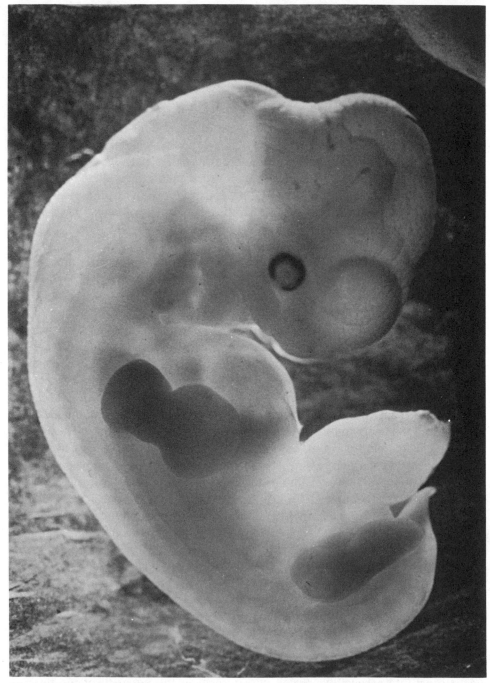

Figure 3.11 The human embryo at 6 weeks. The eye is seen as a dark-rimmed circle. (©Lennart Nilsson, courtesy LIFE Magazine.)

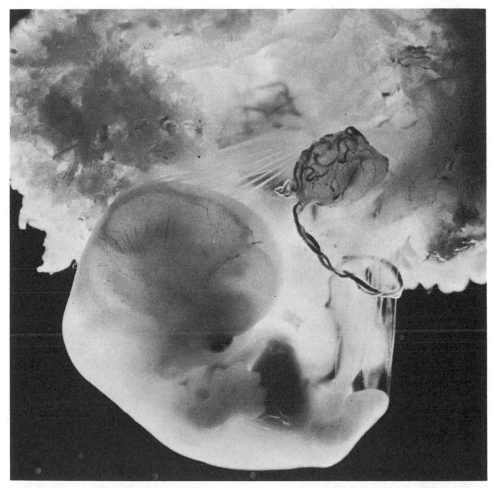

Figure 3.12 The human embryo at 9 weeks. Hands and fingers are now clear. (©Lennart Nilsson, courtesy LIFE Magazine.)

as the mother falling downstairs or an overdose of drugs to the mother) is more likely to cause permanent nervous system damage than a similar disruption at a later date. For example, if the mother should contract German measles during this period, the child is more likely to be mentally deficient than if she should have this illness during the last eight weeks of pregnancy.

The Period of the Fetus

The third period of prenatal development, the period of the fetus, extends from the end of the second month until birth. During this time, the various body systems, which have been laid down in rudimentary form earlier, become quite well de-

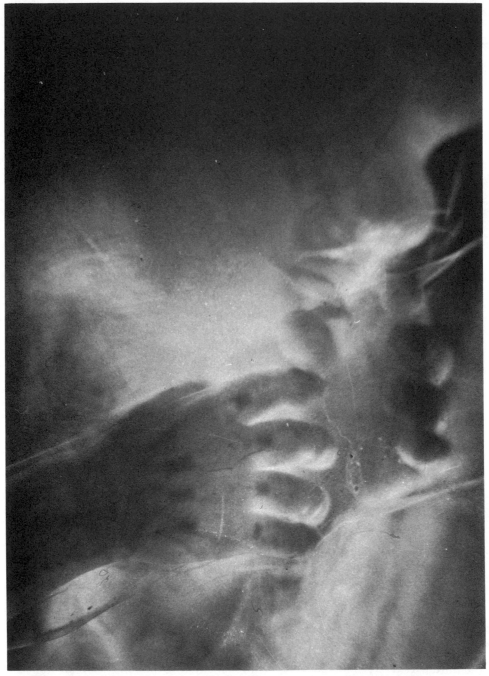

Figure 3.13 A and B (opposite) The 12-week-old human embryo. Reflex movements now appear. The fetus moves its hand to its mouth and makes sucking movements. (©Lennart Nilsson, courtesy LIFE Magazine.)

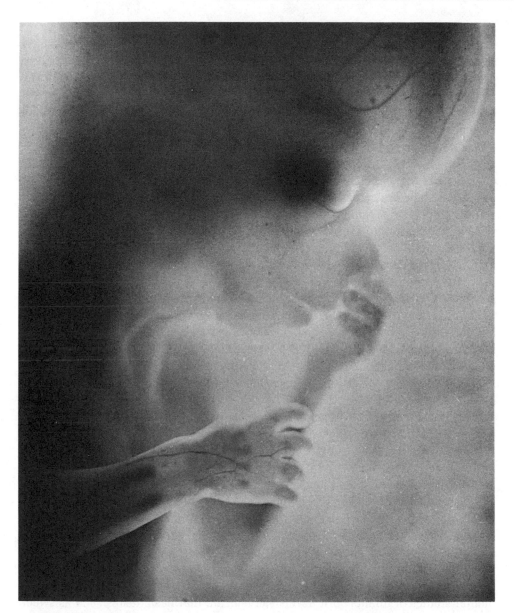

veloped and begin to function. Up until about 8½ weeks, the fetus has led a relatively passive existence, floating quiescently in the amniotic fluid. At this time, however, it becomes capable of responding to tactile (touch) stimulation (60). The trunk flexes and the head extends. From this point on, motor functions become increasingly more differentiated and complex.

Toward the end of the eighth week, the reproductive system begins to develop. The gonads (the ovaries and the testes) initially appear as a pair of blocks of tissue in both sexes. Moreover, it appears that the hormones manufactured by the male's testes are necessary to stimulate the development of a male reproductive system. If the testes are removed or fail to perform properly, the baby that is born possesses a primarily female reproductive system. Evidence from rabbits indicates that if the tiny ovary is removed immediately after its formation, the female fetus develops normally. It appears, therefore, that the anatomy of the female reproductive system is basic—it is the form that will develop if either testes or ovaries are removed or do not function.

By the end of 12 weeks, the fetus is about 3 inches long and weighs about ¾ ounce. It has definitely begun to resemble a human being, though the head is disproportionately large (see Figs. 3.13A and B). Muscles are becoming well developed, and spontaneous movements of the arms and legs may be observed. Eyelids and nails have begun to form, and the fetus' sex can now be distinguished easily. The nervous system is still very incomplete, however. During the next four weeks, motor behavior becomes more complex.

By the end of 16 weeks, the mother can feel the fetus' movements. At this point the fetus is about 4½ inches in length. In the period from 16 to 20 weeks, the fetus increases to about 10 inches in length and 8 or 9 ounces in weight (36). It becomes more human-looking and hair appears on the head and body. The mouth becomes capable of protrusion, as well as opening and closing, a precursor of later sucking movements (25). Blinking of the eyes occurs, although the lids are still tightly fused. The hands become capable of gripping in addition to closing (see Fig. 3.14).

After 20 weeks the skin begins to assume adult form; hair and nails appear, and sweat glands are developed (see Fig. 3.15).

By 24 weeks of age the eyes are completely formed, and taste buds appear on the tongue. The fetus is now capable of "true inspiration and expiration, and of a thin crying noise should he be prematurely born" (25, 71; see Fig. 3.16).

The fetal age of 28 weeks is an important one. It demarcates the zone between viability (the ability to live if born) and nonviability. By this age, the child's nervous, circulatory, and other bodily systems have become sufficiently well structured to stand a chance of being able to function adequately in the extrauterine environment, although, of course, special care is required. At this point, reactions to changes in temperature approximate those of the full-term infant. Experimental studies of infants born at this age indicate that basic tastes such as sweet, salt, sour, and bitter can be differentiated by the fetus (7). Basic odors can also be differentiated. Visual and auditory reactions occur, though not as clearly as in the full-term infant. On the other hand, sensitivity to pain seems to be relatively absent in the premature infant.

The period from 28 weeks to birth at full term (40 weeks) is marked by further development of the basic bodily structures and functions. In the outline which follows, Watson and Lowrey (82) have employed some of the available data on

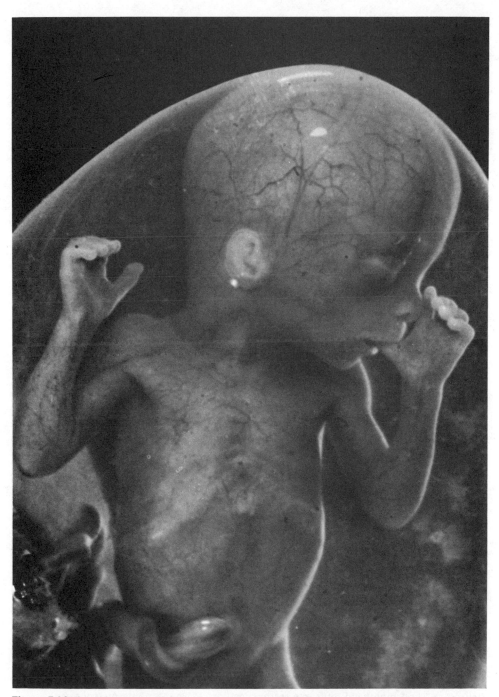

Figure 3.14 The 4½-month-old fetus is shown sucking its thumb. (©Lennart Nilsson, courtesy LIFE Magazine.)

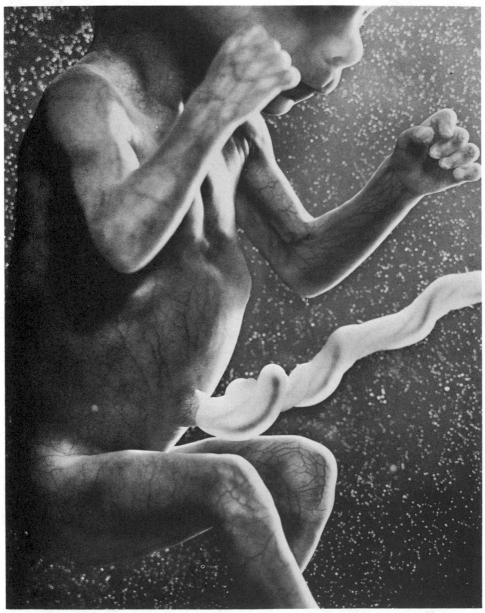

Figure 3.15 The 5-month-old fetus in a resting position. (©Lennart Nilsson, courtesy LIFE Magazine.)

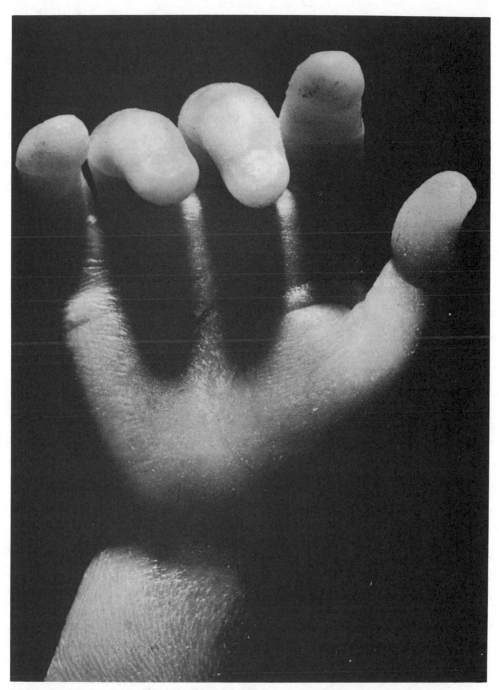

Figure 3.16 The 6-month-old fetus with emerging fingernails (©Lennart Nilsson, courtesy LIFE Magazine.)

premature infants to illustrate the increasingly elaborate behavior which develops between 28 weeks and normal birth.

Fetus at 28–32 weeks

Lack of muscular tone
Mild avoidance responses to bright light and sound
Breathing shallow and irregular
Sucking and swallowing present but lack endurance
No definite waking and sleeping pattern
Cry absent or very weak

Fetus at 32–36 weeks

Muscle tone fair
In prone position turns head, elevates rump
Definite periods of being awake
Palmar stimulation causes good grasp
Good hunger cry

Fetus at 36–40 weeks

Movements active and sustained
Muscle tone good
Brief erratic following of objects with eyes
In prone position attempts to lift head
Definite periods of alertness
Cries well when hungry and disturbed
Hands held as fists much of time, good grasp
Good, strong sucking reflex (82)

PRENATAL ENVIRONMENTAL INFLUENCES

Thus far, we have been discussing what might be called "normal" or typical patterns of prenatal development. But such patterns can occur only when the organism itself and its environment fall within what might be thought of as normal limits.

The discussion of genetic mechanisms emphasized that hereditary factors can affect the individual's development in important ways. We also noted, however, that no trait or characteristic of an individual is entirely hereditarily determined. Heredity may make important contributions to many of the individual's potentialities or limitations, but most of his characteristics are the consequents of complex interactions between genetically transmitted factors and environmental influences. The growth and development of the individual's inherent potential may be actualized, facilitated, and enhanced—or thwarted, mutilated, and limited—depending on the kind of physical, social, and psychological environment he encounters. "The important point to understand . . . is the same genes may be influenced to express themselves differently and to have different end effects as a consequence of the different environments in which they function" (52, 151).

Ordinarily we think of the prenatal environment as constant and similar for all fetuses. Certainly, the fetus' surroundings are relatively simple in comparison with the complex world he will encounter after birth. Nevertheless, there are many variations in prenatal environment, and the pressures to which one fetus is subjected may differ greatly from those exerted on another. Recent research suggests that the mother's physical and emotional status (and consequently the prenatal environment she provides) may exert important influences on the course of fetal development and the subsequent health and adjustment of the child. Some of the more imporant prenatal environmental factors which have been investigated will be discussed in the following sections.

Age of Mother

Advances in medical science have made pregnancy and birth less dangerous and difficult. The total incidence of infant mortality, regardless of the age of the mother, is now low, about 22 deaths per 1000 births. There is some evidence that these mortality rates are higher if the mothers are below 20 or above 35 than if they are between these two ages.

Moreover, mothers under 20 and over 35 tend to have a higher proportion of retarded youngsters than mothers between 20 and 35 years of age (58). These difficulties may be due to the inadequate development of the reproductive system in some younger women and to progressive decline in reproductive functioning in some older ones.

Women who deliver their first infant when they are 35 or over are also more likely than younger women to experience illnesses during pregnancy and longer and more difficult labor. They are also more likely to require operative delivery and Caesarean sections. The older the woman, the greater the likelihood that these problems will arise, but the absolute incidence of serious complications is small.

Diet of the Mother

The expectant mother should have an adequate diet if she is going to maintain her own general good health during her pregnancy and deliver a healthy infant. This appears entirely reasonable when we remember that the growing fetus' food supply comes ultimately from the mother's blood stream, via the semipermeable membranes of the placenta and the umbilical cord. In one experimental investigation of the consequents of malnutrition during pregnancy, the subjects were 210 pregnant women attending a clinic at the University of Toronto (15). All of them had inadequate diets during their first four or five months of pregnancy. In the later phases of pregnancy, the diets of 90 of the women were supplemented and made adequate from a nutritional standpoint. The other 120 maintained their nutritionally deficient diets throughout their pregnancies. By comparing these two groups, the investigators could systematically study the influence of good and poor maternal diets upon the course of pregnancy and the condition of the infant during the first few months of life.

The "good-diet" mothers were in better health throughout their pregnancies. Complications such as anemia, toxemia, threatened and actual miscarriages, premature births, and stillbirths were much more frequent in the "poor-diet" group than in the "good-diet" group. On the average, women in the latter group were in labor five hours less than the women with inadequate diets. Another investigator (80) has also demonstrated that stillbirths, prematurities, and deaths in early infancy were less common among the babies of mothers with nutritionally adequate diets than among those whose mothers had less adequate diets.

Compared with the infants born to "poor-diet" mothers, the babies of "good-diet" women had better health records during the first two weeks of postnatal life. They also had a much smaller incidence of major illnesses (pneumonia, rickets, tetany, anemia) and minor diseases (colds, bronchitis) during the entire first six months.

There is a great deal of concern over potential damage to a fetus caused by severe protein deficiency in the diet of the mother. Babies born to mothers on a chronically low protein diet are more vulnerable to serious diseases. In one animal study it was found that rats born to mothers kept on a very low protein diet had anatomical defects in the central nervous system (12), but it is not known whether this relation between protein insufficiency and the integrity of the brain occurs in man. It is almost impossible in human populations to isolate specific effects of a poor diet—before or after the childs' birth—from the other consequences of living in a community of poverty. The infant from a family of poverty is subject to more disease and more stressful conditions of living. These may be as important as malnutrition in influencing the growth of the central nervous system and the child's intellectual ability.

Study of Indian children living in small Guatemalan villages, most of whom had low-calorie and low-protein diets, reveals that the social status of the family in a particular village was as important a determinant of the child's scores on intellectual tests as physical indexes of malnutrition, like small stature (45). It is likely that assaults on the child's biology, like malnutrition, are most likely to have a detrimental effect on intellectual growth in homes where the child is not encouraged to develop his intellectual skills and where variety of experience is less than optimal.

Drugs

During the last five years doctors and parents have become increasingly concerned about the potentially harmful effects of drugs on the developing fetus. The increased concern comes from two sources. First, scientists no longer believe that there is a completely effective barrier between the mother and the fetus; foreign chemicals in the mother's bloodstream do pass into the fetus' blood stream. Second, there have been many dramatic cases of damage to the fetus as a result of drugs taken by the mother. The most famous of these involved babies born with gross anatomical defects in their limbs, caused by the mothers' taking a drug called thalidomide during pregnancy. Drugs can affect the development of the embryo and the fetus, but we need much more specific information about the relation between fetal malformation and diet and drug use.

There is more certain knowledge about the effects of drugs taken just prior to or during the delivery of the baby, drugs given to ease the mother's distress and pain. These drugs do affect the fetus and the newborn baby, although it is not known how long the effect lasts. Newborn babies delivered from mothers who had been given a depressant (such as pentobarbital) within 90 minutes of delivery looked less at pictures than babies delivered of mothers who had not been drugged within 90 minutes of delivery. Moreover, the closer to the time of delivery the drugs were administered, the less attentive the infant was (75). Although the serious effects of sedation generally seem to be gone by the time the baby is a week old, it is possible that a heavy dosing of the mother with drugs "may so overload the fetal bloodstream as to produce asphyxiation of the fetus at birth, with permanent brain damage of such a kind as to lead to mental impairment" (52, 162).

The rise in drug addiction among young women has led to an increased number of infants who are born with an addiction to drugs. These babies are unusually irritable, tremble, and show frequent vomiting episodes. Pregnant women who are taking drugs are placing an awesome burden on their unborn children.

Irradiation

Radium or roentgen (X ray) irradiation of the pelvis may be therapeutically necessary for the pregnant woman with a pelvic or ovarian tumor or cancer. Small amounts of this irradiation, such as those used in X ray photography, are not known to damage the fetus, but large therapeutic doses may be injurious or precipitate abortions.

Over a third of a group of 75 full-term infants whose mothers had therapeutic irradiation during pregnancy manifested mental or physical abnormalities which could not be attributed to any source other than the treatments. Twenty had severe disturbances of the central nervous system, 16 of them being microcephalic (a clinical type of feeble-mindedness, in which there is an abnormally small, pointed skull and a very small brain); 8 others were extremely small, physically deformed, or blind (54, 55).

The most dramatic illustration of the effect of atomic radiation on the fetus was learned following the dropping of an atomic bomb on Hiroshima, Japan. If a mother pregnant less than 20 weeks was within a half mile of the center of the explosion, she was very likely to give birth to a physically or mentally abnormal child (59).

Maternal Diseases and Disorders During Pregnancy

Since there appears to be only a partially effective barrier between the embryo and its mother's virus or germ organisms, fetal infection from maternal disease can occur. In some cases, infants have been born with smallpox, measles, chicken-pox, or mumps transmitted from the mother (27).

Infection with syphilitic spirochetes from the mother is not infrequent. Spiro-chetes were found in 16 fetuses taken from a group of 67 syphilitic mothers—an incidence of 24 percent (14). These spirochetes may produce abortion or mis-carriage, or, if the child survives, he may be born weak, deformed, or mentally deficient. In some cases, the child may not manifest syphilitic symptoms until several years later. As fetuses under 18 weeks of age are apparently not suscep-tible to the disease, transmission of the spirochetes may be prevented if treatment of a syphilitic mother begins early in her pregnancy.

Rubella (German measles) contracted by the prospective mother in the first three or four months of pregnancy, may damage the fetus considerably, producing deaf-mutism, cardiac lesions, cataracts, or various forms of mental deficiency. There does not appear to be any direct relation between the severity of maternal infection and the degree of fetal involvement. Mild attacks may produce fetal mal-formations as grave as those suffered when the mother is ill for a week or two. About 12 percent of the mothers with rubella during the first three months of pregnancy have defective children (30).

Mothers who are diabetic during their pregnancy often give birth to infants with physical abnormalities that involve the circulatory and respiratory systems (24).

There are also some general disturbances of the mother during pregnancy that may affect the fetus. One of the most common is called toxemia of pregnancy. This disorder, which is of unknown origin, involves swelling of the mother's limbs and is associated with a general dysfunction of the mother's kidneys and circula-tory system. This illness is more common among lower- than among middle-class mothers and could be caused by a combination of poor nutrition and subsequent lowering of resistance to infection. It is possible that the toxemia might affect the fetus in a deleterious way.

Rh Factors

If there are genetically determined differences between the blood types of the fetus and its mother, they may be biochemically incompatible. For example, the child's red blood corpuscles may contain a substance which makes his blood agglutinate or "clump" in response to a specially prepared serum, while his mother's blood may lack this substance. In this case, the child, like 85 percent of the white American population, is "Rh positive"; his mother is "Rh negative" (50).

The Rh-positive fetus produces certain substances called antigens which enter into the mother's circulation through the placental barrier. Toxic substances (antibodies) are then manufactured in her blood and passed back into the fetus' circulatory system. They may do a great deal of damage there, destroying his red blood cells and preventing them from distributing oxygen normally. There may be tragic consequences, including miscarriage, stillbirth, or death shortly after birth from erythroblastosis (destruction of red blood corpuscles). Or, if the child survives, he may be partially paralyzed or mentally deficient, possibly as a result of brain damage from inadequate oxygen supply during a crucial developmental period (51).

Fortunately, these disastrous consequences do not occur in every case of mother-child Rh incompatibility. Erythroblastosis occurs only in about 1 out of every 200 pregnancies (52). First-born children are not usually affected, because it takes time for the mother to develop the antibodies, but subsequent offspring are more likely to suffer if their Rh blood types differ from their mother's.

There are medical techniques now available which, if applied early, minimize the consequences of this incompatibility.

Maternal Emotional States and Attitudes

Despite the fact that there are no direct connections between the mother's and the fetus' nervous systems, the mother's emotional state can influence fetal reactions and development. This is true because emotions such as rage, fear, and anxiety bring the mother's autonomic nervous system into action, liberating certain chemicals (acetylcholine and epinephrine) into the blood stream. Furthermore, under such conditions the endocrine glands, particularly the adrenals, secrete different kinds and amounts of hormones. Cell metabolism is also modified. In brief, the composition of the blood changes, and new chemical substances are transmitted through the placenta, producing changes in the fetus' circulatory system (74).

These changes may be irritating to the fetus. One study (71, 72, 73) noted that bodily movements of fetuses increased several hundred percent while their mothers were undergoing emotional stress. If the mother's emotional upset lasted several weeks, fetal activity continued at an exaggerated level throughout the entire period. When these upsets were brief, heightened irritability usually lasted several hours. Prolonged maternal emotional stress during pregnancy may have enduring consequents for the child (72). The expectant mother's attitude toward her pregnancy may also have some effect on the fetus since that attitude will be reflected in her emotional state during this period. A woman who resents being pregnant is more likely to be emotionally upset than one who is happy about the prospect of having a child.

Emotional tension may predispose the mother to experience more difficult labor and delivery. Moreover, maternal attitudes seem to predict aspects of the young infant's physical adjustment, for maternal emotional tensions may play some role in the development of **colic** in the newborn. Colic is a term applied to a syndrome characterized by a distension of the abdomen, apparent pain, and continuous crying at certain intervals during the day. Mothers of colicky babies were more tense and anxious during pregnancy than the mothers of noncolicky babies (47). The former group also felt more inadequate about their ability to care for the child. Perhaps the mother's chronic concern about her ability to handle the coming baby produced physiological reactions in both mother and baby that predisposed the child to the colic reaction. It is, of course, possible that tense mother-child relations following birth may have led to the development of colic. This study does not permit a differentiation of these alternative explanations, and the student should bear in mind that there are many cases of colic that are not clearly related to maternal tension and anxiety.

The mother's attitude toward the pregnancy and her baby also seems to be a valid predictor of the mother's behavior with her baby after birth. Mothers who were pregnant with their first child were interviewed during the last three months of the pregnancy. They were asked about their attitude toward the baby, their general feeling toward the coming infant, and the degree to which they thought they would seek affection and contact with the baby after its birth. The mothers were then visited in their homes when the babies were 1 month old. These mothers who had the most positive attitudes toward their unborn children spent the most time in face-to-face contact with them at 1 month (52). Similarly, mothers who were hostile during pregnancy had less favorable relations with their children 8 months after delivery (11).

A mother's attitude toward her unborn child has psychological meaning and relates to aspects of her personality and behavior. Because extreme rage, anger, or frustration over an unwanted pregnancy could produce physiological reactions that might influence the fetus, we must at least consider the possibility that the psychological status of the pregnant mother can have consequences for the future psychological integrity of the baby.

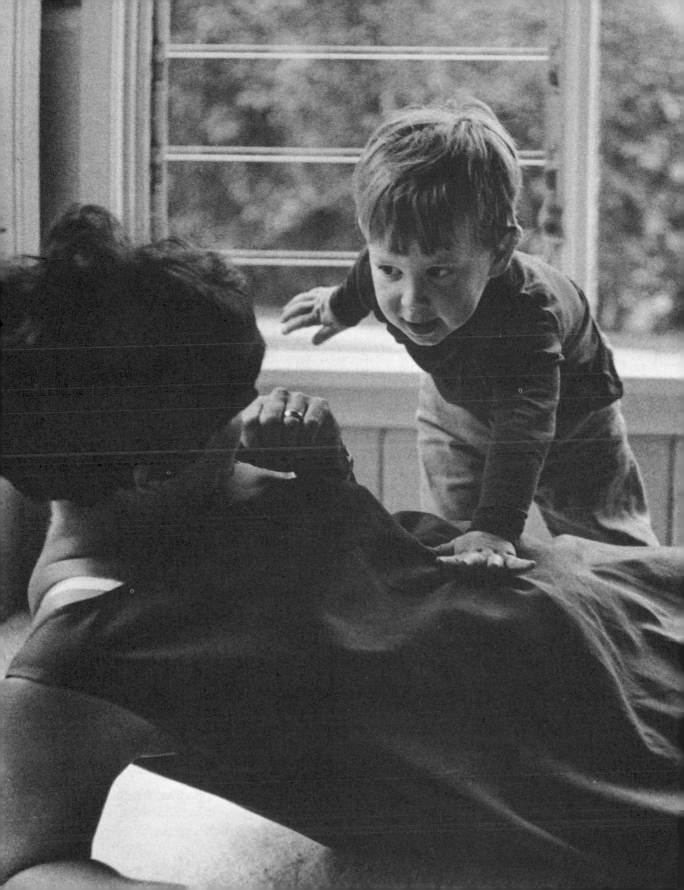

THE BIRTH PROCESS AND ITS CONSEQUENCES

Thus far we have considered the possible effects of events that occur during pregnancy—nutrition of the mother, drugs the mother may have taken, maternal diseases or infections, irradiation, and the mother's attitudes and emotional state. Each tends to influence the fetus during the organization and growth of its organs and the development of its physiological functions. There is a second set of factors that can affect the fetus adversely. They are related to the mechanics of the delivery process—the ease with which delivery occurs and the rapidity with which the newborn begins to breathe. Although there are many dangers associated with this process, the two major ones involve a breaking of the blood vessels of the brain (called hemorrhaging), caused by strong pressures on the head of the fetus, and lack of sufficient oxygen because of the infant's failure to begin to breathe once he is separated from the maternal source of oxygen. Both of these events, hemorrhaging and failure to breathe early, affect the supply of oxygen to the nerve cells of the brain and, in extreme cases, can lead to damage to nerve cells and subsequent psychological defects. The neurons of the central nervous system require oxygen; if they are deprived of oxygen, some cells may die. If too many neurons die, the infant may suffer serious brain damage or, in the extreme, death.

Lack of oxygen (called **anoxia**) in a newborn is likely to cause damage to the cells of the brain stem, rather than to those of the cortex. When the cells of the brain stem are damaged, motor defects are likely to occur. The child may show a paralysis of the legs or the arms, a tremor of the face or fingers, or an inability to use his vocal muscles. In the latter case, he may have difficulty learning to speak. The general term cerebral palsy describes a variety of motor defects associated with damage to the brain cells, possibly as a result of lack of oxygen during the birth process.

Hemorrhaging and respiratory delay, which can deprive nerve cells of a sufficient oxygen supply, can lead to a varied set of defects, most of which are motor (**86**). It is not known whether children who suffer a mild oxygen deficit at birth, but do not show obvious motor paralysis or tremors, have any brain damage which might influence their future psychological development. One way to study this issue is to find a group of infants who experienced mild anoxia during the delivery process and compare them with a group of infants from the same social class and ordinal position who did not experience anoxia. There seems to be some evidence suggesting differences in distractibility between anoxic and normal infants during the first two or three years. With age, however, the differences disappear or become minimal. By the time the child is 7 or 8 years of age it is difficult to distinguish the mild anoxic from the normal child (**9**; see Fig. 3.17).

Anoxic infants are more irritable and show more muscular tension and rigidity than normal infants do during the first week (**29**). In general, infants with

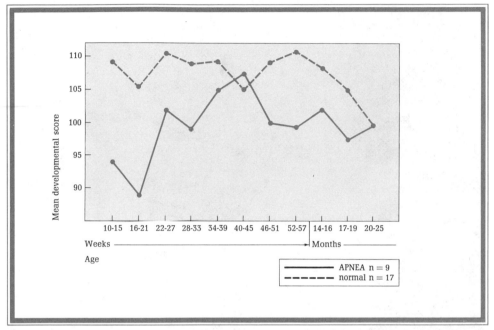

Figure 3.17 Differences in developmental score between normal and anoxic infants. (From G. A. Stechler. A longitudinal follow-up of neonatal APNEA. **Child Development**, 1964, **35,** 343. Copyright 1964 by The Society for Research in Child Development, Inc. By permission.)

mild anoxia score lower on standard tests of motor development during the first year and are less attentive to moving lights (**48;** see Fig. 3.18).

One of the most comprehensive studies of the long-term effects of mild anoxia at birth involved a follow-up assessment of newborns who had suffered anoxia at birth and were tested at both 3 and 7 years of age. At 3 years of age, the anoxic children performed poorly on tests of conceptualization, compared with the normals (**18**). When these children were tested again at age 7, the differences between the normal and anoxic children were less dramatic and their IQ scores were equal. However, the anoxic children had greater difficulty in copying designs placed before them and were more distractible than the normals. A child who does not think about what he is drawing or lets his attention shift to events around him is likely to draw a design poorly, suggesting that the anoxic children may have been less planful.

In sum, mild anoxia can cause damage to the cells of the brain, which, in turn, may disturb motor behavior and produce shorter periods of attentiveness during the first year. With age, the differences between anoxic and normal children become smaller, and there is no firm evidence of serious and permanent intellectual damage at the present time.

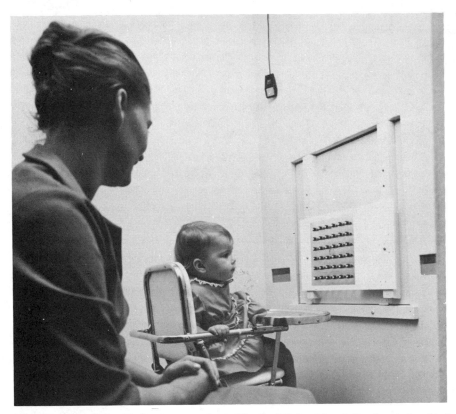

Figure 3.18 The Infant Laboratory conducted by Dr. Michael Lewis for the study of infant attention. A child (approximately 18 months old) sits facing the light matrix. Two of the observation windows flanking the matrix are visible, and it is from these windows that the observers record the infant's behavior. (From M. Lewis, B. Bartels, H. Campbell, & S. Goldberg. Individual differences in attention. **American Journal of Diseases of Children,** 1967, **113.** By permission.)

PREMATURITY

Premature birth is another phenomenon that seems to be predictive of the child's later development. The definition of prematurity should be in terms of the number of weeks of gestational age. An infant born at less than 37 weeks of gestational age (time since fertilization) is classified premature; one born between 37 and 40 weeks would be classified as normal. However, it is difficult to obtain information on the time of conception, and most scientists use the child's birth weight as the index of prematurity. When birth weight is used, an infant born under 5½ pounds is regarded as premature, and an infant born under 4 pounds is classified as severely premature. It is estimated that 7.6 percent of hospital births in the United States are categorized as premature. The premature infant has wrinkled, transparent skin, a disproportionately large head and tongue, poor muscle tone, and prominent and widely spaced eyes. Studies of the development of premature children reveal that these infants remain smaller in height and weight until about 5 or 6 years of age. Prematures also tend to obtain lower scores on general tests of cognitive and motor development during the first 5 years.

An extensive five-year study in Scotland followed 1000 infants, some of whom were born prematurely. As late as at 4 years of age, the prematures of all social classes had lower developmental quotients than the normals, but the premature children from the lowest social-class backgrounds had the poorest scores of all. On the other hand, there were not dramatic differences in overt behavior between the majority of the prematures and the normal children (15).

One study, involving only lower-class black infants born either premature or at term, followed the infants until 1 year of age. The prematures were more likely than the full-term babies to suffer anoxia, a loss in weight, and infection during the opening days of life. The premature infants had much poorer performance than the normals on a test of gross motor development when they were 13 months of age; moreover, within the premature group, the lighter the birth weight, the poorer the performance (4, see Fig. 3.19).

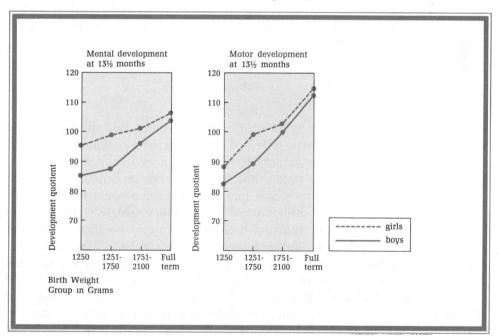

Figure 3.19 Differences in mental and motor development for three groups of varying prematurity and a normal full-term group. (From M. D. S. Braine, C. B. Heimer, H. Wortis, & A. M. Freedman. Factors associated with impairment of the early development of prematures. **Monographs of the Society for Research in Child Development,** 1966, **31,** 139. Copyright 1966 by The Society for Research in Child Development, Inc. By permission.)

In sum, the premature child does differ slightly from the normal. He is likely to be more restless and distractible if extremely premature, and display slightly retarded motor and cognitive development during the first year. At the extreme ranges of prematurity, under 4 pounds, the child is more likely to be brain-damaged so that serious psychological defects will follow. Children with milder levels of prematurity do not differ significantly from normals on tests of motor or cognitive development. There is a suggestion that prematures may suffer mild anoxia, loss of weight, and related physiological disturbances during the early weeks of life, and it is possible that the retarded performance is related to these disturbances.

Finally, we cannot rule out the possibility that the behavioral differences between prematures and normals might be caused, in part, by maternal behavior. The premature infant may be overprotected and isolated by his parents. Because his parents may be afraid of harming an organism they regard as delicate or fragile, they may not stimulate him and fail to encourage his cognitive development as much as they would a normal child. This possibility is supported by an interesting experiment in which some prematures were given tactile stimulation for 5 minutes during each hour of the day for 10 successive days, while other infants were left alone. The infants who had been stroked by the nurses gained more weight and were healthier than those who were left to lie undisturbed in the isolette (70).

THE RELATION OF SEX AND SOCIAL CLASS TO VULNERABILITY IN THE NEWBORN

Although the young fetus can be affected by many factors, two seem unusually important. First, more boys than girls are born with serious abnormalities. In other words, boys seem more vulnerable to anoxia, prematurity, and maternal infection. It is not clear why nature has been so harsh on young males. One possibility is genetic. Males have only one X chromosome while females have two. Since one of the two X chromosomes in the young female is partially inactive, a specific gene on the inactive X chromosome that predisposed a child to a specific defect would be "buffered" because it would be physiologically inactive in half of the bodily cells of the girl. Since the boy has only one X chromosome, that gene would be active in all of his bodily cells. As a result the girl would be less strongly affected by that particular harmful gene than would the boy, and she would be less likely to manifest the disease. Another possibility is that the mother may develop an immunological reaction to male tissue which affects her fetus adversely. These are, at the moment, only speculative interpretations of the higher incidence of male abnormality at birth (67).

A second fact is that the problems associated with pregnancy and delivery are three to four times more frequent among low- than among middle-class families. Toxemias, infections, prematurity, and anoxia are all more likely to occur in the lower-class mother and her infant than in a middle-class parent and her infant.

A recent survey by the National Center for Health Statistics of the U.S. Public Health Service (49) suggests that education of the mother and family income showed a very strong negative relation with the risk of infant damage or death. This risk was between 50 and 100 percent higher in the lower socioeconomic classes than in the middle and upper-middle classes. The factors causing the infant's high risk of death or damage in a family of low social class are the impoverished environment, parental ignorance about child care, and failure to seek professional help. It is believed that 47 percent of the infant newborn deaths in the lowest socioeconomic group were in excess of what should have happened and were therefore in a broad sense, preventable.

The probability that these factors will produce a lasting psychological effect on the child over a period of six or seven years is also higher among poor families than among more affluent ones. However, intellectual retardation is more common among lower-class than middle-class children, even when there is no evidence of any of the above prenatal or perinatal problems. We have, therefore, a positive association among three phenomena: (1) membership in the lower class, (2) prenatal and perinatal complications, and (3) poor performance on measures of intellectual development. But we do not know whether the poorer intellectual scores are caused, in part, by the problems of pregnancy and delivery or are solely the consequent of being raised in a lower-class home, for mother's education is a better predictor of the child's intellectual functioning at age 7 than difficulty of labor, infection during pregnancy, or anoxia (68).

The lower IQ of the lower-class child could be primarily a function of lack of the experiences that result in good performance on IQ tests and have little to do with the prenatal or perinatal factors. On the other hand, the poorer performance on tests of intellectual development could be the consequent of prenatal or perinatal trauma. The results suggest that a child exposed to prenatal or perinatal problems does have a greater likelihood of showing slightly retarded mental and motor development during the early years regardless of his social class. If he is born into a lower-class family, this probability is increased. If he is born to middle-class parents, the probability of permanent intellectual retardation becomes minimal. Many separate factors contribute to intellectual performance. If a child is handicapped by several retarding factors (maternal malnutrition, toxemia, anoxia, prematurity, and minimal intellectual stimulation), the likelihood that he will show retarded intellectual development is increased.

Two facts must be kept in mind, however. First, less than 10 percent of all births in the nation experience any of the problems discussed in this chapter. Fortunately, most infants begin life well within the normal range. Second, the child is extremely malleable, and many children apparently recover from early deficits due either to prematurity or anoxia.

A case study is illustrative. One infant, born with his heart stopped, initially suffered serious anoxia. Within several hours after birth the baby began to show convulsions which lasted for several days. The father, who was a doctor, was concerned that the child would be permanently brain damaged and mentally retarded. However, the convulsions stopped after a few days and when the baby was examined at 8 months of age his psychological development appeared within normal limits. There is an enormous potential for recovery in the newborn and it is difficult to predict later behavior from the reactivity shown during the first few days of life. An extensive study of 75 normal newborns who were also observed during the third year of life found little relation between the sensitivity or strength of the newborn and the child's general behavior two and a half years later. The authors concluded:

> To use an analogy, new born behavior is more like a preface to a book than a table of contents yet to be unfolded. Further the preface is itself merely a rough draft undergoing a rapid revision. There are some clues to the nature of the book in the preface but these are in code form and taking them as literally prophetic is likely to lead to disappointment. In fact, it may well be that the primary meaning of the clues in the preface lies in the extent to which they indicate that the process of revision has lent to the preface a quality of frenzy at one extreme or lethargy at the other extreme (**3,** 132).

SUMMARY

The unborn infant's development can be influenced negatively by a variety of factors, including the adequacy of the mother's nutrition, drugs, X rays, and infection. In general, the younger the fetus, the more susceptible it is to these untoward factors. The most serious threat to the newborn during the birth process is lack of adequate oxygen, which can be caused by both mechanical and chemical factors; this deprivation can damage the cells of the central nervous system. Unfortunately, the majority of the serious problems associated with pregnancy and childbirth are most common among the economically disadvantaged who suffer more from poor health and lack of proper nutrition than the middle class. Although the premature or anoxic infant is different from the normal child during the early months or years of life, these differences become smaller with time, and, at the moment, it is difficult to state the long-term consequences of mild prematurity or mild anoxia.

References

1. Allport, G. **Personality: A psychological interpretation.** New York: Holt, Rinehart & Winston, 1937.
2. Anastasi, A. Heredity, environment and the question "How?" **Psychological Review,** 1958, **65,** 197–208.
3. Bell, R. Q., Weller, G. M., & Waldrop, M. F. Newborn and preschooler: Organization of behavior and relations between periods. **Monographs of the Society for Research in Child Development,** 1971, **36**(1, 2).

4. Braine, M. D. S., Heimer, C. B., Wortis, H., & Freedman, A. M. Factors associated with impairment of the early development of prematures. **Monographs of the Society for Research in Child Development,** 1966, **31**(106), 1–92.

5. Burks, B. S. The relative influence of nature and nurture upon mental development: A comparative study of foster parent-foster child resemblance and true parent-true child resemblance. **In Twenty-seventh Yearbook of the National Society for the Study of Education.** Part 1. Chicago: University of Chicago Press, 1928, Pp. 219–316.

6. Burt, C. The genetic determination of differences in intelligence. **British Journal of Psychology,** 1966, **57,** 137–153.

7. Carmichael, L. The onset and early development of behavior. In L. Carmichael (Ed.), **Manual of child psychology.** (2nd ed.) New York: Wiley, 1954.

8. Cattell, R. B., Stice, G. F., & Kristy, N. F. A first approximation to nature-nurture ratios for eleven primary personality factors in objective tests. **Journal of Abnormal Social Psychology,** 1957, **54,** 143–159.

9. Corah, N. L., Anthony, E. J., Painter, P., Stern, J. A., & Thurston, D. Effects of perinatal anoxia after 7 years. **Psychological Monographs,** 1965, **79,** 1–34.

10. Corner, G. W. **Ourselves unborn: An embryologist's essay on man.** New Haven: Yale University Press, 1944.

11. Davids, A., & Holden, R. H. Consistency of maternal attitude and personality from pregnancy to eight months following child birth. **Developmental Psychology,** 1970, **2, 364**–366.

12. Davison, A. N., & Dobbing, J. Myelination as a vulnerable period in brain development. **British Medical Bulletin,** 1966, **22,** 40–44.

13. DeFries, J. C. Prenatal maternal stress in mice: differential effects on behavior. **Journal of Heredity,** 1964, **55,** 289–295.

14. Dippel, A. L. The relationship of congenital syphilis to abortion and miscarriage, and the mechanisms of intrauterine protection. **American Journal of Obstetrics and Gynecology,** 1944, **47,** 369–379.

15. Drillien, C. M., & Ellis, R. W. B. **The growth and development of the prematurely born infant.** Baltimore: Williams & Wilkins, 1964.

16. Ebbs, J. H., Brown, A., Tisdall, F. F., Moyle, W. J., & Bell, M. The influence of improved prenatal nutrition upon the infant. **Canadian Medical Association Journal,** 1942, 6–8.

17. Eisenberg, L. The intervention of biological and experiential factors in schizophrenia. In D. Rosenthal & S. Kety (Eds.), **The transmission of schizophrenia.** London: Pergamon, 1968. Pp. 403–412.

18. Ernhart, C. B., Graham, F. K., & Thurston, D. Relationship of neonatal apnea to development at three years. **Archives of Neurology,** 1960, **2,** 504–510.

19. Freedman, D. An ethological approach to the genetic study of human behavior. In S. G. Vandenberg (Ed.), **Methods and goals in human behavior genetics.** New York: Academic Press, 1965. Pp. 141–161.

20. Freedman, D. G., & Freedman, N. C. Behavioral differences between Chinese-American and European-American newborns. **Nature,** 1969, **224**(5225), 1227.

21. Fuller, J. C. Experimental deprivation and later behavior. **Science,** 1967, **158,** 1645–1652.

22. Fuller, J. L. & Thompson, W. R. **Behavior genetics.** New York: Wiley, 1960.

23. Gates, R. R. **Human genetics.** Vol. II. New York: Macmillan, 1946.

24. Gellis, S. S., & Hsia, D. Y. The infant of the diabetic mother. **American Journal of Diseases of Children,** 1959, **97,** 1.

25. Gesell, A. **The embryology of behavior.** New York: Harper & Row, 1945.

26. Gesell, A. & Amatruda, C. S. **Developmental diagnosis: Normal and abnormal child development.** New York: Hoeber, 1941.

27. Goodpasture, E. W. Virus infection of the mammalian fetus. **Science,** 1942, **95,** 391–396.

28. Gottesman, I. I. Personality and natural selection. In S. G. Vandenberg (Ed.), **Methods and goals in human behavior genetics.** New York: Academic Press, 1965. Pp. 63–74.

29. Graham, F. K., Matarazzo, R. G., & Caldwell, B. M. Behavioral differences between normal and traumatized newborns. **Psychological Monographs,** 1956, **70**(5).

30. Greenberg, M., Pelliteri, O., & Barton, J. Frequency of defects in infants whose mothers had rubella during pregnancy. **Journal of the American Medical Association,** 1957, **165,** 675–678.

31. Heston, L. L. The genetics of schizophrenia and schizoid disease. **Science,** 1970, **167,** 249–256.

32. Hirsch, J. Behavior genetic analysis. New York: McGraw-Hill, 1967.

33. Honzik, M. P. Developmental studies of parent-child resemblance in intelligence. **Child Development,** 1957, **28,** 215–228.

34. Horner, F. A., & Streamer, C. W. Phenylketonuria treated from earliest infancy. **American Journal of Diseases of Children,** 1959, **97,** 345–347.

35. Horner, F. A., Streamer, C. W., Clader, D. E., Hassell, L. L., Binkley, F. L., & Dumars, K. W. Effect of phenylalanine restricted diet in phenylketonuria: II. **American Journal of Diseases of Children,** 1957, **93,** 615–618.

36. Hurlock, E. B. **Child development.** New York: McGraw-Hill, 1950.

37. Jencks, C. **Inequality.** New York: Basic Books, 1972.

38. Jensen, A. R. How much can we boost IQ and scholastic achievement? **Harvard Education Review,** 1969, **39,** 1–123.

39. Jones, H. E. Environmental influence on mental development. In L. Carmichael (Ed.), **Manual of child psychology.** New York: Wiley, 1946. Pp. 582–632.

40. Kagan, J., & Moss, H. A. **Birth to maturity.** New York: Wiley, 1962.

41. Kallmann, F. J. **The genetics of schizophrenia.** New York: Augustin, 1938.

42. Kallmann, F. J. Genetic aspects of psychosis. In **The history of mental health and disease.** New York: Hoeber, 1952. Pp. 283–298.

43. Kallmann, F. J. **Heredity in health and mental disorder.** New York: Norton, 1953.

44. Kaplan, B. J. Malnutrition and mental deficiencies. **Psychological Bulletin,** 1972, **78,** 321–334.

45. Klein, R. E., Freeman, H. E., Kagan, J., Yarbrough, C., & Habicht, J. P. Is big smart? The relation of growth to cognition. **Journal of Health and Social Behavior,** 1972, **13,** 219–225.

46. Lakin, M. Personality factors in mothers of excessively crying (colicky) infants. **Monographs of the Society for Research in Child Development,** 1957, **22**(64).

47. Landis, C., & Bolles, M. M. **Textbook of abnormal psychology.** New York: Macmillan, 1947.

48. Lewis, M., Martels, B., Campbell, H., & Goldberg, S. Individual differences in attention. **American Journal of Diseases of Children,** 1967, **113,** 461–465.

49. MacMahon, B., & Feldman, J. J. Infant mortality rates and socio-economic factors. National Center for Health Statistics, United States Public Health Service, 1972.

50. McCurdy, R. N. C. **The rhesus danger: Its medical, moral and legal aspects.** London: Heinemann Medical Books, 1950.

51. McGraw, M. B. Motivation of behavior. In L. Carmichael (Ed.), **Manual of child psychology.** New York: Wiley, 1946. Pp. 332–369.

52. Montagu, M. F. A. Constitutional and prenatal factors in infant and child health. In M. J. E. Senn (Ed.), **Symposium on the healthy personality.** New York: Josiah Macy, Jr. Foundation, 1950. Pp. 148–175.

53. Moss, H. A., & Robson, K. S. Maternal influences in early social visual behavior. Paper presented at the annual meeting of the American Orthopsychiatric Association, 1967.

54. Murphy, D. P. **Congenital malformation.** (2nd ed.) Philadelphia: University of Pennsylvania Press, 1947.

55. Murphy, D. P. The outcome of 625 pregnancies in women subjected to pelvic radium roentgen irradiation. **American Journal of Obstetrics and Gynecology,** 1929, **18,** 179–187.

56. Newman, H. H., Freeman, R. N., & Holzinger, K. J. **Twins: A study of heredity and environment.** Chicago: University of Chicago Press, 1937.

57. Parker, M. M. Experimental studies in the psychology of temperament in the adult albino rat. **Abstracts of Doctoral Dissertations,** Ohio State University, 1939(30).

58. Pasamanick, B., & Lilienfeld, A. M. Association of maternal and fetal factors with development of mental deficiency. 1. Abnormalities in the prenatal and paranatal periods. **Journal of the American Medical Association,** 1955, **159,** 155–160.

59. Plummer, G. Anomalies occurring in children exposed in utero to the atomic bomb in Hiroshima. **Pediatrics,** 1952, **10,** 687.

60. Rand, W., Sweeney, M., & Vincent, E. L. **Growth and development of the growing child.** Philadelphia: Saunders, 1946.

61. Rosenthal, D. **Genetic theory and abnormal behavior.** New York: McGraw-Hill, 1970.

62. Scarr, S. Genetic factors in activity motivation. **Child Development,** 1966, **37,** 663–673.

63. Scarr, S. Social introversion as a heritable response. **Child Development,** 1969, **40,** 823–832.

64. Scheinfeld, A. **The new you and heredity.** Philadelphia: Lippincott, 1950.

65. Scott, J. P., & Fuller, J. L. **Genetics of the social behavior of the dog.** Chicago: University of Chicago Press, 1965.

66. Seegmiller, J. E., Rosenbloom, F. M., & Kelley, W. N. Enzyme defect associated with a sex linked human neurological disorder and excessive purine synthesis. **Science,** 1967, **155,** 1682–1683.

67. Singer, J. E., Westphal, M., & Niswander, K. R. Sex differences in the incidence of neonatal abnormalities and abnormal performance in early childhood. **Child Development,** 1968, **39,** 103–112.

68. Smith, A. C., Flick, G. C., Ferriss, G. S. & Sellmann, A. H. Prediction of developmental outcome at 7 years from prenatal, perinatal and postnatal events. **Child Development,** 1972, **43,** 495–507.

69. Smith, R. T. A comparison of socioenvironmental factors in monozygotic and dizygotic twins. In S. G. Vandenberg (Ed.), **Methods and goals in human behavior genetics.** New York: Academic Press, 1965. Pp. 45–61.

70. Solkoff, N., Yaffe, S., Weintraub, D., & Blase, B. Effects of handling on the subsequent development of premature infants. **Developmental Psychology,** 1969, **1,** 765–768.

71. Sontag, L. W. The significance of fetal environmental differences. **American Journal of Obstetrics and Gynecology,** 1941, **42,** 996–1003.

72. Sontag, L. W. War and fetal maternal relationship. **Marriage and Family Living,** 1944, **6,** 1–5.

73. Sontag, L. W., & Wallace, R. F. The effect of cigarette smoking during pregnancy upon the fetal heart rate. **American Journal of Obstetrics and Gynecology,** 1935, **29,** 3–8.

74. Squier, R., & Dunbar, F. Emotional factors in the course of pregnancy. **Psychosomatic Medicine,** 1946, **8,** 161–175.
75. Stechler, G. Newborn attention as affected by medication during labor. **Science,** 1964, **144,** 315–317.
76. Stein, Z., Susser, M., Saenger, G., & Marolla, F. Nutrition and mental performance. **Science,** 1972, **178,** 708–713.
77. Stern, C. **Principles of human genetics.** (2nd ed.) San Francisco: Freeman, 1960.
78. Stewart, A. L., Keay, A. J., Jacobs, P. A., & Melville, M. H. A chromosome survey of unselected live born children with congenital abnormalities. **Journal of Pediatrics,** 1969, **74,** 449–458.
79. Telfer, M. A., Baker, D., Clark, G. R., & Richardson, C. E. Incidence of gross chromosomal errors among tall criminal American males. **Science,** 1968, **159,** 1249–1250.
80. Tompkins, W. T. The clinical significance of nutritional deficiencies in pregnancy. **Bulletin of the New York Academy of Medicine,** 1948, **24,** 376–388.
81. Walzer, S., Breau, G., & Gerald, P. S. A chromosome survey of 2400 normal newborn infants. **Journal of Pediatrics,** 1969, **74,** 438–448.
82. Watson, E. H., & Lowrey, G. H. **Growth and development of children.** Chicago: Year book Publishers, 1954.
83. Watson, J. D., & Crick, F. H. C. Molecular structure of nucleic acids—a structure for deoxyribose nucleic acid. **Nature,** 1953, **171,** 737–738.
84. Weir, M. W., & DeFries, J. C. Prenatal maternal influence on behavior in mice: Evidence of a genetic basis. **Journal of Comparative and Physiological Psychology,** 1964, **58,** 412–417.
85. Weismann, A. **Essays upon heredity and kindred biological problems.** New York: Oxford University Press, 1889.
86. Windle, W. F. Neuropathology of certain forms of mental retardation. **Science,** 1963, **140,** 1186–1189.

Part II
The First Two Years

Chapter 4

Biological Changes in Infancy

The birth of the child is marked by two fundamental changes in his functioning. He is now subjected to states of imbalance, deprivation, or discomfort that must soon be repaired, and he encounters a variety of events and experiences which shape his perception of the environment and his reactions to it. Stated more simply, the newborn experiences states of hunger, heat, cold, and pain from which he was protected during the prenatal period. These states are important psychologically for they force the infant to do something in order to alleviate the discomfort. The infant will typically thrash and cry when hungry, vocalize when excited, thrash his limbs when in pain. These are innate reactions to the sensations he feels, and they typically lead to an important change in the environment. Another person usually comes to tend the child when he cries or thrashes, and with this action the child's development comes under the partial control of the social environment. From the moment a person begins to serve the infant, certain behaviors become selectively strengthened and others weakened—the infant begins his attachment to a human being and is initiated into a system in which human beings are viewed as the basic objects to whom one turns for help and from whom one learns values, motives, and complex behaviors.

This and the next chapter discuss development during the first 18 months, the period that is typically called infancy. "Infancy" ends at about 1½ years, because at this time most children begin to speak meaningful language and are able to comprehend the speech of others. The child's interactions with the world then change dramatically, for he begins to attach symbolic meaning to his experiences. This chapter will concentrate on the perceptual-motor and biological developments of the first 18 months. The next chapter will consider the role of the family and other adults during this period and the child's developing attachment to those who care for him.

BODY GROWTH IN INFANCY

In view of the numerous variations among infants in size at birth and in rate of growth, averages or norms can give only a general picture of development. On the average, full-term male babies, who are slightly larger in all body dimensions than females, are about 20 inches tall and weigh 7½ pounds at birth. It should be noted, however, that the range of "normal" birth heights and weights is large. For example, newborns from poverty-stricken environments, although similarly proportioned, tend to be smaller than those from more favorable environments (3). This is probably caused by nutritional differences and a greater incidence of maternal infection during pregnancy.

The first year of the child's life brings remarkably rapid and extensive growth changes. Body length increases over a third, and weight almost triples, so that by the age of 1, the average baby is about 28 or 29 inches tall and weighs about 20 pounds.

In addition, there are vast modifications in body proportions and in skeletal, neural, and muscular structure. Detailed technical discussions of these developments are beyond the scope of this book, but a condensed description of the major changes follows (88).

Body Proportions

Because "the body does not grow as a whole and in all directions at once" (84, 299), the infant's overall body proportions change rapidly, particularly during the second half of the first year. The differential growth rates of the legs and face illustrate the way in which body proportions change. At birth, the infant's legs are about one-fifth as long as they will be when he is an adult, but from about 8 weeks of age they grow at an accelerated rate. In contrast to this, the head and face grow more slowly than the body as a whole, although skull size and shape become significantly modified. The total length of the head and face of the 3-month-old fetal infant is about one-third of his total body length; at birth this height is about one-fourth; in adulthood, about one-tenth (84; see Fig. 4.1).

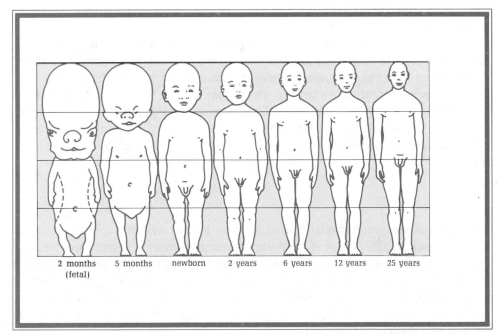

| 2 months (fetal) | 5 months | newborn | 2 years | 6 years | 12 years | 25 years |

Figure 4.1 Changes in form and proportion of the human body during fetal and postnatal life. (From C. M. Jackson. Some aspects of form and growth. In W. J. Robbins, S. Brody, A. F. Hogan, C. M. Jackson, & C. W. Green [Eds.], **Growth.** New Haven: Yale University Press, 1929. P. 118. By permission.)

There are, of course, dramatic differences in body size and proportion among children in various parts of the world. At 1 year, for example, children from different nations can vary as much as 9 pounds in their weight, as much as 5½ inches in their height, and 2½ inches in their chest circumference (62).

Skeletal Development

All of the bones oɩ the body originate from soft cartilage tissue which over a period of time becomes ossified or hardened into bone material by the deposition of minerals. Ossification begins during the prenatal period and continues, for some bones, until late adolescence. As most infants' bones are not ossified to a great extent, they are softer, more pliable, more reactive to muscular pull and pressure, and more susceptible to deformity than those of older children and adults. Fortunately, they are also less subject to breakage.

The timing and rate of ossification differs with the various bones of the body and among individuals. Some of the bones of the hand and wrist ossify very early in life, and by the end of the first year most children have developed 3 of their total (i.e., adult) complement of 28 hand and wrist bones. Other skeletal parts ossify later. The skull of the newborn infant has 6 soft spots (fontanelles) which ossify gradually and do not disappear until the child is about 2 years of age. Other bones develop still later (84).

As with other aspects of development, there are marked individual and group differences in rates of ossification and skeletal growth. Sex differences in skeletal development favoring girls are present at birth and increase with age. Black infants are generally advanced beyond white infants (88). Moreover, broad-framed children tend to have a faster rate of ossification than narrow-framed children. Hereditary factors markedly affect the rate and timing of skeletal development, although illness, allergies, and malnutrition may produce disturbances of ossification.

Muscles

Although the neonate has all the muscle fibers he will ever have, they are small in relation to his size. There is continuous growth in muscle length, breadth, and thickness until, in adulthood, the weight of the muscles is about 40 times what it was at birth. The striped or skeletal (voluntary) muscles of the body are not yet completely under the infant's control during the first year. They fatigue rapidly and recover easily in the early stages of the development of voluntary responses such as sitting and walking (84).

Different muscle groups grow at different rates, and there is a general tendency for the muscles near the head and neck to develop earlier than those of the lower limbs (cephalocaudal development). Finally, infant boys have a greater proportion of muscle tissue than infant girls, and this sex difference holds for males and females at all ages (32, 33).

Finally, it should be noted that there are consistent sex differences in growth dimensions. Girls develop faster than boys and this faster rate of development begins during the fetal period. The body composition of the sexes differs, with infant girls having proportionally more fat and less water than boys. Girls have less muscle tissue and are generally lighter and shorter than boys. But the most intriguing sex difference is that the physical growth of girls is less variable than that of boys. That is, if we pick a particular growth variable, such as number of teeth at age 2, and examine a thousand boys and a thousand girls, the range for number of teeth would be greater for boys than for girls. There would be more boys with many teeth and more boys with few teeth. The range for girls would be smaller (34).

In addition, girls' growth is more stable than that of boys. The rate of skeletal maturity in the 2-year-old girl is a better predictor of her future rate of skeletal development than it is for the boy (1). As we shall see later, this greater stability in bone growth is paralleled by a greater stability in intellectual growth. For example, a girl's vocabulary at age 3 is a better predictor of her adult vocabulary and IQ than a boy's vocabulary is. This interesting parallel between physical and psychological factors is intriguing and suggests the operation of fundamental sex differences in the organization of development. Perhaps before the next edition of this book is written we shall understand this phenomenon more fully.

THE NEWBORN

The Initial Equipment

Surprisingly, the newborn is a remarkably capable organism from the moment he begins to breathe. He can see, hear, and smell, and he is sensitive to pain, touch, and change in position. The only sense modality which may not be functioning immediately at birth is taste, but even this sense develops rather quickly. The infant is biologically ready to experience most of the basic sensations of his species from the moment he is born. This is not true of all mammals. Puppies, as the reader may know, are both blind and deaf at birth.

The newborn's behavioral equipment is also remarkably well developed. He can display a variety of reflexes, some of which are necessary for survival, and many of which are complex. For example, a newborn only 2 hours old will follow a moving light with his eyes if the speed of the light is optimal; his pupils will dilate in darkness and constrict in light; he will suck a finger or nipple inserted into his mouth; he will turn in the direction in which his cheek or the corner of his mouth is touched. He can cry, cough, turn away, vomit, lift his chin from a prone position, and grasp an object placed in his palm. His body will react to a loud sound, and he can flex and extend his limbs, smack his lips, and chew his fingers (21).

One of the important and interesting responses shown by the newborn is called the **Moro reflex.** In this response, the infant throws his arms out to the side, extends his fingers and then brings arms back and hands to the midline, as if he were embracing someone. The infant will normally show this reaction to a sudden change in head position, and often shows it to any event that would surprise him. The best way to demonstrate this reflex is to lay the baby on his back and, when he is quiet, simultaneously hit the sides of the pillow or mattress on either side of the infant's head. This sudden change in stimulation typically elicits the Moro reflex. It is believed that the effective cause of this reflex is either a change in the proprioceptive receptors in the muscles in the neck or stimulation from the vestibular system. This reflex is of developmental importance because, in normal infants, it begins to vanish at 3 to 4 months of age, and by 6 months is difficult to elicit. One interpretation of the disappearance is based on the belief that the newborn's behavior is largely controlled by processes in the brain stem rather than by the cerebral cortex. The brain stem, which lies under the cortex, contains centers that are responsible for the basic biological functions of breathing and circulation, as well as basic reflexes. The cerebral cortex is largely responsible for perception, memory, and thought. The cerebral cortex may not be fully functional in the newborn and may only gradually awaken and begin assuming control of the infant's behavior during the opening weeks of life. As the cortex gains control, it begins to inhibit and modulate the lower brain stem centers that are responsible for the Moro reflex. Neurologists would view with some alarm a 10-month-old infant who was still displaying the Moro response to a change in head position, for this would suggest that there might be some deficiency or damage in the infant's central nervous system.

Table 4.1 lists some of the major reflexes of the newborn and the kinds of stimuli that release them (see Figs. 4.2–4.6).

Contemporary psychology views the newborn with considerably more respect than the scientist of the sixteenth century, who saw the infant as relatively insensitive and helpless. We have exploded the myth of newborn insensitivity and incompetence.

The second myth we must examine is the belief that "the world of the baby is a blooming, buzzing confusion." This idea was probably born from a prejudice that saw the infant as a passive, helpless creature with little power to understand very much about his environment. This description of a buzzing and confusing world is a reasonable conclusion for a harassed urban scientist who must have thought that if his own world was a noisy and confused place, it must be even more chaotic to the more vulnerable infant.

Recent research on attentional processes suggests, however, that the infant's world may actually be quieter than our own. Humans typically attend to one

Table 4.1 **Reflexes of the newborn**

EFFECTIVE STIMULUS	REFLEX
Tap upper lips sharply	Lips protrude
Tap bridge of nose	Eyes close tightly
Bright light suddenly shown to eyes	Closure of eyelids
Clap hands about 18 inches from infant's head	Closure of eyelids
Touch cornea with light piece of cotton	Eyes close
With baby held on back turn face slowly to right side	Jaw and right arm on side of face extend out; the left arm flexes
Extend forearms at elbow	Arms flex briskly
Put fingers into infant's hand and press his palms	Infant's fingers flex and enclose finger
Press thumbs against the ball of infant's feet	Toes flex
Scratch sole of foot starting from toes towards the heels	Big toe bends upward and small toes spread
Prick soles of feet with pin	Infant's knee and foot flex
Tickle area at corner of mouth	Head turns toward side of stimulation
Put index finger into mouth	Sucks
Hold infant in air, stomach down	Infant attempts to lift head and extends legs

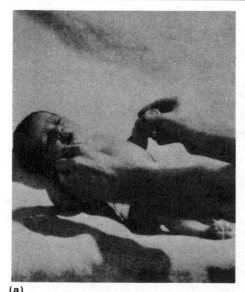 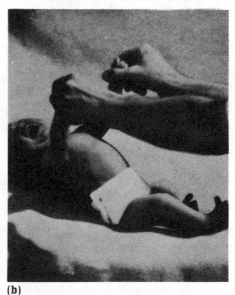

(a)   **(b)**

Figure 4.2 The traction test. (**a**) Initial position. (**b**) Response. The infant's hands are grasped as he is pulled slowly to a sitting position. The normal infant resists as in (**b**). (From H. Prechtl & D. Beintema. The neurological examination of the fullterm newborn infant. **Little Club Clinics in Developmental Medicine,** 1964, Number 12, 46. London: Spastics Society Medical Information Unit and William Heinemann Medical Books, Ltd. By permission.)

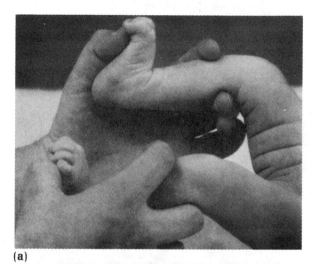

(a)

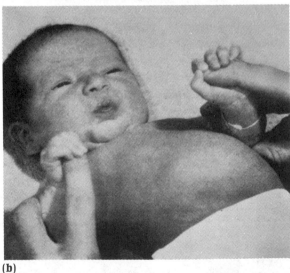

(b)

Figure 4.3 **(a)** Elicitation of ankle clonus. The examiner presses both thumbs against the soles of the foot; the infant's toes flex around the thumbs. **(b)** Testing for the palmer grasp. The examiner presses his finger into the infant's palms and infant's fingers flex around the examiner's finger. (From H. Prechtl & D. Beintema. The neurological examination of the fullterm newborn infant. **Little Club Clinics in Developmental Medicine,** 1964, Number 12, 35. London: Spastics Society Medical Information Unit and William Heinemann Medical Books, Ltd. By permission.)

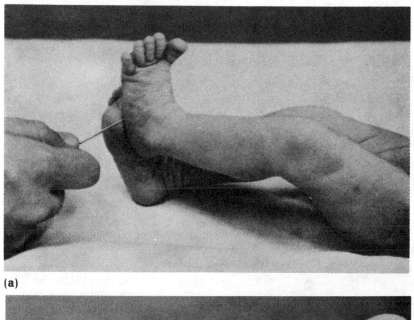

(a)

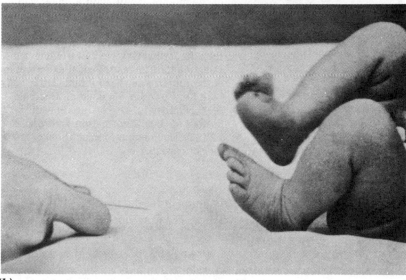

(b)

Figure 4.4 The withdrawal reflex. (a) Stimulation. The examiner pricks the infant's sole with a pin. (b) Response. The infant withdraws his foot. (From H. Prechtl & D. Beintema. The neurological examination of the fullterm newborn infant. **Little Club Clinics in Developmental Medicine,** 1964, Number 12, 40. London: Spastics Society Medical Information Unit and William Heinemann Medical Books, Ltd. By permission.)

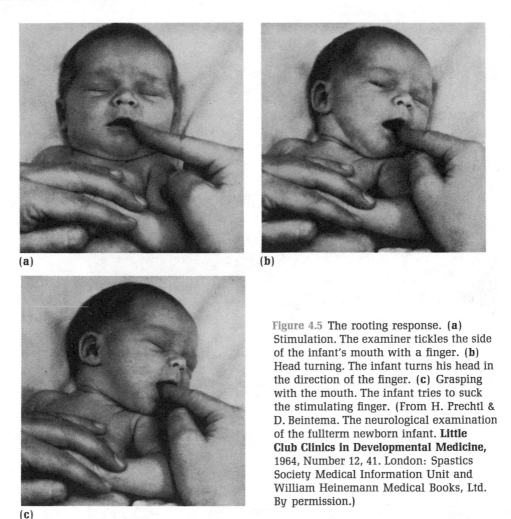

(a)

(b)

(c)

Figure 4.5 The rooting response. (a) Stimulation. The examiner tickles the side of the infant's mouth with a finger. (b) Head turning. The infant turns his head in the direction of the finger. (c) Grasping with the mouth. The infant tries to suck the stimulating finger. (From H. Prechtl & D. Beintema. The neurological examination of the fullterm newborn infant. **Little Club Clinics in Developmental Medicine,** 1964, Number 12, 41. London: Spastics Society Medical Information Unit and William Heinemann Medical Books, Ltd. By permission.)

sensory channel at a time. When we are listening intently to a bird's song, we may not feel a touch, smell a flower, or see a deer. We may not be able to perceive two different auditory messages—one to each ear—coming in at the same time. We choose the one we wish to listen to, and we are temporarily deaf to the other channel (11). We may think we can attend to many channels of sensory information at once because we shift our attention rapidly and frequently from one event to another. This gives us the impression of continuous perception of many things simultaneously. This rapid oscillation of attention is analogous to the electric current in the light bulb that goes on and off 60 times a second. We perceive continuous rather than discontinuous light because the shift in current is so rapid we cannot detect it. It is possible that the newborn cannot change his

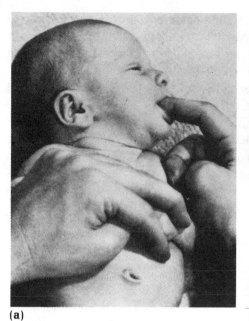
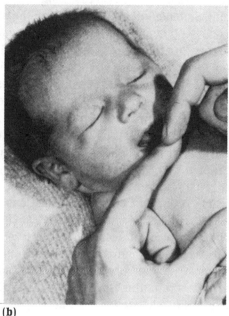

(a)   **(b)**

Figure 4.6 **(a)** Testing sucking. The infant sucks the finger placed into his mouth. **(b)** Elicitation of the jaw-jerk. The examiner delivers a short, sharp tap to the chin and the infant's chin is lifted by contraction of masseteric muscles. (From H. Prechtl & D. Beintema. The neurological examination of the fullterm newborn infant. **Little Club Clinics in Developmental Medicine,** 1964, Number 12, 42. London: Spastics Society Medical Information Unit and William Heinemann Medical Books, Ltd. By permission.)

focus of attention as rapidly as the older child can. When the baby is watching his mother he may not hear sounds around him; when he is attending to a hunger pain he may not feel his mother's touch. His world may be made up of single perceptions and, therefore, be less confused, noisy, and buzzing than our own.

The child begins life with some responses he can make, and a sensory system that functions well. He is now ready to acquire new behaviors and ideas. This process proceeds in stages, not all at once, and psychologists are just beginning to see the outline of these stages for each of the systems that are growing.

MATURATIONAL STAGES IN INFANCY

Although the child's experiences during his first year will determine, in large measure, how active, vocal, and alert he will be when he is 2 or 3 years old, his psychological development is still seriously limited by the growth of his central nervous system. The 2-month-old is not mature enough biologically to benefit as much as a 12-month-old from interaction with objects and people in his environment. Stated another way, although the environment contributes in a major way to the development of social responses and cognitive talents, the child cannot benefit maximally from these experiences until certain biological forces have prepared him for these changes. For example, the child does not become capable of imitating his mother's gestures until the last half of the first year. When that time arrives, there is much the mother can do in her play with the child to encourage and facilitate imitation. She can reward his imitative attempts and initiate interesting responses that will provoke the child to imitate her. It is not clear whether these maternal practices with a 2-month-old will lead the infant to imitate much earlier than he would have had the parent not tried to intervene.

This issue of how much intervention and how early it should be applied has always been, and continues to be, one of the most important and most controversial in developmental psychology. One extreme view maintains that the infant is born with certain capabilities, but from the first day of life it is the environment that assumes primary control of his changing behavior. Until recently, this was the most popular position in the United States. A less popular position, equally extreme, maintains that maturation of the central nervous system is the primary governor of changes in the opening years, and differences in the environment do not exert a strong influence on development.

Neither of these extreme positions is likely to be correct. Of course, the 3-month-old is biologically too immature to speak, and nothing in his environment can make him speak at that age. On the other hand, it is likely that the more talking that occurs between infant and adults during the first year, the more likely the child will become an early talker. For example, in certain parts of Holland and Central America, parents do not talk very much to their infants because they do not believe it is important for development. The ability to comprehend and speak language emerges a little later in these children than in middle-class American children, who experience a great deal of adult verbal interaction (50). Hence, one way to phrase the issue is to say that maturation sets the major direction of psychological growth during the early years, but the environment selectively influences that direction, determining which particular ability will be emphasized and the timing of its emergence in development.

We do not possess a detailed understanding of the changes in brain and spinal cord that permit new capabilities to emerge, but we can describe some of the psychological milestones in the first year, the emergence of new abilities that are likely to be correlated with changes in the central nervous system.

The Newborn Period

The newborn period is considered to cover the first 5 to 7 days. At this time, the infant is recovering from the physiological trauma of delivery and is beginning to establish an equilibrium with his environment. Infants born to mothers who received heavy doses of drugs during labor are groggier and less alert than babies born to mothers given minimal doses of drugs (79). There are dramatic day-to-day changes in the alertness and activity of newborns during the first week due, in part, to recovery from the trauma of birth and physiological adaptations to the new extrauterine environment.

The Period of First Memories

Sometime before he is 10 weeks of age the infant displays some important new abilities. First, he appears to be able to remember an event that occurred moments earlier, for he becomes increasingly bored with a repetition of the same stimulus. In one type of experiment an infant is repeatedly shown a particular visual stimulus, say a checkerboard or a face. Prior to 8 weeks of age the typical infant does not show any sign of boredom following 16 presentations and continues to look as long on the sixteenth presentation as he did on the first. After 8 weeks he becomes bored and looks away after 16 trials. In technical language, the infant becomes **habituated.** Of course, if the experimenter continued to show the stimulus for 100 trials, the infant would look away because of fatigue.

The appearance of habituation implies that the infant is storing a memory of the stimulus. It is likely that this process requires the activity of the cerebral cortex, for a child born without a cortex does not show habituation to repetitions of the same stimulus when he is 10 weeks of age. Absence of visual habituation in a normal 4-week-old implies that the cortex, which inhibits responsivity and stores memories, is relatively inactive. The cortex appears to "wake up" at about 10 weeks of age (7). The capacity to habituate suggests that the infant must be forming some representation of the stimulus. In order to look less attentively at an event on the tenth trial, it is necessary to remember what one has seen earlier.

In a recent study, infants were required to "remember" a particular stimulus over a 24-hour period. One group of infants, either 10 or 16 weeks old, looked at an orange ball moving up and down on a stage for only a few minutes. One day later, these infants, together with those who had never seen the stimulus before, returned to the laboratory and were shown the orange ball stimulus. The first group—who had seen the stimulus a day earlier—became bored more quickly than the second, suggesting that the first group had remembered the event (81).

There is additional proof of the fact that the infant must be creating a representation or schema for what he sees. If an experimenter shows an infant a face for 10 separate trials of 10 seconds each and then substitutes a checkerboard for the face on the eleventh trial, the child's interest increases dramatically. The technical word for this increased attention to a new event following habituation to an old one is **dishabituation.** Obviously, in order for the infant to look longer at the changed stimulus he must have recognized that the new one was different from the one he had been viewing. In order to detect this he must have stored a memory for the older event.

The emergence of the ability to store a representation of an event is mainly a product of maturation. Children born of a pregnancy of normal duration show this ability between 2 and 3 months of age. Premature children born a month early do not behave this way until they are 4 months postnatal, which is the same biological age as the normal 3-month-old. Time since conception is a better predictor of the ability to react to a changed stimulus than how many months the child has been living in a stimulating world (25).

There are other changes that occur at 8 to 10 weeks. If a 5- to 6-week-old is allowed to look at his mother's face, he tends to focus his eyes on the contour line that separates her forehead from her hair, rather than her eyes or nose (5). Apparently, the contrast of the hairline attracts a very young infant. But by 8 or 9 weeks of age he begins to look at her face, especially her eyes, suggesting that he has formed a primitive schema for a human face, and this schema is directing where he looks.

The Smile

By 4 months of age, the infant possesses such a good representation of a human face that he will now smile at a photograph of a face. This is the **smile of recognition,** indicating that the child has been successful in relating an event to his schema of the event. In different places around the world, 4 months of age is the time when infants are most likely to smile at a human face, even a strange one. This fact suggests that the central nervous system has matured enough by 4 months so that the average child is able to relate a new face to his idea of a face.

Fear of Strangers

The next milestone is a natural successor to the earlier period when the child has been creating schemata for the people he encounters. Once schemata for familiar people in his environment are well articulated, the 7- to 8-month-old infant begins to display wariness and fear of strangers (12). The fear reaction involves crying, stiffening of body, and inhibition of play, and at 8 months is apt to be extreme in American children. This phenomenon illustrates the important developmental principle that an event moderately discrepant from a familiar schema alerts the infant and motivates him to try to understand it. The child has schemata for people he knows; strangers represent slight discrepancies. If he cannot relate the new event to one that he knows, he is likely to become afraid.

Thought and Planfulness

A few months after he shows fear reactions to strangers the child becomes capable of simple thought. As we shall see later, he becomes capable of interpreting discrepant events and he activates hypotheses that help him explain why the strange

face looks the way it does. This elementary form of thought occurs at about the same time the child begins to believe in the permanence of objects—the time when he begins to believe that although an object disappears from view it has not ceased to exist. This phenomenon, which has been called **object permanence** by Jean Piaget (65), emerges at 8 to 9 months—a few months before the child utters his first words.

By the end of his first year the child appears to be in greater control of his actions and seems to be able to formulate a plan of behavior; his eyes announce that he has seen an attractive toy across the room, and he scurries directly to it, resisting distraction from other people or attractive objects.

Although the competences described above—habituation, dishabituation, smile, creating schemata, planfulness—appear rather suddenly, they are the result of the continuing development of the foundations of these actions during the prior weeks. There is both a continuity and a discreteness in development. This complementary relation is analogous to the breaking of a wave on the shore. Although there is a discrete moment when the white froth of the wave suddenly appears, the forces that led to its breaking have been building gradually for hundreds of yards out from the shore. If we had been measuring these forces, we would have been able to detect how they gradually built up until the moment the wave broke. Similarly, there are hidden psychological forces that have been gradually changing during the months prior to the first time the child says "da-da" to the sound of his father entering the house. Development is both gradual and discontinuous. Let us now consider in more detail perceptual and motor development during the first 18 months.

PERCEPTUAL DEVELOPMENT

Before discussing the infant's perceptual development we must consider his sensory capacities and the general determinants of attention to stimuli. What are the characteristics of visual, auditory, olfactory, or tactile stimuli that will attract and hold the infant's attention? It is important to appreciate that the aspects of an event that initially attract his attention, like the size and intensity of a stimulus, may not be the same as those that hold his attention (18). An infant may be attracted to a large black circle because of its size and dark color, but once having turned to it he may not spend very much time looking at it. Since the infant's first knowledge of the world grows from his distribution of attention to outside events, we must know the principles that determine what events he usually looks at or listens to with the greatest interest.

Visual Capacities

Although the essential neural mechanisms began to appear in the third week of prenatal life, the neuromuscular apparatus involved in vision is still not perfected when the infant is born. The infant is able to see light, dark, and color at birth and has remarkably good visual acuity. In order to assess the infant's visual sensitivity, we must observe his responses to visual stimuli.

The **pupillary reflex** (contraction of the pupil in response to increased light and dilation in response to decreased light), observed even in premature infants, reveals that the neonate is sensitive to differences in the intensity of visual stimuli. Although the response is somewhat sluggish at birth, it becomes perfected during the first few days of postnatal life (**67, 68**). At first, it can be elicited only by strong stimuli, but with increasing age, less intensity is required.

Infants as young as a few days are capable of **visual pursuit movements.** An infant will follow moving lights, indicating that the eye muscles are sufficiently coordinated to track stimuli. But although eye movements are coordinated, the two eyes do not converge on the same stimulus at birth (**90**).

Convergence of the two eyes, essential for fixation and depth perception, is absent at birth and real convergence, or **binocular fixation,** first occurs at about 7 or 8 weeks. It is initially accomplished by a series of jerking movements which are gradually eliminated and replaced by smooth, continuous convergence.

It appears that for the first month the infant does not make any adjustment to objects at varying distances from his eyes (called **accommodation**). He seems to have a fixed focus at about 8 inches from his face. By 2 months he begins to accommodate to the distance of objects, and by 4 months of age his ability to accommodate is comparable to that of an adult. As early as 16 weeks the infant is capable of making adjustments of his eyes so that he can focus on near and far targets (**45**).

Stimulus Determinants of Attention

Movement, Intensity, and Contour Although the poor accommodation for the first 8 weeks would make the perception of detailed form at a distance difficult, the newborn clearly shows responsiveness to movement of stimuli and to different intensities of light. A 5-day-old baby sucking on a nipple will momentarily stop sucking if a light begins to move in his visual field (**43**), and he will look different amounts of time at stimuli of different brightness (**46**). The infant, therefore, reacts to movement and light intensity from the first day of life.

A third attribute of visual stimulation to which the newborn is reactive is the contrast created by a contour (the edge of a black line on a white background). The infant seems drawn to contours and will focus his attention near the contour more than he will on other parts of the field. If a newborn is shown a black triangle on a white field, his eyes will hover near the sides of the triangle—especially near the vertices of the triangle, the place where the contrast between black and white is maximal (**74**). Moreover, the newborn will detect a black vertical bar in a white visual field and his attention will remain near that vertical stripe, as if he were attracted or drawn to the places that have high contour contrast (**44, 73**).

The young infant's attraction to contour can be used to assess his visual acuity, for he typically looks longest at stimuli that contain a moderate amount of contour. If we show him two stimuli with differing amounts of contour and he looks longer at one of them, we can conclude that he detected the differences between them. Robert Fantz **(26, 27, 28)** has performed experiments of this kind and concluded that, as early as 2 weeks of age, the infant can detect the difference between a gray patch and a square composed of stripes that are only ⅛ inch wide, at a distance of 9 inches from his face. By 3 months of age infants will look longer at (and, therefore, can discriminate) stripes 1/64 inch wide than at a gray patch at a distance of only 15 inches **(28;** see Fig. 4.7).

However, the infant does not always look longest at figures with the greatest

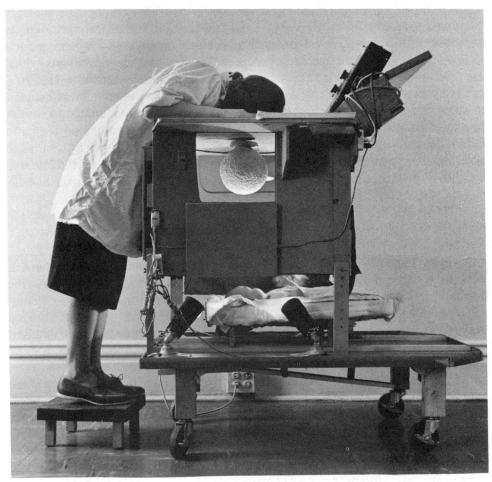

Figure 4.7 Form perception. (From R. L. Fantz. The origin of form perception. **Scientific American,** May, 1961, **204,** 66. Photographer: David Linton. By permission.)

amount of contour. If the figure contains too much or too little contour, because it is too large for him to perceive in one gaze or because it is too finely grained and he cannot perceive all the contour, he will be less attentive to it.

Complexity Amount of contour and movement cannot explain all of the infant's attentional behavior after 2 to 3 months of age. For example, most infants 4 to 8 weeks old look longer at a striped pattern than at a bull's-eye. But after 8 weeks of age they look longer at the bull's-eye than at the striped stimuli. It may be that a bull's-eye has a special retinal effect that holds the infant's attention. It is interesting that several species of birds show an avoidance reaction to stimuli that are circular and composed of concentric circles, such as a bull's-eye pattern (6). Monkeys also show a strong attentive and subsequent fear reaction to a pair of staring eyes, which are, in effect, two bull's-eyes. Thus, there may be special releaser stimuli that innately hold attention as a function of biologically determined neuromotor patterns. We need additional principles to understand the infants' attentional preferences.

One popular hypothesis states that stimuli can be organized on a dimension of complexity, and infants will attend longest to stimuli that are moderately complex. The first question to be raised is, "What does complexity mean?" That is not an easy question to answer. The number of discrete elements in a stimulus is one basis for judging complexity. Thus a checkerboard with 16 black-and-white squares is more complex than a checkerboard with only 9 black-and-white squares. Variety is a second basis for complexity. The more different the elements are in an array, the more complex the stimulus. Thus, a circle that contains 3 stars, 3 squares, and 3 triangles is more complex than a circle with 9 triangles, although each has 9 elements. Experiments in which these definitions of complexity were used have yielded the finding that infants look longer at more complex stimuli as they grow older (9). (See Fig. 4.8).

But there are alternative interpretations of this finding. It is possible that the primary determinants of sustained attention during the opening weeks of life are movement and contour (i.e., lots of black-and-white contrast), combined with an optimal area or optimal length of a contour edge. In general, experiments have indicated that infants devote the longest attention to stimuli that contained a great deal of black-and-white contrast but are of an optimal area (52, 58).

The complexity hypothesis is still controversial; there is no experiment that clearly demonstrates that infants will attend longer to more complex stimuli when the size of the stimulus and the amount of contour are eliminated as factors.

Meaning and Discrepancy Meaning and familiarity of the stimulus clearly affect its attention-getting value. Four-month-old children were shown the four faces in Fig. 4.9 (42). The infants looked longer at the stimuli most similar to a human face than they did at the ones with the most contour or the greatest number of ele-

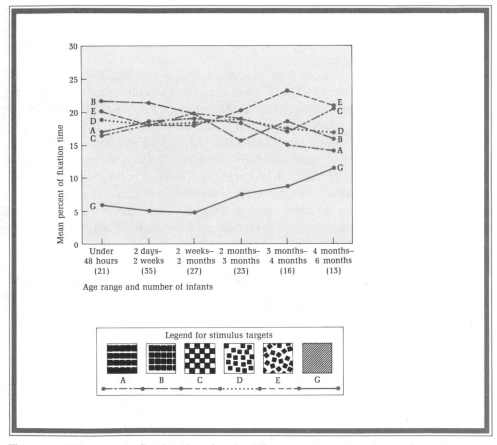

Figure 4.8 Differences in fixation time for six different patterns for infants of varying ages. (From R. L. Fantz, Visual perception from birth as shown by pattern selectivity. Copyright, The New York Academy of Sciences, 1965, **118.** Reprinted by permission.)

ments. More important, faces 2 and 4 were of relatively equal complexity with respect to number of elements, but 2 was more like a face than 4 was. The infants looked longer at 2 than at 4, suggesting that the meaning of a stimulus might be more important than its complexity in holding the infant's attention **(42)**.

In a second study, one group of 4-month-olds were shown the meaningless black-and-white shape in Figure 4.10 and another group were shown the faces in Figure 4.11. Although the nonsense shapes have greater contrast than the faces, the faces attracted longer attention. The 4-month-old infants were reacting to the discrepancy from their established schema for a face. Each of the stimulus faces was clearly different from, yet also similar to, the child's schema for his parent's face **(49)**. (It is interesting to note that by 4 months infants have a smaller change in the dilation of their pupils when they are looking at their mother's face, which is familiar, than when they are looking at the face of a stranger **(30)**). Thus we must add to the power of intensity, movement, contour, and possibly complexity,

Stimulus	Degree of faceness	Amount of detail	Percent fixation time
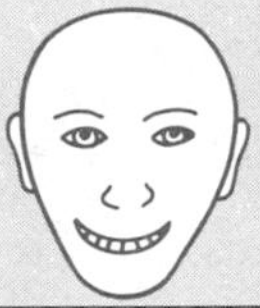	1	3	.33
	2	1	.28
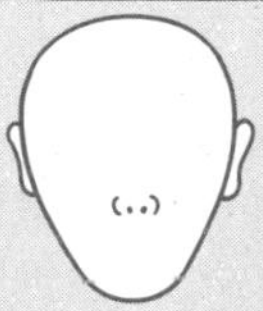	3	4	.19
	4	2	.20

Figure 4.9 Differences in fixation time for four different facial stimuli. (From R. A. Haaf & R. Q. Bell. A facial dimension in visual discrimination by human infants. **Child Development,** 1967, **38,** 895. Copyright 1967 by The Society of Research in Child Development, Inc. By permission.)

still another characteristic of stimuli that can hold attention in the visual mode. **Stimuli that are optimally discrepant from established schemata are likely to maintain attention (51).**

As early as 3 months, the relation of a stimulus to an acquired schema becomes an important determinant of attention. Schema is a hypothetical word which stands for a mental representation of an experience; it is an imageless, languageless memory. Your representation of your childhood home is a schema; your memory of your high school teacher's face is a schema. A schema is not a mental picture or image. We assume that during the first year of life the mental structures the child is acquiring are primarily schemata. After a sufficient amount of experience with a particular object or event, an infant builds up a schema for it. The schema is not a photographic duplicate of the phenomenon. Rather, it is prob-

Figure 4.10 Shape shown to one group of 4-month-old infants.

ably more like a caricature that highlights the most distinctive elements of the event. The most distinctive elements in a human face are probably the oval outline and the two symmetrically placed eyes; it is possible that a 3-month-old infant's schema for the face emphasizes these elements.

A stimulus discrepancy refers to a relation between an event and a schema. A discrepant stimulus is one that is different from a schema, but is not totally dissimilar. It is related to the schema in some way. A picture of a table is not a discrepancy with respect to the schema of a face, but a picture of a face with no eyes is a discrepancy from the schema of a face. A discrepant stimulus is both similar to and different from the original. It preserves some elements of the original.

Moderate discrepancies from established schemata have the greatest power to attract the infant's attention. Changes in shape, orientation, or pattern of the distinctive features of an event can be optimal discrepancies and, as a result, will elicit the most sustained attention.

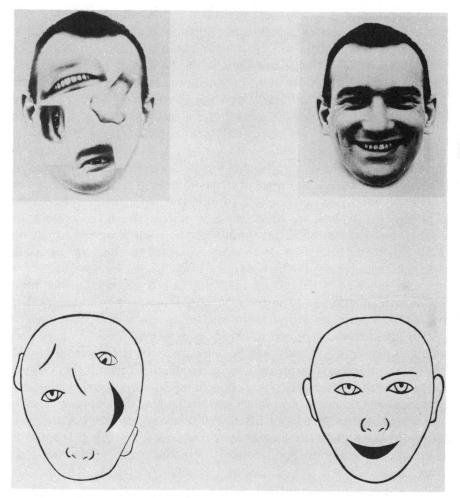

Figure 4.11 Set of achromatic two-dimensional faces shown to 4-month-old infants.

Although we do not yet know what aspects of a complex event are most salient for the infant, pattern appears to be more important than color in the visual mode. In one experiment 3½-month-olds turned their head in order to see a checkerboard pattern. When they became bored the experimenter changed either the color of the checkerboard (from red and white to green and white) or the pattern (from a 4 X 4 to a 24 X 24 checkerboard or the reverse). The infants who saw the change in color did not increase their head-turning. The infants who saw the change in the number of checks slowed their rate of habituation, suggesting that the pattern of the checkerboard was a more important attribute than its color (16), that is, a change in pattern was more readily perceived as a discrepancy than a change of color.

There is no doubt that a discrepant event will increase the child's attentiveness. But there is some controversy over the degree of discrepancy that has the greatest power to hold attention.

There is a good reason to believe that the moderately discrepant event is more likely to elicit and hold attention than the greatly discrepant event. Four groups of infants listened to repetitions of a phrase, spoken in a distinctive rhythm. A different phrase was used for each group. After eight repetitions of the phrase, all the infants heard exactly the same four-syllable phrase. For one group the final phrase was identical with the one they had been hearing, for two groups the final phrase was moderately discrepant, and for the fourth group the final phrase was markedly different from the original. Orientation to the sound source and slowing of heart rate reflect the intensity of attention the infant devoted to the changed phrase. The infants, for whom the final phrase was a moderately discrepant event, displayed a longer orientation and a lower heart rate than the infants who experienced either the identical phrase or the one that was markedly different (a novel event) from the first (54).

Support for this kind of curvilinear relation between discrepancy and attention (greatest attention to moderate discrepancies, less attention to identical or novel events) also occurs in the visual mode. Infants were first shown an arrangement of three colored geometrical objects in a mobile. Some mothers were then given the same mobile to take home to hang above the child's crib for a half an hour a day for three weeks; others were given different mobiles; still others received no mobile at all. Two weeks later all the infants returned to the laboratory to see the same mobile they saw two weeks earlier. But now the laboratory mobile was either minimally, moderately, or maximally different from the one they had been viewing at home. Infants who had seen moderately discrepant mobiles at home paid more attention to the laboratory stimulus than infants who had seen a very novel mobile or a mobile with only minor variations at home. The moderately discrepant mobile attracted more attention than the very familiar or very novel one (51).

The Activation of Hypotheses

Two new facts require the invention of a third hypothetical process that controls attention toward the end of the first year. The first fact is that duration of attention to masks of human faces decreases from 2 to about 12 months, but from 12 to 36 months duration of attention to the same masks increases. This fact holds true not only for American children but also for Guatemalan children living in rural villages and Bushmen children living in the Kalahari desert. If it is discrepancy that exerts the major control over attention, then attention should continue to decrease, not increase, after the first year as the infants' schema for the face become better formed and the masks become less discrepant (51). The increase toward the end of the first year can be explained by the emergence of a new cognitive structure. We call this structure a **hypothesis.** The child tries to mentally transform the discrepant face into the form with which he is familiar, where the familiar one is the schema. It is as if the child implicitly asks of a scrambled face "What happened?" "Who hit him?" "Where is his nose?" One child actually said, "Who threw the pie at him?" while another remarked, "His nose is broken, Mommy. Why is it broken?"

The cognitive structure used in this transformation is a hypothesis. To be able to recognize that a sequence of high-pitched sounds is human speech, rather than bird song, requires a schema for both the human voice and the song. But, the interpretation of why the speech sounds strange requires generation of hypotheses, that is, an attempt to understand why the sound is odd. Hence, there are four processes that affect attention during the first year of life. Each emerges at a different time and its emergence is controlled, in part, by maturation. The power of contrast, movement, discrepancy, and richness of activated hypotheses is probably additive and when the child is 2 years of age the stimulus that has contour-contrast, movement, discrepancy, and activates hypotheses should hold his attention for the longest period of time. The television commercial or a cartoon contains all four characteristics; perhaps that is why nursery school children study the television screen for such long periods.

Perception of Depth and Three Dimensions

A problem that has always baffled psychologists and philosophers concerns the contribution of learning to the fundamental aspects of visual perception, such as the perception of shape and the perception of depth and perspective. Does the human infant have to learn to see things in three dimensions or does he have this capacity from birth? This question is not resolved. Some psychologists assume that the infant has to learn to perceive in three dimensions and that his visual world is two-dimensional. There is some evidence for the learning hypothesis. For example, prior to 10 weeks, infants attend equally long to a two- or three-dimensional black circle; but after 10 weeks of age they will look longer at a three-dimensional sphere than at a two-dimensional circle of the same area, indicating that the infant is reacting to the third dimension. Up to 10 weeks of age most infants will react similarly to two- and three-dimensional faces (a color photograph of the face, versus actual face of a person), but at 3 months he will smile and vocalize more to the actual face than to the two-dimensional representation (66).

However, there is some suggestion that the infant is born with a capacity to appreciate depth. One of the most provocative demonstrations of depth perception during infancy involves an apparatus called the visual cliff. Infants were placed on a center runway that had a sheet of strong glass extending outward on either side. On one side a textured pattern was placed far below the glass, thus giving the illusion of depth (i.e., an adult would perceive depth in this situation). These investigators called this situation the "visual cliff," for the difference between the two sides appeared as a cliff (see Fig. 4.12).

Both 6-month-old infants and terrestrial animals avoided the side which appeared to have the "drop-off" or cliff. Even if the infant's mother stood at the deep side of the apparatus and entreated her child to cross over to her, most infants

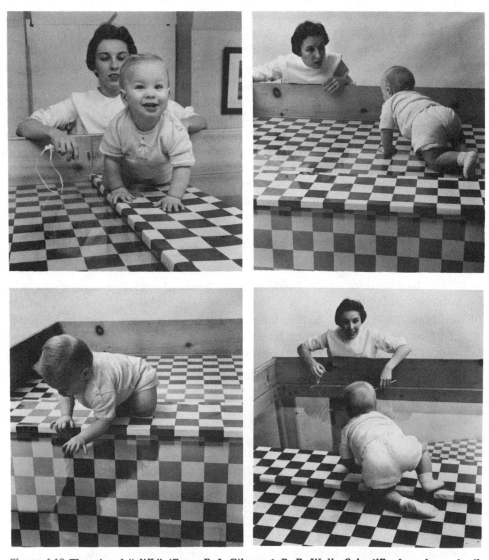

Figure 4.12 The visual "cliff." (From E. J. Gibson & R. R. Walk. **Scientific American,** April, 1961, **202,** 65. Photographer: William Vandivert. By permission.)

would not approach, even though the heavy glass (which they were able to touch) would have made the crossing safe (39). We know that the young infant who cannot crawl must be perceiving something special on the deep side, for he shows a marked decrease in heart rate—indicating attention—when he is placed on the deep side (15).

When a gray pattern was placed on the deep side, making the perception of depth more difficult, many more infants crossed over the deep side to their mothers. Moreover, when the checkerboard pattern on the deep side was brought close to the surface of the glass, thereby reducing the apparent depth, more infants crossed to their mothers (87).

It cannot be concluded that the infant's perception of depth and avoidance of the deep side are unlearned, as these infants were 6 months old when they were tested and had had some opportunity to learn that objects appear at different distances from their eyes. However, work with animals indicates that some species, such as the chicken and goat, are capable of depth perception during the first day of life and will not cross the deep side when tested immediately following birth.

Hearing

Unfortunately there has been less research on hearing and auditory perception than on vision, and much less is known about this sensory modality (especially in the period between 2 weeks and 1 year). Most of the research work has been with newborn infants. The newborn is capable of hearing at birth and is sensitive to location of sound as well as to frequency. In order to study the infant's capacity to make a discrimination, a sound of a given frequency, loudness, or duration is presented for a fixed number of trials (say, 20). By the last trial the infant has become minimally responsive to the tone, that is, he does not show motor movements, babblings, or heart-rate changes that characterize orientation to the source. Then the experimenter presents a new tone which differs from the original in one respect—either loudness, frequency, duration, or location—leaving the other three qualities unchanged. If the infant shows a greater response (a motor action, a heart-rate change, a vocalization, a smile, or a change in breathing) on the twenty-first trial, it could be inferred that the infant discriminated the difference between the last two tones. The experiments that use this general strategy have shown that newborns can detect the difference between tones of 200 and 250 cycles per second (cps), which is approximately equivalent to one step in a musical scale (10).

Babies as young as 1 month old are capable of perceiving the small difference between sounds like **pah** and **bah**. This fact was discovered by giving the sound **pah** as a reinforcement when infants sucked on a nipple at a particular rate. After several minutes the infants became bored with the sound **pah** and began to suck less rapidly. At that point, the **pah** was changed to a **bah**. Most infants began to increase their rate of sucking when the sound changed, indicating they must have perceived the difference between the two auditory stimuli (23, 85). Since infants as young as 4 months can detect the sounds that make up the basic phonemes of their language, it is likely that they are capable of detecting subtle differences among words that are spoken to them.

Psychological Attributes of Sounds The newborn appears to be constructed by nature to react differently to sounds of differing **frequency** or **pitch.** Low-frequency sounds (200 to 600 cps) tend to cause an increase in motor behavior if the child is normally alert and not hyperactive. These low-frequency sounds also inhibit the distress of the child if he is crying. High-frequency sounds (4000 cps, such as a whistle) lead to freezing behavior and a dramatic alerting reaction that makes one think the infant is asking, "What is it?" (24). These different reactions to sounds of varied frequencies resemble the special reaction 8-week-old infants showed to a bull's-eye, and indicate that (in man, just as in lower animals) nature may have built in special behavioral reactions that are more or less specific to particular kinds of stimuli.

A second aspect of sound that affects the newborn is **duration.** Sounds of short duration (less than a second) have a minimal effect. Sounds of 5 to 15 seconds have maximal effect on the infant's level of activity (80). If the sound lasts too long (over several minutes), the infant again becomes less responsive.

A third aspect of sound is the time required to reach maximal loudness, often called **rise time.** An explosion has a very fast rise time; a spoken word has a much slower rise time. Newborn infants heard tones differing in frequency (pitch), intensity (loudness), and rise time (from immediate to 2 seconds). The sounds with fast rise time produced closing of the eyes, as if the startled infant was behaving defensively. The sounds that came on more slowly produced opening of the eyes, as if the newborn was searching for something (53).

A fourth quality of sound is its **rhythmicity.** Newborns become quieter in response to rhythmic sounds than to dysrhythmic sounds. Moreover, if the sound of a rhythmic heart beat is compared with a rhythmic click, the rhythmic heart beat quiets the baby more effectively than the rhythmic click. Low-frequency rhythmic sounds tend to stop a baby's crying. Perhaps this is why leaning over a baby and rhythmically repeating, "hel-lo, hel-lo, hel-lo" in a low voice is often very effective in quieting an upset infant.

There may be some analogy between the data on seeing and hearing. Moving lights elicit more attention than nonmoving lights and this may be related to the fact that rhythmic, intermittent sounds quiet more than steady tones do. In both cases there is a break or discontinuity in the stimulus, which presents a change to the central nervous system. A moderately long contour elicits greater attention than a very short or a very long contour; a sound duration of 16 seconds leads to more reactivity or quieting than one of 1-second or 50-second duration. This comparability suggests some basic relations between the quality of a stimulus, its degree of contrast, rhythmicity, and duration, and the child's attentional behavior.

All of the above-described generalizations are relevant to the newborn, through the first week of life. What about the 6- or 12-month-old infant? What is the effect of learning on his attention to auditory stimuli?

As indicated earlier, attentiveness to auditory stimuli follows the same principles that explain reaction to visual events. Infants seem to be most attentive to sounds, both speech or nonspeech events, that are a little different from those that they know (54). In another study four sets of sentences, varying in both meaning and rhythm, were presented to 8-month-old boys. Some of the sentences were composed of nonsense words read either in a monotone or with normal rhythm. The other two sets of sentences contained meaningful, familiar words, such as baby, smile, and daddy, read in either a monotone or normal rhythm. Each infant heard the stimuli three times in a random order. The set that contained familiar words read with normal rhythm led to more babbling than any of the others, suggesting that the infant was maximally reactive to the characteristics of typical speech (49).

Other Senses

Less is known about olfactory perception than about hearing. The newborn is capable of responding to odors, turning his head away from unpleasant odors such as ammonia or acetic acid The newborn seems to show little discrimination between less distinctive odors, but the presence of odors may provoke more activity than clear air, and greater saturations stimulate greater activity (22). For example, there is a clear relation between the amount of activity and the concentration of vaporized alcohol (72).

The phenomenon of pain sentitivity is somewhat different from that of other sense modalities. First, unlike vision, hearing, or olfaction, there do not appear to be any localized areas in the brain that receive and integrate pain-producing stimulation. Second, the experience that adults call "pain" is highly dependent upon learning. Elaboration of this point is reserved for a later section.

Although there is little systematic information on pain sensitivity in infants, existing evidence suggests that sensitivity to pain is present to some degree at birth, and becomes sharper during the first few days of postnatal life. For example, the number of pain stimuli (pin pricks) necessary to instigate withdrawal of the stimulated area (the original response to pain) decreases between birth and 8 days (76, 77).

There may be constitutional differences among infants in pain sensitivity (57), females being more sensitive than males. As we shall see later, pain plays an important role in the child's acquisition of fear, and individual variation in sensitivity to pain may partially account for differences in susceptibility to fear in older children.

RESPONSE CAPABILITIES

Sensory capacities allow the child to experience differences in quality of sight, sound, taste, smell, and touch, and (as we have seen) the human infant comes into the world with an intact set of sensory receptors for the basic modalities. The infant begins life with a very small set of responses, called **reflexes,** which are not learned. Some of them were discussed in the earlier section on the newborn. Some of these reflexes, such as sucking on a nipple and crying in response to pain, are adaptive and necessary to the baby's survival. Others are not necessary for life but reflect the state of the infant's nervous system. Examples of the latter include the Moro response; shuddering in response to bitter taste; head balancing instigated by changes in bodily position; the grasp reflex (closing hand tightly, usually stimulated by contact pressure on finger or palm); the Babinski reflex (extension of the big toe and fanning out of the other toes when the sole of the foot is stroked); and, in the male, penis erection and raising of the testes, elicited by stimulation of the inner thigh.

Coordination of many parts of the body is involved in the newborn infant's more generalized responses, including: (1) trunk movements (squirming, twisting, arching the back, and drawing in the stomach); (2) body jerks; (3) shivering or trembling; and (4) creeping movements. These responses are present during the first days of life. The responses that are not present at birth are divided into two different types—maturational and learned.

Maturational responses develop with no special tutoring in the formal sense. Given the general opportunity to use limbs and body, every child will creep, stand, walk, sit up, and grab objects. **Learned responses** must be acquired in a specific sense, or they will not appear. These responses include the culturally specific actions that children learn, such as opening a refrigerator, turning on a faucet, sitting on a potty, writing, coloring, singing, skating, playing football, and sailing. Let us consider the maturational responses first, for they tell a dramatic story during the first year.

The Maturation of Motor Development

The child's sitting, crawling, and standing exemplify maturational development. They occur during the first two years of life as a consequence of the opportunity to use the body plus the maturation of certain neural tissues, expansion and increased complexity of the central nervous system, and growth of bones and muscles. In many instances, these seemingly unlearned behavior patterns improve and become better coordinated, more precise, and more accurate after practice.

In this chapter, the emphasis is only on developments in locomotion, reaching, and grasping. No attempt is made to review the whole vast array of responses of the first year; complete surveys may be found in the works of Gesell and Amatruda (37) and McGraw (61).

Locomotion

Sitting The response repertoire of the neonate does not include any reflex sitting posture, but the ability to sit develops early (4, 19, 37, 78). On the average, babies are able to sit for a minute, with support, at the age of 3 or 4 months, and by 7 or 8 months, they can do it without support. Once sitting is achieved, there is rapid improvement, so that by 9 months most babies can sit independently for 10 minutes or longer (37).

Crawling and Creeping There are great individual differences in the ages at which infants reach the various stages of crawling and creeping, but practically all infants go through the same sequence (2).

The first stage, thrusting one knee forward beside the body, appeared in half the infants at 28 weeks or younger. The median age for crawling (that is, moving with the abdomen in contact with the floor) was 34 weeks. At this age, the muscles of the trunk, arms, and legs are not sufficiently strong or coordinated to maintain the body weight. The infants began to creep on hands and knees, which requires new coordination and equilibrium, at a median age of 40 weeks, while creeping on hands and feet, the final stage of prone progression, was attained by a median age of 49 weeks. Infants may skip one or two stages of development, but all of them progress through most of the steps (2).

Walking The ability to walk independently also matures gradually after a series of preliminary achievements. As in other aspects of development, there is a wide range of ages at which the various stages are attained. The median ages for standing while holding onto furniture, walking when led, pulling up to a stand, standing alone, and walking alone were 42, 45, 47, 62, and 64 weeks, respectively, according to Shirley's data on 25 children (78; see Fig. 4.13).

There is considerable evidence (19, 60, 61, 77, 84) that both maturation of the neural and muscular systems, as well as environmental experiences, determine when the child will sit, stand, and walk. For example, Dennis (19) kept a pair of female twins on their backs until they were 9 months old, thus preventing any practice in sitting or standing. When they were given their first opportunities to sit alone at the age of 37 weeks, the restricted twins were not able to do so. Several weeks later, however, they were able to sit alone. Although most children by the time they are 40 weeks old can support their body weight while standing with help, the twins were not able to do this at 52 weeks, when they were given

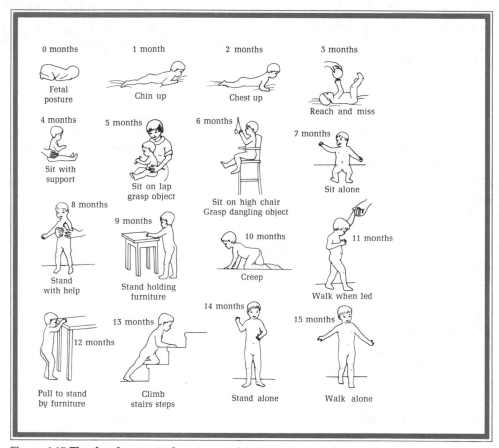

Figure 4.13 The development of posture and locomotion in infants. (From **The First Two Years** by Mary M. Shirley. Institute of Child Welfare Monograph No. 7. Minneapolis: University of Minnesota Press. © Copyright 1933, renewed 1961 by the University of Minnesota. By permission.)

their first opportunity to do so. Within three days, however, both infants could stand with help for at least two minutes.

Generally speaking, although these motor behaviors develop without any special practice or teaching by adults, extreme degrees of environmental restriction on opportunity for motor development can retard the onset of walking (20). Dennis compared the motor development of children (1 to 3 years of age) raised in three different Iranian institutions, only one of which provided its children with opportunities to sit and play in the prone position. The children in this relatively more enriched environment were less retarded in onset of walking than those in the institutions where motor experience was more restricted. Dennis concluded:

> The results of the present study challenge the widely held view that motor development consists of the emergence of a behavioral sequence based primarily upon mat-

uration. . . . These facts seem to indicate clearly that experience affects not only the ages at which motor items appear but also their very form (20, 57).

It is possible to promote walking at an earlier age by giving the very young infant special practice in the walking and stepping reflexes. If a 1-week-old is held by the arms and placed on a table, he will make very primitive walking movements. These reflexes usually fade at about 2 months of age. A group of mothers spent 12 minutes a day having their infants practice the stepping reflex from 2 to 8 weeks. Among these infants the walking reflex did not fade and they showed more walking when held at 8 weeks of age, in comparison with babies who did not have this practice at home. They also walked alone 2½ months earlier—at 10 months of age on the average—than infants who did not have this special experience (92).

Although all normal children will walk eventually, there are slight differences in the rate of the child's physical development or opportunity to practice. African children in Uganda, for example, walk earlier than European children and this precocity in walking is associated with advances in other aspects of motor and physical development during the first year (35). An extensive study of more than 1000 children from five European cities (Brussels, London, Paris, Stockholm, and Zurich) revealed that the Brussels and Stockholm children walked about a month earlier than infants from Paris, London, Zurich, 12½ versus 13½ months (47). Moreover, the Brussels and Stockholm children were taller than the others and more advanced in general motor development at 1 year (47).

How are these differences to be explained? On the one hand, we can argue that children in Uganda, Brussels, and Stockholm are given more freedom and their earlier walking reflects greater opportunity to perfect this skill. On the other hand, as muscle mass in the leg and calf areas and general central nervous system maturation are important in walking, it is possible that genetic or nutritional differences are responsible for such differences among the populations of children. It is not possible at present to decide which of these explanations is better. However, even if it turns out that the Stockholm child develops motor coordination faster than the Parisian child because of genetic differences, this is not equivalent to saying the Stockholm child is generally more intelligent or more advanced in all areas of growth. There is no predictive relation between age of walking or rate of physical development during the first two years and intelligence during the preschool or early school years.

Sensorimotor Coordination and Reaching

One of the interesting maturational developments is a response that typically reaches maturity at about 5 months and has been called **visually directed reaching.** If you place an attractive object in the field of vision of a 1-month-old baby, he will stare at it, but will make no attempt to grab it. By 2½ months of age, he will begin to swipe at it, but will be far off target. By 4 months, the infant will raise his hand in the vicinity of the object, alternate his glance between the hand and object, gradually removing the gap between his hand and the object and then perhaps touching it. By 5 or 5½ months the infant will reach for the object and contact it efficiently. His aim is now perfect.

Although this response goes through a standard set of maturational steps, as walking or standing does, it is subject to alteration through environmental experiences of enrichment. Infants raised in an unstimulating institution where they were deprived of objects to attend to or reach are retarded in their attainment of visual motor reaching. Progress is accelerated for infants who are provided with opportunity for reaching and watching attractive objects (such as mobiles or other objects which can be placed within the child's reach and which he may handle; see Fig. 4.14); they will show visual motor reaching as early as 4 to 4½ months (89).

If the infant is provided with an opportunity to practice and, therefore, to perfect reaching responses, we see earlier manifestation of that behavior—even though the process is basically maturational. Enriching the stimulus environment does not always lead to acceleration of all the child's mental or motor development. The child must be maturationally ready to reach if the enrichment is to help. The child of 3 to 4 months ordinarily studies and swipes at attractive objects, and providing him with some if he has none will direct his attention to them and stimulate him to reach. However, providing stimulation to accelerate responses that the child is not prepared to display may accomplish nothing and in some cases may lead to a retardation. For example, the institutionalized infants placed in the enriched environment described above showed less attentiveness to the colorful environment during the first five weeks. These children were more irritable and fussy than those who did not have the enriched stimulation, as if the enriching stimuli were distressing the child. The presence of a stimulus to which the infant cannot make a response seems to be one cause of distress to the infant. It is possible that the 3-week-old baby is too immature to make any response to the richly colored mobile and becomes more upset than if nothing were present.

Consider a 1-year-old who is not ready to write with a crayon. Giving him crayons or pencils would not necessarily facilitate earlier development of this skill. Indeed, if the child grows tired of the crayons or pencils he may ignore them two years later when he has become maturationally ready to use them. The child can be helped to master skills earlier than he ordinarily would through enrichment, but the timing of the enrichment is important. It may be as harmful to present enriching experiences before the child is ready to benefit from them as it is to deprive the child of these stimulations entirely. It is likely that a two- or three-month retardation or precocity in attaining the skills of standing or walking is of minimal consequence for future development.

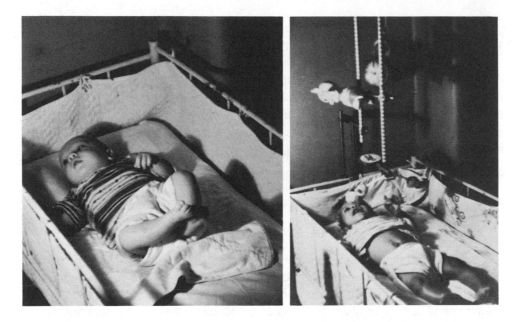

Figure 4.14 A situation in which visual motor coordination is tested. (From B. L. White & R. Held. Plasticity of sensory motor development. In J. F. Rosenblith & W. Allinsmith (Eds.), **Readings in child development and educational psychology.** (2nd ed.) Boston: Allyn and Bacon, copyright © 1966. By permission.)

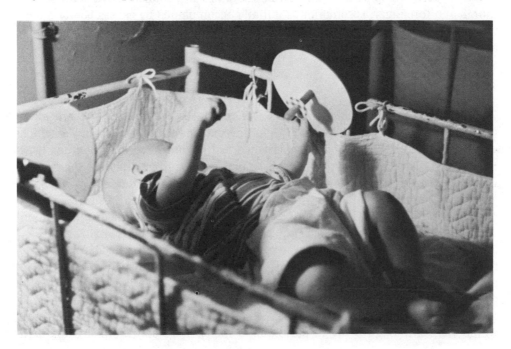

DEVELOPMENTAL TRENDS

First-year sensory and motor developments reflect several general directional trends. The **cephalocaudal** (or head-to-foot) trend is illustrated in the relatively early accomplishment of head movements, visual fixation, and eye-hand coordination, and the relatively late appearance of standing and walking. The limbs and muscles of the upper part of the body become functionally effective before the lower limbs. In walking, appropriate coordination of the arms preceeds that of the legs.

> The principle is well illustrated in the behavior characteristics of the twenty week old infant. His trunk is still so flacid that he must be propped or strapped in a chair to maintain a sitting posture. When he is so secured, however, his eyes, head, and shoulders exhibit heightened activity and intensified tonus. The pelvic zone and the lower extremities at 20 weeks are, in comparison, very immature (**36,** 341).

Progress in the development of motor responses during the first year also follows a roughly **proximodistal** direction, i.e., from the central to the peripheral segments of the body. Thus, in reaching, the shoulders and elbows are used before the wrist and fingers. In both prone and erect locomotion, the upper arm and upper leg are brought under control before the forearm, foreleg, hands, and feet.

The trend **from mass to specific** activities or from large to smaller muscles is also evident in the motor advances of the first year. The gross awkward movements of early grasping are replaced by more precise, refined movements of the thumb and forefinger. Locomotion is initially accompanied by excess bodily movements, but these decrease gradually until only the appropriate muscles and limbs are involved.

Acquired Instrumental Responses

We have thus far considered two kinds of responses—reflexes which are automatically elicited by stimuli without learning and maturational responses which can be retarded or facilitated by experience, but do not have to be learned. Our third category includes complex responses that are acquired. They are learned by the child in order to (1) provide him with sensory feedback (the infant will bang a block or a sphere in order to experience some sensations) or (2) gratify a need or motive (the child will learn to cry when he is alone or learn to turn a doorknob to get out of a room or learn to protest vocally when he is frustrated).

It is now well established that a very young infant, even a newborn, is capable of acquiring a conditioned response, that is, learning to display a behavior to a stimulus that, heretofore, was neutral. In the typical experiment the infant is given a reinforcement, usually food, but often an interesting visual event such as a picture or light, each time he makes a specific response, like turning his head to the right. Although a 7-week-old requires many more conditioning trials than a 4-month-old, due in part to general alertness, he eventually does learn to make the response when the conditioned stimulus appears. Even a newborn's pattern of sucking can be altered if the experimenter rewards one pattern of sucking with milk but not the other (75). The very young infant can be influenced by the arrangement of stimulus events, and his behavior is modified by these events soon after birth.

In order to appreciate the relation between the child's learned responses and the needs and motives that they serve, we must review the needs and motives of the first year. A need is a change in biological or psychological state (a disruption in equilibrium or homeostasis, according to one view). This changed bodily state often leads immediately to unpleasant sensations or to some generalized increase or decrease in behavior or reactivity, but it need not, as in the case of vitamin deficiencies.

BASIC NEEDS

The infant is born with a number of basic physiological drives or needs which must be satisfied if he is to survive. Most of these needs—oxygen, temperature control, and sleep—are usually taken care of in a self-regulatory manner, without any active participation by the infant.

Sleep

At present, there is no completely satisfactory physiological theory to account for the child's need for rest. Sleep seems to be a device by which the body regulates itself, maintains equilibrium in its chemical constitution, and thus preserves the organism's energy for later activity.

The proportion of time spent in sleep decreases as the child grows older. Neonates on the average spend 80 percent of their time asleep, while 1-year-olds on the average spend about 50 percent of their time asleep.

The rhythms and depth of sleep also change rapidly during the first year. For the first 3 or 4 weeks, the average infant takes seven or eight short naps a day, but the number is reduced to between two and four longer periods of sleep by 6 weeks of age. By 28 weeks, most children will sleep through the night, and from then until they are about 1 year old, will require only two or three daytime naps (38). Night sleep also becomes less broken as the child matures—to the considerable relief of weary mothers.

There are great individual differences in sleep needs, and any particular child's requirements may vary from time to time. Many factors influence the quality and quantity of sleep. During the earliest months, intestinal upsets, and later on, wetness, bodily discomfort, noise, or emotional factors (violence, excitement, etc.) may interfere with sound rest. The infant's need for sleep or rest seldom becomes intense, as he will ordinarily sleep as much as is necessary and wake when he is rested. Later on, he will have to learn the culturally approved patterns of sleep and wakefulness, but this is not an important problem during the first year.

There are at least two different kinds of sleep. In one, the person displays short rapid movements of his eyes. In the second these eye movements are absent. In adults, dreams are most likely to occur during the rapid eye movement phase (called REM sleep), but it is not likely that the infant is dreaming when he displays these eye movements. Fig. 4.15 shows the change in proportion of REM and non-REM sleep during the day from the first days of life through old age. REM sleep is most frequent during the first 5 months (40 percent of sleep time), and decreases with age (71).

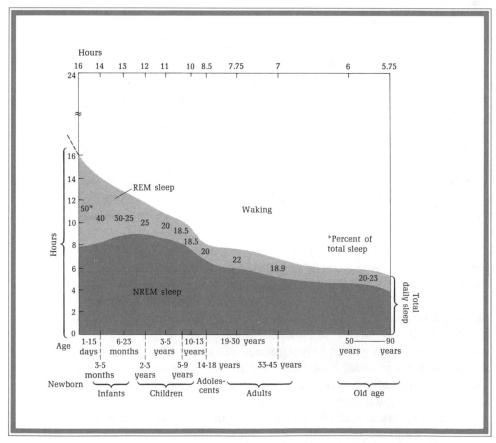

Figure 4.15 Changes (with age) in amounts of total sleep, REM sleep, and non-REM sleep. (From H. P. Roffwarg, J. N. Muzio, & W. C. Dement. Ontogenic development of the human sleep-dream cycle. **Science,** 1966, **152,** 608. Revised since publication in **Science** by H. P. Roffwarg. By permission of the author.)

Need for Elimination

When the neonate's bowel is full, the anal sphincters open reflexively and the contents are expelled. In the same way, when the bladder is swollen, the urethral sphincter is automatically released. These processes are entirely involuntary in early infancy; the neuromuscular equipment necessary for voluntary control has not yet matured. By 8 weeks of age, the average infant usually has only two bowel movements daily, one upon waking and one close to or during a feeding. By 16 weeks, a definite interval between feeding and evacuation has usually been established (38).

Learning to withhold elimination until the proper, that is, socially approved, place and time requires the inhibition or suppression of responses which initially occur automatically. In toilet training, voluntary control must be substituted for reflex actions. This presents a complex and difficult learning problem which requires a great deal of skill and patience in handling, as we shall see later.

Hunger and Thirst

These two needs are not easily differentiated in young infants and hence will be discussed together. From a psychological and social point of view, they are the most important of the neonate's basic drives, for their satisfaction depends on someone else's help rather than on automatic, reflex activities. If the infant's hunger and thirst are not reduced soon, tensions mount, become severe, and provoke a great deal of bodily activity. For this reason, these drives play an important role in the infant's earliest learning. Here we shall review briefly the changes in physiological hunger needs and feeding patterns during the first year. Discussion of the broader social learning implications of the feeding situation, the infant's first interpersonal relationship, is reserved for Chapter 5.

Data on American newborn infants on self-demand schedules (feeding whenever the baby is hungry) indicate that, on the average, neonates take seven or eight feedings per day. By 4 weeks of age, the number has been reduced to five or six. At this time, the average infant's food intake is between 18 and 25 ounces, but this rises to about 35 ounces when he is 6 to 8 weeks old. Within the next few weeks, the number of feedings is further reduced, although total food intake does not change significantly (38).

In our culture, solid foods are often introduced into the infant's menu when he is about 8 weeks of age, and by 20 weeks, cereals and vegetables may form a regular part of his diet. By the time the American child is 1 year old, the three-meal regime has probably become stabilized and he may manifest marked food preferences. The time and manner of weaning the infant to solid foods varies from culture to culture.

Some of the infant's needs lead regularly to the same set of behaviors. When hungry, the infant begins to thrash and cry until gratified. When tired, he is likely to fret. When frustrated, he may protest and thrash. Fretting, crying, protesting, and thrashing are prepotent responses that are elicited by many different needs during the first year. As we shall see in the next chapter, the social development of the cry, protest, or fret depends on how the social environment responds to these actions.

VOCALIZATION

Babbling and vocal sounds are universal responses during infancy. In normal children there is no strong relation between frequency of early babbling and the amount or the time of onset of speech during the second year. Babbling in an infant under 6 months usually occurs when the child is excited by something he sees or hears and is often an accompaniment of motor activity. During the second half of the first year, the child will often quiet while he is listening to a sound. When the sound stops, he will begin to babble. This babbling reflects an excitatory reaction created by processing the sounds he heard.

The expression of meaningful words is a much different phenomenon. Meaningful speech is used to obtain goals and communicate thoughts and is not merely a reflection of general excitement. Speech requires exposure to people who speak a language; babbling does not. The early vocalization of the infant does pass through certain stages, however. Let us review them briefly.

The infant makes two basic sounds. The first includes all sounds related to crying and is present at birth. A second category of sounds emerges during the sixth or eighth week of life and can best be described as a cooing sound (56). Recall that other changes occurring during the sixth to eighth week include increased visual attention, decreased crying, and signs of depth perception. This cooing sound is different from a cry because in cooing the tongue is involved in modulating the sound. This usually does not happen when the baby cries. The babbling that occurs up to 6 weeks is an innate response and is relatively unchanged by experience during this period. The environment seems to affect the frequency and variety of these baby sounds after 8 to 10 weeks. Children raised in homes in which both mother and child engage in reciprocal vocal play with each other vocalize more and with greater variety than infants from homes where such exchange is minimal.

A dramatic demonstration of the role of parental vocal play is seen in a comparison of rural Guatemalan Indian infants with Americans. The American infants, who are spoken to 25 to 30 percent of the time they are awake, vocalize about 25 percent of the time they are awake. Indian infants, who are spoken to very little because their mothers do not believe there is much value in such behavior, vocalize about 7 percent of the time they are awake (50).

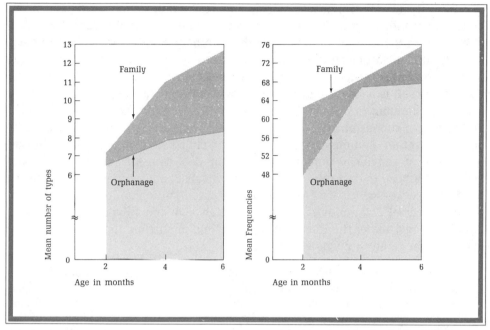

Figure 4.16 Mean frequencies of vocalizing and mean numbers of types of sound in the vocalizing of infants in home and institutions. (From A. J. Brodbeck & O. C. Irwin. The speech behavior of infants without families. **Child Development,** 1946, **17,** 149. Copyright 1946 by The Society for Research in Child Development, Inc. By permission.)

Similarly, babies under 6 months of age living in unstimulating orphanage environments are often retarded both in frequency of vocalizations and number and types of sounds (see Fig. 4.16). During the second half of the first year, infants raised in middle-class homes show more frequent and varied sounds than children of working-class families because middle-class mothers do more vocalizing to their infants which, in turn, stimulates the child's vocal expression. This class difference also holds for 10-month-olds. Observations of the mother-child interaction in the home revealed minimal social class differences with respect to cuddling, physical contact, and general nurturance. However, middle-class mothers were much more likely to talk to their infant and to respond to his babbling with reciprocal speech than were working-class mothers (**86**).

Responding to the 3-month-old child's utterances by smiling and touching his abdomen after each sound leads to an increase in the amount of infant vocalization (**69**). The infant's babbling behavior apparently can be modified through experience and can be increased or decreased, depending on the amounts of social stimulation the child's vocalizations receive. As the vocalizations of infants in institutions are less apt to attract the attention of an adult and are, therefore, not often rewarded, the frequency of such responses among these children is not likely to increase at a normal rate.

Once the elementary speech sounds are acquired, progress in speech consists of using these sounds in a variety of ways and in different combinations. Individual differences in the rates of speech development are apparent from earliest infancy.

One of the intriguing questions that has long baffled psychologists is why infants continue to babble to themselves, even when no one responds to their vocalizations. It is believed that the child's perception of his own voice production acts as a stimulant to further vocalization during the latter half of the first year. The primitive sounds of the 1- or 2-month-old baby, however, appear to be independent of either environmental factors or the child's perception of these noises.

The most convincing demonstration of this fact comes from observations of deaf infants born to deaf mute parents. The vocalizations of these infants during the first 8 weeks—which are heard by neither parent nor child—do not differ from those of normal children with parents who can hear the baby's sounds. After 2 months of age, the environment does play a role in shaping the variety and frequency of the infant's sounds. However,

> [most] present day psychologists seem to agree . . . that new sounds are not learned by imitation of the speech of others, but rather that they emerge in the child's spontaneous vocal play as a result of maturation, and that the child imitates only those sounds which have already occurred in its spontaneous babblings. This view holds that imitation of the speech of others serves only to call attention to new combinations of sounds already used (59, 517).

Relation of Babbling to Later Development

Although frequency and variety of babbling during the opening months are not good predictors of the child's later talkativeness or the size of his vocabulary, there appears to be an interesting sex difference in the predictive power of early babbling between 4 and 12 months of age. Infant girls who babble in response to human faces tend to be more attentive and obtain slightly higher intelligence scores at 1, 2, and 3 years of age than girls who babble very little to human faces (49).

Independent longitudinal studies have reported similar and equally interesting results. Infant girls who vocalized frequently in a testing situation during the first year had higher IQ scores at 2 and 3 years than infant girls who did not vocalize. However, this relation between early vocalization and IQ did not occur for boys (14, 63).

How can we interpret this interesting sex difference found in **three separate longitudinal studies?** There are several possibilities. One explanation assumes that the innate neuromotor organization of boys and girls is basically different. If the central nervous system of girls were structured so that girls were more likely than boys to vocalize when they are attentive to and excited by an interesting event, then the vocalizations of the infant girl would be a good measure of the girl's tendency to invest attention in events around her, and perhaps predictive of her future intelligence. If the innate neuromotor organization of boys did not lead them to vocalize when they were attentive to events, then vocalization in the boy should not be related to future intellectual ability.

A second possible explanation assumes greater stability of cognitive development among girls than among boys. In this case, it is assumed that vocalization to an interesting event reflects advanced mental development for both boys and girls. But because a girl's rate of mental development seems to be more stable than that of the boy, the infant vocalization score is a better predictor of the future intelligence among the girls than boys. It is perhaps a coincidence that physical growth dimensions—such as height, weight, and rate of bone growth—are more stable from year to year among girls than among boys (1). It is possible that the greater predictive power of infant vocalization for girls is another reflection of a more general tendency toward greater stability in girls' development.

A final potential explanation assumes that mothers treat sons and daughters differently, and argues that mothers who are motivated to encourage their daughter's mental development spend a lot of time vocalizing to them—more time than they would with a son and more than mothers who are not concerned with their daughter's rate of development. The mother's face-to-face vocalization should lead to increased levels of babbling in the girl. This mother would also be expected to continue to stimulate her daughter and would probably teach her words early and encourage the development of other intellectual skills. The predictive link between early babbling and later cognitive abilities would then be a function of the continuity of the mother's acceleration of her daughter. The absence of a predictive link between infant vocalization and cognitive development in the boys would require the assumption that accelerating mothers do not preferentially engage in as much vocalization with their sons. Preliminary data support this assumption. Observations of the mother-infant interaction in the home reveal that well-educated mothers engage in more distinctive face-to-face vocalization with their daughters than less-well-educated mothers do, whereas there is no comparable difference among the mothers of sons. Moreover, middle-class mothers are more likely to imitate the vocalization of their 3-month-old daughters than those of their sons (64).

It is not possible at the moment to state which of these explanations is the best. Future research will help to make that decision.

MENTAL DEVELOPMENT

The discussion of the relation of vocalization to mental development leads us to a more general discussion of mental development. Let us be clear about what is meant by this term.

The popular meaning of the word implies that each child is born with a different amount of basic intellectual ability. It is also assumed, implicitly, that the infant with greater mental ability will be ahead on all important psychological skills and, other things equal, will remain ahead unless he suffers a serious illness, serious brain damage, environmental deprivation, or parental rejection. Since this is a simple idea, it is appealing. Unfortunately, there is no firm scientific support for it. Infants who are advanced with respect to walking or sitting are not necessarily advanced in language, learning to read, or drawing of pictures. Moreover, there is an enormous capacity for change in the early years. Rural Guatemalan Indian infants between 12 and 18 months old, who are five months retarded in object permanence and attentiveness, in comparison with American infants, seem to "make up" that retardation during later childhood after they leave the dark hut in which they spend their first year.

An alternative way to view mental development is to consider each of the major stages of growth as characterized by the emergence of new competences. One can determine which infants are ahead and which behind on the skills emerging at that stage. But one must hold in reservation any conviction that there will be a close relation between the skills that emerge from 6 to 12 months and those that begin to appear at 2 to 3 years. Sitting, standing, and stranger and separation anxiety usually appear between 6 and 12 months. Two-word sentences, imitation, and cooperative play emerge at 2 to 3 years of age. These sets of abilities have different foundations and existing evidence suggests no necessary relation between retardation on the first set and retardation on the second.

Although most psychologists agree that there are stages in mental development, that is, different clusters of skills emerging at special times, there is less agreement on whether these stages have a close relation to one another. This controversy forms a bridge to a discussion of Piaget's views of infancy.

Chapter 2 contained a review of Piaget's theory. Let us examine its detailed implications for infancy.

Piaget's View of Intellectual Development in Infancy

During the first year and a half of life, the infant is in the **sensorimotor stage** of development, during which his intelligence is manifested in his actions. When a 1-year-old wants a toy resting on a blanket far from him, he pulls the blanket toward him to get the object. Piaget would regard this as an act of intelligence. The child used the blanket to achieve a goal (the prized toy). Piaget does not call this act an operation, but rather a schema of action. It is a generalized response that can be used to solve a variety of problems. The habit of bouncing in the crib in order to make toys attached to the crib shimmer or move is another example of a schema of action. At every age in infancy the child has a set of such schemata. The infant can suck, hit, bang, and shake, and when a new toy is presented to him he will typically exhibit one of these responses. As indicated earlier, the shaking of a new toy the child has never seen is an example of assimilation. Holding a bottle, shaking a rattle in order to produce a noise, sucking more efficiently, or seeking out a ball that rolls out of sight are examples of the coordinated motor behaviors Piaget calls sensorimotor schemes (65).

The sensorimotor stage is further differentiated into six developmental stages covering the first 18 months of life (65).

During the first stage, that of **reflexes** (birth to 1 month), innate reflexes (such as sucking movements to the stimulus of a nipple) become more efficient. These unlearned responses comprise the major adaptive behavior of the organism. The second stage, called **primary circular reactions,** is characterized by the appearance of repetitions of simple acts that are repeated for their own sake. Examples of primary circular reactions include repetitive sucking, repetitive opening and closing of the fists, and repetitive fingering of a blanket. There seems to be no intent or purpose to this activity, and in contrast to the next stage, the child does not seem to be interested in the effect that his behavior has on the environment.

The succeeding four stages contain more intentional activity, according to Piaget (80). In the third stage, **secondary circular reactions** (4 to 6 months), the child repeats responses which produce interesting results. For example, the child will repeatedly kick his legs in order to produce a swinging motion in a toy suspended over his crib. To a naïve observer it appears that the child has accidentally discovered that a certain act (kicking his legs) produces an interesting change in the external environment (the toy swings), and the child repeats the act in order to see the change in the environment. In the earlier stage of primary circular reactions, the act was repeated for its own sake, rather than to produce an interesting stimulus effect.

In the fourth stage, **coordination of secondary reactions** (7 to 10 months), the child begins to solve simple problems. The infant now uses a response he has already mastered as a means of obtaining a specific goal object. For example, he will now knock down a pillow in order to obtain a toy hidden behind it. In the preceding state (secondary circular reactions) the child might repeatedly knock down a pillow merely to watch it fall. In this later stage, he uses this learned response as a means to obtain a desired goal, and not as an end in itself.

During the fifth stage, **tertiary circular reactions,** the child begins to show active trial-and-error experimentation. During this period (11 to 18 months) the child varies his responses toward the same object or tries out new responses to obtain the same goal. For example, the child who has learned to knock down a pillow with his fist to get a toy may then attempt to knock it down with his feet or use a rattle to push it down. The child is now manifesting the essence of problem-solving behavior.

During this stage the infant discovers (generally accidentally) some novel, interesting, and exciting event that he attempts to repeat and prolong, so that he can continue to enjoy it, for example, kicking a doll hanging above the crib simply to watch it swing. In the secondary circular reaction of the third stage, the repetition is accomplished by rather stereotyped and mechanical actions. But in the fifth stage, the tertiary circular reaction, the child modifies and varies his movements, that is, accommodates, in a "progressively more deliberate fashion" (65). Act and object (means and end) are clearly differentiated.

> The infant gives the impression—and here is the real significance of the tertiary reaction for intellectual development—of really exploring the object's potentialities, of really varying the act in order to see how this variation affects the object, of really subordinating his actions to an object seen as a thing apart, something "out there" (31, 114).

What is most interesting to the child at this stage is novelty per se, the variations that he can produce in the movements he initiates. He becomes active in trial-and-error exploration of his environment, seeking new means of attaining goals and thus discovering new ways of solving problems. In the activities of the fifth stage, the child begins to manifest the constructive, original elements that Piaget regards as characteristic of intelligence. He describes the actions in this way.

> It is therefore a question of innovating. [The child performs] an "experiment in order to see": the child gropes. The only difference is that, now, the groping is oriented as a function of the goal itself, that is to say, of the problem presented . . . instead of taking place simply "in order to see" (Piaget, quoted in 31, 118).

Piaget's observations of his son Laurent illustrate this "discovery of new means through active experimentation" graphically. He records:

> I place my watch on a big red cushion (of a uniform color and without a fringe) and place the cushion directly in front of the child. Laurent tries to reach the watch directly and not succeeding, he grabs the cushion which he draws toward him as before. But then, instead of letting go of the support at once, as he has hitherto done, in order to try again to grasp the objective, he recommences with obvious interest, to move the cushion while looking at the watch. Everything takes place as though he noticed for the first time the relationship for its own sake and studied it as such. He thus easily succeeds in grasping the watch (Piaget, quoted in 31, 117).

The sixth stage of the sensorimotor period, the final and most advanced stage of this period, is achieved at approximately 18 months. It is characterized by "invention of new means through internal mental combinations" (65) and its most striking and significant feature is the development of a primitive form of representation, a kind of imagery that is used in problem-solving. When the child at this stage wishes to obtain some end for which he has no habitual, available means, he invents one. But he does this not by overt, fumbling, trial-and-error explorations, as in the fifth stage. Instead, he operates covertly, by "internal experimentation, an inner exploration of ways and means" (31, 119). Piaget gives some vivid illustrations of activity at this stage.

At 1:6 for the first time Lucienne plays with a doll carriage whose handle comes to the height of her face. She rolls it over the carpet by pushing it. When she comes against a wall, she pulls, walking backward. But as this position is not convenient for her, she pauses and without hesitation goes to the other side to push the carriage again. She therefore found the procedure in one attempt, apparently through analogy to other situations but without training, apprenticeship, or chance. . . .

In the same kind of inventions, that is to say, in the realm of kinematic representations, the following fact should be cited. At 1:10 Lucienne tries to kneel before a stool but, by leaning against it, pushes it further away. She then raises herself up, takes it and places it against a sofa. When it is firmly set there she leans against it and kneels without difficulty (Piaget, quoted in **31,** 119).

The dual processes of representation and invention are the keystones of the sixth stage. The kind of inventiveness demonstrated by Lucienne in the illustrations above clearly requires symbolic images, the ability to symbolize actions or events before acting them out in reality. In short, the child at this stage is capable of imagined representation and, consequently, of a kind of internal manipulation of reality.

The accomplishments of this stage are dramatically reflected in the child's acquisition of the ability to "defer imitation," i.e., to reproduce behavior of an absent model from memory. For example, one day, Jacqueline, another of Piaget's children, saw a child throw a temper tantrum. The next day she tried it herself, although she had never had a tantrum before, producing an obvious imitation of the tantrum she had seen twelve hours earlier.

With the advent of the capacity to represent actions rather than simply to perform them, the sensory-motor period draws to a close and the child is ready for an analogous but even more extended and tortuous apprenticeship in the use of symbols. . . . This does not, of course, mean that the child no longer continues to develop in the sensory-motor sphere. But it does mean that henceforth the most advanced **intellectual** adaptations of which a given child is capable will take place in a conceptual-symbolic rather than purely sensory-motor arena (**31,** 121).

In the course of his work on growth of intelligence, Piaget made some ingenious observations on the development of the permanence of an object. The stages the child passes through in acquiring the idea that objects have permanence will be outlined briefly in order to communicate the flavor of Piaget's observations.

During the first 2 or 3 months of life, the child's visual universe, according to Piaget, is made up of a series of fleeting images without permanence. It is as if the child were on a train watching the world pass before him. He follows a stimulus until it passes out of his line of vision, and he then abandons any search for it, as if he believed that once it disappeared it ceased to exist.

From 3 to 6 months, the child coordinates vision and movements of his arms and hands. He will now grab for objects that he can see, but will not reach for objects outside his immediate visual field. Piaget interprets the child's failure to search for the hidden object as indicating that he does not realize that the hidden object still exists. The infant behaves as if an object out of sight has lost its permanence, that is, it no longer exists.

During the last 3 months of the first year the child advances one step further. He will now reach for an object that is hidden from view, if he has watched it being hidden. Thus, if the child sees the mother place a bottle under a blanket, he will search for the bottle there. Moreover, the 8- to 10-month-old infant will show surprise if he watches an object covered by a person's hand and then notes the object absent when the hand is uncovered. The fact that the child is surprised by the disappearance suggests that he expected the object to be there. He believes in the permanence of the object (17).

During the first 6 months of the second year the child becomes capable of accounting for "spatial displacements" of objects. If an object is hidden under a pillow, the child in the preceding stage will search for it, but if he then sees the object being hidden under a second pillow, he will continue to look for it under the first pillow. In this later stage, however, the child will search for the object under the second pillow, indicating a recognition that objects can be displaced.

In the final stage of acquiring the concept of object permanence, the child will search for objects that he has not actually seen being hidden. For example, if the mother shows the child a toy fish in a box, puts the fish and box under a cover, and then removes the box without the fish, the child will search for the fish under the cover, as though he realized that it must be there. This behavior does not occur during the earlier stages and suggests that the child becomes aware that objects have permanence and do not cease to exist when they disappear from view (65).

From this summary of Piaget's views of mental development in the first year, it can be seen that the coordination of simple motor actions with incoming perceptions (sensorimotor acts) predominate in the mental activity of the child. Precocious development of these behaviors is not necessarily related to the precocious development of vocabulary, comprehension of speech, or the ability to master arithmetic concepts. It cannot be assumed that advanced sensorimotor development at 1 year of age is an index of superior linguistic or numerical ability in later years. Although marked retardation in sensorimotor development at 1 year may be a prognostic sign of retardation in the child, the psychological significance of advanced or precocious sensorimotor development is still largely a mystery.

As a result of Piaget's observations of cognitive process in infants, other investigators have begun to examine the quality of the infants' mental activity. The fruits of these investigations reveal a level of sophistication and complexity that was not expected. One-year-old infants seem to recognize the similarities among objects, suggesting that they possess a form of primitive conceptual skill. Infants 1, 1½, and 2 years of age were seated in an infant chair with a tray. The examiner then placed four yellow cubes (½ inch on each side) and four gray clay balls (the same size as the cubes) on the tray in front of the child. Although the eight objects were arranged in a random and scattered manner in front of the infant, more than 40 percent of the 1-year-olds touched successfully either the four clay balls or the four yellow cubes. Over 70 percent of those in the two older age groups displayed this behavior. That is, if the child first touched or manipulated a clay ball, he was likely to touch the remaining three balls in succession, without manipulating the yellow cubes. The 1-year-old notices the differences in color and shape between the cubes and balls and, what is more important, is predisposed to treat the identical objects in a special way. When the differences between the objects are subtle, infants do not display this primitive conceptual grouping. Thus, when the objects were four elliptical shapes and four parallelograms (of the same color and size), very few infants touched all four identical objects in succession (70). (See pp. 309–318 for Piaget's theory of later cognitive development.)

INDIVIDUAL DIFFERENCES AMONG INFANTS

Thus far, we have been considering primarily general developmental milestones in the average child. But there are many kinds of dramatic individual differences among infants in behavior, in physiological reactivity, and in what is generally called "temperament." Some children walk at 10 months, others at 18; some say their first word at 9 months, others not until 29 months. Thus, norms are misleading, for they describe averages and the average child really does not exist. Individual differences at 1 or 2 years of age may be the result of either environmental differences or heredity, and the environmental effects could be pre- or postnatal. The differences that exist during the first days and weeks are likely to be biological in nature and may have an effect on development in one of two ways. These differences may push the child to develop in one particular direction or they may elicit from the mother different reactions toward the infant. Let us consider first some dimensions of difference among young infants and then suggest what significance they might have for the future.

Infants differ in their physiological reaction to tension or stress. There are at least four physiological systems that can react to increases in tension: the gastrointestinal tract, the skin, the respiratory apparatus, and the cardiovascular system (heart and blood vessels). Newborns differ in the differential responsivity of these systems under stress (41). Some infants show great increases in heart rate or skin temperature when hungry, whereas others show less marked physiological changes in a similar situation. Some babies characteristically vomit when under tension; others break out with a rash; and still others show marked flushing of face or skin indicative of increases in blood pressure and dilation of the small blood vessels near the skin. The major differences among infants are behavioral, however. Although mothers have always recognized that each of their children was "different from the first day," psychologists have only recently begun to look systematically at these initial differences and their potential significance. The term **congenital** refers to characteristics that are present at birth; some of these may be hereditary. There are three obvious kinds of differences among infants that almost all parents notice. They include degree of spontaneous motor activity, irritability, and passivity.

Motor Activity

Some children show frequent and vigorous thrashing of arms and legs, whereas others lie still and quiet. Some infants sleep restlessly, whereas others show minimal activity during sleep (48, 91). Furthermore, there is some evidence that infant boys show higher and more vigorous activity levels than girls (55, 82).

It is reasonable to assume that the child's later development might be influenced by extremely high or low levels of activity. For example, an extremely energetic infant might be more apt to get into closets and upset dishes and, therefore, encounter more maternal restriction and punishment than less active babies. A mother who is easily irritated may be more punitive toward an active child than toward a placid one. An energetic, athletic father may be cross and irritable with a placid boy, but more accepting of an active one.

Irritability

Some infants are easily provoked to crying, whining, and fretting at the least provocation, and are difficult to placate. At the other extreme are infants who rarely cry and seem to have an almost infinite tolerance for frustration. Irritability is not related to level of activity. One possible cause of irritability, but not the only one, is advanced mental development—a tendency to note unusual situations while being unable to understand or react to them. This combination of detection of the strange and having no appropriate coping reaction can evoke fear and crying. The possibility that early irritability reflects precocity was suggested by the fact that 4-month-old girls who cried in a strange laboratory setting, perhaps because they were aware of the strangeness of the room, played more maturely with toys when they were 1 year old (49).

Passivity

Some children generally lie quietly and react with withdrawal, freezing, or inhibition to people or events that are unexpected or slightly frightening. Such infants are called passive because they show passive withdrawal to an intrusion, threat, or new stimulus. At the other extreme are infants who are not only motorically active, but also are likely to approach or to do something in response to a threatening or unusual event. Such infants are called **active copers.** The fact that an infant is passive does not mean that he will be less intelligent or more helpless as an older child or adult.

Other Dimensions of Temperament

There are other dimensions of temperament that are less obvious, but potentially as significant. One group of investigators (83) has suggested nine differences among infants that can be described as early as 3 years old. The first three are activity, irritability, and passivity. The others are (1) rhythmicity or degree of regularity of functions like eating, elimination, and cycles of sleeping and wakefulness, (2) adaptability of behavior to changes in the environment, (3) threshold of response or sensitivity to stimuli, (4) intensity or energy level of response, (5) distractibility, and (6) span of attention and persistence in an activity (see Table 4.2).

The last dimension, span of attention, seems to have significance for future behavior. One group of infants were seen at 4, 8, 13, and 27 months of age. Some of the 4-month-olds showed rapid loss of interest to a set of faces presented to them; a second group of infants showed sustained interest throughout the 16 presentations of the faces. The boys who showed rapid loss of interest were slightly shorter, lighter, and smiled less often than the boys who were slow to habituate. When the boys were seen at 8 months of age, the rapidly habituating group showed more restless and distractible play with toys, shifting from one toy to another. The slowly habituating group tended to play with a toy for a longer period of time before shifting activities (49).

The boys who were extreme at the earlier ages retained their style of play through their second birthday. The light, wiry 4-month-boys who lost interest in the faces quickly and showed frequent shifts in their play at 8 months displayed shorter periods of sustained attentive play with a train or with blocks at 13 and 27 months than the boys who were slow to adapt to the faces and shifted activities less often. One group can be described as having a **fast tempo;** the other group, a **slow tempo.**

Observation of one slow-tempo boy at 13 months illustrates this dimension. The boy was in a room with his mother and he discovered one of the plastic quoits there. For 10 minutes he rolled the quoit around the room, watching carefully as it rolled after each push he gave it, and laughing as it stopped each time. During most of the 10-minute period he was deeply engrossed in the activity, as if he were perceptually addicted to it. The observers who watched him felt that his concentration was so intense that he would have been insensitive to most stimulus changes that might have occurred around him.

The nine dimensions of individual differences listed in Table 4.2 form three basic types: the "easy child," the "difficult child," and the "slow to warm up child."

The easy child, who made up about 40 percent of a group of children studied in New York City usually seems to be in a good mood, has regular sleep and bowel movements, adapts readily to new surroundings, and approaches new events. He is a cheerful infant who is easy to care for and love. The difficult child (about 10 percent of the group) does not establish regular feeding or sleep patterns, reacts intensely to imposition or frustration, and withdraws passively from strange events or people. He seems to require a long time to adjust to anything new and is difficult to rear. The child who is slow to warm up (15 percent of the group) is relatively inactive, withdraws to novelty, is negative in mood, and reacts with low intensity.

The investigators followed some of these infants from infancy to 4 years of age. Of the 141 children studied, 42 of them developed psychological problems requiring psychiatric help. The "difficult" infants comprised the majority of this group. The authors write,   (

> The paramount conclusion from our studies is that the debate over the relative importance of nature and nurture only confuses the issue. What is important is the interaction between the two—between the child's own characteristics and his environment. If the two influences are harmonized, one can expect healthy development of the child; if they are dissonant, behavioral problems are almost sure to ensue (83, 109).

In summary, differences in activity, sensitivity to stimulation, physiological reactions, and other psychological dimensions are apparent during the first weeks of life. Until additional research has been done, it cannot be known whether an infant's characteristic reactions will be stable over long periods of time, although there is some suggestion that some aspects of early temperament may persist until later childhood. Whether these temperamental patterns are hereditary in origin or a result of environmental processes during intrauterine development is a fascinating but still largely unsolved mystery.

SUMMARY

There are several important points to be noted about the first year of life. First, the newborn is a remarkably capable organism with well-functioning sensorimotor systems. He is capable of learning associations between stimuli and responses from the first days of life, and the role of meaning and familiarity of events becomes important before the first half-year is over.

He preferentially attends to visual or auditory stimuli that have sharp on-off characteristics (moving light, intermittent sounds) and are of optimal size or duration. Once he begins to acquire internal representations or schemata for phenomena, his attention is directed to stimuli that resemble the familiar or moderately discrepant stimuli. Still later in the first year, as he matures, he maintains prolonged attention to discrepant events that provoke him to activate hypotheses to aid understanding. His motor actions, like his mental schemata, also develop rapidly, and by 1 year of age he is displaying planned and well-coordinated actions with arms and legs. By 1 year he enters the world of meaning, applying language labels to familiar phenomena.

As the first year ends, the infant is a complicated, knowledgeable, and "thinking" creature who has acquired some knowledge and ideas about the world and ways of dealing with it. The next chapter considers his developing relations with one particular set of objects—the adults who care for him.

Table 4.2

TEMPERAMENTAL QUALITY	RATING	2 MONTHS	6 MONTHS
ACTIVITY LEVEL	HIGH	Moves often in sleep. Wriggles when diaper is changed.	Tries to stand in tub and splashes. Bounces in crib. Crawls after dog.
	LOW	Does not move when being dressed or during sleep.	Passive in bath. Plays quietly in crib and falls asleep.
QUALITY OF MOOD	POSITIVE	Smacks lips when first tasting new food. Smiles at parents.	Plays and splashes in bath. Smiles at everyone.
	NEGATIVE	Fusses after nursing. Cries when carriage is rocked.	Cries when taken from tub. Cries when given food she does not like.
APPROACH/WITH-DRAWAL	POSITIVE	Smiles and licks wash-cloth. Has always liked bottle.	Likes new foods. En-joyed first bath in a large tub. Smiles and gurgles.
	NEGATIVE	Rejected cereal the first time. Cries when strangers appear.	Smiles and babbles at strangers. Plays with new toys immediately.
RHYTHMICITY	REGULAR	Has been on four-hour feeding sched-ule since birth. Regular bowel movement.	Is asleep at 6:30 every night. Awakes at 7:00 A.M. Food in-take is constant.
	IRREGULAR	Awakes at a different time each morning. Size of feedings varies.	Length of nap varies; so does food intake.
ADAPTABILITY	ADAPTIVE	Was passive during first bath; now en-joys bathing. Smiles at nurse.	Used to dislike new foods: now accepts them well.
	NOT ADAPTIVE	Still startled by sud-den, sharp noise. Resists diapering.	Does not cooperate with dressing. Fusses and cries when left with sitter.

1 YEAR	2 YEARS	5 YEARS	10 YEARS
Walks rapidly, eats eagerly. Climbs into everything.	Climbs furniture. Explores. Gets in and out of bed while being put to sleep.	Leaves table often during meals. Always runs.	Plays ball and engages in other sports. Cannot sit still long enough to do homework.
Finishes bottle slowly. Goes to sleep easily. Allows nail-cutting without fussing.	Enjoys quiet play with puzzles. Can listen to records for hours.	Takes a long time to dress. Sits quietly on long automobile rides.	Likes chess and reading. Eats very slowly.
Likes bottle; reaches for it and smiles. Laughs loudly when playing peekaboo.	Plays with sister: laughs and giggles. Smiles when he succeeds in putting shoes on.	Laughs loudly while watching television cartoons. Smiles at everyone.	Enjoys new accomplishments. Laughs when reading a funny passage aloud.
Cries when given injections. Cries when left alone.	Cries and squirms when given haircut. Cries when mother leaves.	Objects to putting boots on. Cries when frustrated.	Cries when he cannot solve a homework problem. Very "weepy" if he does not get enough sleep.
Approaches strangers readily. Sleeps well in new surroundings.	Slept well the first time he stayed overnight at grandparents' house.	Entered school building unhesitatingly. Tries new foods.	Went to camp happily. Loved to ski the first time.
Stiffened when placed on sled. Will not sleep in strange beds.	Avoids strange children in the playground. Whimpers first time at beach. Will not go into water.	Hid behind mother when entering school.	Severely homesick at camp during first days. Does not like new activities.
Naps after lunch each day. Always drinks bottle before bed.	Eats a big lunch each day. Always has a snack before bedtime.	Falls asleep when put to bed. Bowel movement regular.	Eats only at mealtimes. Sleeps the same amount of time each night.
Will not fall asleep for an hour or more. Moves bowels at a different time each day.	Nap time changes day to day. Toilet training is difficult because bowel movement is unpredictable.	Food intake varies: so does time of bowel movement.	Food intake varies. Falls asleep at a different time each night.
Was afraid of toy animals at first, now plays with them happily.	Obeys quickly. Stayed contentedly with grandparents for a week.	Hesitated to go to nursery school at first; now goes eagerly. Slept well on camping trip.	Likes camp, although homesick during first days. Learns enthusiastically.
Continues to reject new foods each time they are offered.	Cries and screams each time hair is cut. Disobeys persistently.	Has to be hand led into classroom each day. Bounces on bed in spite of spankings.	Does not adjust well to new school or new teacher; comes home late for dinner even when punished.

Table 4.2 (Continued)

TEMPERAMENTAL QUALITY	RATING	2 MONTHS	6 MONTHS
THRESHOLD OF RESPONSIVENESS	LOW	Stops sucking on bottle when approached.	Refuses fruit he likes when vitamins are added. Hides head from bright lights.
	HIGH	Is not startled by loud noises. Takes bottle and breast equally well.	Eats everything. Does not object to diapers being wet or soiled.
INTENSITY OF REACTION	INTENSE	Cries when diapers are wet. Rejects food vigorously when satisfied.	Cries loudly at the sound of thunder. Makes sucking movements when vitamins are administered.
	MILD	Does not cry when diapers are wet. Whimpers instead of crying when hungry.	Does not kick often in tub. Does not smile. Screams and kicks when temperature is taken.
DISTRACTIBILITY	DISTRACTIBLE	Will stop crying for food if rocked. Stops fussing if given pacifier when diaper is being changed.	Stops crying when mother sings. Will remain still while clothing is changed if given a toy.
	NOT DISTRACTIBLE	Will not stop crying when diaper is changed. Fusses after eating, even if rocked.	Stops crying only after dressing is finished. Cries until given bottle.
ATTENTION SPAN AND PERSISTENCE	LONG	If soiled, continues to cry until changed. Repeatedly rejects water if he wants milk.	Watches toy mobile over crib intently. "Coos" frequently.
	SHORT	Cries when awakened but stops almost immediately. Objects only mildly if cereal precedes bottle.	Sucks pacifier for only a few minutes and spits it out.

1 YEAR	2 YEARS	5 YEARS	10 YEARS
Spits out food he does not like. Giggles when tickled.	Runs to door when father comes home. Must always be tucked tightly into bed.	Always notices when mother puts new dress on for first time. Refuses milk if it is not ice-cold.	Rejects fatty foods. Adjusts shower until water is at exactly the right temperature.
Eats food he likes even if mixed with disliked food. Can be left easily with strangers.	Can be left with anyone. Falls to sleep easily on either back or stomach.	Does not hear loud, sudden noises when reading. Does not object to injections.	Never complains when sick. Eats all foods.
Laughs hard when father plays roughly. Screamed and kicked when temperature was taken.	Yells if he feels excitement or delight. Cries loudly if a toy is taken away.	Rushes to greet father. Gets hiccups from laughing hard.	Tears up an entire page of homework if one mistake is made. Slams door of room when teased by younger brother.
Does not fuss much when clothing is pulled on over head.	When another child hit her, she looked surprised, did not hit back.	Drops eyes and remains silent when given a firm parental "No." Does not laugh much.	When a mistake is made in a model airplane, corrects it quietly. Does not comment when reprimanded.
Cries when face is washed unless it is made into a game.	Will stop tantrum if another activity is suggested.	Can be coaxed out of forbidden activity by being led into something else.	Needs absolute silence for homework. Has a hard time choosing a shirt in a store because they all appeal to him.
Cries when toy is taken away and rejects substitute.	Screams if refused some desired object. Ignores mother's calling.	Seems not to hear if involved in favorite activity. Cries for a long time when hurt.	Can read a book while television set is at high volume. Does chores on schedule.
Plays by self in playpen for more than an hour. Listens to singing for long periods.	Works on a puzzle until it is completed. Watches when shown how to do something.	Practiced riding a two-wheeled bicycle for hours until he mastered it. Spent over an hour reading a book.	Reads for two hours before sleeping. Does homework carefully.
Loses interest in a toy after a few minutes. Gives up easily if she falls while trying to walk.	Gives up easily if a toy is hard to use. Asks for help immediately if undressing becomes difficult.	Still cannot tie his shoes because he gives up when he is not successful. Fidgets when parents read to him.	Gets up frequently from homework for a snack. Never finishes a book.

References

1. Acheson, R. M. Maturation of the skeleton. In F. Falkner (Ed.), **Human development.** Philadelphia: Saunders: 1966. Pp. 465–502.
2. Ames, L. B. The sequential patterning of prone progression in the human infant. **Genetic Psychology Monographs,** 1937, **19,** 409–460.
3. Bakwin, H., & Bakwin, R. M. Growth of thirty-two external dimensions during the first year of life. **Journal of Pediatrics,** 1936, **8,** 177–183.
4. Bayley, N. The development of motor abilities during the first three years. **Monographs of the Society for Research in Child Development,** 1935(1).
5. Bergman, T., Haith, M. M., & Mann, L. Development of eye contact and facial scanning in infants. Paper presented at the meeting of the Society for Research in Child Development, Minneapolis, April, 1971.
6. Blest, A. D. The function of eyespot patterns in the Lepidoptera. **Behavior,** 1957, **11,** 209–256.
7. Brackbill, Y. The role of the cortex in orienting: Orienting reflex in an anencephalic infant. **Developmental Psychology,** 1971, **5,** 195–201.
8. Brackbill, Y., Adams, G., Crowell, D. H., & Gray, M. L. Arousal level in newborns and preschool children under continuous auditory stimulation. **Journal of Experimental Child Psychology,** 1966, **3,** 178–188.
9. Brennan, W. M., Ames, E. W., & Moore, E. W. Age differences in infants' attention to patterns of different complexities. **Science,** 1966, **151,** 354–356.
10. Bridger, W. H. Sensory habituation and discrimination in the human neonate. **American Journal of Psychiatry,** 1961, **117,** 991–996.
11. Broadbent, D. E. **Perception and communication.** New York: Pergamon, 1958.
12. Bronson, G. W. The development of fear in man and other animals. **Child Development,** 1968, **39,** 409–432.
13. Buhler, C. **The first year of life.** (Trans. by Greenberg and Ripin). New York: Day, 1930.
14. Cameron, J., Livson, N., & Bayley, N. Infant vocalizations and their relationship to mature intelligence. **Science,** 1967, **157,** 331–333.
15. Campos, J. J., Langer, A., & Krawitz, A. Cardiac responses on the visual cliff in prelocomotor human infants. **Science,** 1970, **170,** 196–197.
16. Caron, R. J., Caron, A. J., & Caldwell, R. C. Satiation of visual reinforcement in young infants. **Developmental Psychology,** 1971, **5,** 279–289.
17. Charlesworth, W. Development of the object concept. Paper presented at the meeting of the American Psychological Association, New York City, 1966.
18. Cohen, L. B. Attention getting and attention holding processes of infant visual preferences. **Child Development,** 1973, **44,** in press.
19. Dennis, W. Infant development under conditions of restricted practice and of minimum social stimulation. **Genetic Psychology Monographs,** 1941, **23,** 143–191.
20. Dennis, W. Causes of retardation among institutional children: Iran. **Journal of Genetic Psychology,** 1960, **96,** 47–59.
21. Desmond, M. M., Franklin, R. R., Vallbona, C., Hilt, R. H., Plumb, R., Arnold, H., & Watts, J. The clinical behavior of the newly born: I. **Journal of Pediatrics,** 1963, **62,** 307–325.
22. Disher, D. R. The reactions of newborn infants to chemical stimuli administered nasally. **Ohio State University Studies in Control Psychology,** 1934(12), 1–52.
23. Eimas, P. D., Siqueland, E. R., Jusczyk, P., & Vigorito, J. Speech perception in infants. **Science,** 1971, **171,** 303–306.

24. Eisenberg, R. B., Griffin, E. J., Coursin, D. B., & Hunter, M. A. Auditory behavior in the neonate. **Journal of Speech and Hearing Research,** 1964, **7,** 245–269.

25. Fagan, J. F., Fantz, R. L., & Miranda, S. M. Infants' attention to novel stimuli as a function of postnatal and conceptional age. Paper presented at a meeting of the Society for Research in Child Development, Minneapolis, April, 1971.

26. Fantz, R. L. The origin of form perception. **Scientific American,** 1961, **204,** 66–72.

27. Fantz, R. L. Visual experience in infants: Decreased attention to familiar patterns relative to novel ones. **Science,** 1964, **146,** 668–670.

28. Fantz, R. L. Visual perception from birth as shown by pattern selectivity. **Annals of the New York Academy of Science,** 1965, **118,** 793–814.

29. Fantz, R. L., & Nevis, S. Pattern preferences and perceptual cognitive development in early infancy. **Merrill–Palmer Quarterly,** 1967, **13,** 77–108.

30. Fitzgerald, H. E. Autonomic pupillary reflex activity during early infancy and its relation to social and non-social stimuli. **Journal of Experimental Child Psychology,** 1968, **6,** 470–482.

31. Flavell, J. H. **The Developmental psychology of Jean Piaget.** New York: Van Nostrand Reinhold, 1963.

32. Garn, S. M. Roentgenogrammetric determinations of body composition. **Human Biology,** 1957, **29,** 337–353.

33. Garn, S. M. Fat, body size, and growth in the newborn. **Human Biology,** 1958, **30,** 265–280.

34. Garn, S. M., & Rohmann, C. G., Variability in the order of ossification of the boney centers of the hand and wrist. **American Journal of Physical Anthropology,** 1960, **18,** 219–229.

35. Geber, M. Development psychomoteur de l'enfant africain. **Courier,** 1956, **6,** 17–29.

36. Gesell, A. The ontogenesis of infant behavior. In L. Carmichael (Ed.), **Manual of child psychology.** (2nd ed.) New York: Wiley, 1954. Pp. 335–373.

37. Gesell, A., & Amatruda, C. S. **Developmental diagnosis: Normal and abnormal child development.** New York: Hoeber, 1941.

38. Gesell, A., Halverson, H. M., Thompson, H., Ilg, F. L., Costner, B. M., Ames, L. B., & Amatruda, C. S. **The first five years of life: A guide to the study of the preschool child.** New York: Harper & Row, 1940.

39. Gibson, E. J., & Walk, R. R. The "visual cliff." **Scientific American,** 1960, **202,** 2–9.

40. Grier, J. B., Counter, S. A., & Shearer, W. M. Prenatal auditory imprinting in chickens. **Science,** 1967, **155,** 1692–1693.

41. Grossman, H. J., & Greenberg, N. H. Psychosomatic differentiation in infancy. **Psychosomatic Medicine,** 1957, **19,** 293–306.

42. Haaf, R. A., & Bell, R. Q. A facial dimension in visual discrimination by human infants. **Child Development,** 1967, **38,** 893–899.

43. Haith, M. M. The response of the human newborn to visual movement. **Journal of Experimental Child Psychology,** 1966, **3,** 235–243.

44. Haith, M. M. Visual scanning in infants. Paper presented at the Regional Meeting of the Society for Research in Child Development. Clark University, Worcester, Mass., March, 1968.

45. Haynes, H., White, B. L., & Held, R. Visual accommodation in human infants. **Science,** 1965, **148,** 528–530.

46. Hershenson, M. Visual discrimination in the human newborn. **Journal of Comparative Physiological Psychology,** 1964, **58,** 270–276.

47. Hindley, C. B., Filliozat, A. M., Klackenberg, G., Nicolet-Meister, P., & Sand, E. A. Differ-

ences in age of walking in five European longitudinal samples. **Human Biology,** 1966, **38,** 364–379.

48. Irwin, O. C. The amount and nature of activities of newborn infants under constant external stimulating conditions during the first ten days of life. **Genetic Psychology Monographs,** 1930, **8,** 1–92.

49. Kagan, J. **Change and continuity in infancy.** New York: Wiley, 1971.

50. Kagan, J. Crosscultural perspectives in human development. Paper presented at the meeting of the American Association for the Advancement of Science, Washington, D.C., December, 1972.

51. Kagan, J. Do infants think? **Scientific American,** 1972, **226**(3), 74–82.

52. Karmel, B. Z. The effect of complexity, amount of contour, element size, and element arrangement on visual preference behavior in the hooded rat, domestic chick, and human infant. Unpublished doctoral dissertation, George Washington University, 1966.

53. Kearsley, R. B. The newborn's response to auditory stimulation. Unpublished doctoral dissertation, Harvard University, 1972.

54. Kinney, D. K. Auditory stimulus discrepancy and infant attention. Unpublished doctoral dissertation, Harvard University, 1971.

55. Knop, C. A. The dynamics of newly born babies. **Journal of Pediatrics,** 1946, **29,** 721–728.

56. Lenneberg, E. H. **Biological functions of language.** New York: Wiley, 1967.

57. Lipsitt, L. P., & Levy, N. Pain threshold in the human neonate. **Child Development,** 1959, **30,** 547–554.

58. McCall, R. B., & Kagan, J. Attention in the infant: Effects of complexity, contour, perimeter and familiarity. **Child Development,** 1967, **38,** 939–952.

59. McCarthy, D. Language development in children. In L. Carmichael (Ed.), **Manual of child psychology.** (2nd ed.) New York: Wiley, 1954. Pp. 492–630.

60. McGraw, M. B. **Growth: A study of Johnny and Jimmy.** New York: Appleton-Century-Crofts, 1935.

61. McGraw, M. B. Maturation of behavior. In L. Carmichael (Ed.), **Manual of child psychology.** New York: Wiley, 1946. Pp. 332–369.

62. Meredith, H. V. Body size of contemporary groups of one year old infants studied in different parts of the world. **Child Development,** 1970, **41,** 551–600.

63. Moore, T. Language and intelligence: A longitudinal study of the first eight years. **Human Development,** 1967, **10,** 88–106.

64. Moss, H. A. Sex, age, and state as determinants of mother-infant interaction. **Merrill-Palmer Quarterly,** 1967, **13,** 19–36.

65. Piaget, J. **The construction of reality in the child.** New York: Basic Books, 1954.

66. Polak, P. R., Emde, R. N., & Spitz, R. R. The smiling response: II. Visual discrimination and the onset of depth perception. **Journal of Nervous Mental Diseases,** 1964, **139,** 407–415.

67. Pratt, K. C. The effects of repeated visual stimulation on the activity of newborn infants. **Journal of Genetic Psychology,** 1934, **44,** 117–126.

68. Pratt, K. C. The neonate. In L. Carmichael (Ed.), **Manual of child psychology.** (2nd ed.) New York: Wiley, 1954. Pp. 215–291.

69. Rheingold, H., Gewirtz, J. L., & Ross, H. Social conditioning of vocalizations in the infant. **Journal of Comparative and Physiological Psychology,** 1959, **52,** 68–73.

70. Ricciuti, H. N. Object grouping and selective ordering behavior in infants 12 to 24 months old. **Merrill-Palmer Quarterly,** 1965, **11,** 129–148.

71. Roffwarg, H. P., Muzio, J. N., & Dement, W. C. Ontogenetic development of the human sleep-dream cycle. **Science,** 1966, **152,** 604–619.
72. Rovee, C. K. Psychophysical scaling of olfactory response to the aliphatic alcohols in human infants. **Journal of Experimental Child Psychology,** 1969, **7,** 245–254.
73. Salapatek, P. Visual scanning of geometric figures by the human newborn. **Journal of Comparative and Physiological Psychology,** 1968, **66,** 247–248.
74. Salapatek, P., & Kessen, W. Visual scanning of triangles by the human newborn. **Journal of Experimental Child Psychology,** 1966, **3,** 113–122.
75. Sameroff, A. J. The components of sucking in the human newborn. **Journal of Experimental Child Psychology,** 1968, **6,** 607–623.
76. Sherman, M., & Sherman, I. C. Sensorimotor responses in infants. **Journal of Comparative Psychology,** 1925, **5,** 53–68.
77. Sherman, M., Sherman, I. C., & Flory, C. D. Infant behavior. **Comparative Psychology Monographs,** 1936, **12**(4).
78. Shirley, M. M. The first two years: A study of twenty-five babies. Vol. I. Postural and locomotor development. **Institute of Child Welfare Monographs,** Ser. No. 6. Minneapolis: University of Minnesota Press, 1933.
79. Stechler, G. Newborn attention as affected by medication during labor. **Science,** 1964, **144,** 315–317.
80. Stubbs, E. M. The effect of the factors of duration, intensity, and pitch of sound stimuli on the responses of newborn infants. **University of Iowa Studies in Child Welfare,** 1934, **9**(4), 75–135.
81. Super, C. M. Longterm memory in early infancy. Unpublished doctoral dissertation, Harvard University, 1972.
82. Terman, L. M., & Tyler, L. E. Psychological sex differences. In L. Carmichael (Ed.), **Manual of child psychology.** (2nd ed.) New York: Wiley, 1954.
83. Thomas, A., Chess, S., & Birch, H. G. The origin of personality. **Scientific American,** 1970, **223,** 102–109. Reprinted by permission.
84. Thompson, H. Physical growth. In L. Carmichael (Ed.), **Manual of child psychology.** (2nd ed.). New York: Wiley, 1954.
85. Trehub, S. E., & Rabinovitch, M. S. Auditory-linguistic sensitivity in early infancy. **Developmental Psychology,** 1972, **6,** 74–77.
86. Tulkin, S. R., & Kagan, J. Mother-child interaction in the first year of life. **Child Development,** 1972, **43,** 31–42.
87. Walk, R. D. The development of depth perception in animal and human infants. **Monographs of the Society for Research in Child Development,** 1966, **31**(5), 82–108.
88. Watson, E. H., & Lowrey, G. H. **Growth and development of children.** (3rd ed.) Chicago: Year Book Publishers, 1958.
89. White, B. L., & Held, R. Plasticity of sensory motor development. In J. F. Rosenblith & W. Allinsmith (Eds.), **Readings in child development and educational psychology.** (2nd ed.) Boston: Allyn and Bacon, 1966.
90. Wickelgren, L. W. The ocular response of human newborns to intermittent visual movement. **Journal of Experimental Child Psychology,** 1969, **8,** 469–482.
91. Wolff, P. H. Observations on newborn infants. **Psychosomatic Medicine,** 1959, **21,** 110–118.
92. Zelazo, N. A., Zelazo, P. R., & Kolb, S. Walking in the newborn. **Science,** 1972, **176,** 314–315.

Chapter 5

Social Factors in Infant Development

The infant's response and sensory capabilities allow him to perceive and react to a wide variety of objects and events. One set of important objects to which all infants must react is other people. Moreover, the infant needs other human beings to gratify his drives and, when older, to satisfy his motives. Knowledge of the development of reactions to other human beings is basic to understanding the behavior of either child or adult. In this chapter we will deal with that part of the interpersonal story that occurs during the first two years. By concentrating on the experiences of this period, we will try to shed some light on the emerging social relationships between the infant and adults.

The newborn begins life with very few specific emotional or motivational responses to other people. He has no innate tendencies to love, hate, fear, approach, or avoid people. His experiences with human beings during this first year lay the foundation for his future attitudes toward them. Extreme neglect during this period may result in damage to the child's future capacity for developing satisfying relations with other people. His learned reactions to the person or persons who care for him, in most cases his mother, can form a nucleus for his later behavior towards others.

THE NECESSITY FOR MAKING RESPONSES

We start with a basic fact—from the moment the baby is born, he behaves. Some of his responses are spontaneous; others are reactions to needs. Some of the behaviors are necessary for survival; others are clearly not. As indicated in Chapter 4, the young baby scans the environment, vocalizes, sucks, smiles, cries, and thrashes. As he approaches the third and fourth months of life he begins to cling to objects and to manipulate his fingers, his mother's hair, and toys. What is the role of the caretaker—be it aunt, grandmother, day care teacher, or the biological mother—with respect to this limited set of responses?

Looking

As noted earlier, the infant's attention is attracted to objects that have high black-and-white contrast and move. The eyes of the mother fit these two requirements well. The eyes contain black-white contrast and dart back and forth regularly and quickly. Moreover, if we view the entire face as the effective stimulus for the infant, then the movement of the lips and tongue and the intermittent and changing quality of the voice makes the face a most interesting object—an attractive mobile that makes sounds. We would expect the infant to focus his attention on it. Observations of babies verify this expectation, for infants older than 7 weeks frequently spend long periods of time looking at and scanning their mother's face.

Vocalizing

Babbling is a second spontaneous response that increases dramatically if it provokes a response from another person. Most objects do not produce a sound when the infant babbles. Mobiles, cribs, and hands do not "do something back" to the child when he vocalizes. The caretaker does. The infant babbles, the mother smiles and talks back; the infant babbles again and the mother repeats. This sequence proceeds several minutes with the mother's vocalization and facial reactions maintaining the child's babbling, and often his glee. We have, therefore, a second reason why a human being is a likely object toward which the infant's reactions—in this case, babbling—will be directed.

Smiling

Smiling, like babbling, is another common infant reaction that is often directed at the mother and other adults, especially between 8 and 20 weeks.

When the young infant has acquired a schema for a face, he is likely to smile. At 4 months of age most infants will smile at a still representation of a human face. No movement or voice is necessary, although movement of the face and voice increases the probability that the smile will occur. It appears that 4-month-old infants from various cultural environments are likely to show a smile to a face looking directly at them (see Fig. 5.1).

Gewirtz studied the smiling of three groups of infants raised under different conditions in Israel (16). Institutionalized infants living in residential buildings rarely saw their parents and received routine institutional care. Kibbutz infants lived in collective settlements. They were raised in large houses with professional caretakers but were fed frequently during the first year by their own mothers. Family-reared children were raised in typically western apartments by their mothers. Fig. 5.1 graphs the frequency of smiling to a strange woman's face while the baby lay in the crib. The peak for smiling for the kibbutz- and family-reared infants was a few weeks earlier than the peak for the infants raised in the institution. But the peak age for all infants was very close to 4 months of age (16).

These findings suggest that it takes about three to four months of exposure to people to develop a schema for a human face. The smile at 4 months of age is the infant's way of saying that he recognizes this aspect of a person. The smile and laugh are generally released when the child understands a new event following some mental effort. One-year-olds laugh most often in response to discrepant visual and social events, while 8-month-olds laugh more often to unusual auditory or tactile events (36).

The smile does not always signify recognition of the moderately familiar, however. Many newborn infants smile long before they develop a schema for anything, and 1-year-old babies will smile at anyone who smiles back at them. The smile reflects different messages at different ages.

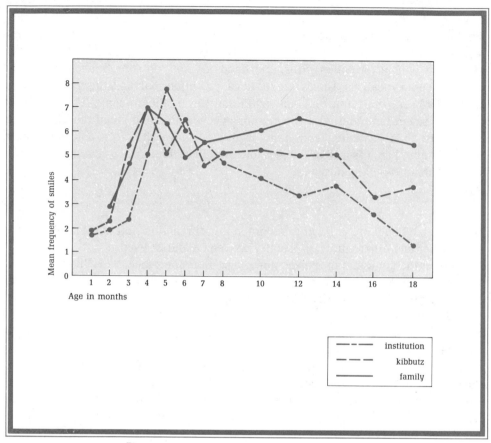

Figure 5.1 Frequency of smiling among infants raised in three different environments. (From J. L. Gewirtz. The cause of infant smiling in four child-rearing environments in Israel. In B. M. Foss (Ed.), **Determinants of infant behavior.** Vol. 3. London: Methuen, 1965. By permission of the publishers and The Tavistock Institute of Human Relations.)

Effect of the Smile on the Mother The infant's tendency to smile a lot or little can affect the nature of the mother-child relation. The mother typically interprets the smile as a sign that her baby is happy and content and, by inference, that she is an effective mother. If her infant is an infrequent smiler she may begin to doubt her maternal competence and worry about her ability to make her infant contented and pleased. Although frequency of smiling can be increased if an adult responds to the child's smile by picking him up **(6)**, there are unlearned differences among infants in the tendency to smile. Even among family-reared infants who have had considerable exposure to a human face, some will show lots of smiling to a strange face or a clay mask, while others will smile very little. These individual differences are also present in newborns. Some premature babies are consistently frequent smilers; others rarely smile **(15)**. Moreover, infant boys who smile frequently tend to be fatter than infrequent smilers, who are often short and wiry. These differences in the readiness to smile may play an important role in the dynamic interaction between the mother and her infant. The smile rewards the mother and increases her involvement with her infant. The mother behaves as if the smile were a reinforcement for her efforts—the infant's way of rewarding the mother for her good works. If some babies are biologically predisposed to be easy and frequent smilers, they are likely to elicit more approach behavior from their mother than nonsmiling infants.

Distress

Crying is a third response of which the infant is capable from the first hours of postnatal life. If the infant is separated from his mother by a few feet or more, crying acts as an effective signal to the mother to retrieve or attend to her baby. This is also true of dogs, monkeys, and kittens. The squeal of a young puppy has the same function as the cry of an infant. It guarantees that the infant will not be in distress for prolonged periods. The infant usually cries in response to either internal distress or a strange event. When the caretaker comes to relieve the distress, the infant typically relaxes his muscles and, when held upright, rests his head on her shoulder and holds her neck.

Feeding

Sucking and the posture assumed when being held are two other responses that involve the caretaker. These responses are obviously part of the experience of children who are nursed. But even if the child is bottle-fed, he is often cradled in the mother's arms while he is feeding, and the sucking, relaxed posture and scanning of the face are selectively directed at the person holding the infant and feeding him.

The Significance of the Feeding Situation It is difficult to differentiate the needs of hunger and thirst in infants—milk will gratify both of them. In order to simplify the discussion, both needs will be referred to as **hunger.** Internal stimuli associated with hunger regularly mount to a high level of intensity several times a day, and the infant is almost completely dependent upon someone else for gratification of this need. If there is a long delay between the first twinges of hunger and their relief the tension may mount considerably. As such delays are unavoidable and occur frequently, hunger is the primary need that is most likely to provoke a high level of sustained discomfort; some of the child's earliest learning will involve this need. Let us consider how hunger might influence behavior directed toward the adult.

Consider what happens during the typical hunger-feeding cycle. The 4-month-old infant begins to feel uncomfortable. He begins to thrash and to cry and after several minutes someone comes to feed him. As the caretaker (usually the mother) feeds him, the infant gradually becomes less active. He studies her face as he feeds and experiences simultaneously the alleviation of the hunger and pain, the tactile contact with his mother, the kinesthetic stimulation from the cradled posture he is assuming, and the olfactory and auditory stimulation the mother presents. As these experiences are occurring simultaneously, the child learns two things. He learns to associate comfortable, pleasant sensations with the visual-vocal-auditory stimuli of the mother, and he learns to make the responses of scanning, babbling, smiling, clinging, and body adjustment in response to the person holding him. In short, he learns an association between the stimuli of the mother and the feelings of plea-sure, and also a tendency to direct the active responses of looking, vocalizing, and postural adjustments to the mother.

The student will note that we have emphasized the distinctive stimulation the mother gives the child, and the complex social interaction involving the two. We have deemphasized the specific feeding practices the mother uses, such as whether she nurses or uses a bottle. This deemphasis of the mode of feeding represents an important theoretical change in psychology's view of what is important in the mother-infant interaction during the first year. There is still some concern, how-ever, with the differences between breast and bottle feeding, and we shall consider this issue briefly.

There have been major shifts over time in the proportion of mothers from par-ticular social, ethnic, or personality groups who choose to breast or bottle feed. Dur-ing the period from 1930 to 1940 lower-class mothers nursed while middle-class mothers used bottles. In the current decade, the situation is the reverse. College-educated mothers prefer to nurse, while lower-class mothers almost exclusively use bottles. The mother's attitude toward the child and the kinds of social interac-tion that occur during feeding are more critical than whether the baby is nursed or fed by bottle. Moreover, as many American mothers tend to stop nursing before the child is 5 months of age, the type of feeding becomes even less important. One can argue that nursing is preferable to bottle feeding because it maximizes the mother's pleasure in the feeding situation and therefore strengthens her attach-ment to her child. Also, when the mother is nursing, she has a better opportunity to hold the child close to her and give him feelings of support, muscle relaxation, and tactile stimulation. The cradling posture the baby assumes when nursing may allow the child to make more active motor responses toward the mother. These actions can occur with bottle feeding if the child is held securely and is stimulated, talked to, and played with. However, bottle feeding will certainly be psychologically less conducive to attachment if the bottle is propped up and the mother leaves the child alone.

There is also concern with whether the child should be fed on demand (when-ever he cries for food) or on a schedule. The advantages of demand feeding are that infants differ in the rate at which they become hungry. Allowing the child to feed when he becomes hungry prevents the build-up of painful hunger tensions. Moreover, if the mother decides to schedule a feeding every three or four hours, it means that the child may sometimes be fed before he desires food, while at other times he may eat only after his hunger pains have become intense, so that eating may be uncomfortable. However, it should be remembered that specific feeding practices assume their major importance because they are embedded in the matrix of the mother-child relationship. The practices employed by the mother should make the feeding situation pleasant and rewarding for the mother and allow the child's attachment to be strengthened. It must be remembered that babies are capable of adapting to the schedule of the mother. For example, D. P. Marquis experimentally investigated the problem of adaptation to a feeding schedule within the first 10 days of life (24). She measured the bodily activities (restlessness) of two groups of infants who were on different feeding schedules. Daily changes in restlessness were used as the criterion of adaptation. One group, consisting of 18 infants, was on a 4-hour feeding schedule throughout the 10-day period. Sixteen other infants were on 3-hour schedules for the first 8 days of their lives but were shifted to 4-hour schedules on the ninth day (24).

After a few days, the infants' bodily activities rose sharply immediately before their next scheduled feeding, the increase being greater and more abrupt in the 4-hour group. This provides some evidence that this group had learned to wait 4 hours for food.

On the day the "3-hour schedule" infants were shifted to the 4-hour schedule, there were marked changes in their activity patterns. At the end of 3 hours, their habitual feeding time, body movements increased abruptly and reached the highest level recorded during the study. Apparently this group had learned to respond to hunger cues at the end of 3 hours. Failure to receive food at this time produced extreme restlessness and activity. It may be concluded that infants just a few days old can modify their behavior in accordance with external demands such as feeding schedules.

In sum, the human infant displays a variety of responses to his caretaker—he scans, sucks, babbles, smiles, cries, reaches, holds, manipulates, and clings.

Other species have slightly different responses that they direct at their mothers. A monkey clings tightly to the hairy underside of the mother, holding her close while she walks or sits. Puppies orient closely to the warm underbelly of the mother and suckle. Precocial birds, like ducks and chickens (i.e., those able to walk at birth), follow their mothers, make sounds at her, and will run to her when frightened or distressed. Hence, for many species, including man, the early unlearned reactions of the infant are usually directed at the biological mother. As a result, the infant, under natural conditions, becomes attached to her, whether the location is a city apartment, a farm house, or a bamboo hut in the mountains of Guatemala.

THE CONCEPT OF ATTACHMENT

The concept of attachment is relatively new in our theorizing about child development, but it has an important connotation that was missing from earlier theoretical discussions. The traditional interpretation of the close emotional relation between an infant and the mother assumed that the relationship was due to a conditioning of positive reward value to the mother. The explanation was usually stated in the following way. Any new stimulus that is associated with a reward (food, warmth, or a pleasant feeling state) acquires reward value itself. Through such conditioning, the mother, as a stimulus, comes to signify pleasure and contentment in much the same way that the buzzer became a sign of food for Pavlov's dogs. The infant learns that to approach this source of pleasure will lead to effective gratification of his needs with minimal delay. The child learns the important response of looking for and approaching his mother when he is hungry.

According to the principle of stimulus generalization, a response learned to one stimulus is likely to occur to stimuli similar to the original one. Other sources of pain and discomfort, (such as injury, cold, and illness), are sufficiently similar to the pain of hunger that the child should make the same response he made when hungry, that is, the child who approaches his mother when hungry should also approach her for nurturance (gratification of needs) when he is in pain and discomfort for other reasons. Further, because the mother is similar to other people, the infant should, in varying degrees, generalize his approach response to other people. In brief, the initial feeding situation was regarded as the basis for learning whether the mother is rewarding, and whether approaching the mother—and, by generalization, other people—leads to gratification.

If the initial feeding experience was not rewarding because the mother was tense, held her baby in an awkward manner, force-fed him, or handled him roughly, the child would experience some pain in association with the stimulus of the mother and the sensations of hunger. If the painful stimuli occurred frequently enough and over a long period of time, the stimulus would acquire a negative or anxiety-arousing value and she would become symbolic of discomfort rather than of pleasure. As an organism's innate reaction to discomfort and pain is withdrawal and avoidance, the infant would learn to avoid rather than to approach the mother. Moreover, the infant would not learn that approaching people in a state of discomfort might lead to gratification of his motives. Another infant, for whom the feeding experience had been predominantly pleasant, will be more likely to look to others for gratification of his needs.

The results of several important experiments have complicated this simple social learning view. One of the most important series of studies was conducted by Professor Harry Harlow and his colleagues at the University of Wisconsin. Harlow placed infant monkeys with "mother" monkeys that were constructed of wire mesh. Some of these infants were fed from a bottle attached to the "chest" of a plain wire-mesh mother. Others were similarly "fed" by a wire-mesh mother that differed in just one respect from the other mother—it was covered by terry cloth (see Fig. 5.2). When the monkeys were given the choice of going to either mother, the animals characteristically chose the terry-cloth mother and spent more time clinging

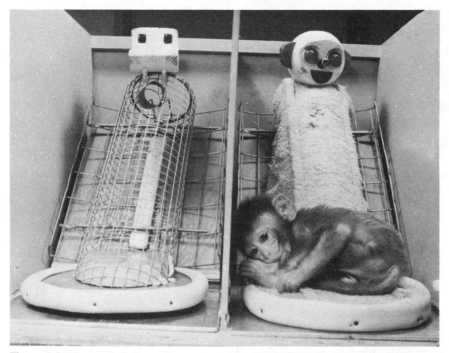

Figure 5.2 Wire and cloth mother surrogates. (From H. F. Harlow & R. R. Zimmerman. Affectional responses in the infant monkey. **Science**, 1959, **130**, 422. By permission.)

to her than to the plain wire-mesh mother. This was also true for infant monkeys fed only from the wire mother, never from the terry-cloth mother. The infant would go to the wire mother only when hungry, feed until satisfied, and then return to the terry-cloth mother for most of the day (**17, 18**).

Because the discomfort associated with hunger is alleviated by the wire but not by the terry-cloth mother, traditional learning theory would predict that the wire mother who supplies the food should be the most rewarding stimulus and, therefore, the one with whom the monkey should spend the most time. The fact that this prediction is incorrect forces us to reassess our basic hypothesis about the events that lead an infant to become related to another figure.

Further, when a fear-provoking stimulus (a large wooden model of a spider) was placed in the cage, the infant monkey ran to the terry-cloth mother rather than to the wire-mesh mother (see Fig. 5.3). The terry-cloth mother was also more effective in reducing the young monkey's fear than the wire mother. When the terry-cloth mother was present, the young monkey was more likely to venture out to explore the fear-arousing stimulus. When the young animal was with the wire-mesh mother, he was more fearful and was less likely to explore the open space around the strange and "threatening" object (see Fig. 5.4).

A series of related studies stimulated by Harlow's original work suggest the

Figure 5.3 Typical response to cloth mother in the modified open-field test. (From H. F. Harlow & R. R. Zimmerman. Affectional responses in the infant monkey. **Science,** 1959, **130,** 430. By permission.)

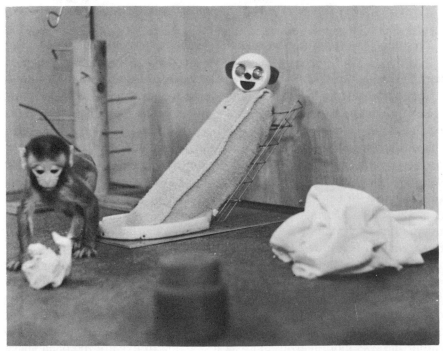

Figure 5.4 Rhesus infant, raised with a cloth surrogate mother, displaying security and exploratory behavior in a strange situation in the mother's presence. (From H. Harlow & M. H. Harlow. Learning to love. **American Scientist,** 1966, **54,** (3), 251. By permission.)

following conclusions. If the young monkey is to develop normally, he must have some interaction with an object to which he can cling during the opening months of life. Another monkey is best, but a terry-cloth surrogate allows the infant to cling and is, therefore, better than the wire surrogate. The clinging response is natural to the monkey, as perhaps scanning and vocalizing are to human infants. In time of stress the monkey runs to the object to which he normally clings. For example, if two chimpanzees are placed in a strange situation, they show increased clinging to each other, as if the clinging reduced fear or distress. As the chimpanzees become familiar with the originally strange situation, the mutual clinging decreases (25). There seems to be a strong similarity between this behavior in the chimpanzee or the monkey and that of a 1-year-old human child who runs to his mother and hides his face in her skirts if a strange person enters the house or an unexpected noise is heard.

Let us consider another example of a close infant-mother relationship before we come to some conclusions. Ethologists have found that if a newly hatched duck first follows a strange object, such as a moving yellow circle or a human being, rather than its mother, it will continue to follow this object for some time. This phenomenon has been called **imprinting** (4). As with Harlow's terry-cloth-reared monkeys we might say that the duck becomes attached to the object, even though it does not alleviate or reduce pain, hunger, or discomfort in any way. In the case

(Elliott Erwitt from Magnum.)

of the duck there does not even have to be any tactile contact between it and the object it follows. How can we explain these phenomena?

One explanation is that each species is provided with a special set of responses that it can emit at birth or soon afterwards. The infant will display these "complex reflexes" in response to the most appropriate stimuli the environment supplies. The objects that elicit these responses are likely to become objects of attachment for the young animal.

In the natural environment of the jungle the young monkey clings to the hairy undersurface of his mother for several months after birth. Nature has supplied the infant monkey with a strong grasping reflex and the monkey becomes attached to those objects that allow him to display this response. The mother is the most effective stimulus for this reaction. The duck or chicken upon hatching typically follows a moving object and under natural conditions the biological mother will be the first moving object the young bird encounters. The chicken becomes attached to the mother because the mother allows the natural response of following to occur.

What of the human infant? What are its naturally strong reactions? As indicated earlier, the infant smiles, sucks, babbles, cries, scans, manipulates, and holds, among other things. In the natural course of events the mother is usually the stimulus that is the target for these responses. The mother talks and stimulates the baby to babble; the mother moves her face and stimulates the child to scan it; the mother allows the baby to play with her hair and permits the manipulative responses to appear. More important the mother alleviates the child's hunger, cold, and pain, and while she is performing these caretaking acts, the infant is studying her face and form, babbling and, occasionally, smiling.

As a result of the daily repetition of these interactions and the infant's behavioral responses to this caretaking, he gradually constructs a well-articulated schema of the mother and any other person who cares for him frequently. Hence, by the time he is 4 or 5 months old, he has differentiated his caretaker from others and now will not allow just anyone to pick him up when he cries, rock him when he is sleepy, or feed him when he is hungry. Only a few special people have earned that privilege. Now the infant is more likely to approach, smile, and play with these caretakers and less likely to be apprehensive and inhibited with them than with other adults. It is during this period of development, from about 2 to 24 months, that the term **infant attachment** has a useful meaning (see Fig. 5.5).

A Definition of Attachment

We shall use the term attachment to refer to the infant's tendency during the first 24 months to approach particular people, to be maximally receptive to being cared for by these people, and to be least afraid when with these people. The primary objects of the child's attachment have the greatest power to placate him and to pro-

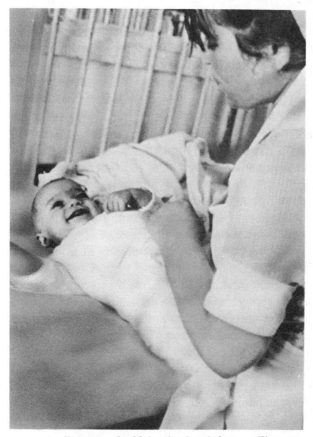

Figure 5.5 Four-month-old institution infant smiling at caretaker while being dressed. (From J. L. Gewirtz. The cause of infant smiling in four child-rearing environments in Israel. In B. M. Foss (Ed.), **Determinants of infant behavior.** Vol. 3. London: Methuen, 1965. P. 217. By permission of the publisher and The Tavistock Institute of Human Relations.)

tect him from fear when he experiences a strange event or is in an unfamiliar situation.

The attachment of infancy is different from the symbolic love relation that exists between a 3- or 4-year-old and his parents. When a child uses symbols consistently, sometime after age 2, he knows which adults "value him" and he wants to maintain an emotionally close relation to these people. It is possible for a 4-year-old child, who did not see his father until he was 3 years old, to believe that his father values him and to have a close relation with the father. This emotional bond can probably develop without a prior attachment during infancy. Moreover, the fact that an infant is attached to his mother during the first two years does not necessarily mean that when he is 4 years old he will be dependent on, secure with, or even emotionally close to her. Imagine two 5-year-olds who had been closely attached to their mothers during infancy. If one mother encouraged and rewarded dependence on her while the other encouraged and rewarded independence from her, it is likely that the former child would more frequently run to his mother in time of stress than the latter, even though both had been equally attached to their mothers as infants. When we say that a 5-year-old is emotionally close to his mother, we are describing a symbolic love relationship that depends on the child's perception of the degree to which his parents value him. That symbolic evaluation may take precedence over the nonsymbolic attachment of the first year. In rural Guatemala, for example, Indian infants are with their mothers continually for most of the first two years and, by our earliest definition, are closely attached. But the preadolescent boys in these villages are hostile to their mothers, relatively independent of them, and do not seek them out in time of distress.

Dr. John Bowlby has a slightly different view of the meaning of attachment (5). Bowlby believes that the goal of the child's attachment behaviors is to keep him close to his mother. When the infant or young child is too far from his parent, both partners become activated to do something until the distance between them is less and the child is again close to his caretaker. Our view is that if the 1-year-old is attached, he will tend to make any one of a number of approach responses toward his mother whenever stress occurs. If he is already near to her, he may display another reaction. For example, if a 1-year-old was holding onto his mother and saw a large animal or felt a painful cramp, he would probably look at his mother or squeeze her hand tightly. The "attachment behavior" is not elicited by the perception of being physically distant from the parent, but rather by any source of uncertainty, fear, or distress.

The gradual differentiation of people into the familiar ones who are targets of attachment (the ones from whom he accepts care, approaches for play, and with whom he feels less afraid) and all others is a product, in part, of the establishment of a schema for his adult caretakers. When that schema is finally articulated, the infant will detect the difference between the familiar caretakers and others and will become afraid of those who are unfamiliar.

This phenomenon is illustrated by detailed study of the imprinting process in ducks, to which we referred earlier. Immediately after hatching, the duck has a strong tendency to approach and to follow a moving object and he will become imprinted on it. However, 13 hours after hatching ,the duck begins to show avoidance responses and will not follow a strange object (4). The time for imprinting is over. It appears that it takes about 13 hours for the duck to develop an articulated schema for the first object it encounters. Now any object that is discrepant from the object of attachment elicits an avoidance reaction and a distress call. Let us now consider the relation of the attachment process to the two prominent fears of the first year—fear of strangers and fear of separation from his caretakers.

The Relation of Attachment and Anxiety

Continued interaction with particular objects leads to the establishment of schemata for those objects. As a result the infant becomes vulnerable to fear when he encounters an event that is discrepant from his schemata. The infant is subject to many instances of fear, but two major classes of anxiety seem to parallel the growth of attachment to adults. One is called **stranger anxiety;** the other, **separation anxiety.**

Stranger Anxiety The response of anxiety to a strange human face is a clear example of a discrepancy reaction. The child at 8 months is sitting in his high chair, playing with his cereal. A strange woman enters the kitchen and stands facing the baby. The infant studies the stranger for 10 seconds; his face tightens, and suddenly he begins to cry. It is clear that the stranger has elicited the cry, for if the stranger leaves, the child becomes happy again. If the stranger reappears, it is likely that the child will cry again. We call this event stranger anxiety and in American children it is typically seen first at about 6 months of age, shows a peak frequency at around 8 months, and then gradually disappears by the time the child is 12 to 15 months. In isolated rural areas, where infants do not see many strangers, the fear reaction to strangers lasts much longer. In infants whose cognitive development is retarded, the fear reaction occurs later, usually at 12 to 14 months. However, the infant is less likely to show fear of the stranger if he is sitting on his mother's lap rather than sitting a few feet from her—much as Harlow's monkeys were less fearful if they were holding the terry-cloth mother than if they were separated from it (26). Proximity to an object of attachment inhibits fear, as if the child feels more secure when near his mother.

Display of fear to an object that partially resembles one for which a schema has been formed can also be seen in kittens. In one study 5-week-old kittens were given one of three treatments (11). One group of kittens was handled and played with by a different person five days a week for four weeks. A second group was given the same handling for the same length of time, but was handled by only one experimenter. The third group of kittens was given no handling at all. At the end of each five-day period during the four weeks of handling, a stranger test was given each kitten. Each kitten was handled by a stranger who did not know to which group a particular kitten belonged. Each week a different stranger was used. The kittens who were either handled by only one experimenter or were not handled at all showed the most fear; they made many attempts to escape or they froze or retreated when called. Apparently the kittens who were exposed to several different people were able to adapt more easily to the stranger because being handled by a stranger was not a discrepant experience. The kittens handled by one person showed little fear of the person to whom they had become accustomed; but they, as well as those handled by no one, showed fear to all strangers—a feline form

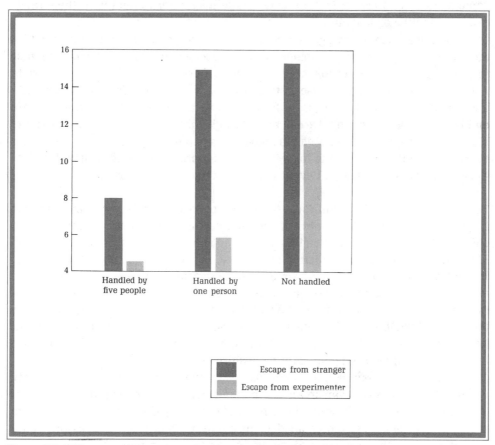

Figure 5.6 Differences in number of escape attempts among kittens raised under three varied conditions. (Adapted from R. R. Collard. Fear of strangers and play behavior in kittens with varied social experience. **Child Development,** 1967, **38,** 883. Copyright 1967 by The Society for Research in Child Development, Inc. By permission.)

of "stranger anxiety"—because the strangers were discrepant stimuli (**11**; see Fig. 5.6).

The sequence of smiling at a strange face at 4 months but displaying anxiety at a strange face at 8 months resembles the imprinting sequence in ducks, for ducks approach a moving object for the first 13 hours of life, but avoid it after that.

The infant, human or bird, initially shows approach responses to the classes of objects encountered most regularly. After a firm schema for an object has developed, the infant may show some temporary fear to stimuli that resemble the original object. Why is this period of fear temporary? Why does it ever develop at all? Is it reasonable to suggest that the infant's reaction to a discrepant event, like a stranger, will depend on whether he has some response to make to it, some way of interpreting it or acting upon it. If the infant has a reaction, he is not likely to become anxious and cry. In fact, he may signify his ability to deal with the strange event by smiling or laughing.

The emergence of stranger anxiety is interpreted as indicating that by 6 to 8 months most infants have developed such a good schema for their mother's face that the stranger is a discrepancy. The infant is alerted. But he is too immature to make any constructive response to this discrepant stimulus. He cannot deal with the strange person and, as a result, he cries. Five months later he is more mature and is able to do something. He can ask, "Who is that, Mommy?" or he can run to his mother. In some instances he may have been exposed to so many strange faces in the interim that his schema for a face will be more generalized. A new face has thus become a less discrepant event than it was five months earlier.

Separation Anxiety A second form of anxiety makes its appearance in American infants at about 10 to 12 months of age, and begins to disappear by the time the child is 20 to 24 months of age (**1, 2, 3, 14**). The event that elicits this fear is different from the one that causes stranger anxiety. For example, a 12-month-old child is playing in the living room with some toys; he sees his mother go to the front door and leave; as the door closes he begins to cry. This is separation anxiety. A 5-month-old American infant would typically not cry in this situation. Why then does the 1-year-old? On the surface, this fear does not seem similar to stranger anxiety. The child has seen the mother leave the house many times and, therefore this event should not be discrepant from an acquired schema.

It should be recognized, however, that the infant is always more likely to cry when his mother leaves him in an unfamiliar place than if he is left in a familiar location. Even in his own home, he is more likely to cry if his mother leaves from a door she rarely uses (the cellar door or a closet) than if she leaves through a typical exit, like the front door. Since the "separation from mother" is the same in both cases and only the familiarity of the exit is different, it seems reasonable to conclude that a primary cause of the crying is the degree of discrepancy of the total event. This interpretation of separation anxiety resembles the one given for stranger anxiety. As the child matures, he establishes a schema for his mother or his caretaker in particular places. The schema is not for the mother as an individual regardless of where she is, but is of the mother in particular contexts—in the kitchen, leaving the bedroom, standing by the sink. If the child is exposed to events discrepant from these representations and is unable to interpret them, he will become afraid. Hence, he is more likely to cry when his mother leaves him in a strange room than if she leaves him in his bedroom.

This argument suggests that the greater the variety of places in which the child has been with his mother and experienced her departure, the later the age at which he will develop a firm idea of his mother in particular places. Therefore, separation anxiety should occur later, if it appears at all.

If the child is with his mother most of the day, as occurs in many parts of

Africa and Latin America, he will be more likely to note her absence and, therefore, become fearful. This prediction is verified by the work of Professor Mary Ainsworth in Uganda (1). Ganda babies are nursed until they are 2 years old and the Ganda mother is usually available to her baby most of the time, carrying the baby most of the day, either straddled across her hip or held in place on her back by a sling of cotton cloth. The Ganda baby does not experience the mother leaving him as often as an American baby who spends most of his first six months in a crib or play pen alone. The Ganda baby shows fear when separated from the mother as early as 6 months of age, which is two to four months before a typical middle-class American infant shows this reaction.

When a familiar person is present in a situation in which a primary caretaker leaves, the child's fear is much less intense and may not even occur. In a recent experiment, child, mother, father, and female stranger were in an unfamiliar room and each of the three adults left, one at a time, on a prearranged schedule. Infants 12 to 18 months rarely became upset if either parent remained in the room when the other parent left. But when both parents were absent and the child was alone with the strange woman, he was likely to cry and stop playing—both signs of fear (22).

An opportunity to make a response that might bring the infant into closer contact with the mother also seems to allay the infant's fear. When 10-month-old children were placed in a strange room away from their mother, they cried. But when 10-month-old infants were placed with the mother in a room which had an open door that led to the strange empty room that had made the other infants cry, the infants often crawled into the empty room, but did not cry when they arrived there. The infants would look around and then crawl back to their mother in the adjoining room. For a short period of time the infants were alone in the same strange room that had made the other infants cry. The difference was that these babies could do something effective if they became apprehensive—they could crawl back to their mother. The infants who cried in the earlier observations could do nothing (30). One reason infants cry less often to maternal departure in the home than in a laboratory is that, in the home, the infant is more likely to crawl toward or run after the mother.

Crying as a response to separation seems to be influenced, therefore, by the child's ability to recognize that he is in an unusual situation and, at the same time, his inability to understand why or to do anything constructive about it. Since the ability to recognize the discrepant quality of the separation experience requires a certain level of cognitive maturity, very young infants should be incapable of separation fear.

It will be recalled that the child begins to activate hypotheses about discrepant events somewhere between 8 and 12 months of age. It is possible that the child may not show separation anxiety until he is able to activate hypotheses about the caretaker's absence, that is, until he is able to fomulate questions such as "What is happening?" "Where is mother?" When will she return?" but be unable to answer them.

Does Separation Anxiety Reflect a Close Attachment?

Some psychologists have used degree of upset in response to separation from the mother as an index of the child's attachment to the parent, where the strength of the attachment was assumed to be related to amount of prior interaction. The previous discussion suggests that separation anxiety is not a sensitive index of intensity of that view of attachment, because it is strongly influenced by the child's cognitive ability—his ability to recognize that the parental departure is unusual and his inability to explain it. Also, some children have a low threshold for becoming fearful and irritable in an uncertain situation, and this dimension also influences the tendency of a baby to cry when he or she sees the mother leave. Let us consider some evidence that casts doubt on the assumption that emotional distress at separation from a parent necessarily measures attachment to that parent.

One-year-old American infants, who typically have many more emotionally toned interactions with their mothers than with their fathers, do not usually become upset when their mother leaves them in a strange room with a strange woman as long as the father remains. Moreover, they become equally upset when either mother or father leaves them alone with a strange woman. If separation anxiety measured intensity of attachment, these children should have become more upset following the departure of mother than father (22, 34). More important, 1-year-old children who interact with their fathers a great deal at home show **less** separation fear when the father leaves them with a stranger than children who interact minimally with their fathers. If frequency of interaction leads to a strong attachment and attachment produces separation fear, then the 1-year-olds who had a great deal of interaction with their father should have cried more, not less.

Perhaps the best evidence that separation fear is not an adequate measure of attachment comes from a comparison of American and Israeli 2½-year-olds in an experimental situation in which their mothers departed (23). The Americans were raised in typical nuclear families in California. The Israeli children lived in a kibbutz and were reared apart from the parents in a group setting. They were cared for by a woman who is called a **metapelet.** In this kibbutz, children live in an infant house during their first year, after which they are transferred to another house until they are about 7 years of age. During the first year, the child's mother visits her infant regularly, but as he grows older, these visits become less frequent. Typically, the mother feeds the child the evening meal and puts him or her to bed. After the child is 1 year old, the metapelet becomes increasingly responsible for his overall care and socialization. Children leave their parents every night to return to their own house, and parent-child separations are much longer than those among typical American families. Many parents are absent from the kibbutz because of special trips, training for jobs, or the army, and one parent may be away for as long as several months.

Almost every kibbutz child in this study had been separated from his parents more often than the American children and had also spent less time with his parents. Consequently, the Israeli child might be expected to be less closely attached. However, when the American and Israeli children were brought into a strange room with the mother, a stranger, and toys, there were no major differences in their reactions when their mothers left them. Both groups of children were equally distressed and about 23 percent of each group cried. The investigators concluded,

> We expected that kibbutz children would be less upset over separation from their mothers than the United States children considering that they have experienced separation as a daily event in their lives, but that they would be more upset over being left alone. In fact, however, the two groups of children were very like each other in their reactions to the two instances of separation that occurred in our series of episodes. The United States and kibbutz children were equally likely to cry both when left with a stranger and when left alone." (23, 79).

The results of these various investigations suggest that differences in frequency of contact between an infant and his caretakers, which might be expected to produce either strong or weak attachments, do not predict differences in fear, crying, or upset to separation. In addition, in spite of differences in rearing, middle-class American as well as poor Guatemalan children show their greatest increase in separation anxiety between 9 and 24 months. It is, therefore, reasonable to conclude that separation anxiety is more closely related to the child's level of cognitive development than it is to the intensity of his emotional bond to his caretaker.

There is one more factor to be added to the mystery of separation anxiety. Regardless of the population in which separation anxiety is studied, it is usually the case that during the first two years of life, between 50 and 60 percent of the children cry at the experience of separation. The usual range is 30 to 70 percent, even though some children are raised in continual contact with their mothers. This fact suggests that children who cry at separation may be temperamentally more prone to fear in an uncertain situation. This suggestion is supported by the fact that 1-year-old children who cry in response to separation also tend to react more irritably to other unusual, nonsocial stimuli and are less likely to smile in response to interesting visual events. This suggests that a temperamental disposition toward fearfulness may be influencing the child's reaction when his parent leaves.

In short, separation fear appears to be much more complex than psychologists had originally surmised. What has seemed to many parents as a cry of "lost love" seems to be influenced more by the child's ability to understand a discrepant event, temperamental disposition toward fearfulness, and inability to make any relevant response that will resolve the discrepancy or bring the child closer to his parent.

Separation anxiety should disappear when the mother's absence is no longer a puzzle or when the child can do something about her absence. Both of these changes occur with age. As a child grows, he experiences more frequent separations from his mother, and becomes increasingly capable of interpreting her absence and reassuring himself of her return. It is important to remember that the cry to separation seen at 1 year does not have the same meaning as the cry of a 3-year-old when his mother leaves him for the first time at nursery school. In the latter case, the child's fears are much more complex. He may be afraid his mother will not pick him up at dismissal; he may be afraid of the children or the teachers in the school. The crying is specific to this situation and does not mean that the child is fearful of heights, strangers, or animals. There seems to be no strong relation among these fears (33).

CONSEQUENCES OF INTERACTION WITH THE CARETAKER

One important consequence of early interaction and the experience of pleasure with the caretaker is that the approach responses the infant makes to the caretaker will generalize to other people. This phenomena was demonstrated in a study of monkeys who were raised under a variety of conditions.

One group was initially reared by a human for 3 weeks and then placed alone in wire cages. These animals had no contact with any monkeys until they were 1 year old. A second group was reared by their natural mothers until 1 year of age. A third group was placed in isolation at birth and could neither see nor touch humans or monkeys until they were 6 months old; then they were put in wire cages until they were 1 year old. During the second year of life, all the monkeys lived in wire cages and had regular opportunities to play with other monkeys each day. When the monkeys were between 2 and 3 years of age, each was placed in a circular chamber with a human on one side and a monkey on the other. The monkey could enter either chamber or stay in the center and approach neither the human nor the monkey. The monkeys who were reared by a human for the first 3 weeks and then isolated for the rest of the first year spent more time with the human than any other group. The early experience with the human apparently led to a preference for a human. The monkeys reared by their mother spent most of their time approaching another monkey. The monkeys reared in complete isolation for the first 6 months spent most of the time in the center of the chamber, approaching neither monkey nor man (37).

This generalization of approach responses from the earliest object of attachment to a similar object also holds for the human infant. The generalization of social responses from a "mother," actually a mother substitute, to other people has been demonstrated in a rigorous experimental study (29). The investigator selected 16 6-month-old infants (the age just prior to the onset of stranger anxiety) who were living in an institution in which many volunteers cared for the children. For 8 of these infants (the experimental babies) the investigator herself played the role of mother 8 hours a day, 5 days a week, for 8 consecutive weeks. During this time, she bathed and diapered them, played with them, smiled at them, and tried to be as good a substitute mother as possible. The other 8 infants (control babies) were cared for in the typical institutional fashion—without individual "mother," but with several women performing these motherly duties in a more routine fashion. Moreover, the experimental babies received **more** nurturance than the controls during the 8-week period. Thus the experimental babies differed from the controls in two ways: they had one person care for them consistently during the 8-week period, and they received more caretaking during this period.

All infants were tested each week during the 8-week experimental period and for 4 additional weeks following the termination of the experimental treatment. The tests administered included tests of social responsiveness to three kinds of people (the experimenter, an examiner who gave them other tests, and, at the end of the 8-week period, a stranger), as well as a postural development and cube-manipulation tests.

The results revealed that the 8 infants who had been cared for by the mother (i.e., the experimenter) showed much more social responsiveness to the experimenter and the stranger than the control children did (29; see Fig. 5.7). That is, when these people smiled or talked to the children, the experimentally treated infants were more likely to smile back or show some facial reaction to the adults than the normally treated children, the effect being most marked in response to the experimenter. These results clearly support the hypothesis that acts learned in response to a nurturant and socially stimulating caretaker can generalize to other people. There were no significant differences in the motor development of the two groups as measured by the cube and posture tests. Apparently, the experience of having the consistently nurturant and stimulating mother figure had minimal effect on simple motor skills, but a dramatic effect on social behavior (29). The investigator believed that the critical factor responsible for the increased social responsiveness of the experimental babies was the reciprocal and playful social stimulation that occurred between child and adult.

The responses of scanning and studying the face, like social responsiveness, can generalize from the mother to a picture of a face. Mothers and their 3-month-old infants were observed in the home and the observers noted how often the mother assumed a face-to-face position with her baby. A week later the infants were brought to the laboratory and shown pictures of human faces and pictures of checkerboards. The infant girls who experienced the most frequent face-to-face contact with their mother at home looked longest at the pictures of faces. The long scanning was specific to the face pictures, because these girls did not look very long at the checkerboards (27).

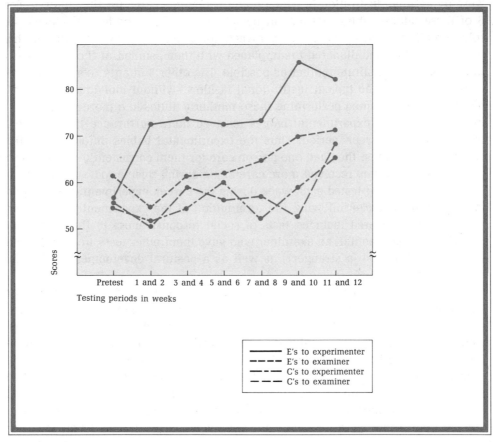

Figure 5.7 The average social responsiveness of the experimental (E) and control (C) infants to the experimental examiner over 12 testing periods. (From H. L. Reingold. The modification of social responsiveness in institutional babies. **Monographs of the Society for Research in Child Development,** 1955, **21,** 23. Copyright 1956 by The Society for Research in Child Development, Inc. By permission.)

Effects of Minimal Interaction with Caretakers

Interaction with adults is an extremely rich source of the varied experiences required for optimal intellectual growth and social responsiveness. It is illuminating, therefore, to examine the development of infants living in poorly run, understaffed institutions. Typically, an adult caretaker in these institutions is responsible for 10 to 20 infants, there are few toys, and the children are likely to be confined to cribs and therefore unable to explore their world. The adults do not conceive of themselves as stimulating psychological growth through play and interaction, but see their role as primarily caring for the infant's basic biological needs of hunger, warmth, and cleanliness. On the basis of our earlier discussion we should expect

Figure 5.8 The monkey raised in isolation shows unusual posture in the cage. (From H. Harlow & M. H. Harlow. Learning to love. **American Scientist,** 1966, **54** (3), 264. By permission.)

children in such settings to be less vocal, less socially responsive, retarded in language, and less alert to changes around them.

Absence of any relation with a living object has grave consequences for the infant monkey and therefore should have a similar effect on human infants. If a monkey is placed in isolation for the first six months of his life, he shows extremely abnormal behavior when he is removed from isolation. He avoids all social contact, appears very fearful, clutches at himself, and crouches (**17**; see Fig. 5.8). If the period of isolation is less than six months, the monkey usually recovers and after a while begins to exhibit normal behavior. If the isolation lasts longer than six months or over a year, the social and sexual behavior of the monkey is abnormal. Monkeys isolated for longer periods show extreme fear (**17**), and some may never recover normal function.

Even the monkeys who are raised with the terry-cloth mothers and who seem secure with them are initially fearful with other monkeys and do not show normal social and sexual behavior when they grow up. After a year of living with other monkeys they gradually recover, but absence of a living mother with whom the infant monkey can interact seriously affects their social behavior. We do not know all the critical actions that a live caretaker performs that produce normal psychological growth. Reciprocal interaction and movement are critical factors. Monkeys raised with a terry-cloth mother who was attached to a motor (the terry-cloth mother moved irregularly in the cage) were less fearful and socially more responsive than monkeys raised with stationary terry-cloth mothers (25). No human child is raised in total isolation, but the effects of lack of responsive caretakers can be studied in infants raised in poorly run institutions.

During the early 1940s Rene Spitz observed the behavior of young children who spent their first year in institutions where care was inadequate and inconsistent (35). During the second half of the first year, 15 percent of the infants began to develop an unusual sequence of behavior. At first they cried continually, but after several months the crying subsided and they began to become indifferent to adults. "The children would lie or sit with wide open, expressionless eyes, frozen, immobile face, and a far away expression as if in a daze, apparently not perceiving what went on in their environment" (35, 314). (It is of more than incidental interest that Harlow's juvenile monkeys who were raised on wire surrogate mothers are described in a way that is similar to Spitz's earlier descriptions of the institutionalized infants.)

Some of these children may have been physically ill, either suffering from serious malnutrition or chronic infectious diseases. However, these observations alerted many psychologists and psychiatrists to the possible psychological consequences of institutional living, and better-controlled studies have corroborated the conclusion that institutionalized babies are markedly different from those raised in families.

Provence and Lipton observed 75 babies living in an institutional environment in the United States where nutrition and bodily care were adequate and the infants were not physically ill, but where interactive play and opportunity to explore were inadequate. The description of the institutional environment will help the reader appreciate the conditions under which these infants lived.

> The younger group of infants (age 4 days to 8 months) occupied cribs placed singularly in glass partitioned cubicles. The room was clean, cheerful and light with adequate heat and ventilation. The infants were fed in their cribs with bottles propped. When cereals, fruits and vegetables were added to the diet they were also given in a propped bottle with a large holed nipple rather than given by spoon. . . . Sometimes a stuffed toy was placed in the crib for the baby to look at. After about 4 months of age, simple rattles, beads and so on, were placed on a string suspended across the crib sides and the single playpen which contained other age appropriate toys. . . . Each infant in this group shared the time and attention of the attendant with 7 to 9 other infants in the same age range for the 8 hour period of the day when she was present. For the remaining 16 hours of the day, there was no person in the nursery except at feeding time when an attendant who also had similar duties in other nurseries heated formulas, propped bottles, and changed diapers (28).

Not only were the infants fed without the presence of an adult, but there was minimal variability in their experience. There were no vocalizations from other people, no reciprocal play, no close relationship between a child's crying and the reaction of someone else.

In considering how these babies were different from those raised in families it should be noted, first, that there were **no** major differences between normal and institutionalized babies prior to 3 or 4 months of age. It is only after 4 months that the differences became evident. The institutionalized babies vocalized very little; they showed no cooing, no babbling, and little crying. Moreover, they did not adapt their postures to the arms of an adult, "they felt something like sawdust dolls; they moved, they bent easily at the proper joints, but they felt stiff or wooden" (28).

These infants were not picked up very often and, therefore, one would not expect them to make the kinds of postural adjustments that babies ordinarily make. By 8 months of age most of these infants were markedly less interested in grasping or approaching toys, and they began to lose interest in their external environment. During the second half of the first year, body rocking became very common and was more frequent than would be observed among family-reared babies. Stranger anxiety was rare, and the infants' facial expressions were bland and clearly not so expressive as those of family-reared infants. If they were frustrated, they would cry passively or turn away; rarely would they make an attempt to conquer a frustration. Finally, language was delayed. There were no words at all at 1 year of age and vocalization and language were the behaviors that were most seriously depressed. The following is a description of one of these babies at 45 weeks of age.

> Outstanding were his soberness, his forlorn appearance, and lack of animation. The interest that he showed in the toys was mainly for holding, inspecting and rarely mouthing. When he was unhappy he now had a cry that sounded neither demanding nor angry—just miserable—and it was usually accompanied by his beginning to rock. The capacity for protest which he had earlier was much diminished. He did not turn to adults to relieve his distress or to involve them in a playful or pleasurable interchange. He made no demands. The active approach to the world, which had been one of the happier aspects of his earlier development, vanished. As one made active and persistent efforts at a social interchange he became somewhat more responsive, animated and motorically active, but lapsed into his depressed and energy-less appearance when the adult became less active with him (28, 134–135).

There were two descriptive comments by observers that seemed to convey the impression Teddy made at this time: one was, "the light in Teddy has gone out"; the other was, "if you crank his motor you can get him to go a little; he can't start on his own"(28).

All of the behaviors that were most likely to be learned as a result of interaction with an adult (clinging, crying to distress, approaching adults for play, and vocalization) were most clearly retarded or absent in the institutionalized children.

Observations in Indian villages in Guatemala, where infants are continually with their mothers and are nursed regularly, reveal the same kind of listless, apathetic infants. This fact suggests that the absence of a single, consistent caretaker is not the critical factor that produces the listlessness and apathy. What then does produce the apparent intellectual retardation?

In both the American institution and the Indian village the child experienced little variety in cognitive and affective experience and had little opportunity to explore the environment, and practice the responses that come so naturally to infants—reaching, manipulating, crawling, and creeping. Moreover, in both contexts attractive toys were absent and there was very little conversation between the adults and infants. Hence, it is likely that the critical factor producing the nonalertness and apparent retardation is lack of variety in experience and the restricted opportunity for exploration and action during the first year.

This conclusion is supported by a study of retardation in institutionalized children in two types of institutions in Iran (12). In the first, called the deprived setting, the child was never placed on his stomach and hence could not practice creeping. He was not held in a sitting position while being fed and had no toys with which to play. In addition, only 1 attendant was provided for every 8 children, so that interpersonal contacts of any sort were severely limited. In the second institution, called the enriched setting, the child was often placed on his stomach, was held while eating, had toys and playthings, and in general received considerably greater attention. In this latter setting, 1 attendant was provided for every 3 children.

The children in both settings typically entered the institution shortly after birth. During the second year of life, the behavior of the 50 children in the deprived setting was compared with the behavior of the 20 children in the enriched setting. While only 42 percent of the deprived children could sit alone, 90 percent of the enriched children could do so. Less than 5 percent of the deprived group could stand or walk while holding on to a support, while over 60 percent of the other children could perform these responses. Finally, no child in the deprived institution could walk alone, while 3 of the 20 children in the enriched setting were able to do so.

The lack of opportunity to learn the motor acts of sitting and walking in the deprived setting was primarily responsible for the observed behavioral retardation of children in this group. The deprived children were not allowed to practice creeping or sitting and, consequently, were retarded in these responses. The deprived children also showed more head-shaking and repetitive rocking of the body and appeared more unhappy than the enriched children.

Although the institutional environment is monotonous, it does contain physical stimulation. Some psychologists have suggested that lower-class children from so-called deprived environments do not have enough sensory stimulation and, as a result, are retarded mentally (see p. 346). Compare the quiet bedroom of a suburban middle-class home in the country with an urban one-room ghetto apartment. If one measured the amount of stimulation in physical terms, the environment of the city child would contain much more stimulus energy than that of the middle-class infant. But the middle-class infant lives in a stimulus environment that is highly variable and distinctive. Moreover, the infant attends to and learns most from distinctive stimulation—stimuli that attract his attention. A mother's voice breaking the quiet of the bedroom and addressed directly to the infant when he is alert has the maximal probability of attracting the young infant's attention and, therefore, of teaching him something. A voice yelling over a television set in a sea of noise is less distinctive and is less likely to recruit the infant's attention.

The importance of **distinctiveness of stimulation** is illustrated in the observations of lower- and upper-middle-class mothers of 4-month-old girls (19). When the upper-middle-class mothers vocalized to their infants, they were likely to be face-to-face with them and not providing any other stimulation. They were not tickling them, touching them, or patting them. The mother's vocalization to the infant was very distinctive. The lower-class mother was apt to talk to her infant when she was feeding, diapering, or burping the baby. As a result, the vocalization was less distinctive, for the infant may have been attending to the tactile or kinesthetic stimuli that accompanied the diapering or burping. It is probably more than coincidence that the upper-middle-class girl produces more variable sounds and shows precocious language development during the first two years of life.

It is helpful to take a relativistic view of the stimulus events that occur during the first year. The issue is not the amount of sensory stimulation the infant receives, but its variety and distinctiveness, that is, its quality rather than quantity. Infants who have greater experiential variety are more alert and perform better on tests of cognitive functioning than infants with minimal variety. In one study one group of institutionalized 2-month-old infants were stimulated with a mobile for two months; a second group received social stimulation; a third group received both the mobile and social stimulation; and a fourth group received no special experience. The infants in the first three groups who received variety had higher developmental quotients when they were 4 months old, suggesting that when the environment is varied, an infant's intellectual performance is enhanced (8).

Similar results have been found with monkeys raised under the following conditions, ordered according to the degree of stimulus variety (31). One group were wild subjects from a natural habitat who were brought to the laboratory somewhere between 1½ and 3 years of age. They experienced the greatest variety. A second group, raised in a laboratory, had access to their monkey mothers and to other young monkeys during the first year. A third group were raised with artificial cloth-covered mothers and had no peer experience until 6 to 8 months of age, after which they were given peer contact. A fourth group lived in complete social and partial sensory isolation for the first six months of life and then were put alone in a wire cage for the remainder of the first year. Finally, a fifth group lived in complete social isolation for the first nine months and then were put in a wire cage for three months. **The greater the degree of stimulus variation present in the rearing condition, the more exploration and motor activity and the less fearful inhibition the older monkeys displayed.** This result matches the observations of human infants raised under conditions of low stimulus variety.

It should be stressed that institutions that provide individualized care for infants and a rich variety of experience do not seem to impair the young child's development and he seems to grow in a manner similar to that of home-reared infants. If a child experiences consistent nurturance and interaction from an adult other than the mother, he will become attached to her and will not necessarily be deficient in intellectual or social reactivity (38). Infants who attend good day-care centers develop attachments to both the mother and the woman who cares for them and show stranger and separation anxiety at the normal times. A comparison of children reared at home and in day care centers concluded that there was no difference between the groups in their attachment to adults at 30 months (9).

Thus the specific nature of the situation in which the child is reared—mud hut, orphanage, or city apartment—is not the important consideration. The mere fact of being in an institution or day-care center is not a major cause of intellectual or social deficiency. In fact, a well-run institution or a good day-care center may produce infants who are precocious compared to those living in inadequate homes. Israeli infants raised in the group care context of a kibbutz have been found to be at the same level of developmental maturity as those reared in middle-class homes, while Israeli infants raised in poor institutions were retarded in comparison with kibbutz children (21).

The potential danger of speaking loosely about the damaging effects of institutionalization, without attempting to specify further the actual variables involved, is well illustrated in a report on two residential nurseries in the Soviet Union where psychological care is adequate (7). In these nurseries, which are maintained primarily for research purposes, children are raised from birth to about 3 years of age. At one nursery, the most prominent feature of the child-rearing program is its stress on physical development, including diet, sleep, and, most particularly, an elaborate schedule of daily massages and exercises in which the child is involved beginning at 60 days of age.

At the other, children spend the first three years of life in a well-equipped nursery which includes such things as specially designed walkers and playpens. According to Brackbill,

> [M]ore usual than its furnishings is the nursery's program for verbal-motor stimulation of its children. This is regarded by the staff as a matter of great importance and something that merits their sustained efforts. As part of the overall plan, every nurse has

specific duties that she performs each day with all infants individually. As an example of "verbal duties," the task for Nurse A might be to ask each infant in turn, "Where is the cat?", "Where is the visitor?", "Show me your ear.", "Show me your hand.", and so on. In each case, the child's answer is followed by appropriate reinforcement. When the mother visits—and she is urged to visit often—she has access to the nurse's list of stimulants and is encouraged to further the verbal and motor training herself.

Attention to verbal and motor development is carried over to the toddler group. But in addition, a new goal is added to their program of upbringing. Staff efforts are now also focused on the child's development of self-help and independence. . . . The one to three year olds are shown how to pick up their toys before midday dinner, how to feed themselves, how to get along socially with their three table companions at dinner time, how to prepare themselves for a nap after dinner (7, 10–11).

No adverse effects of this kind of institutionalization have been evident in the children at either nursery—physically, socially, emotionally, or intellectually.

If one thinks of the negative aspects of institutionalization or day care in terms of such component variables as the absence of close interactions between a child and mother surrogate, minimal opportunities for initiation of play and development of motor responses, and lack of variety in stimulation, then it appears that the Russian nurseries described above meet few of the criteria for an institution. In many respects, in fact, they appear more closely to resemble well-ordered nurturant homes.

Capacity for Recovery

Despite the fact that retardation can result from inadequate variety and opportunity during the first year, the infant retains a vital capacity for recovery. Once the listless, apathetic Guatemalan Indian infants were able to walk (at about 13 or 14 months), they left their dark hut and began to explore the variety of the outside world (20). Their retardation gradually faded, and by 10 years of age they were gay, alert, and intellectually competent children whose performance on memory, perception, and reasoning tests was comparable to those of children in the United States. An equally dramatic recovery was found in institutionalized children living in a Lebanese institution, called the Creche, in which personal care was minimal (13). Although the children 2 to 12 months of age in the institution did not perform as well as normals on standard mental test items, the 5-year-olds were not markedly inferior to normal subjects on some tests of mental ability. The restriction of activity and absence of stimulation temporarily prevented the institutional children from practicing the skills required on the test at 1 year of age, but this retardation was not permanent. The 5-year-olds in the institution were not seriously retarded in memory and drawing, although their language retardation was still present at 5 years of age.

It appears that retardation during the first year is not necessarily predictive of future intellectual functioning during the school years. But that conclusion depends on the environment in which the child is growing up. One must take into account the child's environment during his preschool and early school years. For example, retardation on motor, mental, and social milestones during infancy was predictive of low scores on a standard intelligence test only for infants who continued to grow in low socioeconomic homes. Some of these homes, as we indicated earlier, do not facilitate the skills measured by standard intelligence tests (39).

The dramatic intellectual recovery of the Guatemalan and Lebanese infants is supported by an important study of isolated monkeys (37). Rhesus monkeys were placed in isolation for the first six months of their lives. When these monkeys were removed, they showed the complete array of strange social behavior typical of monkeys reared in isolation. They withdrew in fear, attacked novel stimuli, and displayed bizarre habits. These monkeys were administered therapy by placing them with young infant female monkeys. Since the infant monkeys were immature they did not approach or attack the isolates. Gradually the older monkeys approached and began to interact with them. After only 26 weeks of "therapy" the severely disturbed, isolated monkeys had recovered dramatically and their behavior was similar to that of normal monkeys.

Hence, it seems fair to conclude that human 1-year-olds, whose development is deviant due to inadequate care, retain the capacity to recover. Early retardation due to lack of experiential variety need not doom the child to permanent incompetence, for there is more resilience in early development than psychologists have traditionally believed. The secret is to find the proper environment to overcome the initial handicaps in these children.

CULTURAL DIFFERENCES IN CHILD REARING

There are dramatic differences among cultures in the way young children are reared. In rural Guatemala the infant spends his time in a dark hut with no toys for the first ten or eleven months. In Israel the kibbutz infant lives with his nurse and many other children. In a residential nursery in Czechoslovakia the infant is in a cot in a large room with 25 other infants and experiences a regimented day.

The values and skills older children learn also vary with culture. American children learn how to read and write; Guatemalan children learn to make tortillas, weave cloth, and plant corn. Children in northern India learn to be respectful and obedient; American children learn to be autonomous and individualistic. These differences lead to variety in the child's behaviors. The Indian child is quiet compared with the boisterousness of the American. The Japanese adolescent is obedient compared with the rebelliousness of the American. But, despite these differences there are also similarities in development. Language, reasoning, and laughter develop in similar ways and at similar times, suggesting that there are some basic characteristics of human beings that develop in any environment

where humans care for children and teach them values. Differential conditions of rearing seem to produce major differences among children during the first five years of life and again after adolescence. Children around the world appear to be most similar between 5 and 12 years of age. This is reasonable, for the social play of children is remarkably similar across the world, and age mates have a strong influence on one another at that time.

One important determinant of how the young child is handled is the parents' belief about the basic nature of children and their theory of how one molds a child into the ideal adult. In some cultures parents believe the infant is evil and must be tamed. In India parents believe a child is fundamentally uncontrollable and must never be allowed to be disrespectful. In America it is assumed that a child is relatively helpless and must be pushed, stimulated, and encouraged.

An intriguing study compared 30 Japanese and 30 American mothers and their 3- to 4-month-old first-born infants (10). The Japanese child lives and sleeps typically in the same room with the mother and father and the Japanese mother is always close to her infant. When the infant cries, the mother is apt to respond quickly and feed him soon after he begins to fret. In contrast, the American child usually has a room of his own, and the mother often lets him cry for a few minutes before she comes to feed him. Second, the Japanese mother feels the need to soothe and quiet her baby, while the American mother more often wants to stimulate him and make him vocalize or smile. The American mother plays with her baby and talks to him; the Japanese mother soothes and rarely talks to her baby. The Japanese baby is less active than the American baby and much less vocal. There is, therefore, a reasonable association between the maternal practices and the child's behavior.

The differences in maternal behavior seem to derive from different philosophies, or attitudes, about the infant. The American mother believes that her child is basically passive, and it is her job to mold him—to make him into an active, independent child. As a result, she feels she must stimulate him. The Japanese mother believes her infant is basically independent and active and it is her job to soothe him and make him dependent upon her and the family. She sees "the infant as a separate biological organism, which from the beginning, in order to develop, needs to be drawn into interdependent relations with others" (10).

To put it simply, the American mother sees her infant as fundamentally dependent. She must make him independent and achieving, and she stimulates him to babble and does not rush to soothe him at the first cry. The Japanese mother sees her infant as already independent and she must make him more dependent. Therefore, she soothes him and hastens to care for him as quickly as possible. One could not ask for a clearer example of the importance of cultural attitudes on the rearing practices of the mother and, subsequently, on the behavior of the infant and older child.

Even within our own society there have been major differences in how mothers viewed and handled their infants within a period as brief as fifty years.

In 1914 government pamphlets containing advice to American mothers instructed them to avoid all excessive stimulation of the child because he had an extremely sensitive nervous system. In the 1960s these pamphlets instructed the mother to allow the infant to experience as much stimulation as he wished for that was the only way he would learn about his world. In 1914 the mother was told not to feed or play with the baby every time he cried for such action would spoil him. Fifty years later the mother was told that the child would feel secure if she nurtured him when he cried and she should not be afraid of "spoiling" her baby. The 1914 pamphlet urged the mother to toilet train her child before the first year was over and to prevent thumb-sucking and handling of the genitals. A half-century later she was told to wait until the child understood the purpose of toilet training (at least until the middle of the second year) and not to worry about thumb-sucking or genital touching.

These changes in advice to mothers, which we have good reason to believe were accepted and practiced, reflect the dramatic changes in philosophy regarding ideal traits and views of child development. America is less Puritan in 1973 than it was in 1914 and "enjoying life" is regarded as being as important as having "good habits of character." This change in mood is reflected in the advice given to parents. The way young children are handled is intimately related to the value and belief system of the culture. Since the evidence we have at this time suggests no major difference in the "adjustment" of 5-year-olds in 1914 and 1973, it is reasonable to conclude that children develop adequately under a wide variety of environmental routines and it is not possible to write the perfect recipe for child-rearing.

SUMMARY

The infant is born with the capacity to emit behaviors toward the person caring for it. These responses include clinging, vocalizing, smiling, scanning, and following the caretaker. Moreover, the caretaking adult typically provides pleasant experiences and reduces the infant's pain and distress. As a result, the infant becomes attached to its caretakers and becomes highly receptive to being soothed by the object of attachment. A similar process occurs in many animal species in ways that are markedly similar to the process in the human infant.

In addition to emitting behaviors, the infant is developing schemata about people and objects in the environment and becomes distressed when he encounters objects or people that are moderate distortions of these schemata, especially if he has no response to make to the unusual stimulus. These encounters with a surprising event are one of the most important sources of vigilance and alertness in the infant. If he can interpret or deal with the surprise, he will grow psychologically. If he cannot, he may withdraw or in some cases show panic. Thus the child passes through periods of gaining familiarity with people, objects, and events which permit him, in turn, to understand events at the next level of complexity or difficulty. The repetition of this process is the essence of psychological growth. The institutionalized infant in a monotonous and impersonal environment is likely to be cognitively and emotionally deficient and will not react to human beings in the socialized way so characteristic of family-reared children or those raised in responsive institutions. But the 1-year-old child who may have been a victim of such neglect seems to possess a substantial capacity for recovery, if his environment after the first year allows him the freedom to explore the variety in his world and the opportunity to establish interactive relations with adults and other children.

References

1. Ainsworth, M. D. S. **Infancy in Uganda.** Baltimore: Johns Hopkins Press, 1967.
2. Ainsworth, M. D. S. Object relations, dependency and attachment. **Child Development,** 1969, **40,** 969–1026.
3. Ainsworth, M. D. S., & Bell, S. M. Attachment, exploration and separation: Illustrated by the behavior of one year olds in strange situations, **Child Development,** 1970, **41,** 49–67.
4. Bateson, P. P. G. The characteristics and context of imprinting. **Biology Review,** 1966, **41,** 177–220.
5. Bowlby, J. **Attachment and loss.** Vol. 1. **Attachment.** London: Hogarth (New York: Basic Books, 1969).
6. Brackbill, Y. Extinction of the smiling response in infants as a function of reinforcement schedule. **Child Development,** 1958, **29,** 114–124.
7. Brackbill, Y. **Research and clinical work with children.** Washington, D.C.: American Psychological Association, 1962.
8. Brossard, M., & Decarie, T. G. The effects of three kinds of social stimulation on the development of institutionalized infants. In C. Lavatelli (Ed.), **Readings in child development and behavior.** New York: Harcourt Brace Jovanovich, 1971. Pp. 173–183.
9. Caldwell, B. M., Wright, C. M., Honig, A. S., & Tannenbaum, J. Infant day care and attachment. **American Journal of Orthopsychiatry,** 1970, **40**(3), 397–412.
10. Caudill, W., & Weinstein, H. Maternal care and infant behavior in Japanese and American urban middle class families. In R. Konig & R. Hill (Eds.), **Yearbook of the International Sociological Association,** 1966.
11. Collard, R. R. Fear of strangers and play behavior in kittens with varied social experience. **Child Development,** 1967, **38,** 877–891.
12. Dennis, W. Causes of retardation among institutional children: Iran. **Journal of Genetic Psychology,** 1960, **96,** 47–59.
13. Dennis, W., & Najarian, P. Infant development under environmental handicap. **Psychological Monographs,** 1957, **71**(Whole No. 436).
14. Fleener, D. E., & Cairns, R. B. Attachment behaviors in human infants: Discriminative vocalization on maternal separation. **Developmental Psychology,** 1970, **2,** 215–223.

15. Freedman, D. G. The Effects of kinesthetic stimulation on weight gain and on smiling in premature infants. Paper presented at the annual meeting of the American Orthopsychiatric Association, San Francisco, 1966.
16. Gewirtz, J. L. The cause of infant smiling in four child-rearing environments in Israel. In B. M. Foss (Ed.), **Determinants of infant behavior.** Vol. III. London: Methuen, 1965. Pp. 205–260.
17. Harlow, H., & Harlow, M. H. Learning to love. **American Scientist,** 1966, **54**(3), 244–272.
18. Harlow, H. F., & Zimmermann, R. R. Affectional responses in the infant monkey. **Science,** 1959, **130**(3373), 421–432.
19. Kagan, J. **Change and continuity in infancy.** New York: Wiley, 1971.
20. Kagan, J. The plasticity of early intellectual development. Paper presented at the meeting of the Association for the Advancement of Science, Washington, D.C., 1972.
21. Kohen-Raz, R. Mental and motor development of the kibbutz, institutionalized and home reared infants in Israel. **Child Development,** 1968, **39**, 489–504.
22. Kotelchuck, M. The nature of the child's tie to his father. Unpublished doctoral dissertation, Harvard University, 1972.
23. Maccoby, E. E., & Feld, S. S. Mother-attachment and stranger reactions in the third year of life, **Monographs of the Society for Research in Child Development,** 1972, **37**(Serial No. 146).
24. Marquis, D. P. Learning in the neonate. The modification of behavior under three feeding schedules. **Journal of Experimental Psychology,** 1941, **28**, 263–282.
25. Mason, W. A. Motivational aspects of social responsiveness in young chimpanzees. In H. W. Stevenson, E. H. Hess, & H. L. Rheingold (Eds.), **Early behavior.** New York: Wiley, 1967.
26. Morgan, G. A., & Ricciuti, H. N. Infants' responses to strangers during the first year. In B. M. Foss (Ed.), **Determinants of infant behavior.** Vol. IV. London: Methuen, 1967.
27. Moss, H. A., & Robson, K. S. Maternal influences in early social behavior. **American Journal of Orthopsychiatry,** 1967, **37**, 394–395.
28. Provence, S., & Lipton, R. C. **Infants in institutions.** New York: International Universities Press, 1962.
29. Rheingold, H. L. The modification of social responsiveness in institutional babies. **Monographs of the Society for Research in Child Development,** 1956, 2 (2, Serial No. 63).
30. Rheingold, H. L., & Eckerman, C. O. The infant separates himself from his mother. **Science,** 1970, **168**, 78–90.
31. Sackett, G. P. Exploratory behavior in Rhesus monkeys as a function of rearing experiences and sex. **Developmental Psychology,** 1972, **6**, 260–270.
32. Sackett, G. P., Porter, M., & Holmes, H. Choice behavior in rhesus monkeys. **Science,** 1965, **147**, 304–306.
33. Scarr, S., & Salapatek, P. Patterns of fear development during infancy, **Merrill-Palmer Quarterly,** 1970, **16**, 53–90.
34. Spelke, E., Kagan, J., Zelazo, P., & Kotelchuck, M. Father interaction and separation protest. **Developmental Psychology,** 1973, **9**, 83–90.
35. Spitz, R. A., & Wolff, K. M. Anaclitic depression: An inquiry into the genesis of psychiatric conditions in early childhood, II. In A. Freud et al. (Eds.), **The psychoanalytic study of the child.** Vol. II. New York: International Universities Press, 1946. Pp. 313–342.
36. Sroufe, L. A., & Wunsch, J. P. The development of laughter in the first year of life. **Child Development,** 1972, **43**, 1326–1344.

37. Suomi, S. J., & Harlow, H. F. Social rehabilitation of isolate reared monkeys. **Developmental Psychology,** 1972, **6,** 487–496.

38. Tizard, B., Cooperman, O., Joseph, A., & Tizard, J. Environmental effects on language development. **Child Development,** 1972, **43,** 337–358.

39. Willerman, L., Broman, S. H., & Fiedler, M. Infant development, pre-school I.Q. and social class. **Child Development,** 1970, **41,** 69–77.

Part III
Language and Cognitive Development

Chapter 6

The Development of Language

The use of symbolic speech is uniquely human, man's most distinctive and, perhaps, his most complex achievement. Every human society, however primitive and isolated, has a language, and no animal society has ever developed one. Language may be defined as an arbitrary system of symbols "which taken together make it possible for a creature with limited powers of discrimination and a limited memory to transmit and understand an infinite variety of messages and to do this in spite of noise and distraction" (6, 246).

It is impossible to conceive of a human society functioning without language. Language enables us to communicate an infinite number and variety of messages, meanings, intentions, thoughts, requests, and items of information. We can hear or read a complex, difficult sentence that we have never encountered before, yet we readily interpret its meaning and judge whether it is well-formed or not, that is, whether it is grammatically correct. Poets arrange words in beautiful and entirely novel ways, yet the messages they transmit are understood. And each of us can create, theoretically at least, an infinite number of sentences that have never been said before, and when we say new sentences, we somehow manage to say them in coherent, appropriate, and grammatically acceptable ways.

Culture—society's accumulated knowledge, wisdom, and beliefs—is transmitted from generation to generation largely by means of written or spoken language.

> From an evolutionary point of view the important thing about language is that it makes life experiences cumulative; across generations and, within one generation, among individuals. Everyone can know much more than he could possibly learn by direct experience. Knowledge and folly, skills and superstitions, all alike begin to accumulate and cultural evolution takes off at a rate that leaves biological evolution far behind (7, 212).

Language affects all aspects of human behavior; most of what we know has been transmitted to us through words or symbols. Furthermore, language is generally involved in thinking, memory, reasoning, problem-solving, and planning—in short, in all the higher mental processes.

The study of the acquisition of language is one of the most dramatic and exciting aspects of child development. And, remarkably, all normal children in all cultures acquire language and speak reasonably well by the time they are 4 years old. When the child acquires language and learns to use symbols to represent events, he launches a whole new world of learning and understanding and becomes able to deal with his experiences and his environment in new ways. For instance, after the child learns some names or labels that are applied to objects, such as dog or candy, he is likely to react in the same way to all stimuli that have these labels (approaching and petting four-legged animals called dogs and reaching for things called candy). This is known as **verbal mediation,** and its importance in concept formation, abstraction, problem-solving, thinking, and learning has been demonstrated repeatedly (see pp. 258 ff).

What are the processes underlying the universal human phenomenon of language acquisition? How can this complex achievement be realized in such a short period of time? To what extent is language acquisition determined by innate biological factors and to what extent is it learned? Does man possess a built-in propensity to acquire language, a propensity that is wired into the human organism? How is language related to thought and reasoning? Is thinking entirely dependent on language?

Although these important questions have been asked for centuries, we have only recently begun to understand some of the processes underlying language development. This chapter will review the findings of systematic studies of these problems, most of them from recent research. As we shall see, it is difficult to account for language acquisition solely in terms of learning principles. Biological and cognitive factors loom large in this process.

Before examining the process of language acquisition, however, it is necessary to know something about the nature of language.

MAJOR ASPECTS OF LANGUAGE

Every language has two major aspects: **structure** (the basic units, words and sounds, and rules for arranging them) and **meaning** (conventional, arbitrary signs for referents, for objects and events). The structural aspects consist essentially of the sound system (phonology), rules for formation of words from sounds (morphology), and rules for word combination (grammar or syntax). These aspects, the **linguistic system,** rather than the social-communicative functions of language, are studied by linguists.

The elementary sounds of a language are phonemes—"for the most part, vowels and consonants, . . . [that] correspond roughly to the letters of an alphabetic writing system" (**6,** 247; see pp. 241–242). Phonemes are arranged into larger units called morphemes which are "similar to, but not the same as, words" (**6,** 247) and are the "smallest units of meaning" (**6,** 252). Free morphemes can stand alone, for example, the words **ask** and **cat.** The words **asked** and **cats** are not single morphemes, however. **Asked** is composed of a verb and the ending **-ed,** indicating past time; **cats** is made up of a noun and the ending **-s,** which signifies plurality. These endings are morphemes that cannot stand alone; they are called bound morphemes.

Each language has its own rules governing the combination of phonemes, permitting some combinations and prohibiting others. In English there are no morphemes beginning with **ng** and the sequence **zb** never occurs, although these combinations occur in other languages.

"From morphemes, words are composed by morphological rules and sentences by syntactic rules" (**6,** 252). Grammar, or syntax, refers to the set of rules for creating sentences from words, that is, with syntax, phrases and sentences can be generated.

According to Chomsky, a prominent linguist and linguistic theorist at the Massachusetts Institute of Technology, every sentence, however simple, has a **surface structure** and a **deep structure.** The surface structure refers to what we actually hear, that is, the string of words that make up the spoken sentence, its "sound." The deep structure refers to the basic logical relationships expressed in the sentence, the subject and the object of the verb, for example. It is more abstract and related to meaning. The distinction between the surface and deep structure, which has unnecessarily baffled many people, can be demonstrated by two sentences that have the same surface structure but different deep structures. An oft-cited example is:

1. John is eager to please.
2. John is easy to please.

On the surface, the two sentences are organized in the same way, noun–copular verb (copula)–adjective–infinitive phrase. But in the first sentence, John is clearly the subject, the one of whom eagerness is predicated; he is eager to please someone else. In the second sentence, John is actually the object of the verb in another sentence which is closer to the deep structure: "It is easy to please John." This deep structure has been transformed into the surface structure of sentence 2 above, simply by shifting the object, John, to the front of the sentence, replacing "it."

Surface structure can be misleading and ambiguous. To illustrate, consider the sentence, "Flattering women amused him." This sentence can have two different meanings or deep structures. It could mean, "It amused him to flatter women" or, alternatively, "He was amused by women who were flattering."

Chomsky has proposed a **generative transformational grammar** that ties together what is heard (surface structure) and what is meant (deep structure) specifying how underlying meaning is transformed into the sounds of the sentence. The grammar "attempts to characterize in an explicit way the intrinsic association of phonetic form and semantic content in a particular language" (**13**, 407).

Chomsky's ideas about transformational generative grammar have been very influential and, in the late 1950s and 1960s, psychologists became very much interested in studying the structure of children's language, the grammar of the child's earliest speech. However, after about a decade of research on grammar or syntax, psycholinguists began to feel that highly significant aspects of language were being missed. It became clear that to understand language acquisition, it is necessary to go beyond formal characteristics and to investigate how content and meaning actually develop during early childhood. Significant recent work is concerned "with the child's semantic intentions and with the means by which he deciphers the speech of others" (**39**, 197). There are already some very interesting findings on semantic development.

In later discussions in this chapter we will review empirical data on the beginnings of speech and language development from the points of view of both grammar (syntax) and meaning (semantics). The findings of these studies will be more meaningful if they are placed in the context of theory, so we now turn to theories of language development.

THEORETICAL APPROACHES TO LANGUAGE DEVELOPMENT

Because language is generally considered the most distinctive characteristic of human behavior and because it looms so large in social interactions and in cognitive functioning, psychologists have been concerned with the broad problem of how language develops and functions. Some have attempted to apply their own theories in explaining how children acquire the ability to speak sentences and to communicate meanings and thoughts. As we shall see, no one of the many attempts has produced an entirely satisfactory explanation of these phenomena.

Skinner's Theory

As would be expected, learning theorists have attempted to account for language acquisition in terms of associations between stimulus and response (S-R) and rewards or reinforcements. The most comprehensive effort to apply the principles of reinforcement learning to language development is Skinner's **Verbal Behavior,** published in 1957 (37). There may be some irony in the use of a theory based on research in animal learning to explain a uniquely human ability.

Skinner maintains that language, like other behavioral functions, is learned through operant conditioning. According to his theory, operant conditioning of verbal behavior is based on selective reinforcements of sounds and sound combinations provided by the environment. Infants utter sounds spontaneously, at random, or imitatively. Parents and others in the environment reinforce certain sounds differentially. For example, during the babbling period the infant will make some sounds that have some resemblance to adult speech. These sounds are likely to be rewarded or reinforced immediately by parental attention and praise; hence they become predominant in the child's vocalization.

The child is gradually reinforced for progressively closer and closer approximations to adult speech. Thus, sounds like **kuh** may at first be reinforced with a cookie, **wa** with a drink, and **da** with a smile from Daddy. But as the child matures, closer approximations of the words are reinforced more strongly and immediately and consequently these close approximations become stronger. "Thus, more and more precise . . . speech responses may be gradually shaped up through successive approximation until the child readily emits the speech units involved in everyday language, in other words, finally acquires a repertoire of correct speech responses" (**41,** 121).

This theory also maintains that children learn to imitate the speech responses of their parents through reinforcement. When the mother says "Say cookie," a response that approximates "cookie" will be reinforced immediately. If the child makes some other sound, however, the mother is likely to repeat her request and withhold reinforcement until the child makes a more appropriate sound. Thus, matched or imitated sounds are likely to be reinforced, while failure to match sounds brings no reinforcement; in this way, the child comes to discriminate matched from unmatched sounds.

In addition to learning speech responses, the child must also learn the appropriate situations for each response. In Skinner's terminology, verbal behavior must come under environmental stimulus control. For instance, when the child first says **Daddy** or an approximation of that word, he is likely to be rewarded, whether or not his father is present. The response **Daddy** is therefore likely to be made in the presence of many different men; it is not yet under specific "stimulus control." Soon the child finds that he is reinforced when he uses this response when his father is there, but he will not be reinforced for the overgeneralized response. Thus, the response comes under the precise control of an environmental stimulus, the father.

Critique of Skinner's theory Skinner's approach—and reinforcement theory in general—has not had much influence on the investigation of language development. For many reasons, professional linguists and psycholinguists who study the origins and development of language find S-R learning theory grossly inadequate in explaining language acquisition. This kind of theory, they maintain, takes no account of the contribution of the child to language learning and performance. Rather, the child is regarded as a hollow organism who responds only to external stimulation and reinforcement.

Psycholinguists believe that language is generally acquired without the kinds of reinforcement that Skinner considers necessary. Furthermore, they assert, no reinforcement theory could fully explain the amazingly rapid development of the child's comprehension and use of language or his early mastery of grammatical (syntactic) rules. "Psychological learning theories are constructed to deal with associations of stimuli and responses but what the child acquires in the course of language development is not a collection of S-R connections, but a complex . . . rule system . . . [rules that enable him to generate sentences]" (**38**, 56). As we shall see in great detail shortly, from the very start of sentence-making, babies use appropriate word order, that is, they follow a grammatical rule. If the 18-month-old observes his father going out of the house, he says "Daddy go"; he would never say "Go Daddy."

Social Learning, Imitation, and Language

A less traditional learning approach that does not require reinforcement as an explanatory concept is suggested by social learning theorists, like Albert Bandura, who maintain that much of what the child learns is a result of observation and imitation of a model's behavior, in many cases, without reinforcement. Their research provides substantial evidence that modeling is highly influential in the development of children's social response patterns (see p. 375). Certainly, children cannot acquire vocabulary and grammatical structures without exposure to models. Children listen to language all around them and, even if they do not imitate speech immediately, they are acquiring some information about the language from hearing others. Therefore, according to social learning theorists, some amount of modeling must be indispensable for language acquisition.

While imitation undoubtedly plays an important role in the growth of vocabulary and in learning some things about grammatical structure, social learning theory and imitation cannot explain the remarkable rate of language development. Furthermore, this kind of theory cannot account for a very important fact: children's language is highly **creative.** Careful observers of children's speech point out that, from very early on, children understand novel sentences and, more importantly, construct completely new sentences—sentences they have not heard before and therefore could not be imitations of adult speech, but which are, nevertheless, acceptable as sentences in their own language.

It is interesting to note that in some recent research conducted within the framework of social learning theory the investigators failed to alter young children's grammar—specifically the use of passives and certain prepositions—through modeling. They found no evidence that brief exposure to verbal modeling cues alone had any effect, although modeling **plus** reinforcement did have the effect of increasing the use of these grammatical forms (3).

In a thorough critique of Skinner's **Verbal Behavior,** Chomsky makes some cogent statements that are applicable to all learning theory approaches to language development.

> It is simply not true that children can learn language only through "meticulous care" on the part of adults who shape their verbal repertoire through careful differential reinforcement. . . . It is common observation that a young child of immigrant parents may learn a second language in the streets, from other children, with amazing rapidity, and that his speech may be completely fluent and correct. . . . A child may pick up a large part of his vocabulary and "feel" for sentence structure from television, from reading, from listening to adults, etc. Even a very young child . . . may imitate a word quite well on an early try, with no attempt on the part of his parents to teach it to him. It is also perfectly obvious that, at a later stage, a child will be able to construct and understand utterances which are quite new, and are, at the same time, acceptable sentences in his language. . . . There must be fundamental processes at work quite independently of "feedback" from the environment. [There is] no support whatsoever for the doctrine of Skinner and others that slow and careful shaping of verbal behavior through differential reinforcement is an absolute necessity. . . . (12, 52).

Chomsky's Theory

While it cannot be denied that reinforcement and imitation must play some role in language acquisition, they cannot fully explain the process. Chomsky maintains that something more is needed: the child must have the ability to process the language data he hears from others (input) and to make inferences from these data about correct, acceptable, grammatical forms. In his critique of Skinner's book, he notes:

> As far as acquisition of language is concerned, it seems clear that reinforcement, casual observation, and natural inquisitiveness (coupled with a strong tendency to imitate) are important factors, as is the remarkable capacity of the child to generalize, hypothesize, and "process information" in a variety of very special and apparently highly complex ways which we cannot yet describe or begin to understand. . . . and which may be largely innate, or may develop through some sort of learning or through maturation of the nervous system. The manner in which such factors operate and interact in language acquisition is completely unknown (12, 52).

Chomsky suggests that humans possess a kind of built-in system, which he calls language acquisition device (LAD), a structure that is somehow prewired in such a way that it enables the child to process language, to construct rules, and to understand and produce appropriate, grammatical speech. The device is not actually an organ, of course, but merely an analogy. Here is a diagram of the model.

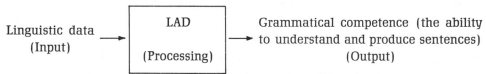

Linguistic data (Input) → LAD (Processing) → Grammatical competence (the ability to understand and produce sentences) (Output)

The device somehow—by the use of some complex means that are not understood —processes linguistic input to the child (the language he hears around him) and constructs a theory about the rules of grammar of the input language. This enables him to understand sentences he hears and to generate new ones. Of course, the LAD must be universally applicable and able to acquire any language.

To summarize, we have briefly reviewed three theories of language acquisition —S-R, social learning, and the "innate mechanism" theory of Chomsky—theories about how children acquire the ability to speak sentences and to communicate their meanings and thoughts. None of the three is completely satisfactory, but Chomsky's has proven the most stimulating and influential to psycholinguists.

Neural Bases of Language

Many psycholinguists have found Chomsky's theory of language acquisition very appealing and have conducted fascinating research that yields data partially supportive of this theory. Their work has brought new vigor and excitement to the problem of language development, as we shall see when we review the findings of psycholinguistic research below.

First, let us turn our attention to neurological evidence that humans have some sort of built-in language processing mechanism. There is a universality and regularity of trends in sound production and in the use of language that suggests that early linguistic development is dependent primarily on maturation and changes in neuromuscular systems. Indeed, neurological research shows that language acquisition is related to increasing specialization in neural structure and functioning, particularly the emergence of **cerebral dominance** or **laterality** of function in the brain.

The brain has two hemispheres and speech is usually more completely represented in the left one; for most people, this region, rather than the right hemisphere is usually dominant in speech, regardless of whether the individual is right- or left-handed. This dominance is not well established in the young child, however. For instance, a newborn or infant with a damaged left hemisphere develops language normally with the right hemisphere. With increasing age, the nervous system becomes less plastic, left hemisphere dominance becomes firmer, and the ability to recover from damage to that hemisphere declines. If a two- or three-year-old suffers damage to the left hemisphere, he loses language to some degree but, since his nervous system is still relatively plastic, he generally recovers quickly with the right hemisphere. Beyond adolescence, however, recovery is likely to be limited or absent; the degree of recovery is correlated with the firmness of cerebral dominance before injury. Specialization in neural structure and functioning, reflected in cerebral dominance, develops and stabilizes after the process of language acquisition has been initiated or sometimes even completed.

The specific cerebral areas involved in symbolic speech were discovered by neurologists working with patients who had lost all or part of their ability to use speech. More information comes from studies in which areas of the cortex are directly stimulated. Damage to **Broca's area,** the anterior speech region of the frontal lobe of the left hemisphere, results in difficulties in **motor speech,** that is, in vocalization and articulation. Destruction or damage in the posterior part of the speech area of the left hemisphere, called **Wernicke's area,** leads to disturbance in the comprehension of speech. Direct stimulation applied to either of these areas produces **aphasic** speech—defects in symbolic speech, such as use of inappropriate words or inability to recall words and names of things.

THE BEGINNINGS OF SPEECH

Early Vocalization

The raw materials of spoken language are elementary sounds or phonemes—the basic vowel and consonant sounds that correspond roughly to the letters of the alphabet. During the first few months, infants vocalize a limited number of sounds including **k, g, x, i** (as in bit), and **u** (as in but). During the so-called babbling period, which begins at about 6 months, many sounds are added and these occur in complex combinations; in fact, during this stage, they produce all the sounds that form the basis of all languages including German gutterals, French trills, and Hebrew **ch** sounds. The early babbling of an Indonesian baby cannot be distinguished from that of a Russian or English infant.

The range of babbled sounds narrows at 9 or 10 months. The baby seems to stop vocal play and concentrates on the elementary sounds that will appear in his first words. It would seem plausible that these sounds are the building blocks of spoken language, but psycholinguists do not believe that they are, because these early vocalizations are not related to structured language.

Regardless of the language to which the infant is exposed, his earliest meaningful sounds are consonants, produced with the tongue in the front of the mouth, such as **p, m, b,** and **t,** and back vowels, produced with the tongue in the back of the mouth, such as **e** or **a.** An English child says **tut** before **cut,** Swedish children say **ta-ta** before **ka-ka,** and Japanese children say **ta** before **ka** (**33**). The early appearance of **m** and **p** in speech sounds may be the reason that **mama** and **papa** are among the first words acquired by all children.

While there are marked individual differences, the average American child says his first word sometime around the end of the first year. Since much of the child's early babbling consists of repetitions of identical or similar syllables, his first word uttered is usually reduplicated monosyllables such as **mama, dada,** or **bye-bye.**

Characteristics of Early Speech

Language acquisition begins with what has been called **holophrastic** or **syncretic speech,** single word utterances which may express complex intentions and meanings (**33**). These very first words, spoken around the end of the first year, are generally labels for persons, objects, or acts, but the child soon begins to use single words to stand for entire sentences, naming an object, describing an action, serving as an imperative or a request, or, with the proper intonation, expressing an emotional state. Thus, the single word "ball" may mean "That is a ball," "I am throwing the ball," "Give me the ball," or spoken while crying, "Help! I dropped the ball and can't reach it."

Children begin to combine words at 18 to 24 months, beginning with such simple "sentences" as "See doggie," "Where Daddy," "Allgone shoe," "Make cake," "More car" (meaning "drive around some more"). Yet most children acquire the syntax (rules of grammar) of their own language almost completely by age 48 to 60 months. Consider the enormous contrast between these two-word sentences of the 18-month-old and the completeness and complexity of the following sentences taken from transcriptions of discussions with two 4-year-old black girls from ghetto neighborhoods: "My momma told us to walk home when church was over. And I walked all the way." "One time I dream about when I was being bad when it was dark time. I dreamed down at the garage and then I dreamed back up in the bed.

Then I dreamed under my dining room table about something coming walking with some green socks and it was saying 'Brenda' and then it was a devil." In other words, in the short period of approximately 30 months, a child progresses from the primitive combination of two words to near-mastery of the complex system of grammar of his own language. This is an enormous intellectual achievement and it seems to occur regardless of the language acquired or of the circumstances under which it is acquired.

> . . . . Such massive regularities of development remind one more of the maturation of a physical process, say, walking, than of a process of education, say, reading. One might even say that children cannot help learning a language, whereas they can easily avoid learning to read.
>
> The acquisition of language thus shows some of the characteristics of physical maturation. Yet, at the same time, it is obvious that language is learned. Without certain linguistic experiences children acquire no language at all—as in the case of congenitally deaf or criminally neglected children (33, 1062).

Psycholinguistic Research Methods

In order to understand what psycholinguists have learned about language development, we must know something about how they do their work. Their basic data are meticulously detailed recordings of young children's spontaneous speech starting at the time that they are just beginning to string words together. In the best known and most thorough of such psycholinguistic studies, Professor Roger Brown of Harvard and his colleagues have conducted a longitudinal study of the development of grammar in three preschool children: Adam, the son of a minister, Eve, the daughter of a graduate student, and Sarah, the daughter of a clerk. The principal data were transcriptions of the spontaneous speech of the child and his mother in conversation at home, and for each child there were at least two hours of speech for every month that he was studied. We have learned a great deal about language development from detailed analyses of these data and from other, independently collected samples of children's speech or speech diaries, as well as from experimental studies of speech.

Children vary greatly in rate of language development, so chronological age is a poor index of linguistic level. According to Brown, the best index of language level during the early period is **mean length of utterance** (MLU) in morphemes (the average number of morphemes used in utterances) and this is the criterion of language level that he and his colleagues used. When speech begins all utterances are single words—"ball," "baby"—and MLU is therefore 1.0 morpheme. As soon as the child begins to combine words, this value rises. For example, the following four utterances contain an average of 1.75 morphemes, so they yield a MLU of 1.75: "Baby walk" (2 morphemes), "Ball" (1 morpheme), "See mama" (2 morphemes), "Baby ball" (2 morphemes). Five stages of early linguistic development were designated, spanning the range from MLU = 1.75 morphemes to the time when MLU = 4.0 morphemes.

Fig. 6.1 shows the curves of linguistic development of the three children through the five stages (10). The curves begin at different points because the children were not of the same chronological age when the study began, although they were at roughly the same linguistic developmental level. Chronologically, Eve was 18 months old, Adam and Sarah were 27 months. Clearly there are marked individual differences in rate of linguistic development. Among the three children, Eve progressed most rapidly and Adam was ahead of Sarah.

In investigating syntactic and semantic development, the researcher needs to attend both to acceptable sentences and to errors—errors of commission as well as

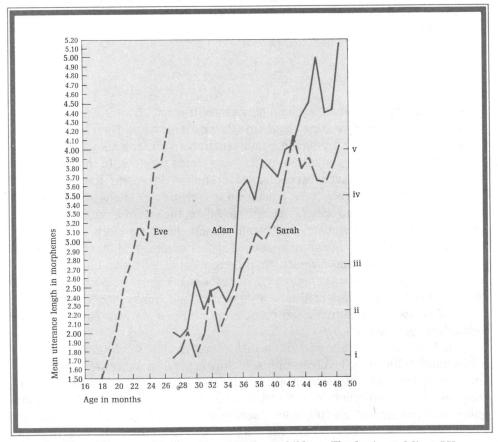

Figure 6.1 Mean utterance length and age in three children. The horizontal lines I-V represent the boundaries of the five stages designated by Brown and his associates. (From R. Brown, C. Cazden, & U. Bellugi-Klima, The child's grammar from I to III. In J. P. Hill [Ed.], **Minnesota Symposia on Child Psychology.** Vol. 2. Minneapolis: University of Minnesota Press, 1969. P. 29.)

omission. If a 2-year-old comments, "Birdies flied away," he reveals that he knows some grammatical rules about word order and forming a past tense by adding **ed,** even though he overgeneralized the rule in this case and added **ed** to a verb that is irregular, an exception to the general rule.

It should be clear from the outset that this and other psycholinguistic research focuses on the **production** of sentences. From the beginning, children give evidence of greater **comprehension,** that is, they understand much more than they can produce. For example, they understand questions, negative statements, and commands, although they can't produce them because they still lack adequate vocabulary and the transformational rules necessary to develop the surface structures expressing them.

First Sentences

As we noted, children begin putting two words together to make simple sentences at about 18 to 24 months of age, on the average. These early sentences are **abbreviated** or **telegraphic** versions of adult sentences ("Where hat?" "Throw ball."). The sentences the child creates are like telegrams in that they are largely made up of nouns and verbs with a few adjectives and generally do not use so-called **functors** —prepositions (for example, in, on, under), conjunctions (and, but, or) articles (a, the), auxiliary verbs (have, has, did), copular verbs (am, is, are, was, were), and inflections (endings to indicate plurals, such as dog**s**, or past or progressive tenses, walk**ed,** walk**ing**).

The adjective telegraphic characterizes the imitative, as well as the spontaneous speech of young children. If you ask a child between 2 and 3 to imitate a simple sentence such as "I can see a cow," he is likely to respond with "See cow" or "I see cow." He omits words, particularly functors, but he does not confuse order; he preserves the word order of the model. This suggests that "the model sentence is processed by the child as some kind of construction and not simply as a list of words" **(8).** At this stage, the child has only limited capacity for processing; hence, he produces only a few words, but these are the most important ones.

Even the child's first two-word "sentences" almost always manifest systematic regularity of word order; from the very start the English-speaking child expresses the basic grammatical relations of subject of the sentence, predicate, and object of the verb. Apparently the baby possesses a simple set of rules for formulating sentences and he puts the subject and object in their appropriate positions (for example, "I getting ball"). There are very few exceptions to well-ordered sentences even at the earliest stage of linguistic development, Stage I in the terminology of Brown and his colleagues.

When children begin to produce strings of more than two words, their sentences become more complex and take on a **hierarchical structure,** that is, they can be analyzed in terms of constituents and subunits. For instance, a child may begin a short sentence and then expand it immediately with a longer sentence, as though he first prepared one component and then "plugged it in" to a more complex sentence. Here are some examples: "Hit ball . . . Jeff hit ball." "Go car . . . Jeff go car."

A little later, the child may expand his sentences into more complex forms: "Sit down . . . Jeff sit down . . . Jeff sit down [pause] chair." Here he seems to have analyzed his sentence into its major grammatical units: subject ("Jeff"); predicate ("sit down chair"); and the predicate is further divided into verb ("sit down") and adverb ("chair," meaning the adverbial phrase "in the chair"). Thus his sentence clearly expresses several grammatical relationships.

> The child's hesitations also provide evidence of his analysis of sentences into units. For example, Brown and Bellugi (9) note the following sort of sentence as evidence that noun phrases function as units in the child speech: "Put . . . the red hat . . . on." In this utterance, "the red hat" seems to function as a single unit which can be placed between the two parts of the verb "put on." It is important to note that hesitations do not tend to occur at other locations in such sentences. For example, Brown and Bellugi report the absence of such utterances as "Put the red . . . hat on" or "Put the . . . red hat on." That is, the noun phrase seems to be maintained as an uninterrupted entity.

> Sentences, then, are not mere strings of words but hierarchies of units organized according to grammatical principles. The child apparently operates on these basic and universal principles even when composing short, idiosyncratic childish utterances (38, 48).

Semantics of Early Speech

Syntactic analysis of a young child's speech gives us no information about the meaning or semantic intention of what he says. Yet it is obvious that in their two- and three-word sentences, youngsters intend to communicate some meaning. The evidence for this is the remarkable consistency with which normal word order is preserved in very early sentences and, in addition, the context in which the utterance is made. The sequential order of words in sentences is almost always correct for the meanings that must be intended, as judged by the context. There are very few violations of normal word order in the early sentences of Brown's young subjects speaking American English.

The early telegraphic sentences of children in all cultures are intended to express a broad range of meanings. Analysis of many samples of early speech, taken from children speaking widely different languages—English, German, Russian, Finnish, Turkish, and Luo (spoken in Kenya)—indicates that "there is a striking uniformity across children and across languages in the kinds of meanings expressed in simple two-word utterances, suggesting that semantic development is closely tied to general cognitive development" (39, 199).

The following range of semantic relations is typical of early speech.

Identification:	**see doggie**
Location:	**book there**
Repetition:	**more milk**
Nonexistence:	**allgone thing**
Negation:	**not wolf**
Possession:	**my candy**
Attribution:	**big car**
Agent-Action:	**mama walk**
Action-Object:	**hit you**
Agent-Object:	**mama book**
Action-Location:	**sit chair**
Action-Recipient:	**give papa**
Action-Instrument:	**cut knife**
Question:	**where ball? (39)**

Even at Stage I, the first stage of linguistic development, children ask questions, but the form of the question is likely to be a statement spoken with a questioning interrogation (Mommie hat?) The subject and verb order characteristic of adult questions (Who has the pencil?) does not appear until later on. Questions about the name or location of referents (What's that? and Where doggie go?) are frequent and the forms do not vary with the number of objects (singular or plural) or with animate or inanimate referents ("Who's this?" might refer to an inanimate object). Many Stage I utterances in all languages have an imperative or commanding nature; they are intended to induce someone to take a certain action.

Speech in Stage II

Stage II in the analyses of language development by Brown and his colleagues is the interval extending from mean length of utterance of 2.00, the upper limit of Stage I, to a mean length of utterance of 2.5. As language develops further and the child's sentences become longer and more complex, a set of little words and word endings (inflections) begin to appear in spontaneous speech: a few prepositions, especially **in** and **on;** an occasional article such as **an;** forms of the copular, such as **is** or **are;** plural and possessive endings on the nouns; and some verb tense inflections such as the progressive (**ing**) and past (**ed**).

These words and inflections, called grammatical morphemes, are not all acquired simultaneously; the child's use of these morphemes improves gradually over a period of two to three years. However, even a year or two after they first use these forms, children do not use all of them perfectly. There may be a considerable period of time between the first appearance of any particular morpheme and the time that it is always supplied where it is grammatically required; "per-

formance does not abruptly pass from total absence to reliable presence" (**8,** 257).
For instance, Brown's subject Sarah added the progressive **ing** ending in half the
instances where it was required when she was 30 months old, but she did not
supply this ending all the time until 16 months later.

Children vary in their rate of acquisition of these forms but the **order** of acquisition is remarkably uniform. For example, all three of Brown's subjects achieved
mastery, or near mastery, of the present progressive **ing** form for verbs, the prepositions **in** and **on,** and plural forms of nouns before they properly used regular and
irregular past tenses and, after that, auxiliary verbs such as **is, was, were.** This degree of constancy is amazing because the basic data are samples of uncontrolled
spontaneous speech. The three children had quite different vocabularies; hence the
records of their speech contain quite different instances of the grammatical morphemes—for example, some plurals formed with **s** sounds (socks), some with **z**
sounds (shoes), others with **es** sounds (matches); **in** could be used in expressions
like "doggie **in** box" and "put it **in** dair." Yet, in spite of the great variety of ways
in which each grammatical morpheme was manifested, there was remarkable constancy in the order in which the morphemes were acquired.

In and **on,** referring to place, are the first prepositions learned and they were
always mastered together by Brown's three subjects. (Prepositional phrases indicating time—**in** June, **on** Wednesday—do not appear until later). This suggests an
early understanding of the semantic distinction between containment and support;
objects may be located in containers (in a box) or on supporting surfaces (on the
table). Again a principle or rule has been learned and, once learned, it is appropriately applied in all instances.

What accounts for the constancy of the order of acquisition of morphemes and
for the other regularities discovered? At present, there is no answer to this puzzling
question; we can only make hypotheses about factors that might be important.
Perhaps there are some built-in mechanisms that enable children to process what
they hear and somehow infer or construct the rules about the use of these forms.
One thing is certainly clear: the constancy of order of acquisition cannot be explained in simple terms. For example, it might be hypothesized that the forms acquired first are the ones used most frequently by the child's parents and, therefore,
most frequently heard by the child. Since Brown had data on the speech of both
children and parents, he was able to test this hypothesis by correlating the frequency of parental use of these morphemes with the children's order of acquisition. There was no correlation between the two, that is, no evidence that the frequency of parental use per se determines the order of the child's acquisition of
these morphemes. This does not necessarily mean that frequency of parental use
makes **no** contribution to the child's order of acquisition of morphemes; it is at
least theoretically possible that this factor, in combination with others, has a significant effect.

Such other possible factors include: **perceptual salience** of the form, that is, does it have some distinctive or attention-getting perceptual qualities, such as greater intensity; **information value,** that is, is the form really necessary to communicate meaning or intention or is it redundant? It is possible that ·the earliest acquired grammatical morphemes are those that are used frequently by parents and also possess distinctive perceptual qualities and/or great information value. Other hypotheses about the effects of combinations of such factors could, of course, be formulated. Some factor, or set of factors, in the child's linguistic environment **must** influence this order of acquisition of grammatical forms. In the present state of our knowledge, however, no one has been able to delineate these factors.

Surprisingly, no specific parental training procedures have been proven to facilitate the acquisition of grammatical knowledge, either. As they interact with their young children, parents often "model" the language by presenting examples of well-formed speech and, frequently, they expand a child's telegraphic sentences by filling in missing functors. For instance, if the child says "Nancy walk," her mother is likely to respond, "Yes, Nancy is going for a walk." Such expansions provide the child with some relevant data from which he can derive some general grammatical rules. Moreover, expansions are given at the ideal time, right after the child has made some statement.

Yet an experimental test yielded no evidence that either expansion or modeling were effective techniques for increasing the child's grammatical knowledge. In the experiment, one group of black children under 3½ years received 40 minutes of intensive and deliberate expansion every school day for three months, while a comparable group was exposed to an equal amount of modeling of well-formed sentences that were not expansions. A control group of children received no special treatment. At the end of the experiment the expansion group did not differ from the control group in any of the measures of linguistic competence used. Modeling was found to have some slight, but not marked, effects on grammatical competence.

Reward and punishment, approval and disapproval, have not been found to be effective means of teaching grammar to young children (see also pp. 237 ff). Brown and his colleagues examined instances of the mother's approving reactions to her child's utterances ("That's right" or "Very good") and signs of disapproval ("That's wrong" or "No").

> Most commonly . . . the grounds on which an utterance was approved or disapproved . . . were not strictly linguistic at all. When Eve expressed the opinion that her mother was a girl by saying **He a girl,** her mother answered **That's right.** The child's utterance was ungrammatical, but her mother did not respond to that fact; instead, she responded to the truth of the proposition the child intended to express. In general, the parents fitted propositions to the child's utterances, however incomplete or distorted the utterances, and then approved or not according to the correspondence between proposition and reality. Thus, **Her curl my hair** was approved because the mother was, in fact, curling Eve's hair. However, Sarah's grammatically impeccable **There's the**

animal farmhouse was disapproved because the building was a lighthouse, and Adam's **Walt Disney comes on on Tuesday** was disapproved because Walt Disney came on on some other day. It seems, then, to be truth value rather than syntactic well-formedness that chiefly governs explicit verbal reinforcement by parents—which renders mildly paradoxical the fact that the usual product of such a training schedule is an adult whose speech is highly grammatical but not notably truthful (**10,** 70).

The evidence, then, does not support the hypotheses that expansions or approval have any marked effect on the development of grammatical competence. Yet, the child's linguistic environment must supply him with basic linguistic data —the input—from which he derives grammatical knowledge, a system of rules for generating sentences. Unfortunately, however, the data presently available do not enable us to state what aspects of that environment or what kinds of training facilitate the acquisition of this competence.

How then can we explain the constancy of order of acquisition of grammatical morphemes or knowledge of the rules of grammar? Certainly not on the basis of any environmental variables studied. Brown suggests that grammatical or semantic complexity may be a critical factor. On a semantic level, some forms have simple and straightforward functional meanings; for example, the use of plurals refers to number only and a simple, irregular past tense, such as **went,** means only that something happened earlier. Other forms, such as the copular **were,** are more complex since they presuppose two other meanings, plurality and earliness. Brown found a significant correlation between complexity and order of acquisition. Thus, the more complex form, **were,** is acquired later than either noun plurals or past irregular verbs. This suggests that the child's grammatical competence is closely linked with his cognitive and intellectual capacities. As the latter increase, the child can learn and use more complex rules appropriately.

Language "Universals"

Most of the findings we have discussed were based on data on American English-speaking children. Can we generalize from these findings? Are there "universals of language development," that is, "similar developmental processes in different sorts of languages?" (**40,** 176). Another prominent psycholinguist, Professor Dan Slobin, asked "is it possible . . . to trace out a universal course of linguistic development on the basis of what we know about the course of cognitive development?" (**40,** 180). For example, one of the earliest semantic relationships expressed in English is that of action (verb) and object (predicate noun), as in **throw ball.** The action-object relationship in English is marked by consistent word order and even the earliest sentences of English-speaking children reflect this word order. In some other languages an inflection (prefix or ending) is used to mark (specify) the object of action. Among children learning such languages, this inflection emerges very early. Thus, among the Luo-speaking children in Kenya, the first inflections acquired are subject and object endings on verbs. Findings such as these offer support for the notion that the first linguistic forms to appear in the child's speech are those that express meanings consistent with the child's level of cognitive development (**40, 181**).

What a child wants to communicate is clearly related to his cognitive level, that is, to his understanding of the world and of the relationships among objects and events in it. But "cognitive development and linguistic development do not run off in unison. The child must find linguistic means to express his intentions" (**40, 182**). But the forms used to express a particular meaning vary from language to language. In some languages a form, for example, the one used to express noun plurals, is simple and easy to learn, while in other languages the corresponding form is complex, difficult to learn, and therefore acquired late. For example, American and Egyptian children probably understand the meaning of plurals at the same time, but the linguistic performance of the two groups, with respect to plurals, differs greatly. Noun plurals are relatively simple in English and are acquired early by English-speaking children, but noun plurals in Arabic have extremely complex forms and are the last aspect of that language to be mastered.

A more compelling example of the influence of grammatical complexity is found in data on young bi-lingual children who speak Serbo-Croatian and Hungarian. These children are able to express directions and positions like **into, out of,** and **on top of** in Hungarian long before they can express these locations in Serbo-Croatian, which has a much more complex form of linguistic structure. Obviously, these children understand the meanings of direction and position, for they can express them in grammatically acceptable ways in one of their languages, although not in the other, more complex, one.

Slobin made comparisons of the grammatical forms for expressing meanings such as the location and position of objects, direction, and plurals in English, Finnish, Serbo-Croatian, and many other languages. He also studied the order of acquisition of these forms by children speaking the various languages. From these analyses, he derived some generalizations or universals about early speech. From these universals, he made some inferences about the **operating principles** or strategies that children might use in processing and understanding linguistic information and in producing grammatical sentences. A few examples illustrate some possible universals and operating principles (**39**).

Consider the acquisition of locative markers such as **in, on, at,** the morphemes that indicate place and position. Children learning languages in which locative markers occur after a verb or noun acquire these forms earlier and more easily than children learning languages in which locatives are placed before verbs or nouns. The developmental universal derived, is: **Locative markers occurring after**

nouns and verbs are acquired earlier than locative markers placed before nouns and verbs. This may be the result of the young child's applying the operating principle of paying close attention to the ends of words as he receives (and processes) linguistic input and searches for cues to meaning.

This may be one of the first operating principles employed in the acquisition of grammar, and it may account for another "universal of language development": **Grammatical expressions of intentions or meanings that are expressed by "endings or suffixes are acquired earlier than those that are in the form of prefixes or prepositions"** (40, 192).

Another early and pervasive operating principle in language acquisition states: **"Pay attention to the order of words and morphemes."** Related to this is another universal: **"Word order in child speech reflects word order in the input language"** (40, 197).

Support for these principles comes from examination of word order in children's sentences and in sentence imitation in different languages. In the English and Samoan languages, word order is fixed; German, Slavic languages, Finnish, and Turkish permit more flexibility of word order. Young children beginning to speak English or Samoan almost always use consistent word orders—for example, the subject of the sentence precedes the verb—while those learning German, Russian, or Turkish do not. Furthermore, when imitating sentences in their own language, English-speaking children retain standard word order, while children who speak Slavic languages frequently change the order of words. Apparently even very young children make inferences about whether or not their own language requires a fixed order of words in a sentence. If it does, he will use this fixed order in his own speech and in imitations. If it does not, he knows that he can change the order of words in his own sentences and he does so.

These are only a small sample of the kinds of operating principles and universals that may be operating in language acquisition. Our understanding of the principles underlying this process is still frankly sketchy; there are undoubtedly a vast number of other cognitive factors and principles operative in processing and producing sentences. Only a few of these can be specified at present. Slobin's work is merely a beginning, "an outline of what someday may evolve into a model of the order of acquisition of linguistic structures" (40, 208). Nevertheless, the approach is very stimulating and it promises to help clarify the relationships between cognitive and linguistic development.

Semantic Development

So far we have centered our attention largely on psycholinguistic research and theory focused on the development of syntax and the relationship between syntax and semantics. Recently psycholinguists have become more concerned with se-

mantic development, with the acquisition of meaning, the problems of how "words are used to **refer** to or represent external objects and events appropriately" (**14,** 65).

By the time he is 2, the average child has an effective vocabulary (words he can use or understand) of over 300 words and, by the time he is 3, this has increased to about 1000. Between the ages of 3 and 5, the child adds over 50 words to his vocabulary each month, on the average. As we would expect, the young child's vocabulary is generally more concrete than the adult's; he has relatively few abstractions or superordinate words such as **action, article, quality,** all of which are common in adult speech (**5**). It could be argued, however, that even though the words seem concrete, they are actually used by the child in rather general ways. One linguist, Eve Clark, maintains that the meanings the child assigns to many of his first words are **overextensions** or **overgeneralizations,** that is, his definitions are broader than the adult's (**14**). For example, he may say "doggie" not only when he refers to dogs, but also when he means cats, cows, horses, rabbits, or other four-legged animals. According to Clark, this kind of overextension reflects the child's tendency to define his terms on the basis of only one or two perceptual features of the stimulus, such as four-leggedness or movement. The adult's definition, in contrast, is likely to be based on a combination of many features. The child narrows down the meaning of his overextended definition as new words are introduced into his vocabulariy and take over parts of the definition. For instance, when the child learns the word **cow,** he adds features like moo-sounds and horns to the criteria four-legged and movement; he can separate the meaning of **cow** from the meaning of **dog** (**14**).

Clark's hypothesis that meanings are originally overextended and gradually narrow down or become differentiated certainly seems plausible; there are undoubtedly many instances of overgeneralizations in the child's early vocabulary. But, as a recent study showed, there are also many instances of **underextension, overdifferentiation,** or **overdiscrimination** (defining words more narrowly than adults do) in young children's use of words. Between the ages of 2½ and 6, both overextension and underextension errors are common (**1**). There are at least two sources of underextension errors. One is failure to include instances in a class because they are unfamiliar and perceptually different from a "typical" instance of the concept; for example, some children did not include praying mantis and worm in the category animal or caviar in the category food. There are also cases in which familiar objects are not considered instances of a general class; for instance, some subjects said, in response to a picture of a dog, "That's a dog, not an animal" (**1**).

With increasing maturity and experience, the child's definitions of words begin to approximate the adult's more closely. Youngsters of preschool age often seem to interpret pairs of antonyms such as **more** and **less, same** and **different, before** and **after** as though the two members of the pair were synonyms, reacting to each member of a pair in the same way. By the time they are 5, however, most children use these opposites as adults do (**15**).

Language Development During the School Years

As we have seen, an impressive amount of data indicates that the young child makes dramatic progress in grammatical competence and semantic knowledge between the time he begins to use two-word sentences, at approximately age 18 months, and the ages of 4 or 5. Within a period of roughly 30 months, he essentially achieves mastery of the exceedingly complex structure of his native language, and this is reflected both in comprehension and production of sentences. In 1963 a psycholinguist maintained that "all the basic structure used by adults to generate their sentences can be found in the grammar of nursery school children" (**34**, 419). This statement seems too strong in the light of recent research which suggests that the child makes important syntactic and semantic advances long after the nursery school years.

A number of important aspects of grammar are only incompletely developed between the ages of 5 and 7 and are not always used appropriately until later. These include the use of **have** as an auxiliary, nominalization (using a verb as a noun as in "Walking is good exercise"), and use of conjunctions with **if** and **so.** In addition, there are some forms used only by children and not by adults; for example, the kind of redundancy manifested in "She picked it up the penny."

While 6-year-olds understand sentences in which the subjects of the deep and surface structures are the same, they have difficulty in comprehending sentences in which the deep and surface structure subjects are not congruent. For example, in the sentence "Lucy was sure to see," Lucy is the subject of both deep and surface structure. However, in "Lucy was impossible to see," Lucy is the object in the deep structure "It was impossible to see Lucy." The children's errors indicate that the difficulty with sentences in this form occurs in the assignment of the incorrect subject to the infinitive verb. From the age of 9, however, children have little difficulty comprehending these statements, and there appears to be an orderly sequence of stages in the acquisition of sentences of this type (**26**).

Comprehension of passive forms, such as "The cart is pulled by the horse," also develops relatively late. Five-year-old children are just beginning to comprehend this construction and almost never use the passive in their own spontaneous speech. When children were presented pictures and encouraged by an experimenter to describe them with passive sentences by focusing attention upon the acted-upon object rather than on the actor, young children did not use the passive form. Not until about the age of 7 could children be induced to give more than 50 percent passive sentences, even after an example was given and the acted-upon object was shown first in the picture. Even then, those who used the passive form tended to be advanced in linguistic ability as shown by independent measures (**43**).

Longitudinal study of language development demonstrates that during the years from kindergarten to ninth grade, speech performance improves, syntax becomes more complete, and children use a greater variety of grammatical patterns and great variation in a structure within sentences, that is, their vocabulary and ordering of words and phrases show greater variety. Written and spoken sentences increase markedly in length and grammatical complexity during this period (**31**). The overall results from several studies indicate that there is a general but gradual consolidation of language skills from kindergarten to the seventh grade, but there are also some abrupt shifts in performance. "Between kindergarten and first grade and between 5th grade and 7th grade are developmental periods when large increases in new grammatical constructions, or sudden increases in the use of constructions previously evidenced at low frequencies, and high error rates on some kinds of constructions, seem to occur" (**35, 416**).

On the semantic level also, children make great advances during the school years. Obviously they continue to add words to their vocabularies at a rapid rate, although many school children assign meanings to a substantial number of words that are quite different from adult definitions. For example, until the age of 8, children misinterpret the verb **ask,** responding to it as if it meant the same as **tell.** When instructed to "Tell X [another child] what to feed the doll," a child of this age will answer, correctly, "A banana." However, when she is told "Ask X what to feed the doll," the child is not likely to ask a question of the other child; instead she simply tells her, "A banana." As in other aspects of speech development, children pass through an orderly, invariant sequence in acquiring full adult comprehension of the words **ask** and **tell (11, 26).**

There are also changes in the use and production of connectives such as **because, therefore, but, although,** and **and,** as well as in the use of prepositions, during the elementary school years. Children's understanding of prepositions was tested in two ways: first, by presenting pictures and asking the child to "show me [the examiner] the girl **behind** the car," and, second, a preposition preference test that asked questions like "Which sounds better: He is holding the door to the lady, or He is holding the door for the lady?" Performance on the first measure improves steadily with age; only 73 percent of the responses of the 3- and 4-year-old children, but about 97 percent of the 10-year-olds', were correct. The greatest increase occurred between 5 and 6 years. Nursery school and kindergarten pupils performed at a chance level on the second test, but at the age of 6 performance jumped to a level that indicated full comprehension of the correct prepositional form (**20**).

Among first-graders words like **because, then,** and **therefore** express time relationships rather than causal ones, that is, all three words are used as if they were semantically synonymous with **then,** with no causal relations implied. At this age children show little comprehension of the meaning of the connectives **but** and **although,** although they occasionally used these words. Even sixth-graders often have little real understanding of the meanings of these words, although they are better than first-graders in recognizing when the words are appropriately used (**23**).

Piaget has pointed out that the meanings of complex relationship terms like

brother and **sister** develop gradually. At the earliest stage, the terms **brother** and **boy, sister** and **girl** may be treated as synonyms. When a 5-year-old was asked "What is a sister?" he replied, "A sister is a girl you know." At the next stage, the children recognize that the use of these terms requires other children in the family. One of Piaget's 9-year-old subjects defined **brother,** "When there is a boy and another boy, when there are two of them." Finally, children realize that **brother** refers to a reciprocal relationship among siblings in addition to sex and other siblings: "A brother is a relation, one brother to another." Apparently the first meanings assigned to kinship terms are derived from perceptual data; later, with increased cognitive development, the child adds social or functional criteria to the definitions (for example, having the same parents or living in the same house). The full, adult meaning of kinship terms includes perceived attributes and, in addition, cognitive factors, knowledge of social structure, roles, and relationships.

Double-function words—words such as **bright, hard, sweet, cold,** which have both physical and psychological meanings—are not understood until after the early years of elementary school (2). Before the age of 7 children apply these words properly only to physical objects, with the possible exception of **sweet,** but they do not believe that these words are applicable to people. Among 7- and 8-year-olds, about half the words are used appropriately to refer to people, although children this age cannot relate the physical meaning of the word to the psychological meaning. By 9 to 10 years of age, half of the children could use all the words in both the physical and psychological context, and they were able to indicate the relationship between the two uses. Eleven- and 12-year-olds showed marked progress in the comprehension of the double function of these words (2). "Children first master the object reference of double-function words and then the psychological sense of these terms as independent meanings, and finally, the dual or relational aspects of the words are acquired" (35, 424).

LANGUAGE AND COGNITION

Are functions like perception, learning, and memory affected by our linguistic capabilities? Does language influence thought, concept-formation, reasoning ability, and problem-solving? Does increased verbal ability enhance mental development? In short, are cognitive functions dependent on language?

These are ancient questions, but there are still no definitive answers. Verbal ability undoubtedly facilitates thinking and problem-solving, but not all cognitive processes are based on language. The child's facility in language increases by leaps and bounds between infancy and the ages of 3 or 4, and, at the same time, the child's cognitive abilities become radically altered (see pp. 309 ff); the 3- or 4-year-old learns, perceives, thinks, reasons, and solves problems in ways that are vastly different from those of the 1- or 2-year-old. However, many deaf children who are very deficient in language solve cognitive problems as well as hearing children do (see p. 260). Therefore, thought and problem-solving ability cannot be entirely dependent on language.

Actually, the issue of the relationship between language and thought and problem-solving is a controversial one. A number of Russian psychologists have maintained that language and thought are closely linked in early childhood, but that, in the course of development, thinking becomes freer of language—at least free of overt speech responses. For example, Luria, a distinguished contemporary Russian psychologist, believes that "in the early stages of child development, speech is only a means of communication with adults and other children. . . . Subsequently it becomes also a means whereby he organizes his experience and regulates his own actions. So the child's activity is mediated through words" (32, 116).

Luria made one fundamental generalization: as the child matures his own speech becomes more powerful in controlling his behavior and at the same time the child shifts from loud, overt speech to covert, primarily internal, subvocal speech.

Advances in language pave the way for progress in complex learning, concept-formation, thinking, reasoning, and problem-solving. These high-level cognitive activities are considerably enhanced by verbal mediation or mediated generalization, and this, in turn, is closely linked to the acquisition of language.

Verbal Mediation

When the child can use speech efficiently for self-instruction, words become mediators of actions. What is a mediator or mediated response? According to Kendler, it "is a response, or a series of responses, which intercedes between the external stimulus and the overt response to provide stimulation that influnces [the] eventual course of behavior. These responses may be overt, but they are usually presumed to be covert" (25, 34).

In mediated generalization, the child may apply the same label to two or more objects and, consequently, react to the objects in the same way. For example, the 4-year-old child has learned to apply the word **candy** to certain stimuli. Because candy stands for something good to eat, he is apt to behave in a predictable way toward all things he labels candy. When an adult introduces a new object the child has never seen and says, "Have a piece of candy," the child will transfer the behavior he has learned for the word candy to this novel stimulus. In all probability he will take this new object and pop it into his mouth. Thus, mediated generalization is usually adaptive and allows the child to behave appropriately to new stimuli on first contact.

A number of excellent experimental studies suggest that verbal mediation is of major help in learning and problem-solving, but it is not essential (22). In transposition experiments, children learn to make choices on the basis of the relationships among stimuli rather than on the basis of their absolute qualities. For example, rewards are given for choosing the largest of three black squares. Later the children are presented with three new squares, the smallest of them being exactly the same size as the largest (rewarded) one in the previous trials. Young children, with limited language ability, find it very difficult to "transpose," that is, to learn to choose in terms of the relative sizes of the new stimuli. Instead, they continue, for many trials, to select the square that had been associated with rewards earlier, although it is the smallest—incorrect and unrewarded—stimulus in this phase of the experiment (27). Kindergarten children can tell themselves "It is the largest one," and respond accordingly, regardless of the absolute magnitude of the stimuli. In other words, they can use words (verbal mediators) and can thus learn transposition or relational problems without difficulty.

Language and Problem-Solving

Simple introspection provides ample evidence that language and labeling (verbal mediation) have a tremendous influence on the process of problem-solving. For example, a subject who is trying to copy a complex design from a model will find it easier to do if he has words and descriptive terms (labels) for the parts of the model; the task may be very difficult if he does not use adequate verbal labels.

In one Russian study, children were shown pictures of butterfly wings and instructed to match them with similar ones in a large sample. The matchings were to be made on a basis of the patterns of wing markings. The children at first found this task difficult and perplexing because they had trouble separating the pattern from the color of the wings. An experimental group was then given labels (the words for spots and stripes) to describe the various patterns, while a control group was not given any descriptive words. After they had learned these labels, the experimental group's performance in matching improved markedly. Even the younger members of the experimental group performed better than the older children of the control group (30). Clearly, attaching labels to these stimuli gave them some distinctiveness and the matching task then became easier.

Furthermore, if young children do not spontaneously use words or labels as mediators in solving cognitive problems, they can easily learn to do so with very little training. For example, in simple recall tests, children are first shown a series of pictures of objects (e.g., a vase, a spoon, a hammer); later they are presented with a large group of pictures and asked to pick out the ones that had been presented earlier. Some children spontaneously label the stimulus objects and rehearse the labels, so that they have relatively good recall. Those who do not spontaneously label the objects or rehearse their names do not do as well in recalling the stimuli, but they can learn to do these things with very little difficulty and with only brief training. After they have learned to rehearse labels, they recall much more (24).

Data such as these demonstrate that verbal labeling often facilitates memory, but they do not indicate that labeling is necessary for recalling events. In fact, a recent study shows that children are able to remember unfamiliar scenes and objects that they cannot lable. Guatemalan children 11 years of age, living in primitive, isolated farming villages, performed as well as urban American children of the same age in a recognition task involving many pictorial stimuli that were completely unfamiliar to them (for example, coasters, telescope, golf club). Clearly, the "representational structures" that these children used to mediate recognition were not dependent on the ability to apply appropriate verbal labels (22, 221).

More complex and difficult problems are also easier to solve if verbal mediators are used. In one experiment, one group of 9- and 10-year-olds was instructed to verbalize while trying to solve difficult problems (moving discs from one circle to another in the smallest number of moves); a control group, trying to solve the problems, did not have these instructions. Those who verbalized during practice solved the problems more quickly and efficiently than those who did not. The experimenters noted the verbalization during practice has the effect of making the subjects think of new reasons for their behavior and thus facilitated "both the discovery of general principles and their employment in solving successive problems" (18, 18).

Verbal mediation (attaching labels) can also help bridge time gaps, thus enhancing our ability to remember objects and events. Formulating verbal rules helps guide performance in reasoning and problem-solving. Nevertheless, we cannot state conclusively that language is necessary for memory, thought, or problem solution. For some children, other kinds of mediators such as images, pictorial representations, or nonverbal symbols may serve the same purpose that language or words do for verbal children. Furthermore, American deaf children who are very deficient in verbal skills and do not learn English until rather late in life perform as well as hearing children do in many intellectual tasks. They can solve difficult cognitive problems as well as children who can hear. The deaf child's cognitive development follows the same course as the hearing child's and they go through the same basic stages, though in some instances the rate of development may be slower. While the kinds of symbols used by the deaf are not known, "successful performance on these tasks [e.g., memory, reasoning, and learning problem-solving] by deaf persons implies an **efficient functioning of a symbolic system other than verbal**" (17, 160, bold type ours). In short, words and labels may be the most commonly used mediators in thinking and problem-solving, but they are not the only possible ones. "Versatile creatures that we are, other symbolic means are apparently exploited when language is denied us, as with the young deaf" (16, 17).

We do not really know the extent to which cognitive abilities, like memory, perception, abstraction, and problem-solving, depend on language. Some researchers in cognitive development, including Piaget and his coworkers, have concluded that language more often reflects, rather than determines, levels of cognitive development. Attempts have been made to accelerate the transition from one cognitive stage or level to another by teaching or training children new ways to talk about problems, tasks, and concepts. These efforts have not proven successful. Until children attain a certain cognitive level, verbal training alone cannot produce real understanding of the principles of logical thinking or of basic concepts such as conservation (the idea that certain properties of matter, such as volume or quantity, are invariant in spite of perceptible alterations in shape; see p. 310).

> Our general systematic conclusions with respect to the effects of language are straightforward. First, language training, among other types of training, operates to direct the child's interactions with the environment and thus to "focus" on relevant dimensions of task situations. Second, the observed changes in the justifications given [by children] for answers in the conservation task suggest that language does aid in the storage and retrieval of relevant information. However, our evidence offers little, if any, support for the contention that language learning per se contributes to the **integration and coordination** of "informational units" necessary for the achievement of the conservation concepts (**21,** 163).

CULTURAL INFLUENCES ON LANGUAGE

Social class differences in language and in verbal facility are apparent beginning early in life. From age 1 through age 5, middle- and upper-class children are superior to those of the lower class in all traditional measures of language ability: vocabulary scores, sentence structure, sound discrimination, and articulation (42). These well-documented differences seem to be attributable largely to the contrast between middle- and lower-class language environments. Do these findings have implications for class and cultural differences in cognitive functioning?

A number of years ago Basil Bernstein, an English educational sociologist, began to study what he called the **restricted language codes** of the lower class and **elaborated codes** or messages of the middle class. In dealing with her child, the lower-class mother uses short, simple, grammatically uncomplicated, and easily understood sentences, primarily denoting things and actions. According to Bernstein, lower-class communication codes "emphasize verbally the communal rather than the individual, the concrete rather than the abstract, the substance rather than the elaboration of processes, the here-and-now rather than exploration of motives and intentions . . ." (**4,** 29). In contrast, mothers in the middle class put great emphasis on the use of language in socializing and disciplining their children, teaching them moral standards, and communicating feelings and emotions. Therefore, the middle-class child becomes "oriented toward universalistic meanings which transcend a given context" (**4,** 28), while the lower-class child's statements are "closely tied to a given context and so do not transcend it" (**4,** 28).

As a result the lower-class child learns only the restricted code, Bernstein maintains, and is therefore more likely to have difficulty in school than the child who has acquired an elaborated code. The restricted code is relatively uncomplicated and rigid and contains few verbal differentiations of feelings and social relationships (although these are perceived and felt). And, according to Bernstein, the restricted code fosters more concrete, and less conceptual, thinking.

Bernstein's work has been severely criticized by a number of researchers in language development because he has not made the important distinction between language **performance** and language **competence;** he is measuring only performance. Other researchers believe that lower-class children may possess the basic competence for the elaborated code, but they do not ordinarily use this code because it is viewed as overly "fancy," effeminate, and too closely associated with school and the values it represents. They may feel that they must uphold the values of their own group, and this requires use of the "tough" and restricted code, even though they know and understand the elaborated code.

There is good evidence that poor boys are in fact competent in the elaborated code. An investigator asked lower-class boys to write two letters, an informal and a formal one. The informal one was to be written to "a close friend" and the boys were instructed to "write **naturally** to him in the way you would if this were a real letter" (**36,** 245). In writing the formal letter, the boys were to imagine that they were applying to a school official for funds to make a trip; only the writers of the best letters would be granted the necessary money. Under the conditions of the formal letter, "virtually no social class differences appeared" (**36,** 250).

> When a formal situation made it necessary for the children to use the elaborated code, they could do so; the necessary competence is available. When the children did not need to use the code, they often did not bother with it and instead reverted to other modes of speech. Thus, the performance of poor children—at least those in England—does not necessarily mirror their competence (**19, 74**).

These findings are particularly relevant to a discussion of a parallel problem in America: differences between the speech of American middle-class whites (standard English) and lower-class blacks (NNE for nonstandard Negro English or BEV for black English vernacular). Many poor, minority group children, particularly blacks, have difficulties with school subjects, such as reading, arithmetic, and English. They also perform poorly in tests of cognitive functions and intelligence (see pp. 345–347).

Some psychologists and educators, following Bernstein's reasoning, have maintained that these difficulties stem from presumed "verbal deficits." Black children's language is said to be grammatically simpler, less differentiated, and more concrete than that used by middle-class whites. Again, such judgments may reflect a failure to differentiate between linguistic competence and performance. A number of prominent professional linguists have made meticulous records of the speech of black children in their homes and neighborhoods and have found no strong evidence that these children show any "verbal deficits" or inadequate language or learning ability. With his family and friends, the black child's language is rich and fluent. Analysis of their linguistic patterns indicates that the language of ghetto black children is no less differentiated, complex, or logical than standard English. According to one investigator, black children "have the same basic vocabulary, possess the same capacity for conceptual learning, and use the same logic as anyone else who learns to speak and understand English" (28, 153–154). In many cases, black children have been alienated from the school system which they view as hostile and threatening. Hence in school—and in interviews and test situations—they behave defensively, ordinarily talking very little and mostly in monosyllables. Unfortunately, the black child's language in school and in interviews, that is, his performance in these situations, has been considered evidence of low levels of linguistic competence and inadequate intelligence. This conclusion is unwarranted.

The following account, taken from a research report, demonstrates that the black child's defensive and inarticulate speech performance may be largely a function of the situation, rather than of his competence in language.

The interviewer was Clarence Robins (CR), a black man raised in Harlem, where the research was conducted. The subject, Leon, was an 8-year-old black boy.

CR: What if you saw somebody kickin somebody else on the ground, or was using a stick, what would you do if you saw that?
LEON: Mmmm.
CR: If it was supposed to be a fair fight—
LEON: I don' know.
CR: You don' know? Would you do anything? . . . huh? I can't hear you.
LEON: No.
CR: Did you ever see somebody got beat up real bad?
LEON: . . . Nope . . .
CR: Well—uh—did you ever get into a fight with a guy?
LEON: Nope.
CR: That was bigger than you?
LEON: Nope.
CR: You never been in a fight?
LEON: Nope.
CR: Nobody ever pick on you?
LEON: Nope.
CR: Nobody ever hit you?
LEON: Nope.
CR: How come?
LEON: Ah 'on' know.
CR: Didn't you ever hit somebody?

LEON: Nope.

CR: (Incredulously) You never hit nobody?

LEON: Mhm.

CR: Aaa, ba-a-be, you ain't gonna tell me that!" (**28,** 159)

The researchers did not believe this interview with Leon gave a valid picture of his verbal ability. So in the next interview they changed the social situation in several ways. Clarence, the interviewer, brought along a supply of potato chips, making the interview more like a party. He also brought along Leon's best friend, 8-year-old Gregory. Clarence got down on the floor of Leon's room, so he was closer to Leon's height, and while interviewing, he used taboo words and introduced taboo topics. As a result of these changes, Leon's responses were strikingly different in volume and in style of speech.

CR: Is there anybody who says **your momma drink pee?**

LEON: (Rapidly and breathlessly) Yee-ah!

GREG: Yup!

LEON: And **your father eat doo-doo for breakfas'!**

CR: Ohhh!! (laughs)

LEON: And they say your father—**your father eat doo-doo for dinner!**

GREG: When they sound on me, I say **C.B.S. C.B.M.**

CR: What that mean?

LEON: Congo booger-snatch! (laughs)

GREG: Congo booger-snatcher! (laughs)

GREG: And sometimes I'll curse with **B.B.**

CR: What that?

GREG: Black boy! (Leon crunching on potato chips) Oh that's a **M.B.B.**

CR: **M. B. B.** What's that?

GREG: 'Merican Black Boy.

CR: Ohh . . .

GREGG: Anyway, 'Mericans is same like white people, right?

LEON: And they talk about Allah.

CR: Oh yeah?

GREG: Yeah.

CR: What they say about Allah?

LEON: Allah-Allah is God.

GREG: Allah—

CR: And what else?

LEON: I don' know the res'

GREG: Allah i—Allah is God, Allah is the only God, Allah . . .

LEON: Allah is the **son** of God.

GREG: But can he make magic?

LEON: Nope.

GREG: I know who can make magic.

CR: Who can?

LEON: The God, the **real** one.

CR: Who can make magic?

GREG: The son of po'—(CR: Hm?) I'm saying the po'k chop God!* He only a po'k chop God! (Leon chuckles).

If you had heard only the first interview, you would have grossly underestimated Leon's verbal capacity. In the second interview, the monosyllabic, noninformative performance disappeared. Instead, the two boys had so much to say that they kept interrupting each other and they had no difficulty in using the English language to express themselves.

> It should be immediately apparent that none of the standard [intelligence and reading] tests will come anywhere near measuring Leon's verbal capacity. On these tests he will show up as very much the monosyllabic, inept, ignorant, bumbling child of our first interview. The teacher has far less ability than Clarence Robins to elicit speech from this child. Clarence knows the community, the things that Leon has been doing, and the things that Leon would like to talk about. But the power relationships in a one-to-one confrontation between adult and child are too asymmetrical. This does not mean that some Negro children will not talk a great deal when alone with an adult, or that an adult cannot get close to any child. It means that the social situation is the most powerful determinant of verbal behavior and that an adult must enter into the right social relation with a child if he wants to find out what a child can do. This is just what many teachers cannot do (28, 163).

Detailed linguistic analyses demonstrate that the language of the black child and other dialects have highly structured grammatical systems through which they can express both emotional and logical thoughts. A number of linguists therefore propose that standard English be taught as a second language or dialect, not as a refinement or superior form of a language that these children already speak. In other words, black children have to be, to all intents and purposes, bilingual, speaking one language in the schools and another in their homes and neighborhoods. The schools must take account of this fact.

> Linguists believe that we must begin to adapt our school system to the language and learning styles of the majority in the inner-city schools. They argue that everyone has the right to learn the standard languages and culture in reading and writing (and speaking, if they are so inclined); but this is the end result, not the beginning of the

---

*The reference to the **pork chop God** condenses several concepts of black nationalism current in the Harlem community. A **pork chop** is a Negro who has not lost the traditional subservient ideology of the South, who has no knowledge of himself in Muslim terms, and the **pork chop God** would be the traditional God of Southern Baptists. He and His followers may be pork chops, but He still holds the power in Leon and Gregory's world (28, 160–161).

educational process. They do not believe that the standard language is the only medium in which teaching and learning can take place, or that the first step in education is to convert all first-graders to replicas of white middle-class suburban children (29, 67).

SUMMARY

Because language is probably man's most distinctive achievement and because it looms so large in social interactions and in cognitive functioning, many psychologists have proposed theories that attempt to explain how language develops. Learning theorists such as Skinner believe that language is acquired largely through the reward or reinforcement of verbal responses, while others emphasize the role of imitation in the development of language. However, psycholinguists studying the development of grammar or syntax (linguistic structure) and semantics (meanings) have been much more stimulated and influenced by the theory of Chomsky. According to his theory, humans possess a built-in or prewired system, a language acquisition device (LAD), that enables the child to process language, to construct rules, and to understand and produce appropriate grammatical speech. Most psycholinguists maintain that neither reinforcement learning theory, direct training, or imitation can account for the amazingly rapid development of the child's comprehension and use of language, his early mastery of grammatical (syntactic) rules, or his ability to generate new, novel, acceptable sentences from very early on.

The raw materials of the spoken language are phonemes, the basic vowel and consonant sounds. During the babbling period, infants produce all sounds that form the basis of all languages. The baby's first word is typically spoken at about the end of the first year and holophrastic speech (single words standing for whole sentences) begins. The child's earliest "sentences," beginning at about 18 months of age, are telegraphic versions of the adult's, consisting largely of essential nouns and verbs plus a few adjectives, but omitting prepositions, conjunctions, articles, and auxiliary verbs.

Yet, approximately 30 months later, when the child is approximately 48 to 60 months of age, he uses full, complex, adultlike sentences that give evidence of near-mastery of the rules of grammar in his own language. Even the child's first two-word sentences generally manifest systematic regularity of word order and, from the very start, the child expresses the basic grammatical relationships of subject, predicate, and object. The telegraphic sentences of children in all cultures are intended to express a broad range of meanings, including such basic semantic relations as identification, location, negation, attribution, agent-action, and agent-object.

As the child's sentences become longer and more complex, he adds some little words and word endings (inflections)—a few prepositions and articles, forms of the verb **to be**, plurals, and possessives. Children vary in their rate of acquisition of these grammatical forms, but there is amazing uniformity in the order in which they emerge. At present, there are no completely satisfactory ways of accounting for this constancy. Cross-cultural research suggests that there may be some "universals" of language development, that is, similar developmental processes in different sorts of languages, and these, in turn, may be related to the course of cognitive development. The meanings that children first assign to words are frequently different from those assigned by adults. Many are overextensions or overgeneralizations (definitions which are broader, more general, than those of adults), while others are underextensions or overdiscriminations (definitions which are narrower, more particular, than those of adults.)

Although children make enormous progress in both the comprehension and production of language during the preschool years, further important syntactic and semantic advances are made throughout childhood. During the years from kindergarten to high school vocabulary increases rapidly, speech performance improves, syntax becomes more complete, a greater variety of grammatical structures is used, and the meanings assigned to words become more adultlike.

Improved verbal ability often enhances cognitive functions such as memory, thinking, problem-solving, and reasoning, but cognitive processes are not completely dependent on language. For instance, many deaf children are deficient in language skills, but solve cognitive problems as well as children who have normal hearing. Verbal mediators such as labels are helpful in many cognitive tasks. However, some children use other mediators (for example, images, pictorial representations, or nonverbal symbols) very successfully in problem-solving.

Middle- and upper-class children perform better than those of the lower class in a number of language measures such as vocabulary, sound discrimination, and articulation. As a consequence, some psychologists and sociologists have maintained that lower-class children are "deficient" in verbal ability compared to those in the middle class. Such judgments may reflect a failure to differentiate between linguistic competence and performance. Linguists who have observed poor black children in their homes and neighborhoods found little evidence of these "verbal deficits" or of inadequate language learning ability. A black child may be inarticulate in school, but his performance there may not reflect any lack of linguistic competence; it may be largely a function of the academic situation.

References

1. Anglin, J. Studies in semantic development. Unpublished manuscript, Harvard University, 1972.
2. Asch, S. E., & Nerlove, H. The development of double-function terms in children: An exploratory investigation. In B. Kaplan & S. Wapner (Eds.), **Perspectives in psychological theory: Essays in honor of Heinz Werner.** New York: International Universities Press, 1960. Pp. 47–60.

3. Bandura, A., & Harris, M. B. Modification of syntactic style. **Journal of Experimental Child Psychology,** 1966, **4,** 341–352.

4. Bernstein, B. A sociolinguistic approach to socialization: with some reference to educability. In F. Williams (Ed.), **Language and poverty: Perspectives on a theme.** Chicago: Markham, 1970. Pp. 25–61.

5. Brown, R. How shall a thing be called? **Psychological Review,** 1958, **65,** 14–21.

6. Brown, R. **Social psychology.** New York: Free Press of Glencoe, 1965.

7. Brown, R. The first sentences of child and chimpanzee. In R. Brown, **Psycholinguistics.** New York: Free Press, 1970. Pp. 208–231.

8. Brown, R. **A first language.** Cambridge: Harvard University Press, 1973.

9. Brown, R., & Bellugi, U. Three processes in the child's acquisition of syntax. **Harvard Educational Review,** 1964, **34, 133**–151.

10. Brown, R., Cazden, C., & Bellugi-Klima, U. The child's grammar from I to III. In J. P. Hill (Ed.), **Minnesota symposia on child psychology.** Vol. 2. Minneapolis: University of Minnesota Press, 1969, Pp. 28–73.

11. Chomsky, C. **The acquisition of syntax in children from 5 to 10.** Cambridge: MIT Press, 1969.

12. Chomsky, N. A review of **Verbal behavior** by B. F. Skinner. **Language,** 1959, **35,** 26–58.

13. Chomsky, N. The formal nature of language. In E. Lenneberg (Ed.), **Biological foundations of language.** New York: Wiley, 1967. Pp. 397–442.

14. Clark, E. V. What's in a word? On the child's acquisition of semantics in his first language. In T. E. Moore (Ed.), **Cognitive development and the acquisition of language.** New York: Academic Press, 1973. Pp. 65–110.

15. Donaldson, M., & Balfour, G. Less is more: A study of language comprehension in children. **British Journal of Psychology,** 1968, **59,** 461–472.

16. Flavell, J. H., & Hill, J. P. Developmental psychology. **Annual Review of Psychology,** 1969, **20,** 1–56.

17. Furth, H. G. Research with the deaf: implications for language and cognition. **Psychological Bulletin,** 1964, **62,** 145–164.

18. Gagné, R. M., & Smith, E. C. A study of the effects of verbalization on problem-solving. **Journal of Experimental Psychology,** 1964, **63,** 12–18.

19. Ginzburg, H. **The myth of the deprived child.** Englewood Cliffs, N.J.: Prentice-Hall, 1972.

20. Goodglass, H., Gleason, J. G., & Hyde, M. R. Some dimensions of auditory language comprehension in aphasia. **Journal of Speech and Hearing Research,** 1970, **13,** 595–606.

21. Inhelder, B., Bovet, M., Sinclair, H., & Smock, D. C. On cognitive development. **American Psychologist,** 1966, **21,** 160–164.

22. Kagan, J., Klein, R. E., Haith, M., & Morrison, F. J. Memory and meaning in two cultures. **Child Development,** 1973, **44,** 221–223.

23. Katz, E. W., & Brent, S. B. Understanding connectives. **Journal of Verbal Learning and Verbal Behavior,** 1968, **7,** 501–509.

24. Keeney, T. J., Cannizzo, S. R., & Flavell, J. H. Spontaneous and induced verbal rehearsal in a recall task. **Child Development,** 1967, **38,** 953–966.

25. Kendler, T. S. Development of mediating responses in children. In J. C. Wright & J. Kagan (Eds.), Basic cognitive processes in children. **Monographs of the Society for Research in Child Development,** 1962, **28**(2), 33–52.

26. Kessel, F. S. The role of syntax in children's comprehension from ages six to twelve. **Monographs of the Society for Research in Child Development,** 1970, **35**(6, Whole No. 139).

27. Kuenne, M. R. Experimental investigation of the relation of language to transportation behavior in young children. **Journal of Experimental Psychology,** 1946, **36,** 471–490.
28. Labov, W. The logic of nonstandard English. In F. Williams (Ed.), **Language and poverty: perspectives on a theme.** Chicago: Markham, 1970. Pp. 153–189.
29. Labov, W. Academic ignorance and black intelligence. **Atlantic Monthly,** 1972, **229** (June), 59–67.
30. Liublinskaya, A. A. The development of children's speech and thought. In B. Simon (Ed.), **Psychology in the Soviet Union.** Stanford, Calif.: Stanford University Press, 1957. Pp. 197–204.
31. Loban, W. D. **Problems in oral English.** (Research Report No. 5.) Champaign, Ill.: National Council of Teachers of English, 1966.
32. Luria, A. R. The role of language in the formation of temporary connections. In B. Simon (Ed.), **Psychology in the Soviet Union.** Stanford, Calif.: Stanford University Press, 1957. Pp. 115–129.
33. McNeill, D. The development of language. In P. Mussen (Ed.), **Carmichael's Manual of child development.** Vol. 1. New York: Wiley, 1970. Pp. 1061–1161.
34. Menyuk, P. Syntactic structures in the language of children. **Child Development,** 1963, **34,** 407–422.
35. Palermo, D. S., & Molfese, D. L. Language acquisition from age five onward. **Psychological Bulletin,** 1972, **78,** 409–428.
36. Robinson, W. P. The elaborated code in working class language. **Language and Speech,** 1965, **8,** 243–252.
37. Skinner, B. F. **Verbal behavior.** New York: Appleton-Century-Crofts, 1957.
38. Slobin, D. I. **Psycholinguistics.** Glenview, Ill.: Scott, Foresman, 1971.
39. Slobin, D. I. Seven questions about language development. In P. C. Dodwell (Ed.), **New horizons in psychology, No. 2.** Baltimore: Penguin, 1972. Pp. 197–215.
40. Slobin, D. I. Cognitive prerequisites for the development of grammar. In C. A. Ferguson & D. I. Slobin (Eds.), **Studies of child language development.** New York: Holt, Rinehart & Winston, 1973. Pp. 175–208.
41. Staats, A. W., & Staats, C. K. **Complex human behavior.** New York: Holt, Rinehart & Winston, 1963.
42. Templin, M. C. Certain language skills in children. **Institute of Child Welfare Monographs.** Serial No. 26. Minneapolis: University of Minnesota Press, 1957.
43. Turner, E. W., & Rommetveit, R. Experimental manipulation of the production of active and passive voice in children. **Language and Speech,** 1967, **10,** 169–180.

Chapter 7

Cognitive Development

The last four chapters have dealt with processes confined to traditional developmental stages—the prenatal period, infancy, and the preschool years. This chapter considers intellectual development across a much longer period, twelve years, from the preschool years through early adolescence. Because psychologists have learned so much about intellectual development during the last decade, it should be more useful to discuss the continuous changes in cognitive functioning across this time period than to organize the discussion in accord with narrower time periods.

This chapter will summarize the major psychological processes and elements involved in cognition in the preschool and school-age child, as they are understood at the present time. The word cognition refers to the interpretation of sensory events, their registration and efficient retrieval from memory; the ability to manipulate schemata, images, symbols, and concepts in thinking, reasoning, and solving problems; and the acquisition of knowledge and beliefs about the environment. Stated in a more formal way, cognitive activity consists, at least, of the active processes of perception, memory, generation of ideas, evaluation, and reasoning. These five cognitive processes, or functions, involve certain cognitive units which are manipulated in thought. The major cognitive units include schemata, images, symbols, concepts, and rules.

THE UNITS IN COGNITIVE ACTIVITY

Schemata and Images

The **schema** is probably the young child's first cognitive unit. The schema is the mind's way of representing the most important aspects, or critical features, of an event. The schema is neither an image nor a photographic copy, but rather like a blueprint. Like all blueprints, it preserves the arrangement of and relations among a set of significant elements. Think of an old childhood friend or playground area near your elementary school. These thoughts will emphasize a few very important elements—perhaps an unusual stairway, the color of the brick, or a particular way your friend wore his hair. For most people, the schema of Abraham Lincoln emphasizes his beard and rugged face; the schema of the Capital building in Washington has the dome as its most outstanding feature. A schema is a little like the cartoonist's caricature of a face, for it exaggerates distinctive features. The following exercise illustrates the meaning of a schema. Look out the window for a few seconds, then turn away and ask a friend to name objects one at a time, some of which are in the outside scene, some of which are not. You have to say whether the objects named by your friend were in the scene. Your accuracy will probably be over 90 percent. The schema, produced by your glance, permitted you to recognize the scene's contents accurately.

The schema is to be contrasted with the **image,** which is a more detailed, elaborate, and conscious representation created from the schema. The schema is the basic skeleton from which the image is actively built.

Only a few children and very few adults in the western world can maintain a complete visual image of a picture so that when it is taken away the person can describe it in detail **(15)**. The child who can do this is said to have **eidetic imagery.** About 5 to 10 percent of the population of American children have eidetic imagery. They can "see" in its original color an image of a picture for 45 seconds after it is taken away from them and can report details of it. However, children and adults among nonliterate groups (the Ibo of eastern Nigeria, for example) have a frequency of eidetic imagery that is close to 20 percent **(7)**. Moreover, occurrence of eidetic imagery among mentally retarded American children is also close to 20 percent **(48)**. The higher frequency of eidetic imagery among the mentally retarded and the Ibo is still not completely understood.

Symbols

Symbols, unlike images or schemata, are arbitrary ways of representing concrete events, characteristics or qualities of objects, and actions. For example, a "skull and crossbones" is a symbol for a dangerous medicine, the orientation of an arrow on an elevator is a symbol for the direction in which the elevator is moving; a yellow light at an intersection is a symbol for caution. The most frequently encountered symbols are, of course, the arbitrary arrangement of lines that we call letters, words, and numbers. The schema and image preserve the physical qualities and relations that are part of a specific perceptual experience; the symbol does not. The child who can name the arbitrary collection of lines that we designate as the letter **m** and can point to an **m** when asked, knows the symbol for that letter. Kindergarten age children usually possess both the schema and the symbol for letters of the alphabet, as well as many objects. They know that a "skull and crossbones" symbolizes danger and that an octagonal sign at the end of a road symbolizes **Stop.** Symbols are part of the fourth unit of thought, the concept.

Concepts

A **concept** stands for, or represents, a common set of attributes among a group of schemata, images, or symbols. The major difference between a symbol and a concept is that the symbol stands for a specific, single event, whereas a concept represents something common to several events. Consider the simple pencil drawing of a house. A 7-year-old child represents the drawing as a schema; a 3-year-old, who may call it a "house," represents it as a symbol. An adult, who regards the picture as potentially representative of all the houses of the world, from log cabin to castle, imposes on the picture a set of complex relations involving the living conditions of man. The adult possesses a concept of "house."

When the child learns to read, he initially represents letters as symbols and only later acquires the concepts for letters. He first learns the letter **b** as the name for a specific sound line design; he later learns that **B** and **b** have a common attribute, that is, they sound the same and are first letters of words like butter and big. Now he has learned the concept of that letter. A child's speech is not always a good clue as to whether he is using a particular word as a symbol or a concept. If he uses **man** to refer only to his father and to no other living creature, the word man is functioning as a symbol. When he uses this word for all males, we infer that he has acquired the concept. The 2-year-old who says he is **bad** only when he wets his pants is using that word as a symbol. When he begins to regard a variety of transgressions like hitting, stealing, and lying as bad, we assume he has acquired the concept.

Concepts represent abstracted characteristics of many events, not a particular event. The concept dog refers to the collection of hair, tail, four feet, elongated face, friendliness to man, and a barking sound. It is not necessary, however, that a concept be always linked to a verbal category. A child can have a concept of friendliness without being able to state its basis. The attributes of beauty are often very difficult to describe, even though we use the concept beautiful when we say that spring and fall days or certain faces are beautiful.

The Attributes of concepts There are several important qualities of concepts, apart from the meanings of their attributes or dimensions. Concepts differ in degree of abstraction, complexity, differentiation, and centrality of their characteristic dimensions.

ABSTRACTION. A concept whose characteristic dimensions are very close to experience is said to be **concrete.** Hence, cups, boys, dogs, and dresses are concrete concepts. Concepts whose dimensions refer to events that cannot be experienced directly, such as intelligence, corruption, or honesty, are **abstract.** The dimensions of concrete concepts are usually physical qualities one can see, hear, or touch. The dimensions of abstract concepts are other concepts. For example, the concept of intelligence rests on other concepts such as language sophistication, alertness, and general learning ability. Each of these three concepts is itself an abstract concept with its own characteristic dimensions.

COMPLEXITY. Concepts also differ in the number of dimensions or simpler concepts that are necessary to define them. Concepts that are based on many dimensions are regarded as more complex than those resting on only a few dimensions. The concept of smoke is simple, for it rests on the three concepts of wispy, gray substance, and rises in the air. The concept of society is complex, for it includes the concepts of schools, courts, churches, customs, laws, and family structure.

DIFFERENTIATION. Concepts also differ in the number of similar concepts they represent. For example, the concept rain is not highly differentiated in English for there are very few words that describe different varieties of 'rain'. Shower, rain storm, and drizzle account for most of the variety in this concept. Concepts like 'hammer' and 'bottle opener' are even less differentiated. By contrast, the concept house is highly differentiated, for it can assume many different forms from hut and cabin to bungalow, house, mansion, and villa.

CENTRALITY OF DIMENSIONS. Some concepts derive their essential meaning from one or two central and critical dimensions. Others rest on a whole set of dimensions, all of them of equal importance. For example, the concept infant rests on the central dimension of age. Although size, type of food eaten, and crying are other relevant dimensions, they are not critical. Infants differ markedly in size, diet, and irritability, but all infants are under 2 years of age. The concept animal rests on several dimensions of approximately equal significance: capacity for reproduction, exchange of oxygen, locomotion, ingestion of food, and egestion of waste.

Thus far, we have been talking only about the nature of concepts. Let us now consider how concepts change with age.

Developmental Changes in Concepts Three attributes of a concept that change with development are validity, status, and accessibility (**12**).

The **validity** of a concept refers to the degree to which the child's understanding of the concept agrees with that of the larger social community. A particular 2-year-old's concept of the word good or mother is often personal and may not be similar to that of other 2-year-olds or adults. As the child becomes older, the meaning of those concepts becomes more similar for all children. In that sense, the concept becomes more valid.

The **status** of a concept refers to its degree of articulation, that is, the clarity, stability, and exactness of its use in thinking. A 3-year-old's concept of size is rather murky, whereas an 8-year-old's understanding of this concept is clearer, more exact, more stable over time—it has an enhanced **status.**

Accessibility refers to how available a concept is for use in thinking and the degree to which the concept can be communicated to others. The child becomes increasingly able to talk about his concepts. Ask a 5-year-old child the meaning of the concept of goodness or of number, and he often says he doesn't know, even though his behavior may indicate that he does have some comprehension of the concepts. On the other hand, a 10-year-old can easily talk about these ideas.

Relative and absolute qualities of concepts One obstacle to the young child's effective use and understanding of concepts is his tendency to regard a concept as absolute rather than relative. The 4-year-old learns the concept dark and regards it as descriptive of an absolute class of colors—black and all other dark hues. The phrase dark yellow makes no sense to him, for dark signifies all dark colors, not relative darkness. He has no difficulty determining which is darker if yellow and black are presented to him, but he will appear confused if turquoise blue and sky blue are presented. He does not understand that the question "Which is darker?" is meant to be a relative one. For the same reason the young child does not understand the relative magnitude of numbers. He believes that 1, 2, and 3 are small numbers, and that 99 and 100 are large numbers. Thus, if he is asked "Which is the larger of the pair 1 and 2?" he may not understand the question.

One difficulty in teaching the young child to see both the absolute and relative qualities of concepts is that he must first believe that the same concept can emphasize different dimensions, that is, he must learn to view the concept from two different points of view. He must see that an orange is a good thing to eat, but a bad ball to bounce; a newspaper is an easy thing to cut, but a difficult thing with which to mend trousers. He is a boy, as well as the son of his father; he is the smallest child in the family, but the largest child in the classroom. The child has to learn that the quality of an object is relative to its context and to the objects with which it is compared. A concept does not always have the same set of critical dimensions.

Rules

Rules are essentially statements about concepts and can be classified according to whether the relation between the concepts is static or dynamic. A rule which describes a simple or static relation between concepts is called a **nontransformational rule;** one which describes a dynamic relation is called a **transformational rule.**

A nontransformational rule states a simple relation between two concepts and is usually a description of one or more of the dimensions of the concept. For example, the rule "water is wet" states a relation between the concepts water and wet. The relation described by a nontransformational rule is always a part of the meaning of the concepts. The rule "bombs are dangerous" states a relation between the concept bomb and danger: a bomb has many characteristics, one of which is the fact that it is dangerous; the quality of danger is characteristic of many objects, one of which is a bomb. The rule does not require us to do anything in order to note the relation. It is present in the meaning of the concepts.

But now consider the rule "place gunpowder and TNT in a metal case with a detonating cap and you have made a bomb." The relation among the concepts gunpowder, TNT, metal case, and detonating cap is not clear until we act upon them and place them in a special relation to one another. The concepts are related by that action. This type of rule which involves a set of procedures, is a transformational rule.

A second way to classify rules is to regard them as informal or formal. **Informal**

rules refer to an imperfect relation between two or more dimensions, that is, the dimensions are shared some of the time or even most of the time, but not all of the time. "Candy is sweet" is an informal rule, for occasionally you find a candy that is sour. Most of our beliefs about the world are informal rules. Snakes are dangerous, sand is dry, men are tall are informal rules that describe one of the characteristic dimensions of the concepts snake, sand and man.

Formal rules state a relation between two concepts that is always true and specifiable. "Oil floats on water" is a formal rule. Similarly, the mathematical rule $6 \times 11 = 66$ states a fixed relation between the dimensions of the concepts 6 and 11 whenever the procedure of multiplication is applied to those concepts. There can be no disagreement with that relation.

There are, therefore, four kinds of rules (see Table 7.1): informal nontransformational (candy is sweet), informal transformational (melt chocolate and let it harden to make candy), formal nontransformational (a triangle has three sides), and formal transformational ($16 \times 11 \div 2 = 88$). Most of our everyday thoughts are informal nontransformational rules. Most of natural science is composed of formal transformational rules. Each of the traditional subjects in school emphasizes one of these kinds of rules. Arithmetic and chemistry favor formal transformational rules; history and social studies favor informal nontransformational rules; poetry relies on informal transformational rules; the axioms of geometry and much of anatomy are composed of formal nontransformational rules, especially when they are learned and recalled by rote.

The delayed appearance of a new stage in the development of rules and reasoning can result from the child's reluctance to replace his old rules with new ones. In Piagetian language, he tries to assimilate new experiences to his old ideas. He stubbornly resists retiring his old beliefs if they have been effective in the past. The child's rules, therefore, are like a scientific theory, for neither is replaced by criticism alone, only by recognition of a better set of rules.

Schemata, images, symbols, concepts, and rules are the primary entities manipulated in thinking. The child is able to understand only information that either matches or is a little in advance of his own cognitive units. If a new scene, idea, equation, or word does not have some association to or relevance for his available

Table 7.1 **Types of rules**

	INFORMAL	FORMAL
Transformational	Routines in construction: "Melt candy to make chocolate."	Routine rules of mathematics and science: "The square root of 144 is 12."
Nontransformational	Experiential rules: "Winters are cold."	Fixed rules: "A quadrilateral has four sides."

cognitive units, he is apt to learn little from it because he will pay minimal attention to it.

COGNITIVE ACTIVITIES

Cognitive activity can be divided, at a very general level, into two types, undirected and directed. **Undirected cognition** refers to free associations, dreams, or reveries, and includes the free flow of thoughts that occur continually as the child walks home or stares out the window. There has not been much inquiry into this exciting and important kind of cognition because it is difficult to study the private, undirected associations of a child (or an adult). If one asks a child to report his free associations or to write them down, the situation is altered, and the undirected thought suddenly becomes directed. The child will view the situation as a problem and will automatically attempt to present an orderly, coherent, and even socially acceptable report of his thinking. The inquiry itself changes the nature of the phenomenon and we do not see the disorder that so often characterizes uncontrolled, free association.

Directed Thinking and the Executive Process

Directed cognition refers to the cognitive processes that occur when the child tries to solve a problem given to him by others or one he sets for himself. The child knows there is a solution to a problem and he knows when he has arrived at the answer. The problem-solving process can be viewed as typically involving the following sequence: perception and interpretation, memory, generation of hypotheses, evaluation, deduction, and, when required, public report. We shall consider each of these processes in sequence. However, it is helpful to keep in mind the general changes that occur during the period between 5 and 12 years of age. The richness of the child's supply of cognitive units increases each year. He becomes increasingly concerned with the degree of agreement between his concepts and those of other children and adults. He becomes more apprehensive about making mistakes. His memory improves dramatically; he has a greater ability to recall more information.

Most important, beginning around 4 to 5 years of age, it is believed that an **executive process** gradually emerges, which, in most children, is firmly in control of cognitive functioning by the time the child is 10 or 11 years old. The functions of this executive process are to monitor and coordinate his perceptions, memory, and reasoning processes, to relate past experiences and future possibilities to the present, to select the best strategies to solve a problem, and to permit the child to be self-consciously aware of his own thinking.

This executive process is similar to an architect supervising the construction of a house. Although some psychologists do not believe it is necessary to assume an executive function—they prefer to view thought as a more or less mechanical interaction of the basic units and processes with the control function inherent in these simpler processes—a simple experiment suggests the necessity of postulating this higher order executive process. Ask a 10-year-old to listen carefully and then say, "cat, cow, pig, dog." Wait about half a minute and then say, "cat, pig, dog," and ask the child which animal was omitted. Most 10-year-olds, but very few 3- or 4-year-olds, will answer "cow." How can we explain this simple event without assuming that a complex psychological process, a little like an executive, emerges at about age 5 to keep an orderly record of experience, making the child aware of what he knows and where to find it.

Process 1. Perception and Interpretation

Perception is the process by which the child extracts meaningful information from the meaningless mosaic of physical stimulation. The difference between **information** and **stimulation** is a little like the difference between what a person and a camera register when each is focused on a scene of a spring meadow. While the camera registers all the colors, shadows, lines, and objects in the scene, the human being selects certain aspects and ignores others. The person makes a bright red flower the central element and the trees and hills background. The camera displays no such favoritism. Second, the person relates what he sees both to what he saw a moment ago and to what he might see a few moments in the future. The person integrates successive exposures; the camera does not. Most important, only the person relates what he sees to what he knows. For example, if on a windless day in a forest a child saw a branch move he might automatically assume that a bird or a rabbit was nearby and begin to search the area near the moving branch for signs of an animal—wings, beak, fur, feet, or tail. If that same branch moved on a windy day, the child would most likely assume it was caused by the wind and not look for an animal.

The goal of perception is to understand events in the world, to match what is sensed to some cognitive unit. The events that are perceived include (1) static, physical things, such as objects, odors, and colors; (2) dynamic events that occur over time, such as a person getting up from a chair in contrast to one that is in the process of sitting down; (3) two-dimensional pictorial representations of objects; and (4) coded symbols, such as letters, numbers, and words.

The very young child usually represents experience by schemata; the older child is more likely to use symbols and concepts, especially words. Consider the following figure: ⊂⊃. If this figure were shown to a 1-year-old, he would most likely represent it as a schema. The 6-year-old is likely to use language; he might say, "It looks like a finger" or "It looks like a pencil." If asked to draw it or select a figure from a set of similar ones, he might make an error that would reveal he

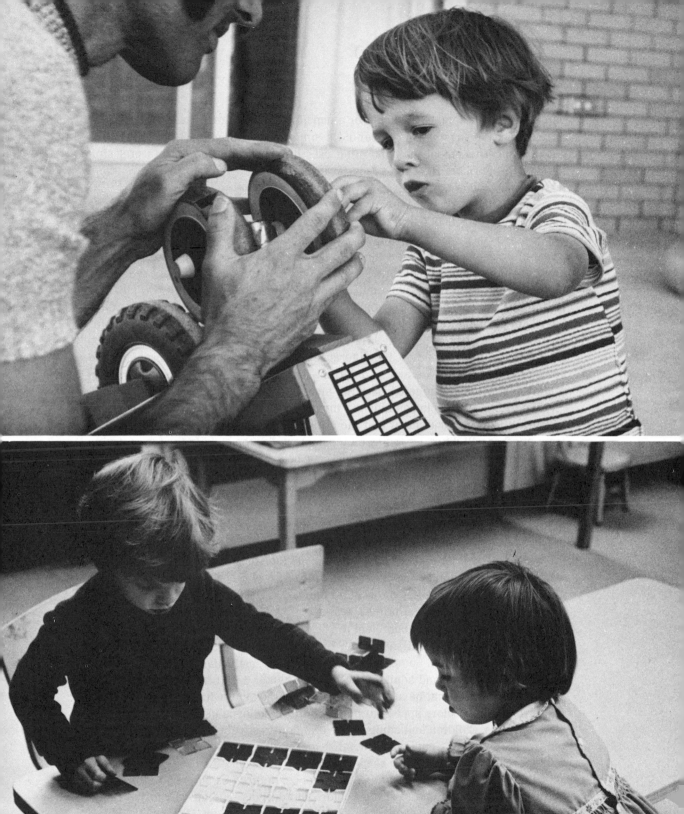

perceived it as resembling a finger or a pencil. He might draw it as ⊏══════⊃ or ⊏══════▷. We say that the 6-year-old assimilated the original figure to his language label. The school-age child often uses linguistic concepts to interpret situations and the richer the child's repertoire of words and concepts, the more likely he will rely on them.

The matching of event to some schema, image, or concept involves, first, the detection of the critical features of the event. In the case of the moving branch on the windless day, the child would begin scanning for the critical attributes of a forest animal—legs, fur, tail. If the moving branch were near the ground he might look for the tail and ears of a rabbit. If the branch were high, he might search for the wings of a bird. If our hypothetical child detected a shadow with two legs and an upright posture, his search would change abruptly, for only bears and humans have that particular form. He would now have a new problem and would look for an entirely new set of features. He would try to determine the presence of fur versus clothing and to detect the difference between the grunts of a bear and the voice of a man. If he were able to determine that the source of the movement was a hunter, he would terminate his search and turn his attention elsewhere.

This simple example contains the important aspects of perception. First, it illustrates the earlier statement that the critical features that disinguish one object from another will differ depending on the context. For the child in the forest, trying to determine whether the moving object is a bear or man, the critical features of a man would be the presence of clothes and sounds of speech. But if the scene is shifted to a dark street in a large city where our hypothetical child hears footsteps behind him, he would want to know if the person in back of him was a boy or a man, for it is unlikely to be a bear. In the context of the dark street, neither the presence of clothes nor the sounds of human speech would be helpful in solving this problem. In order to determine whether the footsteps were of a boy or man he would need information on body size and type of dress. Hence, the critical features for man will differ depending on whether one has to decide if an object is a man or bear or a man or boy. The critical features that distinguish one physical event from another depend on the problem the person is trying to solve.

But this last statement should not be understood to mean that there are no absolutes in perception. Some stimuli are naturally distinctive and salient for all people, both children and adults. Recall from Chapter 3 that all young infants are attracted to designs that have a large amount of black and white contour contrast. Similarly, certain colors appear to have a natural salience in our own as well as other cultures. Children and adults in several cultures will pick the same shade of red as the "best red" and can remember and match shades of red to that "best red" more easily than to other shades. This color happens to be the crimson characteristically printed on Christmas cards. Hence, nature has equipped all humans with a tendency to attend to certain colors and designs. The answer to the riddle "Does my brother see the same red as I do?" appears to be yes (17).

Developmental Changes in Perception

Several important changes in the nature of perception occur between early childhood and adolescence. Increasing knowledge about the world allows the child to be more specific in his search. The child learns that animals can make branches move and that deer are larger than squirrels. Hence, the older child knows what he is looking for and his perception will be faster, more efficient, and, on the whole, more accurate.

The older child is able to focus his attention in a systematic way for a longer period of time. Developmental changes on a variety of intellectual tasks suggest that between 5 and 7 years of age there is a dramatic increase in quality of performance on problems requiring focused and sustained attention. This generalization seems to hold for both American children and those in other cultures. The child under 5 years seems easily distracted and has difficulty maintaining attention for a long time on a problem or communication from another person.

Another related difference between younger and older children is that the younger child may be unable to direct the focus of his attention, that is, he may be unable to shift focus as rapidly as the older one—although the number of sensory events that can be attended to at any one time may be the same.

These psychological changes in cognitive functioning are associated with important biological changes in the central nervous system, including the growth of neural tissue and changes in the electrical potentials generated by the brain. It is possible that an important reorganization of the central nervous system occurs between 5 and 7 years of age, and this reorganization may be partly responsible for the dramatic increase in the child's capacity for sustained attention (51), which is part of the executive function described earlier.

Selective attention is another aspect of perception which seems to show rapid development between 5 and 7. The child's selectivity of attention is also related, in part, to his **expectations.** If a child knows what events are about to happen, that is, if he has an expectancy of what he might see or hear, he can prepare himself better for the event. Often such a preparation aids the accuracy of his perception. School-age children (kindergarten, and grades 2, 4, and 6) listened to a man's voice and a woman's voice simultaneously speaking two-word phrases (for example, dog eat). The voices came simultaneously from two loud-speakers placed 18 inches apart. One speaker was marked with the picture of a man's face, the other with a woman's face. When the child was to report the words spoken by the man's voice, the man's picture was lighted; when the child was to report the words spoken by the woman, her picture was lighted. On some trials the picture of the face was lighted before the voices spoke (the child was given a preparatory signal). On other trials the picture of the face was lighted after the voices spoke. With age, the children became increasingly better at reporting the words spoken by the voice to which they were told to listen. However, when the child was given a preparatory set—when he was

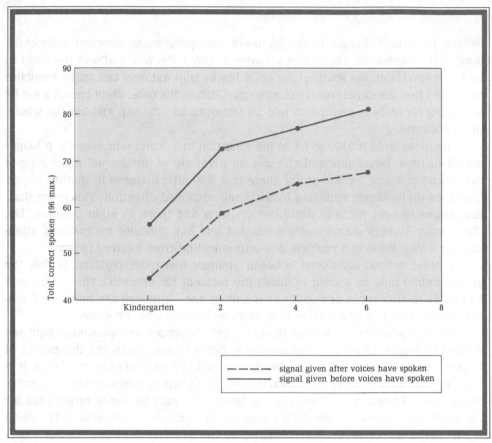

Figure 7.1 Differences in amount of message reproduced as a function of whether the child was told to attend to the voice before or after he heard it. (From E. E. Maccoby. Selective auditory attention in children. In L. P. Lipsitt & C. C. Spiker [Eds.], **Advances in child development and behavior.** New York: Academic Press, 1967. P. 117. By permission.)

told which voice to listen to before the voices spoke—his performance was better than if he was told after the voice spoke (**33;** see Fig. 7.1).

The older child also knows how to interrelate what he perceives and to synthesize it into a more comprehensive cognitive framework. The older child resembles a good detective who knows how to interpret clues and knows the best place to look for them.

Some psychologists believe that the essence of perceptual development is the progressive enriching of cognitive units—schemata, images, or symbols—by associating increasing amounts of information with the original unit. Other psychologists disagree and maintain that with age the child's perceptual units become more differentiated and more distinctive.

In essence, the argument centers on whether the child who decides he has seen a dog when he has only seen its tail does so because he has learned to associate a tail with a dog or because the tail was always part of his perceptual schema of dog, but he has learned that this specific characteristic is a distinctive feature of dogs. The first view sees perceptual development as adding pieces of knowledge together; the second view sees it as the selective extraction and emphasis of particular elements or features. Professor Eleanor Gibson, who favors the second view, says,

> The differentiation theory of perceptual learning is contrasted with an enrichment theory. It holds that perception does not develop by supplementing the stimulation or by associating responses with it, but rather by differentiation of stimulation already rich in information. What is learned are distinctive features, invariants, and higher orders of both which I refer to as structure. The mechanism of perceptual learning is not association but filtering and abstraction. The process is an active one, involving exploration and search. The search is directed by the task and by intrinsic cognitive motives. The need to get information from the environment is as strong as to get food from it and obviously useful for survival. The search is terminated not by externally provided rewards and punishments but by internal reduction of uncertainty. The products of the search have the property of reducing the information to be processed. Perception is thus active, adaptive, and self regulated (**14**, 144).

Support for Gibson's view comes from several sources. If the child learns the distinctive features of an object, then he should be able to recognize a schematic picture of a familiar object even though he has had no previous contact with pictures. He should be able to perceive two-dimensional representations of objects with no special practice. This prediction is verified by two important experiments. In the first (**19**) a child was prevented from seeing any pictures for the first 19 months of his life. When he was 19 months old, he was shown photographs and line drawings of sneakers, skates, and other objects he had experience with in their three-dimensional form. His ability to name these illustrations was better than chance, indicating that he could perceive the distinctive features of two-dimensional representations of objects on his first exposure to them.

In an equally dramatic study, isolated Indian children living in the mountainous area of Guatemala, who had no access to photographs, pencils, or paper, were shown line drawings that merely suggested familiar objects and had to guess the object (see Fig. 7.2). Children 7 to 11 years of age named three-fourths of the items correctly. When the same test was given to American children, who have unlimited access to television, photographs, books, and magazines, their scores were just a little better than the Indians—85 percent versus 79 percent correct (**25**). Moreover, when these same Indian children were asked to detect triangles embedded in much larger pictures (see Fig. 7.3), they were correct 80 percent of the time, which is identical with the performance of American children of the same age. It is likely,

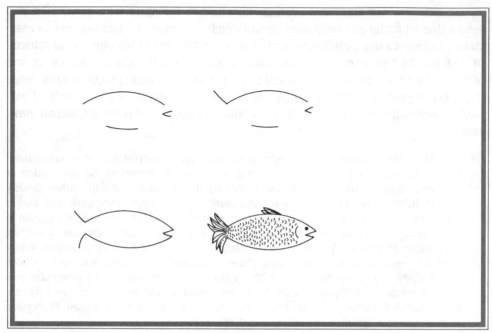

Figure 7.2 Test items shown to a child who has to guess the object from its incomplete form.

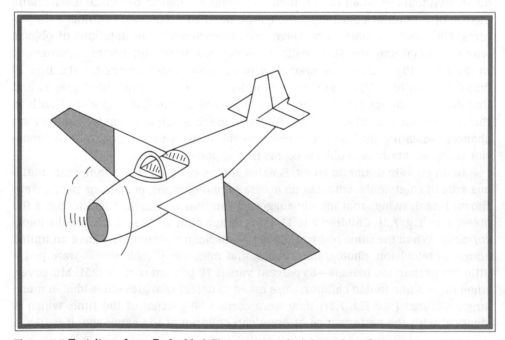

Figure 7.3 Test item from Embedded Figures test administered to Guatemalan children.

therefore, that the ability to analyze two-dimensional pictures and to detect the distinctive features of objects is a natural ability that does not require specific exposure to pictures or specific training.

Support for Professor Gibson's view comes from studies on how children learn to read. The child's first task in reading is to detect the distinctive features of each letter. He has to realize that a, A, H, ꝗ, Ä are to be treated the same way, and he accomplishes this by differentiating the distinctive features of the letter.

Reading, perhaps more than any other skill, illustrates the dual process of extraction of distinctive features which is monitored by a previously acquired set of rules. For example, study the sentence below:

Tŀə pirl wənt ꝺomə ɒn ꝺoʋꞁ ɒꝗo

It probably took less than a minute to read that seven-word sentence even though you never saw words or letters printed that way. Why was it so easy? It was easy because you have learned a set of rules for letters and letter sequences and can detect the distinctive features of an **e** whether it is printed backwards or upside down.

Do Older Children Perceive More? A controversy surrounding age differences in perception starts with the fact that adults report more about an event than children do. If you show a picture of a city street to a child and an adult for about a second and then ask each to say what they saw, the adult always reports more information. This fact leads us to ask if the difference in performance at different ages is due to differences in the initial perception of the scene or to differences in the coding and remembering of the picture. The latter explanation is more likely to be correct.

Adults and children were shown a stimulus with eight simple designs arranged in a circle for a brief period. Following the termination of the stimulus, a "teardrop" indicator appeared under one of the stimuli and the child or adult had to point, on a card containing all eight designs, to the design that was in the location where the teardrop indicator appeared. If the indicator occurred immediately following termination of the stimulus, the children performed as well as the adults. But if there was a 1-second delay between the initial exposure of the designs and the appearance of the teardrop indicator, the children did much more poorly than the adults. It appears that the adults were doing something with the information they perceived. Perhaps the adults were rehearsing their perceptions silently, relating them to prior knowledge, or labeling them. These or other mental strategies could have helped them remember what they perceived (**36**).

In sum, the ability to perceive objects, space, and dynamic events is natural to all children; even the accurate perception of pictures does not require prior experience with photographs. Development brings increased skill at maintaining focused attention on an event without being distracted, and as a result, the child's perceptions become more efficient, more selective, and more accurate. With age the child also learns more of the distinctive attributes of events and acquires the ability to organize these attributes into structures so that it becomes easier to detect an event from partial information. These abilities are wedded to the acquisition of strategies of searching for the information that is needed to make a decision.

Process 2. Memory

Memory refers to the storage of experiences for a period after they have ended. It had been assumed for many years that all perceived events were registered with equal strength. If a person could not remember an event that he perceived, it was assumed that the fault lay with his inability to recall it, rather than with any differences in registration. Recent research suggests that it may be useful to distinguish among three memory processes: **sensory memory, short-term memory,** and **long-term memory.**

In vision, sensory memory refers to the fact that after we see something a representation of it remains vivid for about ¼ second. After this brief ¼ second has passed, it is difficult to retain a complete memory of the object. Sensory memory is probably the same for children and adults, and the differences in memory between younger and older children or between children and adults is due to differences in short-term and long-term memory, not sensory memory (39).

Short-term memory usually refers to a memory trace that is available for a maximum of 30 seconds, and typically for a shorter period of time. The forgetting of a new telephone number after 10 seconds illustrates short-term memory. The child must actively transfer information from short-term to long-term memory if it is to be retained for a longer period of time. Without that special effort, the information will be lost and not retrievable at a later time. Once a name, date, or definition has been transferred from short-term to long-term memory, it is assumed that it is potentially available at any time in the future, even though the person may not be able to "remember" the information on a particular occasion.

Memory is usually measured in one of two ways. The person is asked either to recall an event he saw or heard or to recognize it. In recall the child must retrieve all the necessary information from memory. For example, he may be asked to define the word "shilling" or remember Washington's birthday. In recognition the child is given some information and must decide whether he experienced it in the past or whether it is the information desired. He may be asked to decide if a shilling is a French or a British coin or whether George Washington's birthday occurs in February or July.

Obviously, a child's **recognition memory** is much better than his **recall memory,** and the difference between recall and recognition is more dramatic in younger than in older children. A 10-year-old who has been shown a group of 12 pictures is usually able to recall spontaneously about 8 of them, but he is able to recognize all 12 if they are included in a larger set of photographs and all he has to do is to point to the ones that he saw earlier. His recall is about 30 percent poorer than his recognition. A 4-year-old shown the same pictures will be able to recall only 2 or 3, but will also be able to recognize all 12. The young child's recall is 75 percent poorer than his recognition. Consider a more dramatic example of the difference between recall and recognition memory. A 10-year-old shown 60 different pictures on one day and asked to remember them a day later will recall about 30 percent, but he may be able to recognize over 90 percent of the pictures (26).

Recognition memory is more sensitive than recall because the child has to retrieve all the information in recall and differences in the efficiency of that retrieval process will affect memory performance. In recognition, the information is given and the child merely has to check his perception of the event against his memory.

Factors Affecting Memory The cohesiveness and relatedness of the material affects recall. If the material to be recalled is unrelated (like a string of random numbers), the child will recall much less than if the material is connected, as in a story or sentence. Thus, an average 7-year-old may be able to recall a string of only four different numbers, but will have little difficulty with a sentence of eight to nine different words.

Social class and cultural differences in recall are also greater than class and cultural differences in recognition. When middle-class children from an urban area in Guatemala were compared with isolated village children from the same country, the middle-class city children recalled longer strings of numbers and sentences than the rural children, but the difference between the city and rural children in recognition memory was less dramatic (26). In the recall task the city children activated effective strategies for rehearsal, grouping, and retrieval of the sentences and numbers. The rural children had not yet learned or did not use these strategies, and hence performed more poorly (25). These strategies were of less value on the test of recognition memory.

The use of strategies like rehearsal (repeating or reviewing the item to be remembered soon after presentation), grouping of the information to be remembered, and systematic search of memory during testing helps older children to recall much more than 5-year-olds. Among American children, there is usually a sharp increase around 7 years of age in the length of a string of numbers or words that can be recalled. Professor John Flavell of the University of Minnesota believes that the improved recall is due to the older child's automatic and unconscious use of "tricks" of organizing the information to help him remember (11).

The younger child's memory can be helped if the material to be remembered is organized for him. For example, children in second, fourth, and sixth grades were shown on a screen lists of nine numbers to memorize. The numbers were presented either in a standard way—731246589—or grouped into triplets—731 246

598. The older children performed equally well on both presentations because they had a natural tendency to use the grouping strategy anyway when the numbers were presented. But the younger children, who did not typically activate the grouping strategy, remembered more numbers when they were grouped into triplets (16).

Because young children do not spontaneously organize what they see and hear, the ability of a 5-year-old to answer a question or understand instructions will depend on the amount of information the instructions contain. If the question or instruction contains more than two or three facts or items of information, the kindergarten child may forget it in a few seconds. This forgetting seems due to his failure to rehearse the question so that it stays in long-term memory. In one experiment, children of three ages (kindergarten, second grade, and fifth grade) were exposed to a set of familiar pictures. The experimenter first touched a given number of them (say 3) in a specific order. The experimenter then replaced that set with a new arrangement of the same pictures and asked the child to point to the pictures in the same order as the experimenter had moments earlier. The older children had better memory scores than the younger children; the older children were more likely to rehearse silently the names of the pictures as they were touched or while they were attempting to recall them (as evidenced by distinct movements of the lips). The kindergarten children knew the names of the pictures, but their poor recall was caused by a failure to use the "trick" of saying the names of the pictures to themselves in order to help memory (13). Knowledge of the names for objects is no guarantee that the child will use the names to help him remember information.

Professor Pascual-Leone (41) believes that the improved memory of older children may be due not only to the use of memory tricks, but also to an increase in a basic ability to remember and coordinate information. Pascual-Leone suggests that there is a gradual increase in the absolute number of ideas that the child can manipulate simultaneously. Children of all ages, he believes, have a basic memory capacity which is enhanced by about one unit with each passing year from age 5 until age 11 or 12. "The maximum number of schemes or discrete chunks of information that M (this is the central processor) can attend to or integrate in a single act is assumed to grow in an all-or-none manner as a function of age in normal subjects" (41, 307).

Hence, Pascual-Leone's notions differ slightly from those of Flavell in that he suggests a basic difference in memory ability or capacity between older and younger children. At the same time his ideas about the regular increment of memory capacity deny any abrupt change between 5 and 7 years of age. It is not possible, given current knowledge, to decide which view is correct.

The earlier section on perception suggested that there are no age differences in the capacity to perceive stimuli. Older children perceive more efficiently because they have learned good strategies for scanning stimuli and they have a better idea of what events they may encounter. A similar conclusion may hold for memory. There may be little difference between a 4- and 10-year-old in the basic ability to recognize whether a certain event has happened in the past. Perhaps the older child remembers, or recalls, more simply because he has developed better ways to organize incoming information, consistently transfers that information to long-term memory, and is more efficient at retrieving information when it is necessary. The difference between 5-year-olds and 11-year-olds may be more a product of the "software" of processing and retrieval than the "hardware" of the brain.

This conclusion is supported in an experiment in which children of different ages were shown a set of 24 pictures of objects that belonged to one of four conceptual categories. The four categories were transportation, animals, furniture, and clothing. The pictures were laid on a table randomly and the children were told they would have 3 minutes to study them, during which time they could move them around or do anything else that might help them remember the pictures. They were not told anything about the four categories. The experimenter wanted to determine which children would rearrange the pictures into categories and whether children who do this would recall together the pictures that belonged to the same category. None of the first graders and only a few of the third graders rearranged the pictures by category. However, beginning with the fourth graders, there was an increasing tendency through sixth graders to rearrange the pictures into category groups and to recall pictures of the same category together (38).

As one might expect, if the objects or words are clustered into similar conceptual categories by the experimenter so that the school-age child does not have to organize them, his recall is improved (3). Usually, children show more clustering in their recall for familiar than for unfamiliar categories (49), and school-age children are more likely to remember together words that belong to the same conceptual category (sun-moon) than words that rhyme (sun-fun) or words that bear a grammatical relation to one another (sun-shines). The tendency to remember two words that rhyme or possess a grammatical relation is more characteristic of preschool children (46).

The Role of Anxiety and Motivation in Memory Failure to attend to information, which is an obvious cause of memory failure, can be the result of several factors. The most obvious, and perhaps the most frequent, are interfering thoughts and distracting stimuli. The negative relation between memory and anxiety has been well documented. Anxious children display poorer recall than less anxious children, and it is believed that the anxiety creates distracting stimulation that deflects attention from relevant incoming information and, therefore, impairs memory.

In one study, third-grade boys were divided into three groups. One group was made anxious by causing them to fail on a word problem (35); a second group was allowed to succeed on the same word problem; and a third group was not given the problem at all. Each child was then read the short story that appears below and told to remember it.

> The American horse known as Man of War was a very fine horse. He ran in races in the United States, in France and in Germany. He was brown with a red mane and had very strong legs. Five times a year, he was in horse shows in Boston, where children came to see him trot and run. After watching him, the children were served hot chocolate, biscuits and fudge (35).

Immediately after hearing the story, the children had to recall as much of it as possible. The children who were made anxious had markedly poorer memory for elements of the story than the other two groups, who were equal in their recall scores (35).

In addition to rehearsal, grouping, availability of schemata and labels for categories, and freedom from anxiety and distracting factors, another source of individual differences in memory involves motivational variables. Is the child motivated to recall material or does he stop searching after the first layer of information has been retrieved? Retrieval of information from memory is effortful and the child who works longer is likely to ferret out more information.

The Role of Memory in Learning to Read The task of learning to read, which usually covers a three to four year period, involves a complex set of processes. As we have said, the child must first be able to identify the letters that compose the words. This process involves distinguishing the distinctive patterns of lines that define each of our alphabetic letters. An **o** and a **c** differ in degree of openness of a circle; a **v** and a **u** differ in the degree of curvature or angularity at the bottom of the design; **E** and **F** differ in the number of horizontal lines.

As the child learns to make discriminations necessary to identify the form of each letter, he also learns to name the letters. The sound of the name is his introduction to the sounds the letters represent in words. The child is aided in reading if he automatically associates a sound of the letter with its visual form.

After the child learns this first basic skill, he then faces the most critical problem—the ability to read single words. This is the important obstacle in learning to read, for most children are able to learn to identify letters. The problem in learning to identify words is that the child does not know how to break or analyze the word into its critical parts. Consider the simple word **boy**. The child may know the sound of each letter, but if he says to himself "Bee-Oh-Why," that combination of sounds does not produce a word, that is, it does not sound like boy. Hence, the child has to learn that the letter **o** in that particular set is sounded like "aw" and the **y** is sounded like "ee" and the **b** is sounded like "ba." Second, he has to be able to hold in short-term memory the sound of the **b** while he is working on the **o** and the **y**. If the child cannot hold the sound of the **b** in memory for a second or two, while he is sounding out the **o** and the **y**, he will not be able to read the word, for when he recognizes the **y** he may have forgotten the **b** and will have to start all over again. This is one reason children who have not matured to the point where they are able to hold one or two items of information in memory while they are working on another item and to integrate the previously stored information with the freshly perceived information will have difficulty learning to read.

If the child is mature enough to be able to operate simultaneously on two or three items of information, his first task is to learn the basic sounds of letters and the most frequent combinations in which they appear in words.

The last step in the reading process is learning the rules of word order. The reader comes to know that **the** precedes a noun and that a verb or predicate is about to follow. He also knows that certain predicates are more likely to follow "boy," "dog," "water," or "apple." For example, consider the sentences

The boy spun.
The apple split.
The water spilled.

Although all these three verbs begin with **sp** the child of 9 years, but not the child of 6, will be unlikely to err in reading "spun" for "split" or "spilled" because he knows apples are more likely to split, water to spill, and children to spin.

Finally, it is important to recognize that the strategy of reading after these phases have been mastered—letter recognition, word recognition, and reading of sentences—will differ depending on the goal of the reader. If the reader is primarily interested in the major content, he knows he can skip many words (all the little words, many of the adjectives and adverbs) and he knows which words contain the essential information. By contrast, if the reader is reading for literal facts because he is going to be examined with questions like "What color was the dog?" or "How many boys went to the circus?" he will slow his reading down and attend to many words he might skip in reading for general content. Finally, if a person is proofreading a manuscript for typographical errors, reading proceeds at the slowest rate for he is attending to every letter and probably not processing the meaning at all.

The main implication for teachers of children who are learning to read is to make sure that the child is at a stage of maturity where he can hold previously processed information in memory while he is working on a new item of information—one of the characteristics of the executive process. Since the child is easily discouraged, it is helpful if he can experience success early in the reading process.

Summary Better techniques to store and hold information, a richer store of concepts and schemata to aid storage and retrieval, focused attention, freedom from anxiety, and motivation all lead to better recall during the school years. The basic developmental change in recall appears to involve the ability to organize larger amounts of incoming information and self-consciously transfer it to long-term memory. By contrast, the simple ability to recognize whether a given event has or has not happened may not improve very much from the preschool years to pre-adolescence.

Process 3. Generation of Hypotheses

The perception and interpretation of events and their storage in memory are typically the first two processes activated when the child solves a problem. The third process is the generation of hypotheses or possible solutions, the production of alternative ideas to solve the problem. This process is called the **induction phase** of problem-solving and is related to the notion of creativity.

In order to generate good solutions to problems, the child must (1) have the necessary knowledge or cognitive units, (2) activate that knowledge, (3) have a permissive attitude toward error (the child must not be overly anxious about making a mistake), and (4) possess a less palpable ingredient, insight.

Consider the following problem. A 6-year-old correctly perceives that his mother is sobbing, and he cannot remember ever seeing her crying in the past. This unusual event stirs him to try to explain it and he generates possible solution hypotheses. He thinks of the conditions that make him cry, such as pain, fear, or loneliness. He unconsciously checks the reasonableness of each of these as the cause of his mother's behavior. He is likely to reject the fear interpretation because it contradicts another rule he believes more firmly, namely, that adults are never afraid. He rejects the loneliness hypothesis for the same reason. But he knows that adults can feel pain and decides that hypothesis is correct. He is satisfied. This simple example illustrates the three steps involved in the generation of any explanation. The child first searches his knowledge for possible causes of an event he does not immediately understand and generates possible explanations. The child then checks each explanation for consistency with his older rules about the event. If his new explanation contradicts an older one which he believes more strongly, he will reject it. If the child finds an explanation that both matches his experience and does not contradict an older rule, he will probably accept it as correct. Of course, the child does not go through these steps as systematically and logically as we have described them here, but something like that process probably occurs when a problem is being solved.

The Importance of Critical Attributes The most common intellectual problem a child has to solve is to categorize new objects. The child of 6 has learned a basic set of concepts for the most frequently encountered events in his life—animals, food, clothing, planes, cars, furniture, homes, money, women, men. New he sees a new object, for example, a helicopter, and wants to know—or must decide—to what category it belongs. He makes that decision by trying to decide what known

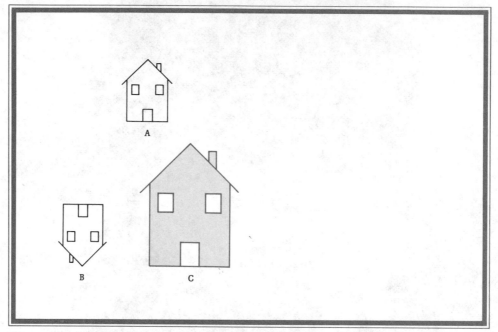

Figure 7.4 Test item to determine whether orientation or size-color is used as primary basis for similiarity.

object the helicopter most closely resembles. The answer to the question of "close resemblance" is not decided by adding up the total number of similarities, but usually depends on a few special, or critical, nodes of similarity. When these critical similarities are physical characteristics, they are the distinctive features discussed in the section on perception (see p. 278). The child's judgment that two objects are similar is partly a function of the degree to which the two objects share the same critical features.

In one experiment 4-year-olds were given a correctly oriented line drawing of a house (Picture A in Fig. 7.4) and then shown two other line drawings of houses, one of the same size and color, but upside down (Picture B), and the other right side up, but of different size and color (Picture C). When asked, "Which is most like Picture A?" a child was most likely to choose Picture B, even though he knows that the house is upside down. He chooses to regard orientation as a less critical feature than size or color (34).

Adults use the term dog to apply to both a chihuahua and a wolfhound because they share the critical attributes of species-typical characteristics of dogs. A chihuahua shares a great number of attributes with a Siamese cat (size, short hair, likelihood of "residence" in a small apartment) but because the chihuahua and the cat do not share the same critical attributes, they are not judged as being members of the same category. In the case of the helicopter, the critical characteristics of movement in the air and large size will tempt the child to call it an airplane, rather than a truck or a bird.

When the points of similarity involve real objects and events, the critical attributes are most important. But often the child must decide on the correct category for a concept or an idea, rather than a concrete, physical event. Now the central dimensions of the concept become important. The child hears his parents talking about candidates for a local election and notes that both feel positively about the candidate who wants to spend more money for schools. The child will be tempted to regard the concept of school expenditure as good, rather than bad, because the candidate his parents regard as a good man favors this action. However, the parents of another child favor the candidate who is opposed to more school expenditures because of the increased taxes it would bring. The child will regard the concept of school spending as bad.

Hence, the critical dimensions of concepts will vary with the child's experiences. Children who learn that social status and prestige are defined by the critical attributes of wealth rather than education will probably, as adults, invest more effort in accumulating material wealth than those children whose definition of social class has education as the critical attribute.

The Concept of Creativity The possession of a rich reservoir of knowledge from which hypotheses can be selected is to be distinguished from the freedom to use that knowledge. Typically, the child with a rich and varied storehouse of schemata, images, concepts, and rules is regarded as **intelligent.** The child who uses these units in both an original and constructive way is called **creative.** Intelligent children can be either creative or noncreative. In one study fifth-grade children were given standard tests of intelligence as well as tests of creativity. The tests for creativity required the child to generate many unusual hypotheses. For example, in one test the child would be told a characteristic and asked to name as many objects as he could that had that characteristic (for example, name all the things that you know that are sharp). The children were also asked to think up varied uses for objects (tell me all the different ways that you would use a newspaper). In a third test the child was shown line drawings (see Fig. 7.5, top) and asked to think up all the things each drawing might be. He was also shown line designs (see Fig. 7.5, bottom) and asked to say all the things these designs made him think of. The child was classified creative if he gave many answers to each of the tests and if some of his answers were very unusual in comparison to the answers given by the other children. The children were grouped into four categories: high intelligence and high creativity, high intelligence and low creativity; low intelligence and high creativity; low intelligence and low creativity.

The girls who were both highly intelligent and highly creative were self-confident in school and were popular with their friends. High-creativity, but low-intelligence girls, on the other hand, seemed to be just the opposite in personality.

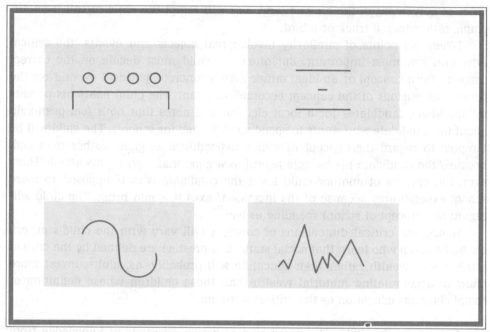

Figure 7.5 Drawings used to test creativity. (From M. A. Wallach & N. Kogan, **Modes of thinking in young children.** New York: Holt, Rinehart & Winston, 1965. Figures 2 and 3. By permission.)

They were cautious, hesitant, and had little self-confidence. The low-intelligence, low-creativity girls were slightly less cautious and hesitant and were more popular and outgoing with their friends than the high-creativity, low-intelligence girls. Finally, the high-intelligence but low-creativity girls were sought out by others, but they often failed to reciprocate such overtures, as if they were a little aloof or cautious with the other girls. Differences in creativity among boys did not relate closely to their social behavior with their peers.

In general, the creative child who was intelligent was willing to take a chance, to risk a "crazy" idea. He seemed to have a less severe attitude toward error. The girl who was both intelligent and creative seemed to be successful both in school and in her relationships with her peers. These children seemed to be confident and free of anxiety over generating unconventional ideas (50).

Obstacles to Creativity There are at least five major obstacles to the generation of good or creative solutions to problems. They are failure to comprehend the problem, forgetting the elements of the problem, insufficient knowledge, firm belief in rules that are inconsistent with the correct hypothesis, and, finally, fear of failure.

FAILURE TO UNDERSTAND THE PROBLEM. A child may be unable to solve a problem not because he is **unable** to perform the task, but simply because he does not understand what he is to do. For example, a 4-year-old is given a red block to hold while a blue block lies on the table in front of him. The experimenter then says, "Make it so the red block is on top of the blue block." The child performs correctly. But, if the child is holding the blue block with the red one on the table and the same instruction is given, the child either does nothing or puts the blue block on the red one. The child's failure in this case is due to his inability to understand the instruction literally; it is not due to an inability to put one block on top of another. One can prove this simple point by first showing the child a red block on a blue, taking away that model, and then repeating the instruction. Now, the child is perfectly capable of holding the blue block and solving the problem correctly (1).

Many children fail to comprehend a question because they do not understand the vocabulary or the grammar used in the posing of the question. A question on a standard intelligence test is "What must you do to make water boil?" Many poor children living in ghetto areas fail to answer correctly because they are not accustomed to the grammatical form "must you do." If the question is rephrased, "What do you do to make water boil?" these children answer correctly—"Put it on the stove."

A second reason for misunderstanding a problem is based on the fact that 6- and 7-year-olds do not appreciate that a problem can be about hypothetical, make-believe objects or events. Many 6-year-olds are **confused** if someone asks them, "A three-headed fish flew 4 miles one day and 3 miles the next day. How many miles did the fish fly all together?" The 6-year-old may refuse to think about this problem because he does not understand it. He knows that there are no three-headed fish and that fish cannot fly. Yet he may be able to add 4 and 3 correctly. The 10-year-old will accept the hypothetical conditions of the problem and produce the answer.

FAILURE TO REMEMBER THE PROBLEM. A second cause of failure to generate a good solution is forgetting the basic elements of the problem. A young child may not remember all the information in the question. As we have said, Professor Pascual-Leone believes that preschool children cannot hold and manipulate more than two items of information in mind at the same time. The preschool child may not be able to solve a problem which requires that he remember three facts. For example, in order to determine if the child can solve Piaget's class inclusion problems (see p. 311) the examiner places six blue buttons and four red buttons on the table and asks, "Are there more blue buttons or more buttons?" At the least, the child has three complex facts to remember: (1) the number of blue buttons, (2) the number of red buttons, and (3) that the examiner said "more blue or more buttons," not "more blue or more red buttons." The 4- or 5-year-old might not remember the exact words used and as a result answer incorrectly. Many new, inexperienced, kindergarten teachers who are not sensitive to the 5-year-old's inability to remember long instructions often misinterpret the child's failure to solve a problem or carry out a request as due to lack of intelligence or hostility, rather than the more innocent explanation that he forgot what he was told.

LACK OF KNOWLEDGE. Assuming that the child both understands and remembers the problem, a third obstacle to correct solution is the lack of appropriate concepts or rules. The child's life experiences help to determine whether he will or will not possess the knowledge necessary to solve a problem.

Suppose the following question were posed to a group of second graders in rural Alabama and to a middle-class group in New York City: "A man is in a log cabin on a cold windy night. All he has with him are some old newspapers and glue. What should he do to keep warm?" The solutions generated by each group can be traced to their specific life experiences. The rural child is more likely than the urban one to say that the newspapers should be glued against the window to keep out the wind, for he has seen this technique used with profit. This suggestion is less likely to come from an urban child because, in his experience, windows are usually intact.

A more dramatic example comes from the replies of isolated Indian children living in poor Guatemalan villages where illness is common. The children were asked to explain "why a man was so happy (for the last few weeks) that he has been singing." American 8-year-olds answer that question by saying that the man probably got a promotion in his job. The 8-year-old Indian child says that "He is crazy, for no one can be happy for that long a time in the village."

Since American children of different social classes have diverse experiences, one would expect them to generate different explanations to problems. Unfortunately, the questions on intelligence tests give credit only for a particular kind of answer. For example, one question on a leading intelligence test is "What should you do if a boy (or girl) smaller than you starts to fight with you?" The middle-class child, who is told never to pick on a smaller child, usually replies he would run home, tell the other child not to fight, or report the incident. The lower-class child, especially in the city, who is told to defend himself when he is attacked or "messed with," usually replies, "I would hit him back." Each child answers the question in perfect accord with what he has been told and has observed. Each has given a "correct" answer. Unfortunately, only the first answer is scored as correct in accordance with the test manual; the second answer receives no credit.

POSSESSION OF OTHER RULES. A fourth obstacle to the generation of good ideas is the firm belief in a rule that contradicts a new, correct explanation. A sixth-grade teacher may ask her class why some young American men went to Canada to avoid the draft. An 11-year-old who believed that these young men were brave would not generate the explanation that some of them may have been afraid of being drafted. That explanation would contradict a strongly held prior belief about the emotional maturity of these men.

Great discoveries in science are rare because most scientists have strong faith in what they were taught as students. It is difficult for them to entertain an idea that challenges one they learned when they were younger. Darwin's bold hypothesis that the animals and plants were not all created at the same time by a divine being, but evolved gradually, so strongly contradicted the dominant belief in the 1860s that he was severely criticized by his scientific colleagues.

FEAR OF ERROR. A fifth obstacle to the generation of good ideas is fear of making a mistake. The average school-age child is not only afraid of criticism from others for failure, but he also wants to avoid self-generated feelings of shame or humiliation for violating his own standards of competence. He does not want to feel the self-doubt that follows failure. The easiest and most frequent reaction to the possibility of failure is to withdraw, to inhibit offering any answer about which one is unsure. Every teacher recognizes the few children in her class who are intelligent, but overly inhibited. These cautious children know more than they are willing to say. They censor good ideas because they would rather forego the possibility of success than risk failure.

Each of the five conditions that stifle the generation of creative or good ideas —lack of comprehension of the problem, memory failure, lack of knowledge, fixed prior beliefs, and fear of failure—is particularly dominant at different stages of development. Most preschool children do not generate creative solutions because they fail to comprehend or forget the problem and because they lack sufficient knowledge. Many school-age children do not generate creative ideas because they fear failure. Adults usually fail to generate good ideas because they hold a set of beliefs that they cannot give up easily and therefore reject a new insightful solution that contradicts an older view. The truly creative child is rare. To be creative, he not only must have much knowledge, but he also must be willing to take a chance; he must be willing to risk failure and criticism for harboring and announcing a strange idea. He must have a permissive attitude toward error.

It is important to realize that a hypothesis generated in response to a problem which is original but unrelated to that problem is not to be regarded as creative. Indeed, it is simply not a solution to the problem. If this textbook were written in ancient Egyptian hieroglyphics and printed upside-down it would certainly be a novel volume, but obviously not a creative one. A creative idea derives from and then improves upon a prior set of explanations and solutions to a problem. It never stands alone, unrelated to earlier solutions. First-grade children are not likely to generate creative hypotheses because they do not have a rich reservoir of ideas from which they might synthesize better solutions. This is not to say that we should belittle originality in the drawings or sayings of young children (or that it is not possible for them to arrive at creative solutions), but we should not confuse the kindergarten child's originality with those products we call creative in the adolescent and adult.

Generation of Hypotheses and Learning Set One of the clearest demonstrations of the importance of developmental changes in the generation of ideas is seen in a phenomenon called learning set or "learning to learn." A **learning set** is the acquired set or attitude that is relevant to solving a particular class of problems, a disposition to attend to the relevant stimuli in the problem and to discard incorrect classes of hypotheses. In brief, the child learns a general solution approach to a specific class of problems. Thus, if a person played 20 Questions each day for 100 days, his efficiency and the quality of his questions would improve daily, even though the specific "secret" object he was trying to guess changed each day. He would be learning to ask better questions and learning not to ask questions that yield little information.

The problems used with children to explore learning set usually involve a series of discriminations in which a pair of objects is presented to the child. The child is told that one of the objects is correct and if he picks the correct one he will get a penny. Suppose that the first pair of objects presented to the child were a red and a yellow cube and that the experimenter had decided that color was to be the key to the solution and that the yellow cube is correct. If the child picks the yellow cube, he receives a penny; if he picks the red cube, he receives nothing. Initially, a 5-year-old might behave as if the position of the cube, whether it is on the right or the left, is the clue to correctness. If the yellow cube were on the right and he picked it and was rewarded, he would likely pick the cube on the right on the next trial even though the yellow cube were on the left. His initial hypothesis to solve this problem is that position is the key to the solution. Eventually the child will solve the problem and pick the yellow cube consistently, regardless of its position. After solving this problem he is presented with a different one. Now he is shown a bird and a four-footed animal of the same size and coloration, and the experimenter has decided that the bird is correct. The key to the solution has nothing to do with color or size, but rather with two versus four feet. The 5-year-old child who has solved the yellow-red cube problem is likely to solve this problem more rapidly as a result of having first had the cube problem. He has learned something from the initial problem; he has learned to disregard more quickly a hypothesis which proves incorrect. He may test the hypothesis of position as a possibility in the new situation, but is likely to reject it after fewer trials and move on to other hypotheses. The more rapidly he eliminates incorrect hypotheses that he ordinarily would try, the quicker he will solve the problem. **Learning to learn** is a combination of disregarding preferred hypotheses that are of no help and attending to the new and relevant aspects of a problem.

In one study **(32)** learning-set problems were administered to preschool children, fifth graders, and college students. Each subject was shown a pair of objects and was told to guess which one was correct. He was given several chances with a specific pair of objects and then was given a new pair of objects and, therefore, a new problem to solve. Each subject was given 10 different problems each day. There was an orderly progression in the efficiency with which a learning set was acquired (see Fig. 7.6). It took the preschool children 6 days (10 problems a day) to learn to solve each new problem quickly. The fifth graders required only 3 days, and the college students only 2 days in order to arrive at a point where they could solve a discrimination problem within one or two trials. The increasing efficiency of the older children was due to (1) greater flexibility in eliminating incorrect hypotheses, (2) the availability of a greater number of hypotheses, and (3) the faith that there is a correct solution—that analysis and attention to the stimuli will result in successful solution.

In addition, the child learns that the content of a problem does not have to be realistic or related to his personal life. The 6-year-old has not yet learned this principle and he occasionally brings in personal items from his own life experiences in solving problems. For example, Scottish children were administered problems of

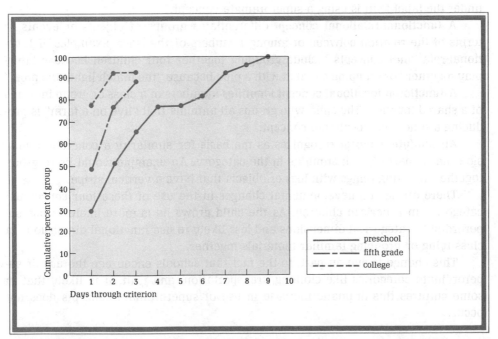

Figure 7.6 Cumulative percentage of age groups reaching criterion on each day of testing. (From B. Levinson & H. W. Reese. Patterns of discrimination learning set in preschool, fifth graders, college freshmen, and the aged. **Monographs of the Society for Research in Child Development**, 1967, **32,** 64. Copyright 1967 by The Society for Research in Child Development, Inc. By permission.)

the following type: "There are three boys, John, Bill and Pete, and they go to three different schools, the North school, the South school, and the West school. John goes to the North school, Bill goes to the South school. Where does Pete go?" A 6-year-old child might say, "Pete goes to the North school because my brother Pete goes there," confusing his own personal experiences with the arbitrary content of the problem. The 10-year-old would realize that West school was correct. Children must learn that a formal problem can be divorced from reality and that a solution can be arrived at logically, through thinking (6).

Generation of Hypotheses in Concept-Sorting Tasks There are important developmental as well as individual differences in the kinds of conceptual categories the child uses to classify information. Normally we are most concerned with the content or particular meaning of the concept (e.g., does the concept deal with people, animals, plants, cars, or school?). However, a second aspect of a concept pertains to its formal qualities, independent of its specific content. Some of the major formal dimensions can be described as follows (27).

A **categorical** or **superordinate concept** represents an abstract attribute shared by objects or events. The child who groups pears, apples, or bananas together under the label fruit is using a superordinate concept.

A **functional-relational concept** differentiates groups of objects or events in terms of the relation between or among members of the class. Examples of functional-relational concepts include grouping together four children because "they play together" or grouping a match with a pipe because "the match lights the pipe."

A **functional-locational concept** identifies members of a class or group in terms of a shared location. The child who groups all animals that "live on a farm" is producing a functional-locational concept.

An **analytic concept** recognizes as the basis for similarity a concrete dimension that is part of each stimulus in the category. An example would be to group together all living things with legs or objects that have a vertical stripe.

There are lawful developmental changes in the use of these four conceptual categories in American children. As the child grows he is more likely to use superordinate categorical dimensions and less likely to use functional dimensions in classifying or grouping familiar materials together.

This change is due, in part, to the fact that schools encourage the use of superordinate categories like clothing, transportation, and fruit. It is likely that in some cultures this dramatic increase in use of superordinate concepts does not occur.

The Meaning and Significance of Analytic Concepts The tendency to produce analytically based concepts with visual stimuli (objects or pictures) also tends to increase with age in American children because of an increased tendency to think before acting, as well as a preference to analyze the stimulus materials. Children

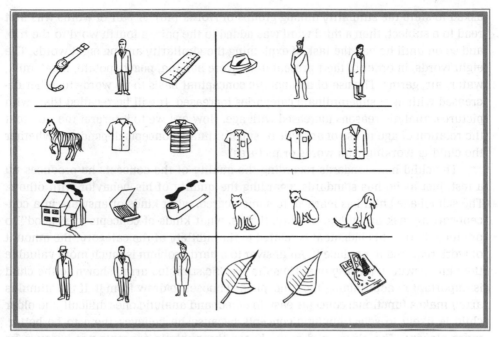

Figure 7.7 Sample items from CST. (From J. Kagan et al., Information processing in the child. **Psychological Monograph**, 1964, 78. Copyright 1964 by the American Psychological Association. By permission.)

6 to 11 years of age were shown a set of three pictures (Fig. 7.7) and were asked to select two pictures that were alike in some way. With age there was an increase in number of analytic concepts. The older children were more likely to say that the watch and the ruler go together because they both have numbers, rather than the watch and the man go together because the man wears the watch. Similarly, the older children grouped the house and the pipe together because they both have smoke coming out, rather than pairing the match and the pipe because the former lights the latter.

Analytic concepts increase with age partly because older children often pause and reflect longer in generating concepts than younger children do. In one experiment one group of school-age children was instructed to wait 15 seconds before telling the examiner the conceptual basis they selected; a second group was told to respond quickly (28). The former group produced more analytic concepts than the latter group.

Effect of Stimuli on Concept-Sorting It is important to realize that the child who uses analytic or relational concepts with pictures may not do so when he is presented with words. The child's strategy of classifying information depends to a great extent on the material being classified. Subjects 6 to 19 years of age were asked to state the similarity among groups of words (40). A pair of words was first read to a subject, then a third word was added to the pair, a fourth word to the trio, and so on until he had the task of explaining the similarity among eight words. The eight words, in order of their presentation, were banana, peach, potato, meat, milk, water, air, germs. The use of an analytic conceptual basis to tie words together decreased with age; superordinate categories increased. It will be recalled that, with pictures, analytic reasons increased with age. How are we to interpret the fact that the relation of age to use of analytic or superordinate concepts depends on whether the child is working with words or pictures?

The child has standards regarding the quality of the concepts he produces on a test, just as he has standards regarding the quality of his behavior with others. The school-age child has learned, to some degree, what kinds of answers in a concept-sorting task are of high quality, that is, what kinds of concepts are "good" to produce. Part of his judgment is related to the subtlety of the category, the amount of work required to produce it. An answer to a hard problem is much more valuable than an answer to an easy one. Thus the specific stimulus array shown to the child is important in determining the concepts he chooses to draw from it. If the stimulus array makes functional concepts easy to detect and analytic ones difficult, the older child is likely to select analytic concepts because he believes them to be better, more elegant. The older child may choose the analytic concepts not because he failed to note the relational aspect, but because he believes them to be "better," more elegant. Hence it is inappropriate to say that a child is analytic or relational without specifying the stimulus materials presented to him.

An illustration of the importance of the stimulus array on ease of conceptualization is contained in a study in which children had to learn either a relational or an absolute categorization of number (52). Children in grades 1, 3, 5, and 8 were presented with pairs of stimuli representing numerical amounts and were told that one stimulus was correct. The children had to learn either a relational (pick the smaller number of the pair) or an absolute (always pick the number 5) conception of number.

One group of children was presented with **perceptual** representations of the numbers (five dots versus seven dots, three dots versus five dots). A second group was presented with **abstract** representations of the numbers in terms of sets (five triangles versus seven squares, three crosses versus five circles). A third group was presented with actual pairs of numerals (the number 5 versus the number 7, the number 3 versus the number 5).

When the stimuli were perceptual and abstract representations, acquisition of the relational concept (pick the smaller) was easier than acquisition of the absolute concept. When the stimuli were numerals, the absolute concept was very easy to attain. The importance of the mode of presentation was clearest among the first-grade children. The relational concept was easy to attain under the perceptual conditions; the absolute response was easy to attain under the numeral condition; but both relational and absolute concepts were very difficult to obtain under the abstract condition. It is not reasonable to conclude, therefore, that first-grade children are preferentially relational or preferentially absolute in the way they think about number concepts. The ease with which they conceptualize number depends intimately on how the material is presented. A preferred conceptual response is rarely independent of the material that is being classified. Similarly, a child is not to be classified as analytic or categorical, for he may be analytic with visual stimuli containing subtle analytic cues, but superordinate when presented with verbal representations of those objects. The descriptive term analytic is like the term prejudiced. In both cases, we must know the target of the attitude.

In trying to understand the kinds of categories the child uses it is important to remember that he is always trying to solve a problem in the most efficient way possible with the concepts and rules he is accustomed to using. It is not "better," in any absolute sense, to categorize an apple, pear, and plum as fruits (superordinate category) than to say "they grow on trees in orchards" (functional-locational) or "they have seeds and a skin" (analytic response).

In certain rural villages in Africa the distinction between domestic animals (like chickens and pigs) and wild animals (like lions) is important and frequently made in the daily conversations of adults. Among African children from the city this domestic-wild distinction is not relevant to everyday life or conversation. In one study African children were shown 17 pictures of animals and were asked to group those that were alike. The rural child grouped them into superordinate categories of wild versus domestic. The urban child used analytic and functional categories (10). It is unreasonable to conclude that the rural child's superordinate concept was better or more mature than the functional or analytic concept produced by the city child. Each child solved the problem with the categories he was familiar with—the categories that were most adaptive for the problems he ordinarily had to solve.

Process 4. Evaluation

The fourth process in problem-solving, evaluation, pertains to the degree to which the child pauses to consider and assess the quality of his thinking. This process influences the entire spectrum of mental work: his initial perception, recall, and hypothesis generation.

Some children accept and report the first hypothesis they produce and act upon it with only the barest consideration for its appropriateness or accuracy; these children are called **impulsive.** Other children devote a longer period of time to consider the merits of their hypotheses and to censor poor hypotheses; they are called **reflective.** This difference among children is evident as early as 2 years of age and seems to be moderately consistent across problems and relatively stable over time **(22, 23, 24).**

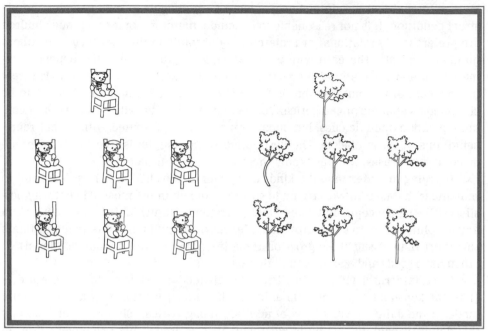

Figure 7.8 Sample items from the Matching Familiar Figures test for reflection-impulsivity in the school-age child.

Testing Reflection-Impulsiveness One of the tests used to assess the tendency of the child to be reflective or impulsive is called Matching Familiar Figures (see Fig. 7.8). A child is asked to select from six variants one stimulus that is identical with the standard. The important variables are the time the child takes to select his first hypothesis and the number of errors he makes. Among American children there is a dramatic decrease in errors and a corresponding increase in response time from 5 to 12 years of age. Moreover, the faster the child's decisions, the more mistakes he makes.

Children who respond quickly and make many errors, in contrast to those who respond slowly and make few errors, tend to retain this disposition over time. This preferred tendency is stable. The reflective children (those who respond slowly and make few errors), in contrast to the impulsive children, wait longer before they describe a picture, delay longer in answering a question posed to them by an adult, are less likely to report words that did not appear in a list that was read to them, are less likely to make errors in reading English prose, and make fewer errors in inductive reasoning tests. In one study first-grade children were given tests of inductive reasoning. On one test the child was told three characteristics of an object and then asked to guess the object (for example, What is yellow, melts in the sun, and you eat it? What has doors, wheels, and moves?). The impulsive children responded more quickly to these questions and made more errors than the reflective children. When the eye-tracking patterns of these two types of children are studied, the reflective children scan the visual stimuli more efficiently and are more likely to search every one of the variants before offering a solution hypothsis (9). The impulsive children adopt a much riskier strategy and answer before they have examined every variant carefully.

A child's disposition to be reflective or impulsive can be modified through training. Some impulsive children were simply told to inhibit their responses on the Matching Familiar Figures test. After several 30-minute sessions of such training in inhibition, they showed longer response times to similar problems than untrained, impulsive children. The impulsive child can be trained to be more reflective, more accurate, and more thoughtful through either reward or punishment or through merely watching other children behave reflectively (5, 45). Since it is more advantageous to be accurate than to make mistakes, it is easier to train an impulsive child to be reflective than it is to make a reflective child impulsive.

The teacher's tendency to be reflective or impulsive can also influence the child. Each of 20 first-grade teachers was classified as reflective or impulsive through use of an adult version of the Matching Familiar Figures task. Then a random group of children from each of the 20 classrooms was tested in the early fall and again in the late spring to determine if exposure to a teacher with a preferred strategy influenced the child's tempo. The children changed in a direction consonant with the teacher's tempo, and the effect was most marked for impulsive boys assigned to teachers who were both reflective and experienced. These boys showed the greatest increase in decision time over the course of the school year. Thus, although the tendency to be reflective or impulsive is stable over time and across varied tasks, it is modifiable (53).

The Basis for Reflection-Impulsiveness One of the major determinants of a reflective or impulsive attitude is fear of making a mistake. The more apprehensive the child is of making an error, the more likely he will be reflective. Reflective children are concerned with error and wish to avoid it at all costs; impulsive children seem minimally apprehensive about making a mistake and respond quickly. The increased tendency among American children to become reflective with age seems to reflect the disposition for American children to grow more cautious with age, to become increasingly concerned with avoiding a mistake (8).

Although fear of being wrong is probably the primary basis for a reflective attitude, there is some reason to believe that some children are born with a temperament that makes it easier for them to become reflective or impulsive (see Chapter 3, pp. 90–92). Observations of infants' play with toys reveal that some children flit from toy to toy, spending 10 to 15 seconds with each object before passing on to the next, while other infants will play with the same toy for a minute or two. The second group do not necessarily play with the toy more creatively, but they do have a slower tempo of play. There is a tendency for the slow tempo children to become reflective preschool children; the fast tempo infants are a little more likely to be impulsive preschool children. As in most basic human traits, both environmental and biological factors interact in producing the final psychological result.

In summary, we can now add one more reason for the offering of incorrect answers to problems. If a child does not think about his hypotheses, does not reflect upon his initial perception, comprehension, or final answer, he is more likely to be wrong, even though he may understand the problem and have the knowledge to solve it.

Process 5. Implementation of Transformational Rules: the Deductive Phase

There are two categories of rules, transformational and nontransformational. During the phase when the child is generating hypotheses, he is usually activating nontransformational rules. For example, in problems where he has to group similar objects, he generates nontransformational rules, such as "apples are fruits," "zebras have stripes," "lions live in a jungle." But some problems require transformational rules, that is, the child must carry out some kind of mental operation in order to arrive at a solution. For example, he may have to multiply two numbers, examine the logic of a geometric proof, or compare the differential appropriateness of several solutions. This phase involves the application of a transformational rule to a set of subordinate rules.

Suppose a 10-year old sees a large animal lying still by a tree. His initial assumption might be that it is sleeping. And if he watches it for a few minutes and notes that the animal remains motionless, he may then generate an alternative hypothesis, perhaps that the animal is dead. He has two incompatible explanations; the animal is either alive and sleeping or dead, and he wants to know which is correct. He may generate a transformational rule—"If I throw a twig at it and it doesn't move, it is probably dead. If it does move, it was sleeping." This rule is different from the rule "Quiet animals are sleeping" in a very important way. The transformational rule involves the activation of a routine, either an action (such as throwing the twig) or a mental process (such as carrying out a multiplication in an arithmetic problem). The routine produces additional information that permits the child to decide, or to deduce, which of two explanations is more likely to be correct. The application of the rules of arithmetic, like addition or multiplication, are transformational rules commonly used in schools.

The activation of appropriate transformational rules shows a dramatic change during the school years. It is possible that during these years the salience of the executive process becomes particularly important. The 5-year-old does not systematically check alternative hypotheses in order to gain further information. Nor does he seem to apply logical rules to select the most likely course of action. These mental processes are characteristic of the late preadolescent and, as we shall see, are signs of Piaget's formal operational stage.

PIAGET'S LATER STAGES OF INTELLIGENCE

As we indicated in Chapter 2, Piaget believes that the child's intellectual growth is characterized by a series of stages culminating in adolescence with the ability to use transformational rules in their most abstract form. We summarized Piaget's first stage of intellectual development—the sensorimotor stage—in Chapter 4. Now we shall consider the next three stages: preoperational, concrete operational, and formal operational.

Preoperational Stages (Ages 1½ to 7)

The child in the preoperational stage has language, and meanings of objects and events are manipulated as well as overt actions. A schema is now symbolic. The 2-year-old will treat a stick as if it were a candle and blow it out, or treat a block of wood as if it were a car and move it around, making a noise as he travels. This ability to treat objects as symbolic of things other than themselves is an essential characteristic of the preoperational stage. Piaget offers an illustration in which a doll is treated as if it were a live baby. "At 2 years 1 month, J put her doll's head through the balcony railings with its face turned toward the street and began to tell it what she saw, 'You see the lake and trees, you see a carriage or houses.' The same day she seated her doll on a sofa and told it what she herself had seen in the garden" (**43,** 127).

Piaget does not believe that the 2- or 3-year-old who collects a group of similar forms (puts all the red blocks in a pile, for example) is necessarily showing categorization or classification. The child, according to Piaget, does not have a mental representation of a set of categories as he sorts and is not aware of any defining characteristic that unites all the members of the class. Thus the act of putting similar things together, which preoperational children often do, is not necessarily evidence for conceptual classification. Moreover, the preoperational child has difficulty taking the point of view of another child or adult. He cannot anticipate how an object will look from the point of view of another person or even realize that a scene he sees may look different in the eyes of another. Piaget regards the preoperational child as egocentric in his perspective.

Although the 3-year-old is symbolic, his words and images are not necessarily organized into firmly articulated concepts and rules. That process happens during the next stage of concrete operations.

Stage of Concrete Operations (Ages 7 to 12)

There are several important differences between the child in the preoperational stage and the 7-year-old who is in the stage of concrete operations; these differences are summarized below:

Mental Representations One major difference between the preoperational and the operational child is that the former does not have a **mental representation** of a series of actions. The 5-year-old can learn to walk four blocks from his home to a neighborhood store, but he cannot sit at a table with a pencil and paper and trace the route he takes. He does not have, according to Piaget, a mental representation of the entire sequence of actions. He walks to the store successfully by making certain turns at certain places along the way, the way a rat runs a maze, but he has no overall picture of the route that he travels. Adults, of course, do have such a mental plan. Try to trace your route, on paper, from your home to a favorite restaurant. Notice how you must have a mental representation of the entire route in order to accomplish this task. According to Piaget, the 4-year-old is incapable of this level of functioning.

Conservation A second deficit of the preoperational stage is the absence of the operation of **conservation.** The notion that liquids and solids can be transformed in shape without changing their volume or mass is manifested only when the child reaches the stage of concrete operations. The 5-year-old believes that if you change the shape of a piece of clay the amount of clay also changes—the quantity of clay is not conserved. For example, a 5-year-old child is shown two balls of clay of equal mass and shape; he acknowledges that they have the same amount of clay. The experimenter then flattens one of the balls so that it resembles a pancake and asks the child which has the greater amount of clay, or whether there is an equal amount of clay in both masses. Typically, the 5-year-old regards the ball and pancake as unequal in quantity. Two years later, he is likely to insist that the ball and pancake have the same amount of clay because "the pancake is thinner but it is wider," indicating that he is aware of the compensatory dimensions; he can also assert, "I can make the pancake into a ball again."

Another example of the absence of the operation of conservation is that the preoperational child does not believe that the length of a stick remains constant despite changes in its relation to another stick or other object. If two sticks of equal length are placed side by side so that their endpoints coincide, the child will admit they are equal. If one stick is moved forward an inch, the 5-year-old will say that it is longer, while the 7-year-old will acknowledge that they are still the same length. The young child does not realize that the attribute of length of an object is constant and not dependent on its perceptual context.

Similarly, the preoperational child does not appreciate the fact that if the number of objects in two arrays is equal, they are equal in quantity regardless of the shape of the arrays. In this experiment, two groups of five buttons each are placed one above the other so that the two rows are of equal length. The child acknowledges that the two rows have the same amount of buttons. But if one row is made shorter (by regrouping the buttons), the preoperational child says that the longer row has more buttons. He behaves as if the word "more" refers to the apparent quantity—the perceptual aspect—and does not refer to the number of items.

Relational Terms The preoperational child does not understand relational terms, such as darker, larger, bigger. He tends to think absolutely, that is, he interprets darker as meaning very dark rather than darker than another object. If he is shown two light objects, one of which is slightly darker, and is asked to pick the darker one, he may not answer. Similarly, concepts such as brother of, left of, and taller than are difficult to apply. These relational expressions are understood as names for absolute attributes of objects, rather than as relations holding between objects. Piaget summarizes the child's conception as follows:

> The conclusion to which we are finally led is this. The child does not realize that certain ideas, even such as are obviously relative for an adult, are relations between at least two terms. Thus he does not realize that a brother must necessarily be the brother of somebody, that an object must necessarily be to the right or left of somebody, or that a part must necessarily be part of a whole, but thinks of all these notions as existing in themselves absolutely (42, 131).

Class Inclusion According to Piaget, a fourth deficit of the preoperational child is that he cannot reason simultaneously about part of the whole and the whole. If a 5-year-old is shown eight yellow candies and four brown candies and asked, "Are there more yellow candies or more candies?" he is likely to say, "More yellow candies." Piaget believes this reply means that the child cannot reason about a part and a whole simultaneously.

Serialization The fifth characteristic that differentiates preoperational children from those in the stage of concrete operations is the ability to arrange objects according to some quantified dimension, such as weight or size, on an ordinal scale. This ability is called **serialization.** The 5-year-old typically cannot arrange eight sticks of differing length in a row according to their length. The student can readily see how critical serialization ability is for understanding the relation of numbers to one another and, therefore, to the learning of arithmetic.

Summary

The child of 7, who has just entered the stage of concrete operations, has acquired an important set of rules that he did not possess a year or two earlier. He believes that length, mass, weight, and number remain constant despite superficial modification in their external appearance. He is able to produce a mental image of a series of actions and realizes that relational concepts such as darker or heavier do not necessarily refer to absolute qualities, but to a relation between two or more objects. Finally, he can reason about the whole and its parts simultaneously and can order objects on a dimension of quantity (such as size or height). In short, he has learned some central rules to aid his adaptation to his environment.

Stage of Formal Operations (Age 12 on)

There are several important attributes of formal operational thinking that differentiate it from the previous stage of concrete operations. First, the adolescent is capable of considering all the possible ways a particular problem might be solved and the possible forms a particular variable might assume. If he is thinking about the shortest way to get to the seashore, he can and will review all the possible routes and he knows when he has exhausted all the possibilities.

Consider the following question put to a 7-year-old and a 13-year-old: "A man was found dead in the back seat of a car which had hit a telephone pole. What happened?" The younger child thinks up a reason that satisfies him and states it: "The man hit a pole and was thrown in the back seat and was killed." The older child is more likely to generate all the possible ways this event might have happened—he could have hit a pole and been thrown into the back seat; he could have been put in the car after it crashed in order to make the scene appear to be an accident; he could have been put in the back seat by his companion after the crash; and so on.

A group of fourth-, fifth-, and sixth-graders were tested repeatedly over a 4-year period on problems requiring the use of transformational rules. One of the tasks resembled the game 20 Questions. The child was shown 16 numbers randomly placed and was told, "I am thinking of one of these numbers, and you have to find out which one I am thinking of by asking me questions which can only be answered yes or no." In a second task the child was given 6 piles of squares of different colors: red, green, yellow, blue, orange, and purple, and was asked to make all the possible pairs of colors. In a third task he was given a shuffled deck of 12 pictures, 4 pictures with a healthy face and a blank microscopic slide, 4 with a sick face and a slide with green germs, 2 with a healthy face and a slide with green germs, and, finally, 2 with a sick face and a blank slide. He was asked whether the evidence on these pictures was sufficient to allow him to conclude that green germs caused the sickness.

The children performed better on these problems as they grew older. The major difference between the younger and older children was that the older children activated a plan of attack for the problem. For example, on the task which required the child to pair all the colors, a child could solve the problem by trial and error or by a transformational rule which systematically paired each color with every other color. Some older children were even able to verbalize the transformational rule they used. Most of the children had difficulty with the disease question, for they could not decide whether the doctor had enough evidence to assume that germs caused the illness (37).

This tendency to generate and explore systematically all the possible solution hypotheses and then to check each carefully for its probable validity is one of the hallmarks of the stage of formal operations.

A second characteristic of formal operations thought is that it is self-consciously deductive and resembles the thought of a scientist. The adolescent can think in terms of hypothetical propositions that may be fanciful and not fit reality. Consider the question "They found a 3-year-old skull of an animal with five feet and three heads that lived to be 50 years. What is silly about that?" The 7-year-old might object to this problem by saying that there are no animals with five feet and three heads; the adolescent is capable of accepting this fanciful hypothesis and attempting to reason out the answer.

A third characteristic of formal operational thought is the organization of operations into higher-order operations—ways of using abstract rules to solve a whole class of problems. For example, consider the problem "What number is 30 less than 3 times itself?" The 7-year-old in the stage of concrete operations is likely to begin the problem by trial and error, trying first one number and then another, using the operations of addition and multiplication until he finally arrives at the correct answer. The adolescent has learned a higher-order operation and may set up the equation $\times + 30 = 3x$ and quickly find the answer of 15. He combines the separate operations of addition and multiplication into the more complex operation of the algebraic equation.

If children are given a bowl of water and a box of objects and are asked to select the ones that float, the older child will not put each object in water one at a time but will apply a simplifying rule. He will first pick out all the wooden objects and may even apply some test (such as knocking them on wood) to see if they are primarily made of wood. These more complex units are called **combinative structures.** To know that one should use the operation of multiplication to solve the problem "How many ways can I pair six color discs with each other?" is an example of a combinative structure, and such structures are necessary to understand algebra and higher mathematics.

Thus, formal thought is basically a generalized orientation toward problem-solving. The basis of this orientation is the tendency to isolate the elements of a problem and systematically explore all the possible solution hypotheses, regardless of how hypothetical they are. Formal thought is rational and systematic. Moreover, the adolescent seems to reflect upon the rules he possesses and is aware of his own thoughts, aware of what he knows. It is not accidental that adolescence is the first time when the child begins to think about himself, his role in life, his plans, and the validity and integrity of his beliefs. The adolescent's concern with "the phoniness" of his own ideals and those of adults is acute in our time, but is rarely seen in childen under 10 years of age. The child in concrete operations tends to deal largely with the present, with the here and now; the adolescent becomes concerned with the hypothetical, the future, and the remote. An adolescent was overheard to remark, "I find myself thinking about my future and then I began to think about why I was thinking about my future, and then I began to think about why I was thinking about why I was thinking about my future." Piaget believes that this preoccupation with thought is the principal component of the stage of formal operations.

Piaget's Views on the Mechanisms of Developmental Change

Piaget believes that several factors influence the child's growth through his stages of intellectual development. They include (1) exercise and activity with objects, (2) detection of the salient aspects of experience, and (3) logicomathematical experiences which result in the discovery of abstract properties of objects that do not belong to the objects themselves. Piaget gives an excellent example of this last process.

> If a child when he is counting pebbles happens to put them in a row and to make the astonishing discovery that when he counts them from the right to the left he finds the same number as when he counts from the left to the right, and again the same when he puts them in a circle. He has thus discovered experimentally that the sum (of the number of objects) is independent of the order (of the number of objects). This is a logical mathematical experiment and not a physical one because neither the order nor the sum was in the pebbles before he arranged them in a certain manner and joined them together in a whole (44, 721).

Evaluation of Piaget

An evaluation of the significance of Piaget's ideas rests directly on the generality of his observations and his theoretical hypotheses concerning the mechanism of intellectual growth. There is little doubt that his statements about the developmental changes in conservation of mass, class inclusion, or seriation are generally true for western children. The provocative suggestion that we theorize about these rules as operations (as interiorized actions that are reversible) is an ingenious and perhaps profitable way to view their gradual acquisition. Piaget's theory implies that a normally endowed child who could not use his arms or legs would have great difficulty growing intellectually, for Piaget assigns an important role to the infant's motor actions. These actions subsequently become internalized as operations. Study of the intellectual growth of thalidomide babies or babies born with paralyzed limbs would furnish an important test of this critical hypothesis.

As we saw in Chapter 4, infants under 1 year seem to be able to generate simple cognitive hypotheses to interpret unusual events, such as the sudden change in the size of a block or the shape of a face, and appreciation of this change does not seem to require a motor component. Furthermore, the 1-year-old infant can have understanding of words like baby and doggie without having established sensory schemes for these objects or words. Hence, Piaget's emphasis on the relevance of sensorimotor schema for cognitive functioning during infancy may be exaggerated.

However, the suggestion that the operation is the "work horse" in cognitive development is more central to Piaget's theory. Let us therefore examine its meaning and potential usefulness. Piaget claims that the 8-year-old can conserve, serialize, and show class inclusion because he has acquired an operation. In the case of conservation of liquid quantities, appreciation of the fact that the amount of water does not change is due to the knowledge that the child can undo the transformation by pouring the water back into the original container.

Quite a different explanation of nonconservation (or conservation) is that the nonconserving child does not relate the original situation of the two containers of equal heights with the final situation containing two containers of unequal heights. He may not realize that the water used in the transformation to make the final pair of containers was the same water that he saw earlier (2). He may think he is being asked two separate and independent questions about two quite different problem situations. Hence it is not clear that the best way to explain conservation is to assume that the child has acquired an interiorized action. The fact that the child gives an answer that implies reversibility (you can pour the water back) may be due to the fact that he is forced to justify his answer to the examiner. That answer is not necessarily the rule that he used to solve the problem. There is no question that an important change in quality of thought occurs during the period from nonconservation to conservation, but it is not yet clear that the psychological differences are best explained as the result of the acquisition of operations.

A third focus of criticism is based on the fact that Piaget and his followers believe that the theory is relevant to all aspects of mental development, not just to the limited phenomena he has studied. Piaget's writings occasionally imply that the 5-year-old child cannot serialize on any dimension; that no 7-year-old can reason on any issue without concrete objects. These stronger statements are still controversial. Most 5-year-olds will state that their father is bigger than a rabbit and a rabbit is bigger than a mouse, and acknowledge that their father is bigger than a mouse, indicating an ability to order objects on a dimension of size. The difference between this problem and those used by Piaget is that the father-rabbit deals with very familiar ideas. When four conservation tasks were given to 5- and 7-year-old children living in rural, agricultural areas of Guatemala (quantity, matter, and area for both farm acreage and cubes) the only test which over half of the 7-year-olds passed was conservation of the area of a farm. It is not coincidental that the area of a piece of land was most familiar to these children who lived in rural areas where corn and beans were planted on well-marked plots of land (31).

If the child does not understand the question that is being put to him, he will obviously perform at an immature level. For example, Piaget suggests that the child of 8 years cannot classify himself on two dimensions simultaneously, that is, he cannot regard himself simultaneously as a member of a city and also as a member of a country. One reason for this deficiency is that the child does not have a complete understanding of the semantic meanings of the words city and country. He does not know that a city is part of a nation. It can be demonstrated that a 5-year-old child is capable of double classification if he understands the two concepts. The 5-year-old knows that he can be both a member of the Jones family and a member of the male sex at the same time.

Piaget is interested in knowing when the child can use, or comprehend, the adult meaning of certain concepts: "Which stick is **longer**?" "Which cup has **more** water?" "Which car traveled for a **longer time**?" The answer the child gives to these questions depends on his understanding of the words longer, more, and time. In the experiment on conservation of quantity the examiner pours water from one jar into a tall thin container and asks which jar has more water. The 6-year-old child points to the tall thin jar. Piaget concludes that the child has not learned that a certain quantity remains constant despite transformation of shape. However, the young child's understanding of the word more in this context may be closely tied to the perception of height (i.e., higher means more). Height is synonymous with quantity for the young child. This point is nicely illustrated in a study on conservation of numbers.

The child was shown two rows of seven buttons, but one row was shorter than the other. The child said that both rows had seven buttons; they both had the same number of buttons. However, when he was asked which row had more buttons, he insisted that the longer row had more buttons (16). For this child, the word was not synonymous with the arithmetic meaning of more.

It is possible that part of the process of acquiring the operation of conservation may involve learning the arithmetic meaning of the words for quantity and giving up other definitions. Piaget has shown that the 5-year-old does not understand the meaning of words such as more, equal, and longer the way adults do. But this conclusion is not only true for the concepts in mathematics or physics; it is also true for the concepts of love, justice, beauty, and evil. The critical attributes of many important concepts in our language change with development, and some of these changes do not seem easily explained in terms of changes in operations.

Piaget's emphasis on the importance of reversibility, class inclusion, serial ordering operations, and combinative structures is most relevant to mathematics and physics and less obviously relevant to many natural phenomena that do not show reversibility or obey class-inclusion rules. The relation between a whole and its parts in mathematics is usually not applicable to living things or the behavior of people. The concept of crowd is more than the sum of the number of people in the crowd. Moreover, the child discovers that death, unlike quantity of water, is not conserved and capable of a reversible operation. When a child kills a butterfly, it is not possible to perform an operation that transforms the insect back to the living state.

Piaget's observations of the squences in cognitive development seem to be essentially correct. The controversy centers on the best way to explain the developmental changes in the child's thinking. Is the ability to conserve quantity best explained as the acquisition of an operation (that is, as an interiorized action that is reversible)? Some studies have successfully trained children to conserve quantity without requiring the child to act on any materials. These children were merely taught—or reminded—that a particular object should be regarded as possessing more than one attribute. For example, 5-year-old children who had not acquired conservation of quantity with clay or water were brought to a room where a woman showed the child various objects and encouraged the youngsters, in a group, to name many characteristics of these objects. Subsequently, the children were shown objects and asked to name all the ways in which they were similar and the ways in which they were different. The following transcript of a training session dealing with multiple attributes of objects conveys the flavor of these interviews (47).

> TEACHER: Can you tell me what this is, Mary?
> MARY: A banana.
> TEACHER: What else can you tell me about it?
> MARY: It's straight.
> TEACHER: It's straight. What else?
> MARY: It has a peel.
> TEACHER: It has a peel. . . . Tom, what can you tell me about it?
> TOM: Ummm . . . It has some dark lines on it.
> TEACHER: Uh-huh.
> TOM: It has some green on it.
> TEACHER: What can you do with it?
> TOM: You can eat it!
> TEACHER: That's right! . . . Now let's see . . .
> CHILDREN: . . .I love bananas!
> TEACHER: What is this?
> CHILDREN: An orange?
> TEACHER: Is it really an orange?
> CHILDREN: Uh-huh. . . . Yes.
> CHILD: Look at it closely.
> TEACHER: It's an artificial one.

CHILDREN: Oh, that's right, it's an artificial one. . . . But, what else can you tell me about it?

TEACHER: You can eat it. . . . It is round . . .

CHILDREN: Uh-huh.

TEACHER: That's right!

CHILD: It has a stem.

TEACHER: Now, look at this one . . . What's this?

CHILDREN: An orange . . . orange.

TEACHER: And what can you do with it?

CHILDREN: You can eat it . . . and it's round . . .

TEACHER: It is round . . .

CHILD: It has a peel . . .

TEACHER: It has a peel. . . . Now, look at these two things. Are they the same?

CHILDREN: No.

TEACHER: What's different?

CHILDREN: This one . . . this one here is pressed in on the side a little . . . this one is lighter.

TEACHER: Do you know what this really is? This is a tangerine . . . and this is an orange. Now tell me in what ways they are alike.

CHILD: This is smaller and that's bigger.

TEACHER: I said, "In what way are they alike?"

CHILD: They are both round . . . they both have a stem . . . both orange (47, 305).

In essence, the children were taught that objects simultaneously possess many characteristics and all should be taken into account. Following several half-hour training sessions, each child was individually tested again on the original tasks for conservation of quantity. After training, most of them were able to conserve quantity, whereas they were unable to do so prior to the training. The experience of noting the multiple attributes of objects facilitates the child's ability to conserve quantity (47). As the training did not teach the child reversibility directly, we are faced with the problem of explaining why the training helped the child to believe in conservation of quantity, for this result is not congruent with Piaget's explanation of the phenomenon. It is important to determine the theoretical validity of Piaget's suggestion that changes in operations are the most profitable way to conceptualize the public phenomena. But regardless of the results of future research on this issue, it is still true that Piaget's contributions have been epochal and his influence on developmental psychology without parallel.

THE ROLE OF MOTIVES AND EXPECTANCY

The heart of this chapter has been devoted to the cognitive factors involved in problem-solving. However, even if the child has all the proper knowledge, he may not use it, and he may not attend to all the relevant information if he is not motivated or expects to fail. Let us consider these issues briefly.

Motives

If a child believes that mastery of an intellectual task will help him obtain a desired goal, the child will work at mastery. At a general level, most children have strong desires for recognition, affection, and approval from adults; dominance over peers; hostility, power, and mastery. If the child believes that working hard at intellectual tasks will help him attain one or more of these goals, he will do so. Some environments teach the child that attainment of athletic skills will lead to power; others teach that intellectual competence will provide the same goal. The specific behaviors the child chooses in order to gratify his motives are obviously a function of the values espoused by his family. The greater the parental emphasis on intellectual mastery, the stronger will be the child's motivation to master these skills. A parent who is accepting but encourages popularity, beauty, or athletic prowess will not foster the development of a desire to excel in school. The child is also motivated to maintain and increase his similarity to desired models. This process of identification can facilitate intellectual mastery. If intellectual competence is one of the model's central attributes, the child will attempt to increase his mastery in order to increase his similarity to the desired model.

Expectancy

Expectancy of success at intellectual tasks is a second factor controlling quality of test performance. As a child approaches his third year he becomes more acutely conscious of his ability—or lack of ability—to complete certain tasks or solve particular problems. He seeks to avoid the unpleasant feelings that accompany task failure. He approaches those tasks he expects to master successfully and avoids tasks he expects to fail. A balance of successes and failures accumulates over time and gradually leads to the establishment of a relatively stable expectancy of success for varied classes of problems. The presence of an excessively competent parent may lead to expectancy of failure if the child cannot identify with the parent. The child is likely to feel that he can never be as powerful or as competent as the parent. Under such circumstances, the child may doubt his ability to succeed and he may withdraw from intellectual challenges.

Anxiety

Finally, the degree of anxiety associated with intellectual mastery is important. Anxiety is most likely to occur under two conditions—when expectancy of success (or failure) is moderate and when motivation is high but expectancy of success is low. In the first instance the child is maximally uncertain about how he will perform on a test and the uncertainty generates anxiety. The child would be much less anxious if he knew definitely he would pass or fail. In the second instance, the child values competence on a particular intellectual task but expects to fail. When there is a discrepancy between a valued goal and the expectancy of obtaining that goal, anxiety is likely to be generated.

Interaction of Psychodynamic Factors

Motives, expectancies, and anxiety are intimately related to each other and both are related to quality of cognitive performance. The most important relation ties expectancy of success with motivation to master the task. If expectancy of success remains low, motive strength often becomes weak; if expectancy of success is high, motivational strength may increase (20, 21).

In one study children 7 to 9 years of age were asked to state whether they could solve mazes and memory tasks of differing difficulty and were later observed in a situation in which observers coded how long each child played with intellectual games and puzzles. The children who had stated that they could solve difficult problems (high expectancy of success) approached the intellectual tasks more frequently that others (4). In general, the child with a high expectancy of success will perform better on an intellectual task than one whose expectancy of success is low.

Expectancy of failure exerts a powerful role on the child's motivation to master or perform on a task, and it can be seen in clear form as early as 2 years of age. Two-year-old children can become very involved in certain problems. If the initial problems are easy and correct solutions come after a brief expenditure of effort, motivation is maintained and signs of delight punctuate the child's performance. But after one failure, or at most two (children seem to know when they have failed without being told), there is a sudden sullen withdrawal from the task which is difficult to overcome. The child knows which answers are correct and which incorrect and he prefers to avoid the pain of possible failure rather than risk the possible delight of success. It is difficult to explain why expectancy of failure is so strong a force in governing the western child's behavior. Perhaps the responses of inhibition and withdrawal are easier to elicit than the acts that characterize task involvement. Moreover, failure leaves the child with no response to make. The child who has failed is uncertain as to what he should do and withdrawal is a likely reaction. Prior to failing, the child had been issuing responses that were accepted and led to positive outcomes. Suddenly these responses are not accepted any more; they do not lead to the expected positive outcome. The child feels pressured to behave, but he does not know what to do. The prepotent reaction in such a situation is to withdraw. This interpretation of withdrawal as a response to failure places the burden of explanation as much on the availability of task-related responses as on the unpleasant feeling generated by failure or disapproval. The western child is driven to avoid failure and the quality of his performance on any cognitive task is continually monitored by his guess as to how well he will perform on the task.

The Significance of the Child's Public Test Behavior

Most of this chapter has been concerned with the child's overt problem-solving behavior—his answers to questions. But an answer, spoken, written, drawn, or acted out in gesture, may not be an absolutely faithful index of the quality of the child's thought. Psychologists and teachers must, of course, use the child's actual performance to make educated guesses about the quality of the child's cognitive processes. But we must view these performances with wisdom. Absence of a correct response does not necessarily mean the child is not capable of the correct answer. If the child says "sheeps" instead of sheep or "wented" instead of went, this error does not necessarily mean that he could not tell you that the latter are correct and the former incorrect. If a child of 4 years is asked to draw a man as best he can, he is likely to draw the arms attached to the head. But if the child is shown a drawing of a well-formed man and a drawing of one with arms attached to the head and is asked to point to the man, the child quickly points to the correct representation, not the incorrect one. He knows much more than he can produce. A child who cannot reproduce a geometric design has no trouble identifying the correct design when it is presented along with a group of similar ones.

Children also differ in their preferred behavioral reactions to difficult problem situations. Some children persist, others directly refuse to go on with the task, still others become quietly passive (neither speaking nor acting). A study compared 3-year-old lower-class Puerto Rican children with middle-class non-Puerto Rican children of the same age (18). There were two interesting differences between the groups in their behavioral reaction to intellectual problems. The middle-class children were more likely to work at a problem than the Puerto Rican children. When problems became difficult, the middle-class subjects were more likely to shake their head or push the material away while the Puerto Rican children just sat passively, saying or doing nothing.

The content of a child's answer, his drawing, or his spontaneous speech are under the control of many factors. A careless attitude toward a drawing can yield a poor reproduction; an inability to coordinate lines can yield a gross pictorial distortion; immature syntax can destroy effective communication of a well-formed idea. Psychologists and teachers have been forced to use the child's actions and speech as the primary sources of information about the quality of his thought because of the absence of more sensitive procedures. But each action is the result of multiple forces. Behavior is the result of motivation, language proficiency, expectancy of success, anxiety, preferred strategies for perceptual analysis, and degree of evaluation, to name only a few elements. The child's final performance is an inadequate index of each of these processes for it is a unique composite of them all. The child has many ways to produce a wrong answer. The invention of procedures which will allow separate evaluation of each of these components of a child's public performance has the highest priority for the future. Perhaps one day we will have more direct access to the child's thoughts and not have to guess their form from his hesitant speech or the cryptic messages he writes on paper.

SUMMARY

Cognitive activity involves the five basic processes of perception and interpretation of information, memory, generation of hypotheses or solutions to problems, evaluation of the accuracy and appropriateness of cognitive products, and deduction. These activities, or mental functions, involve a small set of hypothetical mental entities which we have called schemata, images, symbols, concepts, and rules. In a sense, one can regard these mental functions and entities as the physiology and anatomy of thought. As in physiological and anatomical development, there are important changes in the nature of the interaction between the functions and the mental units. The major changes involve increasing richness of schemata, symbols, concepts, and rules, which, in turn, produce more efficient comprehension, better retention of information, and more flexible and more adequate hypothesis generation. In addition, the rules and concepts become combined into more complicated rules, much as simple chemical elements become combined into complex molecules. As in chemistry, the more complex forms, built from the simpler ones, have unique properties that are not characteristic of the simpler elements. Thus the 12-year-old's realization that he can multiply the speed of a car by the time it travels in order to find the total distance between two points is a forceful and powerful rule that is not given by knowing the meaning of speed or time alone. Perhaps the most important cognitive change that accompanies development from age 3 to 12 is the emergence of an executive process which makes the child conscious of his problem-solving activities, allows him to relate past information to the present problem in a systematic way, and permits him, by the time he reaches adolescence to reason in a systematic and logical fashion. The present task for psychology is to gain more exact knowledge about the separate cognitive functions and how they are combined in thought.

Finally, it must be realized that the quality of a child's performance depends on his motives, fears, and expectations. The relation between the answers he gives in the classroom and the mental processes that produce these answers is still largely a mystery.

References

1. Bem, S. L. The role of comprehension in children's problem solving. **Developmental Psychology,** 1970, **2,** 351–358.

2. Block, S. C. Is the child a scientist with false theories of the world? Unpublished doctoral dissertation, Harvard University, 1972.

3. Cole, M., Frankel, F., & Sharp, D. Dvelopment of free recall learning in children. **Developmental Psychology,** 1971, **4,** 109–123.

4. Crandall, V. J., Katkovsky, W., & Preston, A. Motivational and ability determinants of young children's intellectual achievement behaviors. **Child Development,** 1962, **33,** 643–666.

5. Debus, R. L. Effects of brief observation of model behavior on conceptual tempo of impulsive children. **Developmental Psychology,** 1970, **2,** 22–32.

6. Donaldson, M. **The study of children's thinking.** London: Tavistock, 1963.

7. Doob, L. W. Eidetic images among the Ibo. **Ethnology,** 1964, **3,** 357–362.

8. Draguns, J. G., & Multari, G. Recognition of perceptually ambiguous stimuli in grade school children. **Child Development,** 1961, **32,** 541–550.

9. Drake, D. M. Perceptual correlates of impulsive and reflective behavior. **Developmental Psychology,** 1970, **2,** 202–214.

10. Fjellman, J. S. The myth of primitive mentality. Unpublished doctoral dissertation, Stanford University, 1971.

11. Flavell, J. H. Developmental studies of mediated memory. In H. P. Reese & L. P. Lipsitt (Eds.), **Advances in child development and behavior.** Vol. 5. New York: Academic Press, 1970. Pp. 182–211.

12. Flavell, J. H. Concept development. In P. H. Mussen (Ed.), **Handbook of child psychology.** New York: Wiley, 1970. Pp. 983–1060.

13. Flavell, J. H., Beach, D. R., & Chinsky, J. M. Spontaneous verbal rehearsal in a memory task as a function of age. **Child Development,** 1966, **37,** 284–299.

14. Gibson, E. J. **Principles of perceptual learning and development.** New York: Appleton-Century-Crofts, 1969.

15. Haber, R. N., & Haber, R. B. Eidetic imagery. **Perceptual Motor Skills,** 1964, **19,** 131–138.

16. Harris, G. J., & Burke, D. The effects of grouping on short term serial recall of digits by children: developmental trends. **Child Development,** 1972, **43,** 710–716.

17. Heider, E. R. Focal color areas and the development of color names. **Developmental Psychology,** 1971, **4,** 447–455.

18. Hertzig, M. E., Birch, H. G., Thomas, A., & Mendez, O. A. Class and ethnic differences in the responsiveness of preschool children to cognitive demands. **Monographs of the Society for Research in Child Development,** 1968, **33**(1, Ser. No. 117).

19. Hochberg, J., & Brook, V. Pictoral recognition as an unlearned ability: A study of one child's performance. **American Journal of Psychology,** 1962, **75,** 624–628.

20. Irwin, F. W. Stated expectations as functions of probability and desirability of outcomes. **Journal of Personality,** 1953, **21,** 329–335.

21. Jessor, R., & Readio, J. The influence of the value of an event upon the expectancy for its occurrence. **Journal of Genetic Psychology,** 1957, **56,** 219–228.

22. Kagan, J. Individual differences in the resolution of response uncertainty. **Journal of Personality and Social Psychology,** 1965, **2,** 154–160.

23. Kagan, J. Reflection impulsivity and reading ability in primary grade children. **Child Development,** 1965, **36,** 609–628.

24. Kagan, J. Generality and dynamics of conceptual tempo. **Journal of Abnormal Psychology,** 1966, **71,** 17–24.

25. Kagan, J. Cross cultural perspectives on early development. Paper presented at the meeting of the American Association for the Advancement of Science, Washington, D.C., December, 1972.

26. Kagan, J., Klein, R. E., Haith, M. M., & Morrison, F. J. Memory and meaning in two cultures. **Child Development,** 1973, **44,** 221–223.

27. Kagan, J., Moss, H. A., & Sigel, I. E. Psychological significance of styles of conceptualization. In J. C. Wright and J. Kagan (Eds.), Basic cognitive processes in children. **Monographs of the Society for Research in Child Development,** 1963, **28** (2, Ser. No. 86), 73–112.

28. Kagan, J., Rosman, B. L., Day, D., Albert, J., & Philips, W. Information processing in the child. **Psychological Monographs,** 1964, **78**(1, Whole No. 578).

29. Katz, J. M. Reflection impulsivity and color form sorting. **Child Development,** 1971, **42,** 745–754.

30. Kolers, P. A. Experiments in reading. **Scientific American,** 1972, **227,** 84–91.

31. Lester, B., & Klein, R. E. Unpublished manuscript, Institute Nutrition Central America and Panama, Guatemala City, 1972.

32. Levinson, B., & Reese, H. W. Patterns of discrimination learning set in preschool children, fifth graders, college freshmen, and the aged. **Monographs of the Society for Research in Child Development,** 1967, **32**(7, Ser. No. 115).

33. Maccoby, E. E. Selective auditory attention in children. In L. P. Lipsitt & C. C. Spiker (Eds.), **Advances in child development and behavior.** New York: Academic Press, 1967. Pp. 99–124.

34. McGurk, H. The salience of orientation in young children's perception of form. **Child Development,** 1972, **43,** 1047–1052.

35. Messer, S. B. The effect of anxiety over intellectual performance on reflective and impulsive children. Unpublished doctoral dissertation, Harvard University, 1968.

36. Morrison, F. J. A developmental study on the effect of familiarity on short term visual memory. Unpublished doctoral dissertation, Harvard University, 1971.

37. Neimark, E. D. Longitudinal development of formal operational thought. Unpublished manuscript, 1972.

38. Neimark, E. D., Slotnick, N. S., & Ulrich, T. The development of memorization strategies. **Developmental Psychology,** 1971, **5,** 427–432.

39. Neisser, U. **Cognitive psychology.** New York: Appleton-Century-Crofts, 1967.

40. Olver, R. R., & Hornsby, J. R. On equivalence. In J. S. Bruner, R. R. Olver, & P. M. Greenfield (Eds.), **Studies in cognitive growth.** New York: Wiley, 1966. Pp. 68–85.

41. Pascual-Leone, J. A mathematical model for the transition role in Piaget's developmental stages. **Acta Psychologica,** 1970, **32,** 301–345.

42. Piaget, J. **Judgment and reasoning in the child.** New York: Harcourt Brace Jovanovich, 1928.

43. Piaget, J. **Play, dreams, and imitation in childhood.** New York: Norton, 1951.

44. Piaget, J. Piaget's Theory. In P. H. Mussen, (Ed.), **Carmichael's Manual of child psychology.** (3rd ed.) New York: Wiley, 1970. Pp. 703–732.

45. Ridberg, E. H., Parke, R. D., & Hetherington, E. M. Modification of impulsive and reflective cognitive styles through observation of film mediated models. **Developmental Psychology,** 1971, **5,** 369–377.

46. Rossi, W., & Wittrock, M. C. Developmental shifts in verbal recall between mental ages two and five. **Child Development,** 1971, **42,** 333–338.

47. Sigel, I. E., Roeper, A., & Hooper, F. H. A training procedure for acquisition of Piaget's

conservation of quantity. **British Journal of Educational Psychology,** 1966, **36,** 301–311.

48. Siipola, E. M., & Hayden, S. D. Scoring eidetic imagery among the retarded. **Perceptual Motor Skills,** 1965, **21,** 275–286.

49. Wachs, T. D., & Gruen, G. E. The effects of chronological age, trials, and list characteristics upon children's category clustering. **Child Development,** 1971, **42,** 1217–1227.

50. Wallach, M. A., & Kogan, N. **Modes of thinking in young children.** New York: Holt, Rinehart & Winston, 1965.

51. White, S. H. Changes in learning processes in the late pre-school years. Paper presented at the meeting of the American Education Research Association, Chicago, 1968.

52. Wohlwill, J. F. The learning of absolute and relational number discriminations by children. **Journal of Genetic Psychology,** 1963, **101,** 217–228.

53. Yando, R. M., & Kagan, J. The effect of teacher tempo on the child. **Child Development,** 1968, **39,** 27–34.

Chapter 8

Intelligence

Intelligence is undoubtedly one of the most mysterious, elusive, confused, and controversial words in the English language. Clearly, we need some term or concept to explain differences among people in their "mental capacity," that is, in ability to solve problems they encounter; to acquire, recall, and utilize information; to reason and to make inferences. The term intelligence is used to explain differences in mental ability that are the product of age and maturation—differences between 7-year-olds and 12-year-olds in thinking and problem-solving, for example—as well as differences among children who are the same age and level of maturation—for instance, between "bright" 10-year-olds and those who are considered "dull."

Piaget's theory, which is concerned with age differences in intelligence, is focused on the acquisition of operations that facilitate adaptation—thinking, reasoning, problem-solving, and concept formation. For Piaget, the essence of intelligence is logical thinking or formal reasoning, abilities that are manifested in the stage of formal operations, the ultimate phase of cognitive development (see pp. 312–314). His theory describes regularities or lawful sequences in the development of intellectual functions; slight variations among children of the same age in the solution of cognitive problems are not of central importance in this theory.

The traditional American approach to intelligence, which is much different from Piaget's, has been characterized by interest neither in the sequence of stages in intellectual growth nor in the basic processes underlying cognitive functions. Rather, the explicit emphasis has been practical—a concern with **individual differences** in intellectual ability and the **measurement of these differences.** American psychologists interested in intelligence have typically proceeded by offering a definition of the concept and then attempting to develop tests to measure intelligence as they have defined it. The definition is likely to emphasize concepts such as adaptation, abstraction, generalization, reasoning, and problem-solving, the same functions that concern Piaget. For instance, Wechsler, the author of several very widely used mental tests (see pp. 335–336), defines intelligence as "the aggregate or global capacity of the individual to act purposefully, to think rationally and to deal effectively with his environment" (31, 3). Although it might be assumed that this definition would guide the construction and selection of the items of the mental tests that are used to compare and rank individuals in intelligence, it does not. American intelligence tests do not actually measure these functions in any direct way; rather, as we shall see in detail, to a very large extent they measure **acquired knowledge,** especially language skills. Consider, for example, these test questions from the WISC, the Wechsler Intelligence Scale for Children: What is the color of rubies? What does C.O.D. mean? In what way are pound and yard alike? Could you expect anyone, no matter how great his intellectual potential or "mental capacity," to answer these items successfully if he had not been exposed to the meanings of these words?

It is therefore important to stress that there may be vast differences between performance on a standard test of intelligence and the more global notion of "mental capacity" or "intellectual potential," which cannot be measured directly at present. Unfortunately, there is a rather prevalent tendency to equate scores on an intelligence test, usually expressed as IQ (intelligence quotient), with the general concepts of basic ability or mental capacity or intellectual potential. The score an individual gets on an intelligence test, his IQ, depends largely on his acquiring special kinds of knowledge. For instance, if a child has very little understanding of the words used in a test, he can hardly be expected to do well on that test. Suppose a middle-class white adolescent is given an "intelligence test" made up of items that are familiar to poor urban blacks, but not to middle-class whites. Adrian Dove has suggested the following items: "In C. C. Ryder, what does C. C. stand for? What is a gashead? Whom did 'Stagger Lee' kill in the famous blues legend? What does 'handkerchief head' mean?" (Compare these with the sample Wechsler items listed above.) Obviously, a subject's poor performance on a test made up of these items could hardly be considered an accurate index of his mental capacity, his potential for learning, reasoning, or solving problems.

This is not to imply that existing standard intelligence tests have no value, for, as we shall see shortly, they have proven very useful for predicting school achievement and, to some extent, vocational success. The predictive efficiency of the tests may be severely limited in many cases, however. A child of high mental capacity may perform poorly on the test because he is inadequately motivated or emotionally disturbed. A recently arrived immigrant child or a child from a minority group or ghetto culture may have high mental capacity or intellectual potential—good ability for learning, reasoning, and problem-solving—but he will score low on the test because his language skills are inadequate for this task. After learning the language used in school, he may be very successful in his studies and score higher on the test.

Wechsler and some other authors of intelligence tests consider intelligence to be a unitary characteristic, highly generalized "mental ability," "global capacity," or "ability to adapt." However, other psychologists maintain as strongly that intelligence is made up of many components, specific skills, or dimensions, and they design separate tests to measure these components.

This approach is clearly demonstrated in the work of Professor J. P. Guilford of the University of Southern California. To him, intelligence consists of at least five different types of cognitive processes or operations. These are called recognition, memory, divergent production, convergent production, and evaluation (11, 12, 13, 14).

Recognition involves sensitivity to aspects of the environment, awareness of changes in external stimuli, and the ability to label or name the environment accurately. **Memory** is the ability to remember or retain information. **Divergent production** refers to the individual's facility in generating a variety of hypotheses or hunches in problem situations. **Convergent production** involves grouping divergent ideas into one unifying concept (for example, grouping all women who have children into the conceptual category "mothers"). **Evaluation** refers to the ability to make a decision about a problem without persistent vacillation and to assess the quality of the decision.

Guilford believes that these five basic cognitive processes can be applied to four different kinds of contexts with differing success. The four contexts are **figures, symbols** (letters and numbers), **semantics** (words and sentences), and **behaviors.** Some children are more intelligent with objects, others with numbers, others with ideas. The mechanic, mathematician, and philosopher would be representative of optimal skill with these different types of contexts.

Finally, Guilford suggests that the five processes act on the four units to produce one of six cognitive products. The six products are **units,** a single word or idea; **classes,** a concept that represents a set of units; **relations,** a relationship between or among units or classes; **systems,** an organized sequence of ideas; **transformations,** a change or redefinition of a unit or class; and **implications,** predictions of the future.

Guilford believes that each person is a unique composite of a great many different intellectual abilities. Each intellectual ability, according to Guilford, involves three components: a cognitive operation, a specific content, and a specific product. A child who is exceptionally good at memorizing long poems would illustrate the operation of memory, with a semantic content and a relational product. Guilford visualizes intelligence as a cube containing 120 cells, each cell representing a unique intellectual ability (see Fig. 8.1). This theoretical idea of the cube is, itself, an example of a convergent cognitive process with semantic content and a system as a product.

The differences between Piaget and Guilford stem, in part, from the source of their primary observations. Piaget works with children individually and in a natural context; he infers the concepts they use from their overt behavior and speech. Guilford, on the other hand, administers long paper-and-pencil tests to large groups of adolescents and adults and uses factor analysis (a mathematical procedure) to arrive at his concepts. Unlike Piaget, Guilford does not have an idealized adult state toward which he thinks intelligence is developing, and he is not concerned with the development of intellectual abilities.

Both Piaget and Guilford have produced theoretical and research-based descriptions of the concept of intelligence, despite the differences in their points of view. There is, however, a special meaning of the word intelligence which is more practical than theoretical, and defines intelligence as a score on a test. The test is called the intelligence test and the score is called the IQ.

TYPES OF INTELLIGENCE TESTS

The Concept of the IQ

The concept of the IQ, based on the intelligence test, has gained wide acceptance by Americans. Typical American parents are anxious about their child's IQ, and

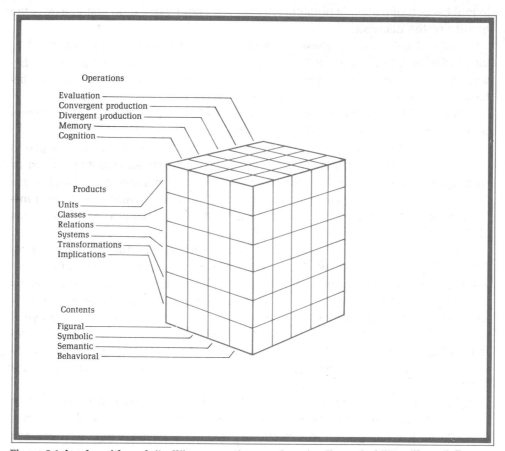

Figure 8.1 A cube with each "cell" representing a unique intellectual ability. (From J. P. Guilford. **The nature of human intelligence.** New York: McGraw-Hill, 1967. P. 63. By permission.)

attribute more value and mystique to a high IQ score than to almost any other individual characteristic possessed by their child. There is a zealous and often fanatic belief in the fundamental nature of the IQ.

Some people believe that a person's IQ is inherited, that an IQ does not change very much over the course of a lifetime, that IQ can be measured in the first year of life, and that a high IQ is associated with a large financial income, mental health, and a happy life. These assumptions are not generally true.

As Guilford, Piaget, and others have suggested, intelligence is best defined as the ability to benefit from experience, the ease with which a child learns a new idea or a new set of behaviors, and the limit to which a person might profit from experience. It is generally assumed that everyone has a ceiling, a point above which he will not be able to profit from experience in a particular activity, and that this ceiling is governed by hereditary factors. However, a psychologist who evaluates a child's IQ by giving him a Stanford-Binet intelligence test does not ask many questions that require the child to learn anything new. The majority of the questions on an intelligence test measure skill or knowledge that the child already possesses, rather than his ability to learn a new skill or fact. The IQ test, therefore, may not measure the basic attribute that most people acknowledge as the central meaning of intelligence.

The reason for this paradox is that the IQ test was invented initially to solve a practical problem, not a theoretical one. At the turn of the century the public schools in Paris were overcrowded and there were many mentally retarded children who could not profit from schooling. The city fathers decided that they needed some practical way to identify the mentally retarded so they could be removed from regular public school classes. They commissioned a psychologist, Alfred Binet, to construct a test that would be a fair and sensitive predictor of the child's ability to profit from academic instruction. The test was constructed with this specific goal in mind. The test that Binet produced did the job for which it was intended. There have been remarkably few basic changes in that early IQ test, and the test used today resembles, in many ways, the one used almost 70 years ago.

The Binet Scale

Construction Binet did not start with a preconceived idea of an entity called intelligence. He started with the fact that on a number of kinds of tasks, some children seemed capable of doing better than others. He further observed that children who did better on one type of test were also likely to do better on others. From these observations he derived a generalized concept of intelligent behavior. He also assumed that individuals differed in their innate capacity for such behavior. His job was to find measures of intelligent behavior that he thought were relatively independent of special training and experiences and differences in motivation, and which would therefore reflect differences in native potential. An additional requirement of the job was to arrive at objective scores which would show the relative ranks of individuals on a continuum from bright to dull.

In standardizing their intelligence tests, Binet and others chose items that were correlated with success in school. Items were included in a test if, and **only** if, they discriminated between children of the same age, for example, 10-year-olds, who had high school grades and those who had low school grades, that is, a significantly higher proportion of good students than of poor students passed the items. Items that were not correlated with school success—those that did not predict academic grades—were eliminated from the test. In view of the criterion used in selecting the items for the intelligence tests, it is hardly surprising that high IQ scores are found to be predictive of high grades in school and college (see p. 342).

Binet published his first intelligence test in 1905 and it consisted largely of items tapping the functions of "reasoning, judgment, and imagination." In 1916

Professor Lewis M. Terman of Stanford University translated the test and adapted it for American use. This is the well-known Stanford-Binet Intelligence Test and it was revised and standardized in a much more careful way in 1937 and again in 1960 (30).

The Stanford-Binet is probably the best known and one of the most widely used intelligence tests for children. It includes a wide variety of verbal and performance items. The 2-year level of the 1960 form has the following tasks: placing simple blocks properly in a three-hole form board; identifying models of common objects, such as a cup, by their use; identifying major parts of a doll's body; and repeating two digits. At later ages, there are items measuring information and past learning, verbal ability, perceptual-motor coordination, memory, perception, and logical reasoning.

The 4-year level items of the test, involving much more language, include naming pictures that illustrate a variety of common objects; naming objects from memory; discriminating visual forms such as squares, circles, and triangles; defining words, such as ball and bat; repeating a ten-word sentence; and counting four objects.

At the 6-year level, the child must define at least six words, such as orange, envelope, and puddle; state the differences between a bird and a dog, a slipper and a boot; recognize parts that are missing in pictures of a wagon, a shoe, a rabbit; count up to nine blocks; and trace the correct path through a maze.

Administration and Scoring After establishing a certain rapport with the child to be tested, the examiner begins with items which are below the expected level of the child and gradually proceeds to those of greater difficulty.

The test is scored in terms of mental age, determined as follows. First, a **basal mental age** is established. This is the year level on the scale at which the child can pass all the test items. For example, a 10-year-old who passed all the items scaled at year 9, but failed some items at year 10, would receive a basal mental age of 9 years. The examiner would then proceed to add to this basal age when items of higher levels are passed. The amount added will depend on the total number of higher items correctly answered. The examiner stops when he reaches an age level at which all items are failed. To illustrate, if the 9-year-old in the above example passed half the items at year 10, one-fourth of the items at year 11, and no items at year 12, he would receive six months credit at year 10, three months credit at year 11, and zero months credit at year 12. Adding these scores to his basal age, he would receive an overall mental age of 9 years, plus 6 months, plus 3 months, or 9 years 9 months.

Since the particular items a child is given on the Binet will depend on the range of his ability, the same items are not given to all children. The test has been developed to cover the years from 2 to adulthood. While some of the items given normal 4- and 5-year-olds would overlap, normal 5- and 12-year-olds would be given completely different items.

Intelligence Quotients

We have already mentioned the term intelligence quotient, or IQ. On the Binet the IQ is simply a ratio of mental age over chronological age multiplied by 100.

$$IQ = \frac{MA}{CA} \times 100$$

Thus a child of 10 years 0 months who obtained a mental age of 10 years 0 months on the Binet would be given a score of 10.0/10.0 × 100, or an IQ of 100. It can be seen that an IQ of 100 will be characteristic of the average child from the group on which the test is based. The 10-year-old previously described, whose mental age was 9 years 9 months, would receive an IQ of 9.75/10 × 100, or 97.5.

Distribution of IQs

Fig. 8.2 shows the distribution of IQ scores for the population used in standardizing the Stanford-Binet. As may be seen, the distribution of scores closely resembles the normal bell-shaped curve with the center of the curve at IQ 100 and with higher and lower IQs about equally common. Table 8.1 shows the percentage of individuals at each IQ level and is probably the most helpful guide to understanding the meaning of a particular score.

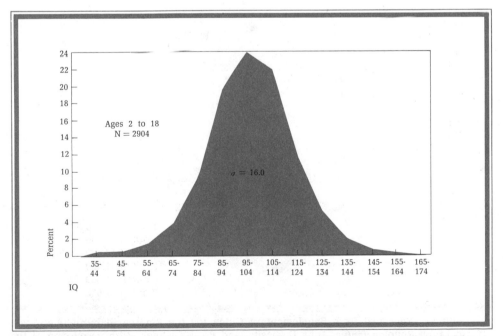

Figure 8.2 Distribution of IQs in the Terman-Merrill standardization group. (From L. M. Terman & M. A. Merrill. **Measuring intelligence: a guide to the administration of the new revised Stanford-Binet tests of intelligence.** Boston: Houghton Mifflin, 1937. By permission.)

Table 8.1 **The meaning of various IQs obtained with the revised Stanford-Binet scale**

THE CHILD WHOSE IQ IS:	EQUALS OR EXCEEDS	THE CHILD WHOSE IQ IS:	EQUALS OR EXCEEDS
136	99 percent	98	45 percent
135	98	97	43
134	98	96	40
133	98	95	38
132	97	94	36
131	97	93	34
130	97	92	31
129	96	91	29
128	96	90	27
127	95	89	25
126	94	88	23
125	94	87	21
124	93	86	20
123	92	85	18
122	91	84	16
121	90	83	15
120	89	82	14
119	88	81	12
118	86	80	11
117	85	79	10
116	84	78	9
115	82	77	8
114	80	76	8
113	79	75	6
112	77	74	6
111	75	73	5
110	73	72	4
109	71	71	4
108	69	70	3
107	66	69	3
106	64	68	3
105	62	67	2
104	60	66	2
103	57	65	2
102	55	65	2
101	52	64	1
100	50	63	1
99	48	62	1
160			1 out of 10,000
156			3 out of 10,000
152			8 out of 10,000
148			2 out of 1,000
144			4 out of 1,000
140			7 out of 1,000

Source: Reprinted from **Supplementary Guide for the Revised Stanford-Binet Scale** (Form L) by Rudolph Pinter, Anna Dragositz, and Rose Kushner. With permission of the Stanford University Press.

Other Types of Intelligence Tests

Two other individual intelligence tests for children, both designed by Professor David Wechsler of New York University–Bellevue Medical School, are also very widely used. These are the WISC (Wechsler Intelligence Scale for Children), published in 1959 and designed for ages 7 to 16, and the WPPSI (Wechsler Preschool-Primary Scale of Intelligence), for ages 4 to 6½. While the items in the Stanford-Binet are grouped by age levels with each level containing a sampling of cognitive functions, the items in the Wechsler tests are divided into two scales and then further grouped into eleven subtests. The verbal scale, made up of six subtests, includes tests of information (items such as "How many weeks are there in a year?"), comprehension ("Why should we keep away from bad company?"), digit span (repeating digits forward and backward), similarities ("In what way are air and water alike?"), arithmetic (simple arithmetic problems), and vocabulary. The **performance scale** has five subtests. In the picture arrangement subtest a story is told in three or more cartoon panels presented in random order; the subject must order them in a way that tells the story. In picture completion each of the pictures presented has something missing from it; the subject must tell what is lacking. In block design the subject arranges small blocks to copy a design that has been presented to him by the examiner. In object assembly the subject is given parts and required to discover how they go together to form such objects as a profile, hand, or elephant (see Fig. 8.3). The coding subtest requires the subject to learn a code symbol for each number and to fill in the code symbol in a series of blank spaces under the numbers. A Verbal IQ and Performance IQ are derived from scores on the verbal and performance scales, and a Full Scale IQ is derived from scores on all the subtests.

The Wechsler tests do not yield a mental age score. Instead, the child's performance on each subtest is scored in terms of the mean for his own age group; a subtest score of 10 indicates that the child's performance is exactly at the mean of his group for that subtest. His IQ, derived from total scores on all subtests, is a function of his percentile rank in comparison with other children his own age in the standardization group. To illustrate, suppose a child of 6 obtains a WISC IQ of 79. This simply means (if one consults the appropriate table in the WISC manual) that this child is at the tenth percentile, that is, he has done better on the test than about 10 percent of 6-year-olds in the standardization group and more poorly than about 90 percent (**32**).

Although there are differences in the test items and in the methods of computation, IQs derived from the Wechsler and from the Binet are highly correlated. Stanford-Binet IQ correlates about +.80 with the Verbal IQ of the WISC, +.65 with the Performance IQ, and +.80 with the Full Scale IQ (**25**). The high correlations are due in large part to the fact that there is much overlapping in specific skills tapped in the two tests. For instance, both contain vocabulary, memory for digits, analogies, and arithmetic items.

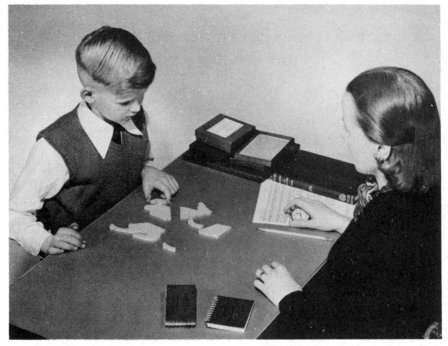

Figure 8.3 Administering the Wechsler Intelligence Scale for Children. (By permission of The Psychological Corporation.)

Group Tests of Intelligence

The intelligence tests described thus far must be individually administered. There are, however, a number of group tests available for use by teachers and others. Such tests have the advantages that they do not require intensive training to administer and they are economical of time.

On the other hand, they also have serious limitations. The results they yield are not so useful for prediction as those from individual tests administered by a skilled clinician. Practical decisions about children who deviate on these tests should not be made without individual follow-up testing by a competent psychologist, together with an investigation of other factors within the individual's life which may be affecting his performance (including his general health and sensory functioning). Too frequently erroneous diagnoses of mental deficiency have been made on the basis of low scores on group intelligence tests.

Infant Tests

The intelligence tests we have been discussing cannot be used with children under 2 or 3 years of age. Yet many believe it would be useful to be able to evaluate the intelligence of infants. The validity of the concept of testing infant intelligence depends on several assumptions about the nature of intelligence. First, we must assume that intelligence is, in fact, a unitary variable which refers to a general factor of "general capacity." Second, we must assume the individual's relative standing in intelligence is manifested early, so that it is measurable in infancy. Third, we must assume that intelligence is stable or continuous, that is, high intelligence in infancy must predict high intelligence in later childhood. If these assumptions are warranted and if valid tests of infant intelligence could be devised, information from these tests would be extremely valuable in dealing with practical problems such as placing infants for adoption with adoptive parents of approximately the same intellectual level. The assessments would also help in detecting mental retardation early, so that parents could be prepared to make special plans for handling their retarded children. In addition, most parents are anxious to have some authoritative reassurance that their children are "normal."

As a result of such considerations, a number of infant intelligence tests have been developed. The first was the Gesell Developmental Schedules. Others, developed after Gesell's, are the California Preschool Mental Scale, Bayley's Scales of Infant Development, Cattell Intelligence Test for Infants and Young Children, Merrill-Palmer Scale, and the Minnesota Preschool Scale.

These tests consist of large numbers of items that presumably sample important aspects of intellectual ability. Each test is "standardized" by trying it out on a large, representative sample of the population from which norms or standards (averages or median ages at which items are passed by infants) are derived. It is then possible to assess the rates of progress of individual children as relatively rapid, average, or slower than average.

Let us look briefly at the newest and best standardized infant intelligence test, Bayley's Scale of Mental Development, which consists of 163 items (2). The following list taken from the scale illustrates the kinds of items used in infant tests. Numbers in parentheses refer to the age placement (months) of the items, that is, the age in months at which 50 percent of the children tested passed the items.

Blinks at shadow of hand (1.9)
Head follows vanishing spoon (3.2)
Recovers rattle, in crib (4.9)
Picks up cube deftly and directly (5.7)
Manipulates bell; interest in detail (6.5)
Fingers holes in peg board (8.9)
Stirs with spoon in imitation (9.7)
Imitates words (12.5)
Builds tower of two cubes (13.8)
Says two words (14.2)
Uses gestures to make wants known (14.6)

Attains toy with stick (17.0)
Imitates crayon stroke (17.8)
Places two round and two square blocks in a board (19.3)
Names two objects (21.4)
Points to five pictures (21.6)
Names three pictures (22.1)
Builds tower of six cubes (23.0)
Names three objects (24.0)
Names five pictures (25.0)

The child's score is based on his performance on these items. Clearly, most of them, like the items of most infant tests, tap sensorimotor and perceptual functions, although many of them involve an elementary understanding and use of language.

Unfortunately, infant intelligence tests have proven to have limited practical utility, although they can distinguish between defective and normal babies. A well-trained, sensitive baby tester may be able to use the tests to diagnose specific disabilities such as deficient social responsiveness or inadequate vision or hearing. On the basis of extensive experience, one clinical researcher concluded that these tests "can succeed in detecting the mentally deviant at a very early age, often before pathology becomes manifest through pediatric or neurological examinations" (7, 120).

A broader, more important question must be asked: Are scores in infant tests predictive of the future mental status of children? Does performance on these infant tests relate to later tests of intelligence? For most infants, the answer is no. The lack of relationship is due, in large part, to the vastly different kinds of abilities sampled at earlier and later ages. Infant tests are made up primarily of items measuring motor skills and sensorimotor development, for instance, placing pegs in a peg board, fitting blocks into a form board, building towers of cubes, obtaining toys that are out of arm's reach with a stick, imitating gestures. In contrast, intelligence tests for older children and adults emphasize verbal ability, cognitive functioning, and abstract thinking. It is easy to see why the correlations between performance on infant tests and scores on adult intelligence tests have not been found to be significant.

In Bayley's longitudinal studies, children were examined at frequent intervals beginning in early infancy. During the first few years, an earlier version of her infant tests (a 185-item scale) was used, and at 6 and 7 the subjects were given the Stanford-Binet. Correlations between scores on the infant tests and on later tests were insignificant. The writer therefore concluded that "scores made before 18 months are completely useless in the prediction of school age abilities" (1, 100).

Moreover, test performance at 21 months gives a negligible prediction of success on the Stanford-Binet at 6 or 7 years (17). These findings emphasize the difficulty of making an accurate prognosis of the future ability of a child on a mental test administered before the age of 2.

CONSTANCY OF IQ

This brings us to the critical problem of the stability of the IQ, the extent to which intelligence test scores at one age predict IQ at a later age. The practical utility of an intelligence test score depends largely on its stability or constancy, that is, upon its capacity for predicting similar scores on subsequent retests. For instance, how confidently can we predict that a child who obtains a superior score at age 5 will obtain a comparable score at a later age, say at adolescence? Fortunately, even though tests given to infants under 2 have little value for the prediction of future intelligence test scores, tests given to older children are more highly predictive.

Evidence for this comes from an extensive longitudinal guidance study conducted at the University of California (17). All subjects in the study were given intelligence tests periodically beginning at age 21 months. During the preschool period the California Preschool Schedule was administered and the Stanford-Binet was given to each subject during later childhood and adolescence. At age 18 the subjects took the Wechsler Adult Intelligence Scale. Table 8.2 shows the correlations between intelligence scores obtained during the preschool and middle-childhood years, on the one hand, and at ages 10 and 18 on the other. As you can see from this table, as children advance in age through the preschool period, their test scores become increasingly better predictors of later performance. During the school years, the correlation between Stanford-Binet test scores given one or two years apart (for example, at ages 8 or 9 and again at 10) is very high, around .90.

Table 8.2 **Correlations between Stanford-Binet IQ during the preschool and middle-childhood years and IQ at ages 10 and 18 (Wechsler-Bellevue)**

AGE	CORRELATION WITH IQ AT AGE 10	CORRELATION WITH IQ AT AGE 18
2	.37	.31
3	.36	.35
4	.66	.42
6	.76	.61
7	.78	.71
8	.88	.70
9	.90	.76
10	—	.70
12	.87	.76

Source: Adapted from M. P. Honzik, J. W. Macfarlane, and L. Allen, The stability of mental test performance between two and eighteen years. **Journal of Experimental Education,** 1948, **17.** By permission.

Moreover, tests given during this period are good predictors of intellectual status in early adulthood, at age 18.

The stability of intelligence test scores is greater for shorter than for longer periods of time; the shorter the interval between tests, the higher the correlation between the IQs derived. For example, the correlation between IQs obtained at ages 3 and 5 is higher than the correlation between IQs measured at ages 3 and 7. Moreover, the IQ becomes more stable (less likely to change) with increasing age. Thus, the correlation between IQs at ages 3 and 5 is .72; the correlation between IQs at ages 8 and 10 is .88 (22).

Benjamin Bloom of the University of Chicago has made a fascinating analysis of these and other longitudinal data (4). He concluded that correlations between early and later intelligence would be much higher if the psychomotor portions of the earlier tests were held constant or suppressed. Thus the correlation between intelligence, when ideally measured, at age 3 (with the sensorimotor portions eliminated) and age 17 is about .65; between intelligence measured at age 5 (psychomotor tasks excluded) and age 17, about .80 (4).

Despite the fact that the IQ becomes more stable at later ages, we must be cautious in using test scores for predicting the future status of individual children because "the correlations are not sufficiently high so that the possibility of marked changes in the IQs of individual children is precluded" (17). Repeated testings of subjects in a longitudinal study between the ages of 6 and 18 revealed that the IQ of over half the children "showed a variation of 15 or more points . . . at some time during the school years, and a third group varied as much as 20 points . . ." (17).

Fig. 8.4 shows the results of successive tests taken by three subjects of the longitudinal Guidance Study at the Institute of Human Development at the University of California. Scores are plotted in standard scores with the mean score of all subjects in this study at each age taken as zero. Notice that the three subjects were quite similar in intelligence, slightly above average, at age 4. However, two of them shifted radically over the years, while the score of the third remained relatively stable. Shifts in IQ may be related to health, emotional stability, and marked environmental changes—either improvements or deterioration. And, as we shall see shortly, there is evidence that personality characteristics affect IQ scores and changes in these scores (see pp. 343–345). Nevertheless, it is very difficult to specify the cause of change in any particular case; simple causal explanations are often inadequate.

For example, the IQ of Case 783 remained relatively stable although he had a poor health history, had difficulties in school, was insecure, and showed some symptoms of emotional disturbance. Case 567 was sickly and shy as a young child but after age 10 her social life expanded and she became much more interested in music and sports. These changes in her situation were reflected in improved intelligence test scores.

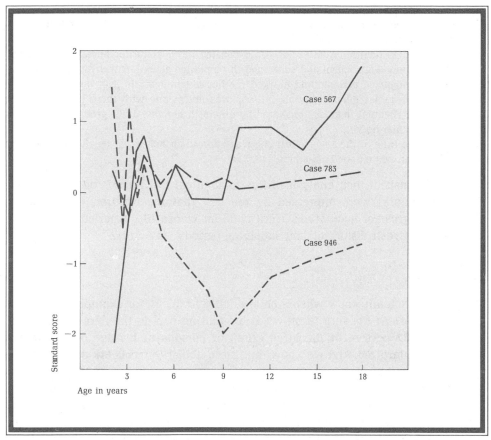

Figure 8.4 Records made by three children on successive mental tests. (From M. P. Honzik, J. W. Macfarlane, & L. Allen. The stability of mental test performance between two and eighteen years. **Journal of Experimental Education,** 1948, **17,** 454–455.)

Case 946, a girl, has varied in I.Q. between 142 (preschool) and 87. . . . [H]er preschool years were clearly higher than later years. Her lowest score (I.Q. 87 . . .), occurred at 9 years, a period of acute body concern and excessive modesty. Immigrant parents of grammar school education, both unstable and involved in chronic, acute marital tension, were divorced when the girl was 7. This child was acutely uneasy around her young stepfather for the first years of her mother's new marriage. Much internal as well as external turmoil has characterized her life (**17,** 314).

The effects of poor health and emotional tension on intelligence test performance were particularly clearly demonstrated in another case.

Case 715, a girl whose I.Q. varies from 121 to 165, presents a history that was characterized by intermittent but severe eczema and asthma throughout the entire testing period. Ages 3 to 7 constituted a particularly bad period; age 9, where there was a drop in I.Q. of 12 points, was a period not only of asthma and poor vision, but of acute economic insecurity and family uneasiness. At age 10, during her highest test period, she was taking two cc. of adrenalin daily to keep her asthma under control.

Added to health strain, social strain became more acute for her at 12 when she entered junior high school and continued through high school. It was a period of over-weight, disfiguring eczema, and marked mother-daughter strain. Not only did the girl belong to a racial minority group, but she was not at one with them because of her marked intellectual interests, unshared by others in her racial age group, at school or in the neighborhood. . . .

At the time of the 18-year test she was very much below par as she was recover-ing from an acute period of asthma (17, 314).

On the basis of their analysis of the longitudinal test records of 252 children, the investigators "were impressed by the fact that the children whose scores showed the greatest fluctuations were children whose life experiences had also fluctuated between disturbing and satisfying periods" (17, 314).

The Usefulness of IQs

What do we actually know when a child obtains an IQ of, for example, 132 on the Stanford-Binet? At the very least, we know that he can do the items on this test better than 97 percent of the large group of persons of his age on whom the test was standardized. And we know that these items are probably representative of segments of knowledge familiar to many people in this society. In this sense, the authors of the test feel justified in calling it a measure of general intelligence. But how useful is such knowledge? Few teachers, for example, are particularly interested in whether a child can solve the particular problems on the Binet. They want to know if he will be able to do satisfactory work in reading, writing, and arithmetic.

The only way of settling the question is by examination of the actual relation-ship between IQ and school success. In general, IQ scores have been found to be fairly good predictors of academic performance. One investigator (5), for example, lists the following correlations between the Stanford-Binet Intelligence Test and school grades.

IQ and reading comprehension	.73
IQ and reading speed	.43
IQ and English usage	.59
IQ and history	.59
IQ and biology	.54
IQ and geometry	.48

Clearly, intelligence test scores are good predictors of academic achievement. As we noted earlier, the high correlation between IQ and school grades is not sur-prising or difficult to explain. First, intelligence test items are selected on the basis of their ability to predict success in schools in traditional school subjects, such as reading, arithmetic, composition; those items that did not differentiate between good and poor students were omitted from the test. A second factor that helps explain the high correlation between IQ and school performance is related to the first. High scores on intelligence tests and good grades in school are, to a large extent, dependent on the same skills, knowledge, and motives—good vocabulary, knowledge of the standard language used in the test, self-confidence, high motivation to succeed in intellectual tasks, reflecting about answers to questions rather than answering impulsively.

EFFECTS OF ENVIRONMENT AND PERSONALITY ON INTELLIGENCE TEST PERFORMANCE

Marked shifts in people's intelligence test scores suggest that environmental factors and personality characteristics may have significant effects on performance in these tests. In considering systematic data about these influences on mental test performance, the reader must keep in mind that the intelligence test does **not** give any direct assessment of "native ability." More than anything else, it is a good measure of what the child knows and what he has taken from his culture; also, the score is strongly influenced by motivational variables, such as the achievement motive. It is a good predictor of the child's grades and test scores in school. If the child has strong motivation to improve the quality of his intellectual skills and has high standards for intellectual mastery, he is likely to have a higher IQ score than a child who is not highly motivated or has low standards. Since middle-class children are more consistently encouraged than lower-class children to learn to read, spell, add, and write, one expects that a child's intelligence test score, social class, and school grades will all be positively related to each other. This is, in fact, the case. Moreover, the personality correlates of school success (i.e., persistence, nonaggression, responsible behavior) are similar to the correlates of social class and IQ.

Children who show large increases in IQ during the early school years tend to be similar in personality and family background to those who have high IQ scores. They work hard in school, obtain good grades, and care about intellectual mastery. Thus, one can use amount of increase in IQ as a rough index of the child's desire to master academic skills.

Investigators at the Fels Research Institute made an analysis of changes in IQ and related these changes to personality variables (23, 29). Their subjects were a group of 140 boys and girls for whom annual IQ scores and behavorial observations were available. Graphs of the Stanford-Binet IQ scores of these children from ages 3 through 12 showed striking differences among children in the patterns of their scores. Some children's scores remained the same, others decreased, and still others increased. Approximately one-half of the group showed a stable IQ pattern with little change over the 10-year period. The other children showed either increases or decreases in IQ score.

What do these changes mean? Are they related to other aspects of the child's psychological functioning? From the total group of 140, the investigators selected 35 children who showed the greatest increase in IQ during the ages 6 through 10, and 35 children who showed the greatest decrease during these years. Ratings based on behavorial observations of these children at home and school during the first 10 years of their lives were then analyzed. A number of interesting discoveries were made.

Twice as many boys as girls showed large increases in IQ. Boys were more likely to gain in IQ score, whereas girls were more likely to lose in IQ. Compared with children who decreased in IQ, those who increased were, according to their behavorial ratings, more independent, more competitive, and more verbally aggressive. While there was no relation between the pattern of IQ changes and the degree of friendliness with age-mates, those who gained in IQ worked harder in school, showed a strong desire to master intellectual problems, and were not likely to withdraw from difficult problem situations. Apparently children who attempt to master challenging problems are more likely to show increases in IQ than children who withdraw from such situations (29).

The mothers of a group of Fels children were rated with respect to the degree to which they encouraged their children to talk and to walk during the first three years of life (21). For the girls, there was a positive relation between maternal concern with the child's early developmental progress and the amount of IQ increase the girls showed during the years 6 through 10. The correlation for boys was positive, but much lower. The lack of a strong relationship between maternal encouragement of walking and talking and IQ increases in boys may be a function of sex differences in the degree of identification with the mother. Girls are more likely than boys to identify with the mother and, hence, more likely to adopt her values. This finding suggests that, although a mother's concern for intellectual mastery influences both boys and girls, this effect may be greater for daughters than for sons. This interpretation is supported by the fact that, even though the relation between mothers' formal education and children's IQ is positive for both sexes, mothers' education is a better predictor of girls' than of boys' IQ scores at ages 3, 6, and 10 (21). For example, the correlation between maternal education and children's IQ at age 10 was .66 for girls, but only .39 for boys. If it is assumed that well-educated mothers are more apt than poorly educated ones to encourage mastery of intellectual skills, it would appear that the mother's emphasis on perfecting intellectual proficiency influences both the level as well as increases in IQ among girls.

How should the IQ score be viewed in the light of this discussion? This question can best be answered by first asking, "What use do we want to make of the IQ score?" If we are interested primarily in predicting the child's success in school

subjects, then this test is the best instrument psychologists have devised, for it does a creditable job of predicting who is likely to obtain good grades in elementary school, high school, and college.

Educators have ordinarily not been interested in predicting nonacademic behaviors from IQ scores. For special skills, such as music or art, there are special tests that are more appropriate. The controversy over the meaning of the IQ concept exists partly because many people assume there is a general factor of intelligence (measured by the IQ test) rather than a set of more specific talents. If Binet had viewed his test as an index of "academic potential" rather than "intellectual potential" there would probably be less controversy.

INTELLIGENCE, HEREDITY, ENVIRONMENT, AND RACE

In our discussion of genetic influences on development in Chapter 3 we noted that several kinds of evidence support the widely prevalent notion that genetic factors play an important role in determining intelligence. You will recall that the correlation between IQs of parents and their natural children is, on the average, about .50, but the correlation between parents and their adopted children is about .25. The IQs of identical twins who have the same genetic make-up correlate about .90. Even the IQs of identical twins who are reared in different environments correlate about .75, which is higher than the correlations between fraternal twins who have different heredities but are reared together (.55). On the basis of these data, many psychologists believe that there are genetic factors in intelligence.

> There can be no question that genetic factors play a substantial role in producing individual differences in . . . [intelligence test performance]. Many research findings testify to the validity of this statement. Perhaps most impressive is the fact that the similarity of identical twins reared apart is clearly greater than that of fraternal twins reared together (**6, 124**).

Because, like almost every human trait observed, intelligence is the product of complex interactions of numerous hereditary and environmental forces, it is almost impossible to separate the effects of the two kinds of influence; hence, most psychologists are unwilling to make a definite statement about the specific amount of the contribution of hereditary factors. Furthermore, the amount of the contribution of heredity to intelligence is somewhat flexible, depending on environmental situations; for instance, without a favorable environment, the individual may never actualize his full intellectual potential.

We have also reviewed some findings that show how experiential, motivational, and environmental factors influence performance on intelligence tests. Obviously, if a child is brought up in an environment in which only very simple language is used, he will not do well in intelligence test items that require a more extensive vocabulary, even if, from a genetic point of view, he has great intellectual potential. Analogously, a child who has not learned basic arithmetic skills will not be able to solve mathematical problems. If a child lives in a suppressive environment, he is not likely to develop achievement motivation or to do as well in intelligence tests as a child who is highly motivated to achieve and to cope with intellectual challenges.

Other environmental factors also affect intellectual development in critical ways. If a mother suffers from protein deficiency during her pregnancy, her offspring may be permanently handicapped intellectually. The infant's diet during the first few months of his life, particularly the adequacy of his protein intake, also appears to be important for later intellectual development. Since poor people are more likely to have deficient diets, we can expect a greater proportion of intellectual deficiency among poor than among middle-class children.

The environmental factors that appear to exert the greatest impact on intelligence test performance are the child's social class and early rearing. Compared with middle-class families, lower-class families, especially in minority groups, typically provide their children with different cognitive and language experience, and they put much less stress on the values of intellectual development and achievement. Compared with lower-class mothers, those in the middle class consistently use more words in responding to their preschool children's questions and in teaching them how to solve problems. They also offer greater cognitive challenges, more "opportunities for labeling, for identifying objects and feelings and adult models who . . . demonstrate the usefulness of language as a tool for dealing with interpersonal interaction and for ordering stimuli in the environment" (**16,** 875). Furthermore, in contrast with lower-class mothers, middle-class mothers use sentences with much more subtle and complex grammar, and their talk contains more abstractions and concepts.

Children apparently learn and emulate their mothers' approaches to problems. In one study, lower- and middle-class mothers and their children solved cognitive problems such as sorting pictures of people into categories or classes. Lower-class children, like their mothers, gave relatively more nonverbal responses and relational responses (for example, "a husband and a wife") than middle-class subjects and fewer descriptive or categorical responses ("all handicapped people"). Lower-class children are not as likely to learn to reflect about alternative solutions to problems nor do they acquire as great a capacity to delay their responses in order to analyze a problem into its component parts.

Of course, categorical or descriptive responses are not inherently superior to relational responses, but intelligence tests are "biased" in favor of the former kind, that is, many tests measure this kind of response in items like "In what way are book, teacher, and newspaper alike?" The middle-class child's training in using categorical responses is likely to aid him in answering such questions correctly and, therefore, in earning high scores on the test. In addition, the correct solutions to many problems posed in intelligence tests demand reflection, weighing of decisions and consequences, and choosing among alternatives; middle-class children are more thoroughly and systematically trained for these responses than lower-class children. In short, the middle-class child's knowledge and his orientation and approach to problem-solving—the cognitive styles acquired by the middle-class child—are conducive to good performance on intelligence tests; the lower-class child's approaches are not (**16**).

Bringing together the results of several different kinds of studies, we are inevitably led to the conclusion that it is not possible to state with any certainty the relative contributions of heredity and environment to performance on intelligence tests. It is virtually impossible to separate clearly the effects of heredity from the effects of environmental factors. After a thorough review of the relevant literature on this matter, Professor Bronfenbrenner of Cornell University, concluded, "It is impossible to establish a single fixed figure representing the proportion of variation in intelligence, . . . independently attributable to heredity vs. environment" (**6,** 124).

Race Differences in Intelligence

While most psychologists would accept this statement of Bronfenbrenner's, the subject of hereditary versus environmental influences on intelligence has loomed large in recent years because a few have argued that differences between blacks and whites in intelligence test performance might be the result of genetic differences between the two races. Studies consistently show that, on the average, blacks score 10 to 15 points below whites on most standard tests of intelligence.

Arthur Jensen, an educational psychologist at the University of California, examined the data on intelligence test resemblances among relatives, particularly between identical twins raised in different environments, and concluded that heredity accounts for approximately 80 percent of the variation in IQ scores (**19**). Heredity, he says, is far more important than anything else in determining the individual's level of intellectual functioning; only 20 percent is left to other factors. Furthermore, Jensen's argument runs, special "compensatory" or remedial educational programs designed to increase the cognitive skills and IQ scores of children from impoverished homes, mostly blacks, have not been successful. He maintains that drastic changes in the environment and in educational programs have little effect on intelligence test scores. Therefore, in his view, intelligence must be determined primarily by genetic factors and the difference between whites and blacks in IQs is the result of the genetic inferiority of blacks (**19**).

Like many other psychologists, we disagree with Jensen's interpretations of the data and with his conclusions. In our opinion, the evidence does **not** support the argument that one race is genetically inferior to another in intelligence. Here are some of our reasons.

Examination of the data on identical twins shows that intelligence, as measured by intelligence tests, **is** influenced by environmental factors. Identical twins reared in drastically different environments do not resemble each other as closely as those reared in more similar environments. In one study 38 pairs of identical twins reared in different environments were found to have an average difference in IQ of 14 points and at least 25 percent of the twin pairs differed more than 16 points in IQ. This average difference is larger than the average difference between black and white populations. On the basis of these data, I. I. Gottesman, a leading behavioral geneticist, concluded, "The differences observed . . . between whites and Negroes can hardly be accepted as sufficient evidence that with respect to intelligence the Negro American is genetically less endowed" (**9, 28**).

As we noted earlier, most psychologists reject Jensen's conclusions that 80 percent—or, for that matter, any specific proportion—of the variation in intelligence is attributable to heredity. But even if we were able to estimate accurately the contribution of heredity to the determination of intelligence test scores in one group, for example, in the white middle-class group from which most of the subjects in the twin studies come, we could not assume that the same estimate holds for other ethnic groups or other social classes.

As every behavioral geneticist knows, the heritability of a behavioral characteristic [the proportion of its variance attributable to genetic factors] is a function of the population in which it is measured. There is no reason to assume that behaviors measured in one population will show the same proportion of genetic and environmental variances when measured in a second population whose distributions of genetic or environmental characteristics, or both, differ in any way from those of the first population. Racial and social class groups are, for many purposes, sufficiently different populations to make a generalization from one to another highly questionable (**26,** 1285)

In fact, a provocative recent study shows that twins from socioeconomically favored families, both white and black, are more similiar to each other in aptitude scores—and hence show higher heritability coefficients—than twins from socio-economically disadvantaged families (**27**).

These findings indicate that for genetic potential to be realized requires an appro-priately complex, sustained, and stimulating environment. In accord with this principle, twins from lower class Black groups, who in our society live in suppressive environ-ments, exhibit lower levels of ability and reduced genetic variability. . . . (**6,** 122).

In contrast, the white middle-class child is more likely to have the cognitive stimu-lation and experiences that produce the motivation, information, and ways of thinking that promote high scores on mental tests.

In interpreting these findings, the investigator noted:

To the extent that children are not given supportive environments for the full de-velopment of their individual genetic differences, changes can be made in their . . . en-vironments to improve both their overall performance and the genetic variance in their scores. If all children had optimal environments for development, then genetic differ-ences would account for most of the variance in behavior. To the extent that better, more supportive environments can be provided for all children, genetic variance and mean scores will increase for all groups (**26,** 1294).

Genetic factors may play an important role in determining intelligence levels **within** groups. Intelligent parents of any race are more likely than unintelligent ones to produce intelligent children. But that fact does not allow us to conclude the IQ differences **between** groups are the result of different genetic constitutions. To clarify this point, consider some data on height, a physical attribute dependent on genetic endowment. Indian children living in rural areas of many Central or South American countries are, on the average, significantly shorter than Indian children living in urban areas of those countries. If one followed Jensen's logic, he would conclude that the shorter stature of the rural children is due to factors in their genetic make-up. This is not the case, however, since both Indian groups come from the same racial stock. The rural children do not grow as tall as those in the cities because they suffer more from disease and malnutrition, both environmental factors. Analogously, the average heights of children in the United States and in many other countries have increased considerably during the past 200 years as a function of better nutrition and immunization against disease; obviously their

genetic constitutions have not been changed. The heritability of height as determined from twin studies is about .90—higher than that for IQ.

> If this high heritability index had been derived in the year 1800, would it then have
> been safe to conclude that height cannot be increased through environmental influ-
> ences? If that conclusion had been drawn, it would have been wrong (8, 302).

> The essential error in Jensen's argument is the conclusion that if a trait is under
> genetic control, differences between two populations on that trait must be due to ge-
> netic factors. This is the heart of Jensen's position, and it is not persuasive (20, 275).

Finally, we do not agree with Jensen's verdict that compensatory education
has failed. The usual traditional preschool, oriented primarily toward children's
play, has not been effective in raising the intelligence levels of children from poor
families, but other, more intensive programs have been quite successful. The effective programs are the ones that make concerted efforts to train children directly in
cognitive skills and in languages; in some of the programs parents are instrumental in the training. We will consider some of these programs in the following
section.

CHANGING COGNITIVE FUNCTIONING

As we noted earlier economically deprived families generally do not provide the
intellectual stimulation that promotes good performance on intelligence tests. Yet,
psychologists maintain, if a child is to realize his full intellectual potential, he
needs to have interesting, cognitively challenging, and rewarding experiences beginning at a very early age.

The question of utmost social significance is: Are the effects of these early conditions fixed and permanent or can they be reversed? If they can be reversed, what
procedures are most effective and at what age must these procedures be applied?
There are not marked class and race differences in intelligence, as measured by
standard infant tests, in babies under 18 months of age. Nevertheless, by the time
they enter school, poor white and black children are at a disadvantage, that is,
they perform more poorly on cognitive tasks and tests of intelligence, on the
average, than middle-class white children. In addition, they frequently manifest a
kind of progressive retardation or cumulative deficit, that is, they fall further and
further behind in tests of intellectual functions as they progress through the
schools. In the interests of social justice and general welfare, these cognitive in-
equalities between social class and racial groups must be reduced or eliminated.
Can this be achieved?

In recent years many governmental and social agencies have concentrated
tremendous amounts of time and effort on proposed solutions to this vast educational and social problem. The goals are very broad ones: to ameliorate the conditions of the socioeconomically disadvantaged, so that children from these back-

grounds can develop competencies and motivational patterns that would enable them to share more fully in our complex society and to reap a fairer share of the social rewards. The question of the reversibility (or irreversibility) of the effects of early deprivation is therefore of paramount importance.

A completed follow-up study and another still in progress provide dramatic evidence that radical environment change, instituted very early in life, can be effective in raising the level of the child's cognitive functioning. The subjects of the older study were 25 infants who had been raised in an orphanage until the age of 2 (28). One group, 13 seriously retarded babies, was transferred from this orphanage to institutions for mentally retarded before they were 3 years old. Each of these children was assigned to an adoptive "mother," an older, mentally retarded girl, who was put in charge of raising the child. The contrast or control group consisted of 12 children matched with the experimental group in age, intelligence, and medical history. These control children remained in the orphanage until adoption at a later age. Approximately two and a half years after the experiment was completed all subjects were tested again. Those who had been individually reared by the mentally retarded "mothers" showed great increases in IQ (average gain of 32 points), while the contrast group showed significant losses (average loss of 21 IQ points).

The two groups were studied again 20 years after they left the orphanage or the institution for the mentally retarded. All who had been in the experimental group with individualized mothering—even though that mothering was given by retarded girls—were self-supporting. They had completed 12 years of school, on the average, and four of them had 1 or more years of college. The mean educational level of the control group was the fourth grade. Many of these subjects were in state institutions and none of them was really self-supporting. Clearly, dramatic transformation in the infants' environment had highly significant, enduring positive effects (28).

An exciting intervention study is currently being directed by Professor R. Heber of the University of Wisconsin (15). Working in a ghetto slum area in which there is a very high prevalence of mentally retarded children, investigators visited all black mothers of newborns and gave these women intelligence tests. Those who had Wechsler IQs of 75 or less, 40 mothers, together with their young infants became the subjects of the study. Each mother-infant pair was assigned at random to either the experimental or control conditions.

The treatment given the experimental group was based on a "comprehensive total family approach to rehabilitation and prevention" (15a, 42). The controls were given no special treatment, but simply were tested at the same time as the experimental subjects.

When a child in the experimental group became a subject, at 3 months of age, he was assigned to a teacher who would be in charge of him for the major part of his waking day, five days a week, until he was 12 to 15 months of age. The teachers are paraprofessionals and the majority of them live in the same neighborhood as the children and thus share a similar cultural background. Most of them are in their mid-20s, but they range in age from approximately 18 to 45. Their educational experience varies from eighth grade to one year of college. They were chosen for their jobs because they were facile in the language, affectionate, and had some experience with infants or young children.

> The teacher who was assigned to an infant was responsible for his total care, including: feeding and bathing, cuddling and soothing, reporting and recording general health as well as organizing his learning environment and implementing the educational program. Within the context of the educational program, the teacher was expected to follow and expand upon a prescribed set of activities. Her job was to make these activities interesting, exciting and varied within the limits of the child's general routine; viz, eating, sleeping and activity. She was also required to "objectively" evaluate and report the child's progress, pointing out areas of apparent difficulty (15a, 50).

When the child was between 12 and 15 months of age, he was gradually paired with other teachers and children. By the time he was 15 to 20 months old, he was grouped with two other children and came into contact with three different teachers. Actually, because of the setting of the experiment each child was in contact with most of the other children and teachers at some time.

The general educational program has a cognitive-language orientation that is implemented through structured learning experiences. Teaching techniques are prescribed on a daily basis (seven hours per day, five days per week). The teachers are carefully instructed in planning and presenting relevant, integrated learning activities; their work is well guided and supervised. After the subjects are 24 months of age, their daily curriculum includes activities that promote the development of skills in language, reading readiness (or reading), and mathematics/problem-solving.

The infant's teacher also has major responsibility of establishing initial rapport with the infant's mother. For the first 6 to 8 weeks she works with the child in his own home until his mother has enough confidence in the teacher to allow the child to go to the center where the major part of the research and teaching takes place. The teachers maintain contact with the parents continuously, reporting on the child's progress and emphasizing his accomplishments and ability.

While the children are having stimulating and challenging learning experiences at the research center, efforts are also being made to bring about some transformations in the home situation. This is accomplished by means of a program designed to improve the experimental mothers' homemaking and child-rearing skills and to prepare them for better employment opportunities. It is assumed that improved employment potential, increased earnings, and increased self-confidence will lead to positive changes in the home environment.

As even this sketchy broad outline indicates, this a complex, comprehensive, and multifaceted program, extremely difficult and expensive to implement. What have these enormous efforts produced? The preliminary results are most encouraging. The cognitive performance of the experimental group is vastly superior to that of the control group and to other children of this age living in the ghetto area.

The Gesell Development Schedule was administered at the ages of 6, 10, 14, 18, and 22 months. The experimental and control groups performed at comparable levels, slightly ahead of the test norm, up to 14 months of age. At 18 months, however, the experimental group began to show superior performance. The difference between the groups was even greater at 22 months when the experimental group was clearly accelerated while the control group was at, or slightly below, the norm for that age.

Intelligence tests (Stanford-Binet, WPPSI, or Cattell) were administered to all subjects every 3 months between the ages of 24 and 48 months, and at 6-month intervals from 48 months on. The experimental and control groups diverged more and more as the children became older. Fig. 8.5 presents these dramatic findings. When the subjects were 5 years of age, the experimental group had a mean IQ of 118, compared to the control group's mean of 92. The discrepancies between the two groups varied from a minimum of 25 IQ points at 24 months to a maximum of 30 IQ points at 66 months. Furthermore, the performance of the experimental

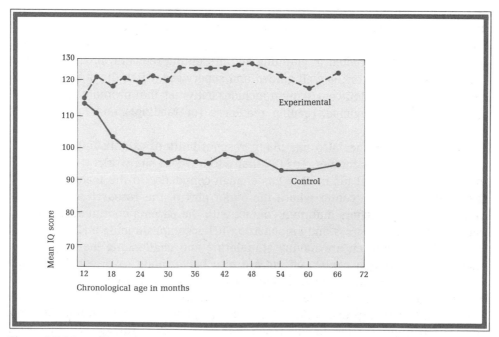

Figure 8.5 Mean IQ performance with increasing age for the experimental and control groups. (From R. Heber, H. Garber, S. Harrington, & C. Hoffman, Rehabilitation of families at risk for mental retardation. Unpublished progress report, Research and Training Center, University of Wisconsin, Madison, Wis., December, 1972, p. 107.)

children was much more homogeneous than that of the controls. At 63 months of age, only 3 controls had ever scored higher than 100 on the WPPSI, while not one experimental subject had scored below 100.

These are indeed impressive findings. Clearly the experimental procedures, the intensive infant stimulation program, resulted in remarkable acceleration in intellectual growth.

What about the cognitive development of children who are reared in deprived, unstimulating environments beyond the infancy years? Can preschool compensatory projects, utilizing less drastic means than transferring the child from his home, raise the cognitive level of these children? Can enriched training programs, during the preschool period, offset early cognitive deficiencies? It is impossible to answer these questions definitively at this time, but a few studies suggest that with conscientious effort, such goals can be achieved. This conclusion is based on the findings of a number of systematic studies. A sample of them will be reviewed briefly here.

The Early Training Project, directed by Gray and Klaus at Peabody College and sponsored by the United States Office of Education, is one of the most successful and suggestive systematic attempts to work with disadvantaged children beginning at the preschool age (3 years) or just before (10). The purpose of the project was "to see whether it is possible, by specially planned techniques, to offset the progressive retardation in cognitive development and school achievement that characterizes the culturally deprived child as he passes through his years of schooling" (10, 887).

The investigators worked with a total of 87 black preschool subjects who came from poverty stricken familes; their parents were unskilled or, at most, semi-skilled workers with only elementary school educations. There were two experimental and two control groups. One of the experimental groups attended three special summer sessions of preschool, while the other attended two such sessions. The controls received no special training.

The experimental subjects participated in a stimulating, concentrated program designed to promote stronger motivation toward achievement and to foster the development of behaviors and characteristics correlated with achievement, such as persistence, ability to delay gratification, and interest in school materials such as books, puzzles, and pencils.

> The materials and activities used in the summer sessions did not differ radically from those of conventional nursery school and kindergarten. The difference lies rather in the way in which materials were used, the self-conscious attempt to focus on the experimental variables—for example, to promote achievement motivation, to stimulate language development, to encourage the child to order and classify the objects and events of his work (10, 892).

In addition, the mothers of the experimental subjects met weekly with a specially trained teacher who attempted to make them aware of children's motives and to encourage them to reward strivings for achievement.

At the end of the training period, the trained children were superior to the controls in tests of vocabulary, language ability, and reading readiness. Follow-up studies of these subjects, after 27 months and again after 5 years, when the children had finished 2 years of public school, showed that the experimental group—the group with special training—had continued to show their early established gains, although the positive effects of early training were less marked than they had been earlier. The controls, on the other hand, showed the usual phenomenon of progressive retardation or cumulative deficit with increasing age. In other words, without special training, children from deprived backgrounds are likely to fall further and further behind in intellectual skills as they become older. The cognitive functioning of specially trained children, however, is likely to improve and at least some of their gains are likely to be maintained (24).

In the Early Training Project just discussed, the mothers of the youngsters were active participants, helping to stimulate the child's achievement motivation and rewarding his intellectual efforts. Another fascinating, well-conducted study indicates that the intellectual performances of disadvantaged nursery-school children may be raised without the mothers' active participation in training, although obviously this participation can be extremely helpful. In this study daily individual tutoring sessions, 15 to 20 minutes per day, produced marked gains in intellectual functioning. In the tutoring sessions, designed to generate an "abstract attitude," the child became actively involved with stimuli "so as to comprehend their significance." The training tasks, conducted by a professionally trained nursery-school teacher, were focused on improving the child's "ability to organize thoughts, to reflect upon situations, to comprehend the meaning of events, and to structure behavior so as to be able to choose among alternatives" (3, 380).

To accomplish each training task the child had to understand and use language, to produce relevant responses independently, and to discuss hypothetical situations related to the task (e.g., past, future, and alternative courses of action). "By structuring the teaching time in this way, the teacher made maximum use of every opportunity to aid the child in developing his budding ability to think and to reflect" (3, 382).

The 22 children in the study, ranging in age from 3 years 3 months to 4 years 7 months, were divided into four groups, matched as closely as possible for IQ, age, and sex. One group was tutored five times a week, and another group received the same training three times a week. There were two control groups: one of them had daily individual sessions with the teacher, but no tutoring, and the other experienced only the regular nursery-school program. The study lasted 4 months and all subjects were tested before and after the training period.

The average IQ gains for the group that had five days of tutoring a week was 15, and for the group that had three days of tutoring per week, 7. The two control groups averaged gains of only 2.0 and 1.3 points. Thus, improvement in intelligence test performance appears to be correlated with the amount of tutoring per week. Some of the children in the tutored groups manifested other dramatic changes in behavior. Several children who were originally excessively withdrawn, spoke incoherently, and manifested symptoms of emotional upset began to speak clearly and coherently, and their symptoms diminished.

> The most striking gains in the program were the apparent joy in learning and the feeling of mastery which the children displayed as the tutoring progressed. The untutored children, even those who received individual attention, showed none of these attitudes. This result is extremely important in that it strongly suggests that exposure to materials, a school-like situation, and an interested adult is not sufficient for learning. Both mastery and enthusiasm for learning will come only when the child can be shown how to become actively involved in the learning process (3, 388).

At the very least, the results of these programs demonstrate that specialized experiences and training can give children from deprived poverty backgrounds a "head start"—some real advantage in cognitive abilities that they would not ordinarily have when they begin school. As a result of such training, these children are better prepared for dealing with schoolwork, and they perform at a higher level in tests and in tasks related to school achievement. We are therefore inclined to agree with the following statement written by Professor J. McV. Hunt in response to Jensen's conclusions.

> Compensatory education has not failed. Investigations of compensatory education have now shown that traditional play school has little to offer the children of the poor, but programs which made an effort to inculcate cognitive skills, language skills, and number skills, whether they be taught directly or incorporated into games, show fair success. A substantial portion of this success endures. If the parents are drawn into the process, the little evidence available suggests that the effect on the children, and on the parents as well, increases in both degree and direction. All this . . . sounds to me like substantial success. . . . Thus, Jensen's opening statement ["compensatory education has apparently failed"] is a half-truth, and a dangerous half-truth. . . . (18, 298).

SUMMARY

American psychologists have traditionally approached the issue of intelligence with a highly practical orientation, a concern with the measurement of individual differences in intellectual ability. Definitions of intelligence emphasize functions such as abstraction, generalization, reasoning, and problem-solving, but the tests devised are, to a large extent, measures of **acquired knowledge,** especially language skills. Consequently, there may be vast differences between scores on standard tests of intelligence, IQs, and more global concepts such as "mental capacity" or "intellectual potential" which are not measured directly.

The ancestor of most intelligence tests was produced at the beginning of the twentieth century by Alfred Binet, a French psychologist. The best known and most widely used descendant of this test is the Stanford-Binet, first published in 1916 and revised in 1937 and 1960. Other widely used American intelligence tests are the WISC (Wechsler Intelligence Scale for Children) and the WPPSI (Wechsler Preschool Primary Scale of Intelligence) which have both verbal and performance scales. In standardizing these tests, the authors selected items that discriminated between children of the same age who were successful academically and those who had low school grades. Since this was the major criterion for including items in the test, it is hardly surprising that IQ scores are highly correlated with grades in school and college. A number of infant intelligence tests have been devised, but, since these measure primarily sensorimotor and perceptual abilities, performance on infant tests is not highly correlated with later measures of intelligence.

Scores on intelligence tests during the later preschool or the elementary school years are generally predictive of future performance. For example, the correlation between Stanford-Binet scores at ages 8 and 10 is around .90, and tests given in middle childhood generally predict intellectual status in early adulthood. Nevertheless, we must be cautious about predicting a particular child's intellectual status because the IQs of many children shift radically over the years. Shifts in IQ may be related to health, emotional stability, and marked environmental changes. Among those whose IQs change significantly, boys are more likely to gain in score, while girls are more likely to lose. Children who increase in IQ have been found to be more independent, more competitive, and more aggressive verbally than those with decreasing IQs, and they work harder in school and show a stronger desire to master intellectual problems.

Most psychologists believe that both hereditary and environmental factors play substantial roles in producing individual differences in intelligence test performance. However, it is virtually impossible to separate the effects of the two or to make a definite statement about the specific contributions of hereditary factors.

The environmental factors that appear to exert the greatest impact on intelligence test performance are the child's social class and early rearing. Compared with the middle class, families in socioeconomically deprived groups typically provide their children with different cognitive and language experiences and put much less stress on the values of intellectual development and achievement.

A few psychologists have maintained that the differences between whites and blacks in intelligence test scores are the result of the genetic inferiority of blacks. The data do not support this conclusion, although on the average poor white and black children do not perform as well as middle-class children on cognitive tasks and tests of intelligence. In recent years, a considerable amount of attention has been centered on the question of whether children from socioeconomically deprived backgrounds can develop competencies and motivational patterns that would enable them to perform better in cognitive and academic tasks.

A number of studies yield encouraging conclusions. Radical environmental changes, instituted very early, can be effective in raising the level of the child's cognitive functioning, especially if direct efforts are made to inculcate cognitive, language, and number skills.

References

1. Bayley, N. Mental growth during the first three years. In R. G. Barker, J. S. Kounin, & H. F. Wright (Eds.), **Child behavior and development.** New York: McGraw-Hill, 1943. Pp. 87–106.
2. Bayley, N. **Bayley's scales of infant development.** New York: The Psychological Corporation, 1968.
3. Blank, M., & Solomon, F. A tutorial language program to develop abstract thinking in socially disadvantaged preschool children. **Child Development,** 1968, **39**(2), 379–389.
4. Bloom, B. **Stability and change in human characteristics.** New York: Wiley, 1964.
5. Bond, E. A. **Tenth grade abilities and achievements.** New York: Bureau of Publications, Teachers College, Columbia University Press, 1940.
6. Bronfenbrenner, U. **Influences on human development.** Hinsdale, Ill.: Dryden, 1972.
7. Escalona, S. The use of infant tests for predictive purposes. In W. E. Martin & C. B. Stendler (Eds.), **Readings in child development.** New York: Harcourt Brace Jovanovich, 1954. Pp. 95–103.
8. Gage, N. L. I.Q. heritability, race differences, and educational research. **Phi Delta Kappan,** 1972 (January), 297–307.
9. Gottesman, I. I. Biogenetics of race and class. In M. Deutsch, I. Katz, and A. R. Jensen (Eds.), **Social class, race, and psychological development.** New York: Holt, Rinehart & Winston, 1968. Pp. 11–51.
10. Gray, S. W., & Klaus, R. A. An experimental preschool program for culturally deprived children. **Child Development,** 1965, **36**(4), 887–898.
11. Guilford, J. P. The structure of intellect. **Psychological Bulletin,** 1956, **53,** 267–293.
12. Guilford, J. P. Three faces of intellect. **American Psychologist,** 1959, **14,** 469–479.
13. Guilford, J. P. **The nature of human intelligence.** New York: McGraw-Hill, 1967.
14. Guilford, J. P. Intelligence has three facets. **Science,** 1968, **160,** 615–620.
15. Heber, R., Garber, H., Harrington, S., and Hoffman, C. Rehabilitation of families at risk for mental retardation. Unpublished progress reports, Research and Training Center, University of Wisconsin, Madison, Wis., (a) October, 1971; (b) December, 1972.
16. Hess, R. D., & Shipman, V. C. Early experience and the socialization of cognitive modes in children. **Child Development,** 1965, **36**(4), 869–886.
17. Honzik, M. P., Macfarlane, J. W., & Allen, L. The stability of mental test performance between two and eighteen years. **Journal of Experimental Education,** 1948, **17,** 309–324.
18. Hunt, J. McV. Has compensatory education failed? Has it been attempted? **Harvard Educational Review,** 1969, **39,** 278–300.
19. Jensen, A. R. How much can we boost I.Q. and scholastic achievement? **Harvard Educational Review,** 1969, **39,** 448–483. 1–123
20. Kagan, J. Inadequate evidence and illogical conclusions. **Harvard Educational Review,** 1969, **39,** 274–277.
21. Kagan, J., & Moss, H. A. Parental correlates of child's I.Q. and height: A cross-validation of the Berkeley Growth Study results. **Child Development,** 1959, **30,** 325–332.

22. Kagan, J., & Moss, H. A. **Birth to maturity: A study in psychological development.** New York: Wiley, 1962.

23. Kagan, J., Sontag, L. W., Baker, C. T., & Nelson, V. L. Personality and I.Q. change. **Journal of Abnormal and Social Psychology,** 1958, **56,** 261–266.

24. Klaus, R. A., & Gray, S. The early training project for disadvantaged children: A report after five years. **Monographs of the Society for Research in Child Development,** 1968, **33**(4).

25. Mussen, P. H., Dean, S., & Rosenberg, M. Some further evidence on the validity of the WISC. **Journal of Consulting Psychology,** 1952, **16,** 410–411.

26. Scarr-Salapatek, S. Race, social class and IQ. **Science,** 1971, **174,** 1285–1295.

27. Scarr-Salapatek, S. Unknowns in the IQ equation. **Science,** 1971, **174,** 1223–1228.

28. Skeels, H. M. Adult status of children with contrasting early life experiences: A follow-up study. **Monographs of the Society for Research in Child Development,** 1966, **31**(3, Whole No. 105).

29. Sontag, L. W., Baker, C. T., & Nelson, V. L. Mental growth and personality: A longitudinal study. **Monographs of the Society for Research in Child Development,** 1958, **23**(68), 1–143.

30. Terman, L. M., & Merrill, M. A. **Measuring intelligence: A guide to the administration of the new revised Stanford-Binet tests of intelligence.** Boston: Houghton Mifflin, 1960.

31. Wechsler, D. **The measurement of adult intelligence.** Baltimore: Williams & Wilkins, 1939.

32. Wechsler, D. **Wechsler intelligence scale for children.** New York: The Psychological Corporation, 1952.

Part IV
The Preschool Years

Chapter 9

Preschool Personality Development

The child's remarkable progress during the preschool period in motor abilities, language, and cognitive function is paralleled by vast changes in his personality characteristics and motives. The preschool child has a much richer, more complex, and more highly differentiated personality than the infant. Personality refers to the total organization or patterning of the individual's characteristics, the ways of thinking, feeling, and behaving that comprise his unique means of relating and adapting to his environment—the individual aspects of behavior that are stable, distinctive, and set him apart from all other people. Systematic study of personality is concerned primarily with individual differences. In the study of personality the descriptive terms used, the traits or dimensions investigated, are the ones that appear to be most salient, that is, the ones that most clearly differentiate people, in the particular culture in which the investigator lives.

In American culture people differ widely in their competitiveness and their degree of dependence on others; hence these are personality traits that American psychologists study. Investigators from other cultures would very likely choose to emphasize other characteristics. In cultures where there is little competition and minimal variability in competitiveness, personality psychologists (if indeed they existed in that culture) would probably not consider competitiveness a major personality trait. In one Guatemalan Indian culture studied by Kagan, almost all 3-year-olds were homogeneously passive; it would probably not be worthwhile to study passivity as a preschool personality trait in this culture.

Casual observation of a group of American nursery-school children at play attests to the striking differences among them in behavior, characteristics, and motives. Some are highly active, outgoing, boisterous, independent, explorative, curious, and adventurous; others appear passive, dependent, shy, unaggressive, and withdrawing. Dominating, creative "leaders" are easily distinguished from suggestible, conforming "followers." Each child manifests his own unique organization of personality characteristics and motivations. The endless variety of such combinations apparent at age 5, in comparison with age 2, is due in large part to the rapid acquisition of new patterns of response, expanding perceptions, increasingly extensive social interactions, and heightened awareness of the social environment. During the preschool years, many new personality characteristics and motives of paramount importance are acquired. For instance, many preschool children give clear evidence, for the first time, of being motivated to solve challenging intellectual problems.

Furthermore, established personal qualities become modified and existing needs may be expressed in new and different ways. Among these characteristics and motives are sexual curiosity, autonomy and independence (or dependence), aggression, competence or mastery, sex typing, anxiety, conscience, cooperation, and altruism. Each of these characteristics is a pervasive one—manifested in many forms, in diverse situations, and affecting many aspects of behavior. As we shall see, some of these traits may become stable and enduring early in life, and thus predictive of subsequent behavior in our culture. For example, the socially anxious 5-year-old is likely to become a shy adolescent (19) and the dependent little girl is likely to become a dependent woman (49, 50).

SOCIALIZATION

Each culture has its own "typical" personality—a particular pattern of motives, goals, ideals, and values—which is characteristic of and valued by that culture and which most children growing up in that culture acquire. Members of the American middle class, especially males, are likely to be vigorous, autonomous, independent, assertive, socially responsive, achievement-oriented, and competitive. In some cultures children are encouraged to act in quite different ways. Even within American society, Mexican-American children in the Southwest are generally trained to be more cooperative and less competitive than Caucasian American children living in the same region. Zuni and Hopi Indian children in America and youngsters on Israeli kibbutzim are also discouraged from competing; their training stresses sharing, cooperation, and egalitarian treatment of others. The Japanese are generally "group oriented," interdependent in their relationships with others, self-effacing, quiet, and outwardly passive. Children in these cultures are less concerned with personal aggrandizement and personal achievement than most children in American middle-class culture.

Socialization is the process by which the individual acquires those behavior patterns, beliefs, standards, and motives that are valued by, and appropriate in, his own cultural group and family. At birth the infant has an enormously wide range of behavioral potentialities open to him. He can, theoretically, become one of many types of adult: aggressive or self-effacing with others, selfish or generous with friends, atheistic or polytheistic, concerned or bored with intellectual achievement, independent of or dependent on parents, honest or dishonest, expressive or inhibited with members of the opposite sex, politically liberal or conservative. The range of possibilities is enormous; yet ordinarily the individual adopts only personality characteristics and behaviors considered appropriate, or at least acceptable, for his own social, ethnic, and religious group. The core problem in studying the process of socialization is to determine **how** people develop the behaviors, beliefs, and motivations that are considered appropriate and in accord with those of the group they take as a reference.

To a considerable extent the culture in which the child grows up prescribes both the **content** and the **methods** of socialization—how he will be trained as well as the personality characteristics, motives, attitudes, and values he should acquire. Certainly there are some universal aspects of socialization. Every culture has to establish an orderly pattern of collective life and provide for satisfaction of the biological needs of its members. In all cultures children must be fed and their dependency needs must be attended to; they must be toilet trained and protected from illness. In all cultures aggressive, sexual, and dependency impulses must be modified to some extent or the culture cannot survive and endure. But cultures differ widely in their permissiveness or restrictiveness with respect to expression of these motives; each has its own ways of handling child rearing. Nevertheless, in each case, the object is to facilitate the acquisition of culturally approved behavior patterns and motives—in other words, to produce individuals who fit into the culture and help to maintain it.

Socialization training becomes more intensive as the child matures, understands more about the world, and is able to think and to solve problems more adequately. In the second year, the child learns to walk, and his motor and manual skills improve. He spontaneously begins "trying out" his abilities, investigating his surroundings, and testing his new capacities. If his parents permit him to explore his world and do not inhibit his curiosity and independence, he will continue to manifest his tendency to explore his environment freely and manipulate objects actively. Under these conditions the child is more likely to develop spontaneity, curiosity, self-assertion, and self-confidence, together with strong drives for autonomy, independence, mastery, competence, and achievement. On the other hand, if parents restrict his freedom of movement severely and inhibit his spontaneous exploratory drive, they are likely to stifle the development of autonomy and independence.

In the following pages the most significant motivations and characteristics that emerge or become modified during the preschool period are defined, examined, and related to socialization training. The "normal" course of development of each characteristic is described, and age changes in the nature and forms of its expression (and conflicts related to overt expression) are specified. In addition, we will discuss basic processes in socialization—learning by rewards and punishments, imitation, and identification—that are involved in the acquisition and development of these traits.

In the last part of the chapter, the focus of attention will shift to the family: the principal and primary determinant, or set of determinants, of personality structure and of individual variations in these characteristics. The child's personality emerges and develops in the context of the earliest complex social relationships, particularly those involving the family. Consequently, the final sections of the chapter will review some significant data on the effects of different types of family atmospheres and parent-child relationships on many aspects of the preschool child's personality and on the patterning and organization of his characteristics and motives.

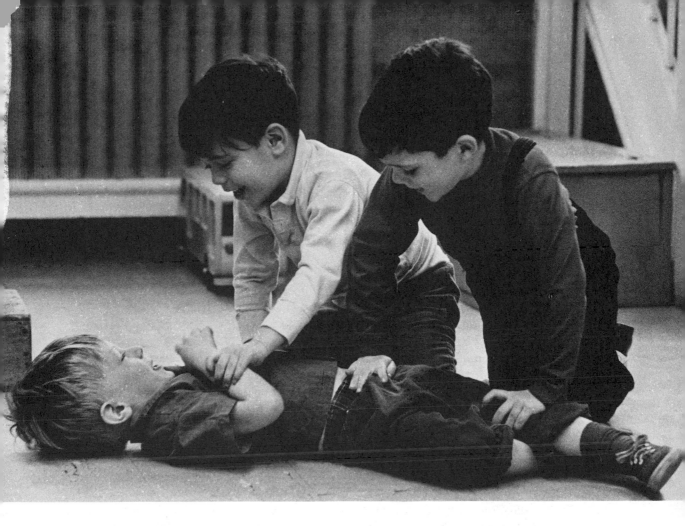

Motives and Behavior

The reader must be alerted to the important distinction between **behavior** and underlying **motives.** We can speak of an aggressive motive (a desire to hurt someone) or aggressive behavior (hitting someone). And, as we shall see, there is not necessarily a direct link between motives and overt responses.

Motives cannot be seen or measured directly. A motive (or need) is a construct or mediating variable referring to the desire for a particular goal. In considering motives, we must usually specify the objects, goals, or targets of the motive. For example, although some children appear to have generalized dependency motives—displaying dependent behavior toward a diversity of targets including mother, sister, friends—the dependency motives of most children, although highly salient, have more specific targets; the child may be dependent on his mother and no one else. Analogously, some children seem to be generally hostile, but more typically there is a particular target of hostility motivation. The child can be hostile toward his older brother, for example, and not toward other people. Some children are highly motivated to achieve in school, in academic subjects, but not in sports; some have the reverse goals.

Motives must be inferred from behavior, and, more specifically, individual differences in the salience of motives are typically inferred from the directionality of the individual's behavior and his perseverance in trying to obtain the desired goal. To illustrate, two boys may desire to achieve an important athletic goal—to set a new record in swimming 100 meters. The boy who practices diligently and persists in his attempts to perform this feat, in spite of handicaps, obstacles, and failures, appears to be more highly motivated for success than the boy who gives up after some perfunctory efforts and a few practice trials.

But, can we be sure that our inferences about the motives of the two boys (based on our observations) are valid? It is not difficult to think of reasons why they may not be. The first boy may want to break the record not because he desires athletic success per se, but because he wants to win the love and approval of his athletic father. This example shows that a particular response may appear to gratify one motive, but may in fact be in the service of another.

The second boy may give up easily, not because he lacks motivation for success in swimming, but because he may be so strongly motivated to achieve this kind of success that he is dreadfully afraid of failure. This case illustrates that (1) a motive can be highly salient and yet not lead directly to behavior that gratifies that motive, and (2) fear or anxiety may inhibit goal-directed behavior in spite of a motive to achieve the goal.

The first boy's most powerful motive was getting approval from his father and he had learned that "trying hard in athletics" brought parental love and approval, the goal he desired. A child readily learns the responses that lead directly to gratification of his motives. Analogously, a girl who is dependent on adults will manifest dependent behavior (e.g., clinging to adults, asking for help) if such behavior leads to gratification of her motive. In short, a motive will be expressed in overt behavior if that behavior effectively gratifies needs, that is, if the child expects to achieve his goals as a result of the behavior. In contrast, another child may have strong dependency desires, but may not approach adults in a dependent way because previous dependent responses have frequently been rejected. Such a child would be anxious about expressing his dependency and would not try to gratify his motives by behaving in dependent ways.

Many of the motives of the 5-year-old involve what is termed an **approach-avoidance conflict.** This means that there will be, on the one hand, a desire to approach a goal and, on the other, anxiety associated with the attainment of the goal. For example, the desire to disobey the mother openly is part of an approach-avoidance conflict. The child wants to rebel against the mother's demand that he drink his milk, but he is anxious about this and fears punishment or disapproval if he refuses her request. There are, therefore, forces impelling him to disobey (approach motives) and counterforces (anxiety and fear) which oppose the direct expression of rebellion (avoidance motives). The actual behavior displayed by the child will be a function of the interaction of these two forces: the desire to gratify the motive and the anxiety that interfered with gratification. Whether the child will attempt to obtain the desired goal will depend on the relative strengths of the approach and avoidance tendencies.

In the course of his socialization training, the child learns that he must inhibit certain forbidden acts and that he must delay the fulfillment of many of his desires. In the 1-year-old child, the arousal of a motive is likely to lead immediately to behavior aimed at gratifying the motive directly. Babies have not yet learned to delay or to inhibit gratification of their needs. The preschool child, however, is expected to exert some control over his aggressive, dependent, and sexual impulses—to modify them and to express them only in acceptable ways. Some kinds of responses, such as physical aggression toward parents, must be inhibited because they will invoke punishment whenever they occur.

The child also learns that the gratification of some motives must be postponed until the appropriate time and place. A 4-year-old girl may find that her nurturant mother generally gratifies her dependency needs (hugging her, helping her) as soon as they arise, but does not do so at all times. For example, if she is engaged in an important discussion with the father, she may postpone her dependency-gratifying reactions toward the child, perhaps telling the little girl, "I'll be with you in just a little while." Under these circumstances, the child learns to postpone or delay gratification until a later time when the mother is able to gratify the child's needs freely. The dependency responses are not inhibited, but the child has learned to delay gratification. This growing ability to delay immediate gratification of a motive is an important aspect of ego development. In brief, the fact that dependent or aggressive behavior occurs infrequently does not always indicate that the child has no dependent or aggressive motivations. Rather, it may only signify the acquisition of controls and inhibitions of these behaviors.

SEXUAL MOTIVES AND CURIOSITY

Sexual motives include many kinds of wishes related to pleasurable, usually genital, sensations. While masturbation and sex-play occur in very young children of both sexes, erotic stimulation from the genitals becomes more intense during the preschool period. Many children discover that stimulation of the genitals produces pleasant sensations and may practice some modified form of masturbation (touching and manipulation of the genitals) during these years. The preschool child is also likely to have opportunities to notice the differences between his own genitals and those of adults and of the opposite sex. The discrepancies elicit curiosity about and interest in the genitals of others, especially those of the opposite sex, and a desire to understand the differences. Questions about sex, particularly about the origins of babies and anatomical sex differences, are common between the ages of 2 and 5 (37).

Many middle-class parents in western culture feel they should suppress signs of sexual activity, interest, or curiosity in their young offspring, spanking or scolding if they discover the child masturbating or running about the house naked (78). If this occurs, the genitals may become the focus for conflict because they supply uniquely pleasant sensations and, at the same time, evoke the anticipation of punishment and anxiety. In more permissive cultures children are much more open and spontaneous in their sexual behaviors. For example, in the Trobriand Islands, where sexual exploration is not punished or restricted, children of preschool age are highly active at a genital level and a large proportion of their play is sexually oriented (57).

Punishment for early sexual activity or curiosity may be a major source of adolescent and adult anxiety about sex, misunderstandings, and handicapping attitudes about sex (see pp. 367 ff). Such adverse effects could be avoided if parents would handle the child's sexual curiosity frankly and realistically, acting neither embarrassed nor secretive about questions or, on the other hand, overwhelming the child with too much information.

HOSTILITY AND AGGRESSION

Aggressive behaviors are actions that are intended to cause injury or anxiety to others, including hitting, kicking, destroying property, quarrelling, derogating others, attacking others verbally, and resisting requests. **Hostility** is the motive or desire to hurt someone. It must be recognized that any particular aggressive act may have different motives or functions; it may or may not be motivated by hostility. For example, a child may hit a playmate as a way of greeting him, because he wants a toy the other will not give him, or because he dislikes the other child. In the first instance, the child's aggressive behavior is motivated by affiliation and is not hostile; in the second, it has an instrumental, not a hostile, purpose —to obtain a nonaggressive goal, a toy. In the third instance, hitting is motivated by a hostile goal, specifically causing injury or pain to the other child. Hostile motivation can be gratified by a wide variety of behaviors, some of which are not obviously aggressive. For instance, a boy who is hostile toward his academically oriented father may do poorly in school because he knows his poor performance will hurt his father's feelings. Yet because poor performance in reading will cause the boy himself shame and anxiety, it does not seem, on the surface, to be an aggressive act.

Social Experience and Aggression

Psychological theory and research are focused on the interpersonal and social factors affecting the child's tendency to behave aggressively. The forms and degrees of aggression a child will exhibit depend on many factors: the intensity of his hostile motivation, the degree of environmental frustration to which he is subjected, the reinforcement received for aggressive behavior, his observation and imitation of aggressive models, and the amount of anxiety and guilt associated with the expression of aggression. Let us turn our attention first to situations that are likely to give rise to aggression.

Frustration and Aggression According to one popular formulation, called the frustration-aggression hypothesis, aggression is a prepotent, if not inevitable, reaction to frustration. While there is no general agreement on a definition of frustration, most investigators and theorists agree that frustrating events are those that block the individual's goal-seeking behavior, threaten his self-esteem, or deprive him of the opportunity to gratify some salient motive. The sources of frustration may be (1) externally imposed barriers that prevent or delay the achievement of an important goal, (2) internal conflicts between incompatible responses, or (3) feelings of inadequacy or anxiety that inhibit or prevent the pursuit of important goals.

There is abundant evidence that aggression is a common reaction to frustration. In nursery school the frequency of conflicts between children increases when the amount of play space is limited and, consequently, the children experience more interferences and frustrations. In experiments children who are frustrated are likely to react with aggressive responses, especially in a permissive situation where such responses do not lead to punishment. In one study preschool boys and girls were observed playing with dolls for two 30-minute sessions **(84)**. During the first session they were allowed to play freely. Before the second session one group of subjects, the failure or frustration group, were given difficult tasks to do; these made them feel unsuccessful and frustrated. The control group was not treated this way before the second session.

In the second session both groups displayed more aggression than they had during the first play period, probably because the permissive atmosphere permitted such expression. However, the frustration group showed significantly greater increases in aggression than the control group. The frustrations experienced by this group elicited intensified aggressiveness **(84)**.

The child's **interpretation** of the frustrating situation, rather than the absolute amount of frustration, is the most salient factor in determining his reaction. An event is considered frustrating only if the child actually feels disturbed or upset by it and believes that some external force or a person was the source of his frustration. For example, if the child cannot open a door that he was able to open earlier, he may be surprised and then become anxious or even apprehensive if he doesn't know why it is locked. But if he believes someone locked him in the room, he is likely to become angry and behave aggressively.

Young children encounter many situations that seem to be frustrating from an adult observer's point of view, but most of these are inconsequential, producing no reaction or only minor, transient responses. Meticulous observations of the incidence, intensity, and duration of interferences and unpleasant events in the everyday lives of children in their natural habitats (home, nursery school, playground) indicated that preschool youngsters experienced more than 90 "goal blockages" per day on the average. However, most of these were "neither sufficient nor necessary conditions for producing states of disturbance in the child" (27, 100). Reactions to these interferences were typically very mild in intensity, and of brief duration, usually less than a few minutes. Minor interferences seldom elicited strong, enduring, or intense reactions. Goal blockages that are really upsetting to the child are more likely to arouse behaviors directed at eliminating the source of the interference or diminishing its effects.

Children differ markedly in their assessments of how frustrating a particular "interference" is. For example, a highly dependent child may be very much frustrated by the brief absence of his mother, which may entail some minor deprivations. However, such a child, being quite passive, may feel very little frustration by another child's domination of social play activities. A more independent child may not feel deprived because of his mother's absence, but may feel very frustrated by another child's "taking over" on the playground.

Situational factors also affect the child's interpretation of the frustration. If a child is tripped by another child, the victim will react with greater hostility if he interprets the action as intentional rather than accidental. The presence of close friends may also reduce aggressive reactions to frustration. In one experiment children were frustrated while playing with friends; their play became more constructive under these conditions. Close friends became more outgoing and cooperative in their play, jointly manifesting aggression towards the experimenter, the source of their frustration (83). Apparently, social cohesiveness and the presence of friends—and the security associated with these—can promote socially desirable reactions to frustration.

Furthermore, there is a range of individual differences in reaction to frustration, both in the intensity and in the form of the reaction. Some children seem to have "low frustration tolerance"; they react immediately and directly to any frustration. Children with "high frustration tolerance" may be remarkably unperturbed by events that most would regard as highly frustrating.

Frustration and Regression Aggression may be a prepotent reaction to frustration, but it is not the only one. Regression (resorting to immature response patterns) is another common immediate consequence. In one highly significant investigation the behavior of nursery-school children was observed under two conditions: first, free-play and, later, frustration. Regression was measured in terms of decreases in productivity, creativity, and constructiveness of play after frustration (7).

In the free-play situation the children played alone for half an hour in a room which contained a standard set of play materials arranged on three large squares of paper. Behavior was recorded and units of play were scored on a 7-

point scale of constructiveness from 2 (superficial examination of the playthings) to 8 (highly original, elaborate game or story involving the toys).

In the frustration situation the child was brought into the experimental room again. This time he found the standard play material of the free-play period incorporated into an elaborate, highly attractive set of new toys. When the child had become thoroughly involved in play with these new toys, the experimenter collected all the less attractive, standard toys. He arranged them, as they had been earlier, on three squares of paper in another part of the room. The child was led to that part of the room and a wire screen separating the standard toys from the new ones was lowered and locked. During this time (30 minutes), the child could play only with the less attractive play materials while the more desirable toys remained visible but inaccessible.

Children's reactions during the second phase of the frustration period differed greatly from their behavior during free play with the same toys. When frustrated, the children displayed a variety of barrier or escape activities, for example, approaching the inaccessible regions, pleading with the experimenter to be allowed out of the room, talking about outside regions, aggressive behavior toward experimenter or barriers. In addition, their play was appreciably less creative and constructive than it had been during free play. In other words, a marked reduction or regression in the level of maturity of play was a consequence of frustration. Furthermore, the children who seemed to be most severely frustrated, that is, those most occupied with barrier and escape behavior during the frustration situation, regressed most in their play (7).

Learning, Imitation, and Aggression

The probability that any particular preschool child will manifest aggression and the strength and intensity of his aggressive behavior depend on a number of factors in his experience. Included are the degree to which he has been rewarded or punished by others for such behavior in the past, the availability and influence of aggressive models, and the degree to which his aggression has been successful in relieving his anger and hostility and in accomplishing the goals he wanted.

The Effects of Rewards Rewards for aggressive responses lead to increases in overt expression of aggression and generalization of aggressive responses to other situations. In one experimental study some preschool children received trinkets as rewards for verbal aggression while playing with dolls (calling the dolls "dirty," "bad"), while a control group was rewarded for nonaggressive verbal responses. All subjects were then observed in another play situation with other toys. The children who had been rewarded for verbal aggression made significantly more of these responses than did the controls, and in the subsequent play period they also manifested significantly greater amounts of nonverbal aggression (hitting dolls, destroying toys; **6**). It is not clear, however, whether these acts were accompanied by increased anger (hostility).

Peers are frequently sources of reinforcement for aggressive behavior and, as parents often complain, many children manifest aggression more frequently after they have attended nursery school than they had before. Aggressive behavior —bodily attack, attack with an object, invasion of territory—is frequently and strongly reinforced by other children in the nursery school, including the victims of aggression. They reward the aggressor's behavior by yielding to his wishes, withdrawing from the conflict, or giving him something (a toy, a place in line), thereby permitting him to attain what he wanted. Thus, peers "provided substantial support for the maintenance of already existing . . . aggressive behaviors" (**68**, 22), and, consequently, "it is unlikely that the nursery school setting will provide a basis for the **extinction** of aggressive behaviors for children who enter the school with these behaviors already at high strength" (**68**, 20).

In fact, the nursery school may provide an efficient program for increasing the frequency of aggressive behavior of some children. Children who are passive or only moderately aggressive when they enter the nursery school show more aggressive behavior during the period of their attendance there if they interact frequently with their peers. At first they are frequent victims of aggression, but eventually they counterattack, and their counterattacks are reinforced. Subsequently, they begin to initiate aggressive actions and their output of these responses increases significantly (**68**). Children who are originally passive and, in addition, do not interact with the other children, do not show significant increases in aggressive initiations; neither do passive children who are unsuccessful in their counterattacks against aggressive peers (**68**).

Permissiveness The effects of permissiveness toward aggression—allowing the child to express aggression overtly and freely—are comparable to the effects of direct reward. Thus, with a permissive adult present, aggressive responses increased from the first half to the second half of a 10-minute doll-play session and from one session to the next (**6**).

If parents clearly permit or reward aggression, children are likely to behave aggressively at home and, by generalization, in other settings where they feel aggression is also permitted, expected, or encouraged. It should be noted, however, that if the child does not regard a particular setting as specifically permissive, he is less likely to manifest overt aggression. This was demonstrated in one study in which children participated in two free-play sessions with a young friend (**79**). For half of the subjects, an adult was present throughout, but for the other half, this was not the case. Two-thirds of the children observed with the permissive adult present showed more aggression in the second session than they had in the first. However, in the adult-absent group, that is, the group without specific permission to be aggressive, all the subjects showed **less** aggression in the second session. Apparently, the accepting adult was seen as granting permission for aggressive expression, but in the absence of an adult the child's own internalized standards (his inhibitions against the expression of aggression) were invoked. The child controls himself when no adult is available to tell him what to do, but abdicates this control when an adult is present—acting as he thinks this adult expects him to.

Modeling and Imitation Exposure to an aggressive model (or models) is likely to elicit imitation of aggression in children. In the stimulating research of Bandura and his associates at Stanford University, preschool children were exposed to aggressive real-life or fantasy (movies or television) models. In one experiment, for example, an adult model was observed by preschool children while she "solved" a discrimination-learning problem (5). During her trials, she made many incidental, irrelevant responses that had nothing to do with the discrimination learning including behaving aggressively toward dolls located on the discrimination boxes. When she was with the control subjects, she did not behave in those aggressive ways.

Subsequently, the subjects were given the same discrimination problem. Ninety percent of the children in the experimental group imitated the aggressive responses of the model, whereas none of the control children displayed such behavior. Mere observation of aggressive models was sufficient to stimulate imitative aggressive behavior in children. Frustration and direct reinforcement are not necessary antecedent conditions for the occurrence of aggressive responses. Again, this behavior—hitting dolls—though called aggressive may not have been motivated by anger or hostility.

Imitative aggressive responses, acquired from a model, as in the experiment described above, may also generalize to other settings. In another experiment some nursery-school children observed models behaving in distinctive aggressive ways toward an inflated balloon painted to resemble a clown. Others observed nonaggressive models. A control group was not exposed to any adult models in the experimental situation.

Following their exposure to the model, the children experienced a mild frustration before being tested for delayed imitation of the model's behavior. Then they spent 20 minutes in a room playing with a variety of toys. The subjects who had been exposed to aggressive models displayed significantly more imitative physical and verbal aggression than the controls or the children who observed nonaggressive models. Other kinds of aggression, not displayed by the model, were also more common among those who observed an aggressive model. Clearly, exposure to human models behaving aggressively has a great deal of influence in eliciting aggressive behavior regardless of whether it is preceded by frustrating experiences.

Punishment for Aggression While reward for aggression, frustration, and observation of aggressive models may stimulate the child's aggressive behavior, punishment for aggression should, according to the principles of learning, lead to inhibition of overt aggression. There is good experimental evidence to support this expectancy.

In one study nursery-school boys were brought into a room in which there was a large clown-shaped doll (Bobo) which they could punch freely for two minutes. The frequency of hitting was automatically recorded. Then each child was rewarded with marbles each time he punched the Bobo doll, for a total of ten trials. After this, the subjects were divided into three groups, each group experiencing a different outcome for punching: one group received no further reward for punching the doll; another group received marbles on half the trials and a noxious buzzer sound following the other half; and the third group received consistent punishment, that is, the noxious buzzer sounded each time they punched the Bobo doll.

All the boys were informed that they could stop the punching game whenever they wished. The measure of aggression was the number of hitting responses that the child delivered before voluntarily ending the game. The results were clear-cut; subjects in the no-outcome group displayed the greatest amount of aggression (the greatest number of punches to the doll), while the consistently punished children showed the least. The inconsistently punished children fell in the intermediate position. Punishment clearly was effective in reducing the amount of aggressive response (67).

Positive reinforcement and punishment of aggression are used in direct ways in **behavior therapy,** a therapeutic technique in which desirable responses are rewarded and undesirable ones punished. These techniques have been used to modify aggression and cooperation among nursery-school boys. The purpose of the experiment was "to control the aggressive behavior of all of the boys in an entire nursery school class, by using as techniques the removal of positive generalized reinforcement (attention for aggression) while giving attention to cooperative acts" (21, 103).

During the training (experimental manipulation), the nursery-school teachers tried, as much as possible, to ignore aggression and to reward cooperative and peaceful behavior by attention and praise. Ratings of the children's aggression were made for a week before the training period began, to determine a base or reference rate of aggressive responses. Similar ratings were made again after the first week of a two-week training period, and again, three weeks later to assess the persistence of the effects of training.

This simple treatment was successful and apparently had enduring effects. The number of acts of physical and verbal aggression decreased significantly in the second week of training, and the number of cooperative acts increased. Although the effects on verbal aggression were enduring, physical aggression increased after the brief training period, decreasing again with further training. The success of the "experiment" was particularly dramatic to the nursery-school teachers, the real "experimenters," who were at first skeptical about its efficacy, because "two extremely aggressive boys became friendly and cooperative to a degree the teachers had not thought possible following the training" (21).

Parental Influences on Aggression During the preschool period, parents control many of the child's experiences of frustration and gratification, determine whether he is reinforced or punished for aggressive behavior, and serve as models for imitation. The findings from studies we have discussed should be applicable to the home situation. If aggression is punished at home, fear and anxiety should become attached to hostile responses, and the child should therefore inhibit such responses at home and, by generalization, in many situations outside the home.

The effects of parental punishment on children's aggressive behavior appear to be more complex, however. A parent who employs physical punishment to inhibit undesirable aggressive behavior is also serving as an aggressive model, demonstrating to the child the power and potential usefulness of aggression.

> When a parent punishes his child physically for having aggressed toward peers ... the intended outcome of this training is that the child should refrain from hitting others. The child, however, is also learning from parental demonstration how to aggress physically and this imitative learning may provide the direction for the child's behavior when he is similarly frustrated in subsequent social interactions (3, 43).

In brief, the child may not only acquire aggressive response patterns but may also fail to learn inhibitions against aggression through imitation of his parents, even though he is presumably being taught that aggression is bad. Hence, the long-term effects of physical punishment may be to enhance aggression (at least in "safe" situations) rather than inhibit it.

Inconsistent handling of the child's aggression may also stimulate aggressive expression. Mothers who permit aggression on some occasions and punish it at other times are likely to have highly aggressive children (78). When parents permit occasional aggression, the child experiences some reduction in anxiety about this response. In addition, inconsistency in discipline creates a frustrating situation which may itself instigate increased aggressive behavior.

Sex and Age Differences in Aggression

The form, style, frequency, and intensity of the child's aggressive responses are, to a very great extent, functions of his social learning experiences. In American culture, as in almost all cultures (24), boys have traditionally received more encouragement (reward) and less punishment for aggressive behavior than girls.

Many parents believe that the ideal boy should be able to fight back and defend himself when attacked (78). Hence boys are not generally made as anxious about aggression as girls and during the preschool years boys express more aggression than girls both in play and fantasy. Physical attacks, fighting, quarreling, tackling, verbal aggression, destructiveness, and temper tantrums are all more common among nursery-school boys (54, 323–324).

Some sex differences become more marked with increasing age during the preschool period. Two-year-old boys and girls hit, scream, and cry with approximately equal frequency, but by the age of 4 boys do more hitting and relatively less screaming than girls do (46). This sex difference reflects the fact that boys are less strongly punished for physical aggression and thus do not learn to inhibit physical aggressive responses as completely as girls do. However, girls are more verbally aggressive than boys (29). A boy is more likely to hit another child; a girl is more apt to scold or insult another.

With increasing age and experience, the child learns to display those forms of aggression that are defined as culturally acceptable and to inhibit aggressive expressions (usually gross, violent types) that are unacceptable. Thus, in doll play, older nursery-school children manifest fewer responses of physical aggression, such as destruction and hitting, than younger children; boys display stronger tendencies toward physical aggression than girls; girls display more verbal aggression, such as expressing disapproval and insults. Because physical aggression by girls is less tolerated in our culture, "it is not surprising . . . that girls develop more indirect means of self expression than boys do" (29).

Stability of Aggressive Expression

There is another critical issue that must be considered in any discussion of socialization and personality development. The concept personality has meaning only if it refers to behavioral characteristics that are enduring or, in other words, relatively stable. More specifically, with regard to aggression, the question is can we predict the amount of the child's later aggressive behavior from his aggressiveness at an earlier period or is aggression so variable from one situation to another that there is little consistency over time? The evidence indicates that there is continuity in aggressive behavior during the preschool years. According to ratings by nursery-school teachers (different teachers independently rating the child's behavior at different times during his period of nursery-school attendance), a child's proneness to aggressive behavior remains relatively stable between the ages of 3 and 5. The child who has many aggressive outbursts at 3 is also likely to have many at 5 (25). Furthermore, the amount of aggression expressed while in nursery school is a good predictor of how much aggressive behavior the child will display in kindergarten (46).

Among the data of the Fels longitudinal study were ratings of aggressive behavior during several periods of childhood (based on observations in their homes, in nursery and elementary schools, and in day camp) and assessments of adult personality. Aggressive behavior was found to be more stable for boys than for girls during childhood and adolescence (**50**). Rage and tantrum behaviors during preschool were predictive of adolescent and adult irritability and aggression for males, but not for females. Boys who showed extreme degrees of aggressive expression during the early school years became men who were relatively easily angered and were verbally more aggressive when frustrated.

The most reasonable interpretation of this finding is that aggressive behavior is a more acceptable component of traditional masculine behavior, that is sex-typed behavior, than it is of feminine behavior. Direct, physical aggression in girls typically meets with more disapproval and punishment than it does in boys, and the role models young girls choose are less likely to be overtly aggressive. For these reasons, most young girls who are aggressive will gradually learn to inhibit these aggressive manifestations, while aggressive boys have more freedom to express their hostile feelings and thus are likely to continue to do so.

Summary

The research reviewed here is centered on aggressive behaviors, which are observable, rather than on hostile motivation. Various conditions and events lead to increased aggressive expression by children: frustrations; reinforcement for and parental permissiveness of aggressive behavior; and observation of aggressive models. Punishment is often effective in reducing the amount of aggressive expression. However, the effects of parental punishment on children's aggressive behavior are complex, because, as the parent physically punishes his child in order to inhibit his aggressive behavior, he is also serving as an aggressive model.

In most cultures boys receive more reward and less punishment for aggressive behavior and consequently express more aggression than girls do. These sex differences become more marked with increasing age during the preschool period. Proneness to aggressive expression is relatively stable and consistent during the nursery-school years, and, in general, aggressive behavior is more stable for boys than for girls over long periods of time.

DEPENDENCY

The dependency motive is the wish to be nurtured, aided, comforted, and protected by others or to be emotionally close to or accepted by other people. The motive is likely to have a specific target, a class of persons such as parents, teachers, or friends. A 3-year-old who wants love and comfort from his mother may not want physical affection from his older sister, his nursery-school teacher, or his playmates. Preschool children manifest numerous types and forms of dependent behavior with different people: seeking assistance, attention, recognition, approval, reassurance, contact; clinging to adults or other children; resisting separation from adults; soliciting affection and support from a teacher.

As in the case of hostility and aggression, there is no one-to-one relationship between dependency motivation and dependent behavior. A child with a strong motive for approval from his father will manifest dependent behavior toward him **if,** and only if, in his experience, these responses have led to gratification and not to punishment, anxiety, or conflict. But a child with dependency wishes may find that his dependent actions bring rejection by his parents who may think that seeking approval is "babyish" and shame him for behaving in this way. Under these circumstances, the manifestation of dependent behavior is likely to make the child anxious, and he will not be likely to exhibit such behavior.

Another 4-year-old boy with strong dependency motivation may be undergoing rather intensive socialization for independence. This may precipitate a conflict because, on the one hand, he wants to ask his parents for help in getting dressed and, on the other (because of his independency motives), he is anxious about expressing this dependency. As a result of this conflict, he is likely to avoid asking for help except in situations in which he desperately needs it.

Investigations of dependency seldom involve efforts to assess motivation. Typically, investigators observe and measure various forms of dependent behavior and then look for the antecedents of this behavior. In the present section we will examine evidence on the development, antecedents, and correlates of dependent behavior during the preschool period. Unfortunately, we can say little about underlying motives.

Changing Forms of Dependent Behavior

While parents in western cultures are likely to begin socializing their children for autonomy and independence in the second year, the young child is still highly dependent upon them. However, the ways of expressing this dependence and the situations that elicit dependent behavior, as well as the targets of dependency, change as the child becomes more mature. Ordinarily the first target of the child's dependency is his mother, and he frequently is insecure and anxious if she is absent. Youngsters 1 year old or just slightly older explore and play freely when they are with their mothers. If a stranger enters the room when the mother is present, the children are not greatly disturbed, although they tend to stay nearer the mother and explore less than they did before. The security-giving function of the mother is clearly reflected in the findings of one study: "The amount of exploratory and play behavior was considerably greater, and the amount of crying considerably less, when the mother was present than when the child was either alone or with the stranger" (**56,** 102).

A process of "spontaneous progressive detachment" begins after the first year.

Children between 1 and 4 years of age were brought into an unfamiliar environment with their mothers and given the opportunity to explore freely. The distance the children went from their mothers increased progressively with age.

In a careful short-term longitudinal study, children's dependency behaviors were observed in a series of episodes with and without their mothers—in an unfamiliar room, in the presence of a stranger, and in a reunion with their mothers—at the ages of 2, 2½, and 3. Intensity of protest about separation from the mother declined substantially between the ages of 2 and 3; 3-year-olds were much less likely to cry when their mother left the room and their crying was more likely to abate when a stranger tried to soothe them. The proportion of children who asked for their mother after she left and when they were with the stranger also decreased with age. Furthermore, in the unfamiliar room, remaining near the mother and touching her or clinging to her also decreased with age. But even the 3-year-old children retreated toward their mothers when a stranger entered the room. It would appear likely "that the children used their mothers as a security base upon the entrance of the stranger to a similar degree at age 3 as they had done earlier" (55, 28).

Other forms of dependency on the mother—looking at her, smiling at her, showing her a toy, and speaking to her—increased with age, especially when a stranger entered the room. At 2 the children interacted with the stranger primarily during the episodes when their mother was present; they interacted with her very little when their mothers were absent and they were alone with her. By 3, however, "the children did not need the mother's presence to permit them to sustain interaction with a stranger" (55, 34).

Observations in nursery school demonstrate that 2-year-olds are likely to be significantly more dependent upon their teachers than upon peers, while among 4-year-olds dependency on peers is more common (38). Comparisons of the dependent behavior of 2-, 4-, and 5-year-olds also show that the forms of dependent expression change with age. Of the three age groups, the 2-year-olds cling and seek affection most frequently, while the 5-year-olds are most likely to seek both reassurance and positive attention from adults. It may be inferred that attention- and approval-seeking are relatively mature forms of dependency expression, while direct bids for affection by clinging, touching, and crying are immature ways of manifesting dependency (34, 348).

In a short-term longitudinal study (25), middle-class nursery-school children were rated by their teachers on a number of behavior scales. Ratings were made each semester of their two years of nursery-school attendance. The scales dealt with dependent behavior, for example, seeks recognition from children, seeks to be near teacher, seeks help from teacher, seeks attention from teacher. The data revealed marked individual stability in manifestations of dependency during this period. Among 3-year-olds, **instrumental dependency** (that is, seeking out the teacher for assistance in obtaining a goal) was highly correlated with **emotional**

dependency behavior (clinging and seeking affection). However, among the 4-year-olds, the two types of dependent behavior were not significantly related. On the other hand, there was no association between instrumental dependency and **autonomy** (independence) among the 3-year-olds, but among 4-year-olds, these attributes were negatively correlated. Apparently by the age of 4, self-reliance and help-seeking are "alternative habits or 'strategies' used by the child in his goal-directed and problem-solving efforts" (25, 23).

Situational Factors Affecting Dependency

While dependency is a fairly stable and pervasive characteristic during the pre-school period, the expression of dependency behavior is strongly affected by the immediate situation. Anxiety-producing settings are likely to elicit more dependency behavior from preschool children, directed toward either the mother or a stranger, while a relaxed situation elicits relatively little. Children who are highly dependent on their mothers frequently generalize their dependency responses, exhibiting greater dependency on others, including strangers, than children low in dependency on their mothers.

These were the conclusions of a study of 64 nursery-school girls who were first observed in interaction with their mothers in the nursery school and divided into high and low dependency groups (71, 72). Half of each group was then assigned to a high anxiety condition and half to a low anxiety condition; each child was observed twice, once with her mother and once with a stranger. In the low anxiety condition, the observation room contained various toys, pictures of smiling faces hung on the walls, and a phonograph played children's songs. In the high anxiety condition, the observation room was a frightening place: a slow-burning alcohol lamp stood on a stainless steel tray; pictures of sad faces hung on the wall; scary noises were heard, including a loud banging on a metal object, a child crying, and a high-pitched shriek.

Under these anxiety or stress conditions, immature kinds of dependency behavior (clinging, staying close) increased in frequency, whether the child was with her mother or with a stranger. However, anxiety did not affect the frequency of the more mature forms of dependency behavior such as seeking attention, approval, and help (71, 72).

Isolation from social contact or reduction in the normal level of social interaction is also likely to intensify dependency behavior. Preschool children, painting at an easel with an adult nearby and consistently attentive, showed relatively little attention-getting behavior; their peers, engaged in the same activity with an adult nearby but busy and relatively unavailable, made many more attention-getting responses (31). Analogously, nursery-school children make more bids for attention from their mothers when their mothers are busy than when she is attentive to them (77). In one study (33) the dependency needs of two groups of preschool

children were experimentally manipulated. One group was consistently nurtured by a female experimenter who played and talked with each child individually. In the second group, each child was first nurtured, and then the nurturance was suddenly withdrawn; it was assumed that this deprivation would increase the children's need for nurturance. Finally each child was asked to learn a simple task and was verbally praised by the experimenter for a good performance. The group that experienced nuturance-withdrawal—and therefore presumably had a stronger need for adult approval and attention—learned the task more rapidly with adult approval than the other group did. Moreover, highly dependent boys were more strongly influenced than relatively independent boys by this treatment. Apparently, the child's need for attention and nurturance was heightened by the experience of nurturance-withdrawal. Consequently, the experimenter's praise, after withdrawal, was a particularly effective reward and led to harder work and faster learning.

Child-Rearing Practices and Dependency

Theoretically, the amount of dependency on a particular target ordinarily manifested by the child will be a function of the extent to which he has been rewarded and punished for such behavior, the salience of his dependency motives, and the imitation of dependent models. A mother who consistently and frequently rewards and rarely punishes dependent behavior should produce a dependent child, while punishment for dependency should discourage this behavior in the child.

A number of studies have yielded data consistent with these expectations. For instance, children reared in an extremely rejecting institutional environment experienced little, if any, nurturant mothering during the earliest years and were rarely rewarded for affiliative and dependent responses. Hence they manifested very little dependent behavior. Evidence from one intensive longitudinal study indicates that, for boys, high levels of early maternal protection are associated with later childhood and adult dependent behavior. The genesis of strong dependency, then, seems to depend in part upon early experiences of relatively consistent gratification and minimal punishment of dependency needs from some other person. Furthermore, "the regular reward of dependent overtures strengthens the child's tendency to make this response in time of crisis. A protective mother prevents the child from learning how to deal with environmental crises on his own and facilitates the development of a feeling of helplessness in the child" (50, 214). However, there is no evidence that parental warmth during the preschool years affects later dependency behavior.

On the other hand, some other child-rearing practices used during the preschool years have been found to be related to frequency of dependent behavior at home. One is the socialization technique that has been labeled "withdrawal of love"—giving love, affection, and approval when the child behaves as the parent wants him to, but withholding affection when the child behaves in disapproved ways. Another is inconsistent discipline. According to clinical studies of overdependent youngsters, their mothers tend to be inconsistent in handling the child's dependency, thus increasing the child's anxiety and eliciting immature dependent responses such as reassurance-seeking. "The implication is that inconsistent nurturance . . . may lead to extreme emotional dependency" (28, 72–73).

These findings are consistent with those of another study of normal kindergarten children. According to interviews with the mothers of these children, punishing dependent behavior and ultimately giving the child the attention or help he demands is likely to increase the frequency of the dependent behavior.

> The situation in which the mother sometimes loses her temper over the child's dependency and sometimes responds sweetly and nurturantly, or in which she becomes irritated but nevertheless turns her attention to the child and gives him what he wants, is one ideally calculated to produce conflict in the child. On the one hand, he anticipates unpleasant consequences to his behavior, and this anticipation produces anxiety. On the other hand, he simultaneously anticipates reward. When he has an impulse to be dependent, the impulse makes him both anxious and hopeful; the fear of the mother's irritation may make him inhibit his impulse temporarily, but the hope of getting the mother's attention through dependent behavior is still there. If eventually the dependent behavior does show itself, it will be exceptionally intense, doubly irritating to the mother, and impossible to ignore (78, 173–174).

Relation of Dependency to Other Aspects of Socialization

Most mothers gradually begin to encourage independence during the preschool period. By the time the child is 5 years old, his mother expects some self-reliance and independent behavior; he should be able to dress himself, to attend to himself in the bathroom, to solve minor problems without help, to initiate and complete some actvities, and to be able to play alone without constant supervision. If the mother is warm, accepting, and nurturant while she encourages independence, her child will be motivated to be more self-reliant, and excessively dependent behavior will diminish.

Many 5-year-olds manifest both strong dependent and independent, autonomous motivations (14, 15, 16, 38). Apparently many children of this age are in conflict about seeking nurturance from others and dealing with the world independently. It is important to recognize that dependent behavior alone may not be an accurate index of the intensity of the child's basic needs for help and support. Some children have learned that it is important to be independent, and they try to inhibit overt help-seeking behavior in many situations.

Like dependency, autonomy or independence has been found to be a general, highly salient motive that has marked stability during the preschool years. Analysis of teachers' ratings of behaviors such as "overcomes obstacles by himself," and "gets intrinsic satisfaction from his work," showed that there is considerable behavioral continuity in these characteristics through the nursery-school years, that is, children tended to maintain their relative standing in these behaviors through-out the four semesters of nursery-school attendance.

During early childhood, manifestations of dependency (and, presumably, dependent motivation) are more frequent and more intense among girls than among boys (23, 25). Moreover, in contrast to aggression, dependent behavior is more stable for girls than for boys from the age of 3 to the age of 14 (49, 50). A dependent 5-year-old girl is apt to become a dependent adolescent and young adult, but it is more difficult to predict adolescent dependency for boys from their preschool behavior. Perhaps this is because girls have less intense anxiety over expressing dependency, traditionally an accepted component of feminine behavior, while conflict over violating sex-role standards may lead to inhibition of this dependent behavior among boys. This trend may change as standards and definitions of appropriate sex-role behavior are modified.

Not surprisingly, highly dependent children become more upset and aggressive when their direct attempts to get help from others are frustrated. On the other hand, when subjected to relatively mild frustration, highly dependent preschool children (as measured by affection-seeking and clinging to the teacher) have been found to be less aggressive than nondependent children (66). A highly dependent child may be less likely to react with aggression because he is anxious about possible rejection or loss of love and nurturance if he behaves in prohibited, aggressive ways.

Similarly, children who are dependent upon peers, seeking them out for help and support, are more compliant when peers request them to do something, and they tend to be nurturant toward other children, giving sympathy and helping others (36). In general, dependence on adults is negatively correlated with the amount of interaction with peers in nursery school, and children who are highly dependent on adults are **not** popular with other children (58).

Summary

Dependency behavior, which must be clearly differentiated from dependency motivation, may be expressed in many different ways. The situations that elicit the expression of dependency, as well as its targets, change with age. Two-year-olds express dependency by direct bids for affection—clinging, touching, and crying—while seeking attention and approval are characteristic dependency expressions of older preschoolers. Anxiety-producing settings, isolation from social contacts, and reduction in normal level of social interaction increase dependency behavior.

Parents who consistently and frequently reinforce dependent behavior and rarely punish such behavior are likely to promote dependency in their children. Disciplining a child by punishing his dependent behavior and then ultimately giving him the attention or help he wants is likely to elevate the level of the child's dependency expression. Girls manifest dependency more frequently and intensely than boys, and girls' dependent behavior is more stable than boys' from the age of 3 through adolescence.

FEAR AND ANXIETY

Everyone sometimes experiences fear and anxiety in one form or another and in varying degrees. The distinction between these emotions is not clear-cut. Both involve a pattern of physiological and psychological reactions, including unpleasant and stressful feelings and emotions. While anxiety and fear are often classified as affects or emotions, they play an extremely important role in human motivation. Like the motives hostility and dependency, fear and anxiety are inferred states, but they are noxious and unpleasant states evoking avoidant behaviors and defenses. Certain conditions or events induce fear and anxiety and subsequently the individual attempts to attain goals—to do something—that will reduce the uneasiness and discomfort accompanying fear and anxiety.

Fear is generally considered the more specific emotion, a response to particular, specifiable objects and stimuli such as fast-moving vehicles or wild animals. Anxiety, a more diffuse, unfocused, and less clearly perceived emotional state, differs from fear primarily in its "free-floating" quality—its lack of objective or realistic foci. However, it is difficult to maintain a rigorous distinction or differentiation between fear and anxiety, particularly in the case of young children, because young children do not differentiate between inner and outer, real and imagined dangers (26).

From a clinician's perspective,

> ... anxiety is not a pathological condition in itself but a necessary and normal physiological and mental preparation for danger. ... Anxiety is necessary for the survival of the individual under certain circumstances. Failure to apprehend danger and to prepare for it may have disastrous results. ... (30, 11).

As we indicated earlier, a child who encounters a frustration he cannot cope with and whose source he does not understand (a door unexpectedly locked) may become anxious and apprehensive rather than angry and hostile. Analogously, a child who frequently manifests dependency behavior toward his mother may become anxious if she refuses to give him help when he feels he needs it; at the same time he is anxious about possible loss of love and nurturance if he becomes aggressive. During the preschool years the child is exposed to many situations and experiences that are potential sources of anxiety. Being closely attached to their parents, many children become anxious about possible loss of parental love because of the birth or adoption of a new baby or because of real or imagined rejection. Other sources of fear and anxiety may be anticipation of punishment, environmental events that seem discrepant with the child's beliefs (for example, finding that the kind father may spank on occasion), and unpredictability of events.

Preschool Children's Fears

Every child develops a variety of fears or sources of anxiety. Some of these serve a "self-preservation" function, that is, fears attached to certain kinds of stimuli (for example, highways, fierce animals, dangerous tools, moving automobiles) motivate effective avoidance responses. Moreover, fears may serve as a basis for learning new and adaptive responses. For example, fear of speeding cars can motivate the child to learn the rules of crossing streets—the appropriate place and the signals to be observed. Fear of wild animals or natural events, such as thunderstorms, may stimulate the child's interest in learning more about nature and about natural science.

But extensive, overly intense, and frequent fear reactions—such as crying, retreating, withdrawing, cringing, trembling, protesting, appealing for help, cowering, clinging to parents—are incompatible with constructive behavior. If the child is to attain adequate emotional adjustment, many of these responses must be replaced by mature, purposeful reactions to stimuli that previously elicited fear.

Fears of actual objects or unusual stimuli such as unexpected movements, strange objects, settings, or people, and the frequency and intensity of the overt signs of fear decline with age during the preschool years. But fears of anticipated, imaginary, or supernatural dangers, such as the possibility of accidents, darkness, dreams, ghosts, increase. Apparently the child's cognitive development—his increased understanding of the world and greater use of representations and symbols—influences his emotional reactions.

Childhood fears are highly unpredictable, and at all age levels there are marked individual differences in susceptibility to fear (45). The same stimulus may be extremely frightening to one child but leave another completely unperturbed. Moreover, a child may be much disturbed by a particular stimulus in one situation but pay no attention to it in another. A 3-year-old may be frightened and anxious if he enters a room full of children he does not know, alone; if he is with his mother, he may be completely relaxed in the situation.

According to parents' reports, half of the preschool child's fears drop out spontaneously about a year or two after they are first manifested and only a third persist in their original form. Many fears become modified in form and they seem to spread by a process of stimulus generalization. A child who was frightened by a balloon used in anesthetizing him for an operation may become fearful of all balloons and objects resembling them. Another, frightened by a mouse running through his bedroom, may fear all scratching sounds at night.

There is a marked tendency for a child to adopt his parents' fears—particularly fears of dogs, insects, and storms (32)—either by identification with the parent or by observational learning. For example, if the mother is afraid of dogs, she cannot do anything to make dogs less fear-provoking for her child. Consequently, he continues to fear the animals and avoids them or, if he sees a dog, he withdraws. This may be tension reducing (reinforcing), for by withdrawing he protects himself from encountering the object of his fears. Consequently, the child becomes more likely to repeat avoidance and withdrawal responses in similar situations, thus preventing the learning of new, more mature reactions to dogs. For these reasons, fears which the child shares with a parent are particularly resistant to treatment and extinction.

Techniques of Eliminating Fears

Children cannot be expected to "outgrow" all their fears automatically; they must learn new responses to fear-eliciting stimuli. The principles of learning theory, particularly the concept of extinction, may be applied with success in reducing children's fears. For example, a stimulus the child fears, such as a snake, may be presented at the same time the child receives something pleasant, such as candy. After several such pairings, the child may begin to have more positive reactions to the object he had previously feared (47). If fear responses fail to occur after many presentations of the stimulus, these stimulus-response connections will be weakened and the response may disappear, that is, be extinguished, eventually.

In one experimental attempt to overcome fears (43), youngsters who were afraid of the dark were accompanied into a dark room by a friendly adult or were encouraged to become active explorers in dark places where they found valuable prizes. In these situations the connections between the feared stimulus (the dark) and the anxiety or fear responses, such as withdrawal, are weakened. In addition, as the child grows older and better able to use language, or verbal mediators, these conditioning techniques may be supplemented with verbal explanations.

The most effective techniques for reducing fears involve the combination of explanation and gradual encouragement of the child's confrontation with the feared situation. Explanation alone is not likely to be successful with young children because they may not yet associate words with the fear-provoking stimuli. On the other hand, when confrontation is accompanied by explanation, the fear-eliciting stimuli become associated with the parent's calming presence, encouragement, and gentle words of explanation. Under these conditions, the child is rewarded for inhibiting fear responses, and new, more mature responses to the stimuli may become dominant over fear responses learned earlier (32).

Peers may also serve as effective models of calm approach responses to feared stimuli. Repeated exposure to a model behaving in this way may be very effective in reducing the observer's fears and avoidance behavior. In one experimental demonstration the subjects were 2- and 3-year-olds, who were fearful of dogs (4). The strength of their original fears was measured by means of a pretest in which the children were required to engage in increasingly intimate interactions with a dog (simply looking at a dog confined in a playpen, patting the dog, walking him on a leash, and, finally, climbing into a playpen and remaining there alone with him).

Each fearful child was then assigned to one of four treatment groups. Group 1, the **model–positive context** group, attended a series of eight enjoyable parties. During each party, a 4-year-old model was ushered into the room and exhibited progressively longer, closer, and more intense interactions with a dog. Group 2, the **model–neutral context** group, observed the same peer model performing the same sequence of approach responses with the dog, but without parties. The other two groups were controls. Group 3, the **exposure–positive context** group, attended parties during which a dog was brought into the room, but did not observe any modeling. Group 4, the **positive context** group, participated in the parties but were not exposed to either the dog or the model.

On the day after completion of the treatment series and also a month later, the children were again given the graded sequence of interaction tasks with two dogs, the one used in the original test and, to test the generalization effects, an unfamiliar one.

Fig. 9.1 shows the performance of the four groups on the pretest, the post-test (given one day after training was completed), and the follow-up (one month later). Subjects in both modeling conditions displayed significantly greater and more stable, lasting reduction in avoidance behavior than the children in the control conditions. In addition, significantly more of the children exposed to models were willing to get into the playpen with the dog even with no one else in the room. The increment in approach responses (or the extinction of avoidance behavior) was generalized from a familiar to an unfamiliar dog. Clearly, then, exposure to peer models coping with feared stimuli produces extensive, enduring fear-reduction outcomes, although the nature of the context of modeling does not have any significant effect (4).

Antecedents of Anxiety

Like fear, anxiety impels the individual to action of some sort. Minimal anxiety may, and often does, serve constructive purposes, acting as a spur to creativity, problem-solution, and inventive accomplishments. However, strong anxiety may be emotionally crippling, evoking a deep sense of helplessness and inadequacy, rendering the person ineffectual and desperate.

According to clinical evidence, intense or excessive anxiety may have its roots in harsh, punitive, or restrictive socialization. This includes parental efforts to impose standards of behavior that are too high; negative evaluations of the child's behavior and accomplishments; and inconsistent treatment of the child, together with frequent changes in mood and in reactions to the child (51, 74). If the child learns to anticipate punishment or rejection from the parents whenever his behavior is unacceptable to them, he begins to distrust his own impulses and he may become anxious and insecure about his parents as sources of love and security. If he is not clear about which actions are acceptable and unacceptable to his par-

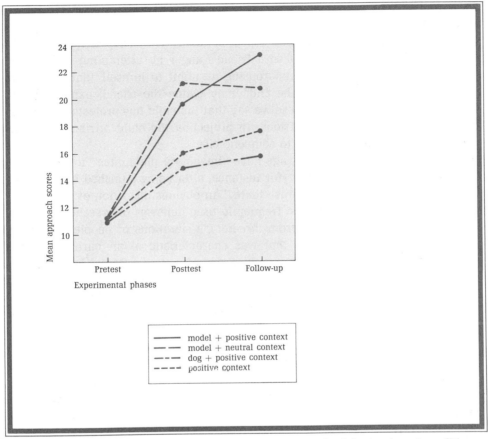

Figure 9.1 Mean approach scores achieved by children in each of the treatment conditions on the three different periods of assessment. (From A. Bandura, J. E. Grusec, & F. L. Menlove. Vicarious extinction of avoidance behavior. **Journal of Personality and Social Psychology,** 1967, **5.** Copyright 1967 by the American Psychological Association. By permission.)

ents, his "safest course of action (or inaction) may be to cling to the parent in submissive passivity and to inhibit all impulses. The long-term effects of socialization anxiety may be evident in the persistence of such symptoms as nightmares or bedwetting" (**28,** 109–110).

Defense Mechanisms

Because anxiety is so unpleasant, the child develops techniques of coping with it or defending against it. These are **coping responses** and **defense mechanisms** that help the child avoid or reduce the painful feelings of anxiety. Typically we are unaware of the presence of the defense mechanism that helps us to avoid anxiety about problems we cannot deal with adaptively and thus enables us to live reasonably comfortably.

When a defense is used, some aspect of reality is usually distorted. For example, a child may have provoked a friend's anger by attempting to dominate him. Because it would be anxiety-arousing to admit to himself that he was responsible for what happened, the child may blame the friend, explaining that "Johnny is a bad boy." In this case we say that the child has projected the blame for the social friction onto his friend. In **projection** the child attributes his own undesirable thoughts or actions to someone else.

Many children of preschool age have "imaginary playmates" to whom they turn for solace in times of crisis (for instance, after being punished by a parent). For some children, the playmate is "there," an obvious distortion of reality.

Withdrawal, one of the most frequently used defenses of preschool children, involves avoidance of or flight from threatening situations or people. **Regression** is the adoption of a response that was characteristic of an earlier phase of development (for example, thumb-sucking or bedwetting). **Denial** is seen in the child's insistence that an anxiety-arousing event or situation, such as the death of a beloved pet, is not true, and he believes his denial is accurate. When **repression** is used, the child refuses to remember the anxiety-producing event. (For further discussion of defense mechanisms, see pp. 453–455).

While everyone uses defense mechanisms, strong dependence on these mechanisms and their pervasiveness in the individual's behavior may be associated with frequent and gross distortions of reality and failure to cope adaptively with psychological problems and with the real world. Used in these ways, the defense mechanisms may have adverse effects on mental health and emotional adjustment.

> When the defensive processes available to a particular individual are varied and flexible, the chances are high that they will be adaptive in most situations. But when an individual's defensive structure is rigid and limited, it follows that his defensive reactions will usually not be appropriate to a particular situation and thus will be maladaptive in the sense that they will interfere with adaptive functioning. Such defensive processes are usually labeled symptoms, although we are learning that even where the defenses are not clearly pathological, they can still interfere with performance if they are inflexible and inappropriate to the particular task (**76,** 31–32).

Highly defensive children—those who use defense mechanisms frequently and inflexibly—typically do not have adequate communication with their parents about either emotional or cognitive matters. They

> do not openly indicate their pleasure or displeasure to their mothers; they do not ask questions about sex nor receive information about it; there is a reluctance by the mothers to discuss death; the mothers don't openly show their own feelings toward the boys. The expression of feelings and curiosity about emotionally tinged topics appears

to be discouraged by the parents, and the motivation to communicate honestly and fully appears to be interrupted (**39,** 66).

MASTERY MOTIVATION

The motives we have discussed so far—sex, aggression, dependency, and anxiety—must be modified and, to some extent, controlled for the sake of the individual's emotional and social adjustment and for the sake of the survival of the culture. Psychologists interested in personality are also seriously concerned with man's motivation to deal effectively with his environment, **effectance motivation,** as it has been labeled by Robert W. White (**80**). The development of competence as an attribute of personality is closely linked to basic and pervasive motives such as curiosity, mastery, and achievement, that is, the child's desire to master problems and increase his skills and abilities (e.g., gross motor tasks, reading, writing, painting).

While mastery may be a basic motive in itself, it must be recognized that mastery behavior may also gratify other motives. Getting good grades in school, one important kind of achievement in our culture, may bring the child recognition from peers, thus helping to gratify his wishes for social status or perhaps for power. Achievement in athletics may bring the boy the love and affection he desires from his parents. Mastery behavior may even, in some cases, help satisfy aggressive motives. A boy who is hostile to his older sister may find that he can hurt her feelings and injure her pride by earning better school grades than she does.

In investigations of mastery behavior, psychologists have arbitrarily delimited the criteria of mastery, usually called achievement, to the areas of intellectual attainment and physical skills. It is, of course, possible to achieve in other areas—in social skills, interpersonal relations, altruism, charity, religious, or political activities—but success and achievement in these areas have not yet been the foci of empirical study.

Correlates of High Achievement Behavior

Preschool children who are highly motivated to achieve in intellectual tasks are also likely to be relatively independent and self-reliant. For example, among the preschool subjects in one study, those who spent most of their time and effort in "intellectual" achievement activities—painting, making clay models, reading books—generally exhibited less dependent behavior toward adults and less frequently sought help and emotional support than peers who were not very much interested in these intellectual activities (**22**). Of course, even children who are highly motivated for achievement sometimes act in dependent ways, but the dependent behavior they exhibit takes the form of attention getting or help seeking, that is, behavior intended to obtain assistance in solving a problem. Children who seem to be motivated for intellectual achievement show considerable adult-role behavior in their play and are likely to be accepted as leaders by other children.

Mothers of the "high achievement" children reward and encourage attempts at achievement from the child's infancy onward and tend to ignore the child's unrealistic requests for excessive help. "Moreover, the mothers who usually spontaneously praised and rewarded their children's achievement efforts, even when the children did not seek approval, had children who displayed especially strong and frequent achievement efforts outside the home" (22, 429).

It is interesting that no sex differences in motivation for intellectual achievement have been noted during the preschool years (23). If older boys in our culture are generally more achievement oriented than girls, the difference may arise because boys are subjected to greater pressure for intellectual achievement during the later school years. Or perhaps girls' intellectual achievement efforts are more frequently disapproved and punished during adolescence and adulthood.

The early development of high achievement motivation during preschool has prolonged and enduring effects. Achievement motivation may be assessed by projective tests in which subjects make up short stories in response to a series of pictures, for example, a picture of a boy looking at a violin, a young man and an older one having a discussion. Those who tell many stories in which the hero is portrayed as accomplishing or trying to accomplish goals of great value (for example, preparing for a major concert or inventing a new type of violin) are considered to have high achievement motivation.

Mothers of boys between 8 and 10 years old with high achievement motivation, as revealed in these projective tests, expect self-reliant and independent behavior at earlier ages, beginning at nursery-school age. From the earliest years, these mothers gave frequent and substantial rewards for independent accomplishments (82, 478). Mothers who encourage their children's early mastery of such basic skills as walking and talking have children with higher levels of school achievement than children whose mothers did not encourage early mastery. Reinforcement for early accomplishment seems to facilitate the development of a general motive for achievement and, more specifically, the desire to learn new intellectual skills and to perform well in school. Clearly, "early training in independence and mastery contributes to the development of strong achievement motivation" (82, 478).

Girls whose intellectual achievements had been rewarded during their first 3 years gained substantially in IQ between the ages of 6 and 10, and personality tests showed that they were highly concerned with mastery and competition. For example, a girl with an achievement-rewarding mother responded to a picture of a boy with a violin by telling a story in which the boy is "practicing the violin and wants to be good so he can play in Carnegie Hall." In contrast, a girl with a nonachievement-rewarding mother said, "The boy doesn't want to practice and wants to go out and play" (59).

Achievement motivation, especially in the intellectual area, is one of the most stable aspects of a child's personality. Girls and boys who show a strong desire to perfect and master intellectual skills during the preschool years tend to retain this motivation during adolescence and early adulthood (59). The child who enters school with high achievement motivation is likely to develop into the adolescent and adult who is concerned with intellectual competence.

Most lower-class children grow up in homes in which they receive less encouragement or reward for intellectual achievements than children in middle-class homes. Understandably, their level of achievement motivation in school is low and, since this motivation is critical for success in school, they are likely to perform poorly there.

IDENTIFICATION

We have frequently used the concepts of reinforcement, punishment, and imitation in explaining the development and modification of aggression, dependency, anxiety, and achievement motivation. But not all behavior and personality characteristics can be explained in these terms. In fact, many highly significant complex patterns of personality characteristics, reactions, personal idiosyncracies, motives, attitudes, and moral standards appear to be acquired by the child spontaneously, without direct training or reward—without anyone's "teaching" and without the child's intending to learn. In short, some acquired characteristics do not seem to yield readily to analysis in terms of reward, punishment, or imitation. A more subtle process, **identification,** is involved.

Identification, a concept derived from psychoanalysis and introduced by Freud, refers to the process that leads the child to think, feel, and behave as though the characteristics of another person (called the **model** or **identificand**)— usually a parent in the case of a young child—belong to him. Identification is not ordinarily a consciously initiated process, like learning to ride a bicycle or to read.

Many events illustrate the complex concept of identification. A 6-year-old boy feels proud as he watches his father defeat a rival in tennis. A young girl feels grown-up when she puts on her mother's apron and attempts to bake a pie. A 10-year-old girl feels ashamed when the police arrest her father or put her mother in a mental institution. In each of these examples, the child acts as if he or she possessed some of the characteristics, feelings, or emotions of the parent with whom he is identified.

Identification with a parent may be a very important source of security for a young child. By means of this identification, the child in effect incorporates in himself the parent's strength and adequacy, that is, the child feels himself to be more adequate and self-controlled. On the other hand, a child identified with an inadequate model (e.g., a psychotic father) feels less secure and more anxious because, in his perception, he believes he possesses the model's undesirable attributes.

Identification, then, is a hypothesized process which leads the child to adopt some of the model's complex integrated patterns of behavior, personal attributes and characteristics, and motives. Moreover, responses acquired by identification seem to be emitted spontaneously, without any specific training or direct rewards for imitation, and they are generally relatively stable and enduring rather than transient.

In concerning himself with identification, Freud was not asking why and how a child might learn an isolated piece of behavior from his parent. He was interested in what he felt to be a more sweeping and powerful phenomenon—the tendency of the child to take on not merely discrete elements of the parental model but a total pattern. Moreover, as Freud saw it, this acquisition was accomplished with an emotional intensity which reflected the operation of motivational forces of considerable power (18, 27).

The Development of Identification

Most behavioral scientists regard identification as a basic process in the socialization of the child. Two conditions are basic to the development and strengthening of identification with a model. Identification begins with the child's perception that he and the model are similar in some ways, that they share some physical or psychological attributes. Once the identification is formed, it will either be strengthened or weakened depending on how attractive and desirable the model is. If the model is attractive, the child is motivated to become increasingly identified with him.

Most children feel that their parents have numerous desirable characteristics, skills, and privileges. They are strong and powerful, and they have abilities and access to pleasures the child envies. In addition, they control important and desirable goal states such as (1) power over the child and other people, (2) mastery of the environment, and (3) love. The child perceives the vast discrepancies between the adults' capabilities and privileges and his own lack of power and mastery. Furthermore, he seems to assume that if he were similar to his parent, he would also possess the parent's desirable psychological characteristics and command of resources: power, affection from others, skills and competencies; he would vicariously enjoy the emotions and pleasures enjoyed by the model. Hence he attempts to acquire more of the parent's attributes, which in turn increases his identification with the parent.

The process of identification is facilitated if the model is an attractive, rewarding person. A nurturant parent is more likely to be taken as a model than a rejecting one. Therefore, the child's imitations of his other actions may, according to some psychologists, also be a source of pleasure and gratification. For example, a 3-year-old girl may cuddle her doll in the same way her mother cuddled the girl. As the child imitates the mother's behavior and characteristics, she tends to experience the feelings and emotions—the warmth, happiness, and pride—that the mother experiences in caring for her. As she acts "as though she were the mother," she feels that she actually possesses the power, skills, and pleasures of the mother. If the mother is highly rejecting, she will not be perceived as a desirable model and the child will not be motivated to practice her actions. Warm and accepting parents are viewed as attractive people and consequently the child desires to increase his similarity to them and to act as much like them as he can.

There are three major ways in which the child may come to feel similar to the model: through perception of actual similarities in appearance (such as hair and eye coloring) and psychological characteristics; through adoption of the model's attributes, behavior, and gestures; and through communications from others who tell the child he is similar to the model. On the basis of these experiences, identification is established and developed; each time the child perceives some similarity with the model, his identification is strengthened.

Furthermore, the child imitates parental behaviors in order to increase the similarity between himself and his parents and thus to possess vicariously the parents' traits, if the parents are regarded as attractive. Many events lead the child to perceive similarities with the model: a little girl notices that she and her mother wear the same kind of dress or cut their hair similarly; sharing the same family name makes her feel more similar to her mother than to mothers with different family names. The child may be told by its grandmother or neighbor, "Mary, you're just like your mother" or "Bob, you have a memory just like your father." These experiences strengthen identification.

When both parents are perceived as nurturant, powerful, and competent, the child will identify to some extent with both of them. Typically, however, the child will perceive greater similarity to the parent of the same sex (in dress, hair, genital anatomy) and will therefore identify with that parent more strongly. As the child's identification becomes stronger, he begins to behave as though he really possesses some of the model's characteristics. The behaviors that he imitated earlier become automatic and are more firmly entrenched aspects of his character and personality.

Finally, it should be emphasized that identification is not an all-or-none phenomenon. Each child identifies, to some degree, with both parents and, as his social contacts become wider, with adults and peers outside the family. As we noted earlier, it is impossible to determine what aspects of personality or what proportions of the individual's vast behavior repertoire are the consequents of identification and what can be attributed to reinforcement learning. A little girl may develop strong dependency needs as a consequence of either reward for dependent behavior, identification with her highly dependent mother, or both. The school-age boy who manifests a high level of motivation for achievement may have been rewarded frequently during early childhood for independent, self-reliant behavior. At the same time, the manner in which he manifests high achievement needs—for example, in striving for academic or social success—may be, at least in part, a product of his identification with his highly educated father. In any case, it is reasonable to infer that identification is a central process in the acquisition of a wide range of behavior patterns and characteristics.

Consequents of Parental Identification

It is believed that there are two major consequents or derivatives of identification that begin to develop rapidly during the preschool period. The first is **sex-typing,** which refers to the adoption of behavior, values, attitudes, and interests generally considered appropriate to the masculine or feminine role in the child's culture. The second is the formation of the **superego** or **conscience,** the internalization of the culture's standards of moral conduct, values, beliefs, and self-control. Both of these are broad, pervasive, multifaceted aspects of the individual's psychological organization.

SEX-TYPING

During the preschool years, sex-typing generally figures prominently in the socialization of the child and most parents pay attention to the sex appropriateness of their children's behavior. Before further analysis of the components and process of sex-typing, it is necessary to make a brief digression. The topics of masculine and feminine behavior and roles and the related topics of male chauvinism, discrimination against women in jobs and salaries, and women's liberation have loomed large in group discussions and in the mass media in recent years. There is no firm evidence that males and females are destined by nature for the arbitrary roles and characteristics frequently assigned to the two sexes in this or any other culture. The behaviors we label masculine and feminine in our culture are **not** inevitable consequences of the biological differences between males and females.

Masculine and feminine behaviors are **culturally** prescribed; youngsters are socialized into the work, activities, and personality characteristics defined as differentially appropriate for males and females in their own culture. These definitions vary from culture to culture. In some cultures, weaving and cooking are women's activities; in others, they are men's. Aggression is a masculine characteristic and passivity a feminine one in most cultures, but in at least a few, women are typically aggressive and men passive.

It is true that in most (but not all) cultures, girls are socialized in ways that encourage the development of nurturance, obedience, and responsibility, while boys are pressured toward self-reliance and independence (8). It is also true that most societies are organized around males rather than females. Men are usually given

authority in legal and moral matters and greater value and prestige are characteristically accorded to the masculine role (24). In most primitive societies and in earlier times in our own culture, physical strength, endurance, motor skills, and speed of movement were major determinants of the assignment of important roles in the community. Because of their superior strength and motor skills, men were given the tasks of hunting, heavy agriculture, domestication of large animals, and defending the group, and in these kinds of activities there was a premium on the development of aggressiveness, assertiveness, and independence. Women, on the other hand, had to be trained for nurturant roles because they were almost entirely in charge of child-rearing, while the men were occupied with caring for animals, agriculture, or defense activities.

In a technologically developed society such as ours, physical strength, speed, and large-muscle motor skills are no longer salient for earning a living or for the preservation of life and the culture. Men and women seem equally capable of performing most activities, and, according to one anthropologist, "we should rear children with only slight regard for sex differences, especially in higher social strata where on-the-job brawn is seldom called for" (44, 311). Clearly, today, "psychological masculinity and femininity . . . are far more complex and overlapping and are less distinguishable from one another than has been the case in earlier generations" (69, 77). As society changes, the notions of appropriate masculine and feminine behavior and characteristics are also likely to change and socialization practices will change accordingly.

> If we want more women to enter science, not only as teachers of science but as scientists, some quite basic changes must take place in the way girls are reared. If girls are to develop the analytic and mathematical abilities science requires, parents and teachers must encourage them in independence and self-reliance instead of pleasing feminine submission; stimulate and reward girls' efforts to satisfy their curiosity about the world as they do those of boys; encourage in girls not unthinking conformity but alert intelligence that asks why and rejects the easy answers (73, 483).

Nevertheless, most parents have rather firm notions about appropriate masculine and feminine behavior; they share the common stereotypes of their culture and transmit these concepts to their children. Many parents encourage their young son to "fight back" if attacked by a peer, but are more likely to punish this same behavior in a daughter (78). If a preschool girl cries after losing a game, her reaction is likely to be accepted as appropriate for girls, but a boy who shows tears is likely to be reminded that "Boys don't cry."

In general, in American society

> . . . females are supposed to inhibit aggression and open display of sexual urges, to be passive with men, to be nurturant to others, to cultivate attractiveness, and to maintain an affective, socially poised, and friendly posture with others. Males are urged to be aggressive in face of attack, independent in problem situations, sexually aggressive,

in control of regressive urges, and suppressive of strong emotions, especially anxiety (48, 143).

By age 5, children are keenly aware of sex-appropriate interests and behavior. Most 3-, 4-, and 5-year-olds prefer toys, objects, and activities (e.g., guns, dolls, cowboys, Indians, kitchen utensils) that are considered appropriate for their own sex (20).

Some idea of the strong parental pressures that foster sex-typing may be found in recent studies in which American mothers and fathers of 3-year-old boys and girls described their child-rearing attitudes and behaviors. Socialization practices used with boys reflect an emphasis on the virtues of the Protestant ethic: encouragement of conformity to conventional standards of achievement and competition, insistence on control of feelings and expressions of emotions. Significantly more parents of boys thought it was important to encourage their child to do his best, to play competitive games, to learn not to cry, to control his feelings. For little girls, on the other hand, emphasis is placed on developing and maintaining the close interpersonal relationships: they are encouraged to talk about their troubles, reflect upon life, and are given comfort and reassurance. Thus, parents of girls felt that it was important to "encourage the child to wonder and think about life," to give her "time to daydream and loaf" (17).

The same investigator asked men and women university students in six western countries—United States, England, Norway, Sweden, Denmark, and Finland—to describe their ideal self, "the kind of person I would most like to be." The cross-cultural stability in masculine and feminine ideals was impressive, that is, the stereotypes appear to be general throughout these countries. The males considered the "ideal self" to be shrewd, practical, assertive, dominating, competitive, critical, rational, reasonable, ambitious, while the females' ideal selves were loving, affectionate, sympathetic, generous, sensitive, helpful, and considerate. Interestingly, American males place greater emphasis than males from other countries on adventurousness, self-confidence, assertiveness, ambition, and competitiveness; American parents place significantly greater emphasis on early and clear sex-typing, including encouragement of boys' competitiveness and expression of aggression. The finding of important differences between American and European sex stereotypes obviously implies that "there **can** be differences, differences that begin to abandon narrow definitions of sex role, definitions held over from harsher and less civilized times" (17).

The child's parents provide considerable reward for displaying the traits considered appropriate for his sex and tend to punish manifestations of traits perceived as appropriate for the opposite sex. Boys are pressured to model themselves after their fathers, girls after their mothers. Older siblings and peers also influence the young child's sex-role training. For example, boys with older sisters are more likely to manifest feminine behavior and characteristics than boys who do not have older sisters, and girls with older brothers will display more masculine characteristics than girls who do not have older brothers. Apparently older siblings can serve as models, just as parents do (69).

The basic components of sex-typing are undoubtedly acquired at home, primarily through identification with and imitation of the parent of the same sex. As we shall see (p. 434), boys who are separated from their fathers for prolonged periods (as a result of the father's military service or because their fathers are sailors and spend long periods of time at sea) are less firmly established in their sex-role behavior and characteristics than boys whose fathers are continually available (53). However,

> In the ideal family constellation, a little boy finds it very natural and highly rewarding to model himself in his father's image. The father is gratified to see this recreation of his own qualities, attitudes, and masculinity; and the mother, loving the father, finds such a course of development acceptable in her son. Tentative explorations, conscious and unconscious, in the direction of being "like mother" quickly convince the boy that this is not his proper or approved destiny; and he speedily reverts to his identification with father. In the well-ordered psychologically healthy household, much the same picture, in reverse, holds for the little girl (60, 596).

It should be noted that psychoanalytic theory does not imply that strong identification with the father will necessarily lead to culturally stereotyped masculine behavior, while identification with the mother will lead to traditional feminine behavor. These consequences follow only if the father and mother themselves personify characteristics congruent with the cultural stereotypes. The daughter of an assertive and achievement-oriented woman will be likely to manifest these characteristics if she identifies with her mother. The son of a socially sensitive man is apt to be socially sensitive if he identifies with his father, even if sensitivity is viewed as "feminine" in his culture. What we are really concerned with in sex-role identity is not sex-role stereotyping, but the child's attitude toward himself, **"the degree to which an individual regards himself as masculine or feminine"** (48, 144).

Theoretically, the degree to which the child adopts a parent's behavior is a function of that parent's nurturance and affection, competence, and power. If the parent did not possess these characteristics, the child would not want to be like him and would not maintain a positive identification with him. The ideal situation for the adoption of adaptive, satisfying sexual identity would be one in which (1) the same-sex parent is seen as nurturant and possessing desirable characteristics and (2) both parents consistently reward evidence of appropriate identification with the same-sex parent.

A number of studies have yielded data supporting these hypotheses. In one, groups of generally nurturant and nonnurturant mothers (categorized on the basis of their responses to an interview on child-rearing practices) served as models, teaching their daughters to solve maze problems (64). During the teaching session, the mother made some novel, irrelevant responses in accordance with directions from the experimenter. For example, she drew her lines very slowly, hesitated at each choice point, made some comment before each trial (e.g., "Here we go"), and made unnecessary marks in her tracing (e.g., loops or curves in her lines). As would be predicted from theory, the daughters of the nurturant group imitated many of their mother's irrelevant responses, but the nonnurtured girls copied relatively few (64).

Studies of the relationship between parental nurturance and sex-typing also show that, as the hypothesis would predict, boys identify with their fathers if the latter are perceived as strong, powerful, and nurturant (62, 63, 65). A group of 5-year-old boys were given a projective test of sex-role preferences. The 10 most "masculine" and the 10 least "masculine" boys were selected for further study on the assumption that the former had strong masculine identifications, based on identification with the father, while the latter were only weakly identified with that parent. These 20 boys participated in doll-play sessions in which they supplied endings to some incomplete stories designed to assess the child's perception of the father as nurturant, warm, punitive, and powerful. The responses of the highly masculine boys, that is, those highly identified with their fathers, indicated that, compared with boys who are low in masculinity, they perceived their fathers as more nurturant and more rewarding.

Analogously, femininity in preschool girls seems to be related to warm, nurturant mother-daughter interactions. In comparison with the other girls, highly feminine sex-typed girls (when judged by scores in a test of sex-role preference) portrayed their mothers in doll-play as significantly warmer, more nurturant, affectionate, and gratifying. According to mothers' reports, the highly feminine girls have more intense and warmer interactions with their mothers than the less feminine girls do.

Kohlberg has added an important dimension to the process of sex-typing, namely, "the child's cognitive organization of his social world along sex role dimensions" (52, 82). The most significant factor in sex-typing, according to Kohlberg, is the child's cognition—his selection and organization of perceptions, knowledge, and understanding of the sex-role concept. The process is said to be initiated by labeling the child as a boy or girl, which occurs very early in life. The child's basic gender self-concept, his categorization of himself as a boy or girl, becomes the major organizer and determinant of his activities, values, attitudes, motives, and ways of thinking. A boy in effect says, "I am a boy, therefore, I want to do boy things," and therefore welcomes the opportunity to emulate males and to do masculine things (and to gain approval for doing them) (52). Sex-typing is thus not viewed as a product of identification; quite the contrary, identification is seen as a consequence of sex-typing. The child's self-concepts about his sex role become stabilized at about 5 or 6 years, according to Kohlberg, and, once established, these basic sex-role concepts generate other sex-typed values and attitudes. Although labeling the child "boy" or "girl" undoubtedly plays a role in sex-typing, Kohlberg's theory cannot explain why some boys are highly masculine and some feminine. All boys learn that they are "boys"; hence other factors, including identification, are necessary to explain individual differences in sex-role identity.

CONSCIENCE DEVELOPMENT AND PROSOCIAL BEHAVIOR

The discussion of sex-role standards leads us naturally to the general issue of values and standards of behavior. The process by which the child acquires standards and beliefs about moral behavior is referred to as superego or conscience development.

During the preschool years the child begins to show evidence of this development, that is, of having a set of standards of acceptable behavior, acting in accordance with these standards and feeling guilty if he violates them. He has, at least to some extent, adopted his parents' moral values and standards for evaluating his own and others' behavior. Freud regarded the development of conscience—or superego as he labeled it—as a product of identification: "When, by the process of identification he demands from himself conformity to a standard of conduct, the superego is said to be making its appearance" (**61**, 543).

The child striving to be similar to the parent will absorb parental moral standards, behaviors, and prohibitions in the same way that he adopts other parental behaviors. The adoption of parental standards makes him feel similar to his parents and, therefore, strengthens his identification with them. He then begins to punish himself whenever he has done something for which he believes his parents might punish him (**81**). According to psychoanalytic theory, ". . . through identification with the parent, he has taken over and incorporated within himself the attitudes of condemnation of those who transgress" (**61**, 541).

Conscience is obviously a broad, pervasive component of the individual's psychological organization. The term subsumes a wide variety of responses, opinions, and judgments: for example, being honest; obeying rules and regulations; resisting temptations to cheat, lie, or steal; acting in kind, considerate, altruistic ways; considering the rights and welfare of others; treating people in egalitarian rather than authoritarian ways; making moral judgments in which justice is tempered with mercy.

The establishment and development of conscience are, of course, complex phenomena and not simply products of identification. Parents who use "power assertive" techniques (physical punishment, severe scolding, threatening) in controlling their child are likely to produce fear of punishment or anxiety in the child, as well as anxiety about loss of love. These may motivate the child to adopt the moral standards and behavior that please the parents (**42**).

Guilt about transgression is frequently used as an index of conscience development and internalized standards of morality. Data from a number of studies show that a child's tendency to feel guilty about "doing something wrong" is related to a number of parental practices such as frequent use of praise, expression of affection, and infrequent use of physical punishment. Maintaining close, affectionate relationships with the child and using training techniques that are "capable of arousing unpleasant-feeling reaction in the child about his misbehavior, independently of external threat . . ." (13, 183) promote the development of a high level of conscience and internalized reactions to transgression (feelings of guilt, self-responsibility, confession).

Among 5-year-old girls, those who actively sought adult approval and nurturance were most likely to imitate adult moral standards, such as instructing another child about the rules of a game or showing interest in another child's safety. These girls also became upset when they committed acts that adults might disapprove. Older boys with internalized standards of morality reported that their parents were affectionate and did not use force or threats in disciplining them, but emphasized the effects of the child's misbehavior on the parents' feelings (42).

The association between high levels of conscience and warm, rewarding, nurturant parent-child relationships is consistent with the hypothesis that conscience development or morality is, at least in part, a consequent of identification. Maternal warmth and acceptance have also been found to be positively correlated with strength of conscience among kindergarten children as measured by their reactions to "doing something wrong." Boys with accepting fathers, with whom they presumably identified, manifested more guilt following wrongdoing and higher levels of conscience development than boys with rejecting fathers. The use of withdrawal of love as a technique of discipline was also associated with strongly developed conscience, but this technique could be effective only if strong, affectionate mother-child relationships had already been established.

> The children most prone to behave in the ways we have considered indicative of having a well developed conscience, were those whose mothers were relatively warm toward them, and who made their love contingent on the child's good behavior. These were the children who truly were risking the loss of love when they misbehaved (78, 388–389).

Altruism

Parental warmth and nurturance are also related to generosity and prosocial behavior, that is, positive, socially oriented actions. In one study nursery-school boys were presented with a bowl of candies and told they could share any or all of them with two friends. Those who shared a substantial portion of their candies revealed in doll-play sessions that they perceived their fathers as warmer, more nurturant, and more rewarding than boys who kept almost all the candies for themselves (75).

This finding is generally supportive of the hypothesis that conscience development is influenced by the nature of the child's interactions with his parents and thus by the strength of his identification with them. But it must be recognized that this is only one of many factors influencing the child's moral judgments and behavior. For example, children become more altruistic after success experiences. In one experiment groups of children experienced success, failure, or a neutral outcome in a game and were subsequently given an opportunity to contribute money to purchase toys for poor children. More of those who had been successful in the games, and thus presumably had more positive feelings, contributed money and they contributed greater amounts of money than those who had failed or experienced a neutral outcome.

Observation of peer or adult models who are behaving generously also enhances children's generosity. In one experimental study children who observed a generous model were significantly more altruistic (shared more of the prizes they won) than control subjects who were not exposed to the model (35). Furthermore, what the model did in the situation proved to be much more important than what he said; what he practiced was more important than what he preached.

> If the model behaves charitably, so will the child—even if the model has preached greed. And conversely, if the model preaches charity, but practices greed, the child will follow the model's behavior and will not contribute to the charity. Behavior in the prosocial area is mainly influenced by behavior, not by words (70, 354).

PERSONALITY AND SOCIAL LEARNING IN THE HOME

Up to this point, we have centered our attention on the development of particular motives, personality characteristics, and social responses, as well as the major processes involved in their development and modification: learning, imitation, and identification. In this last section, we shall examine some broad aspects of the social environment of the home, including parent-child relationships, as they affect the development of traits and motives and the general pattern or structure of personality. This subject is a critical one. Consequently, there have been numerous studies of the relationship between family atmosphere or parental attitudes and the personal and social adjustment of children. Here we will summarize only a few of the many highly relevant investigations.

Methodological Problems in Researching Home Environment

But first, let us digress a bit to consider some methodological problems involved in this kind of research. Investigations of the effects of very early parent-child interactions focus on the mother's role in satisfying the infant's basic needs and in reacting to manifestations of aggression, anxiety, sexuality, and independence. As the child matures, his relationships with his parents become more extensive, more complex, and more subtle. Investigations of parent-child relations during the preschool years focus not on specific interactions in restricted situations, but on broad, global characteristics of the home and parental behavior. Examples of such inclusive, "molar" qualities are parental warmth (or coldness), nurturance, permissiveness and control, expression of affection, democracy and authoritarianism in the home, and ease of communication between parent and child. The study of personality development is concerned with variations in these dimensions as antecedents of children's social behavior, personality characteristics, motives, and attitudes.

These general, comprehensive dimensions are difficult to evaluate and to measure objectively. **Interviews** with parents or **questionnaires** about parent-child relations are the most commonly used methods. But data from these sources are not entirely satisfactory because parents are not ordinarily reliable and objective observers of either their own or their children's behavior. Their reports are likely to be biased, and important information may be forgotten, withheld, or (consciously or unconsciously) distorted. However, because the interview method is, in many ways, efficient and convenient, there have been some interesting attempts to increase the objectivity of interview data, for example by asking a parent to describe in great detail everything that took place between him and the child throughout the day preceding the interview (**40, 41**). Interviews used for research purposes are generally taped and transcribed. The information given may then be coded according to specific categories of behavior, such as parental assertion and child submission, or rated on salient dimensions, such as warmth, affection, communication, and control.

A **home visit** is sometimes used to observe and record family interactions in their natural setting. A home visitor, a specially trained observer, goes to the subject's home for a specified period, say two hours, and watches the family members engaged in their customary activities, presumably interacting naturally and in their habitual ways. The observations are recorded fully and subsequently, as with interview data, coded into categories or rated.

In **structured observation,** a parent and child may be brought together in a standard setting and presented with a task or a problem. For example, the mother may be given instructional material or educational toys and instructed to teach her child how to use these. The spontaneous interactions between parent and child are observed and subsequently coded and/or rated. The situation presumably provides an opportunity to observe the mother's habitual, "natural"

> . . . way of enforcing rules, her directiveness in teaching, her ability to motivate the child and secure his compliance, her use of praise and disapproval in success and failure experiences (the child almost always had both during the teaching period), her methods of dealing with the child's anxiety, her ability to follow and facilitate the child's thought processes and to answer his questions, her degree of involvement with him, her supportiveness, patience, handling of dependency, and her intellectual expectations of the child (**9, 69**).

Unfortunately, most of the studies in this area have used middle-class parents and children as subjects, so it is difficult to know whether the findings can be generalized to members of other social classes. For example, upper-middle-class children may react quite differently from those of the lower class to a rigid, authoritarian home atmosphere. In the middle class, this kind of atmosphere may be relatively uncommon and frequently associated with lack of parental affection. In the lower class, on the other hand, such authoritarian atmosphere may be more usual, but often accompanied by genuine expressions of affection. If this is true, the consequences of authoritarian control might be quite different for children in different social classes.

Another problem in interpreting data in this area of research stems from the fact that the home variables considered most salient—permissiveness, control, democracy, nurturance—are not defined in the same way by all investigators. For instance, in one study high control means authoritarian parental attitudes and arbitrary, dictatorial rules, together with parental domination and lack of permissiveness (1). In another, however, control refers not to authoritarian rules, but rather to "parental acts intended to shape the child's goal-oriented activity; to modify his expression of dependent, aggressive, and playful behavior; and to promote internalization of parental standards. Parental control as defined here is not a measure of restrictiveness, punitive attitudes, or intrusiveness, but is a measure of strict discipline" (11).

Effects of Democratic and Controlled Home Atmospheres

In studies of nursery-school children at the Fels Research Institute, a home visitor visited the children's homes, observed the general family atmosphere and parent-child interactions, wrote a critical summary of the findings, and rated the home on 30 carefully defined scales, such as hostile-affectionate, nonchalant-anxious, dictatorial-democratic, inactive-active, harmonious-conflictful (1, 2).

Taken together, the scales provide objective, well-rounded descriptions of the home and permit systematic examination of the relationships between home environment and children's characteristics. The 30 scales are not entirely independent of each other; many of them are positively intercorrelated. Groups of related variables, called **clusters** or **constellations**, are assumed to measure some common aspect or area of parent behavior.

Two of these clusters, **democracy** and **control**, represent opposite poles of parent-child relationships. The democratic home atmosphere is characterized by general permissiveness, avoidance of arbitrary decisions, and a high level of verbal contact between parents and children (consultations about decisions, explanations of reasons for family rules, supplying answers to satisfy the child's curiosity). Controlled homes emphasize clear-cut restrictions on behavior and, consequently, friction over disciplinary procedures is low.

Nursery-school teachers and observers rated the children's behavior in school. As would be anticipated, children from democratic and controlled homes manifested strikingly divergent personality structures. Those from democratic homes were generally active, competitive, creative, original, and outgoing. They also ranked high in aggressiveness, leadership, playfulness, and cruelty, and tended to be more curious, disobedient, and nonconforming, especially if, in addition to democracy, there was a great deal of parent-child interaction (**activity**) in the home. In democratic, but relatively inactive, homes—characterized by more detachment, fewer verbal interchanges, and less leadership in the parent-child relationship—these effects were less marked.

Children from homes rated high in control presented the opposite kind of personality picture. They showed relatively little quarrelsomeness, negativism, disobedience, aggression, playfulness, tenacity, or fearfulness. Homes characterized by **authoritarian control** (high control together with low democracy) produced quiet, well-behaved, nonresistant children who were socially unaggressive. In these homes conformity, which was associated with restricted curiosity, originality, and fancifulness, was obtained at the expense of freedom of expression. Of course, democratic parents run the risk of producing too little conformity to cultural demands in their children. However, in the groups of homes investigated in this study, there was a positive correlation between democracy and control, that is, most democratic parents practiced enough control to avoid the pitfalls of extreme nonconformity.

> The effect of the democratic home as contrasted to the non-democratic one is to stimulate the child in such a way that he is more actively engaged in peer-centered activities, that he is more successful in those activities, and that he is better able to contribute original creative ideas to the groups with which he interacts (1, 62).

The contrasting personality structures of children from different types of homes may be interpreted as the outcomes of differential patterns of rewards and punishments. In the democratic home the child is rewarded for curiosity and independent activity; for spontaneous, relatively uninhibited expression of ideas, feelings, and opinions; and for participation and self-assertion in family discussions and decision-making. These rewarded responses become strong and habitual at home, and consequently they are generalized to other settings, such as the nursery school and playground. In contrast, children growing up in authoritarian homes may be punished for manifesting curiosity, spontaneity, or self-assertion; they are rewarded for obedience to parents, conformity with parental standards, and suppression of curiosity. Responses of compliance and conformity, therefore, become strong habits, and they generalize to the social world outside the home.

Child-Rearing Antecedents of Competence and Maturity

Studies recently conducted by Diana Baumrind at the University of California at Berkeley were concerned with the kinds of parent-child relationships that enhance the young child's competence (9, 10, 11). Competence was defined in terms of self-reliance, social responsibility, independence, achievement orientation, and vitality. In one study a large group of 3- and 4-year-olds were intensively observed in nursery school and at home and rated on five dimensions intended to measure competence at this age: **self-control; approach tendencies,** the tendency to approach "novel, stressful, exciting, or unexpected situations in an explorative and curious fashion" (9, 52); **vitality; self-reliance;** and **peer affiliation,** "ability and desire to express warmth toward others of his own age."

Three groups of children of different personality structures were selected for further study on the basis of these observations and assessments. Pattern I children were the most mature, competent, content, independent, realistic, self-reliant, self-controlled, explorative, affiliative, and self-assertive. Pattern II children were rated as moderately self-reliant and self-controlled, but relatively discontented, insecure and apprehensive, withdrawn, distrustful, and uninterested in peer affiliation. Pattern III children were the most immature, highly dependent, less self-controlled and less self-reliant than the children in the other two groups, and more withdrawn, that is, they tended to retreat from novel or stressful experiences.

The child-rearing practices of the parents of the three groups of children were investigated by a variety of assessment procedures, including home visits, observations in structured situations, and parental interviews. Four aspects of parental relationships to children were evaluated: **control**, that is, efforts to influence "the child's goal-oriented activity, modify his expression of dependent, aggressive, and playful behavior, and promote internalization of parental standards" (9, 54); **maturity demands,** pressures on the child to perform at the level of his ability intellectually, socially, or emotionally; **clarity of parent-child communication,** for example, use of reason to obtain compliance, asking the child's opinions and feelings; and **parental nurturance,** including both warmth (love, caretaking, and compassion) and involvement (praise and pleasure in the child's accomplishments).

The "scores" of the parents of the three groups of children on these four child-rearing dimensions, assessed on the basis of home visit reports, are shown in Fig. 9.2. The parents of mature, competent children scored uniformly high on all four dimensions. Compared with other parents studied, they were warm, loving, supportive, conscientious, and they communicated well with their children; at the same time, they were controlling and demanded mature behavior from their children. Although they respected their youngsters' independence and decisions, they generally held firm in their own positions, being clear and explicit about the reasons for the directive that they gave. This combination of parental high control and positive encouragement of the child's autonomous and independent strivings was called **authoritative** parental control.

Clearly, such parents provide a learning setting conducive to the acquisition of behavior that is both socialized and independent. They do a great deal of "teaching," integrating attempts to control their children's behavior with giving

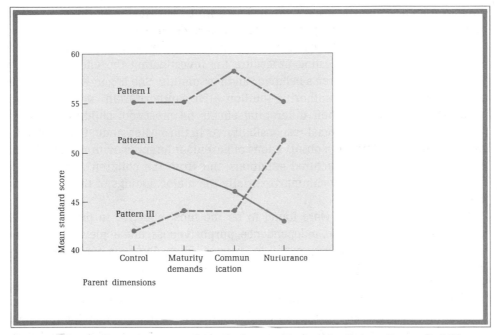

Figure 9.2 Parent dimension scores from the home visit data for three patterns of child behavior. (From Diana Baumrind. Child care practices anteceding three patterns of preschool behavior. **Genetic Psychology Monographs,** 1967, 75. By permission.)

information and reasoning. Thus, they enhance the child's social skills, encourage independence in decision-making, and stress mature ways of thinking and reasoning. Since they are also warm and nurturant, these parents are probably effective reinforcers of the child's mature, independent behavior, using love and approval as rewards. At the same time, they also provide excellent models of competent, decisive, reasonable, calm, self-assertive, and mature behavior.

The parents of children who were somewhat self-reliant, but relatively discontent, withdrawn, and distrustful (Pattern II) were rated as lower on use of rational control and were more coercive; they were less warm, nurturant, affectionate, or sympathetic with their children. They were highly controlling and used power freely; they did not encourage the child to express himself when he disagreed (9). These less warm parents were called **authoritarian.**

The parents of the immature (Pattern III) children—those who were least self-reliant, explorative, and self-controlled—were themselves noncontrolling, nondemanding, and relatively warm. They were not well organized or effective in running their households, were lax both in disciplining and rewarding the child, made relatively few and only weak demands for mature behavior, and paid little attention to training for independence and self-reliance. Consequently, in the nursery-school setting, their children appeared immature, lacking in independence and self-reliance (9). These parents were labeled **permissive.**

In a more recent study, Baumrind (10) studied a large group of parents and children and used a contrasting procedure for investigating the effects of these parental practices on children's behavior and personality. She began with the three basic patterns of parental authority—authoritative, authoritarian, and permissive—and then investigated their differential effects on preschool children's competence, independence, and social responsibility. As in the earlier study, the basic data were derived from intensive observations of parents interacting with their children in their homes and in structured situations and from the children's behavior in the preschool. We can only summarize briefly the major findings of this important study.

Authoritative parents were found to be the most effective in promoting the development of competence, independence, purposiveness, and achievement orientation in girls and social responsibility in boys. High demands for mature performance and firmness in disciplinary matters appear to be associated with both self-assertion and social responsibility in young children of both sexes. According to Baumrind both authoritative and authoritarian parents preach responsible behavior, but only the authoritative ones modeled this kind of behavior for their children. Hence, the children of authoritative parents behaved more responsibly. Authoritarian parents do not practice what they preach, however; they are more concerned with their own ideas and standards than with the child's interests and welfare. "The modelling of socially responsible behavior facilitates the development of social responsibility in young children and more so if the model is seen by the child as having control over desired resources and as being concerned with the child's welfare" (12, 213).

Permissive parents do not demand much of their children, do not reward self-reliant or responsible behavior, and do not discourage immature behavior. Consequently, their sons are also lacking in responsibility and achievement orientation. Neither authoritarian control or permissive lack of control provide the child with the knowledge and experience that he needs if he is to act in independent, self-reliant ways.

The data of all these studies of child-rearing practices indicate that in young children the qualities of competence, independence, affiliation, outgoingness, self-control, and self-reliance are fostered by nurturant, warm home environments in which independent actions and decision-making, as well as responsible and self-reliant behavior, are encouraged and rewarded. Baumrind's data further suggest that in the context of the nurturant home, parental control or firmness, together with high maturity demands, but **not** authoritarian discipline, high punitiveness, high restrictiveness, or overprotection, promote young children's maturity, competence, and social responsibility (9, 10, 11).

Summary

During the preschool years the child's personality becomes richer, more complex, and more highly differentiated. Significant new personality characteristics and motives emerge, while those that are already established may be modified and expressed in new and different ways.

It is important to differentiate between overt behavior and underlying motives; there are not one-to-one relationships between aggressive behavior and hostile motivation or between dependent behavior and dependency motives.

The forms and amounts of aggression a child exhibits depend primarily on his social experiences, including reinforcement received for such behavior, observation and imitation of aggressive models, the degree of anxiety or guilt associated with the aggressive expression. Frustration often produces increased aggression, but children differ widely in the ability to tolerate frustration and in the intensity of their reactions to it. Aggressiveness is a fairly stable characteristic; boys who are highly aggressive during the preschool period are also likely to be highly aggressive in later childhood, adolescence, and adulthood.

Peers are also frequent sources of reinforcement for aggressive behavior and many children become more aggressive as a result of attending nursery school. Parental use of physical punishment for aggressive behavior may actually enhance, rather than inhibit, aggression (at least in "safe" situations) because, by using such punishment, the parent serves as a model of aggression.

The forms of expression of dependency and the situations that elicit dependent behavior, as well as the targets, usually change during the nursery-school years. During the second year, the mother still serves a major security-giving function and the child will explore and play more and cry less when she is present than when he is alone or with a stranger. Intensity of protest about separation from the mother declines substantially between the ages of 2 and 3. Two-year-olds express dependency by clinging and seeking affection frequently, while 5-year-olds are more likely to express these needs by seeking reassurance and attention from adults.

While dependency tends to be a relatively stable characteristic during the preschool years, situational factors, such as an anxiety-producing setting or isolation from social contacts, strongly influence the expression of dependency. Children who are highly dependent on their mothers are more apt to generalize their dependency responses to others, including strangers, than children who are generally low in this motivation.

Inconsistent discipline and use of "withdrawal of love" as a socialization technique—giving love and affection when the child behaves as the parent wants him to, withholding these rewards when he behaves in disapproved ways—produce children who frequently manifest dependent behavior at home.

Dependency, autonomy, and independence tend to be stable characteristics during the preschool years and, for girls, from the preschool years through adolescence. A dependent 5-year-old girl is likely to become a dependent adolescent and young adult, but a boy's adolescent dependency cannot be predicted from his preschool behavior.

Although there are marked individual differences in susceptibility to fear, every child develops some fears or sources of anxiety. Many of the preschool child's fears drop out spontaneously or become modified in form. Successful techniques for reducing fears include explanation combined with gradual encouragement of confrontation with the feared situation and exposure to models who are calm and unafraid when they encounter objects that the child fears. Fears taken over from a parent, either by identification or by observational learning, are particularly resistant to treatment and extinction.

Because anxiety is unpleasant, children develop techniques of coping or defending against it. Projection, withdrawal, regression, denial, and repression are defense mechanisms used frequently by youngsters.

Mastery motivation—the desire to solve problems and increase skills and abilities—may develop early as a consequence of maternal rewards and encouragement of the child's efforts to be independent. Children who are highly motivated for intellectual achievement often emulate adults in their play and are likely to be accepted as leaders by other children. Strong achievement motivation tends to be continuous from the preschool period through adolescence and adulthood.

Many complex, integrated patterns of behavior and personal characteristics seem to be incorporated through **identification** with a model, usually a parent. The degree of identification is, in part, a function of the parent's nurturance, affection, competence, and power. Sex-typing and conscience development are two major products of the process of identification. The child's tendency to feel guilty about transgressions, an index of conscience, is related to parental use of praise, expressions of affection, and infrequent use of physical punishment. Altruism is related to perceptions of the father as warm and nurturant and also to situational factors, including success experiences and observation of a model behaving altruistically.

Homes that are high in control produce children who manifest relatively little negativism, disobedience, playfulness, spontaneity, or fearfulness. Preschool children from democratic home environments tend to be active, competitive, outgoing, aggressive, curious, and nonconforming.

Mature, competent, and independent preschool children have parents who are highly consistent, warm, loving, and secure. These parents respect their child's independence, but hold firm to their own positions, giving clear and explicit reasons for their decisions. Authoritative parental control—a combination of high control and positive encouragement of the child's autonomous and independent strivings—is conducive to the child's development of maturity, competence, contentment, and independence, as well as of self-control, exploration, and an outgoing, social orientation.

References

1. Baldwin, A. L. The effect of home environment on nursery school behavior. **Child Development,** 1949, **20,** 49–62.
2. Baldwin, A. L., Kalhorn, J., & Breese, F. H. The appraisal of parent behavior. **Psychological Monographs,** 1949, **63**(299).
3. Bandura, A. The role of modeling processes in personality development. In W. W. Hartup and N. L. Smothergill (Eds.), **The young child.** Washington, D.C.: National Association for the Education of Young Children, 1967. Pp. 42–58.
4. Bandura, A., Grusec, J. E., & Menlove, F. L. Vicarious extinction of avoidance behavior. **Journal of Personality and Social Psychology,** 1967, **5,** 16–23.
5. Bandura, A., & Huston, A. C. Identification as a process of incidental learning. **Journal of Abnormal and Social Psychology,** 1961, **63,** 311–318.
6. Bandura, W., & Walters, R. H. Aggression. In H. W. Stevenson (Ed.), **Child Psychology.** (62nd Yearbook of the National Society for the Study of Education.) Chicago: University of Chicago Press, 1963. Pp. 364–415.
7. Barker, R. G., Dembo, T., & Lewin, K. Frustration and regression. In R. G. Barker, J. S. Kounin, & H. F. Wright (Eds.), **Child behavior and development.** New York: McGraw-Hill, 1943. Pp. 441–458.
8. Barry, H., Bacon, M. K., & Child, I. L. A cross-cultural survey of some sex differences in socialization. **Journal of Abnormal and Social Psychology,** 1963, **67,** 527–534.
9. Baumrind, D. Child care practices anteceding three patterns of preschool behavior. **Genetic Psychology Monographs,** 1967, **75,** 43–88.
10. Baumrind, D. Current patterns of parental authority. **Developmental Psychology Monographs,** 1971, No. 1, 1–103.
11. Baumrind, D. The development of instrumental competence through socialization: Focus on girls. Minnesota Symposium in Child Development, 1972.
12. Baumrind, D. Socialization and instrumental competence in young children. In W. W. Hartup (Ed.), **The young child: Reviews of research.** Vol. 2. Washington, D.C.: National Association for the Education of Young Children, 1972. Pp. 202–224.
13. Becker, W. C. Consequences of different kinds of parental discipline. In M. L. Hoffman & L. W. Hoffman (Eds.), **Review of child development research.** Vol. 1. New York: Russell Sage Foundation, 1964. Pp. 169–208.
14. Beller, E. K. Dependency and independence in young children. **Journal of Genetic Psychology,** 1955, **87,** 25–35.
15. Beller, E. K. Dependency and autonomous achievement striving related to orality and anality in early childhood. **Child Development,** 1957, **28,** 287–315.
16. Beller, E. K. Exploratory studies of dependency. **Transactions of the New York Academy of Sciences,** 1959, **21,** 414–426.
17. Block, J. H. Conceptions of sex role: Some cross-cultural and longitudinal perspectives. **American Psychologist,** 1973, **28,** 512–529.
18. Bronfenbrenner, U. Freudian theories of identification and their derivatives. **Child Development,** 1960, **31,** 15–40.

19. Bronson, W. The role of enduring orientations to the environment in personality development. **Genetic Psychology Monographs,** 1972, **86,** 3–80.

20. Brown, D. G. Sex-role preference in young children. **Psychological Monographs,** 1956, **70**(421), 1–19.

21. Brown, P., & Elliott, R. Control of aggression in a nursery school class. **Journal of Experimental Child Psychology,** 1965, **2,** 103–107.

22. Crandall, V. J. Achievement. In H. W. Stevenson (Ed.), **Child psychology.** (62nd Yearbook of the National Society for the Study of Education.) Chicago: University of Chicago Press, 1963. Pp. 416–459.

23. Crandall, V. J., & Rabson, A. Children's repetition choices in an intellectual achievement situation following success and failure. **Journal of Genetic Psychology,** 1960, **92,** 161–168.

24. D'Andrade, R. G. Sex differences and cultural institutions. In E. E. Maccoby (Ed.), **The development of sex differences.** Stanford, Calif.: Stanford University Press, 1966. Pp. 173–203.

25. Emmerich, W. Continuity and stability in early social development: II. Teacher ratings. **Child Development,** 1966, **37,** 17–28.

26. Erikson, E. H. Toys and reason. In M. R. Haworth (Ed.), **Child psychotherapy: Practice and theory.** New York: Basic Books, **1964.** Pp. 3–11.

27. Fawl, C. L. Disturbances experienced by children in their natural habitats. In R. G. Barker (Ed.), **The stream of behavior.** New York: Appleton-Century-Crofts, 1963. Pp. 99–126.

28. Ferguson, L. R. **Personality development.** Belmont, Calif.: Brooks-Cole, 1970.

29. Feshbach, N., & Feshbach, S. Children's aggression. In W. W. Hartup (Ed.), **The young child: Reviews of research.** Vol. 2. Washington, D.C.: National Association for the Education of Young Children, 1972. Pp. 284–302.

30. Fraiberg, S. H. **The magic years.** New York: Scribner, 1959.

31. Gewirtz, J. L. A factor analysis of some attention-seeking behaviors of young children. **Child Development,** 1956, **27,** 17–36.

32. Hagman, R. R. A study of fears of children of preschool age. **Journal of Experimental Education,** 1932, **1,** 110–130.

33. Hartup, W. W. Nurturance and nurturance-withdrawal in relation to the dependency behavior of preschool children. **Child Development,** 1958, **29,** 191–201.

34. Hartup, W. W. Dependence and independence. In H. W. Stevenson (Ed.), **Child psychology.** (62nd Yearbook of the National Society for the Study of Education.) Chicago: University of Chicago Press, 1963. Pp. 333–363.

35. Hartup, W. W., & Coates, B. Imitation of a peer as a function of reinforcement from the peer group and rewardingness of the model. **Child Development,** 1967, **38**(4), 1003–1016.

36. Hartup, W. W., & Keller, E. D. Nurturance in preschool children and its relation to dependency. **Child Development,** 1960, **31,** 681–690.

37. Hattendorf, K. W. A study of the questions of young children concerning sex: A phase of an experimental approach to parental education. **Journal of Social Psychology,** 1932, **3,** 37–65.

38. Heathers, G. Emotional dependence and independence in nursery-school play. **Journal of Genetic Psychology,** 1955, **87,** 37–58.

39. Hill, K. T. & Sarason, S. B. The relation of test anxiety and defensiveness to test and school performance over the elementary-school years: A further longitudinal study. **Monographs of the Society for Research in Child Development,** 1966, **31**(2).

40. Hoffman, M. L. An interview method for obtaining descriptions of parent-child interaction. **Merrill-Palmer Quarterly,** 1957, **3**(2), 76–83.

41. Hoffman, M. L. Parent discipline and the child's consideration for others. **Child Development,** 1963, **34,** 573–588.
42. Hoffman, M. L., & Saltzstein, H. D. Parent discipline and the child's moral development. **Journal of Personality and Social Psychology,** 1967, **5,** 45–57.
43. Holmes, F. B. An experimental investigation of a method of overcoming children's fears. **Child Development,** 1936, **7,** 6–30.
44. Honigmann, J. J. **Personality in culture.** New York: Harper & Row, 1967.
45. Jersild, A. T., & Holmes, F. B. **Children's fears.** New York: Bureau of Publications, Teachers College, Columbia University, 1935.
46. Jersild, A. T., & Markey, F. V. Conflicts between preschool children. **Child Development Monographs,** 1935, No. 21.
47. Jones, M. C. A laboratory study of fear: The case of Peter. **Pedagogical Seminary,** 1924, **31,** 308–315.
48. Kagan, J. Acquisition and significance of sex-typing and sex-role identity. In M. L. Hoffman & L. W. Hoffman (Eds.), **Review of child development research.** Vol. 1. New York: Russell Sage Foundation, 1964. Pp. 137–167.
49. Kagan, J., & Moss, H. A. The stability of passive and dependent behavior from childhood through adulthood. **Child Development,** 1960, **31,** 577–591.
50. Kagan, J., & Moss, H. A. **Birth to maturity: A study in psychological development.** New York: Wiley, 1962.
51. Kessler, J. W. **Psychopathology of childhood.** Englewood Cliffs, N.J.: Prentice-Hall, 1966.
52. Kohlberg, L. A cognitive-developmental analysis of children's sex-role concepts and attitudes. In E. E. Maccoby (Ed.), **The development of sex differences.** Stanford, Calif.: Stanford University Press, 1966. Pp. 82–173.
53. Lynn, D. **The father's influence.** Belmont, Calif.: Brooks-Cole, 1973, in press.
54. Maccoby, E. E. (Ed.) **The development of sex differences.** Stanford, Calif.: Stanford University Press, 1966.
55. Maccoby, E., & Feldman, S. Mother-attachment and stranger-reactions in the third year of life. **Monographs of the Society for Research in Child Development,** 1972, **37**(1).
56. Maccoby, E., & Masters, J. C. Attachment and dependency. In P. H. Mussen (Ed.), **Carmichael's Manual of child psychology,** (3rd ed.) Vol. 2. New York: Wiley, 1970. Pp. 73–157.
57. Malinowski, B. Prenuptial intercourse between the sexes in the Trobriand Islands, N. W. Melanesia. **Psychoanalytic Review,** 1927, **14,** 20–36.
58. McCandless, B. R., & Marshall, H. R. Sex differences in social acceptance and participation of preschool children. **Child Development,** 1957, **28,** 421–425.
59. Moss, H. A., & Kagan, J. The stability of achievement and recognition seeking behaviors. **Journal of Abnormal and Social Psychology,** 1961, **62,** 504–513.
60. Mowrer, O. H. **Learning theory and personality dynamics.** New York: Ronald, 1950.
61. Murphy, G. **Personality.** New York: Harper & Row, 1947.
62. Mussen, P. & Distler, L. Masculinity, identification and father-son relationships. **Journal of Abnormal and Social Psychology,** 1959, **59,** 350–356.
63. Mussen, P., & Distler, L. Child rearing antecedents of masculine identification in kindergarten boys. **Child Development,** 1960, **31,** 89–100.
64. Mussen, P., & Parker, A. Mother nurturance and girls' incidental imitative learning. **Journal of Personality and Social Psychology,** 1965, **2,** 94–97.
65. Mussen, P., & Rutherford, E. Parent-child relations and parental personality in relation to young children's sex-role preferences. **Child Development,** 1963, **34,** 589–607.

66. Otis, N. B., & McCandless, B. R. Responses to repeated frustrations of young children differentiated according to need area. **Journal of Abnormal and Social Psychology,** 1955, **50,** 349–353.

67. Parker, R. D., & Deur, J. The inhibiting effects of inconsistent and consistent punishment on children's aggression. Unpublished manuscript, University of Wisconsin, 1970.

68. Patterson, G. R., Littman, R. A., & Bricker, W. Assertive behavior in children: A step toward a theory of aggression. **Monographs of the Society for Research in Child Development,** 1967, **32**(5), 1–43.

69. Rosenberg, B. G., & Sutton-Smith, B. **Sex and identity.** New York: Holt, Rinehart & Winston, 1972.

70. Rosenhan, D. Prosocial behavior of children. In W. W. Hartup (Ed.), **The young child: Reviews of research.** Vol. 2. Washington, D. C.: National Association for the Education of Young Children, 1972. Pp. 340–359.

71. Rosenthal, M. K. The effect of a novel situation and anxiety on two groups of dependency behavior. **British Journal of Psychology,** 1967, **58,** 357–364.

72. Rosenthal, M. K. The generalization of dependency behavior from mother to stranger. **Journal of Child Psychology and Psychiatry,** 1967, **8,** 117–133.

73. Rossi, A. Women in science: Why so few? In B. C. Rosen, H. J. Crockett, & C. Z. Nunn (Eds.), **Achievement in American society.** Cambridge, Mass.: Schenckmann, 1969. Pp. 470–486.

74. Ruebush, B. K. Anxiety. In H. W. Stevenson (Ed.), **Child psychology.** (62nd Yearbook of the National Society for the Study of Education.) Chicago: University of Chicago Press, 1963. Pp. 460–516.

75. Rutherford, E., & Mussen, P. Generosity in nursery school boys. **Child Development,** 1968, **39,** 755–765.

76. Sarason, S. B., Davidson, K. S., Lighthall, F., Waite, R. R., & Ruebush, B. K. **Anxiety in elementary school children.** New York: Wiley, 1960.

77. Sears, R. R. Dependency motivation. In M. Jones (Ed.), **Nebraska symposium on motivation.** Lincoln: University of Nebraska Press, 1963. Pp. 25–64.

78. Sears, R. R., Maccoby, E. E., & Levin, H. **Patterns of child rearing.** New York: Harper & Row, 1957.

79. Siegel, A., & Kohn, L. Permissiveness, permission and aggression: The effect of adult presence or absence on children's play. **Child Development,** 1959, **30,** 131–141.

80. White, R. Motivation reconsidered: The concept of competence. **Psychological Review,** 1959, **66,** 297–333.

81. Whiting, J. W. M., & Child, I. L. **Child training and personality.** New Haven, Conn.: Yale University Press, 1953.

82. Winterbottom, M. R. The relation of need for achievement to learning experience in independence and mastery. In J. W. Atkinson (Ed.), **Motives in fantasy, action and society.** New York: Van Nostrand Reinhold, 1958. Pp. 453–478.

83. Wright, M. E. The influence of frustration upon the social relationships of young children. Unpublished doctoral dissertation, State University of Iowa, 1940.

84. Yarrow, L. J. The effect of antecedent frustration on projective play. **Psychological Monographs,** 1948, **62**(6).

Part V
Middle Childhood

Chapter 10

Development in Middle Childhood

I. Personality Development and Problems of Adjustment

As the child enters the school years, his horizons are expanded, and he is subjected to an ever-widening series of influences—teachers, peers, books, television. Nevertheless, the kind of parents a child has and the kind of relationships he has with them remain, for the average child, the most significant environmental factors in determining the kind of person he will become, the problems he will face in his quest for maturity, and the ways in which he will deal with these problems.

In this chapter, we will turn our attention first to the continuing influences of the family on the child's personality and social development. Following this, we will examine the growth of conscience and moral standards, which assume critical importance during this age period. Finally, we will consider some of the more common problems of adjustment that may occur in the middle-childhood years and their significance.

INFLUENCE OF THE FAMILY IN MIDDLE CHILDHOOD

Parent-Child Relationships

There is probably no area of child development in which public opinion is characterized by more misconceptions and myths than the area of the effects of parental behaviors in childrearing. Thus we frequently hear statements such as: "You can say what you want to about the influence of parents on their children's development, but I know it's really all in the genes they're born with" or "I know psychologists don't believe in discipline, but in my opinion that's what's wrong with today's young people!" From listening to such popular critics, one could easily gain the impression that the field contains no substantive research information and that psychologists are merely responding to shifting fads, in much the same way that women raise or lower the hemlines of their dresses in response to current fashions.

Much popular thinking is deficient in several respects: (1) it oversimplifies the complexities and variations possible in parental behavior; (2) it assumes that any assertion that parental practices affect the child's development is tantamount to declaring that other factors, including individual biological differences, have no effects; and (3) it assumes that it is not possible to investigate the potential effects of parental practices in a systematic, reliable manner. As we shall attempt to show, all of these assumptions are in error. Although we still have much to learn about the interacting effects of various influences on the course of the child's personal and social development—including possible interactions between genetically based temperamental characteristics and parent behaviors (139, 212)—considerable progress has been made in the past decade. Our knowledge of the effects of parent behavior on children has increased substantially.

Dimensions of Parent Behavior As we saw in the case of the preschool child parent behavior is not unidimensional; it does not consist simply of variations along a single axis, as popular oversimplifications sometimes seem to imply. Parents may love their children or they may reject them. They may also, however, be loving and controlling or loving and lax, as well as calm or anxious, confident or insecure, well-adjusted or disturbed. The response of the child will not depend simply on any one aspect of the parents' behavior and personality, but rather on the combined effect of many aspects.

A number of investigators (**7, 193, 194**) have attempted to conceptualize meaningful dimensions of parental behavior and the relationships of the dimensions to one another. There is, of course, no magic in these theoretical models; they are to some extent arbitrary. Furthermore, as we have already noted (see pp. 406–408), even after one has abstracted a potentially meaningful dimension, the task of defining that dimension remains. Nevertheless, as we shall see, these theoretical models may prove extremely helpful both in conceptualizing in an orderly manner variations in the behavior of parents of school-age children and in permitting us to design and interpret meaningful research.

Two major dimensions that consistently emerge in such theoretical schemes are **acceptance-rejection (warmth-hostility)** and **control-autonomy.** Each dimension represents a continuum of parental behavior between characteristics defined as opposite in areas of relationships with children. Furthermore, an increasing number of investigations (**10, 45, 179, 192**) suggest that the control-autonomy dimension is actually comprised of two related, but distinguishable, subdimensions: **psychological autonomy–psychological control** and **firm control–lax control.**

ACCEPTANCE-REJECTION (WARMTH-HOSTILITY). For present purposes, warmth in this dimension of parental behavior is defined by such characteristics as: "accepting, affectionate, approving, understanding, child-centered, frequent use of explanations, positive response to dependency behavior, high use of reasons in discipline, high use of praise in discipline, low use of physical punishment" (**174, 24**). Hostility is defined, in general, by the opposite characteristics.

CONTROL-AUTONOMY. Broadly viewed, control in this dimension is defined as parental efforts (1) to set and enforce rules of behavior and (2) to inhibit the child's development of individuality and autonomy. However, as already noted, it is becoming increasingly clear that these two aspects of control need to be differentiated, since they do not always go together. **Psychological control** (as opposed to **psychological autonomy**) refers to "covert, psychological methods of controlling the child's activities that would not permit the child to develop as an individual apart from the parent . . ." (**192, 555**). **Firm control** (as opposed to **lax control**) refers to the parents' tendency to make "rules and regulations, [set] limits to the child's activities, and [enforce] these rules and limits" (**192, 555**).

A parent may be psychologically intrusive and possessive, preventing the child from developing into an autonomous adult, without explicitly setting forth clear rules for behavior or stressing the importance of standards of conduct. Conversely, a parent may set forth reasonable, age-appropriate rules and standards clearly and firmly and, at the same time, strongly encourage the child to develop in the direction of self-confidence, autonomy, and self-reliance. We have used the term **authoritative** to describe this pattern of parental behavior (see pp. 409–412).

Furthermore, the relationship between these two aspects of parental control may vary with age. Thus a recent study of children's reports of parental child-rearing behavior at grade levels 4 through 8 showed that while **psychological control** steadily decreased throughout this age range, **firmness of control** (rule making and standard setting) increased from fourth to sixth grade, after which it again decreased (see Fig. 10.1). In other words, "as the parents of these children relinquish intrusive and dominating methods of control, they initially compensate through increased overt rule making and limit setting and then, subsequently, also increasingly relinquish these latter forms of control" (**10**, 48).

It is possible to make some limited generalizations about the probable effects on children of variations in parental behavior along one or another of these dimensions considered separately. Thus, hostility on the part of parents tends to produce counterhostility and aggression, either in feelings or behavior, on the part

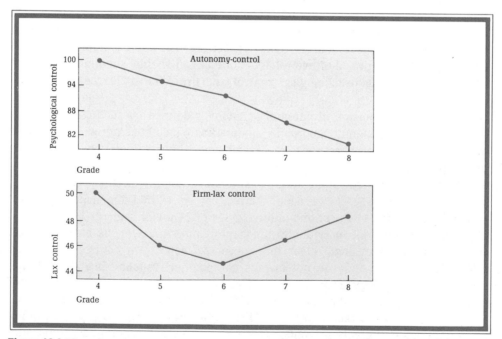

Figure 10.1 Mean factor scores at each grade level. (From J. A. Armentrout and G. K. Burger. Children's reports of parental child-rearing behavior at five grade levels. **Developmental Psychology,** 1972, **7**, 44–48. Copyright © 1972 by the American Psychological Association. By permission.)

of children (**7, 24, 51, 117, 199, 220**). Psychological control (parental intrusiveness and refusal to allow the child to develop as an independent, self-reliant individual) promotes infantile, dependent wishes and behavior (for example, the boy who remains "tied to his mother's apron strings"). Furthermore, children of parents high in psychological control appear to lack direction in developing and pursuing life goals and seem to have difficulty forming mature relationships with same- and opposite-sex peers (**10, 192**). Excessive control of a child's activities, when combined with rigid rule setting and demands for unquestioning obedience, tends to foster inhibited behaviors, while lack of control encourages less inhibited, often impulsive behaviors (**10, 15, 20, 24, 116, 132, 133, 143, 192**).

More precise and more meaningful generalizations become possible when interactions among these dimensions are considered. For example, the child of a hostile, lax parent and the child of a hostile, restrictive parent may both have deep-seated feelings of hostility. But the extent to which (and the directions in which) the hostility is expressed in behavior may vary greatly. The former is likely to express his aggression directly and with little control. The latter may express aggression in certain "safe" areas (for examples, with peers), but his aggression "is more likely to be inhibited and turned against the self; or to be revealed in manifestation of internal conflict" (**24, 198**). It is not likely to be expressed openly or directly against the parents, despite the fact that they may be the primary source of the child's hostile or aggressive feelings.

The "Democratic" Parent We use the term democratic to describe the parent who is warm and accepting, encouraging of autonomy, and low in intrusive psychological control. His child-rearing techniques probably come closest to the popular stereotype of the recommendations of child-rearing specialists—whether this stereotype serves as a source of assurance or outraged alarm. The child of such parents is likely to be rather active, outgoing, socially assertive, and independent (**15, 24, 116, 141, 220**), as well as friendly, creative, and lacking in hostility toward others or himself (**15, 116, 197, 198**). When, in addition to the characteristics mentioned above, the parent is reasonably insistent (and consistent) in setting age-appropriate standards for conduct and activities, the child is also likely to be responsible, self-confident, and purposive in behavior (**10, 20, 24, 26, 225**). On the other hand, if the parent is democratic, but at the same time somewhat lax in instituting age-appropriate controls, the child may be somewhat aggressive and overly assertive, somewhat deficient in orderly pursuit of clearly defined goals, and, on occasion, somewhat disobedient and disrespectful, particularly at home (**15, 21, 134**). However, these aggressive manifestations do not appear to reflect chronic anger and frustration or uncontrollable explosions of deep-seated, repressed feelings of hostility.

In democratic families generally, there tends also to be a high level of communication among family members, a dominant mood of warmth and friendliness, little need for overt support-seeking, an active interest in the views of others, and a tolerance for differences (164).

The Warm-Restrictive Parent A parent who is warm may nevertheless be restrictive in child-rearing practices. Such a parent may tend to be psychologically intrusive as well. It has been found that children reared in warm-restrictive homes, as compared with those reared in warm-permissive homes, were likely to be more dependent, less friendly, less creative, more hostile in their fantasies, and either very high or very low in persistence (24). These results in many ways parallel those of Kagan and Moss (116) in their longitudinal study of the Fels population (see pp. 384–386), although these investigators did not consider restrictiveness specifically in relation to the variable of warmth. In their study, maternal restrictiveness was evaluated by means of extended home observations and interviews, and averaged ratings were obtained for three age periods: birth to age 3, 3 to 6, 6 to 10. Restrictiveness was defined as the degree to which the mother attempted to force the child, through punishment or threat, to adhere to her standards and the degree to which deviations from these standards were punished. In general, it was found that early maternal restrictiveness, particularly during the first three years, tended to have lasting effects upon the child. Children of restrictive parents were more conforming, less aggressive, less dominant and competitive with their peers, and less likely to display mastery behavior. There were, however, a number of interesting variations revealed by this study. First, early restrictiveness (when the child was under 3) appeared to have a much greater inhibitory effect throughout childhood and adolescence than later restrictiveness (ages 3 to 6 and 6 to 10). Second, mothers tended to be more consistent over time in their restrictiveness with girls than with boys. Thus, among girls, early maternal restrictiveness was highly correlated with later restrictiveness, while among boys, it was not (although positive correlations were obtained among **older** age periods). It appears that this difference between boys and girls may be accounted for, at least in part, by the greater sex-role acceptability of restrictiveness and its effects among girls than among boys. Third, restrictiveness at later ages tended to produce more hostility in the child than at earlier ages, regardless of whether this restrictiveness resulted in a conforming, dependent child. In the period between 6 and 10 years of age, maternal restrictiveness toward boys tended to produce both dependency and aggressive reactions to the mother, related to her restrictiveness (116).

Further, consistent data emerge from a study by Maccoby (143) which showed that parents who were both warm and restrictive in the child's early years tended to have sons who, at age 12, were strict rule-enforcers with their peers. These rule-enforcing boys also manifested less overt aggression (based on teacher ratings), less misbehavior when the teacher was out of the room, and greater motivation toward schoolwork, although similar findings were not obtained for girls.

Adequate parental warmth seems to reduce the probability of the more extreme types of behavior disorders, such as neurotic disability or delinquency. However, within the context of warmth, significant differences in behavior may result, depending upon whether the parent is basically autonomy-encouraging or restrictive and intrusive. The child of autonomy-encouraging parents is more likely to be active, outgoing, friendly, creative, independent, and socially assertive; the child of restrictive and intrusive parents is more likely to be submissive to parents, conforming, dependent, compliant, polite, neat, lacking in aggression and competitiveness with peers, and less oriented toward mastery in the assumption of autonomy and independence (116, 149, 198, 221). Further research is needed, particularly in determining differences between boys and girls in their responses to permissiveness and restrictiveness within the context of parental warmth (20, 24, 197).

The Hostile-Authoritarian Parent The parent who is rejecting and at the same time excessively restrictive and demanding tends to promote counterhostility in the child but does not allow the hostility to be expressed. The child may not even be able to admit his hostile feelings to conscious awareness, particularly in cases where parental hostility is covert and disguised, making it difficult for the child to label it and face it for what it actually is without feeling guilty. Consequently, it is not surprising that this parental behavior pattern is often found in the background of neurotic children (7, 117, 185, 186, 200). The combination of low permissiveness or low opportunity for autonomous behavior and high punishment may lead to self-punishment, suicidal tendencies, and accident proneness (7, 198), as well as to shyness and social withdrawal, difficulties in relating to peers, and little confidence in or motivation toward adult role-taking (116, 134, 220). "By and large these studies suggest that the combination of restrictiveness and hostility fosters considerable resentment, with some of it being turned against the self, or, more generally, experienced as internalized turmoil and conflict" (24, 19).

The Hostile-Neglectful Parent The parent who lacks warmth (or rejects the child) and fails to use reasonable, consistent controls appropriate to the child's stage of development is likely to maximize "aggressive, poorly controlled behavior" (24, 193) in the child. As we shall see in our discussion of delinquency (see pp. 629–638), parents of a significant percentage of delinquents are lacking in parental warmth and are neglectful, that is, they fail to exercise appropriate parental control or are highly inconsistent in the use of discipline. When "discipline" is employed, it is likely to be arbitrary and overly severe, often involving physical punishment. Parental discipline in these instances is likely to emerge more as an expression of parental hostility and rejection than as a means of guiding the child and helping him to develop internal controls and appropriate standards of social conduct. The relationships of delinquent children and their parents are frequently characterized by mutual hostility and lack of family cohesiveness and shared goals.

Even among nondelinquent children, those whose parents are rejecting and neglectful, are more likely than other children to engage in aggressive, "acting-out" behavior (149, 199). Lack of parental warmth (or rejection) engenders hostile feelings, while lax, arbitrary, or inconsistent use of controls encourages the expression of these feelings.

Effects of Inconsistent Discipline Perhaps the most frequent question with which parents confront psychologists is "Do you believe in discipline?"—often with the implication that the answer will be "no." In actuality, of course, the question is a meaningless one. The question is not one of discipline or no discipline, but of how much discipline, of what kind, at what stage in the child's development, for what purpose, and in what sort of parental emotional climate. Socialization of the child obviously requires the imposition of controls. Without controls the skills, attitudes, and behaviors necessary for a satisfactory interdependent existence in a complex society could not be learned. However, excessive control and discipline, as we have already seen, threaten the child's development of autonomy, self-confidence, and self-reliance—qualities which are equally necessary for social effectiveness. The studies reviewed above appear to indicate that the most effective balance between cooperative, responsible, disciplined behavior, on the one hand, and self-confidence, autonomy, self-reliance, and emotional freedom, on the other hand, occurs where discipline is flexible but firm and consistent. Discipline is also most beneficial when it is applied only in the child's own interest in terms of his development and only to the extent necessary to achieve its purpose, rather than as an expression of the parents' hostility or need to control or dominate the child.

It appears further that inconsistent or erratic discipline may be as harmful as too little or too much discipline. The inconsistency may stem from parental hostility or indifference (as in the case of the parent who only imposes discipline for his own convenience, e.g., no "back-talk" and keeping quiet or out of the way when father is around) or from parental uncertainty and lack of confidence or from simple mood swings, but whatever its source, inconsistency in parental discipline tends to contribute to maladjustment, conflict, or aggression in the child (24, 188, 190).

Parent-Child Relationships and the Child's Self-Concept

A favorable self-concept (self-esteem) is essential to personal happiness and effective functioning, both in the child and in the adult. Persons who seek psychological and psychiatric help frequently acknowledge that they suffer from feelings of inadequacy and unworthiness (227). They tend to perceive themselves as helpless and inferior (181), have difficulty in either giving or receiving love, and tend to feel isolated and alone (56). They are likely to feel guilty, ashamed, or

depressed, and to derogate their own potential and accomplishments (56). Not surprisingly, a high anxiety level and a negative conception of the self tend to be correlated (32, 44, 67, 135, 165). Furthermore, the anxious child's tendency to derogate himself tends to generalize and affect his image of his bodily integrity and adequacy as well (189, 219). A negative self-concept appears to promote defensiveness in the child's reactions to himself and others (164, 180, 188). Finally, a negative self-concept appears to impair initial school adjustment and subsequent academic progress (32, 62, 74, 168, 197, 221).

While, as we have already seen, the child's self-concept is affected by the way in which his peers and teachers respond to him, it appears likely that for most children the way in which they are treated by parents is of overriding importance in determining their perceptions of themselves (56, 205, 208). How is the child's self-esteem related to the patterns of parental behaviors described above? Some interesting recent studies (56, 184) help to shed considerable light on this question.

What Is Self-Esteem? For purposes of this discussion, "self-esteem is a **personal** judgment of worthiness that is expressed in the attitudes the individual holds toward himself. It is a subjective experience which the individual conveys to others by verbal reports and other overt expressive behavior" (56, 5).

In a study of a large number of preadolescent boys attending the public schools of central Connecticut, Coopersmith (56) found marked differences in the experiential worlds and social behaviors of children differing in self-esteem. Children high in their estimation of themselves approached tasks and persons with the expectation that they would be well received and successful.

They have confidence in their perceptions and judgments and believe that they can bring their efforts to a favorable resolution. Their favorable self-attitudes lead them to accept their own opinions and place credence and trust in their reactions and conclusions. This permits them to follow their own judgments when there is a difference of opinion and also permits them to consider novel ideas. The trust in self that accompanies feelings of worthiness is likely to provide the conviction that one is correct and the courage to express those convictions. The attitudes and expectations that lead the individual with high self-esteem to greater social independence and creativity also lead him to more assertive and vigorous actions. They are more likely to be participants than listeners in group discussions, they report less difficulty in forming friendships, and they will express opinions even when they know these opinions may meet with a hostile reception. Among the factors that underlie and contribute to these actions are their lack of self-consciousness and their lack of preoccupation with personal problems. Lack of self-consciousness permits them to present their ideas in a full and forthright fashion; lack of self-preoccupation permits them to consider and examine external issues.

The picture of the individual with low-esteem that emerges from these results is markedly different. These persons lack trust in themselves and are apprehensive about expressing unpopular or unusual ideas. They do not wish to expose themselves, anger others, or perform deeds that would attract attention. They are likely to live in the shadows of a social group, listening rather than participating, and preferring the solitude of withdrawal above the interchange of participation. Among the factors that contribute to the withdrawal of those low in self-esteem are their marked self-consciousness and preoccupation with inner problems. This great awareness of themselves distracts them from attending to other persons and issues and is likely to result in a morbid preoccupation with their difficulties. The effect is to limit their social intercourse and thus decrease the possibilities of friendly and supportive relationships (56, 70–71).

What patterns of parental characteristics and behaviors distinguished between boys high and low in self-esteem? In general, those with high self-esteem tended to have parents who were also high in self-esteem. These parents, in contrast to parents of boys low in self-esteem, also tended to be more emotionally stable and more self-reliant, resilient, and effective in their attitudes and actions regarding child care. Interactions between the parents of high self-esteem children tended to be marked by greater compatibility and ease, with clearer definitions of each parent's areas of authority and responsibility. While these parents tended to have high expectations of their children, they also provided sound models for them and gave their children consistent encouragement and support.

Mothers of boys high in self-esteem were more accepting of their children and, even more importantly, tended to express their acceptance through specific, everyday manifestations of concern, affection, and close rapport. These mothers were likely to express agreement with such statements as "Children would be happier and better behaved if parents would show an interest in their affairs" and "When you do things together, children feel close to you and talk easier"; and to disagree with such statements as "Children should not annoy their parents with the unimportant problems" and "The trouble with giving attention to children's problems is they usually just make up a lot of stories to keep you interested." In contrast, mothers of children low in self-esteem were "more likely to withdraw from their children, and by their inattentive and neglectful treatment to produce a milieu that is physically, emotionally, and intellectually improverished" (56, 179). Low self-esteem mothers were likely to depreciate their children and to treat them as a burden. Their emotional responses to their children tended to range from hostility to indifference.

Interestingly, mothers of high self-esteem children were **more** likely to enforce established rules carefully and consistently. They used reward as the preferred mode of affecting behavior, but used straightforward and appropriate punishment rather than harsh treatment or loss of love when some sort of punishment was required (56). The fathers of these boys were usually the ones to administer punishment, although they frequently shared that responsibility with the mother. Furthermore, these punishments tended to be perceived as justifiable by the high self-esteem subjects.

In contrast, lack of parental guidance and relatively harsh and disrespectful treatment of children were characteristic of the parents of boys low in self-esteem. Apparently these parents either did not know or did not care to establish and enforce guidelines for their children.

> They are apt to employ punishment rather than reward, and the procedures they do employ lay stress on force and loss of love. The mothers are more likely to administer punishment to these boys, which may have negative connotations and significance for children in this age group. There is an inconsistent and somewhat emotional component in the regulatory behaviors of these parents. They are less concerned, on the one hand, and inclined to employ more drastic procedures, on the other. They propose that punishment is a preferred method of control, yet state that they find it generally ineffective. Their children apparently smart under such a regimen and believe that the control behaviors of their parents are often unwarranted (56, 196–197).

While parents of high self-esteem children were more likely to provide carefully defined standards and limits on behavior for their children, within these limits parental treatment was noncoercive and emphasized the rights and opinions of the child. Typically, the child's views were sought, his opinions respected, and concessions were often granted to him if differences existed. The freedom that prevailed within broad limits permitted the child to enter into discussions as a true participant and to gain confidence from the assertion of his own views. Thus, parents of high self-esteem children were more likely to agree with such statements as "Children should have a say in the making of family plans" and "A child has a right to his own point of view and ought to be allowed to express it." (In the case of the latter statement, 90.3 percent of the parents of high self-esteem children, as compared with only 9.7 percent of the parents of low self-esteem children, were in agreement!) Further, while most parents of high self-esteem children tended to stress "discussion and reasoning" as methods of obtaining the child's cooperation and compliance, most parents of low self-esteem children tended to stress "force and autocratic" measures.

Finally, in their encouragement of independence, parents of high self-esteem boys tended to fall between the parents of children with low self-esteem and parents of those with moderate self-esteem. Parents of boys with high self-esteem seemed to be trying to establish a reasonable balance between protectiveness and encouragement of autonomy. For example, they were less likely than parents in other groups to express anxiety about the child's sleeping outside the home. On the other hand, they were more likely than low-esteem parents and less likely than middle-esteem parents to agree with the statement "A child should be protected from jobs which might be too trying or too hard for him."

Coopersmith's study was limited to preadolescent boys, and the measures of parental attitudes and behavior were obtained concurrently with the self-esteem measures for their children. A recent follow-up study by Robert Sears and his colleagues of a group of sixth-grade boys and girls, whose parents had been studied when the children were 5 years of age, yielded compatible findings, however (**197, 199**). The measure of self-esteem employed was similar to Coopersmith's and was based on the child's self-concepts in a wide range of categories, including physical and mental ability; social relations with peers, parents, and teachers; personal qualities, such as self-confidence and lack of timidity. Parental warmth and acceptance (on the part of both mothers and fathers) were found to be significant antecedents of the self-esteem of both boys and girls. Interestingly, self-esteem was far lower when both parents were cold and unaccepting than when at least one parent displayed warmth and acceptance. Dominating behavior on the part of fathers was associated with lowered self-esteem for boys, though not for girls.

Parent Response to Children's Behavioral Predispositions

Despite general trends, particular patterns of parental behavior do not have identical effects on all children. Furthermore, characteristics exhibited by the child may affect the way that the child is treated by parents, setting up, in effect, a complex feedback system of mutual influence. In addition, some personality characteristics appear more central and more persistent over time than others.

In a longitudinal study at the Institute of Human Development at the University of California at Berkeley (**40, 41, 42**), 45 boys and 40 girls were followed from early childhood through middle adolescence (ages 5 through 16). Two basic dimensions of enduring behavioral predispositions were found: an **emotional expressiveness–reserve** dimension and a **placidity-explosiveness** dimension. How these predispositions will be manifested in specific behaviors appears to be a function of parental patterns of behavior as development proceeds and on the nature of social demands regarding culturally "appropriate" behavior for boys and girls at various developmental stages. For example, the boy who is placid and easy as a toddler and who has an affectionate and rewarding interaction with a calm, stable mother may appear to be in an optimal situation psychologically during this period. However, there appeared to be "some potential long-term limitations of such an apparently ideal experience, since the boy who had been explosive and reactive in early childhood appears as an adult to be a more interesting, perhaps even a more creative individual than his placid contemporary." However, while the placid boy seems to be somewhat penalized when he reaches adolescence, the placid girl appears to be rewarded. She tends to be viewed "as calm and relaxed, intellectually alert, and socially charming; a generally likable, competent, and successful individual" (40, 69).

Similarly, although a boy and girl may both be basically expressive, rather than reserved, this orientation may be reacted to differently by society in the two cases, and hence may lead to different manifestations of this general orientation in specific behaviors. Thus, in the Berkeley study, outgoing assertiveness in boys tended to meet with approval socially, while in girls it tended to be met with ambivalence (40).

At least initially, a parent's affective response to the child and behavior toward him may be determined as much by the child as the converse. In the Berkeley study it was found that: "the mother's affective attitudes develop in the course of her interactions with the expressive or reserved [child] rather than being a factor in bringing about . . . the particular orientation" (40, 40). For example, mothers tended to have a generally positive attitude toward sons and daughters who were expressive in early childhood and more negative feelings toward reserved children. Nevertheless, the closer relationship between a mother and an expressive child would be likely to reinforce the child's outgoing, expressive orientation in later years, while a negative maternal attitude toward a reserved child would be likely to contribute to the child's tendency to withdraw (42). Finally, the salience of a particular parent's attitudes and behaviors is usually a function of age. As the boy grows older (particularly as he approaches adolescence), his relationship with his father is likely to assume increased significance; the same thing is likely to occur in the case of the girl's relationship with her mother (40, 42).

Parental Absence

Thus far we have been discussing the effects of parental influences on the child in the intact family setting. However, families are broken up by death and, increasingly, by divorce, abandonment, or involuntary separation (because of military service, job demands, or other obligations). What are the effects of prolonged parental absence on the child's personality development and adjustment in the middle-childhood years?

Much of the research on parental separation during the early childhood period dealt with separation from the mother—a not surprising fact, in view of the dependency of the young child on direct maternal care. In contrast, most studies of the effects of parental separation upon development during the middle-childhood years have dealt with the effects of father absence, as this is by far the commonest social pattern. In our society children are usually awarded to the mother following divorce or separation of the parents. In socioeconomically disadvantaged families desertion by the father is a far more frequent occurrence than abandonment by the mother; in these families the matriarchal tradition is the stronger. Finally, it is the father who is most likely to be separated involuntarily from the family— through military service, the demands of his job, or even premature death.

Effects of Father Absence on Boys Boys from father-absent homes are more likely than boys from father-present homes to encounter difficulties in social, emotional, and cognitive development. They are more likely to score lower on tests of intellectual performance (**29, 31, 61, 127**) and academic aptitude (**29, 206**) and to perform below grade level on measures of academic achievement (**31, 61, 63**). Interestingly, the patterning of their intellectual performance also differs significantly from that of father-present boys and is more similar to that of girls. For example, father-absent boys are more likely to obtain higher scores in verbal ability than in mathematics, in contrast to the usual male pattern of higher mathematics scores (**48**). The likelihood of "feminine" patterning is greater the longer the absence of the father and the earlier the age at which the separation took place. Father-absent boys are also more likely to display a global (or "field dependent") conceptual style, usually more characteristic of girls, as opposed to an analytical style (**16, 29**). Similar results have been obtained for boys whose fathers are present in the home, but who are ineffective, passive, or neglecting (**27, 31, 48**).

In brief, it appears that having a father present in the home, serving as a competent, effective role model and expressing interest in his son and interacting with him, facilitates the development of intellectual potential and influences its development in a "masculine" direction. In contrast, not having a father or having one who is ineffective or distant from the child is likely to handicap the boy in cognitive development. Obviously, the presence or absence of the father is not the only factor influencing this development, and much of the father-absent boy's ultimate success or failure will depend on the qualities of the mother as the remaining parent.

Boys from father-absent homes are also more likely than those from father-present homes to have emotional and social problems. They are more likely to be impulsive and to have difficulty in delaying gratification and assuming social responsibility (29, 154, 155, 156, 157). It has been suggested that fathers are more likely in our society to represent such values as discipline, order, and punctuality than mothers. Further, mothers whose husbands are absent may be more indulgent and overprotective toward their sons than would otherwise be the case (29, 215).

Boys whose fathers were absent during childhood as a result of World War II behaved in a less masculine way both in fantasy and overt behavior, and they manifested very little aggression (13, 196, 204). Even boys whose fathers had been absent early, but who later returned, continued to be more effeminate in their overt behavior (204). However, there was a marked change in the boys' fantasy expressions. They now produced the maximum amount of aggression in fantasy. The author concludes that father absence during the initial years, followed by later imposition of control by an adult man, tends to produce frustration and conflict over sexual identification.

Similarly, the sons of Norwegian sailors who are often away on extended voyages of two or more years have been studied (46, 98, 216). Among 8- and 9-year-old boys in these sailor families, prolonged absences of the father were linked with lessened adequacy of peer adjustment, infantile and dependent characteristics, and manifestations of conflict over identification through compensatory or overly masculine behavior. Their mothers were more isolated from social contacts, more overprotective, and more concerned with obedience than with happiness and self-realization for their children. This was much less characteristic of father-present households. Father-absent boys are also generally more immature psychologically, have more difficulty in forming satisfying peer relations, and are less popular with their peers (23, 28, 29, 30, 158, 204, 215).

Finally, boys from father-absent homes are significantly more likely than other boys to drop out of school and to become involved in delinquent activities (5, 39, 89, 95, 140). One study showed a significantly higher than average rate of delinquency among boys living with their mothers following the loss of the father through death, parental separation, or divorce (96). When the boy lived with his father following the loss of the mother, however, only an average rate of delinquency was found.

In an effort to explain the relation to delinquency of father absence among boys, a number of investigators "have concluded that the exaggerated toughness, aggressiveness, and cruelty of delinquent gangs reflect the desperate effort of males in lower-class culture to rebel against their early overprotective, feminizing environment and to find a masculine identity" (39, 915).

The age of separation from father also appears to be important. Heatherington (104) found that both early-separated black and white boys (age 4 or earlier) and late-separated boys (after age 6) were more dependent on their peers and somewhat less dependent on adults than boys whose fathers lived at home. But only early-separated boys differed significantly from father-present boys on a number of measures of sex-typing. The former had lower-scores in masculine aggressiveness, masculine sex-role preference, and involvement in competitive, physical contact games. Early-separated boys spent significantly more time in nonphysical, noncompetitive activities, such as reading, working on puzzles, and collecting things. Similar patterns were obtained for both black and white boys, although black boys as a total group showed a somewhat greater involvement in competitive, contact sports than their white peers did. The results of this study suggest that boys who lose their fathers early, before identification can be assumed to have been clearly established, have greater difficulty in establishing a masculine sex-role identification and in acquiring sex-typed traits, while absence of the father after the child reaches age 5 has far less effect.

Effects of Father Absence on Girls The effects of father absence on girls have not been studied as extensively as in the case of boys. Available research data suggest that girls from father-absent homes have higher than average dependency on their mothers (137), especially if the girl has only older sisters as siblings, rather than brothers (29). These girls are also more likely to have emotional problems, to encounter school maladjustment, and to engage in antisocial "acting-out" behavior (105). Father absence during the first ten years of life is associated with deficits in quantitative ability, a finding that appears to parallel the findings for boys in the area of cognitive development (127).

Father-absent girls are also more dependent as adults, but they show little apparent deviation from other women in sex-typed behaviors, in preference for the female role or in relationships with other females (103). As adolescents they do, however, show anxiety about and difficulty in relating to males. Daughters of widows tend to be shy and withdrawn, to become physically tense, and to avoid close proximity to male peers and adults. They also tend to start to date later than other girls and to be sexually inhibited.

In contrast, daughters of divorcees, while also anxious (as evidenced by such behaviors in the presence of males as nailbiting and hair pulling), tend to seek out male peers constantly at the expense of activities with other females. They are also more likely than father-present girls to begin to date earlier and to have sexual intercourse at earlier ages (103, 163).

As in the case of boys, the effects of separation from fathers during early childhood were more marked than those of later separation. Apparently for father-absent girls "lack of opportunity for constructive interaction with a loving attentive father has resulted in apprehension and inadequate skills in relating to males" (103, 324). In general, however, the effects of father absence appear stronger and more pervasive in the case of boys than in the case of girls, possibly due partly to the fact that father-absent girls still have a same-sex identification figure in the home, while father-absent boys do not.

It should be stressed at this point that such effects of absence of either parent are by no means either universal or inevitable. Much depends on the psychological strengths, interests, talents, and skills of the remaining parent. Furthermore, the remaining parent may be able to help to compensate for the other parent's absence by finding parent-surrogates (as in the case of Big Brothers, Brownies, Boy and Girl Scouts, and so on). Several studies have indicated that use of father-surrogates, where the father is absent, ineffective, or antisocial, may help to reduce the incidence of delinquent behavior in boys (29, 89). Continued presence in the home of either parent will do little to help and may, in fact, serve only to hinder the child's development, if the parent is inadequate, rejecting, neglectful, or emotionally disturbed, or if there is extreme tension and conflict between the parents.

Social-Class Differences in the Parent-Child Relationship

Although the extrafamilial environment (teachers and peers) exerts a strong influence on the motives and behaviors of the school-age child, the attitudes and practices of the family are still of major significance. The models that the parents present to the child and the pattern of rewards and punishments they exercise are determined, in large measure, by two sets of factors: the unique personalities of the parents and the values of the social-class setting in which the family lives. Every family belongs to a number of subcultural groups (racial, religious, social class). Members of these groups share many attributes and differ in many ways from the members of other groups. In earlier chapters we reviewed studies indicating that middle- and lower-class families differ in their infant- and child-training practices.

Subcultural influences continue to be effective during middle childhood. Within any particular community, parents of a particular class usually join the same clubs, have similar interests and attitudes, band together against outsiders from other classes, and work together at the same kinds of jobs. Consequently, their ideas about acceptable and unacceptable behavior, including the techniques of child-rearing and discipline, are usually much alike. For example, physical punishment of children is more often condoned among lower-class than among middle-class parents (150) and, therefore, is used more frequently. The reward of artistic interests, on the other hand, is more frequent among middle- than among lower-class families. Honesty, however, is less clearly related to social-class values, being rewarded in all social-class groups. The child's tendency to adopt honesty as a value is, therefore, more dependent upon the degree of honesty displayed by parents (identification) and parental encouragement of this behavior (reward) than upon his social-class membership.

Social-Class Differences in Child-Rearing Practices
Child behavior which is encouraged and rewarded by one social class may be disapproved and punished by

another. Through an intricate system of selective rewards and punishments, parents teach their children the responses, values, and beliefs appropriate for their own social class.

> Class training of the child ranges all the way from the control of the manner and ritual by which he eats his food to the control of his choice of playmates and of his educational and occupational goals. The times and places for his recreation, the chores required of him by his family, the rooms and articles in the house which he may use, the wearing of certain clothes at certain times, the amount of studying required of him, the economic control to which he is subjected by his parents, indeed his very conceptions of right and wrong, all vary according to the social class of the child in question (59, 604).

Most of the evidence indicates that middle-class mothers are more affectionate and less punitive than those of the lower classes. Upper-middle-class mothers "are somewhat warmer and more demonstrative . . . than upper-lower mothers," while the latter "employed physical punishment, deprivation of privileges, and ridicule as techniques of controlling their children more commonly than did upper-middle parents. It appears likely that the upper-middle parents used reasoning and praise more often. . . ." (144, 395). Clearly the basic maternal dimensions of love-hostility and restrictive-permissiveness are associated with the social class of the mother. Differences in personality among children of different classes are no doubt related to these differences in child-rearing practices (22, 46, 144).

Class Differences in Children's Attitudes to Parents If the findings of these studies are valid, lower-class children would be expected to perceive their parents' disciplinary procedures as harsh and punitive, while those in the middle class should see their parents as more lenient. Several investigations indicate that this is so. In one study two groups of fifth-grade children, one lower class and one upper-middle-class, were asked to write compositions concerning a 10-year-old boy's reactions to his younger brother's misbehavior and interference. It was assumed that through the medium of the story, the child would reveal his perceptions of his parents' disciplinary procedures (66).

Twice as many lower- as middle-class children wrote stories involving non-constructive solutions to the problem (e.g., appealing to authority). The vast majority of the solutions suggested by the higher social-class group, but only half of those given by the lower-class children, were constructive, amicable settlements. In general, children of low socioeconomic status were more inclined to use punishment and to avenge misdeeds.

Each subject in this study was also interviewed privately and asked ten questions relating to routine discipline problems in school, at home, or in the neighborhood (e.g., Should children ever talk back to their parents?). The socioeconomically more favored children revealed positive attitudes toward their parents' treatment and toward authority in general. Lower-class children viewed authority, including their parents, as unreasonable and severe. Hence they revealed more rigid compliance and greater fear of deviating from fixed rules and regulations (66).

Somewhat similar results were obtained in another study of the influences of social-class variations in discipline procedures on children's attitudes toward parents (148). The subjects, three groups of 50 children each in grades 5 to 8, were drawn from three schools representing upper-, middle-, and lower-class economic levels. Each child was seen individually and, after good rapport had been established, he was asked to speak out the first ten ideas (associations) that came to him when he thought of his mother and father. Although there was great variability in each group, children of different economic levels generally revealed fairly distinct attitudes toward their parents. For example, as a group, middle-class children manifested pleasant feelings, accepting and respecting their parents, whom they regarded as helpful and permissive. Few of these children appeared to be overly dependent or hostile to their parents.

Lower-class children, on the other hand, had the greatest number of unfavorable reactions. Of the three groups, they were the most ambivalent (had mixed love and hostility) toward the parents and were the most insecure. Although they had relatively few feelings of rejection or overdependence, they felt that their parents were generally repressive and gave them little companionship. The upper-class group was the most variable but as a group they expressed the most severe feelings of rejection and overdependency. Hostility was less common in this group than among the lower-class subjects, but adoration, together with fear and guilt, was more prevalent.

Influence of Siblings

Although the personalities of the parents and their behavior toward the child are of primary importance in shaping his development, the child's relationship with his siblings, if he has any, may also exert some influence on the development of his personality.

More than 80 percent of American children have siblings. In the child's interactions with them, he may learn patterns of loyalty, helpfulness, and protection or of conflict, domination, and competition, and these patterns may be generalized to other social relationships. The number of siblings a child has and his relationship to them constitute an important aspect of the child's learning situation, and hence may strongly affect what and how the child learns at home. For example, the social learning situation encountered by the first-born child obviously differs from that of his younger siblings. Oldest children may be handicapped by the relative inexperience of their parents. They may be pushed too hard to accomplish, or they may have to care for younger children before they are ready for such responsibility. They alone must face the difficult adjustment involved in losing "only child" status. The psychological influence of siblings on the child's development is likely to be felt most keenly when the child is between 3 and 6 years of age. The arrival of a new sibling at this time provides the greatest threat to the first-born. From the perspective of the second-born, it is the time when the older sibling is perceived as an omnipotent and invulnerable competitor, with special privileges and status. Thus each of the ordinal positions carries with it its own set of advantages and disadvantages.

The situation, however, is seldom a simple one. The potential effects of birth order will depend on the sex of other siblings (both older and younger), their proximity in age, the total number of children in the family, and the way in which they are treated by both parents. For example, in Japan and some other traditionally oriented societies first-born males are likely to be treated quite differently from other children in the family (195). They are likely to have more privileges, both financial and social (for example, maintaining the family name and property), as well as greater responsibility. Thus, they may be more likely to achieve more, but also to be more subject to stress (18, 49, 195). In contrast, in contemporary middle-class American families, there is often a conscious effort to try to treat children of both sexes as equally and fairly as circumstances permit.

Nevertheless, birth order appears to have some influence on personality development in our society, even when other relevant factors, such as social class, sex of siblings, and family size are held constant. Thus, first-borns are generally more adult-oriented, more conscientious and prone to feelings of guilt, more achievement-oriented, more affiliative, more concerned with being cooperative and responsible, more conforming to social pressures, and more inclined to choose occupations involving a parent-surrogate role, such as teacher (4, 79, 116, 183, 196, 199). They also appear somewhat more likely to encounter psychological problems than younger siblings, although a number of investigators have exaggerated the extent of this tendency through a failure to properly control for such factors as the greater incidence of first-born children in the population at large (4, 7, 195).

The best designed, most reliable, and most informative studies have been those that control for family size and socioeconomic status and that take into account the effects, not only of birth order, but also of interrelated variables, such as sex and spacing of siblings. In one such carefully controlled investigation, Helen Koch (119, 120, 121) studied 384 subjects, ages 5 to 6, from two-children families. The four types of sibling combinations (older boy–younger girl, older girl–younger boy, two sisters, two brothers) were equally represented, and there were groups of siblings separated by one to two years, two to four years, and four to six years. Teachers of these children observed and rated the children on a variety of traits. All of the major variables—sex, ordinal position, and spacing of the sibling

—influenced the child's personality, with the sex of the sibling being one of the most important determinants of the adoption of sex-typed behaviors.

Sex of Sibling In general, children with brothers had more "masculine" traits than children with sisters. The girls with brothers, as compared with the girls with sisters, were more ambitious, more aggressive, and did better on tests of intellectual ability. Girls with older brothers had more "tomboyish" traits than girls with older sisters. Boys with older sisters were less aggressive and less daring than boys with older brothers. These results would be expected from our knowledge of the identification process and the imitation that occurs between siblings. In many cases, the older sibling is viewed by the younger as stronger, more competent, and in control of important goals that the younger one wants but does not yet possess. The older child can stay up later, eat adult foods, and may even be perceived as the family favorite. The younger sibling would strive, therefore, to become similar to the older by attempting to adopt the latter's behaviors.

Ordinal Position First-born children tended to have stronger consciences than second-borns; they tended to be more responsible, less aggressive, and more intellectually curious. However, the effect of ordinal position is very much dependent on the sex of the siblings and the spacing between them. When siblings were of the same sex and separated by less than two years, there were few differences between them. When the spacing increased to four years or the sibs were of the opposite sex, behavioral differences between them were more marked. For example, if a boy had a brother four years younger, he was less aggressive and more responsible than a boy with a sister four years younger than himself.

Spacing Koch feels that a two- to four-year difference between siblings is the most threatening to the older child. If the first-born is 3 years old when the new baby arrives, he is apt to become anxious over possible loss of nurturance. If the first-born is only 1 year old when the new sib arrives, his self-image is still so diffuse and unclear that he will probably not regard the baby as a major threat or competitor for his mother's affection. If the older child is 7 or 8 when the new sibling arrives, he is much more independent of his parents and is less threatened by the newcomer in the family. Moreover, the older child in this case is more likely than a sibling only two years older to become a hero figure or identification model for the younger child.

It appears that sibling position is an important psychological variable because it duplicates, in microcosm, many of the significant social interaction experiences of adolescence and adulthood. To be first or second, to have high or low power, to side with authority or rebel against it, to feel guilt over hostility, or to be able to "place the blame" are tendencies that begin to be differently strengthened during early childhood as a result of the child's sibling position.

Sibling Rivalry Some degree of sibling rivalry is inevitable in all families with two or more children. Among young children, and particularly first-born children, rivalry and jealousy may be precipitated by the birth of a baby—an unsought intruder who not only demands a share of the parents' attention, but often, at least initially, a disproportionate share. Jealousy of a new arrival is likely to be strongest in the child over 2 and under 5, because he is still very dependent on his parents and has few interests as yet outside the family circle (**202, 205**). But the older child may feel jealousy too, especially if there is a sudden and marked decrease in the parental attention he has become accustomed to receiving. On the other hand, when an older child is not ignored and when there is a great enough age difference, there may be considerable affection and pride in being able to play the role of "big brother" or "big sister."

Among older siblings, the extent of sibling rivalry—frequently manifested in what may seem to the parents like endless "baiting, bantering, bickering, battling, belittling, and bedlam" (**205, 377**)—is most prevalent when children are fairly close in age and are all within the middle-childhood years (**202, 205**). However, even between preadolescent and adolescent siblings, taunting by the younger and belittling by the older are hardly unknown. In general, parents may best alleviate (but not eliminate) sibling rivalry by avoiding comparisons of one child with another, attempting to treat all fairly, and staying out of minor skirmishes.

Sibling Death in Childhood In view of the important role that siblings play in the life of the child and his often strong emotional involvement with them, it might be anticipated that death of a sibling from accident or illness would have a significant traumatic effect on the child. And this indeed appears to be the case, particularly during the middle-childhood period from 6 to 12 years of age (**33**).

Sibling death may precipitate grief and mourning, depression, anxiety, delinquent acting-out, or withdrawal and regression in the child (**25, 86, 107**). There are likely to be "strong and exaggerated feelings in relation to the lost sibling—either hostility or overidealization" (**33, 173**), as well as feelings of loss, guilt, and concern over one's own bodily integrity. The particular kinds of reactions the child is likely to have will, of course, be influenced by the nature of his prior relationship to the sibling, his age, and his cognitive development (**33**). Death of a child imposes on the parents and other adult caretakers an important responsibility to see that the remaining siblings are helped to work out their often complex, confusing, and anxiety-producing feelings before longer term psychological problems are created (**33, 200**). Needless to say, this same obligation applies in the case of a parental death. Even where a child appears to be adjusting well to a sibling or parental death, closer examination will often reveal that he is using the defense mechanism of denial (see pp. 391–392) to avoid confronting his true feelings.

DEVELOPMENT OF CONSCIENCE AND MORAL STANDARDS

While the precursors of conscience and moral standards may be seen in the pre-school years (see pp. 404–406), the middle-childhood years represent a critical period during which conscience develops at a rapid rate. While the older pre-school child may gradually begin to abandon the relative hedonism of the 2- or 3-year-old, whose behavior is pretty much governed by doing whatever he wants to do at a particular moment, his early conscience development tends to be erratic, largely confined to prohibitions against specific behaviors, and based on external rather than internal sanctions. If this situation persisted into later childhood and adult life, we would have to have a host of vigilant authorities keeping an eagle eye on the activities of us all if organized society were to survive. Gradually, however, from about 4 to 6 years on into middle childhood, conscience in most children becomes less confined to specific behaviors and begins to involve the development of more generalized abstract standards; it becomes less exclusively determined by external rewards and punishments and more by internal sanctions; and it begins to involve not only the avoidance of prohibitions, but also the pursuit of what one **should** do.

Piaget believes that from ages 5 to 12 the child's concept of justice passes from a rigid and inflexible notion of right and wrong, learned from his parents, to a sense of equity in moral judgments that takes into account the specific situation in which a moral violation has occurred. For example, the 5-year-old is apt to view lying as bad, regardless of the situation or the circumstances in which it occurs. With increasing age, the child becomes more flexible and realizes that there are exceptions to this strict rule [that is, that there are some circumstances under which lying may be justifiable (**166**)]. Piaget's techniques of investigation included conversing with children and asking them questions about moral issues or about the ethics of characters and events in short stories. For instance, in a conversation with a child he would ask, "Why shouldn't you cheat in a game?" Or, after telling a story about a mother who gives the biggest piece of cake to her most obedient child, he would question the subject about the justice of her action.

Piaget's observations suggest that as the child becomes a member of larger, more varied peer groups, rules and moral judgments may become less absolute and authoritarian, and more dependent on the needs and desires of the group. "Moral relativism," based on cooperation and respect for others, eventually replaces "moral realism": "For very young children, a rule is a sacred reality because it is traditional; for the older ones it depends upon a mutual agreement" (**166**, 192). For example, children between the ages of 6 and 12 were told stories involving a conflict between obedience to parents and a sense of justice or equality, and were asked to solve the conflict. While almost all 6-year-olds chose solutions involving "obedience to adults," the percentage of children choosing this solution decreased steadily with age.

In another phase of this investigation, children were asked to give examples of what they regard as unfair. "Behaviors forbidden by parents" were mentioned by 64 percent of the children between 6 and 8 years of age, but only by 7 percent of those in the 9- to 12-year-old group. On the other hand, inequality in punishment and treatment were mentioned by 73 percent of the 9- to 12-year-olds, but only 27 percent of those 6 to 8 years of age.

On the basis of numerous studies of this sort, Piaget concluded that

> there are three great periods in the development of the sense of justice in the child. One period, lasting up to the age of 7–8 during which justice is subordinated to adult authority; a period contained approximately between 8–11, and which is that of progressive equilitarianism; and finally a period which sets in toward 11–12, and during which purely equalitarian justice is tempered by considerations of equity (166, 314).

Other investigators have repeated or elaborated some of Piaget's studies. For example, in one study boys and girls in the second, fifth, and eighth grades were questioned about the correct thing to do if one child hit a second child (70). The older children were more apt than the younger ones to ask for the particular circumstances of the moral violation and the motive for the aggressive act. In another recent study (210) 55 percent of primary-grade children, but only 7 percent of middle-school children expressed the view that a rule should never be broken. Nine out of ten of the older children gave replies indicating that it depended on the circumstances or the morality of the rule itself. These findings support Piaget's hypothesis that the older child views a rule violation in the total context in which it appears and his reaction is influenced by situational factors, as well as by the morality of the rule.

There is a progressive decline in suggestions for solving conflicts by subordination to adult demands or acceptance of authority (including majority opinion) between the ages of 6 and 13 (129, 130). During the same period, solutions based on moral relativism, reciprocity, and equality increased. Summarizing these changes in moral concepts, Murphy says: "Moral realism yields gradually during childhood to an ethics of reciprocity; what is right is now defined not in terms of self-evident and inherent necessity but in terms of a sense of balance or justice. Rightness is a matter of the mutual consideration of needs" (160, 386).

One investigator attempted to test directly the relationship between the nature of the child's moral concepts and his interactions with parents and peers (138). Moral judgment tests and questionnaires about parents and peers were administered to 244 American boys between 5 and 14 years of age. From the boys' answers to the questionnaire items, the investigator derived measures of several aspects of authority and peer relations.

Analysis of the questionnaire data revealed that boys who were strictly controlled by their parents, currently or in the past, tended to conform rigidly to adult-dictated regulations. Compared with the children of less strict parents, these boys were more likely to make moral judgments primarily on the basis of "such moral prescriptions as . . . respect for property, obedience to teachers, and veracity" (**138, 17**). They were less likely than the other boys to be influenced by the obligations of friendship and peer-group membership.

It is probable that the children of strict parents were more afraid of violating parental prohibitions than were the children of more permissive parents. As we saw earlier, the children who were least likely to be influenced by peer values feared withdrawal of parental acceptance for the commission of prohibited acts.

Kohlberg and his associates (**122, 123, 124, 125**) have studied the development of children's capacity to judge action in terms of moral standards as opposed to prohibitions or punishments. They asked children to evaluate deviant acts which they were told were followed by reward, and conforming acts which they were told were followed by punishment (**124, 321**). A careful analysis of individual responses led the investigators to define six developmental types grouped into three moral levels. At the lowest level ("premoral") the child was guided by an orientation toward punishment and obedience (Type 1) or a naive kind of hedonism (Type 2). At an intermediate level ("morality of conventional rule-conformity"), morality was viewed as a matter of trying to maintain the approval of others and good relations with them, a "good boy-good girl morality" (Type 3) or a reliance on the precepts of authority (Type 4). At the highest level ("morality of self-accepted moral principles"), the child was able to view morality in terms of contractual obligations and democratically accepted law (Type 5) or "morality of individual principles of conscience" (Type 6).

Four-year-olds tended to judge an act as good or bad in terms of its reinforcement, that is, whether it led to punishment or reward, rather than in terms of the rule. The children 5 to 7 years old evaluated the act in terms of its moral label, that is, whether the act itself was considered good or bad, rather than in terms of its reinforcement in the story. However, older children continued to give the possibilities of future punishment as reasons for an act being bad, so that the distinction between badness and situational reinforcement was in terms of long-range as opposed to short-range reinforcement. By preadolescence, a majority of children made "disinterested" moral judgments and formulated some concept of a morally good self (**124**).

Somewhat similar results were obtained in a recent study of children's developing ideas on "rules, justice, and compliance" from kindergarten to college (**210**). When asked, "What is a rule?" children in the period from kindergarten through the second grade tended to emphasize **prohibition,** that is, they defined a rule as a guideline forbidding specific behaviors. Older children, from fourth to eighth grades, increasingly emphasized **prescription,** that is, they tended to define a rule as being "a general, neutral regulatory guideline" (**210, 237**). To a lesser extent, the older children also emphasized what the investigators refer to as its **beneficial/rational** aspect, that is, "a personally or societally purposive, reasonable

guideline" (**210,** 237). For example, a primary-school boy gave this prohibitive response: "A rule is not to run around, not to hit anybody, not to break anything."
But an eighth-grade boy emphasized the prescriptive and beneficial/rational aspects: "Well, a rule is mainly something to keep, to make the place better" (**210,**
237–238).

Similarly, when asked "Why should people follow rules?" primary students
ranked the avoidance of negative consequences first; middle-school children gave
replies indicating that they considered social conformity most important, followed
by an emphasis on acting in accordance with general rational, beneficial, utilitarian principles. College-age youth ranked "rational/beneficial/utilitarian" first,
followed by what Kohlberg would call "principled" behavior (see Table 10.1).

Interestingly, however, when asked further, "Why do **you** [bold ours] follow
rules?" the answers of most middle-school children and adolescents showed a shift
toward earlier, more "primitive" levels, although they were cognitively capable
of understanding loftier reasons and subscribed to these. Thus 60 percent of primary children, 47 percent of middle-school children, and even 25 percent of older
adolescents cited "avoidance of negative consequences"; no primary children, only
7 percent of middle-school children, and 22 percent of older adolescents mentioned rational/beneficial/utilitarian reasons.

Kohlberg views such findings as supporting the general developmental view
of morality espoused by Piaget, although he differs on specifics. In his own work,
he found considerable overlap at various ages in the use of his six moral types
(see Fig. 10.2), although the frequency of the more primitive types declined with

Table 10.1 **Why should people follow rules? (Percentages by age)**[a]

| | EDUCATIONAL GROUP | | | COMPARISONS (BY **T** TEST) | |
CATEGORIES	PRIMARY (1)	MIDDLE SCHOOL (2)	COLLEGE (3)	(1) x (2)	(2) x (3)
Avoid negative consequences	50	13	3	**p** $<$0.01	**p** $<$0.05
Authority	5	—	—		
Personal conformity	35	13	9	**p** $<$0.05	
Social conformity	10	53	25	**p** $<$0.01	**p** $<$0.01
Rational/beneficial/ utilitarian	5	27	51	**p** $<$0.05	**p** $<$0.05
Principled	—	—	5		

[a]This question is multiple coded; therefore, percentages may total over 100 percent.
Where answers were idiosyncratic or uncodable, the categories were omitted from the table.
Source: J. L. Tapp, and F. J. Levine. Compliance from kindergarten to college: A
speculative research note. **Journal of Youth and Adolescence,** 1972, **1,** 233–249. By permission.

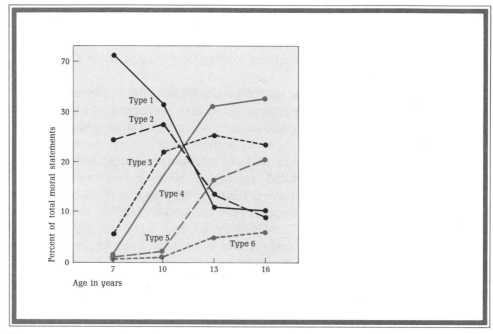

Figure 10.2 Use of six types of moral judgments at four ages. (From L. Kohlberg. The development of children's orientation toward a moral order: 1. Sequence in the development of moral thought. **Vita Humana** [New title: **Human Development**], 1963, **6,** 16. [Karger, Basel/New York 1963.] By permission.)

age and that of the more mature types increased with age. As compared with Piaget's view, "the data suggest that the "natural" aspects of moral development are continuous and a reaction to the whole social world rather than a product of a certain stage, a certain concept . . . or a certain type of social relations . . ." (**124,** 322–323).

Unless a reasonable degree of conscience development takes place during the middle-childhood years, that is, unless standards of right and wrong are established, the child, and later the adult, is apt to yield to asocial temptations offered by others or to his own urges for uncontrolled aggressive, sexual, and regressive behavior. On the other hand, if the learning of internal standards and prohibitions (superego development) is unduly strong, crippling guilt may develop in association with a wide variety of behaviors and thoughts. Furthermore, as we shall see later, defenses erected against painful guilt feelings may lead to the development of psychological and psychosomatic symptoms.

Obviously, mature conscience development requires cognitive maturation, as well as a number of complex psychological processes based on learning. As Kohlberg points out, without the sort of cognitive development described in Chapter 7, the child is unable to carry out the degree of abstract thinking required for the development of generalized standards, as opposed to highly specific, concrete prohibitions (122, 123). Nor would be become capable of shifting from absolute and rigid standards to more flexible and relative ones in which, for example, motivational intent, rather than simply the act itself, is taken into account in assessing blame or determining guilt. Many cognitive functions play a role in conscience development. As the child develops, concepts "of time, of future gratifications, of consequences, of right and wrong, of values and ideals," he becomes increasingly aware of the effects of his actions (124, 58). His perception of the feelings of others also becomes more acute, and he begins to see the logical necessity for people to cooperate with one another in the interests of all (124).

However, conscience development is far from being solely, or even primarily, a function of cognitive maturation. While a child's cognitive development may make him aware of moral values and standards, commitment to following them will depend on other factors, such as parental identification and the probability of experiencing guilt for violations. A variety of studies (3, 11, 106, 108, 133, 199, 218) indicate that the development of conscience—as manifested by internal reactions to transgression in the form of guilt, or by the adoption of moral standards which the child feels responsible for maintaining—is fostered by the presence of parental warmth and love (24). This appears reasonable in terms of two mechanisms that appear to be involved in conscience development: identification and fear of loss of love or approval. If a responsible parent, because of his parental warmth and love, is a rewarding figure for the child to identify with and model himself after, adoption of the parent's standards as his own ("internalization") is more likely to occur, and violations of these standards then become painful and to be avoided because they result in an impaired self-image. The second probable mechanism is more negative in character. If the child has been rewarded by parental love and approval, transgressions against parental standards may produce anxiety based upon fear of parental disapproval or withdrawal of love. Most children have at least some anxiety over possible loss of love from their parents and acquire the standards their parents practice at least partly in order to keep the anxiety low and under control. This process, of course, assumes that the parent, as a socializing agent, has acquired reward value in the first place through parental warmth and nurturance. In other words, fear of withdrawal of love can hardly serve as a motivation when there is no love to lose (3, 24, 106).

It is interesting to note that, contrary to popular stereotypes, children who tend to have internalized standards rather than merely a fear of detection and punishment report that their mothers are less likely to use physical threats of force, deprivation, or direct commands as disciplinary techniques and are more likely to use love-oriented methods (e.g., how much the child's behavior "hurt them"; 108). The former techniques are more likely to produce counteraggression from the child, and while they may sometimes prevent transgressions in the immediate situation out of fear of retribution, they appear relatively ineffective in promoting the development of internal moral standards.

Parenthetically, it has been suggested (24) that love-oriented techniques of discipline may also faciliate the development of conscience by providing a child with a better learning situation for the development of standards—through increased opportunities for identifying the nature of trangressions; providing cues for labeling of transgressions, including self-critical statements; and use of reinforcements carefully geared to the specific behaviors involved (as opposed, for example, to generally punitive parental behaviors, poorly directed parental yelling and screaming, and so on). Becker notes:

> . . . the parent who talks and reasons with the child about his misbehavior is more likely to provide the child with a clear understanding of what he did wrong, so that the anxiety of that misbehavior is connected to the right cues. Secondly, as Aronfreed has suggested, explanations and reasons provide the child with internal resources for evaluation of his own behavior; that is, the child gains explicit training in making moral judgments (24, 185).

It has also been asserted that one of the critical factors involved in love-oriented techniques of discipline may be the reinforcement by the parent of explicit reactions from the child.

> Love-oriented discipline is likely to continue till the child makes some symbolic renunciation of his wrong-doing. Thus self-admission and verbal recognition of wrong-doing may be reinforced by regaining parental approval and ending the punishment. Physical punishment is more likely to occur all at once and be over, and what the child does toward the end of preventing future occurrences is not related to the ending of punishment (24, 18).

Parent-Child Relationships and Conscience Development

From the foregoing, it appears clear that the standards of parents themselves and the nature of parent-child relationships play a crucial role in determining whether a child's developing conscience will be weak, normal, or overly strict and punitive. The parent whose own conscience is defective—either in terms of a deficit or in terms of excessive rigidity and harshness—can hardly serve as an appropriate model for normal superego development in the child. Furthermore, the nature of the parent-child relationship will determine, in large measure, whether adoption by the child of parental standards as his own will be rewarding. Ideally, it would appear that optimal superego development in the child is facilitated (1) if the parent's own conscience and moral standards are mature and reasonable, not overly rigid, harsh, and inflexible, and (2) if adoption of the parent's standards by the child is based on positive identification and modeling. Whether anxiety over loss of love as a mechanism for the child's adoption of parental standards will also be helpful, rather than harmful, will depend in great measure on how this mechanism is employed by the parent. When disapproval and disappointment are confined to the child's transgressions themselves, rather than extended to the child as a whole, and when the disapproval is not extreme, harsh, impulsive, or otherwise inappropriate, socialization may be fostered without crippling effects on the child.

But if it is used, as unfortunately is sometimes the case, as a kind of "emotional blackmail" to control and dominate the child, it may result not only in an overly anxious, superego-ridden child, but a child whose development of autonomy, self-confidence, and self-reliance is impaired.

As we shall see later, the child whose superego development is deficient, either because his parents' standards are themselves deficient or because disturbed parent-child relationships mitigate against identifying positively with parental values, or both, may become delinquent or otherwise lacking in responsible social behavior. Rather than responding to mature internal standards, he may be guided primarily by external considerations of probable reward and punishment. On the other hand the child whose superego is unusually harsh and rigid as a result of strict and emotionally constricting demands on the part of parents who themselves possess rigid, punitive standards, may encounter severe psychological problems. Some of these problems may become especially evident in the later years of middle childhood, as even normal children tend to have difficulty integrating conscience demands into their developing personality structures in this age period.

By about 6 or 7, the child has acquired the capability of feeling guilt. The standards he sets for himself and the particular causes for guilt will continue to change and develop as he grows older.

PSYCHOLOGICAL AND PSYCHOPHYSIOLOGICAL PROBLEMS OF MIDDLE CHILDHOOD

Anxiety, frustration, and conflict are a part of the human condition, and all children will encounter some psychological problems, at one time or another, during childhood. Furthermore, there is some evidence that psychological problems are more frequent at certain ages than at others. For example, referrals to psychiatric and psychological clinics tend to peak in the periods 4 to 7 years and 9 to 11 years, as well as 14 to 16 years for adolescents (7, 182). It has been hypothesized that there may be "certain 'natural' stages and transitions that interrupt the course of development and give rise to temporary imbalances or maladaptations . . ." (7, 704). These stages and transitions may involve accelerations in physical or cognitive development or rapid changes in parental expectations and general social demands (for example, toilet training, beginning school). At all ages prior to puberty, psychological problems are more frequent among boys than girls, which leads some investigators to speak of the "handicap" of being a male (7). For example, during the first grade, boys are referred for clinical help eleven times as frequently as girls for such problems as "social and emotional immaturity, a syndrome characterized by a high rate of absenteeism, fatigability, inability to attend and concentrate, shyness, poor motivation for work, underweight, inability to follow directions, slow learning, infantile speech patterns, and problems in the visual-motor and visual-perception areas" (7, 723). During middle childhood, clinic referrals are consistently several times higher for boys than girls for speech and reading difficulties, personality and behavioral problems, school failure, and delinquency (7, 182). Girls' emotional difficulties are more likely to be manifested in symptoms of anxiety, fearfulness, and timidity; in contrast, among boys, complaints of aggressiveness, destructiveness, and lack of control are more frequent (7).

Most of the more common psychological problems of childhood prove transient and limited in their severity, if the child's neurophysiological functioning is normal, if he is not subjected to abnormally intense traumas in his social environment, and if his parents provide good role models. Such parents are characteristically warm and accepting, consistent and flexible in their disciplinary techniques, and not so controlling or dominating that they thwart the child's development of autonomy, self-reliance, and mastery behavior (see pp. 422–428). The child of such parents will typically have reasonable needs and, in considerable measure, will possess the means for satisfying them. He will have a conscience that can serve as a reliable internal guide to responsible and rewarding personal and social behavior, rather than one which is either seriously defective in providing him with appropriate internal controls or so harsh, punitive, and arbitrary that it conflicts with his normal impulses and needs. Finally, the psychologically favored child will encounter a social environment—in his neighborhood, school, and home, in his peer group, and in society at large—that values him as an individual, provides for his basic needs, and offers an opportunity for optimal development of his potential.

In contrast, the child whose parents and society have seriously failed him in one way or another may be expected to encounter psychological or psychosomatic problems which are more severe, more chronic, and more refractory to treatment. This book is not a treatise on the psychopathology of childhood, and adequate texts are available elsewhere (7, 84, 109, 110, 111, 117, 200). Nevertheless, it may be valuable to discuss briefly some of the more common forms of psychological and psychosomatic symptomatology that may occur in middle childhood.

Some of the manifestations of psychological problems in childhood are relatively easily understood. The child whose efforts at mastery behavior have met consistently with criticism or ridicule for his ineptness may be anxious and uncertain in the face of new and challenging situations and inclined to withdraw and avoid them. The child who has been subjected to an endless series of injustices or rejections, has had only harsh, arbitrary, or inconsistent discipline, and has not developed strong internal superego controls may emerge as angry, rebellious, unmanageable, and generally lacking in conformity to the social patterns one would expect of his age group. The child with overly meticulous, compulsive, overprotective parents who inhibit any evidence of spontaneous emotion and who place great emphasis on being controlled, orderly, and cautious may well end up being overly meticulous, cautious, and lacking in spontaneity himself.

It is not difficult to appreciate, at least in a general sense, the transient depression of the bereaved child or the anxiety and bad dreams of a child who has just been through a terrifying real-life experience. Other kinds of symptoms, however, are not always so easily understood: phobias (strong fears) that seem unrealistic or fantastic and appear to have no basis in actual experience; motoric disturbances, such as tics, in which a child constantly and without apparent awareness blinks his eyes or shrugs his shoulders; obsessional, recurrent, apparently absurd thoughts that won't go away; compulsive behaviors, such as a need constantly to wash one's hands; and psychosomatic symptoms of various sorts.

Anxiety and the Mechanisms of Defense

In most cases, the original source of such symptoms lies in the child's anxiety about something—fear of loss of love or separation; of having angry, hostile feelings; of sexual impulses; of personal inadequacy; of punishment or retribution. The antecedents of his anxiety in the early years were discussed in Chapter 9. Frequently, the anxiety also involves guilt, in that the child's impulses are unacceptable to his conscience, that is, to the internal standards he has developed about what is "right" and "wrong," "good" and "wicked." One of the difficulties in understanding these anxieties arises from the fact that the sources of the child's true concerns are not directly expressed. Instead, the child may unconsciously erect psychological defenses against their expression, because allowing such disturbing impulses and feelings to find conscious expression would produce painful anxiety and guilt, and sometimes even panic. The basic function of these mechanisms of defense (85) is to help the child avoid painful feelings of anxiety. Some defense mechanisms may have the additional advantage of allowing some gratification of unconscious impulses while still allowing the individual to remain unaware of them. Thus the blue-stocking censor of "pornographic" literature may convince himself, by virtue of his dedication to suppressing such literature, that he has no illicit sexual impulses himself, but at the same time he may gain secret satisfactions from having to read this material in order to "protect" others.

The kinds of defenses people are most likely to employ will vary, depending on the individual's personality structure and specific learning experiences. A number of these defense mechanisms are more easily observed in children than in adults, because of the child's relative lack of sophistication and the immaturity of his ego.

In **repression,** the most basic underlying defense, anxiety-producing impulses, memories, and the like are simply kept from conscious awareness. When the individual's associations begin to encroach on such painful areas, anxiety is increased, and the individual's thoughts move off in another direction, with the result that anxiety then decreases. Thus repression as a defense tends to be employed and learned because it is rewarded. The total inability of an individual to recall a particularly painful experience provides one example; the transient block in remembering the name of a familiar person whom one dislikes provides another. In a closely related, but more primitive defense, **denial,** obvious reality factors are treated by the child as if they did not exist; an amusing, if touching, example might be the little girl who, while sobbing her heart out, keeps insisting, "I am not unhappy!"

In denial, the child insists that an anxiety-arousing event or situation is not true, and he believes his denial is accurate. For example, the child who has been openly rejected by his mother may deny that she is hostile and insist that she is a kind and loving person. Some children who have been rejected by their families deny that these people are their parents. The child insists that he is adopted and that his true parents love him.

When repression is used, the child blots out the anxious or frightening event by removing it completely from awareness. Repression is neither a refusal to remember an event nor a denial of its reality. Rather the thought or event has been removed from consciousness by forces beyond the child's control. For example, the child may repress his memory of a violent argument between his parents or of resentful thoughts he has felt toward one of his parents. Although he was clearly aware of these thoughts at one time, after repression the child is unaware of them, and questioning him will not bring them to light.

There is a subtle distinction between denial and repression. In repression the child has no awareness of the frightening or painful thought (for example, he cannot recall his parents' heated argument). In denial, the anxiety-arousing thought is denied (he actively denies having heard the argument).

In projection and displacement, an unacceptable feeling or impulse is acknowledged, but is attributed to other sources. **Projection** is the ascription of an undesirable thought or action to another person, when, in reality, the thought or action applies to oneself. The child of 5 often projects aggression and blame for misdeeds onto other people. For example, a child may be running after a playmate and in so doing bump into an adult. The child may project the blame on the child he was chasing by saying, "He made me chase him. If he didn't make me chase him, I wouldn't have bumped into you." The plea, "He started the fight, Mother, not me," is one of the most common examples of projection in young children.

In **displacement,** the child has the appropriate emotional response, but it is not attributed to its true source, as we shall see in discussing childhood phobias. A child's fear of his father, for example, may be too painful for him to acknowledge, but he **is** fearful, and therefore, he may attribute the fear to an acceptable symbolic substitute for the father (e.g., lions). A little girl's intense fear of snakes, or even perhaps of objects such as pencils, may conceal her underlying fear of masculine sexuality.

Rationalization is a comforting defense that all of us—not only children, but adults as well—engage in. It involves providing oneself with socially acceptable reasons for behavior or attitudes, when the real reason would not be acceptable to one's conscience, and hence would, if permitted into awareness, lead to painful anxiety and guilt. The parent who harshly punishes his child because of his own intense anger toward the child, but who then says he is "doing it for his [i.e., the child's] own good" is engaging in rationalization.

Reaction formation, as it is termed by psychoanalysts, has already been illustrated in the case of the censor of pornographic literature described above. Similarly, the child who is overly preoccupied with being spotlessly clean and tidy may actually be defending himself against strong and unacceptable wishes to be dirty and messy, either literally or symbolically (e.g., sexually). It is as though the child was saying, "I can't have any desire to be messy or dirty, because look how preoccupied I am with being clean." As we shall see, reaction formation frequently plays a role in childhood compulsions.

Behavioral withdrawal is one of the most frequently used defenses of preschool children; it is the direct avoidance of, or flight from, threatening situations or people. The child will hide his eyes or run to his room when a stranger enters the house; he will refuse to approach a group of strange children despite his desire to play with them; he will shy away from a jungle gym if he doubts his ability to climb it successfully.

The withdrawal response temporarily removes the child from the feared situation, but the tendency to withdraw becomes stronger each time the child practices this behavior. This defense is therefore often maladaptive, for the child who refuses to cope with stressful situations may eventually become fearful of all problems and stresses and may never learn to handle adequately the crises that are inevitable in the course of development.

Regression is the adoption—or, more accurately, the readoption—of a response that was characteristic of an earlier phase of development. Thumb sucking or bedwetting are examples of regressive behavior in children who have stopped such behavior for some period of time. In regression, the child is attempting to withdraw from a current anxiety-arousing situation to the more gratifying and less anxious state of infancy.

Regressive behavior frequently occurs when a new baby is brought into the home. Some 4-year-olds are made anxious by the anticipation that a new baby will displace them and obtain the love and attention that they have been receiving. By adopting infantile behaviors they attempt to gain attention and to retain desired parental nurturance.

As already stated, the ultimate function of these and other defense mechanisms is to protect the child from impulses, thoughts, and feelings that would lead to painful anxiety if the child became aware of them.

Fears and Phobias in Middle Childhood

The importance of fears, or sources of anxiety, in the mental life of the 10-year-old child is seen in a study (75) in which children were asked to draw the most important events in their lives. Almost one-third of the drawings illustrated fear experiences. Although many childhood fears are a function of direct experience with frightening events (being bitten by a dog, being hit by a car) or a product of parental warnings about certain objects (stay away from the fire, watch out for snakes), there are also many fears that are symbolic in nature. Many of the fears held by children (about 20 percent) are unrealistic and deal with imaginary creatures, the dark, and being alone (113). Dangerous animals, like lions and tigers, are also frequently named as objects of fear. Responding to questions about their fears, children between 9 and 12 indicated that they were only moderately afraid of immediate and possible dangers, such as getting hit by a car, but were strongly afraid of remote or impossible events, such as a lion attack or ghosts. The remote fears of ghosts, lions, witches, which usually involve being seriously hurt or killed, may be symbolic substitutes of feared parental punishment (68).

Let us elaborate this hypothesis. The typical child learns from the first year of life that a misdemeanor is followed by some form of parental punishment. That is, the child learns that he must pay for the pleasure of a misdemeanor with some form of punishment. Fear of attack by ghosts, snakes, crocodiles, and witches may be symbolic of anticipated parental punishment, rejection, or chastisement—a fear which the child cannot admit to himself directly. The evidence of strong and persistent fears in a 10-year-old, especially when they are excessively unrealistic, may be an index of the amount of guilt and conflict the child is experiencing.

In such cases, a rational attempt to reduce the child's fear of ghosts by pointing out that ghosts do not actually exist is not likely to be successful. After all, the ghosts, in this case, are merely a symbol for the child's unrecognized fear of the parent. Unlike realistic fears (being hit by a car, burned in a fire), unrealistic or symbolic fears can be ameliorated best by attacking the actual source of the fear.

Nightmares and Sleep Disturbances All childhood fears, anxieties, and troublesome feelings are not manifested, either directly or symptomatically, during the child's waking state. Some may remain adequately repressed during the day, only to emerge in nightmares or "bad dreams."

Nightmares tend to reach a peak between ages 4 and 6 (117). According to one investigator, however, more than 25 percent of 6- to 12-year-olds studied were still having nightmares (128). Occasional bad dreams, or even nightmares, need not necessarily be a source of parental alarm, despite the fact that they indicate the presence of at least transient anxiety and conflict in the child—concerns that may be repressed during waking hours, but that emerge when the child's defenses are lowered by sleep. However, when nightmares become frequent, unusually severe, and recurrent, an effort should be made to determine the source of the child's anxiety and to ameliorate it. This course should also be followed in the case of recurrence of an extreme form of nightmare, called night terror or **pavor nocturnus,** following which the child has great difficulty reorienting to reality. He is hard to waken, his panic does not abate, and wakening does not help him to regain control. "In such night terrors, the child is often reliving a traumatic event" (117, 237).

Often the content of nightmares provides some clue as to their source. For example, a child who repeatedly dreams that his father has been killed and who wakes up terrified may well be reflecting hostile wishes toward his father, wishes that he would find too anxiety-producing to be able to admit to himself. The child might also be reflecting a deep fear of losing the father.

Another sleep disturbance that occurs more frequently among children than adults is sleepwalking (80, 117, 200). A child who has been put to bed and has gone to sleep later reappears in the living room where his parents are talking or he is found wandering down a hall or across the lawn. "His parents recognize that he is not 'himself.' His eyes are open and he seems to comprehend the situation partially, but it is evident that he is not really awake and alert" (80, 113). He may be put back to bed and have no recollection, or only a dim awareness, of the event the next morning. In this behavior, often referred to as a "dissociative" state, only a portion of the child's full stream of consciousness is operative, and he is only partially responsive to stimuli in his surroundings (80). It appears as though the child were responding to some need (looking for something about which he is concerned; escaping from an anxiety-producing situation) that disturbs sleep, but that he protects himself from a full awareness of this need (which might itself be anxiety-producing) by not wakening to full consciousness. In this respect, sleepwalking bears some resemblance to other "dissociative" states, such as amnesia or hypnosis. Children who are generally suggestible, histrionic, and emotionally immature appear somewhat more likely than other childen to exhibit sleepwalking. As in the case of other sleep disturbances, the seriousness of sleepwalking depends on its frequency and severity (7, 80, 117, 200).

School Phobias One of the relatively common childhood fears of greatest concern to parents is **school phobia**—a fear, which may approach panic, of leaving home and going to school. While occasional mild reluctance against going to school is common among children of this age—and the source of any number of dubious physical ills that clear up promptly when it is evident that the child can stay home —persistent morbid fear of school is a significant symptom; it indicates a dread of some aspect of the school situation, concerns with leaving home, or, frequently, both. Interestingly, while boys outnumber girls in most child guidance clinics, a majority of clinicians report that school phobias are more common among girls (117). While many problems may be symbolized by a school phobia, the most widely observed pattern involves separation anxiety, a fear of separation shared equally by parent and child (7, 50, 55, 72, 114, 117, 131, 187, 222). Mothers of school-phobic children frequently are threatened by any loss of the child's dependency on them, and many reveal unresolved dependency problems with their own mothers (114). Furthermore, these mothers are themselves likely to see the school as a cold, forbidding place, and go to great lengths to protect their children, not only from it, but from virtually all of the painful facts of existence (117). The child, in turn, perceives—at least unconsciously—the mother's real desire to keep the child dependent and responds to it (72). Further, the child is likely to fear separation from the mother because of both dependent and hostile needs (55, 117).

School phobias may be more common in girls at least partly because of the greater social acceptability of fear and dependency in girls. It should be stressed, however, that while the pattern of parent-child relationships described above appears relatively common, there may be many other factors involved. In a case encountered by one of the authors in his clinical work, an elaborate school phobia in a young boy eventually turned out to involve a vaguely perceived fear of seductive approaches by a male teacher. It has been suggested that school-phobic children commonly overvalue themselves and overestimate their own power and achievements, and then try to hold onto their unrealistic self-image. "When this is threatened in the school situation, they suffer anxiety and retreat to another situation where they can maintain their narcissistic self-image. This retreat may very well be a running to a close contact with mother" (131, 686).

Interestingly, children with school phobias generally have at least average ability (50).

Death Phobias Pronounced fear of death has sometimes been referred to by clinicians as "8-year anxiety" because it tends to occur fairly commonly at this age. Freud was one of the first investigators to note this phenomenon, and he also referred to the eighth year as a kind of "boundary line" separating different periods of childhood. In Piaget's earlier studies, the eighth year was also seen as a boundary line "between the egocentric child with his magical, animistic, 'realistic' tendencies associated with a precausal, prelogical mode of thinking and the 'operational' child who sees the world logically and rationally" (8, 1395). We have already seen that conscience tends to become increasingly severe among children around ages 8, 9, or 10.

In a considerable number of children, there occurs at this age period what James Anthony, a child psychiatrist, refers to as an "existential crisis" (8). The child becomes increasingly preoccupied with ideas that either he or his parents will die. The child's concept of death, like many of his other ideas, develops gradually during the whole period of growth.

> At an early age, death is thought of mostly in animistic terms in which the dead see, hear, and feel. Later it is viewed as separation, or rather desertion, and, still later, death becomes personified as a dreaded figure removing a loved person. Before the age of 7, death is reversible. At about 8 years, death, for many children, becomes irreversible, and, therefore, death wishes, both conscious and unconscious, take on a new emotional coloring. At the time of the crisis, the child becomes aware of a peculiar kind

of helplessness in the face of the inevitability of death, with the additional feeling that no one can help, since everyone also is in the same predicament (8, 1395).

Actual experiences of death may sometimes be instrumental in precipitating a death phobia or may bring it out at an earlier age. However, preexisting conflicts, frequently involving anxiety about separation from parents or fears of punishment and retribution, are usually present. As the condition improves, the sense of personal immunity to death reasserts itself (162).

Depression Because depressive symptoms in children are usually neither as clearly defined nor as severe and persistent as in adults, it used to be thought that children did not develop significant depressions (162, 222). However, recent studies (88, 146, 171) suggest that 10 percent or more of emotionally disturbed children are likely "to suffer depressed moods, apathy, lethargy, or suicidal preoccupation. Additionally, an undetermined portion of disturbed youngsters has been recognized as suffering 'masked' depression" (222, 165). One common form of masked depression in children involves aggressive, delinquent, or antisocial behavior "in which bad conduct is motivated by needs to compensate for a sense of loss" (222, 165).

Depressed feelings may range from normal, and relatively brief, bereavement, as in the case of a loss of a pet dog, to prolonged and apparently inconsolable grief. In most serious cases of depressed reactions, there is, in addition to the feeling of loss, a strong component of anger and, frequently, of guilt (88, 146, 162, 171). Thus, the child who has lost a loved parent is likely not only to miss him or her desperately, but also (at least unconsciously) to blame the deceased parent for deserting him or the remaining parent for allowing this to happen. He may also blame himself, feeling—usually unconsciously and, of course, illogically—that somehow all angry, frustrated feelings toward the parent in the past ("I wish you were dead") have somehow magically been fulfilled. One of the critical responsibilities of those caring for any child who has lost a parent or sibling is to help him to express and come to terms with his painful, confused, and often conflicting emotions (162).

Tics One of the most commonly observed symptoms of psychological tension during the middle-childhood years is the tic. "A tic is a repetitious, involuntary, and seemingly purposeless movement of interconnected muscles" (76, 118). Usually tics involve repeated motor responses of the face, neck, and head, of which the child is largely unaware; the actions may include blinking of the eyes, nose-wrinkling, throat-clearing, yawning, shoulder-shrugging, head-shaking, and the like. Tics frequently are symptoms of repressed needs and conflicts, and sometimes the nature of a tic serves as a clue to the underlying conflict.

Some facial grimaces, for instance, look suspiciously as if the person is aggressively making a face at somebody. The head-shaker is saying "No" to some unconscious wish. Wrinkling of the nose seems to say "something doesn't smell good around here." Blinking the eye seems to suggest an attempt to blot out something which was seen. The child has no awareness either of the tic or the feelings of memory which prompts it. He can neither stop it nor explain it (117, 247).

Tics are more common in tense children with fairly strict parents (200, 202).

> There may be too much pressure at home. Sometimes a mother or father is going at the child too hard, directing him, correcting him whenever he is in sight. Or the parents may be showing constant disapproval in a quieter way, or setting standards that are too high, or providing too many activities. . . . If the child were bold enough to fight back, he would probably be less tightened up inside. But being, in most cases, too well brought-up for that, he bottles up his irritation, and it keeps "backfiring" in the tic (202, 395).

As tics are involuntary, it is important that the child should not be scolded or corrected because of them. Except for brief intervals of awareness, they are practically out of his control. Effort should be made to make the child's life at home as relaxed and agreeable as possible, and with the least possible nagging, and his school and social life should be reasonably satisfying and not overstrenuous. When tics persist, despite such efforts, it is important to seek psychological help in order to gain a more specific understanding of the source of the child's tension, with the aim of ameliorating it.

While tics are isolated disturbances of motility, they tend to be closely related to the fidgeting and restlessness which plague school teachers and parents. These may be no more than a sign of diffuse anxiety, a kind of general movement that is an effort to restore a feeling of ease. However, at other times such restless moving about may serve as a defense against some other motor act which is forbidden, such as masturbation or aggressive behavior. As in the case of tics, generalized restlessness and fidgeting seem to be more common among children subject to strict parental restrictions (117).

Obsessions and Compulsions

Conscience development during the middle-childhood years is likely to pose some difficulty for many children. On the one hand, the child's desires to do what he wants to do when he wants to do it are still strong. On the other hand, his growing conscience, his increasingly internalized set of moral standards, dictates that many of these impulses are "wrong."

Under these circumstances, anxiety is produced in the child. Because unresolved anxiety is a particularly painful state, the child may attempt to erect psychological defenses against it. In the case of conflicts between his needs and the demands of a strict conscience, the child may attempt to ward off his unacceptable impulses, and hence control his anxiety, by the "occurrence of thoughts (obsessions), acts or impulses to act (compulsions), or mixtures of both which are all isolated from the original, unacceptable impulse" (82, 1401). Often the obsessive thought or compulsion serves not only to help control and to prevent awareness of unacceptable impulses, but, as a kind of double insurance, to emphasize the opposite of the unacceptable impulse. Thus a child with desires to be dirty and messy or to indulge in "dirty" sexual practices, such as masturbation, may develop compulsions to be extremely clean or to engage in repeated hand-washing. Obsessive, constantly recurring thoughts about being clean may serve a similar purpose. As previously noted, it is as though the child were saying to himself, "Look, I can't possibly have these impulses to engage in dirty behavior. See how concerned I am with being clean" (reaction formation).

Similarly, in the case of the childhood ritual of avoiding cracks in the sidewalk while chanting "Step on a crack, break your mother's back" the child seems to be saying, "I cannot really be hostile to my mother, because I am carefully avoiding an action which would harm her" (stepping on the crack). Mild obsessions and compulsions are common among children in the middle-childhood years, particularly around ages 8, 9, and 10 (76, 117, 202), and are not necessarily a source of serious concern. Most adults can remember periods when they had "foolish" recurrent thoughts they could not get out of their heads or when they engaged in such activities as touching every third picket in the fence, avoiding cracks in the sidewalk, or having to do some other activity in a special way (202). On the other hand, when obsessions and compulsions are more severe, sustained, or unusual (for example, hand-washing compulsions), psychological or psychiatric help appears indicated. Not unexpectedly, serious obsessive-compulsive neuroses are more frequent in the children of overly strict, fastidious, demanding parents, who pressure the child for accomplishment, hold him to overly severe standards of thought and behavior, and allow him little room for the expression of normal childhood impulses and desires (82, 117). Current research also indicates that the parental milieu most conducive to high guilt is one in which an affectionate relationship between parent and child is combined with withdrawal of love as the most frequent method of socialization. Under these conditions, the child values the parent's nurturance and is made anxious by contemplation of withdrawal of love resulting from any violation, in thought or deed, of strict parental standards.

Conduct Problems

Among the more frequent disturbances of social conduct that may reflect psychological problems, especially during early middle childhood, are lying and stealing. In the case of lying, it is important to distinguish between rather innocuous instances of "stretching the truth" at times, in the interests of wish fulfillment and often in highly imaginative fashion, and more symptomatic behaviors. Sometimes the child may resort to lying because of fear of failure to meet parental or social expectations. To determine the antecedents of such fear it is important to examine whether these expectations are overly rigid and also whether the parents or other adults are overly demanding, punitive, and lacking in warmth or understanding (**88, 117, 200, 202**). Persistent lying may reflect more deep-rooted problems, as in the case of lying that appears arbitrary, lacking in obvious motivation, and unaccompanied by anxiety. This type of behavior may reflect more severe disturbance in conscience development or in the capacity for distinguishing reality from fantasy (**7, 80, 91, 117**).

Stealing, too, may vary in the motivations it expresses, as well as in its seriousness. It may simply indicate a rather thoughtless giving in to an impulse of the moment or going along with the behavior of peers. It may, however, indicate a serious psychological disturbance, for stealing may serve as a symbolic substitute for a perceived lack of love and attention, particularly from parents, or as a means of expressing hostility toward parents by violating their standards and by embarrassing them by getting caught. Stealing and getting caught may serve as an unconscious way for the child to call attention to himself and his problems and to ask for help or to punish himself for real or imagined transgressions. Many of these motivations may also be involved in other childhood conduct problems, such as vandalism, fire setting, and truancy (**200, 222**).

Psychophysiological Symptoms and Hypochondriasis

Psychological problems of the school-age child may also be reflected in real or imagined physical symptoms. In the latter case, referred to as **hypochondriasis,** there is an excessive preoccupation with the functioning of the body, caused largely by anxiety (**117, 200**). While this symptom is more common among adolescents (who are going through dramatic physical changes), it is not unknown in middle childhood (**200**). The child may think that there is something wrong with his heartbeat, breathing, or digestion when these are perfectly normal; or he may exaggerate the significance of minor ailments, such as a slightly stuffy nose or minor stomach upset (**117, 200, 222**). Of course, not all exaggerated physical complaints are determined primarily by anxiety about body functioning. The frequent, and often convenient, complaint of a stomachache or headache among school children on the morning before a test or when homework has not been completed often disappears with amazing rapidity once the impending crisis has been averted. However, although this latter type of complaint is insignificant, anxiety about school performance can lead to physiological upset.

Children who develop frequent hypochondriacal symptoms are likely to come from families that are overly preoccupied with health concerns: "In such families the slightest physical complaint commands everybody's immediate attention and sympathy. Each member of the family has his own particular brand of aches, allergies, and infirmities and his own well-stocked shelf of medicine; family conversations frequently revolve around the current status of everyone's latest malaise" (**222, 164**).

Psychological problems may also be reflected in actual disturbances of physiological functioning. A psychophysiological (or psychosomatic) illness is a bodily disease or disorder in function that is determined, in part, by psychological disturbance. Although constitutional factors appear to play a significant role in predisposing the individual to the development of a psychosomatic disorder, psychological factors often act to bring it about. Such disorders are not limited to any one age period; however, they often occur among school-age children. Indeed, next to acute respiratory illness, they are the most frequent cause of repeated absences from school (200). The most common psychophysiological disturbances during the middle-childhood years are "those characterized somatically by bodily pain (particularly headaches and 'stomachaches,') lack of appetite, overeating and obesity, diarrhea, chronic fatigue, and allergic disorders. Unexplained fever, presumed to be psychogenic, that is, psychologically determined, is not infrequent" (200, 111). Other psychosomatic disorders that may occur during this period include asthma, ulcerative colitis, skin disorders, and rheumatoid arthritis. Interviews with the mother of children with psychosomatic disorders revealed that they were less accepting and more controlling, particularly during their children's first year of life, than the mothers of physically ill or neurotic children (87).

It appears that the likelihood of precipitating a particular psychosomatic condition is influenced by constitutional predisposition and that in any particular symptom complex the relative importance of psychological as contrasted to constitutional factors may vary. Thus, in some children with asthma constitutional factors may be more significant, while in others, psychological factors may play a more important role. Some children with intractable (that is, severe) asthma had a rapid remission in symptoms, even without medication ("rapid remitters") as soon as they were referred to a children's residential treatment center. Other children, however, continued to require maintenance doses of corticosteroid drugs ("steroid dependent") while at the center. A comprehensive series of studies showed that rapidly remitting children reported significantly more often than steroid-dependent children that emotions such as anger, anxiety, and depression triggered their asthma. Furthermore, both mothers and fathers of rapidly remitting children displayed authoritarian and punitive attitudes to a greater degree than the parents of the steroid-dependent children, according to their responses to a questionnaire (173, 174).

The investigators concluded that among rapidly remitting children the symptom of asthma may be more intimately associated with neurotic conflict and affective reactions, while the asthmatic symptom of steroid-dependent children is a response more regularly linked to the influences of allergic and infectious factors. However, "the differences between these groups are regarded as relative rather than absolute" (174).

Many severely asthmatic children become essentially asymptomatic without any medication when they leave their homes and enter the new environment of a treatment center. Most of the rest of these children show substantial, although not so dramatic, improvement. Thus there appears to be clear evidence that removal from the family and placement in a favorable institutional setting often has a profoundly ameliorative effect on asthma in children (**173**).

PSYCHOLOGICAL PROBLEMS OF MINORITY-GROUP MEMBERSHIP

Children of all ethnic groups and all socioeconomic levels may encounter physiological risks, traumatic social experiences, and disturbances in parent-child relationships in the course of their development. However, a relatively small percentage of children may carry an additional psychological burden—membership in a minority group that is vulnerable to hostility and discrimination on the part of majority-group peers and adults. In its report on the mental health needs of children in the 1970s (**115**), the Joint Commission on Mental Health of Children called attention to the damaging effects that poverty and discrimination (which often go together) may have on the psychological adjustment and self-esteem of children and adolescents. An individual who perceives himself as belonging to a group that is subjected to discriminatory treatment and is viewed in derogatory fashion by the majority in a society may become understandably resentful and bitter. Worse still, he may begin, consciously or unconsciously, to accept these views himself, or at least to be in conflict about them, particularly if members of his own group share some of these derogatory views (**52, 203**). The result may be an alienation, not only from society, but also from the self, and the development of what Erikson calls a **negative** identity (**54, 77, 172**).

Self-Image in Minority Groups

Autobiographical or semiautobiographical works of talented and sensitive minority writers (**73, 145, 214**), as well as clinical observation, particularly by minority psychiatrists and psychologists (**38, 97, 167**), attest that this has happened all too often in the past (**19, 38, 172**). As Kenneth Clark, a leading black psychologist and recent president of the American Psychological Association, points out, "The child . . . cannot learn what racial [or ethnic] group he belongs to without being involved in a larger pattern of emotions, conflicts, and desires which are part of his growing knowledge of what society thinks about his [group]" (**52, 23**).

The child's awareness of his racial or ethnic status develops relatively early in childhood, usually by about age 4 or 5 (**52, 203**). What, then, are the disadvantaged minority child's reactions to "society's views?" Does he like his status? Empirical studies suggest that, **in the past at least,** for many children "the answer to this question (ranged) from a qualified to an emphatic 'no' " (**172, 187**). The minority-group child tended to reject his own racial or ethnic group, adopting, quite early in life, the cultural norms and judgments about his group, "learning in a rudimentary way about his limited opportunities and the prejudice against him" (**172, 187**).

For example, in a study by Clark and his wife (**53**), conducted in 1939, 253 2- to 7-year-old black children were shown a variety of black and white dolls and were asked such questions as "Which doll looks nice?" "Which doll looks bad?" "Which doll is a 'nice' color?" A majority of the children picked the white doll as the one which "looked nice" and was a "nice color" and picked the black doll as the one which "looked bad." "While there was a decrease with age in choices of the white doll as 'looking nice' and being a 'nice color,' a majority of subjects at all ages said the black doll 'looked bad' " (**172**, 187). Other earlier studies, using a variety of techniques (playmate selection, drawings, doll play, and picture tests) tended to produce similar results (**101, 159, 172, 203**). For example, young black children between the ages of 3 and 7 perceived children of their own race as aggressive, bad, and those "whom other children fear," significantly more often than white subjects saw white children as possessing these characteristics (**203**). Similarly, Mexican-American children born in the United States were found to perceive themselves as "significantly more emotional, unscientific, authoritarian, materialistic, old-fashioned, poor and of low social class, uneducated, mistrusted, proud, lazy, indifferent, and unambitious" (**60**, 82). In contrast, Mexican-American subjects born in Mexico did not share these stereotypes. The discrepancy was viewed as establishing "the influence of the dominant American value orientation upon native-born Mexican-American self-acceptance and self-stereotyping" (**60**, 82).

Recent Changes Fortunately, an increasing number of recent studies (**17, 19, 38, 57, 81, 112**) suggest that the picture is now changing, at least in some groups and in some areas, with the recent ascendance of racial and ethnic pride ("black is beautiful," the concept of La Raza). At the same time, there has been a growth in understanding and interest in minority groups among many more members of the majority, particularly young people. For example, in a recent repetition of the Clarks' study, conducted in 1969 in Lincoln, Nebraska, a majority of black children now preferred the black doll (**112**). (A control group of white children preferred the white doll by a similar margin; see Table 10.2.) Interestingly, black children who most consistently preferred black dolls were more likely than other black children to have both black and white friends. Apparently children who are most secure and confident in their own racial identification are able, given a favorable social environment, to employ other criteria than race alone in the selection of their friends. That the city of Lincoln offered such a relatively favorable environment was suggested by the fact that 70 percent of black children in the study had white friends and 59 percent of the white sample had black friends.

Similar trends are emerging in studies of older children and adolescents, in a variety of minority groups (**142, 201, 223**). Thus a number of recent studies (**14, 19, 37, 38, 57, 102**) show that the self-esteem of preadolescent and adolescent blacks in a majority of instances equals or exceeds that of whites, although in

Table 10.2 **A comparison of the present results with the Clark and Clark (1939) data**

ITEM	CLARK & CLARK (1939) BLACKS	LINCOLN SAMPLE (1969) BLACKS	x^2 (1939– 1969) BLACKS	LINCOLN SAMPLE (1969)
1. (Play with)				
White doll	67 (169)[a]	30 (27)	36.2[b]	83 (59)
Black doll	32 (83)	70 (62)		16 (11)
Don't know or no response				1 (1)
2. (Nice doll)				
White doll	59 (150)	46 (41)	5.7[c]	70 (50)
Black doll	38 (97)	54 (48)		30 (21)
3. (Looks bad)				
White doll	17 (42)	61 (54)	43.5[b]	34 (24)
Black doll	59 (149)	36 (32)		63 (45)
Don't know or no response		3 (3)		3 (2)
4. (Nice color)				
White doll	60 (151)	31 (28)	23.1[b]	48 (34)
Black doll	38 (96)	69 (61)		49 (35)
Don't know or no response				3 (2)

[a]Data in percentages; Ns in parentheses. Individuals failing to make either choice not included, hence some percentages add to less than 100.

[b]$p < .001$.

[c]$p < .02$.

Source: J. Hraba and G. Grant. Black is beautiful: A reexamination of racial preference and identification. **Journal of Personality and Social Psychology,** 1970, **16,** 398–402. By permission.

some groups and in some areas, this is apparently still not the case (**12, 36, 94, 166**).

Finally, it should be emphasized that other influences, such as socioeconomic status and ability, also play an important role in self-esteem of the minority group child. One such influence, the child's relationship with his parents, is more important than all other influences combined (**14**). The child with warm, understanding parents who are proud of him and actively involved in fostering his development is likely to develop a high level of self-esteem, even in a society where discrimination is still far too pervasive.

The Development of Prejudice

Significant numbers of children have already developed hostile attitudes toward minority groups by the time they enter kindergarten. During the early school years more children acquire these prejudices, which become more crystallized and conform more closely to adult patterns of prejudice (**175, 177**). Children's prejudices are rarely based on their own experiences. Their verbalizations about minorities typically reflect negative attitudes learned from the direct or indirect teaching of adults (175). Parents may make statements in support of democratic values and intercultural education and express opposition to racial or religious segregation in the schools. However, they often have little insight into their own underlying feelings toward minority groups or the implications of their own group membership and make no direct or planned attempts to teach their children ethnic attitudes. Instead, such attitudes are conveyed to the children by restricting social relationships in the home, neighborhood, and school and by disapproving of friendships with members of certain groups (177).

Background and Personality of Prejudiced Children Children may acquire the prejudices of those with whom they identify—parents, peers, their social group. Children of prejudiced parents may become bigoted, while those emulating tolerant parents may develop democratic attitudes. However, more is involved in the development of prejudice than simple imitation of attitudes. Studies of anti-Semitic and antiblack adults show that their prejudices are components of broader patterns of attitudes and are related to basic personality structure. Compared with tolerant people, prejudiced adults tend to be rigid, authoritarian, highly conforming, and overly moralistic (2, 43).

A pioneering study by Else Frenkel-Brunswik "designed to throw light on the determinants of susceptibility to racial or ethnic prejudice and allied forms of undemocratic opinions and attitudes" (83, 295) demonstrated that children's ethnic prejudices are also related to general personality structure. About 1500 California boys and girls between the ages of 11 and 16 were given tests measuring attitudes toward Jews, blacks, Japanese, Mexicans, and out-groups in general. A series of statements about these groups was presented and the subjects were asked to express their agreement or disagreement with each. Some contained sterotypical accusations: Japanese cruelty, black laziness, Jewish radicalism and money-mindedness, etc. Other statements involved sharing activities with minority-group members (eating in the same restaurants, living in the same neighborhood, socializing together). From the larger group, the 120 most and least prejudiced children were selected for further study, including personality tests and interviews.

Ethnocentric (prejudiced) children revealed selfish orientations toward America and indifference toward other countries. They agreed with generally intolerant statements (such as, "Only people who are like myself have the right to be happy"; "We should not send any of our food to foreign countries, but should think of America first") much more frequently than unprejudiced children did.

Other generalized attitudes typical of the prejudiced child, but not the unprejudiced, were: rejection of all that is weak or different; rigid conceptions of appropriate sex roles, together with intolerance of passive or feminine behavior in boys and masculine or tomboyish behavior in girls; admiration of the strong, tough, and powerful and, in the boys, fear of weakness in themselves; rigid conformity to approved social values and moralistic condemnation of others; feelings of helplessness in a world thought to be full of chaos and destruction. All these attitudes were considered indicative of "narrow and rigid personality" (83).

In discussing relationships with parents, the tolerant children frequently mentioned affection, cooperation, and companionship, while the prejudiced children complained of lack of affection and submission to stern, harsh, punitive treatment. Interviews with the parents offered evidence that the tolerant child "learns at home the equalitarian and individualized approach to people, as the ethnocentric child learns the authoritarian and hierarchical way of thinking" (83, 302).

> From the point of view of society as a whole, the most important problem . . . seems to be the child's attitude toward authority. Forced submission to authority produces only surface conformity countermanded by violent underlying destructiveness, dangerous to the very society to which there seems to be conformity. Only a frightened and frustrated child will tend to gain safety and security by oversimplified black-white schematizations and categorizations on the basis of crude, external characteristics. Deliberately planned democratic participation in school and family, individualized approach to the child, and the right proportion of permissiveness and guidance may be instrumental in bringing about the attitude necessary for a genuine identification with society and thus for international understanding (83, 306).

Prejudiced children show significantly poorer self-concepts than unprejudiced children and less satisfaction with their own mental abilities, impaired social relations with members of the same- and opposite-sex, greater dissatisfaction with parents and teachers, and overconcern with their own personality and with school subjects. Interestingly, no relationships were obtained between prejudice and actual school achievement (209, 217).

Such findings are not restricted to the dominant white majority. In a study of black 9- to 18-year-old pupils in three schools in New York City, it was found that black children who were most self-accepting expressed significantly more positive attitudes toward both blacks and whites than did children who were least self-accepting (217).

In another investigation of the relationship between personality and ethnic attitudes, a variety of tests were given to fourth-, fifth-, and sixth-grade pupils (93). Subjects were asked to indicate agreement or disagreement with a variety of statements related not only to minority-group prejudice or acceptance, but also to general tolerance or intolerance. The high correlations obtained between general tolerance and attitudes toward Jews and blacks indicated that there is a generalized prejudiced attitude.

Compared with the tolerant children,

> . . . the more prejudiced child favors his own immediate group over any larger society, he thinks categorically of "weak" and "strong," he declares himself in favor of authoritarianism on the part of teachers, he is suspicious of integrity of others. . . . In general, the picture one gets of the prejudiced child . . . suggests fear and distrust of others, lack of confidence in himself, feelings of guilt and uneasiness, insecurities and doubts

about the larger physical and social world and possibly a reactive hostility toward people who are "weak" or "different" (**93**, 89).

Moreover, intolerant children . . . have cynical, distrustful opinions of others, have fears of being exploited or duped, or have feelings of having been treated unfairly" (**93**, 91).

These two investigations are in essential agreement about the nature of the personality structure of the prejudiced child. In general, personality characteristics associated with intolerance are established in early parent-child relationships.

In a further study of the antecedents of children's prejudices, one team of investigators made a direct test of the hypothesis that "authoritarian and disciplinary attitudes of parents concerning child training practices [which tend to produce repressed or suppressed hostility in the child] would be related to a greater incidence of ethnic bias in the children of these parents" (**99**, 170). The subjects were 154 mothers of children whose attitudes toward minority groups had been tested. The correlations between measures of parental behavior and children's attitude scores generally substantiated the hypothesis.

Prejudice in children appears to be associated with the complex of parental attitudes which is involved in authoritarian handling of control and with lack of tolerance of children's "annoyance value." It appears that attitudes of tolerance and good judgment in child rearing are possibly part of a personality and attitude complex on the parents' part which is associated with freedom from ethnic prejudice in children (**99**, 180).

What children learn is not a specific attitude, but a whole "complex of attitudes and personality characteristics, which reveal themselves in interpersonal relationships of various sorts" (**99**, 180).

Prejudice and Mental Functioning The prejudiced child tends to think in terms of discrete categories. He tends to be rigid in his approach to problems and has difficulty altering his original conception of a problem. Thus we might expect his approach to intellectual tasks to be less effective than that of a less prejudiced child. In one study (**126**), 26 boys and 34 girls, 7 years of age, first designated their agreement or disagreement with statements that contained intolerant or prejudiced statements about Mexicans, Catholics, Jews, and blacks. On the basis of their answers to the test, the children were categorized as prejudiced or unprejudiced. These children were then given a series of tasks to assess their approach to problems and their ability to solve them. For example, in one test a child was confronted with 16 objects that differed in color, shape, and size (4 colors, 3 shapes, and 2 sizes). He was asked to divide the 16 blocks into 2 equal groups. The only correct solution was to divide the blocks on the basis of size. The prejudiced children, in comparison with the unprejudiced, had more difficulty solving the problem; they tended to persist with a poor hunch or hypothesis and showed an inability to make use of the hints that the examiner gave them.

On the basis of this and other tests, the author concluded that the prejudiced child tried to look for simple solutions and had difficulty changing his original approach or idea. The prejudiced child performed poorly when the problems were ambiguous and he had to structure the meaning of the problem. In brief, the rigidity of attitude that is present in maintaining a prejudice is also reflected in an individual's approach to intellectual problems (126).

Modification of Racial Attitudes

As intolerance is related to firmly established characteristics, it might be inferred that intolerance could be reduced only by changing the basic personality structure of the prejudiced person. This, of course, would require intensive clinical treatment.

It would be a serious mistake, however, to assume that there is a one-to-one correspondence between personality and prejudice. If they live among bigoted people, well-adjusted children may learn to behave intolerantly, that is, they will learn to behave in accordance with the standard or accepted attitudes of their own social group. In such cases, prejudice might be viewed as a reflection of the child's identification with his group rather than as displacement of his hostility toward his parents. Perhaps those whose prejudice has this kind of basis, but who in general are well adjusted and not essentially hostile, would become more tolerant if they were transferred to an environment that promoted "democratic living" and an equalitarian philosophy. On the other hand, those who need scapegoats as an outlet for deep-lying aggressive feelings may not be able to relinquish their prejudices, even in a democratic setting. To test these hypotheses, one investigator (161) studied changes in boys' attitudes toward blacks after a four-week vacation at an interracial camp where blacks and whites lived, ate, and played together. The subjects were white New York City boys ranging from 8 to 14 years of age.

An indirect test of prejudice was administered to each boy less than 24 hours before he left home, that is, before intimate contact with black boys at camp. The child was given 12 photographs of boys' faces, eight of them black, four of them white. In the first part of the test the child simply indicated his order of preference for these faces; in the second part, he selected the pictures of boys he would like to go to the movies with, invite home to lunch, etc. The extent of discrimination against the pictures of blacks constituted the measure of prejudice. This test was given again just before the children left the camp.

Personality structure was evaluated by analyzing responses to a picture-story test (the Thematic Apperception Test), in which the subject's underlying needs and attitudes were reflected in the kinds of stories he told. Data about personal and social adjustment at camp were collected from two sources: a brief interview with each child and a camp social worker's report.

Following the camp experience, some of the boys increased significantly in prejudice whereas others decreased. As hypothesized, these changes were related to personality structure. In general, the boys who increased in prejudice were hostile, defiant youngsters who perceived the world as cruel and unpleasant and felt they were frequent victims of aggression. Because, for them, the expression of aggression led to punishment, retaliation, and restraint, they probably did not "act out" their hostile feelings. Hence they had greater needs to displace their aggression by means of antiblack prejudice. Moreover, these boys were dissatisfied with the camp itself, the other campers, and interpersonal relations there. The child who was poorly adjusted socially in the situation and did not find the experience rewarding probably did not identify with the camp or accept its attitudes. Under the circumstances, he may have felt more frustrated and may have become more, rather than less, prejudiced against blacks.

Children who decreased in prejudice presented a sharply contrasting picture. They manifested fewer aggressive needs, less hostility toward the parents, fewer feelings of restraint, and generally favorable attitudes toward society. Consequently, they had little need to displace aggression through prejudice. In the camp, they were well accepted by their peers, and their counselors judged them to be high in "ability to relate to others." They complained less about interpersonal relations, were more satisfied with the camp experience and their fellow campers, and probably formed more intimate friendships (161). It may be assumed that they found the experience rewarding and, consequently, identified more closely with the camp, accepting its tolerant philosophy.

In another extensive study on the modification of racial attitudes (176), more than 1000 children 8 to 13 years of age were observed at a summer camp. Some of the children, both white and black, lived in desegregated cabins for a two-week period. The behavior of the children in the desegregated situation was compared with the behavior of children who lived in segregated cabins.

Signs of tension (enuresis, nightmares, crying, physical symptoms, repeated accidents) were more frequent among the children living in the desegregated cabins. Moreover, the white children initially became vigilant to possible aggression from the black children. As might be expected from earlier work, both the black and white children viewed the latter as more desirable for friends and assigned higher status to the whites. However, there was a general trend for both black and white children to view the blacks as increasingly desirable after the two weeks of desegregated living.

Although the experience of living in a biracial setting decreased suspicion and hostility between the groups, the most important catalyst for change was the counselor. His attitudes and personality, particularly his warmth and personal security, facilitated the establishment of good interpersonal relations between the black and white children.

Apparently both personality and social situational factors are involved in changes in race attitudes. The study suggests that prejudice may be reduced by relatively modest changes in the social milieu and by educational measures, such as encouraging contacts between members of various races. Moreover, this study highlights the importance of the attitudes of authority figures, such as teachers, in promoting more positive feelings toward minority groups in a desegregated setting, whether it is a camp or a school. Modification of the mutual fears, suspicions, and resentments of black and white children is most apt to occur when the adult in charge favors desegregation and is admired and liked by the children (176).

While tensions between various ethnic and cultural groups have come to the surface and emerged into public consciousness in the past decade, hopefully the very acknowledgment of their existence and some of the reasons for them may lead to increased efforts to overcome them. Unfortunately, the question is still an open and very complex one. What is clear, however, is that our society can ill afford continued second-class status for significant minorities of its citizens if it is to survive—socially, politically, or economically (38, 43, 62, 115, 224).

SUMMARY

During the middle-childhood years, the child is exposed to an ever-expanding series of extrafamilial influences. Nevertheless, relationships with parents remain, for most children, the most important factor in determining the kind of person the child will become and the kinds of problems he will face in his quest for maturity.

Parent behavior is not unidimensional. While many theoretical dimensions for conceptualizing parent behavior are possible, the two axes most consistently employed in research to date are **warmth-hostility** and **control-autonomy.** The control-autonomy dimension, in turn, appears to be comprised of two related, but distinguishable, subdimensions: **psychological autonomy-psychological control** and **firm control–lax control.** The child of warm, high autonomy, "democratic" parents is likely to be active, independent, friendly, and socially assertive. Where the parent, in addition, is reasonably insistent (and consistent) in setting age-appropriate standards for conduct without being intrusive, the child is also likely to be responsible, self-reliant, and purposive in behavior. The child of warm-restrictive parents, in contrast, is likely to be more dependent, less creative, more conforming, less dominant and competitive, but more polite and neat. Hostile parents tend to impair the child's adjustment and to arouse counterhostility, whether manifested internally or externally. While restrictiveness combined with hostility tends to maximize self-aggression, social withdrawal, and symptoms of internal conflict in the child, permissiveness or neglect combined with hostility appears to maximize aggressive, poorly controlled behavior, of a kind frequently seen in delinquent or "acting-out" children.

Some personality trends appear more stable throughout the course of de-

velopment than others. Among the more stable dimensions are **emotional expressiveness-reserve** and **placidity-explosiveness.** Another dimension, **dependence-independence,** appears more stable for girls than boys.

The child's development of self-esteem is fostered by parents whose own self-esteem is high, who are warm and accepting and interested in the child's activities, who encourage autonomy without being excessively demanding, and who have definite and consistent standards of conduct for the child, while respecting his rights and opinions.

Absence of either father or mother from the home may make the child's adjustment and development of a clearly defined personal and sexual identity more difficult, particularly when parental absence occurs early in life and when the same-sex parent is absent.

Studies of class differences in child-rearing practices indicate that middle-class mothers tend to be more affectionate and less punitive than those of lower classes; and middle-class children generally have more favorable perceptions of their parents.

Birth order and sibling status also influence the child's personality development, although the relationships are often complex. For example, girls with older brothers have more "tomboyish" traits than other girls. Some degree of sibling rivalry occurs in all multichild families, but it is likely to be greatest when children are fairly close in age. Because of the typically strong involvement of siblings with each other, death of a sibling (as well as a parent) is often a traumatic event for a child, even though he may seem to deny it.

The middle-childhood years represent a critical period for conscience development. According to Piaget, before age 7 or 8 the child's concept of justice is based on rigid and inflexible notions of right and wrong learned from parents. Between the ages of 8 and 11, a progressive equalitarianism develops, and beginning about age 11-12, "purely equalitarian justice is tempered by considerations of equity." Conscience development is dependent upon the child's level of cognitive maturation (Kohlberg) and also upon parental and other influences to which the child is subjected. Optimal conscience development is facilitated if (1) the parent's own conscience and moral standards are mature and reasonable, but not overly rigid, harsh and inflexible; and (2) adoption of the parent's standards by the child is based on positive identification and modeling. Love-oriented discipline appears more effective in fostering conscience development than physical punishment.

All children encounter some psychological problems during middle childhood. These will usually be transient and limited in severity if the child's parents provide good role models, are warm and accepting, and are consistent and flexible in disciplinary techniques, but not so controlling or dominating that they thwart his development of autonomy, self-reliance, and mastery behavior. In contrast, the child whose parents and society have seriously failed him in one way or another may be expected to encounter psychological or psychosomatic problems which are more severe, more chronic, and more refractory to treatment. Many psychological symptoms involve manifestations of defense mechanisms employed to ward off painful feelings of anxiety (repression, denial, projection, rationalization, regression, etc.). Among the most frequent problems of middle childhood are: nightmares and sleep disturbances, school phobias, death phobias, tics, obsessions and compulsions (often related to the child's increasingly strict conscience during this period), conduct problems, hostility to parents, various hypochondriacal and psychophysiological symptoms, and occasionally depression.

Ethnic, racial, and religious identifications become well established during middle childhood, and prejudice can have serious consequences for the child's personality development and self-concept. While prejudiced attitudes among children of this age are typically learned from parents, peers, and society, individual personality factors play a role. In comparison with other children, prejudiced children tend to be more egocentric, rigid, inflexible in mental functioning, fearful of authority, and frustrated; they tend to have poorer self-concepts and poorer relations with peers of both sexes. Modification of racial prejudice is essential for optimal personality development of all children in contemporary society.

References

1. Adelson, J. The political imagination of the young adolescent. In J. Kagan & R. Coles (Eds.), **12 to 16: Early adolescence.** New York: Norton, 1972. Pp. 106–143.
2. Adorno, T. W., Frenkel-Brunswik, E., Levinson, D. J., & Stanford, R. N. **The authoritarian personality.** New York: Harper & Row, 1950.
3. Allinsmith, W. Moral standards: II. The learning of moral standards. In D. R. Miller & G. E. Swanson (Eds.), **Inner conflict and defense.** New York: Holt, Rinehart & Winston, 1960. Pp. 141–176.
4. Altus, W. D. Birth order and its sequelae. **International Journal of Psychiatry,** 1967, **3,** 23–39.
5. Anderson, R. E. Where's Dad? Paternal deprivation and delinquency. **Archives of General Psychiatry,** 1968, **18,** 641–649.
6. Andrews, R. J. The self-concept and pupils with learning difficulties. The **Slow Learning Child,** 1966, **13,** 47–54.
7. Anthony, E. J. The behavior disorders of children. In P. H. Mussen (Ed.), **Carmichael's Manual of child psychology.** (3rd ed.) Vol. 2. New York: Wiley, 1970. Pp. 667–764.
8. Anthony, E. J. Psychoneurotic disorders. In A. M. Freedman & H. I. Kaplan (Eds.), **Comprehensive textbook of psychiatry.** Baltimore: Williams & Wilkins, 1967.
9. Anthony, E. J. An experimental approach to the psychopathology of childhood. **British Journal of Medical Psychology,** 1958, **31,** 211–223.
10. Armentrout, J. A., & Burger, G. K. Children's reports of parental child-rearing behavior at five grade levels. **Developmental Psychology,** 1972, **7,** 44–48.
11. Aronfreed, J. The nature, variety, and social patterning of moral responses to transgression. **Journal of Abnormal and Social Psychology,** 1961, **63,** 223–240.
12. Asher, S. R., & Allen, V. L. Racial preference and social comparison processes. **Journal of Social Issues,** 1969, **25,** 157–165.

13. Bach, G. R. Father-fantasies and father-typing in father-separated children. **Child Development,** 1946, **17,** 63–79.
14. Bachman, J. G. **Youth in transition.** Vol. 2. **The impact of family background and intelligence on tenth grade boys.** Ann Arbor: Institute for Social Research, University of Michigan, 1970.
15. Baldwin, A. L. The effect of home environment on nursery school behavior. **Child Development,** 1949, **20,** 49–61.
16. Barclay, A. G., & Cusumano, D. Father-absence, cross-sex identity, and field-dependent behavior in male adolescents. **Child Development,** 1967, **38,** 243–250.
17. Barnes, E. J. The black community as the source of positive self-concept for black children. **Black Scholars,** 1970, **1,** 166–192.
18. Barry, H., Jr. Birth order: Achievement, schizophrenia and culture. **International Journal of Psychology,** 1967, **3,** 439–444.
19. Baughman, E. E. **Black Americans: A psychological analysis.** New York: Academic Press, 1971.
20. Baumrind, D. Current patterns of parental authority. **Developmental Psychology Monographs,** 1971, **4,** 99–103.
21. Baumrind, D. Child care practices anteceding three patterns of preschool behavior. **Genetic Psychology Monographs,** 1967, **75,** 43–88.
22. Bayley, N., & Schaefer, E. S. Relationships between socioeconomic variables and the behavior of mothers toward young children. **Journal of Genetic Psychology,** 1960, **96,** 61–77.
23. Beck, A. T., Sehti, B. B., & Tuthill, R. W. Childhood bereavement and adult depression. **Archives of General Psychiatry,** 1963, **9,** 295–302.
24. Becker, W. C. Consequences of different kinds of parental discipline. In M. L. Hoffman & L. W. Hoffman (Eds.), **Review of child development.** Vol. 1. New York: Russell Sage Foundation, 1964.
25. Bender, L. Children's reaction to the death of a sibling. In **A Dynamic Psychopathology of Childhood.** Springfield, Ill.: Thomas, 1954.
26. Berens, A. E. Socialization of need for achievement in boys and girls. **Proceedings, 80th Annual Convention of the American Psychological Association,** 1972, **7,** 273–274.
27. Bieri, J. Parental identification, acceptability, and authority, and within sex-differences in cognitive behavior. **Journal of Abnormal and Social Psychology,** 1960, **60,** 76–79.
28. Biller, H. B. **Father, child, and sex-role.** Lexington, Mass.: Heath, 1971.
29. Biller, H. B., & Davids, A. Parent-child relations, personality development, and psychopathology. In A. Davids (Ed.), **Abnormal child psychology.** Belmont, Calif.: Brooks-Cole, 1973, 48–76.
30. Biller, H. B., & Bahm, R. M. Father-absence, perceived maternal behavior, and masculinity of self-concept among junior high school boys. **Developmental Psychology,** 1971, **4,** 178–181.
31. Blanchard, R. W., & Biller, H. B. Father availability and academic performance among third grade boys. **Developmental Psychology,** 1971, **4,** 301–305.
32. Bledsoe, J. C. Self concepts of children and their intelligence, achievement, interests, and anxiety. **Journal of Individual Psychology,** 1964, **20,** 55–58.
33. Blinder, B. J. Sibling death in childhood. **Child Psychiatry and Human Development,** 1972, **2,** 169–175.
34. Bonney, M. E. A study of social status on the second grade level. **Journal of Genetic Psychology,** 1942, **60,** 271–305.

35. Bonney, M. E. A study of the relation of intelligence, family size, and sex differences with mutual friendships in the primary grades. **Child Development,** 1942, **13,** 79–100.

36. Boyton, J. A., Austin, L. J., & Burke, K. R. Negro perception of negro and white personality traits. **Journal of Personality and Social Psychology,** 1965, **3,** 250–253.

37. Bridgette, R. E. Self-esteem in Negro and white Southern adolescents. Unpublished doctoral dissertation, University of North Carolina at Chapel Hill, 1970.

38. Brody, E. B. **Minority group adolescents in the United States.** Baltimore: Williams & Wilkins, 1968.

39. Bronfenbrenner, U. The psychological costs of quality and equality in education. **Child Development,** 1967, **38,** 909–925.

40. Bronson, W. C. The role of enduring orientations to the environment in personality development. **Genetic Psychology Monographs,** 1972, **86,** 3–80.

41. Bronson, W. C. Adult derivatives of emotional expressiveness and reactivity-control: Developmental continuities from childhood to adulthood. **Child Development,** 1967, **38,** 801–817.

42. Bronson, W. C. Early antecedents of emotional expressiveness and reactivity control. **Child Development,** 1966, **37,** 793–810.

43. Brown, A. R. **Prejudice in children.** Springfield, Ill.: Thomas, 1972.

44. Bruce, P. Relationship of self acceptance to other variables with sixth grade children oriented in self understanding. **Journal of Educational Psychology,** 1958, **49,** 229–238.

45. Burger, G. K., & Armentrout, J. A. A factor analysis of fifth and sixth graders' reports of parental child-rearing behavior. **Developmental Psychology,** 1971, **4,** 483.

46. Burton, R. V., & Whiting, J. W. M. The absent father and cross-sex identity. **Merrill-Palmer Quarterly,** 1961, **7,** 85–95.

47. Caplin, M. D. The relationship between self concept and academic achievement and between level of aspiration and academic achievement. **Dissertation Abstracts,** 1966, **27,** 979–980.

48. Carlsmith, L. Effect of early father-absence on scholastic aptitude. **Harvard Educational Review,** 1964, **34,** 3–21.

49. Caudill, W., & Schooler, C. Symptom patterns and background characteristics of Japanese psychiatric patients. In W. Caudill & Tsung-Yi Lin (Eds.), **Mental health research in Asia and the Pacific.** Honolulu: East-West Center Press, 1969.

50. Chazan, M. School phobia. **British Journal of Educational Psychology,** 1962, **32,** 209–217.

51. Chwast, J. Sociopathic behavior in children. In B. B. Wolman (Ed.), **Manual of child psychopathology.** New York: McGraw-Hill, 1972. Pp. 436–445.

52. Clark, K. B. **Prejudice and your child.** Boston: Beacon, 1955.

53. Clark, K. B., & Clark, M. P. Racial identification and preference in Negro children. In T. M. Newcomb and E. L. Hartley (Eds.), **Readings in social psychology.** New York: Holt, Rinehart & Winston, 1947. Pp. 169–178.

54. Conger, J. J. **Adolescence and youth: Psychological development in a changing world.** New York: Harper & Row, 1973.

55. Coolidge, J. C., Tessman, E., Waldfogel, S., & Willer, M. L. Patterns of aggression in school phobia. **Psychoanalytic Study of the Child,** 1962, **17,** 319–333.

56. Coopersmith, S. **The antecedents of self-esteem.** San Francisco: Freeman, 1967.

57. Dansby, P. G. Black pride in the Seventies: Fact or fantasy? In R. L. Jones (Ed.), **Black psychology.** New York: Harper & Row, 1972. Pp. 145–155.

58. Datta, L. Birth order and early scientific attainment. **Perceptual and Motor Skills,** 1967, **24,** 157–158.

59. Davis, A. Child training and social class. In R. G. Barker, J. S. Kounin, & H. F. Wright (Eds.), **Child behavior and development.** New York: McGraw-Hill, 1943.

60. Derbyshire, R. L. Adolescent identity crisis in urban Mexican Americans in East Los Angeles. In E. B. Brody (Ed.), **Minority group adolescents in the United States.** Baltimore: Williams & Wilkins, 1968. Pp. 157–204.

61. Deutsch, M. Minority group and class status as related to social and personality factors in scholastic achievement. **Monographs in Social and Applied Anthropology,** 1960, **2,** 1–32.

62. Deutsch, M., Katz, I., & Jensen, A. R. (Eds.) **Social class, race and psychological development.** New York: Holt, Rinehart & Winston, 1968.

63. Deutsch, M., & Brown, B. Social influences in Negro-white intelligence differences. **Journal of Social Issues,** 1964, **20,** 24–35.

64. Dielman, T. E., Cattell, R. B., Lepper, C., & Rhoades, P. A check on the structure of parental reports of child-rearing practices. **Child Development,** 1971, **42,** 893–903.

65. Dizmang, L. Loss, bereavement, and depression in childhood. In E. S. Shneidman and M. J. Ortega (Eds.), **Aspects of depression.** Boston: Little, Brown, 1969.

66. Dolger, L., & Ginandes, J. Children's attitudes toward discipline as related to socio-economic status. **Journal of Experimental Education,** 1946, **15,** 161–165.

67. Doris, J. Test anxiety and blame-assignment in grade school children. **Journal of Abnormal and Social Psychology,** 1959, **58,** 181–190.

68. Dunlop, G. M. Certain aspects of children's fears. Unpublished doctoral dissertion, Columbia University, 1951.

69. Durkin, D. Children's acceptance of reciprocity as a justice principle. **Child Development,** 1959, **30,** 289–296.

70. Durkin, D. Children's concepts of justice: A comparison with the Piaget data. **Child Development,** 1959, **30,** 59–67.

71. Dworkin, A. Stereotypes and self-images held by native-born and foreign-born Mexican Americans. **Sociology and Social Research,** 1965, **49,** 214–224.

72. Eisenberg, L. School phobia: A study in communication of anxiety. **American Journal of Psychiatry,** 1958, **114,** 712–718.

73. Ellison, R. **Invisible man.** New York: Random House, 1947.

74. Engel, M., & Raine, W. J. A method for the measurement of the self-concept of children in the third grade. **Journal of Genetic Psychology,** 1963, **102,** 125–137.

75. England, A. O. Nonstructured approach to the study of children's fears. **Journal of Clinical Psychology,** 1946, **2,** 363–368.

76. English, O. S., & Finch, S. M. **Introduction to psychiatry.** New York: Norton, 1954.

77. Erikson, E. H. **Identity: Youth and crisis.** New York: Norton, 1968.

78. Escalona, S., & Heider, G. M. **Prediction and outcome: A study in child development.** New York: Basic Books, 1959.

79. Fenton, N. The only child. **Journal of Genetic Psychology,** 1928, **35,** 546–556.

80. Finch, S. M. **Fundamentals of child psychiatry.** New York: Norton, 1960.

81. Fishman, J. R., & Solomon, F. Youth and social action: 1. Perspectives on the student sit-in movement. **American Journal of Orthopsychiatry,** 1963, **33,** 872–882.

82. Freedman, A. M., & Kaplan, H. I. **Comprehensive textbook of psychiatry.** Baltimore: Williams & Wilkins, 1967.

83. Frenkel-Brunswik, E. A study of prejudice in children. **Human Relations,** 1958, **1,** 295–306.

84. Freud, A. The symptomatology of childhood: A preliminary attempt at classification. In **The writings of Anna Freud,** Vol. 7. New York: International Universities Press, 1971.

85. Freud, A. **The ego and the mechanisms of defense.** New York: International Universities Press, 1946.

86. Furman, R. A. Death and the young child. **Psychoanalytic Study of the Child,** 1964, **19,** 321–333.

87. Garner, A. M., & Wenar, G. **The mother-child interaction in psychosomatic disorders.** Urbana: University of Illinois Press, 1959.

88. Glaser, K. Masked depression in children and adolescents. **American Journal of Psychotherapy,** 1967, **21,** 565–574.

89. Glueck, S., & Glueck, E. **Unravelling juvenile delinquency.** New York: Commonwealth Fund, 1950.

90. Gold, M., & Mann, D. Delinquency as defense. **American Journal of Orthopsychiatry,** 1972, **42,** 463–479.

91. Goldfarb, W. Childhood psychosis. In P. H. Mussen (Ed.), **Carmichael's manual of child psychology.** (3rd ed.) Vol. 2. New York: Wiley, 1970. Pp. 765–830.

92. Goodenough, F. L., & Leahy, A. M. Effects of certain family relationships upon the development of personality. **Pediatric Seminars,** 1927, **34,** 45–71.

93. Gough, H. G., Harris, D. B., Martin, W. E., & Edwards, M. Children's ethnic attitudes: I. Relationship to certain personality factors. **Child Development,** 1950, **21,** 83–91.

94. Gregor, A. J., & McPherson, D. Racial attitudes among white and Negro children in a deep south standard metropolitan area. **Journal of Social Psychology,** 1966, **68,** 95–106.

95. Gregory, I. Anterospective data following childhood loss of a parent: I. Delinquency and high school drop out. **Archives of General Psychiatry,** 1965, **13,** 99–109.

96. Gregory, I. Studies of parental deprivation in psychiatric patients. **American Journal of Psychiatry,** 1958, **115,** 432–442.

97. Grier, W. H., & Cobbs, P. M. **Black rage.** New York: Basic Books, 1968. New York: Bantam, 1969.

98. Gronseth, E. The impact of father absence in sailor families upon the personality structure and social adjustment of adult sailor sons. Part I. In N. Anderson (Ed.), **Studies of the family.** Vol. 2. Gottingen: Vandenhoeck and Ruprecht, 1957. Pp. 97–114.

99. Harris, D. B., Gough, H. G., & Martin, W. E. Children's ethnic attitudes. II. Relationship to parental beliefs concerning child training. **Child Development,** 1950, **21,** 169–181.

100. Harris, S., & Braun, J. R. Self-esteem and racial preference in black children. **Proceedings, 79th Annual Convention of the American Psychological Association,** 1971, **6,** 259–260.

101. Hartley, E. L., Rosenbaum, M., & Schwartz, S. Children's use of ethnic frames of reference: An exploratory study of children's conceptualizations of multiple ethnic group membership. **Journal of Psychology,** 1948, **26,** 367–386.

102. Havighurst, R. J., & Dreyer, P. H. **The national study of American Indian education.** Minneapolis: Center for Urban and Regional Affairs, University of Minnesota, 1971.

103. Hetherington, E. M. Effects of father absence on personality development in adolescent daughters. **Developmental Psychology,** 1972, **7,** 327–336.

104. Hetherington, E. M. Effects of paternal absence on sex typed behavior in Negro and white preadolescent males. **Journal of Personality and Social Psychology,** 1960, **1,** 87–91.

105. Heckel, R. V. The effects of fatherlessness on the preadolescent female. **Mental Hygiene,** 1963, **47,** 69–73.

106. Heinecke, C. M. Some antecedents and correlates of quiet and fear in young boys. Unpublished doctoral dissertation, Harvard University, 1953.

107. Hilgard, J. R. Depression and psychotic states as anniversaries to sibling death in childhood. In E. S. Shneidman and M. J. Ortega (Eds.), **Aspects of depression.** Boston: Little, Brown, 1969.

108. Hoffman, M. L., & Saltzstein, H. D. Parent practices and the child's moral orientation. Paper presented at the meeting of the American Psychological Association, Chicago, 1960.

109. Howell, S. J. G. **Modern perspectives in child psychiatry.** Vol. 3. New York: Brunner-Mazel, 1971.

110. Howell, S. J. G. **Modern perspectives in child psychiatry.** Vol. 4. New York: Brunner-Mazel, 1971.

111. Howell, S. J. G. **Modern perspectives in child psychiatry.** Vol. 1. New York: Brunner-Mazel, 1965.

112. Hraba, J., & Grant, G. Black is beautiful: A reexamination of racial preference and identification. **Journal of Personality and Social Psychology,** 1970, **16,** 398–402.

113. Jersild, A. T., Markey, F. V., & Jersild, C. L. Children's fears, dreams, wishes, daydreams, likes, dislikes, pleasant and unpleasant memories. **Child Development Monographs,** 1933, No. 12.

114. Johnson, A. M. School phobia. **American Journal of Orthopsychiatry,** 1941, **11,** 702–711.

115. Joint Commission on Mental Health of Children. **Crisis in child mental health: Challenge for the 1970's.** New York: Harper & Row, 1970.

116. Kagan, J., & Moss, H. A. **Birth to maturity: The Fels study of psychological development.** New York: Wiley, 1962.

117. Kessler, J. W. **Psychopathology of childhood.** Englewood Cliffs, N.J.: Prentice-Hall, 1966.

118. Kliman, G. **Psychological emergencies of childhood.** New York: Grune & Stratton, 1968.

119. Koch, H. L. Attitudes of children toward their peers as related to certain characteristics of their siblings. **Psychological Monographs,** 1956, **70**(426), 1–41.

120. Koch, H. L. Sissiness and tomboyishness in relation to sibling characteristics. **Journal of Genetic Psychology,** 1956, **88,** 231–244.

121. Koch, H. L. Some emotional attitudes of the young child in relation to characteristics of his siblings. **Child Development,** 1956, **27,** 393–426.

122. Kohlberg, L. Development of moral character and moral ideology. In M. L. Hoffman & L. W. Hoffman (Eds.), **Review of child development.** Vol. I. New York: Russell Sage Foundation, 1964. Pp. 383–431.

123. Kohlberg, L. Moral development and identification. In H. W. Stevenson (Ed.), **Child psychology.** Part 1. (62nd Yearbook of the National Society for the Study of Education.) Chicago: University of Chicago Press, 1963.

124. Kohlberg, L. The development of children's orientations toward a moral order: I. Sequence in the development of moral thought. **Vita Humana,** 1963, **6,** 11–33.

125. Kohlberg, L., & Gilligan, C. The adolescent as a philosopher: The discovery of the self in a postconventional world. In J. Kagan & R. Coles (Eds.), **12 to 16: Early adolescence.** New York: Norton, 1972. Pp. 144–179.

126. Kutner, B. Patterns of mental functioning associated with prejudice in children. **Psychological Monographs,** 1958, **72**(460).

127. Landy, F., Rosenberg, B. G., & Sutton-Smith, B. The effect of limited father-absence on cognitive development. **Child Development,** 1969, **40,** 941–944.

128. Lapouse, R., & Monk, M. A. Fears and worries in a representative sample of children. **American Journal of Orthopsychiatry,** 1959, **29,** 803–818.

129. Lerner, E. **Constraint areas and moral judgment of children.** Menasha, Wis.: Banta, 1937.

130. Lerner, E. The problem of perspective in moral reasoning. **American Journal of Sociology,** 1937, **43,** 249–269.

131. Leventhal, T., & Sills, M. Self-image in school phobia. **American Journal of Orthopsychiatry,** 1964, **34,** 685–695.

132. Levin, H. Permissive child rearing and adult role behavior. In D. E. Dulany, R. L. De-Valois, D. C. Beardsley, M. R. Winterbottom (Eds.), **Contributions to modern psychology.** New York: Oxford University Press, 1958. Pp. 307–312.

133. LeVine, B. B. Punishment techniques and the development of conscience. Unpublished doctoral dissertation, Northwestern University, 1961.

134. Levy, D. M. **Maternal overprotection.** New York: Columbia University Press, 1943.

135. Lipsitt, L. P. A self-concept scale for children and its relationship to the children's form of the manifest anxiety scale. **Child Development,** 1958, **29,** 463–472.

136. Lourenso, S. V., Greenberg, J. W., & Davidson, H. H. Personality characteristics revealed in drawings of deprived children who differ in school achievement. **Journal of Educational Research,** 1965, **59,** 63–67.

137. Lynn, D. B., & Sawrey, W. L. The effects of father-absence on Norwegian boys and girls. **Journal of Abnormal and Social Psychology,** 1959, **59,** 258–262.

138. MacRae, D. A test of Piaget's theories of moral development. **Journal of Abnormal and Social Psychology,** 1954, **49,** 14–18.

139. McClearn, G. E. Genetic influences on behavior and development. In P. H. Mussen (Ed.), **Carmichael's Manual of child psychology.** (3rd ed.) Vol. 1. New York: Wiley, 1970. Pp. 39–76.

140. McCord, J., McCord, W., & Thurber, E. Some effects of paternal absence on male children. **Journal of Abnormal and Social Psychology,** 1962, **64,** 361–369.

141. McCord, W., McCord, J., & Howard, A. Familial correlates of aggression in non-delinquent male children. **Journal of Abnormal and Social Psychology,** 1961, **63,** 493–503.

142. McDonald, R. L., & Gynther, M. D. Relationship of self and ideal-self descriptions with sex, race, and class in southern adolescents. **Journal of Personality and Social Psychology,** 1965, **1,** 85–88.

143. Maccoby, E. E. The taking of adult roles in middle childhood. **Journal of Abnormal and Social Psychology,** 1961, **63,** 493–503.

144. Maccoby, E. E., Gibbs, P. K., & the staff of the Laboratory of Human Development, Harvard University. Methods of child-rearing in two social classes. In W. E. Martin & C. B. Stendler (Eds.), **Readings in child development.** New York: Harcourt Brace Jovanovich, 1954. Pp. 380–396.

145. Malcolm X (with Herley, A.). **The autobiography of Malcolm X.** New York: Grove, 1965.

146. Malmquist, C. P. Depression in childhood and adolescence. **New England Journal of Medicine,** 1971, **284,** 887–892, 955–961.

147. Mealiea, W. L., Jr., & Farley, F. H. Birth order and expressed fear. **Proceedings, 79th Annual Convention of the American Psychological Association,** 1971, **6,** 239–240.

148. Meltzer, H. Economic security and children's attitudes to parents. **American Journal of Orthopsychiatry,** 1936, **6,** 590–608.

149. Meyers, C. E. The effect of conflicting authority on the child. **University of Iowa Studies in Child Welfare,** 1944, **20**(409), 31–98.

150. Miller, D. R., & Swanson, G. E. **Inner conflict and defense.** New York: Holt, Rinehart & Winston, 1960.

151. Miller, H., & Baruch, D. W. A study of hostility in allergic children. **American Journal of Orthopsychiatry,** 1950, **25,** 506–519.

152. Miller, T. W. Communicative dimensions of mother-child interaction as they effect the self-esteem of the child. **Proceedings, 79th Annual Convention of the American Psychological Association,** 1971, **6,** 241–242.

153. Miller, W. B. Lower class culture as a generating milieu of gang delinquency. **Journal of Social Issues,** 1958, **14,** 5–19.

154. Mischel, W. Delay of gratification, need for achievement, and acquiescence in another culture. **Journal of Abnormal and Social Psychology,** 1961, **62,** 543–552.

155. Mischel, W. Father-absence and delay of gratification. **Journal of Abnormal and Social Psychology,** 1961, **62,** 116–124.

156. Mischel, W. Preference for delayed reward and social responsibility. **Journal of Abnormal and Social Psychology,** 1961, **62,** 1–7.

157. Mischel, W. Preference for delayed reinforcement: An experimental study of cultural observation. **Journal of Abnormal and Social Psychology,** 1958, **56,** 57–61.

158. Mitchell, D., & Wilson, W. Relationship of father-absence to masculinity and popularity of delinquent boys. **Psychological Reports,** 1967, **20,** 1173–1174.

159. Morland, J. K. Racial acceptance and preference of nursery school children in a southern city. **Merrill Palmer Quarterly,** 1962, **8,** 271–280.

160. Murphy, G. **Personality.** New York: Harper & Row, 1947.

161. Mussen, P. H. Some personality and social factors related to changes in children's attitudes toward Negroes. **Journal of Abnormal and Social Psychology,** 1950, **45,** 423–441.

162. Nagera, H. Children's reactions to the death of important objects: A developmental approach. **Psychoanalytic Study of the Child,** 1970, **25,** 360–399.

163. Nelson, E. A., & Vangen, P. M. Impact of father absence on heterosexual behaviors and social development of preadolescent girls in a ghetto environment. **Proceedings, 79th Annual Convention of the American Psychological Association,** 1971, **6,** 165–166.

164. Odom, L., Seeman, J., & Newbrough, J. R. A study of family communication patterns and personality integration in children. **Child Psychiatry and Human Development,** 1971, **1,** 275–285.

165. Phillips, B. N., Hindsman, E., & Jennings, E. Influence of intelligence on anxiety and perception of self and others. **Child Development,** 1960, **31,** 41–46.

166. Piaget, J. **The moral judgment of the child.** London: Routledge & Kegan Paul, 1932.

167. Pierce, C. M. Problems of the Negro adolescent in the next decade. In E. B. Brody (Ed.), **Minority group adolescents in the United States.** Baltimore: Williams & Wilkins, 1968. Pp. 17–47.

168. Piers, E. V., & Harris, D. B. Age and other correlates of self-concept in children. **Journal of Educational Psychiatry,** 1964, **55,** 91–95.

169. Poussaint, A. F., & Atkinson, C. Black youth and motivation. **Black Scholars,** 1970, **1,** 43–51.

170. Poznanski, E., & Arthur, B. The counterphobic defense in children. **Journal of Youth and Adolescence,** 1971, **1,** 178–191.

171. Poznanski, E., & Zrull, J. P. Childhood depression: Clinical characteristics of overtly depressed children. In S. Chess and A. Thomas (Eds.), **Annual progress in child psychiatry and child development, 1971.** New York: Brunner-Mazel, 1971. Pp. 455–468.

172. Proshansky, H., & Newton, P. The nature and meaning of Negro self-identity. In M. Deutsch, I. Katz, & A. R. Jensen (Eds.), **Social class, race, and psychological development.** New York: Holt, Rinehart & Winston, 1968. Pp. 178–218.

173. Purcell, K. Assessment of psychological determinants of childhood asthma. In P. H. Mussen, J. J. Conger, & J. Kagan (Eds.), **Readings in child development and personality.** New York: Harper & Row, 1970.

174. Purcell, K. & Weiss, J. H. Emotions and asthma: Assessment and treatment. In C. G. Costello (Ed.), **Symptoms of psychopathology.** New York: Wiley, 1971.

175. Radke, M. J., & Trager, H. G. Children's perception of the social roles of Negroes and whites. **Journal of Psychology,** 1950, **29,** 3–33.

176. Radke-Yarrow, M. International dynamics in a desegregation process. **Journal of Social Issues,** 1958, **14,** 3–63.

177. Radke-Yarrow, M., Trager, H. G., & Miller, J. The role of parents in the development of children's ethnic attitudes. **Child Development,** 1952, **23,** 13–53.

178. Rees, A. H., & Palmer, F. H. Factors related to change in mental test performance. **Developmental Psychology Monographs,** 1970, 3(2, Part 2).

179. Renson, G. J., Schaeffer, E. S., & Levy, B. I. Cross-national validity of a spherical conceptual model for parent behavior. **Child Development,** 1968, **39,** 1229–1235.

180. Riley, J. E. The self concept and sex-role behavior of third and fourth grade boys. **Dissertation Abstracts,** 1966, **27,** 680.

181. Rogers, C. R., & Dymond, R. F. **Psychotherapy and personality change.** Chicago: University of Chicago Press, 1954.

182. Rosen, B. M., Bahn, A. K., & Kramer, M. Demographic and diagnostic characteristics of psychiatric clinic outpatients in the U.S.A., 1961. **American Journal of Orthopsychiatry,** 1964, **24,** 455–467.

183. Rosenberg, B. G., Goldman, R., & Sutton-Smith, B. Sibling age spacing effects on cognitive activity in children. **Proceedings, 77th Annual Convention of the American Psychological Association,** 1969, **4,** 261–262.

184. Rosenberg, M. **Society and the adolescent self-image.** Princeton, N.J.: Princeton University Press, 1965.

185. Rosenthal, M. J., Ni, E., Finkelstein, M., & Berkwits, G. K. Father-child relationships and children's problems. **Archives of General Psychiatry,** 1962, **7,** 360–373.

186. Rosenthal, M. J., Finkelstein, M., Ni, E., & Robertson, R. E. A study of mother child relationships in the emotional disorders of children. **Genetic Psychology Monographs,** 1959, **60,** 65–116.

187. Ross, A. O. **Behavior disorders of children.** New York: General Learning Press, 1971.

188. Ruebush, B. K. Anxiety. In H. W. Stevenson (Ed.), **Child psychology.** Part I. (62nd Yearbook of the National Society for the Study of Education.) Chicago: University of Chicago Press, 1963.

189. Ruebush, B. K. Children's behavior as a function of anxiety and defensiveness. Unpublished doctoral dissertation, Yale University, 1960.

190. Sanford, R. N., Adkins, M. M., Miller, R. B., & Cobb, E. Physique, personality and scholarship: A cooperative study of school children. **Monographs of the Society for Research in Child Development,** 1943, 8(1).

191. Scarr, S. The inheritance of sociability. Paper presented at the annual meeting of American Psychological Association, Chicago, September, 1965.

192. Schaefer, E. S. A configurational analysis of children's reports of parent behavior. **Journal of Consulting Psychology,** 1965, **29,** 552–557.

193. Schaefer, E. S. Converging conceptual models for maternal behavior and for child behavior. In J. C. Glidewell (Ed.), **Parental attitudes and child behavior.** Springfield, Ill.: Thomas, 1961.

194. Schaefer, E. S. A circumplex model for maternal behavior. **Journal of Abnormal and Social Psychology,** 1959, **59,** 226–235.

195. Schooler, C. Birth order effects: Not here, not now! **Psychological Bulletin,** 1972, **78,** 161–175.

196. Sears, P. S. Doll play aggressions in normal young children: Influence of sex, age, sibling status, father's absence. **Psychological Monographs,** 1951, **65**(6).

197. Sears, R. R. Relation of early socialization experiences to self-concepts and gender role in middle childhood. **Child Development,** 1970, **41,** 267–289.

198. Sears, R. R. The relation of early socialization experiences to aggression in middle childhood. **Journal of Abnormal and Social Psychology,** 1961, **63,** 466–492.

199. Sears, R. R., Maccoby, E. E., & Levin, H. **Patterns of child rearing.** New York: Harper & Row, 1957.

200. Senn, M. J. E., & Solnit, A. J. **Problems in child behavior and development.** Philadelphia: Lea and Febiger, 1970.

201. Soares, A. T., & Soares, L. M. Self-concept differential in disadvantaged and advantaged students. **Proceedings, 80th Annual Convention of the American Psychological Association,** 1972, **7,** 195–196.

202. Spock, B. **Baby and child care.** New York: Pocket Books, 1970.

203. Stevenson, H. W., & Stewart, E. C. A developmental study of race awareness in young children. **Child Development,** 1958, **29,** 399–410.

204. Stolz, L. M. **Father relations of warborn children.** Stanford, Calif.: Stanford University Press, 1954.

205. Stone, L. J., & Church, J. **Childhood and adolescence: A psychology of the growing person.** New York: Random House, 1973.

206. Sutton-Smith, B., Rosenberg, B. G., & Landy, F. Father-absence effects in families of different sibling compositions. **Child Development,** 1968, **38,** 1213–1221.

207. Swanson, B. M., & Parker, H. J. A child's acceptance by others, of others, and of the self. **Child Psychiatry and Human Development,** 1971, **1,** 243–254.

208. Swift, J. W. Effects of early group experience: The nursery and day nursery. In M. L. Hoffman & L. W. Hoffman (Eds.), **Review of child development.** Vol. 1. New York: Russell Sage Foundation, 1964.

209. Tabachnick, R. Some correlates of prejudice toward Negroes in elementary age children. **Journal of Genetic Psychology,** 1962, **100,** 193–203.

210. Tapp, J. L., & Levine, F. J. Compliance from kindergarten to college: A speculative research note. **Journal of Youth and Adolescence,** 1972, **1,** 233–249.

211. Tapp, J. L., & Kohlberg, L. Developing senses of law and legal justice. **Journal of Social Issues,** 1971, **27,** 65–91.

212. Thomas, A., Chess, S., & Birch, H. G. **Temperament and behavior disorders in children.** New York: New York University Press, 1968.

213. Thomas, A., Chess, S., Birch, H. G., Hertzig, M. E., & Korn, S. **Behavioral individuality in early childhood.** New York: New York University Press, 1963.

214. Thomas, P. **Down these mean streets.** New York: New American Library, 1967.

215. Tiller, P. O. Father-absence and personality development of children in sailor families. **Nordisk Psyckologi's Monograph Series,** 1958, **9,** 1–48.

216. Tiller, P. O. Father absence and personality development of children in sailor families: A preliminary research report. Part II. In N. Anderson (Ed.), **Studies of the family.** Vol. 2. Gottigen: Vandenhoeck and Ruprecht, 1957. Pp. 115–137.

217. Trent, R. D. The relation between expressed self-acceptance and expressed attitudes toward Negroes and whites among Negro children. **Journal of Genetic Psychology,** 1957, **91,** 25–31.

218. Unger, S. M. Antecedents of personality differences in guilt responsibility. **Psychological Reports,** 1962, **10,** 357–358.

219. Walsh, A. M. **Self-concepts of bright boys with learning difficulties.** New York: Bureau of Publications, Teachers College, Columbia University Press, 1956.

220. Watson, G. A comparison of the effects of lax versus strict home training. **Journal of Social Psychology,** 1934, **5,** 102–105.

221. Wattenberg, W. W., & Clifford, C. Relation of self-concepts to beginning achievement in reading. **Child Development,** 1964, **35,** 461–467.

222. Weiner, I. B., & Elkind, D. **Child development: A core approach.** New York: Wiley, 1972.

223. Wendland, M. M. Self-concept in Southern Negro and white adolescents as related to rural-urban residence. Unpublished doctoral dissertation, University of North Carolina at Chapel Hill, 1967.

224. Wilcox, R. C. **The psychological consequences of being a black American: A collection of research by black psychologists.** New York: Harper & Row, 1971.

225. Winterbottom, M. R. The relation of need for achievement to learning experiences in independence and mastery. In J. W. Atkinson (Ed.), **Motives in fantasy, action, and society.** New York: Van Nostrand Reinhold, 1958.

226. Wolman, B. B. Schizophrenia in childhood. In B. B. Wolman (Ed.), **Manual of child psychopathology.** New York: McGraw-Hill, 1972. Pp. 446–496.

227. Wylie, R. **The self-concept.** Lincoln: University of Nebraska Press, 1961.

Chapter 11

Development in Middle Childhood

II. Expansion of Social Environment

During the middle-childhood years, from school-entrance to the beginning of adolescence, the child's social environment expands enormously. At the same time, the child continues to develop physically, and his cognitive abilities increase and become more complex and better differentiated. As a consequence of the continuing interaction between the developing child and his expanding environment, some motives become strengthened and more clearly articulated while others diminish in importance; new standards are set, and the child is confronted with new problems and challenges. If he is prepared to confront and eventually master these problems, his self-image becomes clearer and his self-esteem strengthened. In contrast, if the demands are too great, too sudden, too poorly defined, or inconsistent and contradictory or if the child is too poorly prepared, psychologically, socially, or intellectually, to meet even reasonable demands, crippling conflicts and anxieties may develop and lead to a variety of psychological and psychosomatic symptoms.

Among the major developmental tasks confronting the child during the middle-childhood years are: the development of various intellectual and academic skills and the motivation to master them, learning how to interact with peers, increased autonomy and independence, development of moral standards and conscience, and learning to deal appropriately with anxiety and conflict. These psychological developments are precursors of the problems that adolescents and adults have to face. Thus the ways in which the child handles the tasks of middle childhood will significantly affect his later behavior. The changing adjustments required of him during this period reflect in great measure his movement away from the home as the one central focus of his activities, interpersonal relationships, struggles, and satisfactions, and into the wider world of school, the neighborhood, and, in a more limited sense, society itself. In turn, however, his readiness to take on the new demands of this expanded environment will depend largely on both his prior and his continuing experiences in the family setting.

THE ADJUSTMENT TO SCHOOL

The School Situation

Once a child has entered kindergarten or first grade, school becomes for more than a decade the center of his extrafamilial world, occupying almost half of his waking hours. It would appear difficult to overestimate the potential importance of the child's school experience in his development and, indeed, this is our view. Schooling may serve not only to strengthen some of the social and cognitive responses that the child's parents may be teaching him; it may also teach him many new responses. The number, variety, and complexity of learned responses required of adults in our culture are so great that even the most remarkable parents could hardly accomplish the task of instilling, without assistance, all such responses in their children. As one of the principal socializing agents of our society, the school should be in a uniquely favorable position to supplement, and sometimes to compensate for, parental training. By teaching the child academic skills, by broadening his store of cultural information, by stimulating his needs for achievement and mastery, and by giving him supervised practice in social relationships both with adults and a wider range of peers, the school should make him better able to deal comfortably with the ever-widening range of challenges and opportunities, as well as problems, that lie ahead of him on the road toward psychological maturity.

Nevertheless, the value of schooling has been subject to increasing challenge from a number of directions (110, 112, 225). Most recently, Christopher Jencks and his colleagues at the Harvard University Center for Educational Policy Research have questioned the importance of both schooling and family-background as determinants of adult economic success (136). Their basic argument, based on statistical anlysis of data from a variety of studies, is that differences in these background factors account for only a relatively small proportion of the variations in adult income. Their study is valuable in calling attention to the significance of other factors, such as luck and individual differences in competence (not connected with schooling and family background), but it is subject to a number of questions regarding interpretation (163, 236). In the first place, one may question whether income is a good measure of adult success in our society. Is the poet, child-care worker, or craftsman of modest means necessarily less "successful" than the business executive or, indeed, the well-to-do plumber? Secondly, the measures of income used by these investigators may not be entirely accurate (163). For example, Jencks and his colleagues fail to control for the effects of age on income. But a young management trainee with a potentially large earning capacity may well be earning less currently than a 40-year-old worker whose income has already reached its peak.

Finally, one wonders whether much of the apparently "unexplained" variation in adult income may not have occurred in the broad middle range of the population. Certainly, at the extremes, the effects of schooling and family socioeconomic background on adult income success (as defined by these researchers) appear to be considerable. The economic prospects of the American lower-lower-class child with limited schooling in inferior schools are significantly poorer than those of a typical upper-class child who goes through superior schools and on to college (83, 163, 225). This is true even though individual deprived children may rise above their circumstances, and individual advantaged children may fail to fulfill their potential or become dropouts.

But there is a larger issue involved than that specifically addressed by Jencks, namely, the quality of schooling in general in our society, both for the poor and

for the middle- or upper-class child. How successful are our schools in developing cognitive and social skills and broadening the child's knowledge? From some perspectives the answer appears to be that they are reasonably successful. More young people are going on to complete high school than ever before (approximately four out of five) and more of these go to college (**179, 225, 243**). Furthermore, today's students as a whole obtain higher scores on standardized achievement tests than students of a decade or two ago (**225, 253**).

Nevertheless, the picture is not entirely unclouded. Far too many middle-class schools are oriented toward "education for docility"—an overemphasis on order, discipline, and conformity, at the expense of self-expression, intellectual curiosity, sensitivity, and a concern with values, self-reliance, and independent judgment (**110, 112, 128, 134, 177, 225**). Too often the result is boredom, restlessness, and a failure to develop the individual's full potential. By the same token, many schools for socioeconomically disadvantaged or minority children are involved in "education for inequality" (**65, 154, 157, 225**). Already lacking in many social and economic advantages, many lower-class children go on to schools that are inferior in all ways, physically and academically, to those of their middle-class peers. As we shall see, the consequence frequently is academic frustration and failure, inadequate preparation for life and work, and a loss of self-esteem (**154, 157, 190, 213, 225**). While there is increasing evidence of efforts to decrease the disparity between lower- and middle-class schools and to increase the creative challenge and social relevance of schools generally (**110, 112, 182, 225**), much greater progress is needed. The most dedicated teachers and administrators cannot hope to accomplish these essential goals without the active support and encouragement of the society from which the schools derive their support.

In examining the influence of the school setting upon the child's continuing development, we shall be concerned with the ways in which school adjustment is influenced both by differences among children and by differences in school experiences. As we shall see later, such considerations assume critical importance in any meaningful discussion of the problems of special groups of children, such as the economically deprived.

For many children, school entrance marks the first separation from the mother for a large part of the day, almost every day. The school, therefore, plays an important part in helping the child to reduce his dependent ties to his home. It also presents him with a new adult whom he must obey and whose acceptance he may court. This new adult will require the child to learn certain responses which are not initially rewarding. Hopefully, the school will contribute to the development of a desire to master intellectual skills, to acquire a pride in one's work, to persevere in solving problems, and to formulate long-range goals. Finally, the school provides the child with increased opportunities to establish more extensive and more meaningful relationships with age-mates.

Many new behaviors are learned during the elementary school years. Previously established but inefficient responses (such as crying in stress situations) must be extinguished, while existing motives (such as mastery) are likely to be stimulated and strengthened. The elements involved in this new learning situation and their effects will be analyzed in subsequent sections. In addition, an effort will be made to show how the child's earlier experiences influence his reactions to the school setting.

The Role of the Teacher

Among the situational factors affecting the child's adjustment and progress within the school setting, probably none is as important as the teacher-pupil relationship. This is particularly evident at school entrance. At this stage, the teacher is likely to be the first adult outside the immediate family who plays a major role in the child's life. However, the teacher also continues to have a significant influence on the child's development throughout the school years. The kinds of teachers a child has will determine in great measure whether his school experience will foster his overall development or will simply increase his difficulties and frustrations. Having the right teacher may help a child to overcome handicaps and make the most of his talents and interests, while having a teacher who is ill-suited to working with children generally, or with a particular child or group of children, may have serious and sometimes disastrous consequences. This may be especially true of teachers working with socioeconomically disadvantaged, minority-group children, as will become evident later.

Child's First Teacher as a Substitute Mother The child's first teacher is a woman. She helps the child to dress and undress when necessary; she praises good behavior and punishes bad; she is a source of nurturance; and she encourages honesty, perseverance, and maturity. The teacher's appearance, attitudes, and actions are usually similar to those of the child's mother, especially if teacher and mother are from the same social class. Hence it is not unreasonable to assume that many young children react to the teacher as though she were a substitute mother.

It will be recalled (see Chapter 2) that, according to the principles of generalization, the individual will transfer attitudes and reactions learned in response to one stimulus to others that are viewed as similar to the original. Similarities between teacher and mother in sex, age, and salient behaviors are usually sufficiently numerous to support a high degree of generalization from one to the other. Consequently, the motives, attitudes, fears, and overt behavior that the child has developed in relation to his mother are likely to generalize to the teacher. If the child views his mother as nurturant and accepting, he is likely to approach the teacher with the same positive attitude. If, on the other hand, the child has hostile feelings toward a rejecting mother and has generally behaved aggressively toward her, he may transfer these responses to the teacher. School beginners tend to have similar perceptions of their mothers and teachers. If one is perceived as a disciplinarian or helper, the other tends to be also. Interestingly, this correlation persists throughout the year (98).

Is having the child's first teacher a woman a wise choice? As mothers are generally viewed by young children in our society as more nurturant and less fear-arousing than fathers, there are probably some advantages in having a woman as the child's first contact with an adult in the school environment. Nevertheless, it would appear desirable for both boys and girls to have greater exposure to males as well as females during the early and middle school years. Because most elementary-school teachers are women, children, particularly boys, tend to view school activities as more related to femininity than to masculinity and, therefore, as more appropriate for girls than boys (142, 147). This attitude may increase girls' motivations to master reading and spelling and may help to account for their consistently greater achievement in the early school days, but it may inhibit some boys' involvement in academic work, particularly those who are strongly influenced by sex-role stereotypes (37, 274). Problems in reading, spelling, and conduct are several times as frequent in boys as girls (37, 79, 88), and resistance to a female-dominated school may well be partly responsible, although it seems likely that other developmental factors are also involved (37). Furthermore, there is some evidence that teachers, both male and female, single out boys more often than girls for negative admonitions (174).

Male and female teachers may help to complement each other in meeting children's needs. It may also be useful for children to learn by example early in life that vocational roles in our society need not be as sex-stereotyped as has tended to be the case in the past (22, 274).

What are the major responses to be learned during the first five years of school? There are, of course, the intellectual skills of reading, arithmetic, spelling; the kindergarten and first-grade activities of coloring, painting, and pasting; and the social skills, habits, and attitudes which play an important role in our culture.

In the United States and western Europe the teacher's values are usually middle class in content. She rewards neatness, obedience, cooperation, and cleanliness; she punishes waste, lack of responsibiity, lying, aggressiveness. Many teachers feel that stealing, cheating, lying, and disobedience are the most serious crimes a young child can commit (12). It is easy to see that prior patterns of familial rewards and punishments may facilitate girls' initial adjustment to the teacher's values. For example, as we have seen, neatness and inhibition of aggressive behavior are characteristically feminine typed responses during the preschool years. Sloppiness and mischievous behavior are more often expected of boys, and boys are less likely to be punished for indulging in them. It might be anticipated therefore, that boys will be more frequently subjected to disapproval by the teacher, and friction is more likely to develop between boys and their teachers than between the girls and their teachers. As we shall see, data on social-class differences indicate that lower-class boys, whose backgrounds reflect different attitudes from those of most teachers, are least likely to adopt the values that are encouraged by the traditional middle-class-oriented school (neatness, obedience to a woman, perseverance, desire to master school subjects). Hence it is not surprising that lower-class boys show poorer performance in school than middle-class boys and middle- and lower-class girls.

Despite the formidable adjustments that the child must make upon entering school, the fact is that most children still react to the beginning of school with favorable anticipation, and these positive feeling are maintained by most children at least through the earliest school years (140, 233, 234). Parents, older siblings, and neighborhood chums provide a great deal of information about school ahead of time, and this pervasive "cultural dramatization" of the event stimulates interest and eagerness to begin. Unfortunately, however, in most instances, and particularly in the case of disadvantaged children, the child's enthusiasm for his teacher and for the school tend to decline in the later years of middle childhood. Children in the early grades tend to have rather stereotyped and generally positive feelings about teachers, but those in fourth to twelfth grades have less favorable attitudes and attribute less relative prestige to the occupation of teacher in comparison with others, such as nurse and airline stewardess (2). It is obvious that factors other than simply the quality of teachers and curriculum are at work here, including the influence of parents and the general social environment, and the propensity of children at any particular moment to want to do what they want to—which frequently may not include learning mathematics or how to write a coherent sentence. Nevertheless, the quality of teachers and teaching is vital, and in view of the increased importance of the school in the socialization of today's children, it appears unfortunate that the interest and excitement with which most children begin school cannot be better maintained. The necessity for making education more interesting, challenging, and relevant to children throughout the school years can hardly be overstressed.

Teacher Characteristics and Student Progress What are the relationships between personal characteristics of the teacher and students' academic and social progress at various grade levels? In one preschool study, two types of teachers were differentiated (27, 117, 204, 249). One group tended to be authoritarian and dogmatic in their views, intolerant of complexity or uncertainty, high in ethnocentrism and religiosity, institutionally oriented, and inclined toward platitudes. In contrast, the other group tended to be independent-minded without being negativistic, relativistic in their thinking and moral beliefs, tolerant of complexity and uncertainty, and interested in novelty. In their handling of children, the latter group of teachers were warmer, more relaxed, more innovative, more perceptive of children's needs and interests, and more resourceful and flexible in meeting those needs and interests. They encouraged greater responsibility along with freer expression of feelings and creative efforts and were less oriented to rules and less punitive than the more dogmatic teachers (**117, 204**).

The effects of greater warmth, flexibility, and encouragement of initiative and responsibility on the part of the teacher—as compared with punitiveness, authoritarianism, and an orientation toward obedience to rules—have also been investigated. According to the data of one study (**245**), young children exposed to warmer, more encouraging teachers were more likely to be constructive when faced with possible failure, more ascendant but less destructive, and more involved in class activities. Teachers who are strict disciplinarians and who do not encourage and reward students, foster negative attitudes toward school and teachers, increased tension and aggression, and later difficulties in school adjustment.

Elementary- and high-school students also generally prefer and make greater social, emotional, and academic progress with teachers who are: "warm," high in "ego strength," enthusiastic, able to display initiative, creative, reactive to suggestions, poised and adaptable, planful, interested in parental and community relations, aware of individual differences among children, and oriented toward individual guidance (**3, 34, 101, 123, 155, 173, 212, 215**). In contrast, teachers who are hostile or dominating generally appear to affect pupil adjustment adversely (**4, 5, 6, 7, 8, 9**). The dominating teacher has little concern for the child's needs and a narrower conception of socially acceptable behavior and therefore more frequently frustrates the child in his attempts to satisfy his needs. Because frustrations may produce aggression, the dominating teacher is likely to become a target for hostility rather than a source of reward and is likely to encounter difficulty in attempts to instill socialized responses. He or she may be able to inhibit the pupil's overtly aggressive responses through the use of fear and punishment, but the dominating teacher will not be able to instill a positive desire for cooperation.

It is important to emphasize that the alternative to an authoritarian, dominating approach on the part of the teacher is not passivity, lack of guidance, or "permissiveness." It is important to distinguish between **authoritarianism** and **authoritativeness** on the part of teachers as we did in our discussion of parent attitudes (**21, 23, 24**). The authoritative teacher

> . . . attempts to direct the child's activities in a rational, issue-oriented manner. She encourages verbal give and take, [and] shares with the child the reasoning behind her policy. . . . Both autonomous self-will and disciplined conformity are valued by the authoritative [teacher]. . . . She enforces her own perspective as an adult, but recognizes the child's individual interests in special ways. The authoritative [teacher] affirms the child's present qualities, but also sets standards for future conduct (**21**, 27–28).

Unlike the authoritarian teacher, the authoritative teacher encourages individual initiative, self-esteem, and social responsibility; unlike the permissive teacher, the authoritative teacher provides guidance, ultimate direction, and sets standards and goals.

In summary, most children appear to do best under well-trained democratic teachers, authoritative but not authoritarian, who know their subject matter, are interested in their pupils, and are not overly concerned with their own problems. Such teachers encourage the student to participate actively in the learning process, while maintaining leadership, direction, and, when necessary, reasonable discipline. Optimal academic and personal growth will not be stimulated in most students by the teacher who is either rigidly authoritarian, hostile, or unresponsive to student needs, or the one who is indecisive and uncertain, poorly trained, narcissistic, or preoccupied with his or her own anxieties and personal problems.

Variations in Teacher Effectiveness As might be anticipated, the same teacher may not be equally effective with all kinds of students. The degree of effectiveness involves a relationship between teacher characteristics and student characteristics.

Each student's perception of and reaction to a teacher will necessarily depend on his own intellectual and emotional make-up. For example, **overachieving** students (those whose academic performance is significantly higher than one would expect from measures of their intellectual ability) tend to perceive their teachers as "warm, affable, and deferring [to the student's needs]" (**36, 262**), while **underachieving** students (those performing below their ability level) perceive the same teachers as "cold, unfriendly, and unconcerned" (**262**). Similarly, high-achieving and socially accepted students show a smaller discrepancy between their perceptions of their own teachers and their ideal teacher than low-achieving and rejected students (**63**).

Open-minded, curious students tend to prefer intellectually flexible, innovative teachers and to earn higher grades in their courses (**248**). **Internally oriented** students (those who generally attribute successes and failures in life to their own efforts) tend to perceive their teachers more favorably and to feel that they are better understood by their teachers than **externally oriented** students (those who usually attribute successes and failures to external forces, such as powerful persons, fate, or chance). Internally oriented students are also perceived more favorably by their teachers, who feel that they understand them better and, in turn, are better understood by them (**50, 51**).

Teachers influence their pupils in other ways. First-grade children taught by impulsive teachers tend to become more impulsive and hasty themselves in responding to school tasks; those taught by reflective teachers tend to become more careful, orderly, and slower in their own responses (**270**). The effect is more marked for boys than for girls. It would appear that thought should sometimes be given to tailoring tempo of teachers to tempo of child. Boys have greater difficulty than girls in mastering reading, and this is in part attributable to boys' more impulsive attitudes (**141**). Placement of an extremely impulsive boy with a teacher who is temperamentally reflective might promote the adoption of a more reflective disposition on the part of the boy and facilitate his progress in learning to read.

Similarly, among fourth, fifth, and sixth graders, **self-controlled** teachers are generally more effective than **turbulent** (blunt, impulsive, unpredictable) or **fearful** (insecure) teachers in promoting academic and social progress (**123**). Children taught by self-controlled teachers averaged about half again as much academic progress as those with fearful teachers. Growth in "friendliness" during the school year was also significantly greater under self-controlled teachers than under either turbulent or fearful teachers. However, **conforming** children (possibly already overly self-controlled and orderly) progressed slightly better under turbulent teachers; in contrast, **oppositional** children did far better under self-controlled teachers than under either turbulent or fearful ones (**123**).

The characteristics of the teacher may be especially important for the adjustment and progress of the socioeconomically disadvantaged student, whose needs and social perceptions may differ markedly from those of the average middle-class teacher.

> It may be argued that [lower-class or disadvantaged] pupils have less potent sources of adult warmth and support at home and hence depend more on, and are influenced by, such adult influence at school. The more vulnerable self-concept . . . of the [lower-class] pupil makes him more open to his teacher's influence as a determiner of his attitude toward his teacher (**272**, 281).

Unfortunately, teachers of disadvantaged students appear more likely than teachers of middle-class children to display rigid attitudes toward child control and to be negative and dominating; they are less likely to encourage give-and-take relationships or to manifest a "more permissive, positive, and flexible attitude toward controlling children" (**272, 278**). To make matters worse, such teachers may be further reinforcing negative parental "teaching" behaviors experienced by the child at home.

In an interesting series of experiments in several countries (United States, Israel, and England), Feshbach and her colleagues (**95**) studied the relation of social class to the use of positive and negative reinforcements in the "teaching" styles of children and their mothers, as well as the relationship between reinforcement patterns and reading skills. In the initial experiments, 4-year-olds were asked to teach 3-year-olds how to solve a simple puzzle. Similarly, mothers were asked to teach their 4-year-old children to perform a slightly more complex puzzle. The frequencies of positive rewarding statements and of negative, critical statements were noted in both situations. It was found that middle-class children and mothers generally displayed more positive reinforcement patterns and used fewer negative reinforcements than lower-class children and mothers, although there were some individual variations in reinforcement patterns, depending on nationality, race, and sex of the child.

On the assumption that a predominance of negative, critical reinforcements may interfere with cognitive development and learning, the investigators then went on to compare the "teaching" techniques of middle-class mothers of first-grade problem readers and successful readers. The two groups of children were matched for sex and IQ, and all children were of at least average intelligence with no manifest neurological impairment. Mothers were asked to instruct both their own and other children on relatively simple performance tasks (for example, how to fit cylinders or pegs of different lengths into holes of varying depth so that the pegs would be level across the tops). Interestingly, the mothers of problem readers consistently exhibited significantly more negative reinforcing behaviors, both with their own and other children. Not only were these mothers more likely to make critical statements, they also revealed a greater frequency of controlling and directive statements and were much more likely to intervene verbally or physically in an intrusive fashion when a child made an error or encountered some difficulty. The investigators conclude that it is important, particularly in efforts to improve early cognitive training for socioeconomically disadvantaged children, to pay at least as much attention to the **way** in which a child is taught as to what he is taught.

Variations in Teaching Methods

The effectiveness of different teaching methods will also vary from one child to another (**94, 99, 122, 126, 146, 150, 180, 207, 214, 232, 242**). High levels of anxiety tend to impair academic achievement, and in general, moderate levels of compulsivity in children would appear to foster academic achievement. The compulsive child tends to be careful, orderly, conforming, concerned with meeting adult expectations, and attentive to detail (**109**). But the effects of anxiety and compulsivity upon the child's performance may depend in great measure on the type of teaching he experiences.

Traditional Versus Student-Oriented School Setting Highly anxious or highly compulsive children have been found (**109**) to be more dependent than less anxious or less compulsive children on highly structured approaches to teaching reading. (The structured approach stresses phonics, as compared with the less structured word-recognition, approaches). Analogously, adolescents who were low in anxiety performed better in more informal, student-centered classes (in which active student participation was encouraged at all times); students high in anxiety performed better in more formal, structured, teacher-centered classes (**86**).

Traditional schools place primary emphasis on acquiring established knowledge and view academic competence as the essential goal. The teacher functions largely as an authority figure, maintenance of order is heavily stressed, and motivation for learning is assumed to rest largely on teacher approval, competition with peers, and differential rewards for achievement.

"Student-oriented" schools place greater emphasis on the total development of the child—intellectually, socially, and psychologically. Attempts are made to excite the child's curiosity and imagination through the use of varied instructional methods emphasizing exploration, experimentation, and discovery. In these settings teachers attempt "to carry their authority role in a relatively flexible way" (182, 7), and active dialogue, questioning, and cross-questioning between teachers and students are encouraged. Creative arts are considered as essential supplements to traditional subjects.

One recent longitudinal study (182) attempted to compare the effects of these two kinds of schools. While there were few consistent differences in standard cognitive skills, there were differences in the pupils' self-images. Children from more student-oriented schools appeared more differentiated in their perceptions of themselves, more accepting of their own negative impulses, "more invested in their childhood status, and more open in their conceptions of social sex roles. We found their traditionally schooled counterparts to be more consistently impersonal, future-oriented, and conventional in their images of roles and development" (182, 372-373).

Although this study was not focused on the effects of particular training approaches for particular kinds of children, it is interesting that a number of bright children in the least structured, most student-oriented school "floundered unproductively and appeared unable or unwilling to mobilize and express themselves even in their own terms" and whose "performance skill seemed erratic . . ." (182, 406). It appears that for some children in this school, greater emphasis on freedom and individuality served as an intellectually and psychologically liberating experience, while for others it was a source of stress (182).

While the results of this study appear reasonable, it should be observed that the investigators were not able to control for the motivation of parents in seeking one or another type of school for their children and so the effects of home influences may be confounded with those of type of school.

Taken together, the findings of these studies serve as a needed corrective to the natural tendency of both students and teachers to assume that a technique that seems to work for them individually (or for their school) would automatically be good for others as well.

Influences of Children's Textbooks

While the teacher's own attitudes and behavior probably exert a more profound effect on the child's development than the texts she uses, the texts do play an important role. It is, of course, obvious that textbooks contribute to a child's development of academic skills. What has probably been less evident, at least until recently, is that they may also influence his development of social and emotional attitudes (71, 72, 102).

Within the past five years there has been increasing emphasis on investigating the content as well as the formal characteristics of children's readers. This interest has been stimulated by a variety of factors, including a greater interest in the special educational and social needs of socioeconomically disadvantaged, urban children (257, 258) and by a growing awareness of and concern with the far higher incidence of reading difficulties among boys than among girls (37, 183).

It appears reasonable to hypothesize that the desire to learn to read and to continue reading will be influenced by the interest aroused by elementary readers and that the degree of such interest will be a function of the age- and sex-appropriateness of the content of the reader, its meaningfulness in relation to the child's everyday life experiences, and its appeal to his personal need systems, including fantasy needs. It also appears reasonable to assume that the course of the child's socialization—his developing view of the world, the strengthening of some motives and the weakening of others, the encouragement or discouragement of sex-role identifications—will also be influenced by the content of the books to which he is exposed in the early school years.

Before examining specific hypotheses about the effects of textbooks, however, it may be useful to discuss briefly the general tone of typical elementary school readers. Comprehensive historical reviews of children's readers (275, 276) present a generally discouraging picture to anyone concerned with the educational requirements of our pluralistic society. Despite the growing need for all children, both dominant middle class and the disadvantaged, to gain a better understanding of and sympathy for cultural diversity and for their own and others' real-life problems, the average children's reader still presents a world that is largely unrelated to the real needs and experiences of children (not only children with special problems, but all children). Unfortunately, despite some encouraging recent trends, a majority of children's early readers are still primarily of the "Dick and Jane" variety.

> Dick and Jane's world is a friendly one, populated by good, smiling people who are ready and eager to help children whenever necessary. Strangers, therefore, are not to be mistrusted but are viewed as potential helpmates. Human nature and physical nature are also cooperative and friendly rather than competitive and conspiring. There are no evil impulses to be controlled. Instead, free rein and encouragement is given for seeking more and more fun and play. Life in general is easy and comfortable; frustrations are rare and usually overcome quite easily. Combining work with play, seeking out new friends, and giving generously are all amply rewarded by nature, adults and one's peers (275, 331).

In addition, "despite the fact that 60 percent of Americans now live in cities, city life is largely ignored in these readers" (137). And it is not only the urban or lower-class or racially different child who is ignored in the sunny, Caucasian, suburban world of children's readers: "Kids from large families, or one-parent homes, children who wear glasses, youngsters who are short, tall, slim, or stocky—they all belong in any but a falsely glamorized fantasy world" (181). Finally, as Sara Zimet

(275) has observed, "And if all this isn't bad enough, it is also felt that unnecessary barriers to the intellectual development of children are perpetuated by the adherence to out-dated vocabulary lists and readability formulas, as well as to the proliferation of anthropomorphism and animism in the content of the readers" (275; see also **153**).

To understate the case, it hardly appears that readers such as those described above are likely to broaden the contemporary child's understanding of the pluralistic, complex world in which he will have to live, nor do they seem likely to help him to understand and to struggle more effectively with his own needs, anxieties, and conflicts.

While a number of publishers have attempted recently to overcome some of the obvious liabilities of traditional readers for urban, racially mixed schools by producing texts which "would focus on the life of a working-class family, living in a typical, racially mixed, urban neighborhood" (**176**, 305), their success to date has not been striking. Studies of such readers (**256, 257**) indicate that with a few notable exceptions, we still see the "same Pollyannaish stories about essentially the same sunshiny, idealized middle-class situations" (**257**, 8). It appears that only the color and shape of the faces have been changed to provide the illusion of multiethnic relevance. In the case of black-oriented, supposedly "urban" readers, "what is depicted is a Negro family living in a happy, stable, white suburban neighborhood" (**38**, 179).

The narrow approach of the readers is also seen in their portrayal of rigid sex-typed behavior. Thus story themes involving active or aggressive play, pranks, and work projects are generally related to boy activity. Quiet activities, school, folk tales, and "real life with positive emotions" (i.e., "Pollyannaish" themes) are related to girl activity. One survey (**38, 64**), found twice as many girl activity stories (63 percent) as boy activity stories (37 percent) involved school activities. Although literacy and formal education were primarily masculine prerogatives in the early period of American history, this is no longer the case, as is reflected in readers of that era and the contemporary association of school with girl activities in children's readers; this appears inappropriate if we are concerned with promoting positive relationships between school and boy-associated activities. The fact that female teachers predominate in the elementary school years only heightens the need for encouraging boys to view school activities as appropriate for males.

Furthermore, the feelings, personal characteristics, and activities of the male and female characters in the stories are also different (**38, 64**). Compared with males, females are more frequently portrayed as sociable, outgoing, kind, timid, easily frightened, but inactive, unambitious, and uncreative. "To the extent that boys identify with male characters and girls with female characters, this difference both in itself and as a reflection of facts that hold true of many sources of influence on children, must have a profound significance for the differential development of personality in the two sexes" (**64**). Not surprisingly, the inculcation of rigid sex stereotypes has attracted criticism from current feminist groups. It has also led to specific suggestions for change from investigators broadly concerned with the whole problem of establishing sexual identity:

> In accomplishing the developmental task of establishing a sexual identity, the growing child makes extensive use of identification with adults and older children. Thus, a more balanced distribution of characters of different ages and of both sexes, involved in a greater variety of age-appropriate activities is strongly recommended. For example, stories concerning the function of adults (other than being parents) need to be present in far greater numbers than currently exist. Occupational, recreational and social adult models outside the family setting have been virtually absent from these texts. By presenting sex-disassociated career possibilities and role functions to children as young as first graders, long before they begin to accept the stereotyped sex-role work and home models as unchangeable facts of life, the textbook will reflect both **what is** as well as **what should be.** For example, women characters would be engineers, doctors, reporters, scientists, taxi drivers, letter carriers, secretaries, teachers, nurses and store clerks, **as well as** mothers, maiden aunts, sisters and daughters. On the other hand, men would be nurses, teachers, secretaries, cooks, waiters, store clerks, lawyers, mechanics and carpenters, **as well as** fathers, bachelor uncles, brothers, and sons. Inside the home, married and/or unmarried women and men would both carry out the household and/or nurturant roles in a way that would not detract from a man's competence or emphasize a woman's incompetence" (**274,** 43).

Effects of School Size

Many people today are concerned about the effects of "bigness" on the quality of contemporary life. Does school size affect the personality and academic achievement of children and adolescents? Teachers in large schools with large classes frequently rely on the use of control, restraint, and direct guidance, emphasizing rules of social living. In contrast, teachers in small schools with smaller classes are less likely to impose restrictive rules of behavior and their relations with the children tend to involve greater interaction in a freer and more intimate atmosphere (**205**).

Students in small high schools, as compared with their peers in large schools, report more internal and external pressure to participate in school activities (**264**). The former engage in more different kinds of activities and hold more positions of responsibility in these activities, that is, they are active participants rather than merely nominal participants or spectators (**264**). Even though large schools may offer a greater total number of activities, the number per student is usually higher in the small school. Since in smaller schools fewer students are available for various school activities (clubs, student council, sports), there is likely to be more encouragement of active student participation for the purpose of keeping a satisfying activity going.

What are the consequences of the greater involvement of more students in more activities in the small school? Students in small schools are more likely than those in large schools to report that involvement in school activities has helped them to develop skills or abilities, to increase confidence in themselves, to prove themselves, to feel needed, to gain a sense of accomplishment, and to work closely with others (264).

Of particular interest are findings relating to the involvement of **marginal students** (those whose IQs, academic performance, and home background appear "relatively unsuited for academic success"; (113, 2). It was found that where there were relatively few students available for activities, marginal students felt a sense of obligation to participate in these activities that was similar to that of their schoolmates. However, in the large school the marginal students were a group apart and felt little, if any, sense of obligation to participate. In fact, "it would appear that the small-school marginal students were not experientially and behaviorally marginal, while their large-school counterparts were a group of relative outsiders" (265, 1257-1258).

Partly because of their experience of greater participation in school activities and their greater sense of being needed and being important to the success of these activities, marginal students in small schools are less likely to drop out of school than marginal students of comparable IQs, grades, and home backgrounds in large schools (113).

The principal advantage of large schools is, of course, the greater variety of educational experiences they offer. However, many of the offerings of the large school tend to be used by only a limited number of students. "Although opportunities in the large school seem great, it is the small school that does a better job of translating opportunities into actual experiences for the total student body" (113, 4). In school, as in so many other areas of contemporary society, it appears that the traditional American slogan "bigger is better" is open to considerable question.

SOCIOECONOMIC STATUS, EDUCATIONAL ASPIRATION, AND SCHOOL ACHIEVEMENT

Not surprisingly, the socioeconomic status of a child's family is significantly related to his level of educational aspiration and to school achievement. Children of relatively high socioeconomic status have traditionally aspired to higher educational levels than their lower-middle- and lower-class peers. Parents and children from higher socioeconomic levels tend to view education as having intrinsic values quite apart from its function of increasing vocational opportunities and economic rewards (13, 14, 30, 44, 158, 244, 246).

Social-class and minority-group disparities in educational aspirations, opportunities, and actual performance have been shrinking somewhat recently. The total number of young people completing high school and going on to college has risen and increased (though still inadequate) efforts have been made to provide greater opportunities for economically and culturally disadvantaged children and youth. Nevertheless, a recent study of a representative national sample of tenth-grade boys (14) showed that the individual's self-concept of his ability is significantly related to his socioeconomic status—the higher the socioeconomic status, the more favorable the self-concept of school ability. This held true even when other relevant predictive factors, such as actual intelligence and family background, were controlled. Positive attitudes toward school are also more frequent, and negative attitudes less frequent, among boys of higher socioeconomic status.

At all grade levels, socially and economically favored children and adolescents score somewhat higher than their "working class" peers, and much higher than seriously deprived peers, in both school grades and standard tests of academic skills (30, 56, 81, 82, 106, 168). This difference is partly a function of such factors as broader cultural and educational opportunities and fewer health and nutritional problems (32, 241). But other, more subtle factors also operate to limit the educational aspirations and accomplishments of "working class" and deprived young people, including broad, class-related customs and values and the individual influence of parents and peers.

Parental Values and Academic Motivation

From school entrance on, middle- and upper-class parents typically display a marked interest in their children's academic careers—urging greater effort, praising indications of progress, and, not infrequently, providing "more tangible rewards, in the form of movies, bicycles, or spending money for accomplishments in school" (189, 561). These parents are likely to view education as the solution to a wide range of economic, social, and personal problems.

Parental interest in the school has traditionally been less common among lower-middle and upper-lower socioeconomic groups, where school has been looked upon largely as a way of getting children ready for adulthood (120, 121, 189). Parents in these groups have not been great believers in education per se, but have seen it as necessary for vocational success. Nevertheless, all these groups, in contrast to lower-lower-class groups (particularly those subject to ethnic segregation and discrimination), have reinforced the value of school to some extent because they expected the school to do something for their children (189).

As we are beginning to see in the increasing activism of economically deprived and minority group parents, a significant part of their traditional lack of interest in and suspiciousness of the school has not been simply a function of a lack of belief in the value of education per se. Rather, it has stemmed in considerable measure from a disenchantment with the kind of education offered to them and their children—an education that they were convinced (often rightly) was largely irrelevant, if not actually damaging, to the real needs of their children (see pp. 507–510).

The more positive attitudes toward academic success shown both by young people and adults of higher socioeconomic levels are related to the fact that most school programs have actually been more "relevant" to their needs, customs, and expectations (**169, 189**). Indeed, one of the school's principal functions has traditionally been to prepare (indoctrinate?) succeeding generations of young people for admission to a middle-class dominated and controlled society (**189, 190, 230**). As Boyd McCandless comments, "schools succeed relatively well with upper- and middle-class youngsters. After all, schools are built for them, staffed by middle-class people, and modeled after middle-class people" (**169, 295**).

Other factors also play a role in the formation of the more positive attitudes traditionally displayed by socioeconomically favored parents and their young. For one thing, the school child's social-class identification tends to be strong, and threats to his membership status in a particular social class may be tremendously anxiety-producing. School success is still more important in maintaining class membership in the higher socioeconomic classes than in the lower, and thus children of these classes are likely to be motivated toward success in school. They are able to see for themselves the delayed future rewards to which academic skills may lead, by noting the important part that they play in the success of a doctor-father or a businessman-uncle. Moreover, parents of higher socioeconomic status are more likely to encourage their children to work hard in school, not simply because of their interest in the child's academic progress, but also because of the threat to their own social status of having a child who "couldn't make the grade."

Finally, socioeconomically favored children are more likely to see their parents and their parents' friends engaged in intellectual work, as in the case of the son or daughter of a doctor, lawyer, architect, or engineer. Thus, middle-class parents are often intellectual models for identification, that is, they not only encourage intellectual goals for the child, but also value them in their own lives. They practice what they preach. Lower-class parents, on the other hand, are less likely to engage in intellectual activities and, consequently, may fail to provide models for intellectual interests or mastery.

Despite popular stereotypes, social-class differences in parental attitudes toward school are not restricted to the WASP majority in our society; class values do cut across racial, ethnic, and other minority-group lines. For example, among middle- and upper-class blacks, the concern of parents for their child's scholastic success and, consequently, their approval of his successful efforts are, if anything, stronger than among middle-class whites. Furthermore, there are differences in attitudes toward education even when socioeconomic level is held constant, as can be seen in the emphasis on education which is traditional among Jews.

PARENTAL AND PEER INFLUENCES ON EDUCATIONAL ASPIRATION

There are, of course, wide individual differences within all socioeconomic, ethnic, racial, and other subgroups, and these differences, as expressed in parental and peer relationships, are perhaps more important than general group standards in determining each child's level of educational aspiration (159, 169, 189). When parents are truly interested in their children and want them to succeed academically and when relevant educational opportunities exist in the community, the effects of parental influences may override the limiting effects of lower socioeconomic status or the negative influence of peers. For example, a study of high school boys (143) showed that working-class boys whose parents encouraged and supported educational and occupational mobility had higher aspirations than middle-class boys whose parents did not encourage such striving. Similarly, a national study of tenth-grade boys (13) found that family relations were a significantly better predictor of school attitudes than socioeconomic status. Boys whose family relations were positive and rewarding (as measured by closeness to parents, parent-child interaction and consultation, and lack of parental punitiveness) showed more positive and fewer negative attitudes toward school. They also had significantly better self-concepts of their school ability than boys with poor family relationships, even when the effects of other relevant variables, such as socioeconomic level and intelligence, were controlled (see Fig. 11.1).

Parents of academically motivated, achieving children are likely to place a high value on autonomy and independence, rather than dependence and conformity (10, 193), and on mastery, competence, and achievement generally (26, 31, 43, 170). These parents tend to be democratic and to encourage an active "give-and-take" interaction with their children (85, 185); they exhibit curiosity and a respect for knowledge (26, 185, 246). In contrast, parental dominance of the child, particularly maternal dominance, **and** parental submissiveness both adversely affect the development of autonomy and academic motivation (89, 90, 242).

Peer Influences on Educational Aspiration

Gaining acceptance by peers is one of the strong needs of children and adolescents. Depending upon the particular values of the peer group generally, and of close friends in particular, educational aspirations may be either strengthened or reduced. The educational aspirations of children and adolescents are clearly consonant with those of their peers (114, 143, 172, 226), and the degree of agreement with peers is directly related to the intimacy of the relationship. Among high school students (143), friendship pairs characterized by greater intimacy and more frequent contact showed closer agreement on academic aspirations and goals. Furthermore, "agreement is higher with school friends who are also the adolescent's very best friend overall (outside school as well as in school) than with those school friends who are not" (143, 221).

Relative Influence of Parents and Peers It is often assumed that in educational aspiration, as well as in most other matters, irreconcilable differences are likely to arise between parents and peers and that peer values are likely to win out over

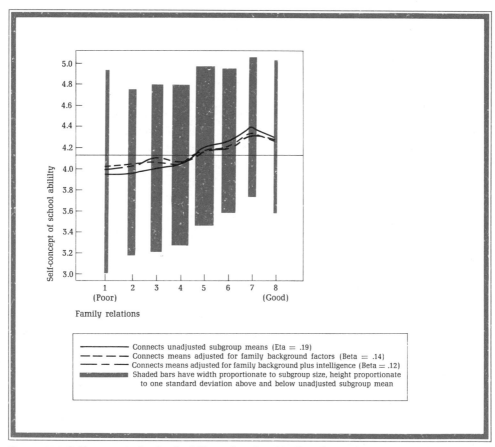

Figure 11.1 Self-concept of school ability related to family relations. (From J. G. Bachman, **Youth in transition.** Vol. 2. **The impact of family background and intelligence on tenth-grade boys.** Ann Arbor: Institute for Social Research, University of Michigan, 1970 p. 99. By permission.)

those of parents **(69)**. Actually, however, there is usually considerable overlap between the values of parents and peers because of commonalities in their backgrounds—social, economic, religious, educational, even geographic. With respect to educational goals, in many middle- and upper-class groups, scholastic success, or at least the absence of scholastic failure, is positively valued and explicitly rewarded, not only by teachers and parents, but also by young people themselves. Thus, among middle-class children and adolescents, the most popular in school are also better students and are rated as more conforming and cooperative **(39, 42, 188)**. Lower-class, and particularly slum children, are far less likely to be rewarded either by parents or peers for scholastic achievement.

While peer influences may predominate in some current customs and tastes, particularly during the high school years, parental influence is likely to be predominant in more fundamental areas, such as life goals, "underlying moral and social values, and understanding of the adult world" (**76,** 1129; **85**). Concordance between the aspirations of adolescents and parents has been found to be greater than that for peers generally and even for best school friends (**143**).

The majority of the high school students (57 percent) in one study had educational plans that were in agreement with those of their parents **and** their friends. Furthermore, adolescents who agreed with their parents were more likely to be in agreement with their peers (76 percent) than those who disagreed with their parents (59 percent). "In the area of future life goals, no polarization seems to exist either toward parents or peers" (**143,** 217). Obviously, however, there are exceptions to this general finding, as in some cases where deviant peer-group pressures are unusually strong and homogenous. In addition, where communication between parents and their children has broken down, parental influence is correspondingly vitiated.

Parental Practices, Anxiety, and Academic Achievement

Parents who create a high level of anxiety in their children about failing to measure up in evaluative situations may affect the child's overall adjustment and self-concept as well as his intellectual performance and academic achievement. Many individuals have an unusually intense fear of failure; they doubt their ability to pass a test and to solve problems (**33, 170**). For some, this anxiety can be so intense that it interferes with clear thinking and results in withdrawal of interest from academic tasks. There are, therefore, many bright children who possess a strong desire to improve their intellectual skills but fail to do so. Strong anxiety and doubts about their ability interfere with their effectiveness on tests, cause them to become easily discouraged, and, therefore, make concentration and new learning difficult (**59, 78, 87, 94, 99, 101, 108, 207, 217, 218, 221, 235, 268**).

This is not to say that the existence of any anxiety will necessarily have negative effects on the child's performance and motivation. A moderate degree of anxiety over performance may help to motivate learning and achievement, as long as it is not strong enough to be disruptive. In fact, there appears to be a curvilinear relationship between amount of anxiety and school achievement (**93, 218, 221**): Among 15- to 17-year-olds, students with moderate anxiety levels had significantly higher levels of achievement than students who were either very low or very high in anxiety (see Fig. 11.2).

The relationship between anxiety and performance becomes greater as the child grows older (**126**). Also, increases or decreases in the child's anxiety are frequently paralleled by changes in test performance; the test performance of children who become more anxious declines and performance improves with decreases in anxiety (**126**). Thus parents who create excessive anxiety in their children as a result of their desire to have their children excel, whether in school or in other areas, may, ironically, achieve the opposite effect.

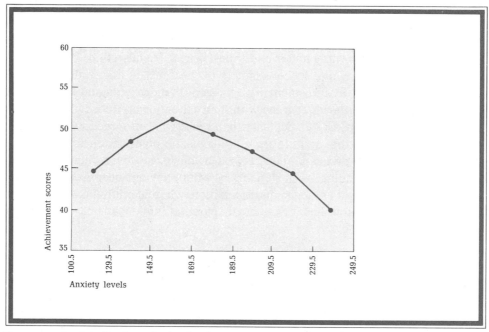

Figure 11.2 Anxiety levels and school achievement. (Adapted from S. Sharma. Manifest anxiety and school achievement of adolescents. **Journal of Consulting and Clinical Psychology,** 1970, **34**(3), 403–407. Copyright © 1970 by the American Psychological Association. By permission.)

THE SCHOOL AND THE DISADVANTAGED STUDENT

The socioeconomically disadvantaged student is likely to be poorly prepared to enter and to progress in the traditional school setting. Largely as a result of developmental influences in the family and his social milieu, which are markedly different from those of the middle- and upper-class child, he is likely to be handicapped in approaching academic tasks requiring a variety of specific cognitive abilities **(70)**. In particular, the kinds of language skills possessed by the socioeconomically disadvantaged child may not prepare him as well as those of the middle-class child for traditional academic demands (see pp. 261–266).

By the end of first grade, more than one-half of children who will be failing in arithmetic in sixth grade can be identified on the basis of their socioeconomic status, their intelligence test scores, and their achievement in arithmetic. By the end of the second grade, two-thirds of such children can be identified **(237)**.

In general, it would appear that disadvantaged children "tend to depend more on real life encounters than on symbolic experience in developing ideas and skills" **(106, 15)**, and their ability to attend to and concentrate on sustained academic tasks tends to be poorer **(81, 83, 106, 225, 263)**. In addition, as we have already seen, they are likely to be less highly motivated and to have lower aspirations for academic achievement than middle-class children, and they receive little academic encouragement from either parents or peers. The lower-class child's progress in school may also be further limited by feelings of inadequacy and a depressed self-concept resulting from the greater difficulties he encounters and from feelings of not "belonging" in a social setting characterized by unfamiliar goals and codes of behavior (**106, 107, 160, 198, 254**).

Another problem encountered in efforts to provide academic continuity and a feeling of participation for socioeconomically disadvantaged children and adolescents in the school setting, particularly in the changing urban environment, is that of transiency (**139, 164**). As people become more affluent and move out of urban slums, their places are taken by a constant stream of newcomers, largely from poor rural backgrounds: blacks, Appalachian whites, Puerto Ricans, Chicanos, Latinos, and others. In many ghetto schools the turnover of pupils may approach 100 percent in a single year (**75, 83, 164, 225**).

Given the problems that the disadvantaged child faces in meeting traditional academic demands, it seems reasonable to conclude that, if anything, he should be provided greater assistance in school than the better prepared middle-class youth. Yet the fact of the matter is that the reverse is usually the case. The school the poor or minority group child attends is far more likely to be physically deteriorated (often to the point of posing real dangers to his health and safety), overcrowded, lacking in essential physical facilities (such as playgrounds, shops, laboratories, cafeterias, even adequate lavatories), inadequately staffed, and lacking in the most basic kinds of equipment, such as teaching aids and books (**70, 75, 149**).

It would be a mistake, however, to assume that what is required to meet the educational needs of socioeconomically deprived children and adolescents is simply more of what has traditionally been provided the average middle- and upper-class child. Certainly, the disadvantaged child, like all children, needs decent physical surroundings and educational facilities and dedicated, skillful teachers. But he also needs new and imaginative kinds of approaches to education and curricular development; to vocational, social, and personal guidance; and to community involvement with the schools. All of these things are necessary, not merely to help the disadvantaged child to compensate for his general academic deficiencies, as judged by traditional measures of performance, but also to respond to his specific life problems and, it should be added, to take maximum advantage of his particular assets and aptitudes, whether they fit traditional middle-class patterns or not (**81**). "The big mistake most schools have made is showing reluctance to meet the child in his home territory and then take him for the ride. Until now we have been asking the child to meet us in **our** territory and then begin the ride from there" (**225**, 97).

Above all, schools need to provide an atmosphere that makes learning a rewarding and relevant experience, one that promotes self-confidence, self-respect, and a sense of cultural identity—particularly in the case of minority students. Too often at present the schools serve only to reinforce already existing negative self-concepts and feelings of inadequacy and frustration (61).

Improved and innovative programs need to begin early, preferably at the pre-school level or earlier, and continue throughout the entire course of the young person's educational experience (15, see pp. 350–359). Finally, if school programs for poor and minority children are to work, they must gain the confidence of parents and community (106, 149, 225).

These are challenging assignments, and the difficulty of carrying them out successfully should not be underestimated. Nevertheless, the fact is that at all educational levels **some** schools, led by imaginative administrators and enthusiastic, dedicated teachers, are succeeding, often against seemingly insurmountable odds (92, 111, 124, 190, 225). In schools as in laboratory experiments, "it is the successful experiment which is decisive and not the thousand-and-one failures which preceded it. More is learned from the single success than from the multiple failures. A single success proves it can be done" (225, 95).

The John H. Finley elementary school in Harlem has a student body that "is 89 percent black, 10 percent Puerto Rican, and 1 percent 'other,' i.e., white" (225, 99). Despite the fact that all of the entering students at this school, in a recent survey, scored below the national median in reading readiness, by the end of the second grade more than three-fourths of these same students scored above the national median. "More important, the children continue to learn; their reading scores do not dip in the upper grades, as is the case in most ghetto schools" (225, 100).

How are such results achieved? Several factors appear to play a major role. (1) "The atmosphere is a good bit warmer and more humane, and the environment both freer and more supportive, than in most schools" (225, 103); kindness and gentleness are evident throughout the school, and unkindness on the part of staff is not tolerated. (2) Disruptive behavior is handled more gently and more positively. (3) There is "a conviction that 'disadvantaged' children can learn" (225, 105), and the principal and teachers hold themselves accountable if their students fail. (4) Innovative, imaginative, pupil-centered approaches to the development of reading and other skills are flexibly employed. (5) Strong efforts are made "to involve parents in their children's education" (225, 110). (6) Every opportunity is taken advantage of to enhance the child's self-esteem and pride in his cultural identity.

Schools such as Finley—the "experiments that succeed"—demonstrate that it is possible to reach even seriously disadvantaged students. But unless the number of such schools is expanded significantly, and soon, there is a real question, as the National Advisory Commission on Civil Disorders points out, as to whether democracy as we know it can survive (209). At the least, unless adequate steps are taken, millions of children will enter adulthood unprepared to lead reasonably happy, self-sustaining, and productive lives.

SCHOOL DROPOUTS

In a society characterized by rapid technological change, increasing automation, and ever greater specialization, the school dropout, particularly the early dropout, is likely to be seriously disadvantaged in the social and economic world. At the present time, the percentage of dropouts from high school is decreasing—800,000 in 1971, as contrasted with approximately 1,000,000 in 1960 (192). However, the fact that more young people are completing high school or going beyond it may add to the problems of those who do not finish school by increasing the stigma in our society of being a dropout.

Antecedents of Dropping Out

Both sociological and psychological factors appear to be involved in the adolescent's leaving school prematurely. The dropout rate is higher among the poor than among the more well-to-do, and it is highest among ethnically segregated youth living in urban and rural slums (31). The proportion of dropouts among upper-middle-class youth is one in six. Among lower-middle- and upper-lower-class youth, it is one in four. At the bottom of the socioeconomic ladder, one in two lower-lower-class youth drops out prior to completing high school (61). Nevertheless, a variety of investigations indicate that economic need per se is not ordinarily the major factor in dropping out (65, 73, 255). Thus, in one study of a large number of youths who dropped out of school in a large urban community, only 3 percent withdrew primarily because of financial need or because they were required at home (61).

School Experience and the Dropout

A greater number of dropouts than graduates are below average in intelligence test performance, and the probability of dropping out of school prior to completion of high school varies inversely with IQ (61, 64, 225, 255). Almost 33 percent of dropouts, but only 10 percent of high school graduates, have IQ scores below 85 (255). In contrast, 48 percent of dropouts have average IQ scores (90-109), and 6 percent have above average scores (110 or more). These findings suggest that a high level of intellectual skill favors graduation, but that intellectual ability is not in itself a decisive factor in many cases of dropping out of school, since a majority of dropouts are of at least average IQ.

A qualification should be added, however. Early dropouts, students who drop out in the seventh grade, have much lower intelligence test scores than dropouts at all later grade levels (255). While approximately one-third of later dropouts have IQ scores below 85, three-fourths of early dropouts score below this level.

School difficulties, both academic and social, play a prominent role in the history of most dropouts. The typical dropout, even though of average IQ, is retarded two years in reading and arithmetic by the time he reaches the seventh grade, and a majority of his grades are below average. Again, the grades of early dropouts are significantly lower than those of later dropouts (255). Dropouts are likely to have failed one or more school years (31, 61, 255).

It has been found that dropouts and graduates differed significantly in academic performance even in the early school years (58, 61). In the second grade, for example, only about 10 percent of future graduates scored below grade level on measures of reading and spelling in one study, while about 90 percent of future dropouts performed below grade level (58). Students "dropped out earlier and more abundantly in direct ratio to their low scholastic ranks" and in direct proportion to the number of times that they had been held back in grade level (58).

Interestingly, as the above findings suggest, the percentile level of dropouts in reading achievement is characteristically lower than their overall level of intelligence (84). Obviously, there are a variety of reasons for discrepancies between the potential dropout's intelligence and his basic academic skills: deficiencies in home background, in motivation, in emotional adjustment, in the appropriateness of his teaching, and the like. Once academic difficulties have developed, however, they exert a formidable influence of their own.

The student who cannot keep up academically or who finds much of the curriculum puzzling and irrelevant to his needs is likely to find his school experience frustrating, unrewarding, and in a significant number of instances, humiliating. A frequent theme expressed by dropouts in various studies is "feeling goofy" with those "little kids." In such a situation, the decision to drop out is at least as likely to be guided by a desire to escape from the burdens of his school experience as by any positive attraction of external goals.

For many lower-class youth (among whom the largest numbers of dropouts are found), school is an unrewarding experience socially as well as academically. They do not participate to the same degree as other youth in the social life and activities of the school; they do not share the values of their largely middle-class teachers; and they are likely to feel inadequate or resentful when confronted with the social, as well as the academic, demands of the school setting (165). Even while still in school, future dropouts tend more frequently than other students to associate with peers who have already dropped out and to avoid participation in school activities (61, 91).

One conclusion appears inescapable at this juncture, namely, that "the school experience, as currently constituted, is failing to meet the needs—personal, social, and vocational—of an increasing number of our youth, particularly in the lower-class large urban ghettos" (188, 732). And the situation for these young people is continuing to deteriorate. This is not to say the fault lies solely with the schools themselves. Obviously, much wider social and personal factors are also involved.

Influence of Family and Peers

Not all dropouts come from deprived backgrounds, and many students who come from such backgrounds (over 50 percent) successfully complete high school. In one study dropouts were matched in age, sex, school background, family socioeconomic status, and minority-group membership with students who graduated. The groups differed significantly in family and peer influences and in personality characteristics (**60, 61**). Communication between parents and children and mutual acceptance and understanding among family members were all significantly poorer in the families of dropouts than of graduates. For example, when asked, "Would you say that your whole family both understands and accepts each other?" 85 percent of dropouts gave responses classified as "little" or "very little," while 82 percent of graduates gave replies ranging from "moderate" to "very much" (**60**).

When asked further, "Would you say that your family both understands and accepts **you**?" 79 percent of the dropouts replied in terms similar to those used by Dan, a 17-year-old dropout, who confessed that he had never felt understood or accepted: "I always felt left out. But really I think I need the time that the others got. . . . It's just that I felt left out. It seems when I was little I was always left out. I wasn't one of the family, really" (**60,** 220). In contrast, 84 percent of the graduates expressed the view that they were both understood and accepted by their families.

There also appeared to be far less communication within the families of dropouts than within those of graduates, and the families of graduates were far more likely to share leisure-time activities as a family. The families of dropouts also tended to be more unhappy and isolated socially than those of graduates. They had fewer friends, and their friendships tended to be more superficial; friends were simply viewed as people you "can have fun with" or "who will help you." In contrast, families of graduates tended to view friendships more in terms of reciprocal assistance and mutual understanding.

Psychological Characteristics of Dropouts

Data from several studies show that dropouts, compared to graduates, tend to be more troubled emotionally, less confident of their own worth, lower in self-esteem, more lacking in a clearly defined self-image and sense of identity, and less likely to have structured values and personal, social, or occupational goals (**14, 60, 61**). They are more likely to have hostile, angry feelings and to be resentful of authority in any form—"home authority, civil authority, intellectual authority, occupational authority" (**61,** 192). Influenced more by frustrations from which they are trying to escape than by goals toward which they are striving, these adolescents tend to live more for the moment, responding impulsively, planning little, showing little sustained, goal-directed activity, and seeking immediate gratification (**14, 61**).

Male high school graduates scored significantly higher than dropouts on measures of tidiness, calmness, vigor, self-confidence, cultural interests, emotional maturity, and sociability; dropouts scored higher than graduates on impulsiveness and, to a lesser extent, interest in leadership. Similarly, among females, graduates significantly exceeded dropouts in all of the measures differentiating males, and in social sensitivity as well. On none of the measures, did female dropouts score higher than graduates.

According to projective tests and interview material, dropouts are more likely to view the world as an unpredictable place, characterized by violence, hostility, strife, cheating, faithlessness, and exploitation of other people (61). In a world such as this long-term goals seem relatively meaningless. Plans are likely to go astray or to be doomed from the start; ". . . the mind of the dropout seems to exhale feelings of inadequacy, worthlessness, frustration, and failure. A dropout, by that very fact, is more clearly cast in the role of outcast and pariah" (61, 192-193).

Dropping Out—Problem or Symptom?

It should be obvious at this juncture that many dropouts' later problems—higher unemployment rates, more personality problems, lower aspiration levels, and a higher incidence of delinquency—are reflections of the kinds of problems that led them to drop out in the first place. A recent extensive national four-year study of what happens to high school dropouts (14, 191) showed that the act of dropping out itself did not appear to further aggravate their problems. "The difficulties experienced by the dropouts we studied—the low aspiration and accomplishment, and even the limitations in self-esteem and self-concept—were already present or predictable by the start of the tenth grade, and there is little evidence that dropping out made matters worse" (192).

Indeed, in one area, self-esteem, the scores of the dropouts improved somewhat after dropping out, although they still did not reach the level of the graduates (14). Furthermore, the investigators found that unemployment "is better predicted using background and ability measures than by using dropout data—[although] the best prediction is made when the two are combined" (191, 7).

Dropping out of school is more likely to be the result of an adolescent's problems than their cause. The greatest challenge is to ameliorate the conditions that lead to dropping out in the first place, beginning as early as possible in the child's life. Nevertheless, for those who have already dropped out and who are unable to find jobs or to manage their lives in a constructive and adaptive fashion, we need to develop more appropriate and more extensive vocational, educational, and personal opportunities than we have to date (240).

RELATIONS WITH PEERS

The child of school age is confronted with two new socialization agents: teachers and peers. As we have already seen, the teachers that a child is exposed to may have a significant effect on his subsequent development. The peer group, too, plays an increasingly important role in influencing developments as the child moves out of the home for a greater percentage of his waking hours—a percentage which increases steadily from kindergarten to high school (53).

The peer group provides an opportunity to learn how to interact with age-mates, how to deal with hostility and dominance, how to relate to a leader, and how to lead others. It also performs a psychotherapeutic function for the child in helping him deal with social problems. Through discussions with peers the child may learn that others share his problems, conflicts, and complex feelings, and this may be reassuring. For example, the discovery that other boys are also angry at their fathers or are concerned with sexuality may relieve tension and guilt somewhat.

Finally, the peer group helps the child develop a concept of himself. The ways in which peers react to the child and the bases upon which he is accepted or rejected give him a clearer, and perhaps more realistic, picture of his assets and liabilities.

> It is fair to say that the crucial arena for self-esteem is the arena of one's age-mates. At home there is an age hierarchy. Even the siblings are bigger or smaller, so that differences of competence are expected. The home, moreover, continues to be the source of love and provision of basic wants, even when the child ventures forth to playground and school. At home he must be **love-worthy:** this may include being competent but it is heavily weighted on the side of being good, obedient and affectionate. On the play-ground the values are different; he must be **respect-worthy,** able to command respect because he shows competence and handles himself with ease. It is a sharp strain for many children when they pass from the atmosphere of a child-centered home into the competitive realities of even a friendly play group. They must show what they have in the way of physical prowess, courage, manipulative skill, outgoing friendliness, all in direct comparison with other children of their age. The penalties for failure are humiliation, ridicule, rejection from the group (**261,** 144–145).

The influence of the peer group as a socializing agent appears stronger in American culture at the present time than in some other societies or than in our own society in earlier eras (**53**). For example, it has been found that Mexican youth (**178**) and Chinese youth living in Hawaii (**130**) are far less under the "tyranny of their peers" than American youth because, in comparison with the American child, they "live far more in the family and less in peer society" (**53,** 295). The same is true of many European youth. In contrast, however, children living in an Israeli kibbutz or within the Soviet educational system are, through conscious design on the part of society, reared under maximal peer, rather than family contact (**231**).

However, in these settings, peer influences are less likely to deviate from adult standards, and the child is more likely to resist deviant pressures when they occur. Urie Bronfenbrenner and his colleagues, who have studied the role of the peer group in children's socialization in a variety of countries (**45, 46, 47, 115**), found that Russian children were significantly more resistant to deviant peer pressure than American and German children, while English children were least resistant. Significantly, it was also found that English children spent less time with their parents, less time alone, and more time with peers than American or German children, and their time with peers was more likely to be unstructured and free of adult supervision or direction than was the case for Soviet children. Finally, among English, German, and American children, time spent with peers (particularly time spent with gangs) was negatively related to orientation toward adult influences.

The rapidity of social change within American society enhances the influence of the peer group by "creating a hiatus between one generation and the next, thus contributing to the role of age mates in the socialization process" (**80**, 523). Keniston makes a similar observation: "the relations between the generations are weakened as the rate of social innovation increases (**148**, 153). This change will become especially evident in our later discussions of adolescence and the relationships between generations (see pp. 574–578).

Peer Culture in Middle Childhood

In a very real sense, the child lives in two worlds, that of his parents and other adults and that of his peers. Even when these worlds exist side by side, there is often remarkably little overlap between them. The world of peers is a subculture of its own, influenced in many ways by the larger culture of which it is a part, but also having its own history, its own social organization, and its own means of transmitting its folklore from one generation to another.

Much of the ritual of the childhood years is transmitted by peers, not by parents, even though the rituals themselves may have changed little over the years (**238**). When adults overhear children at their games, they are likely to be nostalgically reminded of their own childhood years. Much the same thing appears to apply to the changing nature of children's groups over the middle-childhood years and to their sometimes amusingly elaborate, though frequently violated, rules, regulations, and initiation ceremonies.

The changing adult culture may act to set limits on peer associations. Thus the suburban, middle-class, Protestant white child or the urban, lower-middle-class black child may each have little opportunity for interaction with children of other cultural, ethnic, or socioeconomic backgrounds, often to the detriment of both. Parents may restrict, even among available opportunities, the other children with whom they allow their children to associate. Segregation of boys and girls in peer groups in the middle-childhood years may be partially encouraged by the adult culture in its efforts to promote sex-typed identification. However, within the limits set by the social circumstances of the larger adult culture, the structure, function, and membership of children's groups and their changes with age tend to occur in a largely autonomous fashion, with marked similarities from generation to generation.

During the early years of middle childhood, informal groups, formed by the children themselves, predominate, and the school-age child is likely to refer to "the gang." The gang has few formal rules for governing itself, and there is a rapid

turnover in membership. Expediency plays a large role in determining group membership.

Later, however, between the ages of 10 and 14, there is a tendency for children's groups to become more highly structured and more cohesive (115). Aspects of formal organization, such as special membership requirements and elaborate rituals for conducting meetings, appear. Even so, the personnel may change frequently and the group itself may not last long. At this time, formal organizations such as the Boys' Clubs or Campfire Girls become more important, especially for middle-class children.

The group play of children from 7 to 11 years differs in important ways from that of children 5 to 6 years of age. In the younger period, a boy may play, or fight, with either boys or girls. In terms of cultural stereotypes, their games may be "feminine" (playing house) or "masculine" (playing ball or building). Beginning at age 7 or 8, however, children in our society begin to associate primarily with same-sex peers. Age also plays an important role in determining the nature of peer group relations (53, 62, 127, 250). Both boys and girls tend to associate primarily with peers of the same age, although prepubertal girls, with their earlier growth spurt, may begin to express an interest, however tenuous, in somewhat older boys.

The child needs the experience of interacting with other children of his own age and level of cognitive development who share his interests, needs, abilities, skills, and problems (166). Increasingly, as the child moves away from his relatively exclusive ties with his parents during the early school years, he needs a compensatory feeling of belongingness in a peer group in which he can feel comfortable.

Sex cleavages in interests and activities become increasingly evident throughout the school years. While there is still much overlap—for example, girls show an increasing interest in masculine games and activities from third to sixth grades (239)—there is nevertheless growing separation of interests, activities, and concerns of boys and girls during these years. Boys tend to be somewhat more involved with gang and other peer-group activities than girls, who tend to remain somewhat more closely tied to parents during these years. However, girls tend to have more intimate, individual interpersonal relationships than boys even at these ages—a precursor, perhaps, of later lifelong interpersonal orientations.

Social Status With Peers

Because of the important role that the peer group plays during middle childhood, not simply in providing the child with immediate satisfactions, but in implementing his integration into the broader social world, the youngster who is accepted by his peers clearly has an advantage over one who is rejected. But what determines whether a child will be popular in his group, treated indifferently, or avoided by others? On what basis are friendships among children formed? What variables are related to leadership? What are the consequents of high or low social standing in the group?

Several techniques of measurement have been used in studies of the social status of children. The most common, however, is the sociometric approach, in which youngsters are asked to list their preferences and rejections among the other children of the group with respect to some definite criterion. For example, each child in a camp cabin might be asked to name three children he would like to have as teammates, as swimming buddies, or as neighbors at home. From these data, a composite diagram of all the children's choices, known as a sociogram, can be constructed. The sociogram shows the relative social status of each child, from the highest in social acceptance (most frequently chosen) to the "social isolates" (never chosen).

In one investigation classmates and teachers rated the 20 most popular and 20 least popular children on a battery of 20 personality variables. The children highest in social acceptance were rated much higher in socially aggressive and outgoing characteristics. In general, they manifested either of two personality syndromes (groups of characteristics which go together). The first syndrome was composed of strong, positive, aggressive characteristics such as leadership, enthusiasm, and active participation in recitations. The second, which was less definite, involved cheerful disposition and friendly attitudes (tidy, good-looking, frequent laughter, happy, and friendly) (40, 41). Other studies of school-age children indicate that peer acceptance is also related to "lack of withdrawal" as perceived by peers (267), the frequency with which "kindness" is expressed to peers (228), self-confidence (54), sensitivity to the social overtures of other children (115, 152), adjustment to and cooperation with group rules and routines (115, 184), being a "good sport" and being able to take a joke on oneself (115, 152), willingness to both give and receive friendly overtures, and willingness to respond positively to the dependent behavior of peers (54). Increased sharing of rewards with peers increases positive ratings on sociometric evaluations (115, 144). By and large, the characteristics associated with popularity showed a great resemblance to those which have been found to be the consequents of gratifying and rewarding early interactions in the family setting.

The relationships between particular attributes and popularity varies somewhat with sex and age. For example, among first-grade girls popularity is closely associated with such characteristics as "being quiet," "not quarrelsome," and "not bossy." By the fifth grade, good looks, good sportsmanship, friendliness, tidiness, and lack of quarrelsomeness are most highly correlated with girls' popularity.

The most highly esteemed first-grade boys tend to be those whom their peers consider good sports, good at games, "real boys," not bashful, and daring. Fairness in play and leadership ability are the most important correlates of popularity among third-grade boys. Fifth-grade boys with high prestige also tend to be viewed as best friends, good-looking, not bashful, and "real boy." In this group, friendliness, good sportsmanship, and tidiness were somewhat less closely linked to popularity. Characteristics such as "not bossy," "doesn't get mad," "not quarrelsome," and "doesn't fight" had little to do with prestige position.

In the area of skills and abilities, "the picture continues to build up that the more intelligent and creative are generally more accepted by their age mates; the slow learners and the retarded, less well accepted" (53, 305; see also 16, 17, 103, 115, 186, 195, 199, 202, 220, 269). Significant relationships have also been obtained between peer status and reading achievement, arithmetic ability, and general academic achievement at every socioeconomic level of the school community (125, 129, 131, 202, 219, 229). Body size, muscular strength, and athletic ability also influence social acceptance among boys (67, 68, 115, 251).

The attributes of low-status or rejected children have been found to include anxiety, excessive emotional dependence on adults, uncertainty, social indifference, withdrawal, rebelliousness, aggressiveness, and hostility (74, 115, 116, 125, 129, 194, 228, 247, 267). Physical liabilities, such as obesity and facial disfigurement, are also associated with rejection (210).

Finally, it appears that the extent to which a boy's or girl's behavior is rewarding to others influences the way in which they treat him in return and the extent to which he is accepted by others. For example, one investigator (208) found a positive correlation between acceptance of others and acceptance by others among fourth-, sixth-, and eighth-grade children. Popular children are more able to make subtle inferences about the causes of other children's behavior and to be socially sensitive to and accepting of their needs (54, 104, 115).

Status with Peers and Social Behavior

The child's status among his peers strongly affects the course of his socialization. A study of boys and girls, aged 11 to 15, in a summer camp demonstrated that children who were accorded high status by their peers felt more secure and accepted in the group and were able to sway the behavior of others by means of both direct and indirect techniques (201). Others responded by following their leads, thus rewarding their leadership activities.

Children with high status were less likely than the average child to accept others' commands and suggestions, but they were more attuned to and responsive to group trends in mood and behavior. Because they were secure in their group, they were free to "pick up" contagion if they wished, but could also resist direct attempts at influencing them. Their peers, aware of the high-status children's position in the social hierarchy, more frequently made indirect rather than direct approaches to them when attempting to influence their behavior.

By and large, those children to whom prestige position is attributed are aware of the fact; their awareness is facilitated by the behavior of others toward them in a variety of ways including, among other things, a readiness to be influenced either directly or "contagiously." They tend to act on the basis of this awareness by making more direct attempts at influencing, and by other behavior indicative of freedom to act spontaneously in the group (201, 334).

While the greatest influence on others is possessed by high-status children and interest understandably tends to focus on them, influence is not entirely confined to such children. A single impulsive child, given the right potential situation, may be an important determiner of group action. A "contagious" response which extends rapidly throughout the group may result when the impulsive child "triggers off an action that the group is ready for, but has not yet done" (53, 313). Such children may exert a surprisingly dramatic influence in stressful situations when their expressive emotionality parallels needs of the group at the moment (201).

Effects of Adults and Situational Factors on Peer-Group Relationships

While many children's groups are informal and relatively independent of adult influence, there are other situations in which adults may be involved and in which they can exert significant influences both on general group atmosphere and effectiveness and on individual peer relationships—for good or ill. The roles played by adult leaders can significantly affect the outcome of peer-group efforts (97, 167, 271). One investigation of racial desegregation in preadolescent campers (271) showed that adults significantly affected the young campers' reactions to the initial ambiguity of the interracial situation "by structuring activities, defining behavioral possibilities, and setting the tone of affective relations" (53, 314). In another study of tenth-grade students (97), the teacher restricted praise for participants in a discussion session to students sitting in odd-numbered seats; the method was not known to the participants. Subsequent sociometric ratings by the children indicated that the praised students received more positive choices.

Environmental factors may also influence peer relationships and peer acceptance (53, 115, 151). In a classic series of experiments (222, 223, 224) preadolescent male campers who had previously been associating informally were broken up into two new groups; each group was assigned separate living quarters and given its own program of activities. The effects were then unobtrusively observed. Prior friendship patterns between boys who were now in different groups began to dissolve and new within-group friendships began to form. Hierarchical social structures of leaders and followers within each group rapidly emerged. Perhaps most significantly, there began to be much talk within each group of "we" and "they," accompanied by mildly derogatory and competitive attitudes toward the other ("they") group, but without outright hostility.

When instances of intergroup competition were created by adult leaders, however, through a series of contests, intergroup hostility and within-group solidarity increased markedly (222, 223). Conversely, when the investigators reshuffled situational factors so that the two groups needed to work cooperatively to accomplish salient goals (for example, restoring the camp's water supply), intergroup conflict decreased, stereotyped views of the other group diminished, and across-group friendships increased.

Needless to say, these findings among children have obvious adult parallels in the factors governing friendship or enmity between social or ethnic groups and between nations. They also have numerous practical implications for children's development, both as members of groups and as individuals. External or situational influences that tend to define a child as a member of a group can ease his acceptance by peers and help to diminish the likelihood of rejection. Many socially isolated children could be helped to gain self-confidence and to begin to initiate socially successful behavior if they were provided assistance in gaining admission to peer-group settings through appropriate structuring of these settings (**115, 222, 224**). Similarly, cooperative settings with close physical and social proximity, rather than competitive settings with physical and social distance, could help to diminish hostility and cultural stereotyping between social, ethnic, or sex-linked groups (see pp. 470–472).

Socialization Functions of the Peer Group

The peer group obviously provides an opportunity for boys and girls to gain many immediate satisfactions. Here they find companions who can keep up with their restless energy in a way that weary fathers or mothers with aching joints never could. They find others of their own level of intellectual and social development with whom to talk and to compare notes. And they find the personnel necessary for group sports, games, and other activities.

It would be a mistake, however, to dismiss the peer group as simply a way of keeping children happy during this period, for it serves much more extensive purposes in their socialization. One of the major functions of the peer group involves changing some of the child's attitudes. The peer group may strengthen existing attitudes, establish new ones, or weaken those that are in conflict with peer-group values (**115**). When peer-group values are in conflict with existing attitudes, the child's susceptibility to change will depend on the relative importance of peer acceptance.

Some children appear particularly susceptible to peer-group influences that conflict with parental values. The child who comes from a cold or rejecting home will be insecure and will have a strong need for acceptance and nurturance by others. In such a case, the child will not be too anxious about disappointing his parents, for they have not been nurturant. If the group will accept the child, he may adopt their values eagerly. Furthermore, the boy or girl who lacks adequate parental models of appropriate social behavior will be more strongly motivated to adopt the attitudes, social norms, and behaviors of peer-group leaders.

Children will be most likely to resist peer group values that contradict parental values if they have identified with parents who are nurturant, and are therefore anxious about violating parental standards, (**76, 115, 162**). Moreover, children who feel that they are not popular with peers are more subject to adult persuasion than children who feel liked and accepted by peers (**115, 162**). A child who views his parents as accepting and the peer group as rejecting is more likely to agree with the opinions and values of adults.

Conformity to Peers

Conformity, that is, the tendency to adopt the values and attitudes of others, is a personality characteristic that varies with age and is of different strength in different children. The special power of the peer group during middle childhood was clearly demonstrated in one study in which children were shown a single, black line (standard) and three black lines of different lengths (reference lines) and asked to state which of the three reference lines was equal in length to the standard (**29**). When tested alone, most children were accurate in their judgments. Some time after being tested alone, however, each child was placed in the same test situation with eight other peers who were "stooges." The subject was not aware that all the stooges had been instructed ahead of time by the experimenter to report aloud the wrong answer. The child under study was seated in the room so that five of the stooges reported their judgments before the subject did. Under these conditions all children showed an increased tendency to "go along" with the majority and make objectively inaccurate judgments. The young children (ages 7-10) were more influenced by the incorrect majority than the older children (ages 10-13).

In a second experiment with different children, a teacher served as the "stooge" instead of peers. The teacher first made her judgment aloud, after which the child responded. It was found that these children were less influenced by a single teacher than the first group had been by a group of eight peers. Again, however, the younger children were much more influenced than the older children.

While conformity behavior increases during the middle-childhood years (**29, 77, 133, 171, 200**), preschool children "are generally impervious to normative pressure from their peers" (**115, 407**). Younger preschoolers show no evidence of conformity to group norms (**115**), and only a small minority (12 percent) of kindergarten children show any shift in the direction of group norms (**132**). Such data strongly support Piaget's description of these years as a presocial and egocentric stage.

In most situations, girls have been found more conforming to peer-group pressures than boys (**53, 57, 115, 133, 175, 197, 216, 252**), perhaps reflecting a generally greater interpersonal orientation and need for social approval among girls. When sex-typed norms become strongly involved, however, the picture becomes more complex. Thus, for example,

> . . . situational factors arousing motives that are salient for males (e.g., achievement, aggression) wipe out or reverse this difference in conformity behavior. . . . Situational

factors, if they elicit sex-typed behavior, can serve either to reduce this sex difference or reverse it" (**115, 414**).

Finally, individual personality factors play a role in determining the strength of a child's conformity tendencies (**135, 206, 260**). In middle childhood and adolescence the peer-conforming individual "resembles the conformity-prone adult—he manifests low ego-strength, repression of impulse, low self-esteem, and high social sensitivity" (**115, 418**). Conforming children tend to be more dependent (**135**) and anxious (**260**); on the other hand, hyperaggressive boys are more rigid and less susceptible to influence than normal boys (**206**).

> The reasonable implication is that "conformity" is not solely the province of the anxious, the dependent, the maladjusted; unwitting conformity in the face of ambiguity may be so, but conformity to the socially accepted demands of clearly defined situations seems a perfectly healthy response for a child (**53, 312**).

SUMMARY

The child's social environment expands markedly during the middle-childhood years. In the continuing interaction between the developing child and his expanding environment, some motives become strengthened and more clearly articulated, while others diminish in importance; new standards are set; and the child is confronted with new problems and challenges. The changing adjustments required of him during this period reflect in great measure his movement away from home as the one central focus of his activities. Beginning with kindergarten or first grade, the school becomes the center of the child's extrafamilial life, occupying almost half of his waking hours. The kinds of teachers he has, the teaching methods he encounters, and the types of textbooks he is exposed to, will have important effects not only on his academic progress, but upon his general capacity to meet and master new problems and challenges, and consequently his self-confidence and self-esteem. Teachers, teaching methods, and textbooks vary widely not only in overall quality, but in their appropriateness for individual children. While children generally prefer teachers who are kind, cheerful, fair and consistent in discipline, and enthusiastic, some children may progress better with a quiet, self-controlled teacher, while others may benefit more from a gregarious, outgoing, and less orderly teacher. Similarly, highly compulsive and highly anxious children may respond differently to highly structured teaching methods than children low in compulsivity and anxiety.

Students in small schools participate in more activities than those in large schools, and they are more likely to report that their involvement helped them develop skills or abilities, increase self-confidence, feel needed, and gain a feeling of accomplishment. Academically marginal students are particularly likely to benefit from small school size.

The child's school progress is also influenced by his family background. Parental interest in school and rewards for school achievement occur more frequently among middle-class than among lower-class parents. In addition, the middle-class child, having been exposed to a higher degree of intellectual activity in the home, is likely to enter school better prepared to profit from the learning experiences to which he will be exposed.

In contrast, the socioeconomically disadvantaged student, deprived of such experiences, is likely to be handicapped in approaching academic tasks. He tends to be limited in language development and cognitive skills. In addition, both he and his parents may be less highly motivated and have lower aspirations for academic achievement. The disadvantaged child's progress in school may be further limited by feelings of inadequacy and a depressed self-concept resulting from the greater difficulties he encounters and from feelings of not "belonging" in a social setting characterized by middle-class goals and codes of behavior. There is an urgent need for the development of curricular approaches geared to the needs of disadvantaged students; better preparation of teachers for working with these children; and much more adequate physical facilities and supportive services (e.g., remedial reading, speech pathology, psychological counseling, cultural enrichment and early admission programs).

The child's contact with his peers also expands greatly during the school years. The peer group provides an opportunity to learn to interact with age-mates, to deal with hostility and dominance, to relate to a leader, to lead others, to deal with social problems, and to develop a concept of himself. The child whose school experiences and interactions with peers are constructive and rewarding and whose relationships with parents are favorable will develop a clearer self-image, increased competencies, and enhanced self-esteem. Unfavorable experiences in any of these areas are likely to limit the child's development of his potential and to foster crippling conflicts, anxieties, and an impaired self-image.

The influence of the peer group appears stronger in America than in some other societies, where children live more in the family and less in peer society. The current rapidity of social change also affects the influence of the peer group, creating a hiatus between one generation and the next, and thus contributing to the role of age-mates in the socialization process. During the early years of middle-childhood, informal groups, such as "the gang," formed by children themselves, predominate; between 10 and 14, however, children's groups tend to become more highly structured. Beginning at age 7 or 8, children begin to associate primarily with same-sex peers. This persists through middle childhood, although prepubertal girls may begin to express a tenuous interest in somewhat older boys. Sex cleavages in interest and activities also become increasingly evident throughout the school years, despite considerable overlap. Boys tend to be more involved with gang and other peer-group activities, while girls tend to have more intimate, individual interpersonal relationships.

Children having high social status with peers tend to be more socially aggressive, outgoing, enthusiastic, cheerful, intelligent, and friendly. In contrast, anxiety, uncertainty, social indifference, withdrawal, and hostility emerge as attributes of low-status or rejected children. The relationship of other attributes to popularity varies with sex and age. Peer-group status is also related to social class, with lower-class children generally having lower status than their middle-class peers. Finally, a number of studies indicate that the roles played by adult leaders can significantly affect the likelihood of a child's profiting from peer-group experiences. Many socially isolated children could be helped to gain group acceptance and self-confidence if provided proper assistance.

While there is a general tendency for children to conform to the values and attitudes of other members of the peer group, there are wide variations in the strength of this tendency. Girls are more likely to conform to peer-group suggestions than boys, and low-status group members are more likely to conform than leaders. Furthermore, individual personality factors may play a role. On the one hand, dependent and anxious children are more conforming than nondependent, nonanxious peers; on the other hand, hyperaggressive children are more rigid and less susceptible to influence than normal children. Conformity should not be associated with only negative traits such as low status, high anxiety, high dependency. It is true that extreme, unquestioning conformity to social values and behavior and fear of not conforming may be indicative of maladjustments, but reasonable conformity to accepted social standards of behavior during the middle-childhood years is a healthy, adaptive response.

References

1. Alexander, L., et al. Achievement as a function of teacher-initiated student-teacher personal interactions. **Psychological Reports,** 1971, **28,** 431–434.
2. Allen, B. H. Development of children's stereotype of the female school teacher. **Dissertation Abstracts,** 1962, **23,** 231–232.
3. Anderson, H. E., White, W. F., & Wash, J. A. Generalized effects of praise and reproof. **Journal of Educational Psychology,** 1966, **57,** 169–173.
4. Anderson, H. H. An experimental study of dominative behavior and integrative behavior in children of preschool age. **Journal of Psychology,** 1937, **8,** 335–345.
5. Anderson, H. H. Domination and integration in the social behavior of young children in an experimental play situation. **Genetic Psychology Monographs,** 1937, **19,** 341–408.
6. Anderson, H. H., & Anderson, G. L. Social development. In L. Carmichael (Ed.), **Manual of child psychology.** (2nd ed.) New York: Wiley, 1954.
7. Anderson, H. H., & Brewer, J. E. Studies of teachers' classroom personalities. II. Effects of teachers' dominative and integrative contacts on children's classroom behavior. **Applied Psychology Monographs,** 1946, **8,** 33–122.
8. Anderson, H. H., Brewer, J. E., & Reed, M. F. Studies of teachers' classroom personalities. III. Follow-up studies of the effects of dominative and integrative contacts on children's behavior. **Applied Psychology Monographs,** 1946, **8,** 101–156.
9. Anderson, H. H., & Brewer, J. E. Studies of teachers' classroom personalities. I. Dominative and socially integrative behavior of kindergarten teachers. **Applied Psychology Monographs,** 1945, **6,** 109–152.

10. Argyle, M., & Robinson, P. Two origins of achievement motivation. **British Journal of Social and Clinical Psychology,** 1962, **1,** 107–120.

11. Ausubel, D. P. How reversible are the cognitive and motivational effects of cultural deprivation? Implications for teaching the culturally deprived child. **Urban Education,** 1964, **1,** 16–38.

12. Ayers, L. P. The effect of physical defects on school progress. **Psychological Clinics,** 1909, **3,** 71–77.

13. Bachman, J. G. **Youth in transition.** Vol. 2. The impact of family background and intelligence on tenth-grade boys. Ann Arbor: Institute for Social Research, University of Michigan, 1970.

14. Bachman, J. G., Green, S., & Wirtanen, I. **Dropping out—problem or symptom.** Ann Arbor: Institute for Social Research, University of Michigan, 1972.

15. Bachman, J. G., Kahn, R. L., Mednick, M. T., Davidson, T. N., & Johnston, L. D. **Youth in transition.** Vol. 1. **Blueprint for a longitudinal study of adolescent boys.** Ann Arbor: Institute for Social Research, University of Michigan, 1967.

16. Baldwin, W. K. The social position of the educable mentally retarded child in the regular grades in the public schools. **The Exceptional Children,** 1958, **25,** 106–108.

17. Barbe, W. B. Peer relationships of children of different intelligence levels. **School and Society,** 1954, **80,** 60–62.

18. Barker, R. G. Ecological units. In R. G. Barker & R. V. Gump (Eds.), **Big school, small school.** Stanford: Stanford University Press, 1964. Pp. 11–28.

19. Barker, R. G. Ecology and motivation. In M. R. Jones (Ed.), **Nebraska symposium on motivation.** Lincoln: University of Nebraska Press, 1960. Pp. 1–49.

20. Barker, R. G., & Barker, L. S. Structural characteristics. In R. G. Barker & P. V. Gump (Eds.), **Big school, small school.** Stanford: Stanford University Press, 1964. Pp. 41–63.

21. Baumrind, D. A critique of radical innovation as a solution to contemporary problems of education. Unpublished manuscript, University of California, Berkeley, March, 1972.

22. Baumrind, D. From each according to her ability. **School Review,** February 1972, 161–197.

23. Baumrind, D. Current patterns of parental authority. **Developmental Psychology Monographs,** 1971, 4(Part 2).

24. Baumrind, D. Child care practices anteceding three patterns of preschool behavior. **Genetic Psychology Monographs,** 1967, **75,** 43–88.

25. Beck, J. M., & Saxe, R. W. (Eds.) **Teaching the culturally disadvantaged pupil.** Springfield, Ill.: Thomas, 1965.

26. Bell, G. D. Processes in the formation of adolescents' aspirations. **Social Forces,** 1963, **42,** 179–195.

27. Beller, E. K. Research in teaching: Organized programs in early education. In R. Travers (Ed.), **Handbook for research on teaching.** New York: Rand-McNally, 1972.

28. Bereiter, C., & Englemann, S. **Teaching disadvantaged children in the preschool.** Englewood Cliffs, N.J.: Prentice-Hall, 1966.

29. Berenda, R. W. **The influence of the group on the judgments of children.** New York: King's Crown Press, 1950.

30. Berman, G., & Eisenberg, M. Psycho-social aspects of academic achievement. **American Journal of Orthopsychiatry,** 1971, **41,** 406–415.

31. Bertrand, A. L. School attendance and attainment: Function and dysfunction of school and family systems. **Social Forces,** 1962, **40,** 228–233.

32. Birch, H. G., & Gussow, J. D. **Disadvantaged children: Health, nutrition and school failure.** New York: Grune and Stratton, 1970.

33. Birney, R. C., Burdick, H., & Teevan, R. C. **Fear of failure.** New York: Van Nostrand Reinhold, 1969.

34. Blake, M. T. Factors influencing teacher success. **Dissertation Abstracts,** 1966, **27,** 990.

35. Blanchard, R. W., & Biller, H. B. Father availability and academic performance among third-grade boys. **Developmental Psychology,** 1971, **4,** 301–305.

36. Bledsoe, J. C., Brown, I. D., & Strickland, A. D. Factors related to pupil observation reports of teachers and attitudes toward their teachers. **Journal of Educational Research,** 1971, **65,** 119–126.

37. Blom, G. E. Sex differences in reading disability. **Reading Forum.** 31–46 (NINDS Monographs No. 11). Washington, D.C.: National Institute of Neurological Diseases, National Institute of Health, 1970.

38. Blom, G. E., Waite, R. R., & Zimet, S. G. Ethnic integration and urbanization of a first grade reading textbook: A research study. **Psychology in the Schools,** 1967, **4,** 176–181.

39. Bonney, M. E. Relationships between social success, family size, socioeconomic home background, and intelligence among school children in grades III to V. **Sociometry,** 1944, **7,** 26–39.

40. Bonney, M. E. Sex differences in social success and personality traits. **Child Development,** 1944, **15,** 63–79.

41. Bonney, M. E. The constancy of sociometric scores and their relationship to teacher judgments of social success and to personality self-ratings. **Sociometry,** 1943, **6,** 409–424.

42. Bonney, M. E. A study of the relation of intelligence, family size, and sex differences with mutual friendship in the primary grades. **Child Development,** 1942, **13,** 79–100.

43. Bordua, D. J. Educational aspirations and parental stress on college. **Social Forces,** 1960, **38,** 262–269.

44. Boyle, R. P. The effect of the high school on students' aspirations. **American Journal of Sociology,** 1966, **131,** 628–639.

45. Bronfenbrenner, U. **Two worlds of childhood: U.S. and U.S.S.R.** New York: Russell Sage Foundation, 1970.

46. Bronfenbrenner, U. Response to pressure from peers versus adults among Soviet and American school children. **International Journal of Psychology,** 1967, **2,** 199–207.

47. Bronfenbrenner, U., Devereux, E. C., Suci, G. J., & Rodgers, R. R. Adults and peers as sources of conformity and autonomy. Unpublished manuscript, Cornell University, 1965.

48. Brophy, J. E., & Laosa, L. M. Effect of male teacher on the sex-typing of kindergarten children. **Proceedings, 79th Annual Convention of the American Psychological Association,** 1971, **6,** 169–170.

49. Brown, O. H., Fuller, F. F., & Richek, H. G. A comparison of self-perceptions of prospective elementary and secondary school teachers. **Psychology in the Schools,** 1967, **4,** 21–24.

50. Bryant, B. K. Student-teacher relationships as related to internal-external locus of control: Implications for the role of school psychologists. **Proceedings, 80th Annual Convention of the American Psychological Association,** 1972, **7,** 567–568.

51. Buck, M. L. The culturally disadvantaged child and level of school achievement as related to the internal versus external and classroom behavior, and parental attitudes. **Dissertation Abstracts International,** 1970, **30,** 3312–3313.

52. Burton, R. V., & Whiting, J. W. M. The absent father and cross-sex identity. **Merrill-**

Palmer Quarterly, 1961, **7,** 85–95.

53. Campbell, J. D. Peer relations in childhood. In M. L. Hoffman & L. W. Hoffman (Eds.), **Review of child development research.** Vol. 1. New York: Russell Sage Foundation, 1964. Pp. 289–322.

54. Campbell, J. D., & Yarrow, M. R. Perceptual and behavioral correlates of social effectiveness. **Sociometry,** 1961, **24,** 1–20.

55. Campbell, W. J. Some effects of high school consolidation. In R. G. Barker & P. V. Gump (Eds.), **Big school, small school.** Stanford: Stanford University Press, 1964. Pp. 139–153.

56. Caplin, M. D. The relationship between self concept and academic achievement. **Journal of Experimental Education,** 1969, **37,** 13–16.

57. Carrigan, W. C., & Julian, J. W. Sex and birth-order differences in conformity as a function of need affiliation arousal. **Journal of Personality and Social Psychology,** 1966, **3,** 479–483.

58. Carrino, C. Identifying potential dropouts in the elementary grades. **Dissertation Abstracts,** 1966, **27,** 343.

59. Castaneda, A., McCandless, B. R., & Palermo, D. S. The children's form of the Manifest Anxiety Scale. **Child Development,** 1956, **27,** 317–327.

60. Cervantes, L. F. Family background, primary relationships, and the high school dropout. **Journal of Marriage and the Family,** 1965, **5,** 218–223.

61. Cervantes, L. F. **The dropout: Causes and cures.** Ann Arbor: University of Michigan Press, 1965.

62. Challman, R. C. Factors influencing friendships among preschool children. **Child Development,** 1932, **3,** 146–158.

63. Cheong, G. S. C., & DeVault, M. V. Pupils' perceptions of teachers. **Journal of Educational Research,** 1966, **59,** 446–449.

64. Child, I. L., Potter, E. H., & Levine, E. M. Children's textbooks and personality development: An exploration in the social psychology of education. **Psychological Monographs,** 1946, **60**(3).

65. Clark, K. B. Alternative public school systems. **Harvard Educational Review,** 1968, **38,** 100–113.

66. Clark, K. B. **Dark ghetto.** New York: Harper & Row, 1967.

67. Clarke, H. H., & Greene, H. W. Relationships between personal-social measures applied to 10-year-old boys. **Research Quarterly of the American Association for Health, Physical Education, and Recreation,** 1963, **34,** 288–298.

68. Clarke, H. H., & Clarke, D. H. Social status and mental health of boys as related to their maturity, structural, and strength characterisics. **Research Quarterly of the American Association for Health, Physical Education, and Recreation,** 1961, **32,** 326–334.

69. Coleman, J. S. **The adolescent society.** New York: Free Press, 1961.

70. Coleman, J. S., et al. **Equality of educational opportunity.** Washington, D.C.: U.S. Government Printing Office, 1966.

71. Collier, M. J., & Gaier, E. L. The hero in the preferred childhood stories of college men. **American Imago,** 1959, **16,** 177–194.

72. Collier, M. J., & Gaier, E. L. Adult reactions to preferred childhood stories. **Child Development,** 1958, **29,** 97–103.

73. Combs, J. & Cooley, W. W. Dropouts: In high school and after school. **American Educational Research Journal,** 1968, **5,** 343–363.

74. Commoss, H. H. Some characteristics related to social isolation of second grade children. **Journal of Educational Psychology,** 1962, **53,** 38–43.

75. Conant, J. B. Social dynamite in our large cities. In **Social dynamite: The report of the conference on unemployed, out-of-school youth in urban areas.** Washington, D.C.: National Committee for Children and Youth, 1961.

76. Conger, J. J. A world they never knew: The family and social change. **Daedalus,** Fall 1971, 1105–1138.

77. Costanzo, P. R., & Shaw, M. E. Conformity as a function of age level. **Child Development,** 1966, **37,** 967–975.

78. Cotler, S. The effects of positive and negative reinforcement and test anxiety on the reading performance of male elementary school children. **Genetic Psychology Monographs,** 1969, **80,** 29–50.

79. Critchley, M. **Development dyslexia.** London: Heinemann, 1964.

80. Davis, K. The sociology of parent youth conflict. **American Sociological Review,** 1940, **5,** 523–535.

81. Deutsch, M. The disadvantaged child and the learning process. In A. H. Passow (Ed.), **Education in depressed areas.** New York: Columbia University Press, 1963. Pp. 163–179.

82. Deutsch, M. Minority group and class status as related to social and personality factors in scholastic achievement. **Monographs in Social and Applied Anthropology,** 1960, **2.**

83. Deutsch, M., Katz, I., & Jensen, A. R. (Eds.), **Social class, race, and psychological development.** New York: Holt, Rinehart & Winston, 1968.

84. Division for Youth, **The school dropout problem: Rochester, Part I.** Albany: State of New York, 1962. Pp. 14–16.

85. Douvan, E., & Adelson, J. The psychodynamics of social mobility in adolescent boys. **Journal of Abnormal and Social Psychology,** 1958, **56,** 31–34.

86. Dowaliby, F. J., & Schumer, H. Teacher-centured versus student-centered mode of college classroom instruction as related to manifest anxiety. **Proceedings, 79th Annual Convention of the American Psychological Association,** 1971, **6,** 541–542.

87. Duffy, E. **Activation and behavior.** New York: Wiley, 1962.

88. Eisenberg, L. The epidemiology of reading retardation and a program for preventive intervention. In J. Money (Ed.), **The Disabled Reader.** Baltimore: Johns Hopkins Press, 1966.

89. Elder, G. H., Jr. Family structure and educational attainment: A cross-national analysis. **American Sociological Review,** 1965, **30,** 81–96.

90. Elder, G. H., Jr. Family structure and the transmission of values and norms in the process of child rearing. Unpublished doctoral dissertation, University of North Carolina at Chapel Hill, 1961.

91. Elliott, D. S., Voss, H. L., & Wendling, A. Dropout and the social milieu of the high school: A preliminary analysis. **American Journal of Orthopsychiatry,** 1966, **36,** 808–817.

92. Featherstone, J. **Schools where children learn.** New York: Liveright, 1971.

93. Fein, L. G. Evidence of a curvilinear relationship between IPAT anxiety and achievement at nursing school. **Journal of Clinical Psychology,** 1963, **19,** 374–376.

94. Feldhusen, J. F., & Klausmeier, H. J. Anxiety, intelligence, and achievement in children of low, average, and high intelligence. **Child Development,** 1962, **33,** 403–409.

95. Feshbach, N. D. Cross cultural studies of teaching styles in four year-olds and their mothers: Some educational implications of socialization. Paper presented at the Minnesota Symposia on Child Psychology, Minneapolis, October, 1972.

96. Feshbach, S., & Adelman, H. S. An experimental program of personalized classroom instruction in disadvantaged area schools. **Psychology in the Schools,** 1971, **8,** 114–120.

97. Flanders, N. A., & Havumaki, S. The effect of teacher-pupil contacts involving praise on the sociometric choices of students. **Journal of Educational Psychology,** 1960, **51,** 65–68.

98. Franco, D. The child's perception of "The Teacher" as compared to his perception of "The Mother." **Dissertation Abstracts,** 1964, **24,** 3414–3415.

99. Frost, B. P. Intelligence, manifest anxiety, and scholastic achievement. **Alberta Journal of Educational Research,** 1965, **11,** 167–175.

100. Furfey, P. H. Some factors influencing the selection of boys' chums. **Journal of Applied Psychology,** 1927, **11,** 47–51.

101. Gage, N. L. Desirable behaviors of teachers. **Urban Education,** 1965, **1,** 85–95.

102. Gaier, E. L., & Collier, M. J. The latency-stage story preferences of American and Finnish children. **Child Development,** 1960, **31,** 431–451.

103. Gallagher, J. J. Social status of children related to intelligence, propinquity, and social perception. **Elementary School Journal,** 1958, **58,** 225–231.

104. Gold, H. A. The importance of ideology in sociometric evaluation of leadership. **Group Psychotherapy,** 1962, **15,** 224–230.

105. Gordon, E. W. Educational achievement in the Prince Edward County Free School, 1963–1964. In E. W. Gordon & D. A. Wilkerson (Eds.), **Compensatory education for the disadvantaged. Programs and practices: Preschool through college.** New York: College Entrance Examination Board, 1966.

106. Gordon, E. W., & Wilkerson, D. A. (Eds.), **Compensatory education for the disadvantaged. Programs and practices: Preschool through college.** New York: College Entrance Examination Board, 1966.

107. Greenberg, J. W., Gerver, J. M., Chall, J., & Davidson, H. H. Attitudes of children from a deprived environment toward achievement-related concepts. **Journal of Educational Research,** 1965, **59,** 57–62.

108. Greer, D. R. Test anxiety, psychological arousal and test performance of first grade children. **Dissertation Abstracts,** 1966, **27,** 953.

109. Grimes, J. W., & Allinsmith, W. Compulsivity, anxiety, and school achievement. **Merrill-Palmer Quarterly,** 1961, **7,** 247–269.

110. Gross, B., & Gross, R. (Eds.) **Radical school reform.** New York: Simon and Schuster, 1969.

111. Gross, R. (Ed.) **The teacher and the taught: Education in theory and practice from Plato to James B. Conant.** New York: Dell, 1963.

112. Gross, R., & Osterman, P. **High School.** New York: Simon and Schuster, 1971.

113. Gump, P. V. **Big schools, small schools.** Moravia, N.Y.: Chronicle Guidance Publications, 1966.

114. Haller, A. O., & Butterworth, C. E. Peer influence on levels of occupation and educational aspiration. **Social Forces,** 1960, **38,** 289–295.

115. Hartup, W. W. Peer interaction and social organization. In P. H. Mussen (Ed.). **Carmichael's Manual of child psychology.** (3rd ed.) Vol. 2. New York: Wiley, 1970. Pp. 457–558.

116. Hartup, W. W., Glazer, J. A., & Charlesworth, R. Peer reinforcement and sociometric status. **Child Development,** 1967, **38,** 1017–1024.

117. Harvey, O. J., et al. Teachers' belief systems and preschool atmospheres. **Journal of Educational Psychology,** 1966, **57,** 373–381.

118. Harvey, O. J., & Consalvi, C. Status and conformity to pressures in informal groups. **Journal of Abnormal and Social Psychology,** 1960, **60,** 182–187.

119. Harvey, O. J., & Rutherford, J. Status in the informal group: Influences and influencibility at differing age levels. **Child Development,** 1960, **31,** 377–385.

120. Havighurst, R. J., & Breese, F. H. Relation between ability and social status in a mid-western community. III. Primary mental abilities. **Journal of Educational Psychology,** 1947, **38,** 241–247.

121. Havighurst, R. J., & Janke, L. L. Relations between ability and social status in a midwestern community. I. Ten-year-old children. **Journal of Educational Psychology,** 1944, **35,** 357–368.

121. Havighurst, R. J., & Janke, L. L. Relations between ability and social status in a midwest-**tion of the American Psychological Association,** 1972, **7,** 503–504.

123. Heil, L. M., & Washburne, C. Characteristics of teachers related to children's progress. **Journal of Teacher Education,** 1961, **12,** 401–406.

124. Henssenstamm, F. K. Activism in adolescence: An analysis of the high school underground press. **Adolescence,** 1971, **6,** 317–336.

125. Hill, K. T. Relation of test anxiety, defensiveness, and intelligence to sociometric status. **Child Development,** 1963, **34,** 767–776.

126. Hill, K. T., & Sarason, S. B. The relation of test anxiety and defensiveness to test and school performance over the elementary-school years: A further longitudinal study. **Monographs of the Society for Research in Child Development,** 1966, **31**(2), 1–76.

127. Hollingshead, A. B. **Elmtown's youth: The impact of social class on youth.** New York: Wiley, 1949.

128. Holt, J. **How children fail.** New York: Pitman, 1964.

129. Horowitz, F. D. The relationship of anxiety, self-concept, and sociometric status among fourth, fifth, and sixth grade children. **Journal of Abnormal and Social Psychology,** 1962, **65,** 212–214.

130. Hsu, F. L. K., Watrous, B. G., & Lord, E. M. Culture pattern and adolescent behavior. **International Journal of Social Psychiatry,** 1960–1961, **7,** 33–35.

131. Hudgins, B. B., Smith, L. M., & Johnson, T. J. The child's perception of his classmates. **Journal of Genetic Psychology,** 1962, **101,** 401–405.

132. Hunt, R. G., & Synnerdale, V. Social influences among kindergarten children. **Sociology and Social Research,** 1959, **43,** 171–174.

133. Iscoe, I., Williams, M., & Harvey, J. Modification of children's judgments by a simulated group technique: A normative developmental study. **Child Development,** 1963, **34,** 963–978.

134. Jackson, P. W. **Life in classrooms.** New York: Holt, Rinehart & Winston, 1968.

135. Jakubczak, L. F., & Walters, R. H. Suggestibility as dependency behavior. **Journal of Abnormal and Social Psychology,** 1959, **59,** 102–107.

136. Jencks, C., and associates. **The social determinants of success.** New York: Basic Books, 1972.·

137. Jennings, F. Textbooks and trapped idealists. **Saturday Review,** January 18, 1964, 57–59, 77–78.

138. Jersild, A. T. Characteristics of teachers who are "liked best" and "disliked most." **Journal of Experimental Education,** 1940, **9,** 139–151.

139. Justman, J. Academic aptitude and reading test scores of disadvantaged children showing varying degrees of mobility. **Journal of Educational Measurement,** 1965, **2,** 151–155.

140. Kabasakalian, L. The grade school from childhood reality to school reality. **Dissertation Abstracts,** 1964, **25,** 615.

141. Kagan, J. Reflection-impulsivity: The generality and dynamics of conceptual tempo. **Journal of Abnormal Psychology,** 1966, **71,** 17–24.

142. Kagan, J. The child's sex role classification of school objects. **Child Development,** 1964, **35,** 1051.

143. Kandel, D. B., & Lesser, G. S. Parental and peer influences on educational plans of adolescents. **American Sociological Review,** 1969, **34,** 213–223.

144. Karen, R. L. Operant conditioning and social preference. Unpublished doctoral dissertation, Arizona State University, 1965.

145. Katz, L. Teaching in preschools: Roles and goals. ERIC No. 70706-E-AO-U-26, 1969.

146. Keller, E. D., & Rowley, V. N. Anxiety, intelligence, and scholastic achievement in elementary school children. **Psychological Reports,** 1962, **11,** 19–22.

147. Kellogg, R. L. A direct approach to sex-role identification of school-related objects. **Psychological Reports,** 1969, **24,** 839–841.

148. Keniston, K. Social change and youth in America. **Daedalus,** Winter 1962, 145–171.

149. Kerber, A., & Bommarito, B. (Eds.) **The schools and the urban crises.** New York: Holt, Rinehart & Winston, 1966.

150. Kestenbaum, J. M., & Weiner, B. Achievement performance related to achievement motivation and text anxiety. **Journal of Consulting and Clinical Psychology,** 1970, **34,** 343–344.

151. Kiesler, C. A., Zanna, M., & DeSalvo, J. Deviation and conformity: Opinion change as a function of commitment, attraction, and presence of a deviate. **Journal of Personality and Social Psychology,** 1966, **3,** 458–467.

152. Klaus, R. A. Interrelationships of attributes that accepted and rejected children ascribe to their peers. Unpublished doctoral dissertation, George Peabody College for Teachers, 1959.

153. Klineberg, O. Life is fun in a smiling, fair-skinned world. **Saturday Review,** February 16, 1963, 75–77, 87.

154. Kohl, H. **36 children.** New York: New American Library, 1967.

155. Kosier, K. P., & DeVault, M. V. Effects of teacher personality on pupil personality. **Psychology in the Schools,** 1967, **4,** 40–44.

156. Kounin, J. S. **Discipline and group management in classrooms.** New York: Holt, Rinehart & Winston, 1970.

157. Kozol, J. **Death at an early age.** Boston: Houghton Mifflin, 1967.

158. Krauss, I. Sources of educational aspirations among working-class youth. **American Sociological Development,** 1964, **29,** 867–879.

159. Kriesberg, L. Rearing children for educational achievement in fatherless families. **Journal of Marriage and the Family,** 1967, **29,** 289–301.

160. Lefevre, C. Inner-city school—as the children see it. **Elementary School Journal,** 1966, **67,** 8–15.

161. LeShan, L. L. Time orientation and social class. **Journal of Abnormal and Social Psychology,** 1952, **57,** 589–592.

162. Lesser, G. S., & Abelson, R. P. Personality correlates of persuasibility in children. In I. C. Janis, C. I. Hovland, et al. (Eds.), **Personality and persuasibility,** New Haven, Conn.: Yale University Press, 1959. Pp. 187–206.

163. Levin, H. Schooling and inequality. The social science objectivity gap. **Saturday Review of Education,** 1972, **55,** 49–51.

164. Levine, M., Wesolowski, J. C., & Corbett, F. J. Pupil turnover and academic performance in an inner city elementary school. **Psychology in the Schools,** 1966, **3,** 153–158.

165. Lichter, S. O., Rapien, E. B., Seibert, F. M., & Slansky, M. A. **The drop-outs.** New York: Free Press, 1962.

166. Linton, R. Age and sex categories. **American Sociological Review,** 1942, **7,** 589–603.

167. Lippit, R., & White, R. K. An experimental study of leadership and group life. In T. M. Newcomb & E. L. Hartley (Eds.), **Readings in social psychology.** New York: Holt, Rinehart & Winston, 1947. Pp. 315–330.

168. Little, J. K. Occupations of non-college youth. **American Educational Research Journal,** 1967, **4,** 147–153.

169. McCandless, B. **Adolescents: Behavior and development.** Hinsdale, Ill.: Dryden, 1970.

170. McClelland, D. C. **The achieving society.** New York: Van Nostrand Reinhold, 1961.

171. McConnell, T. R. Suggestibility in children as a function of chronological age. **Journal of Abnormal and Social Psychology,** 1963, **67,** 286–289.

172. McDill, E. L., & Coleman, J. S. Family and peer influence in college plans of high school students. **Sociology of Education,** 1965, **38,** 112–116.

173. McKeachie, W. J., et al. Student affiliation motives, teacher warmth, and academic achievement. **Journal of Personality and Social Psychology,** 1966, **4,** 457–461.

174. McNeil, J. D. Programmed instruction versus usual classroom procedures in teaching boys to read. **American Educational Research Journal,** 1964, **1,** 113–119.

175. Maccoby, E., & Masters, J. C. Attachment and dependency. In P. H. Mussen (Ed.) **Carmichael's Manual of child psychology.** (3rd ed.) Vol. 2. New York: Wiley, 1970.

176. Marburger, C. L. Consideration for educational planning. In A. H. Passow (Ed.), **Education in depressed areas.** New York: Columbia University Press, 1963. Pp. 298–321.

177. Martin, E. C. Reflections on the early adolescent in school. **Daedalus,** Fall 1971, 1087–1104.

178. Maslow, A. H., & Diaz-Guerrero, R. Delinquency as a value disturbance. In J. G. Peatman & E. L. Hartley (Eds.), **Festschrift for Gardner Murphy.** New York: Harper & Row, 1960. Pp. 228–240.

179. Mayer, L. A. New questions about the U.S. population. **Fortune,** February 1971, 82–85. (Source: U.S. Census, 1970.)

180. Meyers, J., & Dunham, J. L. Anxiety x aptitude interactions in concept learning. **Proceedings, 80th Annual Convention of the American Psychological Association,** 1972, **7,** 485–486.

181. Michalak, J. City life in primers. **New York Herald-Tribune,** January 26, 1965.

182. Minuchin, P., Biber, B., Shapiro, E., and Zimiles, H. **The psychological impact of school experience.** New York: Basic Books, 1969.

183. Money, J. (Ed.) **Reading disability: Progress and research needs in dyslexia.** Baltimore: Johns Hopkins University Press, 1962.

184. Moore, S. G. Correlates of peer acceptance in nursery school children. In W. W. Hartup and N. L. Smothergill (Eds.), **The young child.** Washington, D.C.: National Association for the Education of Young Children, 1967. Pp. 229–247.

185. Morrow, W. R., & Wilson, R. C. Family relations of bright high-achieving and underachieving high school boys. **Child Development,** 1961, **32,** 501–510.

186. Muma, J. R. Peer evaluation and academic performance. **Personnel Guidance Journal,** 1965, **44,** 405–409.

187. Murrow, C., & Murrow, L. **Children come first.** New York: Harper & Row, 1971.

188. Mussen, P. H., Conger, J. J., & Kagan, J. **Child development and personality.** (3rd ed.) New York: Harper & Row, 1969.

189. Myerhoff, B. G., & Larson, W. R. Primary and formal aspects of family organization: Group consensus, problem perception, and adolescent school success. **Journal of Marriage and the Family,** 1965, **29,** 213–217.

190. Namenwirth, J. Z. Failing in New Haven: An analysis of high school graduates and dropouts. **Social Forces,** 1969, **48,** 23.

191. **Newsletter,** Institute for Social Research, University of Michigan, 1971.

192. **New York Times,** November 6, 1971.

193. Norman, R. D. The interpersonal values of achieving and nonachieving gifted children. **Journal of Psychology,** 1966, **64,** 49–57.

194. Northway, M. L. Outsiders: A study of the personality patterns of children least acceptable to their age mates. **Sociometry,** 1944, **7,** 10–25.

195. Northway, M. L., & Rooks, M. McC. Creativity and sociometric status in children. **Sociometry,** 1956, **18,** 450–457.

196. Offer, D. **The psychological world of the teen-ager: A study of normal adolescent boys.** New York: Basic Books, 1969.

197. Patel, A. E., & Gordon, J. E. Some personal and situational determinants of yielding to influence. **Journal of Abnormal and Social Psychology,** 1960, **61,** 411–418.

198. Pavenstedt, E. A comparison of the child-rearing environment of upper-lower and very low lower-class families. **American Journal of Orthopsychiatry,** 1965, **35,** 89–98.

199. Peck, R. F., & Galliani, C. Intelligence, ethnicity, and social roles in adolescent society. **Sociometry,** 1962, **25,** 64–72.

200. Piaget, J. **The moral judgment of the child.** Glencoe, Ill.: Free Press, 1932.

201. Polansky, N., Lippitt, R., & Redl, F. An investigation of behavioral contagion in groups. **Human Relations,** 1950, **3,** 319–348.

202. Porterfield, O. V., & Schlichting, H. F. Peer status and reading achievement. **Journal of Educational Research,** 1961, **54,** 291–297.

203. Portuges, S. H., & Feshbach, N. D. The effects of teacher's reinforcement style upon imitative behavior of children. Paper presented at the meeting of the American Educational Research Association, Chicago, February, 1968.

204. Prather, M. Project Head Start teacher-pupil-parent interaction study. In E. Grotberg (Ed.), **Review of research 1965 to 1969.** Washington, D.C.: Project Head Start, Office of Economic Opportunity, 1969.

205. Prescott, E., et al. Group day care as a child-rearing environment: An observational study of day care programs. Pasadena, Calif.: ERIC Research in Education, Pacific Oaks College, 1967.

206. Raush, H. L., Farbman, I., & Llewellyn, L. G. Person, setting and change in social interaction: II. **Human Relations,** 1960, **13,** 305–322.

207. Reese, H. W. Manifest anxiety and achievement test performance. **Journal of Educational Psychology,** 1961, **52,** 132–135.

208. Reese, H. W. Relationship between self-acceptance and sociometric choice. **Journal of Abnormal and Social Psychology,** 1961, **62,** 472–474.

209. **Report of the National Advisory Commission on Civil Disorders.** New York: Bantam, 1968.

210. Richardson, S. Personal communication.

211. Riessman, F. **The culturally deprived child.** New York: Harper & Row, 1962.

212. Rosenthal, T., Underwood, B., & Martin, M. Assessing classroom incentive practices. **Journal of Educational Psychology,** 1969, **60,** 370–376.

213. Rothman, E. P. **The angel inside went sour.** New York: McKay, 1971.

214. Ruebush, B. K. Children's behavior as a function of anxiety and defensiveness. **Dissertation Abstracts,** 1966, **27,** 971.

215. Ryan, D. G. **Characteristics of teachers.** Washington, D.C.: American Council on Education, 1960.

216. Saltzstein, H., Rowe, P. B., & Greene, M. E. Spread of social influence on children's judgments of numerosity. **Journal of Personality and Social Psychology,** 1966, **3,** 665–674.

217. Sarason, S. B., Hill, K. T., & Zimbardo, P. G. A longitudinal study of the relation of test anxiety to performance on intelligence and achievement tests. **Monographs of the Society for Research in Child Development,** 1964, **29**(7).

218. Sarason, S. B., & Mandler, G. Some correlates of test anxiety. **Journal of Abnormal and Social Psychology,** 1952, **47,** 810–817.

219. Sears, P. S. **The effect of classroom conditions on the strength of achievement motive and work output on elementary school children.** (U.S. Department of Health, Education, and Welfare, Office of Education, Cooperative Research Project, No. 873.) Stanford, Calif.: Stanford University Press, 1963.

220. Sells, S. B., & Roff, M. Peer acceptance-rejection and personality development. Final Report, Project No. OE 5-0417. U.S. Department of Health, Education, and Welfare, 1967.

221. Sharma, S. Manifest anxiety and school achievement of adolescents. **Journal of Consulting and Clinical Psychology,** 1970, **34,** 403–407.

222. Sherif, M., & Sherif, C. W. **Reference groups.** New York: Harper & Row, 1964.

223. Sherif, M., Harvey, O. J., White, B. J., Hood, W. R., & Sherif, C. W. **Intergroup conflict and cooperation: The Robbers Cave experiment.** Norman: University of Oklahoma Press, 1961.

224. Sherif, M., & Sherif, C. W. **Groups in harmony and tension.** New York: Harper & Row, 1953.

225. Silberman, C. E. **Crisis in the classroom: The remaking of American education.** New York: Random House, 1970.

226. Simpson, R. L. Parental influence, anticipatory socialization, and social mobility. **American Sociological Review,** 1962, **27,** 517–522.

227. Smith, A. J. A developmental study of group processes. **Journal of Genetic Psychology,** 1960, **97,** 29–30.

228. Smith, G. H. Sociometric study of best-liked and least-liked children. **Elementary School Journal,** 1950, **51,** 77–85.

229. Spaulding, R. L. Personality and social development: Peer and school influences. **Review of Educational Research,** 1964, **34,** 588–598.

230. Speedie, S., Hobson, S., Feldhusen, J., & Thurston, J. Evaluation of a battery of noncognitive variables as long-range predictors of academic achievement. **Proceedings, 79th Annual Convention of the American Psychological Association,** 1971, **6,** 517–518.

231. Spiro, M. E. **Children of the kibbutz.** Cambridge, Mass.: Harvard University Press, 1958.

232. Stakenas, R. G. Evaluative stress, fear of failure and academic achievement. **Dissertation Abstracts,** 1966, **27,** 401.

233. Stendler, C. B. Social class differences in parental attitudes toward school at grade 1 level. **Child Development,** 1951, **22,** 36–46.

234. Stendler, C. B., & Young, N. Impact of first grade entrance upon the socialization of the child. Changes after eight months of school. **Child Development,** 1951, **22,** 113–122.

235. Stevenson, H. W., & Odem, R. D. The relation of anxiety to children's performance on learning and problem-solving tasks. **Child Development,** 1965, **36,** 1003–1012.

236. Stinchcombe, A. L. The social determinants of success. **Science,** 1972, **178,** 603–604.

237. Stodolsky, S. S., & Lesser, G. Learning patterns in the disadvantaged. **Harvard Educational Review,** 1967, **37,** 546–593.

238. Stone, L. J., & Church, J. **Childhood and adolescence.** (2nd ed.) New York: Random House, 1968.
239. Sutton-Smith, B., Rosenberg, B. G., Morgan, E. F., Jr. Development of sex differences in play choices during preadolescence. **Child Development,** 1963, **34,** 119–126.
240. Taber, R. C. The critical dilemma of the school dropout. **American Journal of Orthopsychiatry,** 1963, **33,** 501–508.
241. Tanner, J. M. Physical growth. In P. H. Mussen (Ed.), **Carmichael's Manual of child psychology.** (3rd ed.) Vol. 1. New York: Wiley, 1970.
242. Taylor, R. G. Personality traits and discrepant achievement: A review. **Journal of Counseling Psychology,** 1964, **11,** 76–82.
243. **The American almanac for 1972 (The statistical abstract of the United States, 92nd ed.).** New York: Grosset and Dunlap, 1973.
244. **The American almanac for 1971 (The statistical abstract of the United States, 91st ed.).** New York: Grosset and Dunlap, 1971.
245. Thompson, G. E. The social and emotional development of preschool children under two types of education programs. **Psychological Monographs,** 1944, **56.**
246. Toby, J. Orientation to education as a factor in the school maladjustment of lower-class children. **Social Forces,** 1957, **35,** 259–266.
247. Toigo, R. Social status and schoolroom aggression in third-grade children. **Genetic Psychology Monographs,** 1965, **71,** 221–268.
248. Tuckman, B. W. Study of the interactive effects of teacher style and student personality. **Proceedings, 77th Annual Convention of the American Psychological Association,** 1969, **4,** 637–638.
249. Tuckman, B. W., Forman, N., & Hay, W. K. Teacher innovativeness: A function of teacher personality and school environment. **Proceedings, 79th Annual Convention of the American Psychological Association,** 1971, **6,** 527–528.
250. Tuddenham, R. D. Studies in reputation: I. Sex and grade differences in school children's evaluation of their peers. **Psychological Monographs,** 1951, 66(1).
251. Tuddenham, R. D. Studies in reputation: III. Correlates of popularity among elementary school children. **Journal of Educational Psychology,** 1951, **42,** 257–276.
252. Tuma, E., & Livson, N. Family socio-economic status and adolescent attitudes to authority. **Child Development,** 1960, **31,** 387–399.
253. U.S. Department of Health, Education and Welfare, **Toward a social report.** Washington, D.C.: U.S. Department of Health, Education and Welfare, 1969. Pp. 66–70.
254. Vosk, J. S. Study of Negro children with learning difficulties at the outset of their school careers. **American Journal of Orthopsychiatry,** 1966, **36,** 32–40.
255. Voss, H. L., Wendling, A., & Elliott, D. S. Some types of high-school dropouts. **Journal of Educational Research,** 1966, **59,** 363–368.
256. Waite, R. R. Black and white families in a multiethnic urban primer. In S. G. Zimet (Ed.), **What children read in school.** New York: Grune and Stratton, 1972. Pp. 55–69.
257. Waite, R. R. Further attempts to integrate and urbanize first grade reading textbooks: A research study. **Journal of Negro Education,** Winter 1968, 62–69.
258. Waite, R. R., Blom, G. E., Zimet, S. G., & Edge, S. First-grade reading textbooks. **Elementary School Journal,** 1967, **67,** 366–374.
259. Walberg, H. J. & Ahlgren, A. Predictors of the social environment of learning. **American Educational Research Journal,** 1970, **7,** 153–167.
260. Walters, R. H., Marshall, W. E., & Shooter, J. R. Anxiety, isolation, and susceptibility to social influence. **Journal of Personality,** 1960, **28,** 518–529.

261. White, R. W. **The abnormal personality: A textbook.** New York: Ronald, 1948.
262. White, W. F., & Dekle, O. T. Effect of teacher's motivational cues on achievement level in elementary grades. **Psychological Reports,** 1966, **18,** 351–356.
263. Whiteman, M., & Deutsch, M. Social disadvantage as related to intellective and language development. In M. Deutsch, I. Katz, & A. R. Jensen (Eds.), **Social class, race, and psychological development.** New York: Holt, Rinehart & Winston, 1968.
264. Wicker, A. W. Undermanning, performances, and students' subjective experiences in behavior settings of large and small high schools. **Journal of Personality and Social Psychology,** 1968, **10,** 255–261.
265. Willems, E. P. Sense of obligation to high school activities as related to school size and marginality of student. **Child Development,** 1967, **38,** 1247–1260.
266. Wilson, R. S. Personality patterns, source attractiveness, and conformity. **Journal of Personality,** 1960, **28,** 186–199.
267. Winder, C. L., & Rau, L. Parental attitudes associated with social deviance in preadolescent boys. **Journal of Abnormal and Social Psychology,** 1962, **64,** 418–424.
268. Wood, C. G., Jr., & Hokanson, J. E. Effects of induced muscular tension on performance and the inverted U function. **Journal of Personality and Social Psychology,** 1965, **1,** 506–510.
269. Yamamoto, L., Lembright, M. L., & Corrigan, A. M. Intelligence, creative thinking, and sociometric choice among fifth-grade children. **Journal of Experimental Education,** 1966, **34,** 83–89.
270. Yando, R. M., & Kagan, J. The effect of teacher tempo on the child. **Child Development,** 1968, **39,** 27–34.
271. Yarrow, L. J., & Yarrow, M. R. Leadership and interpersonal change. **Journal of Social Issues,** 1958, **14,** 47–50.
272. Yee, A. H. Source and direction of causal influence in teacher-pupil relationships. **Journal of Educational Psychology,** 1968, **59,** 275-282.
273. Yellott, A. W., Liem, G. R., & Cowen, E. L. Relationships among measures of adjustment, sociometric status and achievement in third graders. **Pschology in the School,** 1969, **6,** 315–321.
274. Zimet, S. G. The messages in elementary reading texts. **Today's Education,** 1973, **62,** 43ff.
275. Zimet, S. G. American elementary reading textbooks: A sociological review. **Teachers College Record,** 1969, **70,** 331–340.
276. Zimet, S. G. Sex role models in primary reading textbooks of the United States: 1600–1966. Unpublished doctoral dissertation, University of Denver, 1968.

Part VI
Adolescence

Chapter 12

Adolescence

I. Physical Change, Sex, and Social Development

Adolescence has traditionally been viewed as a critical period in development, not only in America but in many other cultures as well, particularly the more technologically advanced societies. References to the "storm and stress" of the years between childhood and nominal adulthood have been common, both in popular discussion and in the writings of novelists, dramatists, and poets. Behavioral scientists have also tended to agree that adolescence represents a period of particular stress in our society. Some, particularly the more biologically oriented, have emphasized the adjustments required by the physiological changes associated with puberty, including increases in sex hormones and changes in body structure and function. Others have tended to hold the culture primarily responsible for the adolescent's difficulties, emphasizing the numerous, highly concentrated demands which our society has traditionally made upon youth at this time—demands for independence, for heterosexual and peer adjustments, for vocational preparation, for the development of a basic, guiding philosophy of life. In many cultures in which these demands are neither as complex nor as restricted to one limited age period as in our society, adolescence is not viewed as a particularly difficult period of adjustment.

While we encounter differences of opinion regarding the relative importance of biological, social, and psychological factors, there is nevertheless general agreement that the adolescent period has traditionally presented special adjustment problems in our society. There is, however, a good deal of disagreement, even among acknowledged authorities in child development, about whether the problems of adolescents have become more acute in recent years, with a consequent heightening of difficulties and conflicts with the adult culture. Magazines, newspapers, and television programs are replete with conflicting accounts of the values, attitudes, and behavior of today's adolescents.

We are told by some alarmed observers that youth today is more rebellious, more troubled emotionally, more promiscuous sexually, less idealistic, more critical of the values and standards of the adult culture, and more "disengaged" from those values than youth in earlier times. All manner of plausible sounding "evidence" has been cited in support of this "distressing" state of affairs: demonstrations on college and high school campuses; lack of respect for authority; confrontations with police and public officials; riots in minority-group ghettos; increased use of drugs, from "pep" pills and glue sniffing to marijuana, "speed," LSD, and even "hard" narcotics; pregnancy among adolescent girls; venereal disease; and suicide. Even adolescent music and fashions in dress and personal appearance have been cited as examples of this presumably deteriorating state of affairs.

In contrast, we are told by other observers, and with equal assurance, that adolescents today are brighter and better informed than their parents; less sentimental, but more genuinely idealistic; more serious; no more promiscuous in sexual behavior than their elders were at adolescence, but more open, honest, and tolerant; and less hypocritical, obsessed, or troubled in their sexual attitudes and beliefs. We are informed that youth are more concerned about the fundamental purposes of education and less satisfied merely to "get by" with acceptable grades; that they feel a greater sense of social responsibility and concern for the welfare of others; and that, if anything, they come closer to having a sense of their own identity and are less emotionally conflicted than their parents were at the same age.

Still another group of observers feel that presumed differences—good or bad—between today's adolescents and those of earlier generations are largely illusory and more a matter of form than of substance, or that they stem from unwarranted generalizations based upon the behavior of vocal, but relatively small, numbers of atypical youth. Protagonists of this view remind us that every generation of adults has viewed its successors with alarm, and that there have always been differences between generations in social and political beliefs, tastes and fashions, and fundamental liberalism or conservatism.

It will be one of our major aims in this and the following chapter to examine the evidence for these conflicting views and to try to arrive at a balanced judgment about the problems confronting adolescents and their responses to these problems. In order to approach this task, however, it will be necessary to consider separately the problems facing youth in general and those confronting special subgroups of adolescents within American culture. In our opinion, much of the current confusion regarding adolescence stems from the widespread tendency to assume that all adolescents are alike, face the same problems and demands, and react to them in similar fashion. Thus, if some late adolescents engage in conspicuous demonstrations against the dominant values of the adult culture, it is frequently concluded that a majority of today's youth are in active rebellion against society to a degree unprecedented in earlier generations. Or if an adolescent crime wave occurs in one of our larger urban ghettos, we can anticipate a sudden rash of television programs and articles in the popular press mantaining that an entire generation stands on the brink of lawlessness.

Available evidence, however, does not support such deceptive oversimplifications. It is certainly true, as we shall see, that adolescents share a number of common experiences and problems. All undergo the physiological and physical changes of puberty and later adolescent growth. All face the need for establishing an identity of their own—some kind of personal answer to the age-old question, "Who am I?" All are ultimately confronted with the need to earn a living and to make their own way as independent members of society.

But the fact remains, despite such similarities, that adolescents clearly are not all alike and do not all face the same environmental demands. The problems confronting a socioeconomically deprived youth from a broken home living in a segregated urban ghetto are vastly different from the problems faced by an economically favored adolescent from a loving and protective suburban family; and the responses of youths from such widely disparate environments may differ significantly.

An appreciation of the problems and developmental demands facing adolescents in general and of those confronting particular subgroups in our society is necessary if we are to avoid misleading oversimplifications regarding adolescent behavior and adjustment. In this chapter our attention will be directed primarily to considerations of adolescent growth and development, the adjustment demands facing youth generally in our culture, and the responses of adolescents to these demands. We shall consider the development of independence, sexual maturation, peer relations, and preparation for a vocation. In the final chapter, we shall examine the problems confronting young people generally in developing a system of values and a sense of ego identity, as well as the special problems of those who for one reason or another—social, psychological, economic, or ideological—find themselves outside the mainstream of adolescent culture in America.

PHYSICAL DEVELOPMENT IN ADOLESCENCE

Among the most dramatic of all developmental events to which all youth must adjust is the host of interrelated physiological and morphological changes occurring during the early adolescent period from about 11 to 15 years of age. The term puberty derives from the Latin word **pubertas** (meaning "age of manhood") and refers to the first phase of adolescence when sexual maturation becomes evident. Strictly speaking, puberty begins with the gradual enlargement of the ovaries (and such related organs as the uterus) in females and the prostate gland and seminal vesicles in males. For convenience in research and clinical practice, however, it is frequently dated from the beginning elevation of the breasts or the onset of menstruation (the menarche) in girls and the emergence of pigmented pubic hair in boys (181).

Endocrinological Factors in Development

The physiological and bodily changes that occur at this time are due, in part, to an increased output of activating hormones by the anterior pituitary gland, which is located immediately below the brain. Pituitary hormone stimulates the activity of the gonads or sex glands, thus increasing the production of sex hormones and the growth of mature sperm and ova in males and females. These sex hormones, including testosterone in males and estrogen in females, in combination with other hormones of the body, stimulate the growth of bone and muscle and lead to the growth spurt (132, 180).

Adolescent Growth Spurt

The term growth spurt refers to the accelerated rate of increase in height and weight that occurs with the onset of adolescence. This increase varies widely in intensity, duration, and age of onset from one child to another, even among perfectly normal children—a fact often poorly understood by adolescents and their parents and, consequently, too often a source of needless concern.

In boys the growth spurt may begin as early as 10½ years or as late as 16 years (**179**). For the average boy, however, rapid acceleration in growth begins at about 13 years, reaching a peak rate of growth at about 14 years, and then declining sharply to pregrowth-spurt rates by around 15½. Further slow growth may continue for several years thereafter (see Fig. 12.1; **179, 180, 181**).

In girls the adolescent growth spurt may begin as early as 7½ years of age or as late as 11½ (**179, 180, 181**). For the average girl rapid acceleration in growth begins about age 11, reaches a peak at about 12 years, and then decreases rapidly to pregrowth-spurt rates by about age 13, with slow continued growth for several additional years (**132, 180, 181**).

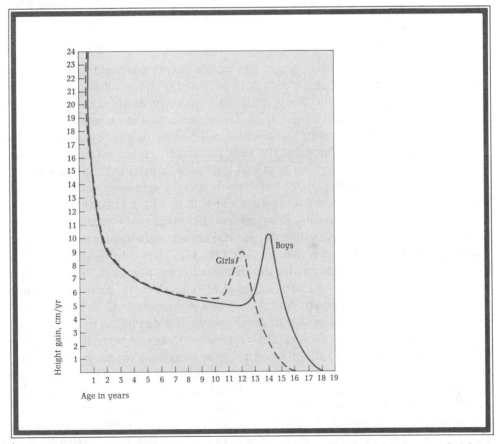

Figure 12.1 Typical individual velocity curves for supine length or height in boys and girls. These curves represent the velocity of the typical boy and girl at any given instant. (From J. M. Tanner, R. H. Whitehouse, M. Takaishi. Standards from birth to maturity for height, weight, height velocity and weight velocity; British children, 1965. **Archives of the Diseases of Childhood,** 1966, **41,** 455–471. By permission.)

The popular belief that girls mature earlier than boys stems primarily from the fact that girls obtain their adult height and weight about two years earlier than boys. During the adolescent growth spurt, boys increase only slightly more than girls in height. The greater eventual height of males results primarily from their being older and, therefore, taller at the beginning of their adolescent growth spurt (**132**).

> Practically all skeletal and muscular dimensions take part in the spurt, though not to an equal degree. Most of the spurt in height is due to acceleration of trunk length rather than length of legs. There is a fairly regular order in which the dimensions accelerate; leg length as a rule reaches its peak first, followed by the body breadths, with shoulder width last. Thus a boy stops growing out of his trousers (at least in length) a year before he stops growing out of his jackets. The earliest structures to reach their adult status are the head, hands, and feet. At adolescence, children, particularly girls, sometimes complain of having large hands and feet. They can be reassured that by the time they are fully grown their hands and feet will be a little smaller in proportion to their arms and legs, and considerably smaller in proportion to their trunk (**179**, 911).

Along with the increases in height and weight during this period, less obvious physical changes are occurring, too. In both boys and girls muscular development proceeds rapidly as height increases, reaching a peak rate of growth slightly after the point of peak velocity in height. Boys, however, show a more rapid rate of increase than girls, with the result that their overall gain in muscle tissue during this period is greater than that for girls (**179, 180**), an advantage they retain throughout the adult years. Conversely, both boys and girls show a decline in the rate of development of fat during the adolescent growth spurt, a decline which reaches its maximum velocity at the point of maximum growth in height (**180, 181**).

The acceleration of muscular development that takes place during this period is accompanied by increases in strength, as measured by such indices as pulling and pushing strength in the arms (**69, 78, 99, 126, 131**). Not surprisingly, relative strength increases are much greater in the case of boys than girls. While, for the most part, prepubescent boys and girls are similar in strength, after adolescence boys are, and remain, much stronger. While this greater strength in boys is principally a function of greater muscular development, it is due partly to a number of other related developmental factors. Thus, relative to their size, boys develop larger hearts and lungs, a higher systolic blood pressure, a greater capacity for carrying oxygen in the blood, a lower heart rate while at rest, and interestingly, "a greater power for neutralizing the chemical products of muscular exercise, such as lactic acid" (which makes itself felt in fatigue) (**180**, 95). Increases in strength during adolescence are reflected in the greater emphasis on athletic activities (as well as general physical restlessness) that is likely to occur at this time, particularly in boys (**97**, 124).

Unlike the skeletal structure and most other bodily organs, there is relatively little further growth in brain size during adolescence. While the average child has acquired about 50 percent of his **total** adult weight by the age of 10, the beginning adolescent has already acquired 95 percent of his total adult brain weight (**180**).

Sexual Maturation As in the case of the growth spurt in height and weight, there are marked individual differences in the age of onset of puberty. Among girls the beginning elevation of the breast, the so-called "bud stage" which is usually the first obvious sign of sexual development, may vary from about 8 to 13 years. Among boys increases in the size of the testes may begin as early as 9½ or as late as 13½ years (see Fig. 12.2).

Interrelationships Among Growth Factors

Although the age of onset of the overall developmental sequence may vary widely, the maturational factors all appear to operate together. Thus the correlation between age of height spurt and beginning testes growth is .86. The correlation between age of menarche and beginning breast-bud appearance is also .86, and the correlation between age of menarche and time of appearance of pubic hair is .70. These correlations suggest that in any one adolescent there is likely to be a close correspondence between the age at which he reaches his maximum rate of growth in height and weight and the age at which he reaches puberty (**42, 170, 171**). Thus the boy who shows the growth spurt early will develop pubic hair early; the girl who has early menarche will show early breast development. Figure 12.2 shows the maturational sequences for average adolescent boys and girls.

Even before maximum growth rate is achieved, measures of skeletal activity are predictive of age of menarche (**171**). During the preadolescent period, the bones of the legs, arms, hands, and feet increase in length and begin to join together or fuse. The rate at which this fusion of the bones occurs is closely related to the reproductive maturity of the adolescent. There is a close correspondence between age of menarche in the girl and the age at which the bones of the fingers become fused (**81**). Similarly, appearance of pubic hair in boys is closely associated with skeletal development of the hand (**81**). Similar relationships seem to hold among other aspects of skeletal and muscle growth and primary and secondary sexual development. In brief, there tends to be a general "going togetherness" of various maturational factors at this period of the individual's life (**144**).

From a psychological viewpoint, it is most important that all girls and boys be aware of the fact that maturational age, including age of sexual maturation, varies widely among normal young people with no associated physical abnormalities. There may be somewhat less concern in these matters among contemporary adolescents than there was in earlier generations, because of better information, less secrecy, and a healthier attitude toward sexual development generally. But the fact remains that anxiety among adolescent girls and boys could be reduced if there were more widespread awareness that such variations are perfectly normal and do

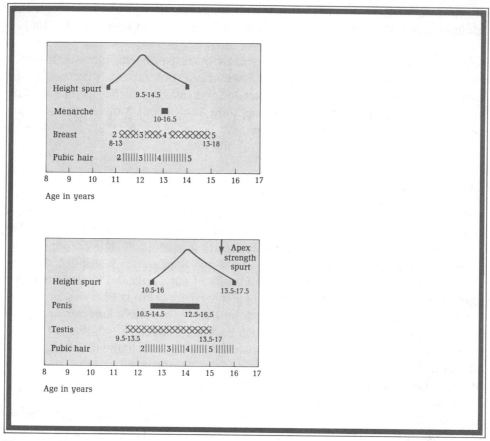

Figure 12.2 Diagram of sequence of events at adolescence in boys and girls. The average boy and girl are represented. The range of ages within which each event charted may begin and end is given by the figures placed directly below its start and finish. (From W. A. Marshall & J. M. Tanner. Variations in the pattern of pubertal changes in boys. **Archives of the Diseases of Childhood,** 1970, **45,** 13. By permission.)

not presage later difficulties in either general physical development or specific sexual development and functioning.

PSYCHOLOGICAL ASPECTS OF ADOLESCENT GROWTH AND DEVELOPMENT

Many adults, having managed to repress potentially anxiety-producing memories of the needs, desires, and fears associated with their own adolescence, have only a vague realization of how acutely aware the average adolescent is of the entire growth process. The development of one's own identity as a person (what Erikson has called **ego identity**) requires a perception of the self as separate from others (despite ties to them) and a feeling of "wholeness," that is, a feeling of **self-consistency,** not only in the sense of internal consistency at a particular moment, but also over time. The adolescent, and particularly the younger adolescent, is faced with rapid increases in height, changing bodily dimensions, and the objective and subjective changes related to sexual maturation. Obviously, all of these developments threaten his feeling of self-consistency, and the adolescent needs time to integrate them into a slowly emerging sense of a positive, self-confident ego identity.

While the very fact of developmental changes tends to focus adolescent concerns upon physical aspects of the self, the nature of these concerns is influenced by a number of additional factors. With the onset of adolescence and the accelerated shift away from dependence on the family and toward the peer group as a major source of security and status, conformity, not only in social behavior, but in appearance and physical skills, becomes increasingly emphasized (142). While there have been recent and hopeful signs of a greater tolerance of diversity among some groups of today's youth, deviance from group norms in rate of development and physical appearance can still be an agonizing experience for many adolescents.

Marked deviations from idealized norms of physical appearance, skills, and interests—norms that conform largely to the culture's stereotypes of masculinity and femininity—may adversely influence how the adolescent is treated by others and what he thinks of himself (52). It should be stressed, however, that the adolescent's self-perceptions are not always simply a result of objective realities. An adolescent's perception of his physical self (his "body image") may be influenced by prior experiences that have led him to view himself as attractive or unattractive, strong or weak, masculine or feminine, regardless of the actual facts of his adolescent physical appearance and capabilities.

For example, a boy who is physically of average size and strength may view himself as smaller and weaker than he is. Adolescent girls tend to be even more interested and concerned about their physical development than boys (50, 53, 97). A girl who, in terms of current cultural stereotypes, is really quite beautiful, may view herself as unattractive because she has been told for years that she "looks just like" a parent or other relative whom she resents or that others have denigrated.

Psychological Aspects of Menstruation

Menstruation means much more to the adolescent girl than just a simple physiological readjustment. It is a symbol of sexual maturity and the capacity for having children of her own. Because the reactions of the girl to menstruation may be generalized so broadly, it is vital that her initial experience with it be as favorable as possible.

Many girls look forward calmly to the onset of menstruation, and some receive it proudly, as a sign of increased status. Unfortunately, because many notions concerning shamefulness or even dangerousness of menstruation have persisted in our time, there are other girls who fear and hate it (142). If a menstruating girl's parents and friends act as though she requires sympathy for her "plight"—an attitude implied in such prevalent euphemisms for menstruation as "the curse" and "being unwell"—the girl herself is likely to adopt similar attitudes toward her menstruation. A girl who has been unable to establish a satisfactory feminine identification "may be disturbed by having her attention bluntly directed by the onset of menstruation to the fact that she is a woman and can do nothing about it" (142, 617).

Negative reactions to menstruation may also stem in part from physical discomfort (164). During the early years of menstruation, when the menses are likely to be quite irregular, a number of girls experience disturbing symptoms, such as headaches, backaches, cramps, in relation to their menstrual period, although the extent to which these are organically determined or psychosomatic is often difficult to determine (1, 95, 146). However, such initial disturbances tend to disappear as puberty progresses and menstruation becomes more regular.

Many of these negative reactions to menstruation could be avoided or alleviated if parents employed a wise and understanding approach to the problem. By seeing that the girl receives adequate medical care in the case of physical difficulties, by explaining to her the naturalness of the phenomenon, and by showing pride and pleasure in her greater maturity, the parents—particularly the mother—can help to make the onset of menstruation a happy, rather than a feared or hated event. This, of course, will have consequent benefits for the girl's whole future sexual and social role as a woman.

Nocturnal Emission

Just as the onset of menstruation may cause concern to the pubescent girl, so may the appearance of nocturnal emission surprise and worry the pubescent boy. Nocturnal emission is the ejaculation of the seminal fluid during sleep. Approximately 83 percent of males report experiencing nocturnal emissions at some time in their lives, tending usually to begin a year or two after the onset of puberty. Frequently, but by no means always, these emissions are accompanied by erotic dreams (111, 156). The female equivalent of nocturnal emissions, nocturnal dreams with orgasm, is far less frequent (probably never exceeding 10 percent) and tends not to reach a peak until after adolescence.

Boys as a group worry less about nocturnal emissions than girls do about menstruation, perhaps partly because boys are more often able to talk freely among themselves about such matters. It also appears that contemporary adolescents are better informed and less likely to be concerned about nocturnal emissions than were boys of earlier generations. Nevertheless, many boys, especially in the early and middle years of adolescence, do not gain proper instruction from their peers or parents and torture themselves with unnecessary fears (152).

Early Versus Late Maturation

As we have already seen clearly, maturational rates vary widely among normal adolescents. At age 15, one boy may be small, with no pubertal development of reproductive organs or pubic hair. Another boy of the same age may appear to be "virtually a grown man, with broad shoulders, strong muscles, adult genitalia, and a bass voice; he could easily be mistaken for a 17- or 18-year old" (180, 173). Are such dramatic physical differences reflected in differences in personal development and social behavior and, if so, in what manner?

According to the data of one intensive study of boys aged 12-17, later maturers were rated as less attractive in physique, less well-poised, more "immoderate" in their behavior, more affected and more tense in manner, and more eager. They tended to engage in more attention-getting behavior, were more restless, talkative and bossy, were less popular with their peers, and fewer of them were leaders (100, 101, 103). In contrast, early maturers emerged as more reserved, more self-assured, more matter-of-fact, more likely to engage in well-modulated, socially appropriate behavior, and more able to laugh at themselves.

Personality tests showed that later maturers revealed more feelings of inadequacy, negative self-conceptions, feelings of rejection and domination, and persistent dependency needs, coupled, perhaps paradoxically, with a seemingly rebellious searching for autonomy and freedom from restraint (143).

Many of these differences appeared to persist over long periods of time. In a follow-up study of subjects from the original samples at age 33, late maturers were relatively less self-controlled, responsible, and dominant and more inclined to turn to others for help and support (102).

In another study comparing early-, average-, and late-maturing college students on several personality measures (193), late-maturing boys scored significantly higher in feelings of guilt, inferiority, depression, and generalized anxiety, and in needs for encouragement, sympathy, and understanding from others than either early- or average-maturing boys. The late-maturers were significantly lower in needs for leading, controlling, or dominating others, but they were more anticonventional, mildly rebellious, and autonomy-oriented; the later maturers' personality "suggests a prolongation of the typically adolescent independence-dependence conflict" (193, 840).

Whereas for boys early or average maturation consistently appears advantageous and late maturation disadvantageous, the picture in girls is more complicated. In general, it appears that differences between early- and late-maturing girls may not be as great as in the case of boys. Furthermore, the advantages or disadvantages of early versus late maturation may vary over time.

For example, among sixth-grade girls early maturation (as determined by age of menarche) tended to be a social handicap (71). At this grade level, when most girls were themselves prepuberal, prestige-enhancing personality traits were most frequently ascribed by their peers to prepuberal girls. However, beginning with the seventh grade, when most girls had begun to cope with the demands of puberty, and continuing throughout junior high school, the picture shifted. At the seventh grade, postpuberal girls scored most favorably, and at eighth and ninth grades, girls who were already late adolescents (4-6 years beyond menarche) scored most favorably.

> . . . it appears that prestige is more likely to surround those in the sixth grade who are developmentally "in phase" (prepuberal), whereas during the junior high school years being ahead of the group developmentally seems to be an advantage. . . .
>
> This discontinuity suggests that for girls neither physical acceleration or physical retardation is consistently advantageous. It is not until the junior high school years that the early-maturing girl "comes into her own" and reaps the benefit of her accelerated development. Until that time her precocious development is somewhat detrimental to her social status. The adjustments which inevitably must be made to losses and gains in status during the adolescent period may be partly a function of this discontinuity in the relationship between development maturity and prestige during the adolescent period (71, 97, 98).

In attempting to account for such sex differences in the effects of differential maturation rates, one investigator commented:

> In our society the cultural sex-role prescription for males is relatively unambiguous and is one which places a high value upon attributes associated with physical strength and athletic prowess, especially in the adolescent and young adulthood years. As Lynn (125) pointed out, however, the feminine sex-role prescription is much less definite and stereotyped; consequently it is less likely to be closely tied to any specific pattern of physical attributes (193, 485).

EFFECTS OF ADOLESCENT MENTAL GROWTH ON PSYCHOLOGICAL DEVELOPMENT

As we have seen in Chapter 7, the young person's cognitive ability also continues to develop, both quantitatively and qualitatively during the adolescent years. The importance of the changes taking place during this period, most notably the advent of the stage of formal operations, would be difficult to overestimate (see pp. 312–314). These changes play a critical role in helping the adolescent to deal with increasingly complex educational and vocational demands. It would be virtually impossible to master such academic subjects as calculus or the use of metaphors in poetry without a high level of abstract thinking—the capacity that Piaget has referred to as "second-degree operations," or the ability to think about statements that have no relation to real objects in the world.

Further reflection, however, should make it clear that many other aspects of adolescent development are also dependent on the cognitive advances occurring during this period. Changes in the nature of parent-child relationships, emerging personality characteristics and psychological defense mechanisms, planning of future educational and vocational goals, mounting concerns with social, political, and personal values, even a developing sense of ego identity, all are strongly influenced by these cognitive changes.

One of the most important aspects of the emergence of formal operational thought is the ability to entertain hypotheses or theoretical propositions that depart from immediately observable events. In contrast to the child who is preoccupied, for the most part, with learning how to function in the world of "here and now," the adolescent is able "not only to grasp the immediate state of things but also the possible state they might or could assume" (**63,** 152). The implications of this change alone are vast (**43, 62**).

For example, the adolescent's new-found and frequently wearing talents for discovering his previously idealized parents' feet of clay—for questioning their values, for comparing them with other "more understanding" or less "square" parents, and for accusing them of "hypocritical" inconsistencies between professed values and behavior—all appear at least partly dependent on the adolescent's changes in cognitive ability. "The awareness of the discrepancy between the actual and the possible also helps to make the adolescent a rebel. He is always comparing the possible with the actual and discovering that the actual is frequently wanting" (**63,** 152).

The relentless criticism by many adolescents of existing social, political, and religious systems and their preoccupation with the construction of (often elaborate or highly theoretical) alternative systems is similarly dependent on their emerging capacity for formal operational thought. The fact that such concerns tend to be most characteristic of our brightest young people appears due at least as much to their greater cognitive capability, as to their more "permissive upbringing," "affluence," or other favorite whipping boys of politicians and the popular press.

A good deal of an adolescent's apparently passionate concern with the deficiencies of parents and the social order and with the creation of "viable alternatives" often turns out to be primarily verbal, more a matter of word than deed. This is perhaps a reflection of the fact that this stage of cognitive development is still relatively new and not yet fully integrated into the adolescent's total adaptation to life (**62**).

At the same time, it is important to recognize the positive aspects of the adolescent's newly acquired ability to conceptualize and reason abstractly about hypothetical possibilities and instant convictions.

> To reason is for the young person a need and a pleasure; the "constructs of the mind" are a delight. He reasons every which way, about subjects that are most unreal and farthest from his experience. . . . The arrival at abstraction permits the individual to delve into the systems of collective representation that are offered to him by the culture in which he is growing up, and he will gradually be carried away by ideas, ideals, and values (**147,** 15).

While the younger adolescent's enthusiasm will often appear initially to have little order or system, as though it were an uncritically accepted game of ideas, it is important for adults to recognize that the exercise is, nevertheless, a vitally important and productive one.

> Everything will be food for thought, for spoken thought, for passionate discussion, for endless discussions, for preemptory affirmation, and the adult, losing his footing a little in this tidal wave, will often fail to perceive that what he takes to be vain rehashing or sterile questioning of old worn out problems corresponds in reality, for the youngster, to youthful explorations and true discoveries (**147,** 15).

Cognitive Aspects of Adolescent Personality Development

Adolescent cognitive development is reflected not only in attitudes and values with respect to parents and society, but also in attitudes toward the self and in the personality characteristics and defense mechanisms likely to assume prominence during this period. With his increasing ability to consider hypothetical possibilities and to "take his own thought as object and reason about it" and guided by the irresistible, and sometimes painful, self-awareness that stems from the rapid physical, physiological, and psychological changes of this period, the adolescent is likely to become more **introspective** and **analytical.** Many adolescents at this stage are concerned with such issues as whether the world that they perceive "actually" exists and, indeed, whether they themselves are "real" or a product of "consciousness." Many readers will probably feel a nostalgic empathy for the young adolescent who remarked, "I found myself thinking about my future, and then I began to think about why I was thinking about my future, and then I began to think about why I was thinking about why I was thinking about my future" (**48,** 367). Such preoccupation with thought itself is characteristic of the emergence of the stage of formal operations.

The adolescent's thought and behavior may appear **egocentric.** Although he can conceptualize the thoughts of others, "he fails to differentiate between the objects toward which the thoughts of others are directed and those which are the focus of his own concern" (**64,** 1029). And since the focus of the adolescent's concern during this period of rapid change is likely to be upon himself, he is likely to conclude that other people are equally obsessed with his behavior and appearance. "It is this belief that others are preoccupied with his appearance and behavior that constitutes the egocentrism of the adolescent" (**64,** 1029).

As David Elkind notes, one of the consequences of the adolescent's egocentrism is a feeling that he is "on stage" and much of his time is spent "constructing, or reacting to, **an imaginary audience**" (**64,** 1030). It is an audience because the adolescent feels that all eyes are focused upon him and, fortunately or unfortunately, it is imaginary because this is so seldom the case. The construction of such imaginary audiences helps to account, at least to some degree, for a variety of adolescent behaviors and experiences, including the adolescent's sometimes excruciating self-consciousness (64). When the adolescent is feeling self-critical, he is likely to anticipate that this "audience" will be similarly critical.

By the same token, when the adolescent is in an ebullient, self-admiring mood, he may project these feelings as well onto his peers or adults. The younger adolescent boy who stands before the mirror flexing his muscles and admiring his profile, or the girl who spends hours applying her makeup or trying one hair style or one dress after another, may be dreaming of the dramatic impression that he or she will make on a date or at a party that evening (64). It is perhaps one of the minor tragedies of adolescent life that when these young people actually meet, each is likely to be more preoccupied with himself than with observing others. "Gatherings of young adolescents are unique in the sense that each young person is simultaneously an actor to himself and an audience to others" (64, 1030).

The adolescent's frequent use of irony—of the sometimes elaborate "put on" or "put down"—while clearly serving many motivations, can be partly understood as an exercise of his new talents for thinking at the symbolic level of the metaphor, the "as if," and the manifestly absurd. The delight of the younger adolescent (and some rather adolescent adults) in the use of "double-entendres" appears to represent not merely an exhilarating tasting of forbidden fruit, but an opportunity to demonstrate a new cognitive skill. The same may be said of the older adolescent's appreciation of political and social satire and his skill "in making the apparently innocent yet cutting remark" (61, 35).

It also appears that the emerging awareness of how things might be, in contrast to how things are, may help in part to explain some of the "recurrent adolescent feelings of depression and dissatisfaction ('Weltschmerz')" (63, 152). It is most often in adolescence, for example, that adopted children are likely to feel compelled to seek out their real parents. Similarly, "it is only in adolescence that previously happy, cheerful and 'gutty' handicapped and crippled children experience their first real depression" (63, 152).

The adolescent's cognitive development also plays an important role in the emergence of a well-defined sense of ego identity. It seems likely that the degree of differentiation and definiteness that an individual is able to achieve in the development of a sense of identity will depend upon his cognitive capability.

The psychological defense mechanisms (see pp. 453–456) employed by the adolescent may also reflect his level of cognitive development. **Asceticism** and **intellectualization** are two defense mechanisms that are more likely to emerge in adolescence than at other ages (13, 14, 75). Asceticism involves "an attempt to deny entirely the instinctual desires" (83, 25). An adolescent boy or girl may, perhaps in the name of religious dedication or simply "self-discipline," seek to avoid any semblance of "giving in" to sexual desire, tastes in food or drink, sometimes even such basic bodily needs as sleep or protection from cold.

It is as though the disruptions of psychological equilibrium and previously workable controls, and the increases in drive (e.g., sexual, aggressive) that accompany the onset of puberty create conflicts and anxieties that the young person attempts to counteract by making avoidance of all such basic impulses a **positive** value (38).

Intellectualization may also be employed by some adolescents to deal with troubling anxieties that may be too painful to deal with directly. Thus, apparently impersonal, highly intellectual discussions of the philosophical basis of free-love versus marriage, of the role of aggression in human affairs, of responsibility versus freedom, of the nature of friendship, of the existence of God may, in fact, more nearly reflect deep-seated personal concerns. For example, they may indicate strong concern with how to handle the unfamiliar and insistent stirring of sexual or aggressive feelings or how to resolve conflicts between childlike gratification of desires and an increasingly demanding conscience.

In contrast to denial and other more childlike defenses, defenses such as intellectualization and asceticism are dependent upon a reasonably advanced degree of cognitive development and are, in fact, most frequent among intelligent, sensitive adolescents. Furthermore, while much of the motivation for the use of these defenses may be to avoid anxiety, they may also provide the adolescent with important practice in exercising his capacity for abstract thought and for formulating and testing hypotheses.

DEVELOPMENTAL TASKS OF ADOLESCENCE

As we have seen, physical and intellectual maturation play a necessary and vital role in the adolescent's transition from childhood to adult status in our society. But meaningful social and psychological maturity cannot be achieved unless the adolescent is also able to master successfully a number of critically important, interrelated developmental tasks. If the adolescent is to become truly adult, not just physically mature, he must, in the few short years between childhood and nominal adulthood, gradually achieve independence from his family; adjust to his sexual maturation; establish cooperative and workable relationships with his peers, without being dominated by them; and decide on and prepare for a meaningful vocation. In the process, he must develop a philosophy of life, that is, a set of guiding moral beliefs and standards which can lend some order and consistency to the many decisions he will have to make and the actions he will have to take in a diverse, changing, sometimes chaotic world. And he must develop a sense of his own identity. Before the adolescent can safely abandon the security of childhood dependence on others, he must have some idea of who he is, where he is going, and what the possibilities are of getting there.

In many ways, the question "Who am I?" is the central problem of adolescence, a problem celebrated in poetry, in novels, and autobiographies over many centuries.

Recently, however, it has become the focus of increased psychological concern through the writings of the gifted psychoanalyst, Erik Erikson, who has discussed the problem in terms of "ego identity." Perhaps it is no coincidence that Erikson came to psychoanalysis with a broad background in literature and the arts. In Erikson's words:

> The identity the adolescent seeks to clarify is who he is, what his role in society is to be. Is he a child or is he an adult? Does he have it in him to be someday a husband and father? What is he to be as a worker and an earner of money? Can he feel self-confident in spite of the fact that his race or religious or national backgrounds make him a person some people look down upon? Overall, will he be a success or a failure? By reason of these questions adolescents are sometimes morbidly preoccupied with how they appear in the eyes of others as compared with their own conception of themselves, and with how they can make the rules and skills learned earlier jibe with what is currently in style . . . (**68**, 9).

The danger of this developmental period is self-diffusion. As one of the characters in the play **Death of a Salesman** puts it, "I just can't take hold. I can't take hold of some kind of a life." A boy or girl can scarcely help feeling somewhat diffuse when the body changes in size and shape so rapidly, "when genital maturity floods body and imagination with forbidden desires, when adult life lies ahead with such a diversity of conflicting possibilities and choices" (**68**, 9). Thus a sense of ego identity is necessary for a secure footing in life, for it leads to "a sense of knowing where one is going, and an inner assuredness of anticipated recognition from those who count" (**66**, 118–119).

Let us consider in detail the major developmental tasks facing the adolescent in our society—the establishment of independence, sexual adjustment, peer relations, and preparation for a vocation. However, as we shall see in the next chapter, the individual adolescent's ability to meet each of these requirements, the directions he takes, and the degree of success he has in integrating these complex and varied demands will be intimately related to his success in establishing a workable set of personal values and a strong sense of his own ego identity. That some adolescents succeed while others fail, for personal, social, or other reasons, will become painfully evident in the final chapter's discussion of alienated youth.

THE DEVELOPMENT OF ADOLESCENT INDEPENDENCE

The development of independence is central to any discussion of the tasks of adolescence, especially in American society, with its relatively strong emphasis on individual self-reliance. An adolescent's failure to resolve the conflict between a continuing dependence and the newer demands (and privileges) of independence will lead to difficulties in most other areas as well. Without the achievement of a reasonable degree of separation and autonomy, the adolescent can hardly be expected to achieve mature heterosexual or peer relationships, confident pursuit of a vocation, or a sense of identity, which requires a positive image of himself as separate, unified, and consistent over time.

Establishing true independence from parents is seldom a simple matter because motivations and rewards for independence and for continued dependence are both likely to be strong, thus leading to conflict and vacillating behavior. However, the degree of difficulty that the adolescent will encounter in establishing independence will depend in large measure upon (1) the consistency, the rate, and the extent and complexity of independence training sanctioned by the society as a whole and (2) the child-rearing practices and models of behavior provided by his parents. There are wide variations in patterns of independence training, both from one culture to another and from one set of parents to another.

Establishing Independence in Other Cultures

In many preliterate societies (though by no means all), and even in some areas of more technologically advanced societies, the task of establishing independence may be less difficult than it is in our own complex, socially fragmented, and rapidly changing culture. Among the Mountain Arapesh people of New Guinea, for example, there is a very gradual transition from a rather high degree of dependence and indulgent care in infancy and early childhood to increasing independence as the child grows older, with no discernible spurt during puberty or adolescence; "the mildness of the transition in this case is facilitated by the fact that the change is not very great" (136).

The Arapesh adolescent begins to take over much of the responsibility for supporting and managing the household, but there are few marked changes in basic family relationships at this time. The Arapesh girl does not suddenly leave home during adolescence to go to live in a strange household with strange people, in order to undergo the joint uncertainties of married life, sex, and childbearing (136). In this society, the girl has been chosen as a wife by her husband's parents many years prior to the consummation of the marriage, and she has been allowed during the interim to wander confidently back and forth between her own home and her future husband's. By the time her marriage is consummated she has come to think of her parents-in-law as an additional mother and father. She has known her husband almost as an older brother, whose responsibility it has been to look after her, to feed her, and to help her grow up (136).

As time goes by, the Arapesh girl takes on increasing responsibility in her new home. Many of the problems which occur frequently in contemporary American marriages do not exist in Arapesh culture. There is none of the atmosphere of confusion, of sudden separation from parents, of moving into a new house, often in a distant city, and beginning a separate existence with a relatively unknown male and bearing and caring for her children largely by herself—all of which are likely to characterize today's increasingly isolated young "nuclear" families in our society.

Similarly, the independence problems faced by the Arapesh boy are likely to be less severe than those faced by American boys. Once the Arapesh youth has passed through the initiation ceremony following pubescence, he assumes added responsibility. "From one who has been grown by the daily carefulness and hard work of others, he now passes into the class of those whose care is for others' growth" (136, 76). He takes on new responsibilities toward those "who after years devoted to his growth are now growing old themselves, and toward his younger brothers and sisters, and his young betrothed wife" (136, 76). But he does not need to go out into a new community on his own, obtain an unfamiliar job, and complete his emotional independence from his parents. He continues, but with new responsibility, to till the family's garden. He still sees his parents daily, and when at last he consummates his marriage, it is with a girl he has known, whom he has cared for, and to whom he has adjusted his personality over a long period of time (136, 142).

In contrast to societies like the Arapesh, children and adolescents in some other preliterate societies may find the establishment of independence a stressful and anxiety-producing task. The extent of the shift from dependency to independency required by a particular society may be relatively great (a shift from extreme dependency and indulgence early in life to equally extreme demands for independence in later childhood, adolescence, or adulthood) or the transition from dependence to independence may be compressed into a relatively short period of time or characterized by sharp breaks or discontinuities. Sudden, rapid shifts may occur following puberty rites intended to mark the transition from childhood to some degree of adult status or the problem of establishing independence may be increased in complexity and stressfulness by other factors.

The Mundugumor adolescent of the South Seas, for example, finds the problem of orderly transition from dependence on the parents to the setting up of an independent household extremely difficult, largely because "Mundugumor social organization is based on a theory of a natural hostility between all members of the same sex . . ." (136, 176). Fathers and sons view each other almost as natural enemies, as do mothers and daughters. Moreover, relations between husband and wife are notably poor. Fathers band together with daughters, while mothers band together with sons, and rivalry and distrust between the two subfamily groups are typical.

Consequently, the Mundugumor boy approaches adolescence close phychologically only to his mother, hostile toward his father, and distrustful of girls his own age. The girl, on the other hand, has strong ties to her father, resentment toward her mother, and distrust of her male contemporaries. In addition, the girl's problem is magnified because of the jealous father's attempts to keep his hold on her as long as possible.

There seems little doubt that Mundugumor children early develop a kind of hardy independence that prepares them somewhat for the demands they must face in adolescence. But this advantage is virtually negated by the fact that the independence demanded of the Mundugumor adolescent is so much more extreme than in most cultures. The prospect of establishing independence is unpleasant, and in many ways threatening. In fact, its only really attractive aspect seems to be escape from the hostility of the same-sex parent (142).

Establishing Independence in American Culture

The American adolescent of today (and his counterparts in other technologically advanced nations) clearly encounters greater stress in establishing independence than the Arapesh youth, although, at least in most families, he is spared much of the hostility of the Mundugumor's struggle for independence. The American adolescent is expected, in the limited period between puberty and adulthood, to pass from a state of relatively great dependence on his family to one of considerable independence (139, 197, 198). Strong societal demands for independence, in the face of incompatible and well-established dependent responses, are likely to produce conflict. And the fact that this conflict is timed to coincide with so many other developmental demands related to puberty and adolescence only tends to increase its stressfulness. Moreover, no clear pattern of transition from dependence to independence is spelled out for the adolescent by our society as a whole. There is little agreement as to the forms this greater independence should be allowed to take. We have no formalized procedures in our culture comparable to the puberty ceremonies or **rites de passage** of many primitive cultures which can serve as guides to parents and to the adolescent as to when and how independence should be granted and assumed.

About all that our society has in the way of institutionalized patterns of recognizing the adolescent's increasing independence is a variety of laws. These laws are often internally inconsistent and, furthermore, they vary a great deal in their content from one area of the culture to another. Thus, there are significant variations from state to state in the age at which a young person can drink alcohol, drive a car, marry, and own property. One of the ironies of our time is that, until 1971, young people who were considered old enough to fight a war for their elders in Indochina were not considered "mature" enough to vote (70).

As a consequence, the adolescent who must face the problems of transition from childish dependency to adult independence is likely to be impressed, not with the solidarity of the expectations of adult society, but with their confusion and divisiveness. In one instance, or with one set of people, he is likely to find that independent responses are rewarded. In other instances, or with other people, he may find that these responses are punished. The church, the school, the members of the various social classes, even the adolescent's own parents may have different notions as to the time when adult protection and guidance should be relinquished in favor of greater individual responsibility.

The contemporary adolescent is likely to observe that some of his peers are allowed by their parents to decide how to earn and spend their own money, to obtain a car, to choose their companions, to go off alone on dates, to take trips by themselves or with friends, and to make their own educational and vocational plans. In contrast, other adolescents, even of the same age and social group, may be allowed to do none of these things (**142**).

Furthermore, today's adolescents often find inconsistencies in the way in which people react to them as individuals. The young high school student's employer usually expects him to be independent and responsible more often than his parents do. Even within one family, a mother and father may have differing independence expectations with regard to their young. Finally, either or both parents "may possess mixed feelings over their child's growing independence. These mixed feelings are likely to be reflected in inconsistent patterns of parental behavior—as, for example, demanding independence and at the same time punishing it when it occurs" (**142,** 627).

But not all problems of achieving independence stem from inconsistencies on the part of society or parents. The adolescent himself is conflicted. He may really desire to be a free agent, but he may just as strongly want the security and lack of responsibility that are associated with continuing dependence (**142**).

Parent-Child Relationships and the Development of Independence The relative ease or difficulty of establishing independence depends in great part upon prior and continuing parent-child relationships. The parent who provides a successful model of independence with which the child can identify and who balances controls and realistically age-graded opportunities for independent behavior will make the task a great deal easier.

Adolescents from "democratic" families (in which the adolescent freely participates in family discussion about issues relevant to his behavior and may even make decisions, but where parents retain ultimate control) are likely to consider their parents fair and reasonable in their "ideas, rules, or principles about how you should behave." This is not as true of the adolescent children of either autocratic parents or permissive or neglectful parents (**55, 58, 59**). Democratically reared adolescents are also far less likely to report feelings of having been unwanted as children (about 10 percent) than the children of autocratic parents (about 40 percent; **59**).

Some parents attempt to make their exercise of power "legitimate" (**58**) by explaining their rules of conduct and expectations; others do not. The children of democratic and permissive parents, who also frequently provide explanations, are relatively high in both confidence and independence. Lack of confidence and independence more frequently characterize the children of autocratic parents who infrequently provide explanations of parental rules of conduct and expectations (**2, 58, 151, 161**). Confidence and self-esteem are highest among adolescents whose parents express strong interest in and knowledge about their opinions and activities and who encourage autonomous behavior and active participation in family affairs (**161**).

In brief, it appears that democratic practices, with frequent explanations by parents of the reasons for their rules of conduct and expectations, foster the earning of responsible independence in several ways: (1) by providing opportunities for increasing autonomy, guided by interested parents who communicate with the child and exercise appropriate degrees of control; (2) by promoting positive identification with the parent, based on the love and respect the child receives; and (3) by providing models of reasonable independence, that is, autonomy within the framework of a democratic order. In contrast, the child of autocratic or neglectful parents is not presented with models of responsible, cooperative independence; rejection or indifference are likely to limit his positive identification with adults; and he is not given age-graded experiences in the orderly assumption of responsible autonomy (**6, 7, 175**).

The democratic child-rearing structure, which provides for perceptions of parental fairness, for feelings of personal security and being wanted, and for the development of both responsibility and increasing autonomy, seems especially important in today's turbulent social climate. Autocratic authoritarian patterns of parental behavior may have been more workable in cultures where the adolescent could expect to be successful simply by following in his father's or mother's footsteps, assuming similar tasks and responsibilities in the same manner and at the same ages. Under such cultural conditions, the society also provided carefully defined channels for coping with the greater intergenerational hostility that an autocratic structure may provoke.

Furthermore, in such situations the autocratic posture of the parent, though frustrating to the adolescent, was more "legitimate," in the sense that the parent really did "hold all the cards" and had most of the relevant power and skills that the adolescent was seeking. Today, however, parents may be able to provide models of autonomous, flexible, problem-solving behavior, as well as love and a fundamental underlying security, but they cannot provide detailed blueprints for mastering the changing demands of a society in rapid transition.

The laissez-faire or ignoring parent—permissive but uncommunicative, and frequently not emotionally involved with his child—also makes the task of achieving responsible independence especially difficult in today's world. Neither peers, the older adolescent youth culture, nor the adult world can provide adequate or consistent guidelines for assuming the kind of responsible independent behavior required by our changing times. Where there is a systematic, consistent, supervised effort by adults to employ the peer group as models in adult standard setting, peers may play such a role. Such is the case with Soviet and Israeli Kibbutz children and adolescents (26), but it is not the prevailing situation in countries like the United States and England.

Sex Differences in Independence-Dependence Conflicts

Girls in our culture appear to experience fewer and less stressful conflicts over the development of independence than boys, particularly during the earlier years of adolescence (3, 50). Girls are more likely than boys to consider their parents' rules to be fair, right, or lenient (50). They are also more likely to progress from an initial childhood acceptance of parental authority to a more independent identification with that authority without an intervening phase of defiant assertion of their own values and controls before moving closer to those of the parents (50).

The girl's lesser degree of conflict with parents and within themselves may be due in part to the greater cultural reinforcement, in the years prior to adolescence, of dependency and compliance in girls and of independence, self-assertiveness, and aggression in boys (3, 4, 49, 92, 104, 128, 142, 163). Also, puberty may bring a greater, more sudden, and qualitatively somewhat different increase in the strength of sexual and aggressive impulses in boys and, consequently, a greater need for establishing independent control of these impulses and a greater likelihood of rebellion and conflict with parents (3, 50).

It is important not to exaggerate these relative differences. Although adolescent girls may remain somewhat more dependent and have fewer acute conflicts over the development of independence, extreme and generalized dependence is not socially adaptive in contemporary society in either boys or girls and typically reveals a lack of independent self-esteem (3, 49, 51, 92, 163).

Furthermore, dependency is not necessarily a one-dimensional trait. Judith Bardwick makes useful distinctions between "**instrumental** dependence, in which objective help is sought; **emotional** dependence, in which affection, support, and comfort are the goals; and **aggressive** dependence, in which the objectives are negative and manipulative" (3, 119).

Emotional dependence still remains fairly acceptable for girls in our society, but it is far less so for boys (128); in boys it "is likely to take oblique or derivative adult forms because the stereotype of the male is to be strong and independent" (3, 119). On the other hand, sex differences in instrumental dependency are smaller. Instrumental dependency (for example, dependence on a parent or other adults for obtaining objective help in mastering skills) is more acceptable in boys than emotional dependency (3, 128), and excessive instrumental dependency (for example, not being able to handle her own affairs in a competent fashion) is not adaptive for girls, even though they may be more emotionally dependent on others. Indeed, if a girl is lacking in sufficient instrumental independence, or is overly emotionally dependent, she is likely to resort to what Bardwick calls "the tyranny of the weak," using dependency as a means for controlling and manipulating others and for avoiding responsibility for her own actions.

Finally, it should be recognized that dependency is most likely to be selective. A mature, well-adjusted girl may be more emotionally dependent on a small number of trusted individuals than her male counterpart, but she is unlikely to behave in accordance with the common, but misleading stereotype of "a high **generalized** dependence" (**3**, 123). In turn, while adolescent boys may be less dependent than girls on parents, they may be quite dependent on male peers, at least partly as a means of aiding the process of detachment from the family and establishing their own independence (**3**).

SEXUAL ATTITUDES AND BEHAVIOR IN THE ADOLESCENT

Increased sexual drive, influenced by hormonal and anatomical changes, is, of course, a major physiological concomitant of adolescence. However, the forms it takes and the manner in which it is expressed will vary depending on the sex of the adolescent and also upon a wide variety of psychological and cultural forces. There is little question that for most boys the rapid increase in sexual drive which accompanies adolescence is difficult, if not impossible, to deny. In boys this drive is "imperious and biologically specific. . . . He must confront [it] directly, consciously, find within himself the means of obtaining sexual discharge without excessive guilt, and means of control without crippling inhibitions" (**50**, 110).

Among girls sexual drive is likely to be more diffuse and ambiguous. For many girls a limited temporary denial of sexual impulses may not only be feasible, but may also often provide a comfortable adaptation (**50**). Regardless of the underlying reasons for these sex differences, sexual impulses among girls appear to be more easily transformed and displaced into a great many other disguises: "Sexuality is then not experienced as such; it very easily becomes spiritualized, idealized, etherealized" (**50**, 111). Obviously, as adolescence proceeds, girls experience a greater increase in conscious awareness of sexual impulses, but, even then, for most girls erotic gratification as such is likely to remain secondary to, or at least closely related to, the fulfillment of other needs such as self-esteem, reassurance, affection, and love. The overall relationship with the individual boy whom she loves—the extent to which this relationship is characterized by trust, concern, and a mutual sharing of life experencies—takes precedence over specific sexual release. Consequently, control of impulses is likely to constitute a considerably less urgent problem for girls.

Virtually all available data indicate that the specifically sexual interests and behavior of both sexes increase significantly during adolescence, although there are sex differences. Sexual activity in general, and masturbation in particular, is considerably greater among boys than girls (**110**, **111**, **156**). Furthermore, girls typically display more conservative attitudes toward sexual matters, such as pre-marital intercourse or pornography (202, 205). These findings themselves are not surprising, but the underlying reasons for the differences are far from clear. A number of theories have been advanced—some primarily physiological in nature, others primarily cultural. One hypothesis is that females are less likely than males to discover sexual responses spontaneously because the girl's sexual organs are less prominent and hence less subject to spontaneously learned manipulation (3, 136, 137).

It has also been asserted that there may be basic physiological differences between males and females in the levels of their sexual drive and responsiveness or in the capacity of various stimuli to arouse them or both (21). For the Victorians, of course, the question was not even considered to be open to discussion; it was simply assumed that "normal" women did not have strong sexual drives or responses.

A majority of today's adolescent girls, however, do not subscribe to such views. More than two-thirds of adolescent girls, aged 13 through 19, express the belief that "women enjoy sex as much as men" (94, 96). Only one out of every ten adolescent girls believes that "women have innately less capacity for sexual pleasure than men" (94). This predominant contemporary view receives strong support from William Masters and Virginia Johnson, the gynecologist-psychologist team of investigators, who have been the first scientists to study human sexual responses comprehensively and objectively (133, 134). They comment that the female's basic "physiological **capacity** [bold ours] for sexual response . . . surpasses that of man" (133, 219–220). It has also been clearly documented (110, 111, 134) that sexual behavior (for example, frequency of orgasm) may vary over much wider ranges among girls than among boys, and even within a particular girl at different times.

A still more complex question than the relative physiological **capacity** of males and females for sexual response involves the conditions under which **arousal** of the response is likely to occur. It has been argued that boys are more easily aroused than girls by a wider variety of external "psychosexual stimuli," such as provocative behavior, erotic art, films, and literature (28, 111, 131, 134, 149, 185, 201, 202, 205, 206). Here, too, however, simplistic hypotheses appear inadequate. A wide-ranging series of experimental investigations showed that while males still emerge as more responsive in an overall survey, the differences are smaller than originally supposed (185, 205). Furthermore, in some situations, some groups of adolescent and young adult females, that is, the younger, more liberal, and more sexually experienced, reported greater "sexual excitement" in response to various kinds of sexual stimuli than some groups of males, that is, the older, more conservative, more inhibited, and less experienced (110, 185, 201, 202).

It may well be that sexuality is more intimately bound up with total personality in the case of girls and, therefore, the conditions that must be satisfied if psychosexual stimulation is to produce arousal may be more complex than is generally the case for boys. Stimulation that cannot be related to the self as a total person, because it is perceived as threatening, conflicts with existing value systems, is impersonal, or is aesthetically offensive, may be more likely to "turn off" the average adolescent girl than her male peer (**168, 169, 170**).

It may also well be that the greater sexual aggressiveness generally manifested by adolescent males than females is related, at least in part, to vastly greater increases in testosterone levels among males at puberty. It has been demonstrated that this hormone increases sexual and aggressive behavior in both sexes under experimental conditions (**21**).

Regardless of the ultimate significance of these and other factors, it appears abundantly clear that the lesser sexual activity of female adolescents, and probably to some extent its qualitatively different nature, is **at least partially** attributable to our culture's more restrictive social attitudes toward sexual gratification for girls (**133**).

Cultural Influences on Sexual Attitudes and Behavior

Learning appears to play a critical role in determining the sexual response patterns that are adopted to satisfy sexual drives (**21, 74, 110, 111**). Hence, we would expect to find rather wide variations in sexual attitudes and behavior from one culture to another. "Human sex behavior finds expression within the context of culture, the patterned ways of living that characterize social life" (**73**, 306). There are some widespread generalities, even universals, which reflect commonalities in the human condition, for example, some form of incest taboo, but there are also marked differences between cultures, not only in the amount and type of sexual behavior that is socially accepted, but also in the consistency of the society's sexual standards as development proceeds.

Some cultures are restrictive with regard to sexual activity throughout childhood, adolescence, and even to some extent in adulthood. Others are thoroughly permissive at all ages. Still others are highly restrictive during childhood and adolescence, and then suddenly become much more permissive about, and even demanding of, sexual activity in adulthood.

Among the Cuna of the northwest coast of South America, children "remain ignorant of sexual matters (as far as adult information is concerned) until the last stages of the marriage ceremony. They are not even allowed to watch animals give birth" (**74**, 180). The Ashanti of the west central coast of Africa believe that sexual intercourse with a girl who has not undergone the puberty ceremony is so harmful to the community that the offense is punishable by death for both partners (**74**).

In contrast, sexual experience in some societies is carefully nurtured from early childhood on. The Chewa of Africa believe that unless children begin to exercise themselves sexually early in life they will never beget offspring. "Older children build little huts some distance from the village, and there, with the complete approval of their parents, boys and girls play at being husband and wife. Such child matings may extend well into adolescence, with periodic exchanges of partners until marriage occurs" (74, 190). Similarly, the Lepcha of India believe that girls "will not mature without benefit of sexual intercourse. Early sex play among boys and girls characteristically involves many forms of mutual masturbation and usually ends in attempted copulation. By the time they are eleven or twelve years old, most girls regularly engage in full intercourse" (74, 191).

Among the Siriono of central South America, intercourse before puberty is forbidden, but premarital relations are customary once the girl has menstruated (74). Somewhat the reverse occurs among the Alorese of Oceania. Here the young child enjoys relatively complete sexual freedom. Alorese mothers may fondle the genitals of their infants while nursing them, and young boys and girls are allowed to masturbate freely and occasionally they may imitate intercourse. But as these children grow older, "sexual activity is frowned upon and during late childhood such behavior is forbidden to both boy and girl" (74, 189).

In our own society sexual behavior has traditionally been viewed as appropriate only between marriage partners, and, consequently, all forms of sexual behavior have been discouraged among children and adolescents. There is increasing evidence currently that cultural attitudes are becoming somewhat more liberal, but in many segments of society parents still spend a great many years teaching children and adolescents to inhibit sexual responses, presumably in order to prepare them for a time when they will be expected to make these responses! Children are taught to respond to sex with anxiety, and then, upon marriage, are expected to be able to respond without anxiety. What we have tended to teach, in fact, is not sexual adaptation, but rather sexual conflict.

Societies also vary widely in the relative acceptability of various forms of sexual behavior (for example, heterosexual versus homosexual), generally and at different stages in the life cycle. In some societies, such as the Rwala Bedouins of Eurasia, homosexuality is so strongly opposed that both male and female offenders are put to death; in other societies, such as the Mbundu of Angola, it is simply considered immature and ridiculed; in still others, it is considered an essential part of sexual and social maturation. For example, among the Siwans of Africa, all men and boys engage in homosexual intercourse, and although assuming a feminine role is strictly limited to sexual situations "males are singled out as peculiar if they do not indulge in these homosexual activities" (74, 131–132).

Sexual Attitudes in Relation to Broader Cultural Values The kind and timing of sexual training that a boy or girl receives during childhood and adolescence can be of major importance in determining whether he will show great or little interest in sexual behavior. His sex training also determines whether he will tend to view sex as a pleasant and matter-of-fact affair, as sinful and dangerous, as extremely exciting, or as a manifestation of aggressive conquest, or even rape. Socialization practices with respect to sex may also have broader and more generalized effects upon the adolescent's or adult's personality and his perceptions of the world about him.

In societies which begin training in inhibition of heterosexual behavior relatively late in childhood and avoid using excessively severe training methods, people are less likely to show propensities toward guilt about sex than members of societies which institute early and relatively harsh training. Individuals in more permissive societies also have significantly less fearfulness of other persons as adolescents and adults (198).

Such relationships between sexual training and broader characteristics of the individual and of his culture are not unidirectional. Sex training practices may be generalized to affect other aspects of social behavior, and, at the same time, they are affected by and reflect broader cultural attitudes. Thus, among the Zuni, the relations—sexual and otherwise—between husband and wife tend to be pleasant, cooperative, and untainted by feelings of guilt. Sexual intercourse is a cooperative, rather than a competitive, matter to the Zunis, "not simply because of specific sex training, but because cooperation is an integral part of the whole Zuni way of life" (12). In societies such as the Mundugumor aggression and competition play an important part in the individual's sexual relations largely because they pervade the whole Mundugumor way of life (136).

Sexual Attitudes and Values of Contemporary American Adolescents

If one asks American adolescents whether they think there is now a new "sexual morality," the answer, at least among middle- and upper-class youth—definitely appears to be yes. In one nationwide study of adolescents, aged 13 to 20, 75 percent stated that they were developing a new sexual morality. However, they did not view this change as a lowering of morals; most viewed their morals as "no lower than their parents'" (184, 48). In the words of one adolescent girl, "Adults are just plain phonies about sex."

What does the "new morality" involve for the average adolescent? Most clearly, it appears to involve a desire for greater openness and honesty about sex (87, 170, 203). For example, 98 percent of a large sample of middle-class adolescent girls, aged 13 to 19, wanted broadly inclusive sex education in school (94). Although these girls were concerned about biological information and about sex techniques, they wanted even more to learn "about 'the meaning of sex in and out of marriage' and 'the relationship between sex and love'" (94, 133).

In addition to a greater emphasis on openness and honesty, there appears to be a growing tendency to view decisions about individual sexual behavior as more a private and less a public concern. Increasing numbers of young people campaigned during the past decade against the imposition of regulations regarding

visiting privileges of opposite-sex peers and sign-in hours in student dormitories and rooming houses. More have demanded the right of access to contraceptive information and devices, whether or not they individually wish to avail themselves of the opportunity (**38**).

Yet most young people today are not promiscuous and do not approve of promiscuity. Rather, in their opinion, the acceptability of heterosexual behavior is highly dependent on the degree of closeness of the relationship shared by the couple involved (**123, 149, 160**). Thus, according to the data of one large study, high school and college students agreed that premarital intercourse when the couple is engaged or in love is more acceptable than petting when no particular affection is felt. In contrast, adults found intercourse, even between engaged couples, far less acceptable than petting, even when affection is absent (**160**). Obviously, these students (both males and females) place a greater emphasis on the meaningfulness of the personal relationship between the partners than on what they view as arbitrary social standards of right and wrong.

Other studies (**123, 149**) show that most United States students disapprove of premarital sexual relations between persons who are merely "casually attracted" or "good friends," regardless of their ages; only 37 percent of males and 11 percent of females sanctioned sexual relations under these conditions. A majority of the males felt that couples should at least be "going steady." Girls went further, a majority believing that the couple should also be at least officially engaged, with four in ten believing that they should be married. Certainly these results do not support the view that today's young people are exponents of promiscuous and unrestrained hedonism. It should be noted that no study shows a majority of either younger or older adolescents approve of premarital sexual relations for couples who are not in love or engaged (**94, 160**).

> Many felt that everything depended upon the quality of the "relationship" between the two people. If the two people feel that it is right and meaningful for them and they are prepared to meet the consequences, then it is all right and it is no one else's business. The respondents seemed to want to eschew traditional labels on stages of relationship (**149**, 161).

Variations in Adolescent Attitudes Toward Sexual Behavior While such findings reflect overall attitudes of contemporary youth, they do not reflect the diversity in attitudes occurring in different sectors of the adolescent and youth population (**60, 123, 149**). Factors such as age, sex, socioeconomic and educational level, race, religion, and even geographical area all appear related to sexual attitudes and values.

Contrary to much popular thinking, the attitudes of younger adolescents, as a total group, still appear more conservative than those of older adolescents and youth (**77, 87, 94**). College youth are significantly less conservative, at least in their attitudes, than their noncollege peers. For example, one study of American youth, 17 and older, found that those in college were significantly more likely than their noncollege peers to believe that "sexual behavior should be bound by mutual feelings, not by formal ties," and they were more likely to express a desire for "more sexual freedom" (203).

In general, students from the east and west coasts are less conservative than those from the midwest (123, 149, 159). More midwestern than eastern students, both male and female, responded affirmatively to the question, "Do you feel that ideally it is still true that a man and a girl who marry should have their first full sexual experience together?" Similarly, three-fourths of girls at midwestern schools, but less than one-third of those at eastern schools, agreed that "coitus was reasonable 'only if married' for possible participants . . . in the 21- to 23-year age group" (149, 163). Students at "permissive," liberally oriented colleges are less conservative than those at more traditional colleges (77, 149).

The sexual attitudes and values of girls tend to be significantly more conservative than those of males (149). Career-oriented girls have been found to be less concerned with confining sexual intercourse to marriage than girls not oriented to careers (149). In general, while there are fairly wide social-class variations, black youth (both boys and girls) appear significantly less conservative than white youth in sexual attitudes (156, 160). Not surprisingly, religious and politically conservative youth are consistently more conservative than their nonreligious and activist peers (149, 176, 177, 202, 203).

It would appear from these data that adolescent attitudes and values regarding sex are changing, although the extent of the change varies widely from one segment of the youth population to another. Indeed, as in other areas of social concern, the differences between some subgroups of youth appear wider than those between youth in general and adults in general. There is a real and often ignored danger in generalizing too widely from specialized subgroups (a particular college campus or a particular urban high school) to all youth.

Parent-Child Differences in Sexual Attitudes There are some generational differences in sexual values between parents and their adolescent young, but the size of the differences appears to have been exaggerated.

Parents tend to express more conservative and more traditional attitudes than their adolescent sons and daughters on such topics as necking, petting, and premarital intercouse (11, 203). They also differ regarding the ages and circumstances under which sexual intimacies are acceptable (11, 149, 160). The largest single difference between generations involves the acceptability of full sexual relations for engaged couples. Although a majority of youth of both sexes believe that sexual relations are morally acceptable for engaged couples (particularly if they are 20 years of age or older), only a minority of adults agree (110, 111). Youths' charges of adult "hypocrisy" appear to gain some support from the fact that the size of the minority of adults expressing approval is considerably smaller than the percentage of these same adults who had premarital intercourse (110, 111).

Sexual Behavior of Contemporary Adolescents

Some observers (150, 158, 170) argue that the sexual behavior of today's adolescents, while more open and in some respects probably freer, is not strikingly different from that of their parents at the same age. Conversely, others assert that, in addition to dramatic attitudinal changes, there have also been significant changes in sexual behavior (150). What do the data reveal? The answer appears to depend on what behaviors one is referring to, among which adolescents, and how recently.

In Kinsey's original investigation (111, 156) about 25 years ago, 95 percent of boys reported having their first orgasm by age 15, two-thirds of them through masturbation. As adolescence progressed, the average boy's frequency of orgasm increased, reaching a lifetime peak of about 3.4 times per week between 16 and 17 years of age. This frequency tended to persist with only slight diminution until the age of 30, after which there was a gradual tapering off.

In contrast, fewer girls than boys experienced orgasm in adolescence. Only 23 percent of girls had experienced orgasm by age 15, and only 53 percent by age 20. The cumulative incidence did not reach a lifetime maximum of around 90 percent until age 35. The maximum average frequency of orgasm (1.8 per week) did not occur until the period of 26-30 years (110, 111).

Girls also reported much more variability in frequency of masturbation than boys. Some girls reported never masturbating; others reported a frequency of masturbation as low as once or twice a year; still others masturbated as many as 10 to 20 times a week (110, 111, 156).

Recent studies indicate that there has been relatively little, if any, change in the past few decades in the incidence of either male or female masturbation (3, 152, 153, 167, 168, 173). However, anxiety, conflict, and guilt about masturbation have decreased and there is increased objectivity and scientific information.

Petting does appear to have increased somewhat in the past few decades, and it tends to occur slightly earlier (110, 111, 123, 148, 156, 158, 173). The major change has probably been in frequency of petting, degree of intimacy in terms of techniques involved, the frequency with which petting leads to erotic arousal or orgasm, and, certainly, frankness about this activity (11, 123, 148, 170, 173).

Premarital Intercourse The greatest amount of public discussion (and of parental and social apprehension) centers about the incidence of premarital sexual intercourse among contemporary adolescents. Yet, inconceivable as it may seem to many of today's adolescents, if anything that could properly be called a sexual revolution has occurred in this century, it was probably initiated by their parents and grandparents. For example, Kinsey's data indicate that only 2 percent of females born before 1900 had premarital intercourse prior to age 16, 8 percent prior to age 20, and only 14 percent prior to age 25. In contrast, for the mothers of today's adolescents, the corresponding figures were 4 percent, 21 percent, and 37 percent, respectively (110, 111).

How does the incidence of premarital intercourse among today's parents compare with that of their adolescent sons and daughters? A recent representative national study (173) of adolescents, aged 13 to 19, found that 44 percent of boys and 30 percent of girls have had sexual intercourse prior to age 16. These figures increase to 72 percent of boys and 57 percent of girls by age 19. When compared with females of their mothers' generation in Kinsey's investigation (only 3 percent of whom had engaged in premarital intercourse by age 16, and less than 20 percent by age 19), this represents a very large increase, particularly at the younger age level. When compared with males of their fathers' generation (approximately 39 percent of whom had engaged in premarital intercourse by age 16, and 72 percent by age 19), contemporary adolescent boys as a whole, show a much smaller change, mainly a tendency to have first intercourse at a slightly younger age.

It is important to note, however, that Kinsey's data showed marked socioeconomic influences on the incidence of premarital intercourse, especially among boys. Thus, while only 50 percent of college-educated fathers of today's adolescents had intercourse by age 21, the incidence among grade-school educated fathers was 84 percent (110, 111). In contrast, among contemporary 21-year-old college males, incidence of premarital intercourse approached 80 percent in 1972—nearly as high as that of grade-school educated males of their fathers' generation (125, 150, 176, 177). (The comparable incidence of premarital intercourse for contemporary college females is 56 percent).

All the available evidence indicates strongly that the greatest percentage increase in premarital intercourse in recent years has been among higher socioeconomic adolescents and youth, and particularly among better educated middle- and upper-class girls (173, 176, 177, 204), both in the United States and other western nations, such as England and the Scandinavian countries (33, 34, 85, 106, 121, 145, 150, 158). Of course, it is in these socioeconomically favored groups that most other manifestations of the so-called youth revolution, or counterculture, have been centered.

In a majority of cases, however, there is little evidence of promiscuity among these young people. Most are having intercourse with only one partner, in most cases a boy or girl of their own social group with whom they are seriously involved emotionally (148, 150, 176). In contrast to the prevailing situation twenty years ago, there has been a spectacular decline in involvement with prostitutes. While in the earlier period, 20 to 22 percent of college-educated males had been involved with prostitutes (111, 158), less than 4 percent (148, 150) of current youth have had such experience.

ADOLESCENTS AND THEIR PEERS

Peers play an important role in the psychological development of most adolescents. Indeed, the current popularity of such terms as "youth culture" and "generation gap"—and the looseness with which they are frequently employed to "explain" everything from changing standards of social and sexual behavior to alienation, drug use, and delinquency—suggests that, if anything, the **relative** importance of the peer group has been exaggerated. There is widespread confusion, both about the kinds of influences that peers exert and the ways in which they are exerted. Hopefully, some of this confusion can be dispelled and the issues clarified.

Interactions with peers perform many of the same functions for the adolescent that they do for the child (see pp. 516–518). But the role peers play in adolescence is an even more important one for a variety of reasons. Relations with both same- and opposite-sex peers in this period come closer to serving as prototypes for later adult relationships, in social relations, in work, and in interactions with members of the opposite sex. The young man or woman who has not learned how to get along with others of his own sex and to establish satisfactory heterosexual relationships by the time he reaches adulthood faces serious obstacles.

Adolescents are also more dependent than young children upon peer relationships simply because ties with parents become progressively looser as greater independence from parents is achieved. Furthermore, relationships with family members are frequently so charged with conflicting emotions during the adolescent period—dependent yearnings existing alongside independent strivings, hostility mixed with love, and conflicts over cultural values and social behavior—that many areas of the adolescent's inner life and outward behavior become difficult to share with parents. Also, it appears that parents themselves, having finally come to terms with their own prior adolescent struggles to achieve a sense of ego identity and impulse control, tend frequently to "let the past bury its dead." They may not desire or, in most cases, be capable of reviving the intense, shifting, and sometimes painful feelings of adolescence. Reawakening such feelings may be discomforting and may also endanger the arduously achieved repression of underlying impulses and feelings which appear inappropriate to an adult role (50). Consequently, parents may have difficulty in understanding and sharing the problems of adolescents, even though they may make an effort to do so.

And yet the adolescent needs, perhaps more than at any time in his life, to be able to share his strong and often confusing emotions, his doubts, and his dreams. Adolescence is generally a time of intense sociability, but it is also often a time of intense loneliness. Merely being with others does not solve the problem; frequently the adolescent may feel most alone in the midst of a crowd, at a party or a dance (97). Under such circumstances, being accepted by his peers generally and, especially, having one or more close friends may make a great difference in the life of the adolescent.

Finally, the role of the peer group in helping the individual to define his own identity assumes particular importance at adolescence because at no other stage of his development is his sense of identity so fluid. No longer a child, but not yet fully accepted as an adult, the adolescent must prepare, with few clear guidelines, to meet society's demands for social independence, for vocational competence, for a responsible role as a citizen, for marriage and a family, and for a workable philosophy of life.

These problems have been compounded in recent years by rapid social change. Even in simpler, more stable societies, however, where the adult culture can present a more unified, more clearly defined image of itself, the adolescent still needs the guidance, support, and communion of his peers. For no matter how stable the adult culture is, no matter how "understanding" parents may be, one incontrovertible fact limits the role that adults are able to play in relation to the adolescent: the adolescent and his peers still face the struggle to achieve adult status; adults are already there. Furthermore, the adolescent is also struggling to discover, interpret, and control a self that is changing rapidly, both physiologically and psychologically (**65, 67**). Under such circumstances, the adolescent may gain considerable reassurance from affiliation with his peers and from adoption of the principle that, as it were, "Fifty million Frenchmen can't be wrong." He may not know how he is going to achieve ultimate adult identity and status nor, indeed, how his friends are going to, but he knows that, as a group, adolescents do "make it," generation after generation. If he and his peers, who are, after all, "all in the same boat," can stick together, he is likely to reason, they (and he) can make it too.

Conformity to Peer Culture

The heightened importance of the peer group during adolescence is an important factor in the increased motivation for conformity to the values, customs, and fads of peer culture which is characteristic of this period (**15, 19, 60, 188**). There appears to be a rather rapid rise in conformity needs and behavior during the preadolescent and early adolescent years, followed by a gradual, but steady decline from middle through late adolescence.

Parents are frequently mystified, and sometimes deeply threatened, by the shifting external trappings of adolescent peer culture, from fashions in clothes and music to special and rapidly changing vocabularies. Parents may wonder why adolescents need to look so "different" and act so "bizarrely." But, of course, that is one of the principal reasons for the existence of adolescent fads: to establish, at least superficially, a clear line of demarcation from adults.

Having left the world of childhood forever, but not yet accepted as adults, adolescents are virtually forced to create at least a semblance of an "interim culture" of their own. And, obviously, if it is to serve its purpose, this culture, whatever its form (and forms are likely to change with breathtaking speed), must be unambiguously recognizable as different from that of adults. Once adults have recovered from their anguished cries of imminent disaster and have, rather ironically, gone on to incorporate adolescent fashions and tastes into their own culture (as is currently happening in dress, in music, and even to some extent in language), adolescents have to turn to new fads to preserve their separateness.

It appears to us that parents and other adults might actually take some comfort from the presence of these outward signs of the "differentness" of adolescents. By achieving the semblance of a group identity of their own in these relatively superficial ways, adolescents may satisfy some of the need to be different from their parents and therefore not strive to be different in more fundamental matters (50). While, as we shall see, adolescent values and behavior are changing and are different to some degree, sometimes to an important degree, from those of adults, most adolescents show a fundamental continuity in many of the values and beliefs of parents and children that is often overlooked.

Parental and Peer Influences—A False Dichotomy?

The widespread view that parental and peer group values are necessarily mutually incompatible and that there is inevitably a sharp decline in parental influence during adolescence is misleading, at least in the case of most adolescents. There is usually considerable overlap between the values of the adolescent's parents and peers because of social, economic, religious, educational, even geographic commonalities in their backgrounds. A white, Catholic, lower-middle-class, "ethnic," blue-collar adolescent's peers in one of our larger cities are likely to share more common values with his parents than with upper- or upper-middle-class WASP contemporaries (60). In this sense, then, peers may actually serve to reinforce parental values. We should be cautious about overemphasizing differences and underemphasizing similarities; the differences observed may be relatively conspicuous, but actually rather superficial (e.g., musical tastes, fashions, fads).

Another factor that limits the potential conflict between parental and peer influences is the uncertainty of many parents as to the behavior they should expect from adolescents.

> [Parents] . . . are likely to be impressed (probably over-impressed) by social change, likely to feel that parent and child live in different worlds, and that they themselves lack the experience to teach the child how to meet and manage his world. We have here something similar to a self-fulfilling prophecy. Half believing he cannot really guide his child, the parent helps the child in his turn to the peer group (50, 200).

Furthermore, many parents, particularly upper- and middle-class parents, place a great emphasis on popularity and success, and thus strengthen the adolescent's motivation to conform to peer expectations (142).

Neither parental nor peer influence is monolithic, extending to all areas of adolescent decision-making and behavior (22, 24, 117). The weight given to either parental or peer opinion will depend to a significant degree on the adolescent's appraisal of its relative value in a specific situation. For example, peer influence is more likely to be predominant in such matters as tastes in music and entertainment, fashions in clothing and language, patterns of same- and opposite-sex peer interaction, and the like. Parental influence is more likely to be predominant in such areas as underlying moral and social values and understanding of the adult world (**39, 50**).

An unusually dominant role of the peer group in the life of an adolescent may be due to the lack of attention and concern at home, as much as, if not more than, the inherent attractiveness of the peer group. Adolescents who are strongly peer oriented were found more likely than those who are adult oriented to hold negative views of themselves and the peer group (**37**). In interviews, these adolescents

> . . . expressed a dim view of their own future. Their parents were rated as lower than those of . . . adult-oriented children both in the expression of affection and support, and in the exercise of discipline and control. Finally, in contrast to the adult-oriented group, the peer-oriented children report engaging in more antisocial behavior such as "doing something illegal," "playing hooky," lying, teasing other children, etc. . . . The peer-oriented child is more a product of parental disregard than of the attractiveness of the peer group . . . he turns to his age-mates less by choice than by default. The vacuum left by the withdrawal of parents and adults from the lives of children is filled with an undesired—and possibly **undesirable**—substitute of an age-segregated peer group (**26,** 96).

Parental influence is greatest where "parent-adolescent affect" (that is, the quality of the parent-child relationship, as measured by parental interest and understanding, willingness to be helpful, and amount of shared family activity) is highest (**117**). Furthermore, adolescents with high parent-adolescent affect are significantly less likely than those with low affect to see a need to differentiate between the influence of their parents and their best friends (**117**).

Parental influence appears greatest at the sixth-grade level and least at the twelfth-grade level. At the seventh-grade level the extent of parental influence is only minimally a function of the quality of the parental relationship. However, at later grade levels, where the potential impact of peer-group influence has increased significantly, parent-adolescent affect assumes markedly increased importance as a determinant of parental influence (**117**). In short, a mother or father may be making a serious mistake if he thinks that just because he can influence his children at the beginning of adolescence, even if he isn't concerned with the quality of his relationship with them, he will automatically continue to be able to do so in middle and later adolescence.

Finally, we tend to overlook the important fact that the need for rigid conformity to either parents or peers varies enormously from one adolescent to another (**23, 60, 108, 130, 187**). More self-confident, more autonomous adolescents may be able to profit from the views and learning experiences provided by both parents and peers, without being strongly dependent on either or unduly troubled by parent-peer differences (155). Ironically, the adolescent who has gained most self-confidence (largely as a result of the child-rearing techniques used by his parents), who is least concerned with popularity, "and goes his own way may find that his peers flock around him as a tower of strength" (174).

Social Acceptance, Neglect, and Rejection

In general, adolescents of both sexes who are accepted by their peers (as measured by sociometric tests) are perceived as liking other people and being tolerant, flexible, and sympathetic; being lively, cheerful, good-natured, and having a sense of humor; acting "naturally" and self-confidently without being conceited; and possessing initiative, enthusiasm, drive, and plans for group activity (16, 86, 96, 109, 118, 119, 186, 191). Adolescents who are viewed favorably tend to be those who contribute to others by making **them** feel accepted and involved, by promoting constructive interaction between peers, or by planning and initiating interesting or enjoyable group activities (107, 142).

In contrast, the adolescent who is ill-at-ease and lacks self-confidence, who tends to be timid, nervous, or withdrawn, is likely to be neglected by his peers and to emerge as a social "isolate" (142). The one who reacts to his discomfort by a compensatory overaggressiveness, conceit, or demands for attention is likely to court active dislike and rejection. Similarly, the adolescent who is self-centered and unable or unwilling to meet the needs of others, who is sarcastic, tactless, inconsiderate, and contributes little to the success of group efforts, is likely to receive little consideration in return.

There are, of course, many other factors which may affect an adolescent's acceptance or rejection by his peers, including his intelligence and ability, special talents, socioeconomic status, and ethnic-group membership. Other factors being equal, intelligence is positively and significantly related to acceptance by peers (86). Awareness that he or she is of below-average ability and is having school difficulties may lead an adolescent to develop personality characteristics—insecurity, withdrawal, compensatory demands for attention, or aggressiveness—that may lead to rejection (142).

In the past, members of ethnic minorities were less likely to be accepted by others, including members of their own groups (25, 35, 154). However, with the current emphasis, particularly among adolescents and young adults, on ethnic pride and cultural traditions, acceptance and popularity with members of one's own ethnic group appear to be increasing rapidly (5, 25, 93). Hopefully, the growth of genuine confidence and pride in one's own cultural identity and in oneself as an individual human being may lead to a lack of defensiveness—of a need to "protest too much"—among young people of all cultural, racial, and ethnic groups, majority and minority. If this occurs, future adolescents will become increasingly free to

select friends and acquaintances on the basis of compatible personal characteristics and shared interests, outlooks, and goals, including, but not restricted to, shared ethnic cultural interests.

Few adolescents are unaffected by social neglect or rejection. A few "rugged individualists," confident of their own goals and interests and possessed of a strong sense of their own identity, may not need or seek the approbation of peers. But most adolescents, still judging their own worth to a considerable extent in terms of others' reactions to them, are dependent on the approval and acclaim of prestigeful peers.

Unfortunately, the unpopular adolescent is likely to be caught in a vicious circle. If he is already emotionally troubled, preoccupied with himself, and lacking in a secure self-concept, he is likely to meet with rejection or indifference from his peers. In turn, awareness that he is not accepted by his peers and lack of opportunity to participate in and learn from peer-group activities only further undermine his self-confidence and increase his sense of social isolation. The result is likely to be still further inappropriateness in his behavior with peers. In our opinion, there is currently an overemphasis, particularly among upper- and middle-class parents, on the pursuit of popularity for their children. David Riesman has suggested that people in our culture are too much the products of "other-directedness"—concerned with "fitting-in," with superficial appearances, with "not rocking the boat" in an organization-minded society, rather than with pursuing their own private, "inner-directed" dreams and goals (157).

There is some encouraging evidence that a number of today's adolescents may be beginning to swing the pendulum back in the direction of a more tolerant individualism, wherein each person is freer "to do his own thing." But to expect the average adolescent—unsure of his own identity and unclear about the demands that will be made upon him in a confused, rapidly changing society—to be immune to the favor of his peers would be unrealistic. Most adolescents, at one time or another, feel that they "do not belong," and the pain, even if temporary, is very real. Parents' overdetermined insistence on "popularity" can only further compound the adolescent's difficulties.

VOCATIONAL CHOICE

The problem of deciding on a vocation represents one of the critical developmental tasks of adolescence. Despite recent explorations of "alternative life styles" by a growing minority, most adolescents, particularly boys, and their parents are committed to the belief that future financial security and status rest primarily in his own hands. Boys are more likely than girls to have to go to work for the greater portion of their adult lives. And in most cases a family's standard of living, its place in the community, and its financial security depend largely on the earning capacity of the husband and the kind of position he has. Consequently, parents, teachers, and even peers are likely to place considerable pressure on the boy to make a vocational decision during this period. The extent and the kinds of pressure exerted will, of course, vary with social class and ethnic group, as well as with a number of other factors.

Vocational Orientation of Girls

Significant changes are currently taking place in the vocational orientation of increasing numbers of girls, as a consequence of changes in the nature of male-female relationships, in the family as an institution, and in society generally (3, 40, 89, 135). There is increasing evidence that more young women are working prior to marriage, are delaying marriage longer, and are returning to work sooner and in greater numbers following the birth of children (see Table 12.1). Male-female differentials in amount of education have steadily declined in recent decades, so that by 1969, they were identical (12.1 years). More young women are insisting on entrance into jobs, both professional and nonprofessional, that previously were largely male preserves and are also insisting, with convincing justification, upon equal pay for equal work.

However, for most women, identification with an adult role still involves primarily assuming successfully the roles of wife and mother, and only secondarily, if at all, that of breadwinner (3, 50, 135). It is probably at least partly for this reason that girls still generally set their sights lower than boys in their vocational aspirations and have less commitment to vocational goals, although there are many notable exceptions (3, 50).

Affiliation Versus Aggression: A "Fear of Success?" There is another significant reason for the average girl's lesser motivation for vocational achievement (4, 92). According to traditional sex-role stereotypes, aggressive, competitive behavior is more likely to be viewed as masculine, while affiliative, nurturant, interpersonally oriented behavior is more likely to be viewed as feminine. Most vocational "achievement situations," especially high-status positions, are competitive, and because competition may be seen as a sublimated form of aggression, a girl who

Table 12.1 **Percentage of women workers in the labor force**

	1950	1960	1970 (Est.)
All women	31.4%	34.8%	42.5%
All married women, husband present	23.8	30.5	40.5
With children under 6 years	11.9	18.6	29.5
With children 6-17 years only	28.3	39.0	49.5
With no children under 18 years	30.3	34.7	42.0

Source: Bureau of Labor Statistics, 1971.

engages in vigorous vocational competition, particularly with male competitors, may be viewed by others—and equally importantly, by herself—as "unfeminine." "This creates conflict for the female, evidenced by her higher anxiety level which is then reflected in her behavior" (3). As a consequence, rather than fearing failure, she may come to fear success. Margaret Mead reflected a similar view when she suggested that traditionally in our culture, "boys are unsexed by failure and girls by success" (3, 137).

Fear of success is more characteristic of women than of men (4, 92). The subjects of one study of freshman and sophomore college students were asked to write a story to the cue, "After first-term finals, Anne (or for men, John) finds herself (himself) at the top of the medical school class." Women's stories tended to be characterized by three principal themes: the **fear of social rejection, concern about one's femininity,** and **denial** (for example, misinterpreting the cue). An example of fear of rejection is the following.

> Anne has a boyfriend, Carl, in the same class, and they are quite serious. Anne met Carl at college, and they started dating about their sophomore year in undergraduate school. Anne is rather upset and so is Carl. She wants him to be higher scholastically than she is. Anne will deliberately lower her academic standing the next term, while she does all she subtly can to help Carl. His grades come up and Anne drops out of med school. They marry and he goes on in school while she raises their family (92, 60).

As had been predicted, the response of fear of success occurred significantly more frequently for women. Of the 90 women in the study, 50 presented stories reflecting this fear; of the 88 men, only 8 showed this fear. Many women, "especially those high in the motive to avoid success, will explore their intellectual potential to full measure only when they are in a non-competitive setting and least of all when competing against men" (92).

A very recent replication of this study has shown a sharp increase in rejection of success by men, to a level now equal to that of women (89). However, in men this is due primarily to a belief that singleminded pursuit of success is not worth the sacrifices involved, rather than to fears of rejection or concern with sexual identity, which still characterize women.

A significant minority of talented young women are confronted with culturally induced conflicts. They face the problem of working out a more satisfactory resolution of needs for both traditionally feminine goals (that is, marriage, home, children) and intellectual and vocational achievement consistent with their individual interests and abilities. As Germaine Greer recently observed, "We know what we are, but not what we may be, or what we might have been" (80). While increasing numbers appear to be succeeding despite the problems involved (3), recent investigations (3, 4, 162) indicate that many others are left feeling frustrated and somehow lacking in personal fulfillment.

Psychological Determinants of Career Choice

A vocation may offer adolescents a socially approved way to achieve direct or indirect satisfaction for strong motives that are not fully gratified in other ways. Thus, motives such as dominance over others, aggression, nurturance, and, occasionally, sexual curiosity can be at least partially gratified in one or another occupation, such as army officer, policeman, social worker, physician, or nurse.

The choice of a vocation and subsequent participation in it may help to crystalize and reinforce an adolescent's self-concept (**17, 31, 178, 207**). Indeed, in our culture, vocational identity often plays a major role in the individual's sense of identity. "Working gives [most people] a feeling of being tied into the larger system of society, of having something to do, of having a purpose in life" (**127, 141**).

Vocational Adjustment in American Culture

In many nonliterate societies, the vocational problems of the adolescent are much simpler than in our own culture. The number of vocations supported by the culture are fewer, and the adolescent is already likely to be familiar with them, either through observation or apprenticeship. The Arapesh youth, for example, gradually takes over from his father responsibility for tilling the family garden as he enters adolescence (see pp. 558–560). Furthermore, many, but by no means all, nonliterate societies lack the involvement in aggressive competitiveness and concern with social status characteristic of American culture.

The typical adolescent in our own society knows that, not only his survival, but many of his important satisfactions will depend on his ability to find and keep a job. His chances for full emancipation from his parents, for acceptance as an equal by his peers, and for getting married and maintaining a home are all related to vocational success. Yet he typically has only a vague idea of the nature of the various jobs available in the society. He does not know which he would be able to do successfully and would enjoy doing, the prior training required for a specific job, or the present or future demands for various occupations.

This problem, rather than becoming easier, is becoming increasingly difficult as our entire society grows more complex, more specialized, and more technologically oriented. The kinds of skills society requires are changing ever more rapidly as new technologies are developed. With the growth of automation, there is less and less room for the unskilled or semiskilled worker; prior education and training are becoming increasingly necessary for admission to the world of work. Further, as machines take on more of the jobs formerly performed by workers, there is a significant movement away from production and into service occupations. We shall have more to say later about some of these critical problems and their implications for the adolescent, including the socioeconomically deprived youth. For the present, we only wish to emphasize the increasing difficulties faced by most adolescents today in planning for their vocational futures.

Ordinarily, as the adolescent leaves his childhood behind, and the time when he must support himself approaches, he begins to spend more of his time thinking about vocational goals. He also becomes progressively more realistic about these goals. As a child, he is likely to have preferred occupations which seemed active and exciting to him, such as those of cowboy, fireman, airplane pilot, or detective. The social status of his preferred occupation is not likely to have much influence on him. However, as he grows older, he is likely to begin to prefer occupations of marked prestige in the adult world—being a famous doctor, scientist, or lawyer. Finally, as adulthood approaches, he is likely to settle upon some occupation that represents a realistic reconciliation between what he would like to do and what he thinks he might actually be able to do (84, 140).

As the child's vocational interests become progressively more realistic, more influenced by status and less by glamor and excitement, they also become more stable. For example, the older the adolescent, the more stable his vocational interests become (as measured by vocational interest tests repeated after a given interval of time) (32). By age 25, practically complete stability is achieved.

Despite the increasing stability and realism of the adolescent's vocational interests, there is considerable evidence that he cannot be left simply to his own devices in dealing with his vocational problems. In a complex society such as ours, in which the actual requirements of most jobs and their availability in the labor market are not matters of common knowledge, the adolescent needs help.

The young person's vocational interests usually develop in a rather unsystematic fashion, guided by such influences as parental desires, relationships with parents, accidental contact with various occupations, and the kinds of jobs his friends choose. Class and sex-typed standards also play a role.

Socioeconomic Status and Vocational Goals

The individual's social-class membership partially determines the kinds of occupations with which he will be familiar and be likely to consider in formulating his occupational aims. It also determines the social acceptability, that is, the reward value, of various occupations. Certain types of occupations are considered appropriate to the members of a particular social class, others inappropriate. The very young upper-class boy who wants to be a cowboy or fireman or truck driver may be indulged or even encouraged. After the attainment of adolescence, however, when vocational choice becomes a serious problem with practical implications, the child's parents are not likely to find such notions amusing. Choices of lower-status occupations run counter to the parents' ideas about appropriate behavior for a member of their social class and consequently are likely to be discouraged (142).

Many otherwise tolerant and reasonably flexible upper- and middle-class parents react strongly to the announcement that their adolescent daughter intends to raise vegetables and take in sewing on a communal farm or that their son intends to take part-time laboring jobs in order to devote as much time as possible to writing poetry. Parents may also fear that such choices will lead to general social disapproval of their child and, indirectly, of themselves.

Recently, all graduating seniors in Wisconsin's public and private high schools were asked to state the occupations that they hoped eventually to enter. Their choices were then assigned "prestige scores." Very few subjects in the lower third in socioeconomic status aspired to high-prestige occupations; many students in the upper third aspired to high-prestige occupations. Furthermore, the later actual occupational attainments of students of lower socioeconomic status "were close to their expectations" (122).

The socioeconomically disadvantaged adolescent usually has little opportunity for training in upper-level occupations such as medicine or architecture. In addition, social-class factors are also likely to influence the adolescent's chances of obtaining certain jobs, even if he is qualified. Persons in a particular social class tend to pick others from the same social class as their colleagues and successors, although they may do this without conscious awareness. An employer may say that a person from another social class does not have the right sort of personality for a particular job, when he means that he does not have the same sets of social traits—learned as a member of a particular social class—as others holding that position.

Somewhat similar arguments may also be used to justify racial, ethnic, or sex-related discrimination, despite the fact that substantial numbers of minority group individuals and women are currently doing well in previously nearly all-white, male occupations and professions (135, 183).

Parental Influences on Vocation Choice

Parental motivation is a significant factor in the adolescent's vocational choice, and there is a good deal of variation in parental motivation in all social classes. Parental motivation has been found to be significantly related to student's aspiration level, even when social-class status and IQ are held constant. A working-class boy is relatively likely to seek advanced education and occupational mobility if his parents urge him to; he is unlikely to do so if they do not exert pressure in this direction (172; see also 18, 72, 105, 115).

According to the data of one study (172), **ambitious middle-class boys** showed the highest percentage of parental support; **mobile working-class boys** ranked a close second. In contrast, **unambitious middle-class boys** and **nonmobile working-class boys** ranked far behind in percentage of parental support.

In general, if parents have high aspirational motivations for their children, hold high educational and occupational goals for them, and reward good school work, their children will have high aspiration levels themselves. This positive relationship was found particularly strong among students scoring high on personality measures of authoritarianism and conformity. Apparently, nonauthoritarian and nonconforming adolescent males are less susceptible than their more dogmatic, conforming peers to parental influences and goals.

Father's occupation also exerts a significant influence on the career choice of sons, though generally not of daughters (**194, 195**). For example, 43.6 percent of physicians' sons choose medicine and 27.7 percent of lawyers' sons choose law. Similar results have been obtained with the sons of physical and social scientists (**194**). This can probably be accounted for on several grounds, including (1) greater opportunity to become familiar with the father's occupation, as compared with others; (2) greater likelihood of access to the occupation; (3) strong parental motivation—and sometimes pressure—for the son to enter that occupation; and (4) identification with the parent, encouraging the development of similar interests, values, and goals.

Fifteen-year-old boys whose fathers provided strong **and** positive role models—occupationally or overall—tended to achieve higher levels of vocational adjustment than those whose fathers were absent or provided weak or negative role models. Interestingly, however, vocational adjustment was generally better where the father provided a negative role model than where he was absent or provided a weak model.

> [I]t is possible that "negative" role models can . . . be helpful in . . . identity striving. It may be as important to have in one's environment those with whom one perceives a dissimilarity, whose attitudes or values one refuses to adopt, or whom one would wish not to imitate (**9**).

Peer Group and School Influences

The adolescent's career choice will also be affected by his school environment, his teachers and, in particular, the peers with whom he associates (**8, 10, 46, 171, 189, 200**). A boy from a lower-class home is more likely to have upwardly mobile educational and vocational aspirations if he attends a largely middle-class school than if he attends one whose students come primarily from a lower-class background (**20**).

Even within a particular school setting, those lower-class boys who associate frequently with middle-class boys are more likely to aspire to higher status, including a college education and a prestige career. Working-class boys who engage in a substantial number of extracurricular activities that bring them into contact with middle-class interests and values are more likely than those not so engaged to seek higher-status careers. Increased contact with middle-class peers appears to foster "anticipatory socialization" into middle-class values (**10, 172**). In general, however,

parental influence is more strongly related to career aspirations than is peer influence (172).

Vocational Values and Social Change

Much has been made recently of a presumed revolution in vocational values and goals among today's adolescents. Young people, it is asserted, are no longer interested in such traditional goals of the American work ethic as power and material success. Such blanket generalizations should be viewed with considerable caution. In many respects, the variations among adolescents in their vocational values, goals, and beliefs appear at least as wide as differences between the average adolescent and his counterpart of earlier eras or between the average adolescent and adult of today.

There is no doubt that limited numbers of contemporary adolescents are profoundly disenchanted and "turned off" by a vocational world that they view as exploiting its own workers and the public, remaining indifferent to the ills of society, or unduly restricting personal freedom and individual expression (see pp. 614–615).

Nevertheless, a majority of young people still hold many traditional beliefs commonly associated with the Protestant work ethic" (see pp. 609–611), such as the beliefs that "competition encourages excellence" and that "everyone should save as much as he can regularly and not have to lean on family and friends the minute he runs into financial problems" (165, 203). Approximately two out of three contemporary adolescents express the view that hard work leads to "success and wealth" and believe that these goals are worth striving for (203).

Such findings may appear to provide considerable reassurance to ardent establishment ideologues, but it would be a mistake to conclude that there have been no changes in the vocational values of the average adolescent (112). Even the majority who intend to work within the system appear to be seeking somewhat different job satisfactions than stereotypes of the "success ethic" might imply. Thus, when asked "What factors are most important in choosing a job?" a majority of both younger and older adolescents in a recent representative national survey cited the following (in order of importance): enjoyable work, pride in job, pleasant working conditions, and creative satisfaction (87). The following factors were cited as least important: short hours, recognition by society, and achieving status (87). College youth are relatively more concerned than their noncollege peers with having an "opportunity to make a meaningful contribution" and with "stimulation of the job," and they are less interested in "prestige and status of the job" (54).

Most young people are willing to work hard (less than a third would welcome "working less hard"), but they consider "doing work that is more than just a job" very important (54, 87, 203). Two out of three state that they could accept the power and the authority of the "boss" in a work situation, but at least that many could not easily accept "being treated impersonally on the job" or having to engage in "outward conformity for the sake of career advancement" (203).

Vocational Opportunities in a Changing World

In the long run, the most critical problem for American society may not be the refusal of some young people to participate in "the system," but rather the capacity of that system to provide the numbers and kinds of jobs that an expanding population of young adults will need. Overall unemployment among youth in early 1972 exceeded 17 percent, as contrasted with 4.4 percent for adult males (192). Unemployment rates for minority youth were more than twice as high as among youth generally (98).

The problem, of course, is not simply one of numbers of jobs, but also of the kinds of jobs that will be needed in the 1970s and 1980s. As has been apparent for more than a decade, automation and rapid technological change, the consolidation of small businesses and farms into larger ones, and increased urbanization are producing significant shifts in employment patterns. These trends are expected to continue through the decade of the 1970s. The number of jobs available to unskilled and farm workers will continue to decline, while those for professional and technical workers and those engaged in service occupations and clerical and sales positions will continue to rise.

Clearly, poorly educated youth with few skills will find themselves increasingly penalized in the years ahead. Opportunities will be much greater for youth who have managed to obtain increased skills and education. However, the relationship between job opportunity and amount of education and training is not a simple one.

The extent of an individual's education and specialized skill can no longer be directly and proportionately related to vocational opportunity because of factors like the recent economic recession, greatly reduced federal, state, and private support for education, scientific research, and many social services, as well as previous overproduction in many professional, scientific, and technical fields (for example, teachers, aerospace engineers and physicists, biochemists). One of the economic problems of a highly technological society appears to be that, on the one hand, it demands highly specialized, frequently nontransferable skills, while, on the other hand, it also generates rapid shifts in technology and in the economy generally. Under these conditions many skills become obsolete in a relatively short period of time.

The problem of finding appropriate employment for young people is extremely complex and is likely to become more so in the future. Our entire society is growing more competitive, more specialized, and more technologically oriented. But unless the problems can be resolved—unless some better match can be found between vocational opportunities, on the one hand, and the needs, educational preparation, talents, skills, and values of young people, on the other—both society and its youth will be in serious trouble. If present trends continue, any "revolt of the young" may well stem more from the failure of society to provide adequate avenues for admission to the economic and social order, than from any loudly deplored rejection by youth of the society and its values.

References

1. Ausubel, D. P. **Theory and problems of adolescent development.** New York: Grune and Stratton, 1954.
2. Bachman, J. G. **Youth in transition.** Vol. 2: **The impact of family background and intelligence on tenth-grade boys.** Ann Arbor: Institute for Social Research, University of Michigan, 1970.
3. Bardwick, J. **Psychology of women: A study of bio-cultural conflicts.** New York: Harper & Row, 1971.
4. Bardwick, J. M., Douvan, E., Horner, M. S., & Guttman, D. **Feminine personality and conflict.** Belmont, Calif.: Brooks-Cole, 1970.
5. Baughman, E. E. **Black Americans.** New York: Academic Press, 1971.
6. Baumrind, D. Authoritarian vs. authoritative control. **Adolescence,** 1968, **3,** 255–272.
7. Baumrind, D. Effects of authoritative control on child behavior. **Child Development,** 1966, **37,** 887–907.
8. Beilin, H. The pattern of postponability and its relation to social class mobility. **Journal of Social Psychology,** 1956, **44,** 33–48.
9. Bell, A. P. Role modeling of fathers in adolescence and young adulthood. **Journal of Counseling Psychology,** 1969, **16,** 30–35.
10. Bell, G. D. Processes in the formation of adolescents' aspirations. **Social Forces,** 1963, **42,** 179–195.
11. Bell, R. R. Parent-child conflict in sexual values. **Journal of Social Issues,** 1966, **22,** 33–44.
12. Benedict, R. Continuities and discontinuities in cultural conditioning. In W. E. Martin & C. B. Stendler (Eds.), **Readings in child development.** New York: Harcourt Brace Jovanovich, 1954. Pp. 142–148.
13. Blos, P. **The young adolescent: Clinical studies.** New York: Free Press, 1970.
14. Blos, P. **On adolescence.** New York: Free Press, 1962.
15. Blos, P. **The adolescent personality: A study of individual behavior.** New York: Appleton-Century-Crofts, 1941.
16. Bonney, M. E. A sociometric study of some factors relating to mutual friendships on the elementary, secondary, and college levels. **Sociometry,** 1946, **9,** 21–47.
17. Bordin, E. S. A theory of interests as dynamic phenomena. **Educational and Psychological Measurement,** 1943, **3,** 49–66.
18. Bordua, D. J. Educational aspirations and parental stress on college. **Social Forces,** 1960, **38,** 262–269.
19. Bowerman, C. E., & Kinch, J. W. Changes in family and peer orientation of children between the fourth and tenth grades. **Social Forces,** 1959, **37,** 206–211.
20. Boyle, R. P. The effect of the high school on students' aspirations. **American Journal of Sociology,** 1966, **71,** 628–639.
21. Brecher, E. M. **The sex researchers.** New York: New American Library, 1971.

22. Brittain, C. V. A comparison of rural and urban adolescents with respect to parent vs. peer compliance. **Adolescence,** 1969, **13,** 59–68.

23. Brittain, C. V. Age and sex of siblings and conformity toward parents versus peers in adolescence. **Child Development,** 1966, **37,** 709–714.

24. Brittain, C. V. Adolescent choices and parent-peer cross-pressures. **American Sociology Review,** 1963, **28,** 358–391.

25. Brody, E. B. **Minority group adolescents in the United States.** Baltimore: Williams & Wilkins, 1968.

26. Bronfenbrenner, U. **Two worlds of childhood: U.S. and U.S.S.R.** New York: Russell Sage Foundation, 1970.

27. Burnstein, E. Fear of failure, achievement motivation, and aspiring to prestigeful occupations. **Journal of Abnormal Social Psychology,** 1963, **67,** 189–193.

28. Cairns, R. B., Paul, J. C. N., & Wishner, J. Sex censorship: The assumptions of anti-obscenity laws and the empirical evidence. **Minneapolis Law Review,** 1962, **46,** 1009–1041.

29. Campbell, J. D. Peer relations in childhood. In M. L. Hoffman & L. W. Hoffman (Eds.), **Review of child development research.** Vol. 1. New York: Russell Sage Foundation, 1964. Pp. 289–322.

30. Caro, F. G. Social class and attitudes of youth relevant for the realization of adult goals. **Social Forces,** 1966, **44,** 492–498.

31. Caro, F. G., & Pihlblad, C. T. Aspirations and expectations: A reexamination of the bases for social class differences in the occupational orientations of male high school students. **Sociology and Social Research,** 1965, **49,** 465–475.

32. Carter, H. D. The development of interests in vocations. In **Adolescence.** Part I. (43rd Yearbook of the National Society for the Study of Education.) Chicago: University of Chicago Press, 1944.

33. Chesser, E. **The sexual, marital, and family relationships of the English woman.** London: Hutchinson, 1956.

34. Christenson, H. T., & Carpenter, G. R. Value-behavior discrepancies regarding premarital coitus in three Western cultures. **American Sociological Review,** February, 1962, **27,** 66–74.

35. Clark, K. B., & Clark, M. P. Racial identification and preference in Negro children. In T. M. Newcomb and E. L. Hartley (Eds.), **Readings in social psychology.** New York: Holt, Rinehart & Winston, 1947. Pp. 169–178.

36. Coleman, J. S. **The adolescent society.** New York: Free Press, 1961.

37. Condry, J. C., Jr., Siman, M. L., & Bronfenbrenner, U. Characteristics of peer- and adult-oriented children. Unpublished manuscript, Department of Child Development, Cornell University, 1968.

38. Conger, J. J. **Adolescence and youth: Psychological development in a changing world.** New York: Harper & Row, 1973.

39. Conger, J. J. A world they never knew: The family and social change. **Daedalus,** Fall 1971, 1105–1138.

40. Cooper, D. **Death of the family.** New York: Pantheon, 1970.

41. Coopersmith, S. **The antecedents of self-esteem.** San Francisco: Freeman, 1967.

42. Costanzo, P. R. Conformity development as a function of self-blame. **Journal of Personality and Social Psychology,** 1970, **14,** 366–374.

43. Cottle, T. J., Howard, P., & Pleck, J. Adolescent perceptions of time: The effect of age, sex and social class. **Journal of Personality,** 1969, **37,** 636–650.

44. Crites, J. O. Parental identification in relation to vocational interest development. **Journal of Educational Psychology,** 1962, **53,** 262–270.

45. Davis, G. A. Teaching creativity in adolescence: A discussion of strategy. In R. E. Grinder (Ed.), **Studies in adolescence.** (2nd ed.) New York: Macmillan, 1969.

46. Day, S. R. Teacher influence on the occupational preferences of high school students. **Vocational Guidance Quarterly,** 1966, **14,** 215–219.

47. Dennis, W. The adolescent. In L. Carmichael (Ed.), **Manual of child psychology.** New York: Wiley, 1946. Pp. 633–666.

48. **Developmental psychology today.** Delmar, Calif.: CRM Books, 1971.

49. Douvan, E. New sources of conflict in females in adolescence and early adulthood. In J. M. Bardwick, E. Douvan, M. S. Horner, and D. Guttman, **Feminine personality and conflict.** Belmont, Calif.: Brooks-Cole, 1970. Pp. 31–43.

50. Douvan, E., & Adelson, J. **The adolescent experience.** New York: Wiley, 1966.

51. Douvan, E., & Gold, M. Model patterns in American adolescence. In M. L. Hoffman and L. W. Hoffman (Eds.), **Review of child development research,** Vol. 2. New York: Russell Sage Foundation, 1966. Pp. 469–528.

52. Dwyer, J., & Mayer, J. Variations in physical appearance during adolescence. Part 1. Boys. **Postgraduate Medicine,** 1967, **41,** 99–107.

53. Dwyer, J., & Mayer, J. Variations in physical appearance during adolescence. Part 2. Girls. **Postgraduate Medicine,** 1967, **42,** 91–97.

54. Editors of **Fortune. Youth in turmoil.** New York: Time-Life, 1969.

55. Elder, G. H., Jr. Adult control in family and school: Public opinion in historical and comparative perspective. **Youth and Society,** 1971, **49,** 5–34.

56. Elder, G. H., Jr. Achievement motivation and intelligence in occupational mobility: A longitudinal analysis. **Sociometry,** 1968, **31,** 327–354.

57. Elder, G. H., Jr. Occupational level, motivation, and mobility: A longitudinal analysis. **Journal of Counseling Psychology,** 1968, **15,** 1–7.

58. Elder, G. H., Jr. Parental power legitimation and its effect on the adolescent. **Sociometry,** 1963, **26,** 50–65.

59. Elder, G. H., Jr. Structural variations in the child rearing relationship. **Sociometry,** 1962, **25,** 241–262.

60. Elder, G. H., Jr. Family structure and the transmission of values and norms in the process of child rearing. Unpublished doctoral dissertation, University of North Carolina at Chapel Hill, 1961.

61. Elkind, D. Measuring young minds. **Horizon,** 1971, **13**(1), 35.

62. Elkind, D. **Children and adolescents: Interpretive essays on Jean Piaget.** New York: Oxford University Press, 1970.

63. Elkind, D. Cognitive development in adolescence. In J. F. Adams (Ed.), **Understanding adolescence: Current developments in adolescent psychology.** Boston: Allyn and Bacon, 1968. Pp. 128–158.

64. Elkind, D. Egocentrism in adolescence. **Child Development,** 1967, **38,** 1025–1034.

65. Erikson, E. H. **Identity: Youth and crisis.** New York: Norton, 1968.

66. Erickson, E. H. Identity and the life cycle. **Psychological Issues,** 1959, **1,** 1–165.

67. Erikson, E. H. The problem of ego identity. **Journal of the American Psychoanalytic Association,** 1956, **4,** 56–121.

68. Erikson, E. H. **A healthy personality for every child. A fact finding report: a digest.** (Mid-century White House Conference on Children and Youth.) Raleigh, N.C.: Health Publications Institute, 1951. Pp. 8–25.

69. Espenschade, A. Motor performance in adolescence. **Monographs of the Society for Research in Child Development,** 1940, 5(1).
70. Faulkner, W. **Go down, Moses.** New York: Random House, 1942.
71. Faust, M. S. Developmental maturity as a determinant in prestige of adolescent girls. **Child Development,** 1960, **31,** 173–184.
72. Floud, J. E., Halsey, A. H., & Martin, F. M. (Eds.) **Social class and educational opportunity.** London: Heinemann, 1956.
73. Ford, C. S. Culture and sex. In A. Ellis and A. Abarband. **The encylopedia of sexual behavior.** Vol. I. New York: Hawthorn, 1961. Pp. 306–312.
74. Ford, C. S., & Beach, F. A. **Patterns of sexual behavior.** New York: Harper-Hoeber, 1951.
75. Freud, A. **The ego and the mechanisms of defense.** New York: International Universities Press, 1946.
76. Frisch, R. E., & Revelle, R. Height and weight at menarche and a hypothesis of critical body weights and adolescent events. **Science,** 1970, **169,** 397–399.
77. Gallop poll, **Denver Post,** May 21, 1970.
78. Garrison, K. C. Physiological changes in adolescence. In J. F. Adams (Ed.), **Understanding adolescence: Current developments in adolescent psychology.** Boston: Allyn and Bacon, 1968.
79. Graduates and jobs: A grave new world. **Time,** May 24, 1971, 49–59.
80. Greer, G. **The female eunuch.** New York: Bantam, 1971.
81. Greulich, W. W. The rationale of assessing the developmental status of children from roentgenograms of the hand and wrist. **Child Development,** 1950, **21,** 33–44.
82. Grinder, R. E., & Schmitt, S. S. Coeds and contraceptive information. **Journal of Marriage and the Family,** 1966, **28,** 471–479.
83. Group for the Advancement of Psychiatry. **Normal adolescence.** New York: Scribners, 1968.
84. Gunn, B. Children's conceptions of occupational prestige. **Personnel Guidance Journal,** 1964, **42,** 558–563.
85. Hall, P. L., & Wagner, N. N. Initial heterosexual experience in Sweden and the United States: A cross-cultural survey. **Proceedings, 80th Annual Convention of the American Psychological Association,** 1972, **7,** 293–294.
86. Hallworth, H. J., Davis, H., & Gamston, C. Some adolescents' perceptions of adolescent personality. **Journal of Social and Clinical Psychology,** 1965, **4,** 81–91.
87. Harris, L. Change, yes—upheaval, no. **Life,** January 8, 1971, 22–27.
88. Heilbrun, A. B., & Gillard, B. J. Perceived maternal childbearing behavior and motivational effects of social reinforcement in females. **Perceptual and Motor Skills,** 1966, **23,** 439–446.
89. Hoffman, L. W. The professional woman as mother. Paper prepared for the Conference on Successful Women in the Sciences, New York Academy of Sciences, New York, New York, May 11–13, 1972.
90. Holland, J. L. Explorations of a theory of vocational choice. Part I. Vocational images and choice. **Vocational Guidance Quarterly,** 1963, **11,** 232–239.
91. Hollingshead, A. B. **Elmtown's youth: The impact of social classes on youth.** New York: Wiley, 1949.
92. Horner, M. S. Femininity and successful achievement: A basic inconsistency. In J. M. Bardwick, E. Douvan, M. S. Horner, and D. Guttman. **Feminine personality and conflict.** Belmont, Calif.: Brooks-Cole, 1970. Pp. 45–73.
93. Hraba, J. & Grant, G. Black is beautiful: A reexamination of racial preference and identification. **Journal of Personality and Social Psychology,** 1970, **16,** 398–402.

94. Hunt, M. Special sex education survey. **Seventeen,** July 1970, 94ff.

95. Israel, S. L. Normal puberty and adolescence. **Annals of the New York Academy of Science,** 1967, **142,** 773–778.

96. Jennings, H. H. Leadership and sociometric choice. **Sociometry,** 1947, **10,** 32–49.

97. Jersild, A. T. **The psychology of adolescence.** (2nd ed.) New York: Macmillan, 1965.

98. **Jobs for blacks.** New York: NAACP Legal Defense Fund, Inc., 1971.

99. Jones, H. E. **Motor performance and growth: A developmental study of static dynamometric strength.** Berkeley: University of California Press, 1949.

100. Jones, H. E. The California adolescent growth study. **Journal of Educational Research, 1938,** 31, 561–567.

101. Jones, M. C. A study of socialization patterns at the high school level. **Journal of Genetic Psychology,** 1958, **92,** 87–111.

102. Jones, M. C. The later careers of boys who were early or late maturing. **Child Development,** 1957, **28,** 113–128.

103. Jones, M. C., & Bayley, N. Physical maturing among boys as related to behavior. **Journal of Educational Psychology,** 1950, **41,** 129–148.

104. Kagan, J., & Moss, H. A. **Birth to maturity: The Fels study of psychological development.** New York: Wiley, 1962.

105. Kahl, J. A. Educational and occupational aspirations of "common-man" boys. **Harvard Educational Review,** 1953, **23,** 186–203.

106. Karlsson, G., Karlsson, S., & Busch, K. Sexual habits and attitudes of Swedish folk high school students. Research Report No. 15, Department of Sociology, Uppsala University, Uppsala, Sweden, 1960.

107. Keislar, E. R. Experimental development of "like" and "dislike" of others among adolescent girls. **Child Development,** 1961, **32,** 59–66.

108. Kelley, H. H., & Volkart, E. H. The resistance to change of group-anchored attitudes. **American Sociological Review,** 1952, **17,** 453–465.

109. Khana, A. A study of friendship in adolescent boys and girls. **Manus, Delhi,** 1960, **7,** 3–18.

110. Kinsey, A. C., Pomeroy, W. B., Martin, C. E., Gebhard, P. H. **Sexual behavior in the human female.** Philadelphia: Saunders, 1953.

111. Kinsey, A. C., Pomeroy, W. B., & Martin, C. E. **Sexual behavior in the human male.** Philadelphia: Saunders, 1948.

112. Kleiber, D. A., & Manaster, G. J. Youths' outlook on the future: A past-present comparison. **Journal of Youth and Adolescence,** 1972, **1,** 223–231.

113. Kuhlen, R. G., & Bretsch, H. S. Sociometric status and personal problems of adolescents. **Sociometry,** 1947, **10,** 122–132.

114. Kuhlen, R. G., & Lee, B. J. Personality characteristics and social acceptability in adolescence. **Journal of Educational Psychology,** 1943, **34,** 321–340.

115. Kuvelsky, W. P., & Bealer, R. C. The relevance of adolescents' occupational aspirations for subsequent job attainment. **Rural Sociology,** 1967, **32,** 290–301.

116. Lansky, L. M., Crandall, V. J., Kagan, J., & Baker, C. T. Sex differences in aggression and its correlates in middle-class adolescents. **Child Development,** 1961, **32,** 45–58.

117. Larson, L. E. The relative influence of parent-adolescent affect in predicting the salience hierarchy among youth. Paper presented at the annual meeting of the National Council on Family Relations, Chicago, October, 1970.

118. Latham, A. J. The relationship between pubertal status and leadership in junior high school boys. **Journal of Genetic Psychology,** 1951, **78,** 185–194.

119. Laughlin, F. **The peer status of sixth and seventh grade children.** New York: Columbia University Press, 1954.
120. Lewin, K. Field theory and experiment in social psychology. **American Journal of Sociology,** 1939, **44,** 868–897.
121. Linner, B. **Sex and society in Sweden.** New York: Pantheon, 1967.
122. Little, J. K. The occupations of non-college youth. **American Educational Research Journal,** 1967, **4,** 147–153.
123. Luckey, E., & Nass, G. A comparison of sexual attitudes and behavior in an international sample. **Journal of Marriage and the Family,** 1969, **31,** 364–379.
124. Lund, F. H. Adolescent motivation: Sex differences. **Journal of Genetic Psychology,** 1944, **64,** 99–103.
125. Lynn, D. B. A note on sex differences in the development of masculine and feminine identification. **Psychological Review,** 1959, **46,** 126–135.
126. MacCurdy, H. L. **A test for measuring the physical capacity of secondary schoolboys.** New York: Harcourt Brace Jovanovich, 1953.
127. McCandless, B. R. **Adolescents: Behavior and development.** Hindsdale, Ill.: Dryden, 1970.
128. McCandless, B. R., Bilous, C. B., & Bennet, H. L. Peer popularity and dependence on adults in preschool age socialization. **Child Development,** 1961, **32,** 511–518.
129. McDonald, R. L., & Gynther, M. D. Relationship of self and ideal self descriptions. **Journal of Personality and Social Psychology,** 1965, **1,** 85–88.
130. McGhee, P. E., & Teevan, R. C. Conformity behavior and need for affiliation. **Journal of Social Psychology,** 1967, **72,** 117–121.
131. Mann, J. Experimental induction of human sexual arousal. In W. C. Wilson, et al., **Technical report of the Commission on Obscenity and Pornography.** Vol. I. **Preliminary Studies.** Washington, D.C.: U.S. Government Printing Office, 1971. Pp. 23–60.
132. Maresh, M. Variations in patterns of linear growth and skeletal maturation. **Journal of the American Physical Therapy Association,** 1964, **44,** 881–890.
133. Masters, W. H., & Johnson, V. E. **Human sexual inadequacy.** Boston: Little, Brown, 1970.
134. Masters, W. H., & Johnson, V. E. **Human sexual response.** Boston: Little, Brown, 1966.
135. Mayer, L. A. New questions about the U.S. population. **Fortune,** February 1971, 82–85. (Source: U.S. Census, 1970.)
136. Mead, M. **From the south seas: Part III. Sex and temperament in three primitive societies.** New York: Morrow, 1939.
137. Mead, M. **Male and female.** New York: Morrow, 1939.
138. Minahan, N. Relationships among self-perceived physical attractiveness, body shape, and personality of teen-age girls. **Dissertation Abstracts International,** 1971, **32,** 1249–1250.
139. Minturn, L., Lambert, W. W., and associates. **Mothers of six cultures: Antecedents of child rearing.** New York: Wiley, 1964.
140. Montesano, N., & Geist, H. Differences in occupational choice between ninth and twelfth grade boys. **Personnel Guidance Journal,** 1964, **43,** 150–154.
141. Morse, N. C., & Weiss, R. S. The function and meaning of work and the job. In D. G. Zytowski (Ed.), **Vocational behavior.** New York: Holt, Rinehart & Winston, 1968. Pp. 7–16.
142. Mussen, P. H., Conger, J. J., & Kagan, J. **Child development and personality** (3rd ed.). New York: Harper & Row, 1969.
143. Mussen, P. H., & Jones, M. C. Self conceptions, motivations, and interpersonal attitudes of late and early maturing boys. **Child Development,** 1957, **28,** 243–256.

144. Olson, W. C., & Hughes, B. O. Growth of the child as a whole. In R. G. Barker, J. S. Kounin, & H. F. Wright (Eds.), **Child behavior and development.** New York: McGraw-Hill, 1943. Pp. 199–208.

145. Oskamp, S. International attitudes of British and American students: A fading double standard. **Proceedings, 80th Annual Convention of the American Psychological Association,** 1972, **7,** 295–296.

146. Osofsky, H. Somatic, hormonal changes during adolescence. **Hospital Topics,** 1968, **46,** 95–103.

147. Osterrieth, P. A. Adolescence: Some psychological aspects. In G. Caplan and S. Lebovici (Eds.), **Adolescence: Psychosocial perspectives.** New York: Basic Books, 1969.

148. Packard, V. . . . and the sexual behavior reported by 2100 young adults. In **The sexual wilderness: The contemporary upheaval in male-female relationships.** New York: Pocket Books, 1970. Pp. 166–184.

149. Packard, V. The sexual attitudes of 2200 young adults. In **The sexual wilderness: The contemporary upheaval in male-female relationships.** New York: Pocket Books, 1970. Pp. 152–165.

150. Packard, V. **The sexual wilderness: The contemporary upheaval in male-female relationships.** New York: Pocket Books, 1970.

151. Pikas, A. Children's attitudes toward rational versus inhibiting parental authority. **Journal of Abnormal Social Psychology,** 1961, **62,** 315–321.

152. Pomeroy, W. B. **Boys and sex.** New York: Delacorte, 1969.

153. Pomeroy, W. B. **Girls and sex.** New York: Delacorte, 1969.

154. Proshansky, H., & Newton, P. The nature and meaning of Negro self-identity. In M. Deutsch, J. Katz, and A. R. Jensen (Eds.), **Social class, race, and psychological development.** New York: Holt, Rinehart & Winston, 1968.

155. Purnell, R. F. Socioeconomic status and sex differences in adolescent reference-group orientation. **Journal of Genetic Psychology,** 1970, **116,** 233–239.

156. Reevy, W. R. Adolescent sexuality. In A. Ellis and A. Abarband (Eds.), **The encyclopedia of sexual behavior.** Vol. 1. Englewood Cliffs, N.J.: Hawthorn, 1961. Pp. 52–68.

157. Reisman, D. **Individualism reconsidered.** Glencoe, Ill.: Free Press, 1954.

158. Reiss, I. L. How and why America's sex standards are changing. In W. Simon and J. H. Gagnon (Eds.), **The sexual scene.** Chicago: Trans-action Books, 1970. Pp. 43–57.

159. Reiss, I. L. (Ed.) The sexual renaissance in America. **Journal of Social Issues,** 1966, **22,** No. 2.

160. Reiss, I. L. The scaling of premarital sexual permissiveness. **Journal of Marriage and the Family,** 1964, V, 188–199.

161. Rosenberg, M. **Society and the adolescent self-image.** Princeton, N.J.: Princeton University Press, 1965.

162. Schaeffer, D. L. (Ed.) **Sex differences in personality: Readings.** Belmont, Calif.: Brooks-Cole, 1971.

163. Schaeffer, D. L., & Eisenberg, J. Cognitive conflict and compromise between males and females. In D. L. Schaeffer (Ed.), **Sex differences in personality: Readings.** Belmont, Calif.: Brooks-Cole, 1971.

164. Schonfeld, W. A. The body and the body-image in adolescents. In G. Caplan and S. Lebovici (Eds.), **Adolescence: Psychosocial perspectives.** New York: Basic Books, 1969.

165. Seligman, D. A special kind of rebellion. In Editors of **Fortune, Youth in turmoil.** New York: Time-Life, 1969.

166. Shuttleworth, F. K. The physical and mental growth of girls and boys, age six to nine-

teen, in relation to age at maximum growth. **Monographs of the Society for Research in Child Development,** 1939, **4**(3).

167. Simon, W., Berger, A. S., & Gagnon, J .H. Beyond anxiety and fantasy: The coital experiences of college youth. **Journal of Youth and Adolescence,** 1972, **1,** 203–221.

168. Simon, W., & Gagnon, J. H. Psychosexual development. In W. Simon and J. H. Gagnon (Eds.), **The sexual scene.** Chicago: Trans-action Books, 1970. Pp. 23–41.

169. Simon, W., & Gagnon, J. H. The creation of the sexual in early adolescence. Unpublished manuscript, 1970.

170. Simon, W., & Gagnon, J. H. (Eds.) **The sexual scene.** Chicago: Trans-action Books, 1970.

171. Simmons, K. The Brush Foundation study of child growth and development: II. Physical growth and development. **Monographs of the Society for Research in Child Development,** 1944, **9**(1).

172. Simpson, R. L. Parental influence, anticipatory socialization, and social mobility. **American Sociological Review,** 1962, **27,** 517–522.

173. Sorenson, R. C. **Adolescent sexuality in contemporary America: Personal values and sexual behavior ages 13–19.** New York: World, 1973.

174. Stone, L. J., & Church, J. **Childhood and adolescence: A psychology of the growing person.** (2nd ed.) New York: Random House, 1968.

175. Straus, M. A. Conjugal power structure and adolescent personality. **Marriage and Family Living,** 1962, **24,** 17–25.

176. Student survey, **Playboy,** September 1971, 118 ff.

177. Student survey, **Playboy,** September 1970, 182 ff.

178. Super, D. E., Starishevsky, R., Matlin, N., & Jordaan, J. P. **Career development: Self concept theory.** New York: College Entrance Examination Board, 1963.

179. Tanner, J. M. Sequence, tempo, and individual variation in the growth and development of boys and girls aged twelve to sixteen. **Daedalus,** Fall 1971, 907–930.

180. Tanner, J. M. Physical growth. In P. H. Mussen (Ed.), **Carmichael's manual of child psychology.** (3rd ed.) Vol. 1. New York: Wiley, 1970.

181. Tanner, J. M. **Growth at adolescence.** (2nd ed.) Oxford: Blackwell Scientific Publications, 1962. (Philadelphia: Davis.)

182. Tanner, J. M., & O'Keefe, B. Age at menarche in Nigerian school girls, with a note on their heights and weights from age 12 to 19. **Human Biology,** 1962, **34,** 187–196.

183. **The American almanac (The statistical abstract of the United States, 92nd ed.).** New York: Grosset and Dunlap, 1972.

184. The open generation. **Look,** September 20, 1966, **30,** 52 ff.

185. **The report of the Commission on Obscenity and Pornography.** New York: Bantam, 1970.

186. Tryon, C. M. Evaluation of adolescent personality by adolescents. **Monographs of the Society for Research in Child Development,** 1939, **4**(4).

187. Tuddenham, R. D. Correlates of yielding to a distorted group norm. **Journal of Personality,** 1959, **27,** 272–284.

188. Tuma, E. & Livson, N. Family socioeconomic status and adolescent attitudes to authority. **Child Development,** 1960, **31,** 387–399.

189. Turner, R. H. Sponsored and contest mobility and the school system. **American Sociological Review,** 1960, **25,** 855–867.

190. Valenstein, E. S. Steroid hormones and the neuropsychology of development. In R. L. Isaacson (Ed.), **The neuropsychology of development: A symposium.** New York: Wiley, 1968. Pp. 1–39.

191. Van Krevelen, A. Characteristics which identify the adolescent to his peers. **Journal of Social Psychology, 56,** 285–289.
192. **Wall Street Journal,** January 17, 1972.
193. Weatherley, D. Self-perceived rate of physical maturation and personality in late adolescence. **Child Development,** 1964, **35,** 1197–1210.
194. Werts, C. E. Paternal influence on career choice. **Journal of Counseling Psychology,** 1968, **15,** 48–52.
195. Werts, C. E. Social class and initial career choice of college freshmen. **Sociology and Education,** 1966, **39,** 74–85.
196. What people think of their high schools. **Life,** May 16, 1969, **66,** 23–33.
197. Whiting, B. B. (Ed.) **Six cultures: Studies of child rearing.** New York: Wiley, 1963.
198. Whiting, J. W. M., & Child, I. L. **Child training and personality.** New Haven, Conn.: Yale University Press, 1953.
199. Whiting, J. W. M. **Becoming a Kwoma.** New Haven, Conn.: Yale University Press, 1941.
200. Wilson, A. B. Residential segregation of social classes and aspirations of high school boys. **American Sociological Review,** 1959, **24,** 836–845.
201. Wilson, W. C. (Ed.) **Technical report of the Commission on Obscenity and Pornography.** Vol. 1. **Preliminary studies.** Washington, D.C.: U.S. Government Printing Office, 1971.
202. Wilson, W. C. (Ed.) **Technical report of the Commission on Obscenity and Pornography.** Vol. VI. **National survey.** Washington, D.C.: U.S. Government Printing Office, 1971.
203. Yankelovich, D. **Generations apart.** New York: CBS News, 1969.
204. Zelnik, M., & Kantner, J. E. **National Survey for the Commission on Population Growth and the American Future.** Washington, D.C.: U.S. Government Printing Office, 1972.
205. Zubin, J. & Money, J. (Eds.). **Contemporary sexual behavior: Critical issues in the 1970s.** Baltimore: Johns Hopkins University Press, 1973.
206. Zuckerman, M. Physiological measures of sexual arousal in humans. In W. C. Wilson (Ed.). **Technical report of the Commission on Obscenity and Pornography.** Vol. I. **Preliminary studies.** Washington, D.C.: U.S. Government Printing Office, 1971. Pp. 61–102.
207. Zytowski, D. G. (Ed.) **Vocational behavior.** New York: Holt, Rinehart & Winston, 1968.

Chapter 13

Adolescence

II. Identity, Values, and Alienation

Central to the task of becoming an adult is the development of a sense of one's own identity, of a definition of oneself as a person. This conception of oneself need not be all positive; it can contain negative elements as well (72). But there must be something there to provide a frame of reference within which the individual can view with some perspective the varied, sometimes seemingly random, influences and events of a rapidly changing, often chaotic world. Without some sense of his own identity, of who he is and where he is headed, the adolescent faces virtually insurmountable odds in attempt-to cope with the demands of adolescence—the demands for independence, for integrating his new-found sexual maturity, for establishing meaningful and workable relations with peers of both sexes, and for deciding on his life work and his goals.

The problem of identity cannot be separated from that of values. We live in a period of accelerated technological transformations and a continually shifting population. Speaking of Americans, Erik Erikson comments, "This is the country of changes; it is obsessed with change" (72, 29). To maintain some stability in his conception of himself and in his internal guides to action in a changing world, the individual must be faithful to some basic values. He may have to adopt new ways of implementing these values to meet changing circumstances, but if the values are there and if they are sound, he will be able to adapt to change while remaining constant in his conception of his own identity. However, ". . . without the development of a capacity for fidelity the individual will either have what we call a weak ego, or look for a deviant group to be faithful to" (53, 72).

In this final chapter, we will examine some of the antecedents and correlates of a sense of identity, and then turn to the problem of values—both for the average adolescent and for those youth who in one way or another have become alienated from the dominant values of contemporary American society.

IDENTITY

The adolescent or adult with a strong sense of identity sees himself as a distinctive individual in his own right. Indeed, the very word "individual," as a synonym for "person," implies a universal need to perceive oneself as somehow unique and separate from others, even though we share motives, values, and interests with others. Closely related to the need for separateness is the need for self-consistency —for a feeling of "wholeness." When we speak of the integrity of the self, we imply both separateness from others and unity of the self—a workable integration of one's needs, motives, and patterns of responding. Finally, in order to have a clear sense of ego identity, the adolescent or adult must perceive the stability of the self, that is, that he is separate and self-consistent not only at a particular moment, but also over time. He needs to perceive consistent links between the person that he is today and the person he was yesterday.

Any developmental influences which contribute to a confident perception of oneself as separate and distinct from others, as reasonably self-consistent and integrated, and as having a continuity of the self over time contribute to an overall sense of ego identity. By the same token, influences which impair any of these self-perceptions foster ego diffusion (confusion).

Many adolescents find themselves playing roles which shift from one situation or from one time to another and worry about "Which, if any, is the real me?" They also self-consciously try out different roles in the hope of finding one which seems to "fit." An adolescent girl who had three distinctly different handwriting styles was asked why she did not have one consistent style. She replied, "How can I only write one way till I know who I am?" (62).

The problem of identity becomes acute at adolescence for a variety of reasons. The changes that occur during the middle-childhood years are, for the most part, relatively gradual and regular, without abrupt shifts from day to day or month to month. During adolescence, however, change is very rapid. Confronted with a physiological revolution within himself and with the varied intellectual, social, and vocational demands of adulthood that lie directly ahead, the adolescent is concerned with how he appears in the eyes of others compared with how he feels he actually is, and with the question of how to connect the roles and skills cultivated earlier with the demands of tomorrow.

Achieving a well-defined sense of individual identity is also partially dependent upon the capacity of the individual to conceptualize himself in abstract terms, at times almost like a spectator—"to take his own thought as object and reason about it." This capability aids the adolescent in his search for an individual identity but, at the same time, increases its difficulty. According to Erikson, "such cognitive orientation forms not a contrast but a complement to the need of the young person to develop a sense of identity, for, from among all possible and imaginable relations, he must make a series of ever-narrowing selections of personal, occupational, sexual, and ideological commitments" (70, 245).

Identifications and Identity

The ease with which the adolescent boy or girl is able to achieve a clear sense of identity will depend on many factors. Among these are the kinds of previous identifications he has developed and his ability to integrate these identifications with his sexual maturity, the aptitudes and skills he has developed out of his ability and experience, and the opportunities provided by changing social roles (71, 172). Perhaps most critical is the kind of relationship the boy or girl has had, and continues to have, with parents (50).

Establishing a strong sense of identity is facilitated by a rewarding, interactive relationship between the adolescent and both parents—a same-sex parent who serves as an adequate model for personally and socially effective behavior and an opposite-sex parent who is also an effective individual and who manifests approval of the model provided by the same-sex parent (**24, 71, 114, 116, 117, 159, 160, 164, 172, 173, 176, 179, 180, 193**). An adolescent or young adult with parents of this sort is likely to have favorable and clearly defined self-perceptions. He is also likely to have fewer conflicts, and be able to deal with those he does encounter, between self-perceptions, on the one hand, and the internal demands of approaching sexual maturity and the external demands of society, on the other.

Adolescent boys with nurturant fathers perceive themselves as having a greater role-consistency, that is, as responding in similar ways to parents, friends, employers, casual acquaintances, children, and members of the opposite sex (**113**). If they view themselves as being relaxed or formal, warm or indifferent, independent or dependent in one kind of relationship, they tend to view themselves as responding in similar fashion in other relationships (**113**).

Late adolescent girls who score high in identification with their mothers tend to perceive themselves as "calm," "reasonable," "reserved," "self-controlled," "confident," and "wise." In contrast, those scoring low in identification tend to view themselves as "changeable," "impulsive," "rebellious," "restless," "dramatic," "touchy," and "tactless" (**24**). In Erikson's terms, the former self-descriptions are more characteristic of emerging ego identity, while the latter indicate ego diffusion, or what he now calls confusion. Futhermore, adolescent girls who see themselves as more like their mothers (that is, are identified with their mothers) perceive their actual and "ideal" selves as more similar and consistent than girls who are less identified with their mothers (**24**).

Sex-Typing and Sexual Identity

We are all aware of current controversies regarding sex-typing of behavior—controversies which in many instances have generated a good deal more heat than light (see pp. 398–404). In discussing sex-typing, two points must be emphasized. Appropriate behavior as a man or woman does not mean rigid conformity to sex-role stereotypes. Further, identification with the same-sex parent does not necessarily lead to the adoption of traditional or exaggerated sex-role stereotypes. Each of these points will be considered briefly in turn.

Adolescent boys with traditional, highly "masculine" interests show more positive self-conceptions and more self-confidence than boys with traditionally feminine interests (**171**). They are more carefree, more contented, more relaxed, more exuberant, happier, calmer, and smoother in social functioning than those with less masculine interests (**171**).

However, by the time they are young adults, those who were highly masculine adolescents are less confident in their perception of themselves and more

... lacking in qualities of leadership, dominance, self-confidence, and self-acceptance. In general, there seems to have been a shift in the self-concepts of the two groups in adulthood, the originally highly masculine boys apparently feeling less positive about themselves after adolescence; and, . . . the less masculine group changing in a favorable direction (**170**, 440).

Apparently, personality traits associated with a high degree of masculinity of interests are highly rewarded in the culture of the adolescent peer group, which emphasizes stereotyped masculine behavior and interests. In adult social and vocational roles, less value is given to conformity to superficial stereotypes of "masculinity"—although this may be more the case in some settings than others (e.g., a complex, cosmopolitan urban environment, as contrasted with a rural, "frontier-type" ranching community).

Admittedly, vocational roles, such as ballet dancer, interior decorator, or woman's hairdresser, continue to be viewed as "feminine" in our society. But many vocational roles that combine demands for "masculine" independence and aggressiveness and demands for "feminine" nurturance, sensitivity, and interpersonal orientation (for example, physician, psychologist, teacher, personnel director) are highly rewarded in adulthood. Personality characteristics that may have developed partly as defenses among less stereotypically masculine adolescents—such as efforts to be sociable and sensitive to the needs of others, introspectiveness and inner resourcefulness, and a need to prove oneself—may contribute to social and vocational success. This success, in turn, may result in increased security and a more confident adjustment.

In short, stereotyped masculine identification does not guarantee a stable, long-term sense of ego identity, even in one's role as a male. Perhaps the most desirable identification, under most conditions in contemporary society, is one that, while basically masculine, allows for flexibility and avoids constricting stereotypes (**172**). Adolescent boys whose fathers provide a moderately masculine role model and who are moderately nurturant have less difficulty in establishing appropriate and effective behavior than boys whose fathers are either extremely masculine or very low in masculinity (**115**). Furthermore, the social behavior of the sons of moderately nurturant fathers is more congruent with their expressed social values.

The situation with respect to sex-typing and identity is even more complex for girls (**14, 62, 114, 159**). There are more ways in which adolescent girls can successfully establish feminine ego identities in contemporary society than is the case with boys, although they may have as much or more difficulty. As a child, the girl is permitted considerably more freedom than a boy to engage in cross-sex behaviors (**14, 62, 114, 132**). There is a wider range of feminine than of masculine sex-role attributes and personality qualities "because the culture, by not defining the female role as rigidly as the male, permits greater variance. Female role expectations become more specific in adolescence, but by that time it is rather late to impose stringent criteria for acceptable personality traits and behaviors" (**14**, 144).

The traditional feminine role is undoubtedly in a state of transition (**14, 172**). Hence, the young girl may be exposed to conflicting social rewards and punishments "no matter whether she assumes the traditional feminine role or the 'modern' masculinized role" (113, 352). The development of a relatively conflict-free sexual identity (as distinguished from the acquisition of a highly stereotyped sex-role) depends, in considerable measure, upon the kind of parental identification on which it is based and on congruence between one's role behavior and basic biological nature as a girl or boy (of course, as we saw in the previous chapter, peers may also play a significant, and sometimes corrective, role in helping the adolescent to achieve a satisfying social and sexual identity.)

For example, the girl who is identified with a traditional "feminine" mother and the girl who is identified with a socially assertive, intellectual, highly independent mother may both achieve a relatively conflict-free adjustment and a strong sense of identity. On the other hand, a girl whose sex-role behavior is based on rejection of a nonnurturant mother (regardless of whether the mother is "traditional" or "modern") may have difficulty in establishing a stable, secure ego identity. So, too, may a girl whose sex-role behavior is based on identification with a mother who rejects her basic biological identity (that is, a mother who resents her sexual nature or her childbearing capability or who is hostile to her own or the opposite sex).

One study of a variety of groups of adolescent girls (62) found that girls with a strong, uncomplicated, traditional feminine sex-role identification were clearly identified with their mothers and had close and amiable relationships with strong, traditional parents. Compared with other girls, they most often chose their mother or some other feminine relative as an adult ideal and reported fewer disagreements with their parents. The traditional feminine girl expressed a clear sense of her own identity:

> She gains self-esteem from helping others and playing a succorant role; she typically chooses an adult ideal on the basis of interpersonal warmth and sensitivity. She shows little motivation for personal achievement. She prefers security to success, she does not daydream about achievement, but rather exclusively about popularity, dating, marriage, and family goals (62, 244).

In contrast, girls with antifeminine identifications were least likely to choose **any** women as ideal adults. Their parents were more likely to be traditional, restrictive, and considerably more punitive than the parents of any other group. The girls responded more often with resentment against their parents' regulations and rejected the feminine role model, which they perceived as restricting freedom, requiring attention to clothes and grooming, and, in some cases, as "subjecting" the girl to feminine biological functions, such as menstruation and childbirth. In general, they were lower in self-esteem and more insecure and self-rejecting. They displayed fewer interests, had difficulty forming friendships, had a low activity level, and frequently appeared to have a poorly defined sense of their own identity (62).

Falling between these two extremes was a third group of girls who, although strongly feminine, could and did recognize attractions in the traditionally masculine role. They were similar to the strongly traditional feminine girls in their interest in marriage and motherhood, but they also maintained a lively interest in personal achievement and individual development. These girls appeared to be modeling themselves after parents with whom they had positive, generally rewarding relationships. Their mothers were likely to be ambitious and highly educated women who worked outside the home and encouraged their daughter's independence and self-reliance (62).

The great majority of contemporary adolescent girls fall into either the traditional feminine sex-role category or this third category. Relatively few (not more than 5 percent) fall into the antifeminine group. Up to the present time, the most typical and socially encouraged pattern of identity formation has been that of the traditional feminine girl. Initially, this pattern may permit the fewest role conflicts, since it is functional for these girls' future success as wives and mothers (14). And as long as circumstances do not change markedly, it may produce both a relatively satisfying adaptation and adequate sources of self-esteem and a sense of achievement. The girl in this category who finds a mate with whom she is happy and who becomes engaged in rearing a family, may continue to find the traditional feminine identification a rewarding one (14, 198). On the other hand, her relatively greater dependence on others and lack of alternate sources of personal fulfillment may leave her more vulnerable to the effects of disruptions in her basic relationships as, for example, failure of a marriage or the departure of adolescent children from the home (20, 119).

The more or less traditional feminine pattern continues to predominate and seems to be preferred by a majority of young women (14, 57, 62, 198). However, an increasing number of adolescent girls are seeking a more flexible, less traditionally stereotyped sex role. Among this group, there is increasingly greater commitment to academic and vocational interests—especially in fields that combine "feminine" opportunities for nurturance with more "masculine" opportunities for achievement—combined with a commitment to more traditional feminine goals, including marriage and a family (14). For such girls, "interpersonal success and traditional behaviors remain important while . . . achievement success becomes equally important" (14, 187).

MORAL DEVELOPMENT AND VALUES

At no time in his life is the average person as likely to be concerned about moral values and standards as he is during adolescence. The adolescent's accelerated cognitive development makes him more aware of moral questions and values and more capable of dealing with them in a relatively sophisticated fashion. Furthermore, social demands upon him are changing rapidly, and this requires a continuing reappraisal of moral values and beliefs. To complicate matters further, the adolescent may engage in thinking about broad philosophical and moral issues, not simply for their own sake, but as a way of struggling with more personal problems. For example, a strong philosophical concern about the problem of violence may serve as a way of helping the adolescent to deal with his own aggressive impulses. In brief, increased adolescent concern with the problem of moral values and standards is likely to involve cognitive, social, and intimate emotional aspects.

Cognitive Growth and Moral Development

By the time the average child reaches preadolescence, his thinking about moral issues has shifted away from rather simplistic **preconventional** modes (see pp. 444–450) and is more apt to be influenced by **conventional** moral reasoning (**148**). He has a "good boy" orientation, that is behavior approved by others is perceived as "good" and "right." At this stage, the child is likely to be concerned with conforming to the social order and with maintaining, supporting, and justifying this order (**147, 148, 149**).

Only with the onset of adolescence proper, however, and the further development of formal operational thought is the young person likely to reach the **postconventional** stages of moral development. These stages are characterized by "a major thrust toward autonomous moral principles which have validity and application apart from authority of the groups or persons who hold them and apart from the individual's identification with those persons or groups" (**148**, 1066–1067). At this juncture many adolescents, particularly the brighter and more sophisticated, may no longer be able to adopt without question the social or political beliefs of their parents (**65, 66, 67, 172**). They think about moral behavior in terms of general rights and standards which have been examined and agreed upon by society as a whole. There is a new-found "relativism of personal values and opinions and a corresponding emphasis upon procedural rules for reaching consensus. . . . The result is an emphasis upon the legal point of view, but with an emphasis upon the possibility of changing law in terms of rational considerations of social utility . . ." (**148**, 1067). As adolescence proceeds, orientation toward inner concerns and the individual's own conscience may increase—the individual may become less other-directed and more inner-directed—but still without clear rational or universal principles.

While many adolescents do not proceed beyond this stage, some go on to achieve what Kohlberg views as the highest stage of moral reasoning. At this stage, there is an effort to formulate and be guided by "abstract ethical principles appealing to logical comprehensiveness, universality, and consistency" (**148**, 1068), for example, the Golden Rule, Kant's categorical imperative in which "good" is no longer defined in conventional moral terms of approved behavior; a personal motive or action can be considered "good" only if its adoption by all other persons would work out successfully. The motivation for conformity to such principles is not social approbation, but rather consistent internalized moral standards; the principled individual conforms to these in order to avoid self-condemnation. When asked whether a husband should steal an expensive black-market drug from an exploitative druggist to save his wife's life, Steve, age 16, answered, "By the law of society he was wrong but by the law of nature or of God the druggist was wrong and the husband was justified. Human life is above financial gain. Regardless of who was dying, if it was a total stranger, man has a duty to save him from dying" (**147,** 244).

Only about 10 percent of young people over age 16 showed "clear principled" thinking, "but all these 10 percent were capable of formal-operational logical thought" (**148,** 1071). The attainment of an appropriate cognitive stage "is a necessary but not sufficient condition for attainment of the [corresponding] moral stage" (**148,** 1071).

Changing Societal Demands

Younger children live in a world which is relatively more homogeneous, more focused on the present, and more limited than that of adolescents. The younger child faces fewer demands for making moral choices; his life is circumscribed by a set of rules, established for the most part by his parents. Of course, he must learn to establish internal controls, but he does not ordinarily have to make value decisions (**62,** 172).

In contrast, the adolescent boy or girl must make choices. Not only is he himself changing, but his immediate social world and his relations with it are changing too. As he moves further into adolescence, the young person is confronted with an increasingly diverse world in which the opportunities and the necessity for choice are multiplied. He finds, for example, that there are many ways to live his life and that he must make choices. How is he going to earn a living? What sort of person does he eventually want to marry, if, in fact, he wants to marry at all? Such choices cannot be made independently of personal values. If an adolescent is strongly oriented toward helping others, he is likely to make a different career choice than if he places a high valuation on material success. If he believes more in freedom and autonomy, his choice will be different from that of a youth who is primarily concerned with security.

Moral Values and Intrapsychic Conflicts

Value conflicts are often " 'chosen' by adolescents for internal and usually unconscious reasons" (**62,** 85). Preoccupations with the moral issues of war and peace, for example, may stem from perfectly rational concerns with these important matters. But they may also reflect conflict about being able to handle the stronger aggressive impulses that are likely to accompany adolescence, particularly in boys. Analogously, an adolescent girl may develop a highly intellectualized philosophy of "free love," principally as a way of reassuring herself that she should not feel guilty about her own sexual impulses. Conflicts with parents about moral or political values and beliefs may reflect efforts to establish an independent identity or to express a deep resentment toward hostile or indifferent parents.

Consider the following case of an intellectually gifted adolescent boy who suddenly lost interest in his schoolwork, opted for the "hippie" life, and was preparing to go on the road.

> When he was taken to a psychological clinic by his parents, he offered a compelling indictment of the fakeries of the "Organization" society, . . . and the intake interviewer (also **au courant** in these matters) was persuaded that this was a social-philosophical rather than a personal crisis. The clinic staff thought something was fishy, nevertheless, and urged a more searching interview, which revealed that the boy's loss of interest had been preceded by a homosexual seduction by one of his teachers. Going on the road was simultaneously a flight from homosexual arousal, an unconscious seeking to repeat and master the trauma, a way of punishing the "elders," a self-punishment for having yielded, and no doubt much else. This tale is not told to debunk [the belief] that the prevailing ideology of adolescent discontent tells a great deal about the culture and about those adolescents attracted to it; nor is it meant to refute the "reality" of the protest or of adolescent values in general. Rather we mean to caution against simplistic appraisals of parent-peer conflicts, which are always a mixture of the social" and "psychological," the real and the unreal, the objective and the personal (62, 86).

In summary, the increased preoccupation with moral values and beliefs that characterizes many adolescents is likely to have its roots in expanded cognitive development; in increased, often contradictory, societal demands; and in intimate, often unconscious, intrapsychic concerns and conflicts.

Changing Religious Beliefs

The adolescent's religious beliefs also tend to reflect his accelerated cognitive development, becoming more abstract and less literal between the ages of 12 and 18 (39, 105, 151, 172, 202). For example, God comes to be considered more frequently as an abstract power and less frequently as a fatherly human being. Religious views also become more tolerant and less dogmatic (151, 172), and belief in the importance of religion, at least formal religion, declines (105).

Today's adolescents seem to place a somewhat greater emphasis than previous generations on personal, rather than institutionalized, religion (99, 105, 202, 239). This is consistent with their greater stress generally on personal values and relationships and on individual moral standards, accompanied by less reliance on traditional social beliefs and institutions. Even the young person who remains within the church is more likely than earlier generations to want to get away from rigid dogma and traditional forms (105).

An interesting, though still minor, recent movement involves the return to a fundamentalist religion among some young people, including some highly educated middle- and upper-middle-class adolescents. The increase in the number of "Jesus Freaks" (99, 212) may be related, at least partly, to disillusionment with more rationalistic approaches as "spiritually empty," and a turning back to a seemingly more comfortable, secure **conventional** mode of moral thought.

The Growth of Political Ideas

Ordinarily the boy or girl "begins adolescence incapable of complex political discourse—that is, mute on many issues, and when not mute, then simplistic, primitive, subject to fancies, unable to enter fully the realm of political ideas" (1, 1013).

By the end of adolescence, however, a dramatic change is frequently evident; many adolescents' grasp of the political world is recognizably adult. During the course of adolescence there is a significant shift in the direction of greater abstractness of political thought, a decline in authoritarian approaches to political questions, and an increase in the capacity for developing a reasonably consistent political ideology (1, 2, 3). For example, when confronted with questions about handling violations of the law, younger adolescents tend to be simplistic and authoritarian in their answers, stressing punishment and, if that does not work, more punishment. In contrast, older adolescents are more concerned with individual rights and consider alternative solutions to punishment, such as reform and rehabilitation. They also question the usefulness and fairness of the law or custom violated, distinguish between behavior and intent, and note the possibility that illegal acts may be a symptom of more fundamental problems.

When asked what is the purpose of laws, one 12-year-old replied, "If we had no laws, people could go around killing people." In contrast, one 16-year-old replied, "To insure safety and enforce the government," and another commented, "They are basically guidelines for people. . . ." (1, 1015).

Current Trends in Adolescent Values

Adolescent concerns with moral standards and values vary not only with age, but also from generation to generation. While there are important continuities in values between parents and children, it is also obvious that values become modified over time. Not all moral values are held with equal intensity. Some values give way to expediency when the pressure for compromise is great. More strongly held, central values, however, may be much more resistant to external pressures.

Significant, and probably growing, minorities of contemporary adolescents have become profoundly disillusioned by American society and its values, which they view variously as unjust, cruel, violent, hypocritical, superficial, impersonal, overly competitive, or immoral. Nevertheless, the average adolescent still retains many traditional values (81, 239). For example, a substantial majority of today's adolescents subscribe to such beliefs as the following: "competition encourages excellence," "the right to private property is sacred," "depending on how much character a person has, he can pretty well control what happens to him," "society needs some legally based authority in order to avoid chaos," and "compromise is essential to progress" (239). Approximately two out of three contemporary adolescents express the view that hard work leads to material success and that such success is worth striving for (10, 11, 105, 239).

However, even though the average adolescent has retained many traditional values, he is not overly impressed with the current state of society and its principal institutions (37, 105, 239). For example, only 22 percent of adolescents have a "great deal" of confidence in the government's ability to solve the problems of the 1970s, 54 percent have "some confidence, but not a lot," and 22 percent have "hardly any" confidence (239). A substantial majority believe that most of our social institutions, including big business, the military, political parties, and the mass media, are in need of reform (37, 239). It should be noted, however, that only a portion of this skepticism reflects a "generation gap." Although today's young are more critical of these institutions than their parents, adults have also shown an attitude shift recently in the direction of greater skepticism (10, 11, 108, 199).

The current generation of adolescents appears to have a greater concern than previous generations of young people with such issues as socioeconomic discrimination, racial prejudice, and pollution of the environment; and less concern with such matters as military preparedness and space exploration (11, 106). They are increasingly favorable to school integration and to having blacks or other minority group members as neighbors (10, 11, 108, 172). Their attitudes seem to reflect flexibility, tolerance, and lack of prejudice, more than crusading zeal.

This attitude of relative tolerance, of a greater willingness to let others "do their own thing," pervades much of adolescent thinking, younger and older alike, and is accompanied by a high valuation of open, honest, and "meaningful" interpersonal relationships. For instance, adolescents are more tolerant than their parents of premarital sexual relationships in which love and commitment are present, but they appear generally opposed to promiscuity, both in principle and in behavior (see pp. 569–572). Today's adolescents reveal a pervasive need for a world in which there is more true friendship and love (105, 239). Indeed, no other values are as strongly and consistently held.

Most adolescents are interested in job success as conventionally defined, but they are less concerned with achieving status and recognition by society in their future jobs than earlier generations were. They want to find work that is "meaningful" and enjoyable and in which they can have pride (see pp. 588–589).

Two other characteristics of current adolescents deserve brief mention, although they are difficult to document. Despite their often impressive intellectual capability, many adolescents today appear less knowledgeable about the past and less convinced that there are lessons to be learned from history. They are more inclined to view the future as either unpredictable or, at best, full of options that need not be explored yet. Relatively, though only relatively, they do appear to be more of a "now" generation (51).

In addition, although both older adults and adolescents are confronted currently with a society in turmoil, many adults, using their own childhood experiences as a frame of reference, view this unhappy state of affairs as a deviation from a subjective conception of "normality." In contrast, having no such frame of reference, their children view the uncertainties of the world as "normal," not as a deviation from prior expectancies, for they have "always" existed (51). Adolescents between 13 and 17 describe the world they live in as "warlike," "impersonal," "competitive," "fast-moving," and fraught with constant change (107).

While parents frequently cling nostalgically to the symbols of a simpler, more rational past, the "now" generation looks for ways of living in the present, for finding meaning in uncertainty and irrationality (51). They look for meaning in seeming meaninglessness—"happenings," elaborate "put-ons" in dress and manner, distortions of "reality" in light shows and movies, the recent preoccupation with astrology (50, 51).

ALIENATION

It has become fashionable in recent years to speak of youth who in one way or another do not "fit in" as being "alienated." By such labeling we may gain the illusion that we have said something significant, but all we have really done is to imply that "something is wrong somewhere," that some relationships have been lost. Unless we can go further and specify what the alienated individual has lost, what he is alienated from, we have accomplished little (142). Has the alienation been imposed on the individual largely by external forces or does it originate primarily within himself? We need to know what new relationships, if any, have replaced those which have been lost and how the alienation is expressed.

> In one sense the revolutionary and psychotic are both highly alienated from the norms and values of their society—both reject these norms and values. Yet there is a vast difference in the way their rejection is expressed: the revolutionary actively attempts to transform his society; the psychotic has undergone a regressive self-transformation that leaves his society relatively unaffected (142, 454).

One major way of classifying alienations is, therefore, according to their mode—whether they involve an attempt to transform the world or whether they involve self-transformations.

Varieties of Alienation

Some aspects of alienation tend to be relatively widespread in a particular culture, while others tend to be more limited to particular subgroups. At present, there is a rather widespread feeling of alienation from formal religious faith and from the notion of a meaningful and orderly universe, with a personal God at its center. This feeling of "existential outcastness" (142), of the essential lack of any absolute meaning in the universe as a whole, can be painful indeed and may result in feelings of deprivation and outrage.

Many adolescents also share what have been called **developmental estrangements:** a sense of alienation or loss that comes with the abandonment of childish ties to one's parents, one's childhood self, and, indeed, the whole world of childhood —an egocentric world which seems to have been created specifically for the child. Alienation may also take the form of a sense of estrangement from what is vaguely felt to be one's "real self," and much of what one does therefore appears empty, flat, and devoid of meaning (142).

Probably the most prominently discussed form of alienation among today's adolescents and youth, however, involves an "explicit rejection of traditional American culture" (142, 465). Most of the adolescents we will discuss in the remainder of this chapter share a common disillusionment with the goals, values, practices, and accomplishments of contemporary society. Nevertheless, there may be important differences in the sources of alienation and in the ways in which it is expressed. The economically favored middle- or upper-class youth may be reacting against what he perceives as the ultimate futility of materialistic rewards and social status as well as the shallowness and hypocrisy of many of the values and practices of contemporary society.

In contrast, for lower-class minority and poor white youth who have suffered economic deprivation and ethnic discrimination, alienation is, to a great extent, imposed by society. Quite simply, these youth are prevented by the accident of birth and by discrimination from sharing in the affluent society that they see all about them and on the ever-present television screen that often occupies a central place in even the poorest homes. The great majority of adolescents in these disadvantaged groups (e.g., blacks, Spanish-speaking persons of Mexican-American or Puerto Rican heritage, Appalachian whites, American Indians) are born into the "culture of poverty," whether in urban ghettos, in rural slums, or on reservations.

Poorly prepared intellectually, psychologically, and socially, the disadvantaged child enters overcrowded, run-down schools. Under these conditions, he may fail to make normal school progress and may drop out of school as soon as he is able to. Few jobs are likely to be available at his skill level, and if he is also a member of an ethnically segregated minority, he may find himself discriminated against even in jobs for which he is qualified. For such a youth, the idea of the American dream becomes merely a nightmare.

Still worse, such a young person may become alienated, not only from the dominant American culture, but from himself; he may be cut off from the possibility of developing a clearly defined, self-confident, normally assertive personal and cultural identity. Even while resenting the discrimination to which he has been subjected by the dominant majority in society, he may come to accept, at least

partially, many of its attitudes, values, and beliefs. This may result in a loss of self-esteem, a negative identity (50, 70, 71), and an alienation from the self (43, 59, 64, 70, 129, 177, 188, 211). Fortunately, with the recent ascendance of racial and ethnic pride, particularly among young people, negative perceptions of one's own minority or ethnic group appear to be declining (16, 34, 49, 75) and self-esteem is increasing (16, 162, 177, 188, 230).

The "New" Alienation

In contrast to the alienation of the poor or the victims of racial or ethnic discrimination, there is a special kind of alienation that has increasingly affected the "nonrejected" in the past decade. A significant minority of middle- and upper-class youth have not been "going along" with prevailing social values and practices, despite their privileged socioeconomic status. The roots of the alienation of some young people derive to an important degree from particular kinds of developmental experiences, such as disturbed parent-child relationships, that would be likely to result in alienation in most societies (142, 172). The special characteristics and conflicts of contemporary society play a major role in the alienation of others.

For some youth the alienation may be quite specific; it may involve rejecting a specific aspect of the culture, such as the recent war in Indochina, racial and economic discrimination, while still accepting the climate of society as a whole.

For others alienation may be both deep and pervasive. Obviously, too, there are differences in the individual's response to alienating aspects of society. Some youth may find positive substitutes for alienation, for example, social service or political activities, and may pursue them within the framework of the established social order. Others may feel that the only way to attack and modify the social structure lies outside the traditional processes of social change (172).

Still other youth may respond to their alienation by withdrawing from the society as a whole. This sometimes may involve deep despair, apathy, or defeat, without any meaningful alternative commitment to relieve their feelings of alienation. A number of the youthful psychiatric casualties of our time fall in this category. Others may find only a blind, angry, disorganized, self-defeating striking back—if this can properly be called an alternative—as in the case of some kinds of delinquents (see pp. 633–636).

Still other youth may, while expressing their alienation from society, continue to search for meaningful private alternatives within themselves or within a separate subculture of like-minded individuals. Here one may find youth who, while perhaps outwardly inconspicuous, are attempting to find meaning as individuals in inner exploration, in meditation, in Eastern religions, in the private pursuit of art, music, or poetry, or in a return—or an escape—to the "simple life" of farm or rural commune (50, 51, 120).

Alienation and Adolescent "Counterculture"

According to a recent nationwide survey (239), more than one-fifth of all youth (and more than one-third of college youth) expressed the belief that their "own personal values and point of view" are **not** "shared by most Americans today." An additional one-third were "not certain." Approximately two young people in five think that ours is a "sick society," and the majority of these express doubts about the ability of the "system" to make needed changes peacefully through normal channels (87, 105, 240).

These adolescents and youth view themselves as confronted by a "technocratic" (194), "postindustrial" (85), or "mass" society—one in which the goals of technological progress and economic affluence are relentlessly pursued without regard to the human costs or "the quality of the environment" (50). This society often seems to them to value things more than people, achieving affluence for the few at the expense of the disenfranchised poor (50). The impersonal, highly specialized, status-oriented, hierarchical organizations (big business, government, education, the military) are regarded as inimical to values they hold strongly (50).

Values of Alienated Middle-Class Youth Among the most strongly held values of this group are: intimacy ("love," both individual and communal), individuality (freedom to know and to be oneself), autonomy (freedom from coercion and freedom to act independently), and honesty (lack of pretense). Conversely, these young people tend to question or reject such values and practices as relentless competition and status seeking, "role-playing games" that involve dissimulation and manipulation of others for one's own ends, and respect for authority as authority (that is, based on power or assigned status, rather than on competence, talents, wisdom, or experience).

In their thinking they emphasize immediate experience, rather than delayed gratification—the more traditional, middle-class Protestant ethic of struggle and sacrifice now for a presumably brighter tomorrow. There are, of course, other values and approaches that distinguish this youthful counterculture. These may include an ahistorical orientation, skepticism about intellectualism or even **rationality** for its own sake, and a corresponding attraction to feeling, sensory stimulation, mysticism, the "camp" or absurd (50).

Such trends appear to characterize large numbers of the disenchanted minority of advantaged adolescents and youth, but differences in relative emphasis obviously occur in different subgroups—social and political activists, the "culturally alienated," hippies and other "social dropouts," even some delinquents. The nature of some of these differences will be explored in succeeding sections.

ALTERNATIVE LIFE STYLES: ACTIVISM VERSUS DROPPING OUT

In recent years considerable attention has been focused both upon youthful activists (particularly left-oriented, political student activists) and upon social dropouts (such as the "beats" of the 1950s and the hippies and related groups of the 1960s). While current distinctions between activists and social dropouts are not as tidy or clearcut as they appeared in the middle and late 1960s (50, 139), there are still fundamental differences in their modes of response.

Activist Youth: Self-Destructive Rebellion or a "Striving to Thrive?"

Some observers (58, 74) regard youthful activism and dissent, particularly student activism, as basically self-destructive and socially harmful, more a manifestation of personal maladjustment than a mature response to social pathology. Others, equally competent, consider the opposite to be the case. They believe that salvaging a "sick society" depends on the efforts of dedicated youthful activists, who are not "sick" but unusually intelligent, mature, psychologically resilient, and socially effective (18, 25, 140, 141, 197).

Studies of activist students of the 1960s indicated that, in general, they were brighter than their nonactivist peers, more successful academically, more flexible, more individualistic, and more autonomous (118, 207, 225). They were also more anxious, more imaginative, more tolerant of ambiguity, more concerned with reflective and abstract thinking in the areas of art, literature, music, and philosophy, and more liberal and less conventional in religious values (77, 118). They came largely from upper-status, professional families with a relatively high income (77, 219) and high levels of parental education (225). Student activism was clearly not a response to social rejection and exploitation. Moreover, parents of activists emerged from these studies as more permissive than those of nonactivists, and according to their activist sons and daughters were milder, warmer, more lenient, and less strict in their child-rearing practices (77). The likelihood of parents "intervening strongly" in the decisions of their adolescent sons and daughters was found to be greater among nonactivist parents.

The views of activist students, rather than being in opposition to those of their parents, tended to parallel them. For example, the attitudes of the fathers of activist sons, as reflected in their responses to questions on various social issues, were more liberal than those of the fathers of nonactivist sons. Activist sons appeared to share their father's liberal values, but to carry them further and to act on them in a more militant or "radical" fashion (77).

Many of these earlier studies suffered from a variety of practical limitations: (1) they were restricted largely to college youth, and often to those from "elite" colleges and universities; (2) they were largely restricted to one (early) time period in a rapidly changing social climate; and (3) perhaps of greatest importance, many studies only compared the more visible, liberal, or left-oriented activists with students in general (50). Consequently, it was not possible to determine whether the characteristics of these liberal or left-oriented activists were primarily a function of their ideology (whether activist or not), their activism (regardless of ideological orientation), or some combination of the two.

More recent studies (22, 23, 144, 145, 155, 239, 240) have attempted to overcome some of these limitations, and their findings suggest the wisdom of more cautious and qualified generalizations. In one such investigation (143) activist students (regardless of ideological orientation) were found to be more autonomous, ascendant, and assertive than nonactivist students and to value leadership more. They also emerged as more sociable and less in need of support and nurturance.

Ideologically disparate students (regardless of whether they were activist or not) differed from one another in several ways. Left-oriented students placed relatively little value on conformity and recognition, but relatively great value on independence. "In not valuing conformity, they stood together with middle-oriented students, whereas in valuing independence, they stood together with rightist students" (144, 81). Right-oriented students valued leadership more highly than those who were either middle- or left-oriented. Left-oriented students were more sensitive and subjective and manifested more concern for the welfare of others than middle-of-the-road students, who in turn showed more concern than right-oriented students (23, 155).

The activism-ideology subgroups did not differ significantly on measures of intelligence, responsibility, seriousness of purpose, perseverance, or emotional stability.

The notion that left activists approach being "psychological noblemen," as posited by [some investigators] (**19, 135**), or the opposite notion put forth by less sympathetic sources that left activists are maladjusted and playing out authority conflicts, are both probably exaggerations and oversimplifications (**145**, 80).

Radical Dissent versus Socially Oriented Activism

Left-of-center activists, who were among the subjects in one study, fell into two groups, **radical dissenters** ("revolutionaries") and **moderate reformers.** Revolutionary youth agreed on the need for radical, even violent change, feeling that the "social system is too rotten for repair" (**239**). Moderate reformers, in contrast, tended to feel that most social institutions are badly in need of reform, but that change is possible without destroying these institutions. Many of this group were committed to positive efforts to ameliorate social ills by their individual efforts.

As a group, the revolutionaries rejected all traditional values of American culture. They opposed any interference with their personal freedom or social constraints imposed for "moral" reasons. They felt that personal dress and grooming are exclusively personal matters and that drug use, abortion, homosexuality between consulting adults, and premarital or extramarital relations are not moral or public issues.

Moderate reformers felt strongly that big business "is overly concerned with profits and not with public responsibility," that "economic well being in this country is unjustly and unfairly distributed," and that we are basically "a racist nation." However, unlike the revolutionaries, the moderate reformers did not believe that traditional social institutions should be done away with.

The moderate reformers' position on more personal values was also less extreme than the revolutionaries'. While a majority felt that abortion and much sexual behavior were not moral issues, they felt that extramarital relations were wrong, and said they could "accept easily" prohibitions against LSD and other drugs (excluding marijuana).

The same study included subjects classified as **conservative.** As would be expected, a larger percentage of this group subscribed to traditional values. They believed strongly that competition encourages excellence, that people should provide for themselves and not lean on friends, and that the right to private property is sacred. Of all subgroups, conservatives expressed least concern about the social restraints imposed by society; the majority stated that they could "accept easily" requirements for conformity in matters of dress, prohibitions against marijuana, LSD, and other drugs, and the power and authority of the police and employers. Substantial majorities of conservative youth rejected, as morally wrong, abortion, relations between consenting homosexuals, and premarital relations. At least three-fourths said that "patriotism," "living a clean, moral life," education, and religion are "very important."

Nevertheless, like other young people, the great majority of conservatives stated that they would welcome more emphasis on friendliness and neighborliness, love, and privacy (see pp. 609–610). Less than half said they could "easily accept" abiding by laws they didn't agree with, having little decision-making power in the first few years of a job, or having to show outward conformity for the sake of career advancement.

Parent-Child Relationships, Activism, and Dissent

Undoubtedly many activist youth have had positive and rewarding relationships with liberally oriented parents, and their activism may reflect, to varying degrees, identification with and extensions of parental values. However, there is little justification for assuming that this is nearly always the case or, indeed, for assuming that other groups of young people, including nonactivists, have not had their share of positive and rewarding parent-child relationships and identification with parental values. Several extensive recent investigations (**22, 239, 240**) show that conservative and middle-of-the-road youth are just as likely as activists and social dissenters to get along well with parents, share their basic values, and report close childhood ties with them. Furthermore, activists, even left-of-center activists, are by no means a homogeneous group.

> . . . there are obviously many individuals with . . . healthy characteristics who are not activists, just as there are many within the group of activists who do have definite

psychopathologies. A variety of individuals with highly diverse talents and motivations are bound to be involved in any social movement; global descriptions are certain to be oversimplified (**197,** 182).

The Social Dropouts

Contrary to much popular opinion, the "social dropout" is not a new phenomenon. In every society there are people who do not share the values of the dominant social order and who elect to find their own way of life outside it. Early American history contains numerous examples of individuals and groups, for example, some of the early communal settlements, who in Thoreau's words, "hear a different drummer." In our own time, the "beat" generation antedated that of the hippies (**206**). The alternatives sought by social dropouts may be purposeful and well-defined or they may be aimless, confused, and defined at least as much by what is being escaped from as by what is being sought.

"The Hippie Modality" There was, and is, no single type of hippie. Even in the relatively early years of the movement in the late 1960s, there were those who were more philosophically oriented, as well as the "groovers" and teeny-boppers who drifted aimlessly, searching principally for "kicks" (**50, 206, 241**). As the movement became publicized and commercialized, there were increasing numbers of pseudohippies and "plastic" or part-time (usually younger) "summer" hippies.

Despite such wide variations, a number of salient features characterized a majority of the original or "true" hippies. Most of them were white, ranged in age from about 18 to 26 years (with an approximate mean of 22 years for males and 20 years for females), and came from middle- or upper-middle-class urban or suburban backgrounds (**38, 184, 186, 241**). Their parents tended to be socially active, politically moderate, and success-oriented—in short, "pillars of the community" (**184**).

Nevertheless, these young people showed a common aversion to what they perceived as the aggressive, highly competitive, conformity-demanding nature of modern society, with its emphasis on social status and material success (**50**). Not only did they view these values as hollow and meaningless, "a real hang-up," but as inimical to other values that they held: love; gentleness; honesty; an immediate relatedness and sharing between people, unencumbered by competition or role-playing; an emphasis on individual self-expression ("doing your own thing"); heightened sensory awareness, typically aided by drugs; an appreciation of nature and direct experience; an antirational, antiintellectual orientation; and a presumed lack of social or sexual inhibitions (**7, 36, 60, 172, 185, 186**).

Obviously, many of these are values that many adults either admire or envy, but which they find difficult or impossible to express or fulfill (**50**). Many adults subscribe to the principles of "love thy neighbor as thyself," "thou shalt not kill," and "peace on earth to men of good will." And, many who have struggled long and hard to achieve financial security and social status in a highly competitive society have discovered, after they achieved these goals, that they are not enough to produce a sense of meaningful personal fulfillment (**50**).

This, then, is one side of the coin. The obsessional and frequently excessive concern of many adults with the hippie movement probably tells us more about the deficiencies of our society than about the hippies themselves. But there is another side.

The most laudable values of the hippie movement have proven no easier to achieve outside of the organized social system than within it. Further, hippie culture had several inherent flaws. It was essentially parasitic, that is, it depended basically upon the continued existence of the society it rejected. Like other mortals, hippies must eat, and this meant that most either had to obtain part-time jobs in the "system," panhandle, or solicit money from "square" parents back home (**36, 206**). A few hippies came close to "having it both ways"—notably the more sucessful acid-rock musicians and some artists and craftsmen—but most did not. In its ultimate dependence on the continuation of a society it claimed to reject, the hippie movement probably contained the seeds of its own destruction.

Another central characteristic of the hippie culture from its inception was its dependence on drugs; it has always been a drug culture—a fact appreciated by hippies themselves, but frequently not fully grasped by outsiders (**36**). Among 200 hippies surveyed in San Francisco's Haight-Ashbury district, the average number of psychedelic trips on LSD was 26. The average hippie had smoked hashish or marijuana 6.7 times per week, with some having smoked as many as 35 times. About two-thirds said they had also used stimulants such as methedrine and dexadrine (**36**).

Aside from the dangers of some of these drugs (see pp. 622–629), there is a real question as to whether there is any chemical shortcut to true creativity and meaningful, heightened inner experience. For the chronic drug user, it is often too easy to confuse self-indulgence, impulsivity, apathy, and lack of intellectual discipline with creativity.

Further, the proclaimed values of the hippies, such as love, cannot always be taken at face value. Certainly some hippies, particularly the more mature, did indeed appear to display "love" in the traditional Judeo-Christian sense, through gentleness, tolerance, and concern for the welfare of others. But in many cases, "love" seems to have emerged in practice more as a matter of simple tolerance or dependent, narcissistic gratification, or sometimes even indifference, regarding others. Often it meant simply a way of relating directly to others with a minimum of competitive role playing, and by sharing common experiences: turning on with drugs, listening to music, walking in the park. A stranger might be welcome to drop into someone's pad, such food or drugs as there are might be shared with him, and no one would demand to know who he was or where he was from. However, this same stranger might leave a day, a week, or a month later, and there would be little feeling of loss. Many hippies have proclaimed, as one stated, that

"Christ was a very groovy cat" (36), but too often they have appeared to lack the self-discipline, the stable sort of psychological commitment, and the capacity for true identification and emotional involvement with others that being "your brother's keeper" or "loving others as yourself" requires.

The apparent, proudly proclaimed happiness of the original hippie—the assertion that everything was "groovy"—was, in many cases, a matter of self-deception and was destined to become more so with the passage of time. The hippies' off-beat clothes, the gay beads, the psychedelic designs, the flowers, the put-ons, the sometimes perceptive humor (e.g., "better living through chemistry," "kill for peace"), the leisure, the self-indulgence, the frequently proclaimed (but not as frequently achieved) sexual freedom, the drug highs, and the freedom from "the rat race" might be misleading.

Many of the hippie subjects of one study were characterized by "ego deficits," manifested by an "inability of these subjects to understand, organize, or integrate the events of their lives" (184, 22). Despite their relatively high intelligence test scores (ranging from bright-normal to superior, with a mean IQ of 119) and generally good earlier academic records (184), many of these young people displayed deficiencies in cognitive functioning—in recalling the events of their childhood, in sustaining attention, tendencies toward both "overconcreteness" and "overabstractness" in their thinking, and a marked lack of critical judgment (38). In addition, a majority showed little frustration tolerance, preferring to avoid "hassles" (often with the aid of drugs), rather than facing up to emotionally difficult situations.

Most striking, however, was the frequency of inadequacies in establishing interpersonal relationships: "A universally reported experience of our subjects is a profound sense of psychological distance from others which often dates back to their earliest memories of childhood" (38, 7). Despite their "normal" middle-class backgrounds, these young people had typically been subjected to unusually high degrees of stimulation, stress, and trauma (184, 186, 213), particularly during middle childhood—intense conflicts between parents; accidents and serious illnesses; a loss of parents or siblings through death, divorce, or desertion; chronic parental illness or alcoholism; frequent changes of residence; sexual molestation; exposure to violence. "What particularly characterizes their accounts of childhood . . . is their sense of living amidst great confusion, chaos, and disorganization, and their inability to escape for even brief periods to a calmer and more benign environment" (184, 15).

What has happened to the original hippies? An ongoing investigation (221) of the subsequent fate of a sample of a large number of hippies, begun shortly after 1967, shows that, as a group, they have "outwardly disengaged themselves from the hippie culture in terms of residence, occupation, and educational pursuits" (221, 4). Most have moved out of hippie neighborhoods, and 75 percent are currently employed at least part-time (as contrasted with 17 percent at the beginning of the study). Approximately one-third have returned to school. Drug use, particularly of the stronger hallucinogens and amphetamines ("speed"), has declined somewhat, reflecting a "general trend away from mind-altering drugs to those with a greater effect on mood and affect" (221, 7).

At the same time, it would be a mistake to conclude that these young people have reembraced "establishment" attitudes. They tend to have minimally stressful jobs, below the level expected from their educational achievements (221). Those who are back in college are primarily in such areas as the arts and humanities and, to some extent, the "helping" occupations, rather than the natural sciences or business. Most still continue to be regular users of marijuana, hashish, and alcohol (221). They "refuse to participate in political activities and see organized politics as a farce" (221, 9), and most reject all forms of western religion. In brief, although their life styles appear to have become more conventional, "their ideology remains hip" (221, 9).

ADOLESCENTS AND DRUGS

There is probably no other area in which there is as wide a "generation gap" between some groups of adults and some groups of adolescents as there is in attitudes toward various drugs (9, 102). If an investigator reports that effects of a particular drug appear to be minimal, some groups will react to this information with a sense of outrage, accusing the investigator of promoting moral decay. If, on the other hand, he finds a drug to have potentially serious consequences for health or psychological well-being, other groups will discredit the results, accusing the investigator of "copping out" to the "establishment."

Evaluation of the effects of drugs often involves not only scientific knowledge, but value judgments as well. The current emotion-laden controversy over drugs in our society is not merely a dispute about the specific effects of various drugs. It also reflects a deep division on fundamental social values, of which drugs may serve as a convenient, tangible symbol (102, 130).

Drug Use in Contemporary Society

Drug use in our culture is not new. Our society has for some years now been becoming increasingly a "drug culture." One-quarter to one-third of all medical prescriptions now written in this country are for "pep" pills (amphetamines) or tranquilizers, far in excess of what many responsible physicians consider medically justifiable (50, 79). Television currently bombards viewers with insistent messages that relief for almost anything—anxiety, depression, fatigue, restlessness—is just "a swallow away." The commercial slogan "Better living through chemistry" appears to have been adopted by our society in more ways than were intended.

The adult who is smoking cigarettes, drinking two martinis at lunch, taking amphetamines to restore his energy, tranquilizers to relax, and barbiturates to sleep is just as surely a product of a "drug culture" as the adolescent drug user seeking a new "high" (50). Elementary and high school students whose parents take tranquilizers are twice as likely to smoke marijuana and three times as likely to use stronger hallucinogens as those whose parents do not (190, 191, 205).

Marijuana

Among the growing number of adolescents who have experimented with one or another illicit drug, marijuana users account for the greatest percentage by far. Most adolescents appear to have gotten the messages that LSD can be "a bad trip," "Speed kills," and heroin and other "hard" narcotics are, in the words of one ghetto 14-year-old, a "one-way trip to nowhere" (50, 191, 214, 215, 239).

According to an authoritative survey conducted in 1972 (190, 191), at least 24 million persons in this country had tried marijuana and an estimated 8 million still use it. The largest percentage of those who have ever used marijuana fall into the category of "experimenters," while the smallest percentage fall into the category of "heavy users." Marijuana usage is most frequent among youth, although increasing numbers of adults, particularly young adults, are using or have used it (see

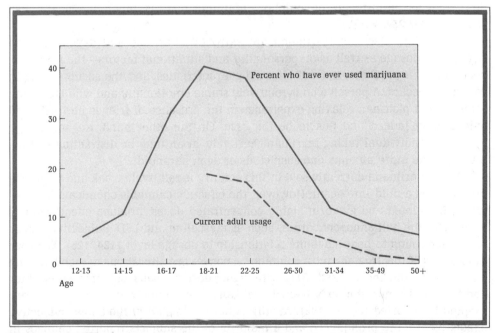

Figure 13.1 Marijuana experience by age. (From R. P. Shafer et al. **Marihuana: a signal of misunderstanding. The official report of the National Commission on Marihuana and Drug Abuse.** New York: New American Library, 1972.)

Fig. 13.1). The incidence is higher among males, those with more education, and those in the east and west, as opposed to the midwest and south (**28, 29, 30, 88, 191**).

Overall incidence is considerably higher among college students than the population at large. A 1967 Gallup survey showed that 5 percent of all college students had tried marijuana (**86**); by 1969 this figure had risen to 22 percent; by 1970, it had almost doubled again to 42 percent (**169, 215**); by 1972, 51 percent of all college students reported having tried marijuana at least once (**86**).

Effects of Marijuana Marijuana is not a narcotic and not physiologically addictive (**101, 102, 190, 191**); nor does it appear likely to lead to the use of hard drugs, such as heroin (**190, 191**). Its short term physical effects in normal dosage levels are not particularly remarkable (**50, 101, 102, 227**): an increase in pulse rate, some alteration of blood pressure, and some minimal loss in muscle strength and steadiness (**101, 190, 227**). Perhaps the most dramatic physical effect is a marked increase in appetite 30 to 60 minutes after ingestion (**102, 227**). There is no evidence of genetic damage or long-term physical effects, except possibly lung damage in chronic users (**101, 134, 190, 191**).

The degree of impairment of cognitive and psychomotor performance tends to be related to strength of the dose and there are wide individual differences. At low dosage levels, impairment is usually minimal on simple or familiar tasks; at higher dosage levels, performance of complex, unfamiliar tasks is impaired (**50, 101, 190, 226, 227, 233, 234, 235**).

Subjective effects of marijuana are extremely variable and depend on the strength of dosage as well as on personality and situational factors—the user's expectations, his psychological and physical characteristics, and the social setting in which use occurs. A person who is relatively stable emotionally and who is looking forward to a pleasant, relaxing experience in the presence of friends he trusts and enjoys, may indeed find this to be the case. On the other hand, an anxious or suspicious individual taking marijuana furtively in an ugly or distracting setting, may become more anxious and suspicious or even paranoid.

Most marijuana currently sold in this country is relatively weak and functions primarily as a mild intoxicant. However, the effective **cannabis** chemicals in marijuana, if isolated and given in highly concentrated doses, produce effects similar to those of the hallucinogenic drugs, such as mescaline and LSD. Subjective effects have been found to bear a definite relationship to dosage level (**124, 125**). For very mild levels of the drug, the most common responses are alterations in mood, feeling happy, gay, silly, and relaxed (**31**). With higher dosage levels, colors seem brighter and hearing keener, the body feels lighter, and alterations in time perception are frequently reported (**33, 35, 102**). At still higher levels, "all of the above subjective effects were more pronounced and a majority of the subjects reported changes in body image, illusions, delusions, and hallucinations—toxic reactions which occur with excessive dosage of many chemicals which affect the nervous system" (**174, 99**).

Marijuana smoking by psychologically unstable individuals or under unfavorable circumstances (when there are "bad vibrations") may lead, at least temporarily, to suspiciousness, terror, paranoia, or depression (33, 190). Further, marijuana, especially in larger doses, may produce changes in one's body image and subjective sensations, as well as a feeling of "loss of bodily boundaries" or fusion with the surroundings (33, 35). While many users view this as pleasurable or even a philosophically important goal, others who fear loss of control—or more seriously, have only a tenuous contact with reality—may experience extensive psychological distress (50). Acute toxic psychotic reactions are rare, especially at low dosage levels, but they can and sometimes do occur in physiologically or psychologically susceptible individuals (137, 191, 217, 234). In rare instances, marijuana apparently serves as a triggering mechanism for a return of symptoms, including hallucinations, experienced by LSD users on a previous "trip."

Although marijuana is not addictive, psychological dependence upon the drug can become a serious problem for a minority of users. Probably not more than 5 percent of marijuana users are chronic users or "potheads." However, for such a person, marijuana can present real dangers, comparable in severity to those of the chronic alcoholic (33, 50, 190, 191, 214, 215).

Personal Characteristics of Marijuana Users Intermittent marijuana users and experimenters are generally conventional in most respects, liberal politically and socially, and interested in education for personal improvement rather than for recognition or high grades. They are likely to be self-expressive, intellectually and culturally oriented, creative, and flexible, interested in searching for new experiences (104, 191). In contrast, heavy users seem to need the drug experience more often. Their marijuana use appears motivated not only by curiosity and an urge to share a social experience, but also by a desire for "kicks," "expansion of awareness and understanding," and relief of anxiety or boredom (191). Generally, the heavy marijuana users' life style, activities, values, and attitudes are unconventional. They tend to be pessimistic, insecure, irresponsible, restless, nonconforming, immature, resistant to authority, impulsive, pleasure-seeking, and oriented toward immediate gratification and individual expression (191). At the same time, however, they tend to be "curious, socially perceptive, skillful and sensitive to the needs of others, and possess broadly based . . . interests" (191, 45–46). Very heavy users tend to lose interest in almost all activities and are characterized by extreme lethargy and increasing deterioration of social behavior (191).

Other Drugs

Young people are considerably more wary of other drugs than they are of marijuana (191, 214, 215, 239). While approximately half of all college students have tried marijuana, less than one in five had tried amphetamines (speed), barbiturates, LSD (acid), or hard drugs. Only 1 percent or less stated that they used barbiturates, LSD, or hard drugs frequently, as compared with 13 percent for marijuana (214, 215). Only a very small minority appear to have used barbiturates and amphetamines in massive doses for "kicks"—amphetamines or speed ("uppers") to get high and barbiturates ("downers") to come down from a trip. In contrast, LSD and other potent hallucinogens tend to be used primarily either for a mystical experience ("greater insight into myself") or for "kicks." Use of heroin and other hard drugs by middle-class college students is still relatively rare.

Among high school and junior high school students use of marijuana, amphetamines, LSD, mescaline, and peyote is lower than among college students, but use of heroin is twice as great (191). Over 1.5 million Americans 17 and under, or 6 percent, have at least tried heroin, compared to 3 percent for college students and less than 5 percent for all persons 18 and older (191, 214, 215, 239). In our view, younger adolescent drug users are the greatest single source of concern. Their ego development and search for an identity of their own is at a critical stage, and they generally possess poorer judgment and less knowledge. For these reasons, they may be more susceptible to extremely dangerous and ill-considered practices. Youth workers are encountering increasing numbers of multiple, indiscriminate, almost constant drug use, even including heroin, among preadolescent "teeny boppers," "mini-flower children," and youthful runaways.

The "Pills" The problems posed by the "pills"—barbiturates, tranquilizers, and amphetamines—vary from one category to another. All these drugs are clearly overused, both by adolescents and adults.

The barbiturates (sleeping pills) account for over 3000 accidental or intentional deaths a year in this country alone, but habituation and addiction are far greater problems (26, 89). As nonspecific general depressants (174), barbiturates do not provide a true "high" and, after a brief period of relaxation and apparent freedom from tension, they provide only physical and mental lassitude. Barbiturate addiction is characterized by intellectual impairment, self-neglect, slurred speech, tremor, defective judgment, drowsiness, emotional lability, bizzare behavior, and muscular incoordination (82, 89, 98, 174). Barbiturates are taken for "kicks" mostly by younger, more indiscriminate users.

The amphetamines ("pep" pills, "speed") "produce effects resembling those resulting from stimulation of the sympathetic nervous system" (174, 88). These drugs are not physiologically addictive, but they may be psychologically habituating and extremely dangerous physically. Increased dosage levels may be necessary to maintain feelings of energy and well-being and result in marked increases in nervousness and insomnia (174). Hence, an alternating vicious cycle between amphetamines and barbiturates frequently characterizes heavy users. Continued heavy usage may produce impairments of judgment and intellectual functioning, aggressive or violent behavior, incoordination and hallucinations (33, 89, 98, 174), extreme irritability, and suspicious or paranoid feelings (21, 41, 174). In the words of one "speed freak,"

> I make lots of plans, but I don't ever carry any of them out. I get into this megalomaniac bag about 5 hours into speed, and I'll build these mountainous castles in my mind, all the far-out things I'm going to do, and all the money I'm going to make. I'll be driving a Rolls Royce and have two speed labs going at once, a heroin refining plant, my own private two-engine plane . . . and when I start to come down I realize that none of it is going to exist and it's like someone pulled the bottom out of your brain. I feel empty and suicidal in about 4 or 5 hours (21, 22).

Overdoses (frequently resulting from "mainlining," or injection of the drug into a vein) may lead to convulsions, coma, and cerebral hemorrhage (174). As the hippies succinctly, and correctly, state, "speed kills."

LSD and Other Hallucinogens The hallucinogens vary from mild (aeroplane glue, nutmeg, marijuana, morning glory seeds) to moderate (psilocybin, mescaline, peyote—the Indian ceremonial drug) to highly potent (LSD-25).

There appear to be two broad extremes of users of hallucinogenic drugs. One consists of intellectuals, artists, and other creative (or pseudocreative) people who view hallucinogens as providing aesthetic, religious, and mystical experiences (an "expansion of consciousness" and a deepening of insight into themselves). At the other extreme are nonacademic, rootless adolescents who see these drugs simply as an explosive way of becoming "high" or "getting their kicks."

Use of LSD may lead to experiences of a sense of timelessness, vivid panoramic visual hallucinations of fantastic brightness and depth, a heightening and blocking of sensory experience, the feeling that superior and lasting insights are emerging, and feelings of a loss of individual identity, together with a feeling of unity with other human beings, animals, inanimate objects, and the universe in general. While there is little doubt that many LSD users sincerely have these feelings, there is also no evidence that its use increases creativity or artistic productivity.

The effects of LSD vary from one individual and from one situation to another and are highly unpredictable. An LSD "trip" may also produce bizarre and frightening images, a sense of isolation and depersonalization, acute panic, and paranoia. In psychologically unstable individuals, it may sometimes precipitate an acute psychosis (46, 174, 233).

Further, there is still very little understanding of the long-term physiological or psychological effects of LSD "trips" (33, 47, 174, 233). Long-term, steady users of LSD tend to view themselves as less constricted, less anxious, more relaxed, more creative, more loving, and generally more "open" to experience. On the other hand, to outside observers, many of these presumed assets are viewed differently; many long-term users appear to others as showing "poor judgment insofar as they are overly trusting and euphoric" (27, 267). Not only may they be less anxious in responding to what previously were neurotic sources of anxiety; they may also fail to respond appropriately to more realistic sources of concern or danger, for example, the possibility of arrest, loss of a job, exploitative or aggressive intents of others, physical danger. Their "creativeness" may involve increased preoccupation with the self and with inner experience, and with a somewhat impulsive openness to the experiences of the moment, rather than with increased creativity as demonstrated in disciplined aesthetic productions.

Among many users of LSD and related hallucinogens, there has been a vocal, and at times monotonous, insistence upon direct and "meaningful" experiences and open, honest interpersonal relationships characterized by "love." However, to an observer who views love primarily as a heightened concern for the welfare of all, the "love" extolled by the LSD disciple may seem more like psychological dependency on others with similar views, accompanied by withdrawal from an active confrontation of social problems into greater passivity, narcissism, and a reduction in socialized anxiety (27, 28, 29, 30, 50).

Heroin

Until very recently, use of heroin (a semi-synthetic derivative of the opium poppy) and other "hard" narcotics was confined largely to the most depressed sections of our society. Indeed, heroin has been aptly described as "the drug of despair"—a drug used not to "turn on" to the neglected beauty of the surrounding world or to "expand one's consciousness," but rather to shut out physical pain, mental anguish, and a sense of emptiness. The drug produces a brief euphoria and release of tension, characterized by apathy, listlessness, and inertia.

The use of heroin has recently spread from the ghettos to middle-class, suburban high schools and junior high schools in many parts of the country (33, 63, 127). One and a half million, or 6 percent of all young people aged 12 through 17, acknowledge having at least tried heroin (191). While the numbers of users of hard narcotics still appear to represent a small minority of total adolescents, the dangers can hardly be exaggerated.

Tolerance for the drug develops quickly and ever increasing doses may be needed to maintain its effects, with consequent increased danger of addiction. If the individual becomes addicted, the "habit" can become tremendously expensive, costing up to a hundred dollars a day. For many youthful users, this means a resort to criminal activity—most frequently robbery, muggings, small-time drug pushing, and prostitution. Furthermore, overdoses of heroin (and substances with which it is mixed) among youthful users are being reported with increasing frequency (79, 88). It is critically important that young people be made aware of the fact that heroin is an extremely dangerous drug with which to experiment and always carries the danger of becoming a "one-way road to nowhere."

Why Do Adolescents Take Drugs?

Against the background of the "drug culture" in which we all live, drug use by adolescents may serve a number of special motivations. There may be an urge to rebel against adult constraints by using disapproved drugs or simple curiosity—this is a reflection of the adolescent need to take risks of many kinds and to explore new experiences. Some adolescent drug users reject the values of an adult society that they perceive as increasingly impersonal ("don't fold, spindle, or multilate"), often cruel, and lacking in general concern for the individual. Instead, they turn inward to the self-preoccupied world of mind-altering drugs, such as LSD, marijuana, and mescaline, seeking a renewal of wonder, trust, beauty, and meaning. Other, more "disadvantaged" adolescents may give up the search for meaning and a sense of ego identity entirely and seek escape in oblivion of the "hard" narcotics, such as heroin.

Although drugs may produce oblivion or temporary escape or even, in more positive instances, a feeling of greater appreciation for simple beauty in the world, there is little evidence that they foster true creativity. In fact, drug use often impairs creativity. Nor have drugs produced a better or more responsible world. The challenge to adolescents is not to "turn on with drugs and drop out" of life, but to find a way to make life itself more just, more creative, and more meaningful, so that, without drugs, the individual can turn on to life itself and drop out of social isolation, personal anonymity, hopelessness, and despair.

JUVENILE DELINQUENCY

Delinquency is basically a legal concept, defined in different ways in different times and places. Thus, drinking, fighting, and some forms of sexual behavior might be called delinquent at one time in a particular culture, but may be sanctioned at another time or in another culture. In our society, the term juvenile delinquent is generally applied to young persons under 16 or 18 years of age who exhibit behavior which is punishable by law.

Incidence of Delinquent Behavior

The number of young persons who are detected, reported, or charged in connection with delinquent behavior began to increase substantially after 1948 and has continued to rise ever since (73, 218). Part of this rise is accounted for by rapid increases in the number of older children and adolescents in the population during this period, a pattern that will be reversed in the decade of the 1970s (by 1980, there will be more than a million fewer persons age 10-19 than in 1970). Unfortunately, however, the incidence of reported delinquency has been rising faster than the youthful population, and, consequently, a reduction in the rate of delinquency during the coming decade appears highly unlikely (see Fig. 13.2; **73, 163, 218**). According to recent estimates, at least 12 percent of all young people (and 22 percent of boys) are likely to turn up in juvenile court records before the end of adolescence. Although most delinquents are adolescents when they come to the attention of authorities, closer examination reveals that for many, delinquent behaviors actually began during middle childhood (**92, 93, 94, 128**).

There are striking sex differences in the incidence of recorded delinquency. For many years the ratio of boy to girl offenses was four or five to one (**94, 128, 218**). The most frequent complaints against boys involved active or aggressive behaviors, such as joyriding, burglary, malicious mischief, larceny, and auto theft (**73, 94, 128, 200, 218**). Girls, on the other hand, were more likely to be reported for such offenses as running away from home, "incorrigibility" (parental inability to "control" the girl), and illicit sexual behavior.

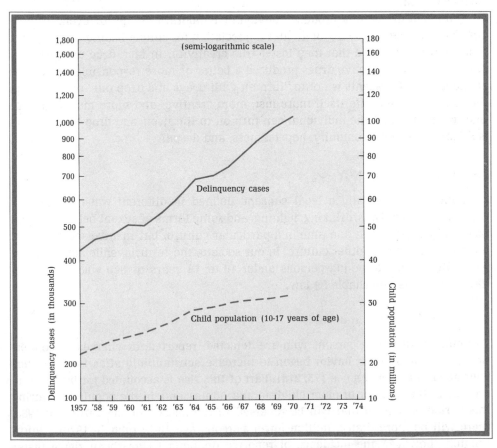

Figure 13.2 Trend in juvenile court delinquency cases and child population, 10–17 years of age, 1957–1970. (From **Juvenile Court Statistics 1970.** Washington, D.C.: National Center for Social Statistics, U.S. Department of Health, Education, and Welfare, 1972.)

Recent evidence suggests that the disparity between the sexes in delinquency rates is narrowing. Delinquency among girls has increased more than among boys every year since 1965, and from 1969 to 1970 the rate of increase was more than twice that of boys (131). Particularly dramatic has been the increase over the past decade in the incidence of more serious "aggressive" offenses among girls. "Between 1960 and 1970, arrests of girls under 18 years of age increased by 276 percent for 'violent' crimes and by 255 percent for 'property' crimes; for boys the percentage increases were 159 percent and 75 percent, respectively" (131, 3–4). Consequently, the ratio of boys' to girls' offenses has now been reduced to about three to one (131). It appears that the recent rise in girls' delinquency is at least partially attributable to increased aggressiveness and independence among girls in our society, and also to increased running away from home and drug use, which may lead to crime-related activity to gain income (131). Indeed, among both boys and girls, drug use has played a significant role recently in increased numbers of arrests, either for illicit drug use itself, or for crimes motivated by a need for money to buy drugs.

Reported delinquency rates are also higher among youths of lower socio-economic status, particularly those living in urban ghettos (53, 56, 92). At least some of the statistics on reported delinquent behavior may be misleading (10, 94, 95). In particular it appears that much behavior that is technically in violation of existing laws either goes undetected, or if detected, is not recorded and does not result in filing of charges (94). Official statistics showing large social-class differences in delinquency may sometimes be distorted. For example, there may be discrimination against lower-status youth by juvenile authorities and/or, greater difficulty in finding nonlegal solutions to the problems posed by the delinquent behavior of the lower-class child (50, 52, 94, 128). A lower-class youth may be remanded to the custody of the court when an upper-class youth with a similar offense may be remanded to his parent's custody, without formal charges (50, 94, 128).

Social Change, Deprivation, and Delinquency

The increased rate of delinquency in recent years is related at least in part to changes in the structure of society: increased mobility of the population, with a consequent disruption of well-established cultural patterns and family ties; increased population growth and social disorganization in large metropolitan areas; and lack of a clear sense of national purpose and concern with social problems. Increases in delinquency are most likely to occur where a sense of community solidarity and of the integrity of the extended family have been most seriously disrupted, for example, in urban ghettos and some of our more affluent, "swinging," suburban "bedroom" communities. Such increases are least likely where these have been preserved, as in some traditional, stable, rural or semirural small towns and cities (50, 51). In the past decade, the greatest increase in the juvenile crime rate has oc-

curred in the suburbs (73, 200) and in communities and among families characterized by a high degree of social and geographic mobility and a lack of stable ties to
other persons and social institutions (181, 182).

Nevertheless, delinquency rates are still highest in deteriorated neighborhoods near the centers of large cities (92, 93, 128). In such areas, characterized by
economic privation, rapid population turnover, and general disorganization, delinquency is often an approved tradition and there are many opportunities for learning antisocial behavior from delinquent peers (44, 68, 182).

A disproportionate share of delinquents come from broken or economically
substandard homes (150, 238), and delinquency rates are about twice as high
among the children of immigrants as among those of native-born parents (172, 200).
In native-born minority groups, such as blacks and Spanish-Americans, delinquency
rates are higher among the children of parents moving from a relatively simple
rural environment to crowded cities than among children of parents already long
established in the city environment. Children of parents who are relatively new in
the city experience a great deal of conflict about the contrasting customs of their
homes, on the one hand, and the neighborhood and school, on the other. The prestige of these children and their parents in the community may be relatively low
(50). In addition, such families are more likely to live in deteriorated neighborhoods, where the children are more likely to be exposed to delinquent practices.
Finally, in all too many cases, such parents may themselves lack the knowledge
and necessary skills to deal successfully with their environment and hence may
not provide adequate role models.

Traditionally, lower-class youth in urban ghettos have been likely to join delinquent gangs (45, 146, 168, 195, 203). These gangs often helped in meeting needs
common to all youth—a sense of personal worth, a meaningful social life and peer-
group acceptance (42, 44. 45), and self-preservation (96, 195, 206).

There is some indication of a decline recently in the importance of large-scale
organized gangs in some ghetto areas and a rise in small group and individual
crime (210), partly due to increased availability of cheap hand-guns and to the
disruptive effects of drugs (210). Consequently, the world of many delinquent
ghetto youth now promises even fewer satisfactions (such as the former feeling of
group belongingness and prestige) and more hazards (less protection). What kind
of life is this for a young adolescent? In the words of one 14-year-old boy, "The
human race stinks, man. I'm glad I ain't in it" (210, 91).

Of course, even in high delinquency areas, many adolescents do not become delinquent. Conversely, many adolescents who are not economically deprived, who
come from well-established middle-class homes, and whose parents are neither
culturally displaced nor members of struggling minority groups, do become delinquent (68, 131, 172, 200). Indeed, while the absolute rate of delinquency remains
lower among middle-class suburban youth, the greatest increase in rate in recent
years has occurred in this group.

Personality and Delinquency

Why does one child from a particular neighborhood, school, social class, and ethnic background become delinquent, whereas another, apparently subject to the same general environmental influences, does not? In approaching this problem, investigators have typically used a research design in which delinquents and nondelinquents from the same general background are compared with respect to personality characteristics and parent-child relationships at various ages. The average delinquent scores somewhat lower on tests of intelligence (**40, 52, 166**), and there is a slightly greater incidence of mental retardation among delinquents than in the population at large. Nevertheless, most delinquents are of at least average intelligence (**166**). Inasmuch as the average IQ difference between delinquents and nondelinquents is not large, and there is a great deal of overlap between the two groups, low intelligence, in and of itself, cannot be considered a major factor in determining most cases of delinquency (**40, 52, 166, 172**).

More significantly, delinquents have generally been found to be more likely than matched groups of nondelinquents to be socially assertive, defiant, ambivalent to authority, resentful, hostile, suspicious and destructive, impulsive, and lacking in self control (**4, 52, 92, 97**). Many of these traits appear defensive in nature, reflecting impaired self-concepts and feelings of inadequacy, emotional rejection, and frustration of needs for self-expression (**4, 52, 53, 96, 112**). Delinquents are significantly more likely than nondelinquents to perceive themselves, consciously or unconsciously, as "lazy," "bad," "sad," and "ignorant."

According to their own self-concepts, delinquents are "undesirable people; they tend not to like, value, or respect themselves. In addition, their self-concepts are confused, conflictual, contradictory, uncertain and variable" (76, 81). Furthermore, the differences between nondelinquents and delinquents in social behavior and personality characteristics are likely to be manifested early in their development, even though clearly defined delinquent behavior may not begin until later.

Delinquent Boys According to the data of one extensive longitudinal study (52, 53), these differences emerge in the early school years and continue and, indeed, expand over the years. By the end of the period from kindergarten through third grade, future delinquents were already viewed by their teachers as more poorly adapted than their classmates. They appeared less considerate and fair in dealing with others, less friendly, less responsible, more impulsive, and more antagonistic to authority. In return, they were less liked and accepted by their peers.

In their schoolwork, they were much more easily distracted, daydreamed more, and, in general, had greater difficulty in maintaining attention and sticking to the task at hand until it was completed. They were less likely to display any special ability or interest. Not surprisingly, these social and academic problems appeared to reflect underlying emotional problems, and in the opinion of their teachers, future delinquents more often came from a disturbed home environment, and were considered overly aggressive.

Although this general picture continued into the period covering fourth to sixth grades, some additional differences and some changes in emphasis emerged. Thus in the middle school years inconsistent academic performance among delinquents became increasingly evident. They were more likely to be viewed as underachieving and showed poorer work habits. Future delinquents demonstrated less leadership ability and had a narrower range of general interests—although, relatively, they were becoming more and more attention-seeking. On the other hand, resentment toward and rejection of school authority began to differentiate less clearly between delinquents and nondelinquents at this age, "possibly because problems with authority are **generally** more common at this age than among school beginners" (52, 186).

By the end of the ninth grade, when these boys were entering the period in which delinquent acts are most common, the delinquents manifested differences from their nondelinquent peers in virtually every area of personality functioning and behavior measured through either personality tests or teacher ratings and comments. They continued to display significantly less respect and consideration for the rights of others than the nondelinquents. Not surprisingly, they were much less cooperative in observing school rules and regulations and in meeting their responsibilities as members of a social group. Moreover, at this age the delinquents showed a much greater antagonism toward authority in comparison with nondelinquent peers than was true in fourth to sixth grades. Apparently in the years between middle childhood and adolescence the attitudes of the nondelinquents toward authority improved considerably, while among delinquents, they continued to deteriorate.

Peer relations remained significantly poorer among the delinquents in adolescence. The delinquents were less friendly and pleasant toward classmates and, in return, were less well liked and accepted by their peers. In their academic activities, the delinquents continued "to have greater difficulty than their nondelinquent matches. Their work habits were still significantly poorer; they were more careless in their work, appeared more often to be working below their capabilities, and needed much more supervision from teachers. Attendance was more often a problem among these youths" (52, 187). The delinquents appeared more distractible; they manifested much less capacity for sustained attention, daydreamed more, and, when challenged academically, tended to give up more easily.

In adolescence, the delinquents were rated as less well adjusted generally, more lacking in self-confidence and self-respect, less cheerful and happy, less able to get along with members of their own and the opposite sex, and were more attention-seeking. Again, delinquents were much more likely to have a "disturbed home environment" mentioned spontaneously by their teachers as a significant problem.

Interestingly, these impressions of poorer adjustment among the delinquents seemed to find support in the reports of the boys themselves, as judged from the psychological testing at the end of junior high school. In the various group tests, the delinquents emerged as clearly less well adjusted.

In particular, they appeared to feel less capable of establishing close personal relationships with either peers or adults, especially the latter. They described themselves as having fewer interests in life, and emerged as generally lacking in enthusiasm. Not unexpectedly, they appeared significantly less impressed by the dominant ethical values and goals of American middle-class culture than their nondelinquent matches.

Perhaps somewhat more surprisingly, in the areas of emotional stability, general maturity, and behavior symptomatology, the delinquents also tended to view themselves in much the same way as their teachers had pictured them. Thus the delinquents emerged in the testing as more: egocentric, childishly demanding, inconsiderate, thoughtless, and given to petty expressions of pique (although they might not have cared to use these particular labels for the implicit and explicit attitudes they expressed). They also acknowledged feelings of depression and discouragement, mood swings, daydreaming, and oversensitivity more frequently than their nondelinquent peers. And they admitted more often to a variety of somatic and behavioral expressions of anxiety and hypochrondriacal preoccupations. Finally, they also appeared significantly more likely than the nondelinquents to respond to environmental pressures (particularly from parents or other authority-figures) with hostility, rejection, or simply withdrawal from the situation, rather than by acceptance, either for their own sake or that of others (52, 188).

Delinquent Girls Somewhat similar results were obtained for girls, significant differences between future delinquents and nondelinquents becoming evident as early as the period from kindergarten to the third grade. Increasingly, it became evident that future delinquents were significantly less well adjusted socially, emotionally, and academically than their nondelinquent matches. They were less poised and more unstable emotionally; less likely to be cheerful, happy, or friendly; and less likely to possess "a good sense of humor." They had more difficulty in relating to same- and opposite-sex peers. They were less likely to show respect and consideration for the rights of others and, in return, were less well liked and accepted by others.

The delinquent girls also displayed significantly more antagonism toward adult authority of any kind, including the school, and were much less cooperative in observing rules and regulations. At the same time, they appeared to have greater difficulty in learning to think for themselves and in developing a clear set of values of their own or realistic, planful goals. They showed less creative ability generally and fewer special abilities or interests. Their work habits were significantly poorer than those of their nondelinquent peers.

Many of these differences are similar to those obtained for boys. There did, however, appear to be some variations of emphasis. Thus the largest differences between delinquent and nondelinquent girls appeared in the areas of emotional adjustment and conformity; among boys, the largest delinquent-nondelinquent differences occurred in the areas of conformity, creative ability, self-reliance, and relations with peers. Furthermore, though differences were somewhat smaller, negative affect (i.e., feelings of unhappiness, moodiness, humorlessness, and discouragement) differentiated significantly for girls, but not for boys, while leadership ability differentiated for boys but not for girls. On self-reports (group psychological tests), many more differences emerged for boys than for girls. This is consistent with the findings of other investigators (109) that delinquent girls are more likely than delinquent boys to be aware of social expectations and to respond on self reports and psychological tests in terms of these expectations—even though their actual behavior, feelings, and attitudes may be quite different.

Parent-Child Relationships

The single most predictive indicator of adolescent delinquency is the young person's relationships with his parents (10). The better an adolescent gets along with parents, the less delinquency. With rather remarkable consistency, investigations indicate that the early parental disciplinary techniques used with delinquents are likely to be lax, erratic, or overly strict and to involve physical punishment, rather than reasoning with the child about misconduct (4, 13, 54, 55, 92, 161, 187, 216, 231). Parent-child relationships of delinquents are far more likely than those of nondelinquents to be characterized by mutual hostility, lack of family cohesiveness, and parental rejection, indifference, dissension, or apathy (4, 13, 92, 161, 187, 237). Parents of delinquents are more likely to have minimal aspirations for their children, to be hostile or indifferent toward school, to have a variety of personal problems and police records of their own (4, 50, 56).

Fathers of delinquents are more likely than those of nondelinquents to be rated by independent observers as cruel, neglecting, and inclined to ridicule their children (particularly sons); and less likely to be rated as either warm, affectionate, or passive (13, 92, 161, 187). In turn, their delinquent young, especially sons, are likely to have few close ties to their fathers and to consider them wholly unacceptable as models for conduct (92).

Mothers of delinquents are more likely than those of nondelinquents to be rated as careless or inadequate in child supervision and as hostile or indifferent; and less likely to be rated as loving (161, 187, 224). Among girls, delinquents, especially recidivists, more frequently acknowledge hostility to their mothers and report that their mothers spent less time with them (224).

Broken homes are significantly associated with a higher incidence of delinquent behavior (4, 237). However, the likelihood of adolescent delinquency is far higher in **nonbroken** homes characterized by mutual hostility, indifference or apathy, and a lack of cohesiveness than in **broken** homes (usually mother only) characterized by cohesiveness and mutual affection and support (4).

Prevention and Treatment of Delinquency

Efforts to prevent or treat delinquency have not yielded encouraging results. Neither psychiatric nor psychological treatment (32, 228), work-study programs (4, 167), family case-work (187, 216), the use of "street-corner" youth workers (204, 209), foster home placement (216), recreational programs (4, 216), or combinations of these or other approaches (health care, legal aid) have had widespread success. More traditional approaches, such as punishment or imprisonment in "correctional" institutions have generally tended only to make matters worse. These approaches subject the young person to psychologically traumatic and embittering experiences, while providing little or no psychological, educational, or vocational help; and, at the same time, they serve as "finishing schools" for future criminal behavior (126, 165, 192).

Future efforts to reduce delinquency will probably have to emphasize prevention and will have to begin much earlier. Futhermore, they will have to be part of a much larger program of comprehensive psychological and physical care, education, and training, aimed at optimal development for children and adolescents in all areas. In the last analysis, delinquency is not a disease, but a symptom of more fundamental problems—social, psychological, economic, educational, vocational, physical, even philosophical.

"Patchwork" approaches—attempts to salvage particular groups of children—

appear destined to have only limited success as long as our society does little to ameliorate the social conditions that are the breeding ground of delinquency. We refer, of course, to poverty; urban decay; ethnic and socioeconomic discrimination; the breakdown of an effective sense of community among all classes of citizens; and the increasing paralysis of fundamental social institutions, such as the schools and agencies of government. Without a sense of real commitment to attacking such problems, we are likely to find that the rate of delinquency, already staggering, will rise still further.

SUMMARY

An essential element in the task of becoming a mature adult is the development of a sense of one's own identity. The adolescent or adult with a strong sense of ego identity sees himself as distinctive and separate from others, but also as self-consistent, with a workable integration of his own needs, motives, and patterns of responding. The problem of ego identity becomes particularly acute at adolescence, partly as a function of the rapid physical and physiological changes of puberty, but also because of increased and changing social demands. The ease with which a strong and stable sense of ego identity and a relatively conflict-free sex-role adjustment is achieved in adolescence will depend to an important degree on the nature of previous parent-child relationships. This task will also be made easier or more difficult, depending upon the values, expectations, and opportunities of the society in which the youth is expected to adjust.

The problem of ego identity cannot be separated from that of values, and adolescents are particularly concerned with issues of conscience and with moral values and standards. The nature of these concerns, however, varies from generation to generation. The average current adolescent tends to view society as becoming more fast-paced, competitive, conflicted in its values and beliefs, complex, and impersonal. Nevertheless he intends to remain in the mainstream of society, is interested in "success" as conventionally defined, and is reasonably happy.

In achieving such adjustment, the average adolescent has tended to rely somewhat more than earlier generations on such values as: honesty and "openness" in interpersonal relationships with members of both the same and opposite sex; a belief in the importance and dignity of the individual; a greater emphasis on personal, relativistic, and individualized codes of morality and behavior; and less emphasis on the institutionalized, arbitrary, and frequently inconsistent dictates of contemporary society. Today's average adolescent appears more ready than his more self-conscious predecessors of earlier generations to put into practice the philosophy of "live and let live" and of pragmatic idealism. More than his counterparts in earlier generations, he appears to be a sophisticated and critical exponent of the art of the possible—not illusioned, but not disillusioned either. One commentator has termed today's adolescents a generation of "flaming moderates."

In contrast, important minorities in the adolescent subculture have become alienated from the values and practices of contemporary society. In some instances, alienation is imposed primarily from without, and represents a reaction of frustration and resentment to deprivation and discrimination imposed by the larger society (as in the case of the socioeconomically deprived and the school dropout). This sort of alienation is more traditional and has been a part of society over many centuries.

However, there has recently been a "new" alienation taking place among economically and socially favored middle-class youth, based upon an explicit rejection of contemporary American culture, with its emphasis on competition and materialistic values, and its apparent lack of concern for social justice, equality of opportunity, and civil rights, as well as its continued involvement in wars, both hot and cold. Some of these middle-class youth react by trying to change "the system," either within or outside traditional political mechanisms (e.g., student activists); while others attempt to establish a more compatible way of life for themselves outside the system (e.g., social dropouts and hippies). Still others, partly as a result of disturbed parent-child relationships in the past as well as current social conditions, are far too pessimistic, nihilistic, and despairing to look for a new way of life, either within the system or outside of it.

A problem of mounting concern is the increasing use of drugs among adolescents—marijuana, highly potent mind-altering drugs such as LSD, amphetamines, and heroin and other hard narcotics. For some adolescents, the use of drugs may simply reflect an urge to rebel against adult constraints or to seek novelty. For others, drug use may represent a rejection of contemporary society and an attempt to seek a creative subjective experience, to restore a sense of beauty and wonder, or to find meaningful personal values. For still others, such as the slum-dwelling user of the "hard" narcotics such as heroin, drug use may simply reflect an attempt to escape into oblivion from an intolerable existence. However, the fact remains that drugs, while they may produce a temporary escape, frequently create new problems, have never been shown to increase creativity, and, in fact, have frequently impaired it.

Another problem of major concern is the rising incidence of juvenile delinquency. This phenomenon has both sociological and psychological roots. While delinquency rates are higher among youth who grow up in poverty, live in deteriorating neighborhoods of large cities, and have culturally and economically deprived parents, not all such youth become delinquent. Conversely, many children who are not deprived, who come from well-established middle-class homes, and whose parents are neither culturally deprived nor members of struggling minorities, do become delinquent.

Obviously, personality characteristics and parent-child relationships are also important in the development of delinquency. For example, as compared to nondelinquents, delinquents have been shown to be more poorly adjusted generally and more lacking in self-confidence; more impulsive, distractible, aggressive, unhappy, and resentful; and less well liked and accepted by their peers. In general, parents of delinquents are less afffectionate and more indifferent or hostile toward their children. They are also likely to provide less supervision, to be more erratic or unduly harsh in discipline, and to lack cohesion as a family unit.

References

1. Adelson, J. The political imagination of the young adolescent. **Daedalus,** Fall 1971, 1013–1050.
2. Adelson, J., Green, B., & O'Neil, R. The growth of the idea of law in adolescence. **Developmental Psychology,** 1969, **1,** 327–332.
3. Adelson, J., & O'Neil, R. The development of political thought in adolescence: A sense of community. **Journal of Personality and Social Psychology,** 1966, **4,** 295–308.
4. Ahlstrom, W. M., & Havighurst, R. J. **400 losers.** San Francisco: Jossey-Bass, 1971.
5. Alexander, F. From adolescence to adulthood. **Mental Health Bulletin** (Illinois Society for Mental Hygiene), 1948, **26,** 1–4.
6. Alkire, A. A. Enactment of social power and role behavior in families of disturbed and nondisturbed preadolescents. **Developmental Psychology,** 1972, **7,** 270–276.
7. Allen, J. R., & West, L. J. Flight from violence: Hippies and the green rebellion. **American Journal of Psychiatry,** 1968, **125,** 120–126.
8. Andry, R. G. Paternal and maternal roles in delinquency. In **Deprivation of maternal care.** (Public Health Paper No. 14.) Geneva: World Health Organization, 1962. Pp. 31–43.
9. Auchincloss, K., et al. Marijuana: Time to change the law? **Newsweek,** September 7, 1970, 20–32.
10. Bachman, J. G. **Youth in transition.** Vol. 2. **The impact of family background and intelligence on tenth-grade boys.** Ann Arbor: Institute for Social Research, University of Michigan, 1970.
11. Bachman, J. G., & Van Duinen, E. **Youth look at national problems: A special report from the youth in transition project.** Ann Arbor: Institute for Social Research, University of Michigan, 1971.
12. Baltes, P. B., & Nesselroade, J. R. Cultural change and adolescent personality development. **Developmental Psychology,** 1972, **7,** 244–256.
13. Bandura, A., & Walters, R. H. **Adolescent aggression.** New York: Ronald, 1959.
14. Bardwick, J. **Psychology of women: A study of bio-cultural conflicts.** New York: Harper & Row, 1971.
15. Barglow, P., Bornstein, M. B., Exum, D. B. Wright, M. K., & Visotsky, H. M. Some psychiatric aspects of illegitimate pregnancy during early adolescence. **American Journal of Orthopsychiatry,** 1967, **37,** 266–267.
16. Baughman, E. E. **Black Americans: A psychological analysis.** New York: Academic Press, 1971.
17. Baumrind, D. Current patterns of parental authority. **Developmental Psychology Monographs,** 1971, 4(1, Part 2), 1–103.
18. Bay, C. Political and apolitical students. In E. E. Sampson and H. A. Korn (Eds.), **Student activism and dissent: Alternatives for social change.** San Francisco: Jossey-Bass, 1970. Pp. 60–88.

19. Bay, C. Political and apolitical students: Facts in search of theory. **Journal of Social Issues,** 1967, **23,** 76–91.

20. Birnbaum, J. L. A. Life patterns, personality style and self esteem in gifted family oriented and career committed women. Unpublished doctoral dissertation, University of Michigan, 1972.

21. Black, J. The 'speed' that kills—or worse. **New York Times Magazine,** June 21, 1970, 14–28.

22. Block, J. H., Haan, N., & Smith, M. B. Socialization correlates of student activism. **Journal of Social Issues,** 1969, **25,** 143–177.

23. Block, J. H., Haan, N., & Smith, M. B. Activism and apathy in contemporary adolescents. In J. F. Adams (Ed.), **Understanding adolescence: Current developments in adolescent psychology.** Boston: Allyn and Bacon, 1968. Pp. 198–231.

24. Block, J., & Turula, E. Identification, ego control, and adjustment. **Child Development,** 1963, **34,** 945–953.

25. Blom, G. E. A rebuttal to Bruno: Student unrest as striving to thrive. Unpublished manuscript, Department of Psychiatry, University of Colorado Medical School, 1970.

26. Blum, R. H. Mind-altering drugs and dangerous behavior: Dangerous drugs. In **Task force report: Narcotics and drug abuse.** Washington, D.C.: The President's Commission on Law Enforcement and the Administration of Justice, 1967.

27. Blum, R. H. **Utopiates: The use and users of LSD-25.** New York: Atherton, 1964.

28. Blum, R. H., and associates. **Horatio Alger's children.** San Francisco: Jossey-Bass, 1972.

29. Blum, R. H., and associates. **Society and drugs.** Vol. 1. **Social and cultural observations.** San Francisco: Jossey-Bass, 1970.

30. Blum, R. H., and associates. **Society and drugs.** Vol. 2. **College and high school observations.** San Francisco: Jossey-Bass, 1970.

31. Bonier, R. J., & Hymowitz, P. Marijuana and college students: Set, setting, and personality. **Proceedings, 80th Annual Convention of the American Psychological Association,** 1972, **7,** 417–418.

32. Bowlby, J. Forty-four juvenile thieves. **International Journal of Psychoanalysis,** 1944, **25,** 1–57.

33. Brenner, J. H., Coles, R., & Meagher, D. **Drugs and youth: Medical, legal, and psychiatric facts.** New York: Liveright, 1970.

34. Brody, E. B. **Minority group adolescents in the United States.** Baltimore: Williams & Wilkins, 1968.

35. Bromberg, W. Marihuana intoxication. **American Journal of Psychiatry,** 1934, **91,** 303–330.

36. Brown, J. D. (Ed.) **The Hippies.** New York: Time-Life, 1967.

37. Bryant, B. E. **High school students look at their world.** Columbus, Ohio: Goettler, 1970.

38. Calef, V., Gryler, R., Hilles, L., Hofer, R., Kempner, P., Pittel, S. M., & Wallerstein, R. S. Impairments of ego functions in psychedelic drug users. Paper presented at the Conference on Drug Use and Drug Subcultures, Asilomar, Pacific Grove, Calif., February 11–15, 1970.

39. Campus '65. **Newsweek,** March 22, 1965, 43–54.

40. Caplan, N. S., & Siebert, L. A. Distribution of juvenile delinquent intelligence test scores over a thirty-four-year period (N = 51, 808). **Journal of Clinical Psychology,** 1964, **20,** 242–247.

41. Carey, J. T., & Mandel, J. A San Francisco Bay Area "speed scene." **Drug Dependence** (National Institute of Mental Health), 1969, No. 2, 20–29.

42. Clark, J. P., & Wenninger, E. P. Socio-economic class and area as correlates of illegal behavior among juveniles. **American Sociological Review,** 1962, **27,** 826–834.
43. Clark, K. B., & Clark, M. P. Racial identification and preference in Negro children. In T. M. Newcomb and E. L. Hartley (Eds.), **Readings in social psychology.** New York: Holt, Rinehart & Winston, 1947. Pp. 169–178.
44. Cloward, R. A., & Ohlin, L. E. **Delinquency and opportunity: A theory of delinquent gangs.** New York: Free Press, 1960.
45. Cohen, A. K. **Delinquent boys: The culture of the gang.** Glencoe, Ill.: Free Press, 1955.
46. Cohen, S. A classification of LSD complications. **Psychosomatics,** 1966, **7,** 182–186.
47. Cohen, S., & Edwards, A. E. LSD and organic brain impairment. **Drug Dependence** (National Institute of Mental Health), 1969, No. 2, 1–4.
48. Coles, R. The weather of the years. **Daedalus,** Fall 1971, 1139–1157.
49. Coles, R. **Children of crisis: A study of courage and fear.** Boston: Atlantic-Little, Brown, 1967.
50. Conger, J. J. **Adolescence and youth: Psychological development in a changing world.** New York: Harper & Row, 1973.
51. Conger, J. J. A world they never knew: The family and social change. **Daedalus,** Fall 1971, 1105–1138.
52. Conger, J. J., & Miller, W. C. **Personality, social class, and delinquency.** New York: Wiley, 1966.
53. Conger, J. J., Miller, W. C., & Walsmith, C. R. Antecedents of delinquency, personality, social class and intelligence. In P. H. Mussen, J. J. Conger, & J. Kagan (Eds.), **Readings in child development and personality.** New York: Harper & Row, 1965.
54. Craig, M. M., & Glick, S. J. **A manual of procedures for application of the Glueck Prediction Table.** New York: New York City Youth Board, 1964.
55. Craig, M. M., & Glick, S. J. Ten years' experience with the Glueck Social Prediction Table. **Crime and Delinquency,** 1963.
56. Cressey, D. R., & Ward, D. A. **Delinquency, crime, and social process.** New York: Harper & Row, 1969.
57. Davis, R., & Olsen, V. The career outlook of professionally educated women. **Psychiatry,** 1965, **28,** 334–345.
58. Dempsey, D. Bruno Bettelheim is Dr. No. **New York Times Magazine,** January 11, 1970, 22 ff.
59. Derbyshire, R. L. Adolescent identity crisis in urban Mexican Americans in East Los Angeles. In E. B. Brody (Ed.), **Minority group adolescents in the United States.** Baltimore: Williams & Wilkins, 1968. Pp. 157–204.
60. Didion, J. The hippie generation: Slouching towards Bethlehem. **Saturday Evening Post,** 1967, **19,** 27–31, 88–94.
61. Dishatsky, N. I., Loughman, W. D., Mogan, R. E., & Lipscomb, W. R. LSD and genetic damage. **Science,** 1971, **172,** 431–439.
62. Douvan, E. A., & Adelson, J. **The adolescent experience.** New York: Wiley, 1966.
63. Dunbar, E. Campus mood, spring, '68. **Look,** 1968, **7,** 23–27.
64. Dworkin, A. Stereotypes and self-images held by native-born and foreign-born Mexican Americans. **Sociology and Social Research,** 1965, **49,** 214–224.
65. Elkind, D. **A sympathetic understanding of the child from six to sixteen.** Boston: Allyn and Bacon, 1971.
66. Elkind, D. **Children and adolescents: Interpretative essays on Jean Piaget.** New York: Oxford University Press, 1970.

67. Elkind, D. Cognitive development in adolescence. In J. F. Adams (Ed.), **Understanding adolescence.** Boston: Allyn and Bacon, 1968. Pp. 128–158.

68. Empey, L. T. Delinquency theory and recent research. **Journal of Research in Crime and Delinquency,** 1967, **4,** 28–42.

69. English, O. S., & Finch, S. M. **Introduction to psychiatry.** New York: Norton, 1954.

70. Erikson, E. H. **Identity: Youth and crisis.** New York: Norton, 1968.

71. Erikson, E. H. **Childhood and society.** New York: Norton, 1950.

72. Evans, R. I. **Dialogue with Erik Erickson.** New York: Harper & Row, 1967.

73. Federal Bureau of Investigation. **Uniform Crime Reports, 1960–72.** Washington, D.C.: U.S. Department of Justice.

74. Feuer, L. S. **The conflict of generations.** New York: Basic Books, 1969.

75. Fishman, J. R., & Solomon, F. Youth and social action: 1. Perspectives on the student sit-in movement. **American Journal of Orthopsychiatry,** 1963, **33,** 872–882.

76. Fitts, W. H., & Hammer, W. T. **The self-concept and delinquency.** (Research Monograph No. 1.), Nashville, Tenn.: Nashville Mental Health Center, 1969.

77. Flacks, R. The liberated generation: An exploration of the roots of student protest. **Journal of Social Issues,** 1967, **22**(3), 52–75.

78. Fleck, S. Pregnancy as a symptom of adolescent maladjustment. **International Journal of Social Psychiatry,** 1956, **2,** 118–131.

79. Fort, J. The drug explosion. **Playboy,** September 1972, 139–142.

80. Fort, J. The problem of barbiturates in the United States of America. **Bulletin of Narcotics,** 1964, **16,** 17–35.

81. Fredrickson, L. C. Value structure of college students. **Journal of Youth and Adolescence,** 1972, **1,** 155–163.

82. Freedman, A. M., & Wilson, E. A. Childhood and adolescent addictive disorders. **Pediatrics,** 1964, **34,** 283–292.

83. Freud, A. Adolescence as a developmental disturbance. In G. Caplan and S. Lebovici (Eds.), **Adolescence: Psychological perspectives.** New York: Basic Books, 1969.

84. Freud, A. **The ego and the mechanisms of defense.** New York: International Universities Press, 1946.

85. Galbraith, J. K. **The new industrial state.** Boston: Houghton Mifflin, 1967.

86. Gallup college drug survey. **New York Times,** February 6, 1972.

87. Gallup, G. H., Jr., & Davis, J. O., III. Gallup poll, **Denver Post,** May 26, 1969.

88. Gallup poll. **New York Times,** October 26, 1969, 75.

89. Gershon, S., & Angrist, B. Drug-induced psychoses. **Hospital Practice,** 1967, **2,** 50–53.

90. Glaser, H. H., & Massengale, O. M. Glue sniffing and children. **Journal of the American Medical Association,** 1962, **181,** 300–303.

91. Glueck, S., & Glueck, E. T. **Physique and delinquency.** New York: Harper & Row, 1956.

92. Glueck, S., & Glueck, E. T. **Unraveling juvenile delinquency.** New York: Commonwealth Fund, 1950.

93. Glueck, S., & Glueck, E. T. **One thousand juvenile delinquents.** Cambridge, Mass.: Harvard University Press, 1934.

94. Gold, M. **Delinquent behavior in an American city.** Belmont, Calif.: Brooks-Cole, 1970.

95. Gold, M. Undetected delinquent behavior. **Journal of Research in Crime and Delinquency,** 1966, **3,** 27–46.

96. Gold, M., & Mann, D. Delinquency as defense. **American Journal of Orthopsychiatry,** 1972, **42,** 463–479.

97. Goldberg, L., & Guilford, J. S. Delinquent values: It's fun to break the rules. **Proceedings, 80th Annual Convention of the American Psychological Association,** 1972, **7,** 237–238.
98. Goldstein, R. **1 in 7: Drugs on campus.** New York: Walker, 1966.
99. Greeley, A. Jesus freaks and other devouts. **New York Times Book Review,** February 13, 1972, Part II, 4 ff.
100. Grier, W. H., & Cobbs, P. M. **Black rage.** New York: Basic Books, 1968. (New York: Bantam, 1969.)
101. Grinspoon, L. **Marijuana reconsidered.** Cambridge, Mass.: Harvard University Press, 1971.
102. Grinspoon, L. Marihuna. **Scientific American,** 1969, **221**(6), 17–25.
103. Grossman, D. S. Variables associated with marijuana use in college students. **Proceedings, 80th Annual Convention of the American Psychological Association,** 1972, **7,** 601–602.
104. Grossman, J. C., Goldstein, R., & Eisenman, R. Openness to experience and marijuana use: An initial investigation. **Proceedings, 79th Annual Convention of the American Psychological Association,** 1971, **6,** 335–556.
105. Harris, L. Change, yes—upheaval, no. **Life,** January 8, 1971, 22–27.
106. Harris, L. Profile of the new voter. **Newsweek,** October 25, 1971, 38–49.
107. Harris, L. The teen-agers. **Newsweek,** March 21, 1966, 57–72.
108. Harris, L., and associates. What people think of their high schools. **Life,** May 16, 1969, 32.
109. Hathaway, S. R., & Monachesi, E. D. (Eds.) **Analyzing and predicting juvenile delinquency with the MMPI.** Minneapolis: University of Minnesota Press, 1953.
110. Hauser, S. T. Black and white identity development: Aspects and perspectives. **Journal of Youth and Adolescence,** 1972, **1,** 113–130.
111. Hauser, S. T. **Black and white identity formation: Studies in the psychological development of lower socioeconomic class adolescent boys.** New York: Wiley, 1971.
112. Healy, W., & Bronner, A. F. **New light on delinquency and its treatments.** New Haven, Conn.: Yale University Press, 1936.
113. Heilbrun, A. B., Jr. Identification and behavioral ineffectiveness during late adolescence. In E. D. Evans (Ed.) **Adolescents: Readings in behavior and development.** Hinsdale, Ill.: Dryden, 1970.
114. Heilbrun, A. B., Jr. Conformity to masculinity-femininity stereotypes and ego identity in adolescents. **Psychological Reports,** 1964, **14,** 351–357.
115. Heilbrun, A. B., Jr. Parental model attributes, nurturant reinforcement, and consistency of behavior in adolescents. **Child Development,** 1964, **35,** 151–167.
116. Heilbrun, A. B., Jr., & Gillard, B. J. Perceived maternal childbearing behavior and motivational effects of social reinforcement in females. **Perceptual and Motor Skills,** 1966, **23,** 439–446.
117. Heilbrun, A. B., Jr., & Fromme, D. K. Parental identification of late adolescents and level of adjustment: The importance of parent-model attributes, ordinal position and sex of the child. **Journal of Genetic Psychology,** 1965, **107,** 49–59.
118. Heist, P. Intellect and commitment: The faces of discontent. In O. W. Knorr & W. J. Minter (Eds.), **Order and freedom on the campus: The rights and responsibilities of faculty and students.** Boulder, Colo.: Western Interstate Commission for Higher Education, 1965. Pp. 61–69.
119. Horner, M. S. Femininity and successful achievement: A basic inconsistency. In J. M.

Bardwick, E. Douvan, M. S. Horner, & D. Guttman, **Feminine personality and conflict.** Belmont, Calif.: Brooks-Cole, 1970. Pp. 45–73.

120. Houriet, R. **Getting back together.** New York: Avon, 1971.

121. Hungerford, D. A., Taylor, K. M., Shagass, C., LaBadie, G., Balaban, G. B., & Paton, G. R. Cytogenic effects of LSD-25 therapy in man. **Journal of the American Medical Association,** 1968, **206,** 2287–2291.

122. Hunt, M. Special sex education survey. **Seventeen,** July 1970, 94 ff.

123. Huyck, E. E. (Ed.) **White-nonwhite differentials in health, education, and welfare.** Washington, D.C.: U.S. Department of Health, Education, and Welfare, 1965.

124. Isbell, H., et al. Studies on tetrahydrocannabinal. I. Method of assay in human subjects and results with crude extracts, purified tetrahydrocannabinal and synthetic compounds. Unpublished manuscript, University of Kentucky Medical Center, 1967.

125. Isbell, H. Gorodetsky, C. W., Jasinski, D., Claussen, U., Von Spulak, F., & Korte, F. Effects of $(-)\triangle^9$ trans-tetrahydrocannabinal in man. **Psychopharmacologia** (Berl.), 1967, **11,** 184–188.

126. James, H. **Children in trouble: A national scandal.** New York: Pocket Books, 1971.

127. Janssen, P., and associates. High schools in trouble. **Newsweek,** February 16, 1970, 66–67.

128. Johnson, A. M. Juvenile delinquency. In S. Arieti (Ed.), **American handbook of psychiatry.** New York: Basic Books, 1959. Pp. 840–856.

129. Johnson, C. S. **Growing up in the black belt.** Washington, D.C.: American Council on Education, 1941. (Republished: New York, Shocken, 1967.)

130. Johnson, L. **Drugs and American Youth: A report of the youth in transition project.** Ann Arbor, Mich.: Institute for Social Research, University of Michigan, 1973.

131. Juvenile Court Statistics 1970. Washington, D.C.: National Center for Social Statistics, U.S. Department of Helath, Education, and Welfare, 1972.

132. Kagan, J., & Moss, H. A. **Birth to maturity: The Fels study of psychological development.** New York: Wiley, 1962.

133. Kandel, D. B., & Lesser, G. S. **Youth in two worlds.** San Francisco: Jossey-Bass, 1972.

134. Kaplan, J. **Marijuana: The new prohibition.** Stanford, Calif.: Stanford University Press, 1970.

135. Katz, J. The student activists: Rights, needs, and powers of undergraduates. Report prepared for the U.S. Office of Education, 1967.

136. Keasey, C. T., & Keasey, C. B. Formal operations and moral development: What is the relationship? **Proceedings, 80th Annual Convention of the American Psychological Association,** 1972, **7,** 113–114.

137. Keeler, M. H. Adverse reactions to marihuana. **American Journal of Psychiatry,** 1967, **124,** 674–677.

138. Kendall, R. F. Psychosis and psychedelics. Paper presented at the annual meeting of the California State Psychological Association, Coronado, Calif., January 31, 1971.

139. Keniston, K. **Youth and dissent: The rise of a new opposition.** New York: Harcourt Brace Jovanovich, 1971.

140. Keniston, K. **Young radicals: Notes on committed youth.** New York: Harcourt Brace Jovanovich, 1968.

141. Keniston, K. The sources of student dissent. **Journal of Social Issues,** 1967, **22**(3), 108–137.

142. Keniston, K. **The uncommitted: Alienated youth in American society.** New York: Dell, 1960.

143. Kerpelman, L. C. **Activists and nonactivists: A psychological study of American college students.** New York: Behavioral Publications, 1972.

144. Kerpelman, L. C. Student activism and ideology in higher education institutions. Unpublished manuscript, Department of Psychology, University of Massachusetts, 1971.

145. Kerpelman, L. C. Student political activism and ideology. **Journal of Counseling Psychology,** 1969, **16,** 8–13.

146. Klein, M. W., & Crawford, L. Y. Groups, gangs, and cohesiveness. **Journal of Research in Crime and Delinquency,** January 1967, 63.

147. Kohlberg, L. Moral education in the schools: A developmental view. In R. E. Grinder, **Studies in adolescence: A book of readings in adolescent development.** New York: Macmillan, 1969. Pp. 237–258.

148. Kohlberg, L., & Gilligan, C. The adolescent as a philosopher: The discovery of the self in a postconventional world. **Daedalus,** Fall 1971, 1051–1086.

149. Kohlberg, L., & Kramer, R. Continuity and discontinuity in moral development from childhood to adulthood. **Human Development,** 1970, in press.

150. Kris, E. **Psychoanalytic explorations in art.** New York: International Universities Press, 1952.

151. Kuhlen, R. G., & Arnold, M. Age differences in religious beliefs and problems during adolescence. **Journal of Genetic Psychology,** 1944, **65,** 291–300.

152. Kuhn, D., Langer, J., & Kohlberg, L. The development of formal operational thought: Its relation to moral judgment. Unpublished paper, Harvard University, 1971.

153. Kvaraceus, W. C., Miller, W. B., and associates. **Delinquent behavior: Culture and the individual.** Washington, D.C.: National Education Association, 1959.

154. Lefeber, J. A. The delinquent's self-concept. Unpublished doctoral dissertation, University of Southern California, 1965.

155. Lipset, S. M. The activists: A profile. **The Public Interest,** Fall 1968, 39–51.

156. Lipsitt, P. D., & Lelos, D. Relationship of sex-role identity to level of ego development in habitual drug users. **Proceedings, 80th Annual Convention of the American Psychological Association,** 1972, **7,** 255–256.

157. Loughman, W. D., Sargent, T. W., & Israelstein, D. M. Leukocytes of humans exposed to lysergic acid diethylamide: Lack of chromosomal damage. **Science,** 1967, **158,** 508–510.

158. Luce, J. End of the road. **Behavior: San Francisco Sunday Examiner and Chronicle,** November 8, 1970, 8–10.

159. Lynn, D. B. **Parental and sex-role identification: A theoretical formulation.** Berkeley, Calif.: McCutchan, 1969.

160. McBride, B. E. The parental identifications of adolescence. **Alberta Journal of Educational Research,** 1962, **8,** 204–210.

161. McCord, W., McCord, J., & Zola, I. K. **Origins of Crime.** New York: Columbia University Press, 1959.

162. McDonald, R. L., & Gynther, M. D. Relationship of self and ideal-self descriptions with sex, race, and class in southern adolescents. **Journal of Personality and Social Psychology,** 1965, **1,** 85–88.

163. Mayer, L. A. New questions about the U.S. population. **Fortune,** February 1971, 82–85. (Source: U.S. Census, 1970.)

164. Medinnus, G. R. Adolescents' self-acceptance and perceptions of their parents. **Journal of Consulting Psychology,** 1965, **29,** 150–154.

165. Menninger, K. **The crime of punishment.** New York: Viking, 1968.

166. Merrill, M. A. **Problems of child delinquency.** Boston: Houghton Mifflin, 1947.
167. Miller, D. **Growth to freedom: The psychosocial treatment of delinquent youth.** Bloomington, Ind.: Indiana University Press, 1964.
168. Miller, W. B. Violent crimes in city gangs. **Annals of the American Academy of Political and Social Science,** March 1965, **358,** 110.
169. Mizner, G. L., Barter, J. T., & Werme, P. H. Patterns of drug use among college students. **American Journal of Psychiatry,** 1970, **127,** 15–24.
170. Mussen, P. H. Long-term consequents of masculinity of interests in adolescence. **Journal of Consulting Psychology,** 1962, **26,** 435–440.
171. Mussen, P. H. Some antecedents and consequences of masculine sex-typing in adolescent boys. **Psychological Monographs,** 1961, **75**(506).
172. Mussen, P. H., Conger, J. J., & Kagan, J. **Child development and personality.** (3rd ed.) New York: Harper & Row, 1969.
173. Mussen, P. H., Young, H. B., Gaddini, R., & Morante, L. The influence of father-son relationships on adolescent personality and attitudes. **Journal of Child Psychology and Psychiatry,** 1963, **4,** 3–16.
174. Nowlis, H. H. **Drugs on the college campus.** New York: Anchor, 1969.
175. Nye, F. I. **Family relationships and delinquent behavior.** New York: Wiley, 1958.
176. Pable, M. W. Some parental determinants of ego identity in adolescent boys. **Dissertation Abstracts,** 1965, **26,** 3480–3481.
177. Parsons, T., & Clark, K. B. (Eds.) **The Negro American.** Boston: Houghton Mifflin, 1966.
178. Perlman, I. R. Delinquency prevention: The size of the problem. **Annals of the American Academy of Political and Social Science,** 1959, **322,** 1–9.
179. Pietz, K. R. Parent perception and social adjustment among elementary and high school students. **Journal of Clinical Psychology,** 1968, **24,** 165–171.
180. Pikas, A. Children's attitudes toward rational versus inhibiting parental authority. **Journal of Abnormal and Social Psychology,** 1961, **62,** 315–321.
181. Pine, G. J. The affluent delinquent. **Phi Delta Kappan,** December 1966, 138–143.
182. Pine, G. J. Social class, social mobility, and delinquent behavior. **Personnel Guidance Journal,** April 1965, 770–774.
183. Pittel, S. M. Psychological effects of psychedelic drugs: Preliminary observations and hypotheses. Paper presented at the meeting of the Western Psychological Association, Los Angeles, June 21, 1969.
184. Pittel, S. M., Calef, V., Gryler, R. B., Hilles, L., Hofer, R., & Kempner, P. Developmental factors in adolescent drug use: A study of psychedelic drug users. Paper presented at the meeting of the American Academy of Child Psychiatry, Denver, Colo., October 17, 1970.
185. Pittel, S. M., Wallach, A., & Wilner, N. Utopians, mystics, and skeptics: Ideologies of young drug users. Unpublished manuscripts, Department of Psychiatry, Mount Zion Hospital and Medical Center, San Francisco, Calif., 1970.
186. Polk, F. F., et al. Symposium on current research in psychedelic drugs, California Psychological Association, Coronado, Calif., January 31, 1971.
187. Powers, E., & Witmer, H. **Prevention of delinquency: The Cambridge-Somerville youth study.** New York: Columbia University Press, 1951.
188. Proshansky, H., & Newton, P. The nature and meaning of Negro self-identity. In M. Deutsch, I. Katz, & A. R. Jensen (Eds.), **Social class, race, and psychological development.** New York: Holt, Rinehart & Winston, 1968. Pp. 178–218.

189. Reiss, A. J. Social correlates of psychological types of delinquency. **American Sociological Review,** 1952, **17,** 710–718.

190. **Report of the National Commission on Marijuana and Drug Abuse.** Washington, D.C.: Superintendent of Documents, U.S. Government Printing Office, 1972.

191. Response Analysis Corporation. Survey on drug use. Report prepared for the National Commission on Marijuana and Drug Abuse, Washington, D.C., May, 1972.

192. Richette, L. A. **The throwaway children.** New York: Dell, 1969.

193. Rosenberg, M. Parental interest and children's self-perceptions. **Sociometry,** 1963, **26,** 35–49.

194. Roszak, T. **The making of a counter culture: Reflections on the technocratic society and its youthful opposition.** New York: Anchor, 1968.

195. Salisbury, H. E. **The shook-up generation.** New York: Harper & Row, 1959.

196. Sampson, E. E. (Ed.) Stirrings out of apathy: Student activism and the decade of protest. **Journal of Social Issues,** 1967, **23**(3).

197. Sampson, E. E., and Korn, H. A. (Eds.) **Student activism and dissent: Alternatives for social change.** San Francisco: Jossey-Bass, 1970.

198. Sanford, N. **The American college.** New York: Wiley, 1962.

199. Scammon, R., & Wattenberg, B. J. **The real majority.** New York: Coward-McCann, 1970.

200. Sebold, H. **Adolescence: A sociological analysis.** New York: Appleton-Century-Crofts, 1968.

201. Sheldon, W. H., Hartl, E. M., & McDermott, E. **Varieties of delinquent youth: An introduction to constitutional psychiatry.** New York: Harper & Row, 1949.

202. Shepherd, J. The **Look** youth survey. **Look,** September 20, 1966, 44–49.

203. Short, J. F., Jr., & Strodtbeck, F. L. **Group process and delinquency.** Chicago: University of Chicago Press, 1965.

204. Slack, C. W. Experimenter-subject psychotherapy: A new method of introducing intensive office treatment of unreachable cases. **Mental Hygiene in New York,** 1960, 238–256.

205. Smart, R., & Fejer, D. Drug use among adolescents and their parents: Closing the generation gap in mood modification. **Journal of Abnormal and Social Psychology,** 1972, **79**(2), 153–160.

206. Smith, D. E., & Luce, J. **Love needs care.** Boston: Little, Brown, 1971.

207. Somers, R. H. The mainsprings of the rebellion: A survey of Berkeley students in November, 1964. In S. M. Lipsett & S. S. Wolin (Eds.), **The Berkeley student revolt.** New York: Anchor, 1965. Pp. 530–537.

208. Sparkes, R. S., Melnyk, J., & Bozzeti, L. P. Chromosomal effect in vivo of exposure to lysergic acid diethylamide. **Science,** 1968, **160,** 1343–1344.

209. Spergel, I. **Street gang work: Theory and practice.** Reading, Mass.: Addison-Wesley, 1966.

210. Stevens, S. The "rat packs" of New York. **New York Times,** November 28, 1971, 29 ff.

211. Stevenson, H. W., and Stewart, E. C. A developmental study of race awareness in young children. **Child Development,** 1958, **29,** 399–410.

212. Streiker, L. D. **The Jesus trip: Advent of the Jesus freaks.** New York: Abington, 1971.

213. Stubbs, V. M. Environmental stress in the development of young drug users. Paper presented at the annual meeting of the California State Psychological Association, Coronado, Calif., January 31, 1971.

214. Student survey, **Playboy,** September 1971, 118 ff.

215. Student survey, **Playboy,** September 1970, 182 ff.

216. Tait, C. D., Jr., & Hodges, E. F. **Delinquents, their families, and the community.** Springfield, Ill.: Thomas, 1962.

217. Talbott, J. A., & Teague, J. W. Marihuana psychosis. **Journal of the American Medical Association,** 1969, **210,** 299–302.

218. **The American almanac for 1971 (The statistical abstract of the United States, 91st ed.).** New York: Grosset and Dunlap, 1971.

219. Trent, J. W., & Craise, J. L. Commitment and conformity in the American college. **Journal of Social Issues,** 1967, **22**(3), 34–51.

220. Vroegh, K. Masculinity and femininity in the elementary and junior high school years. **Developmental Psychology,** 1971, **4,** 254–261.

221. Wallach, A. Varying fates of young drug users. Paper presented at the annual meeting of the California State Psychological Association, Coronado, Calif., January 31, 1971.

222. Waterman, A. S., & Waterman, C. K. Relationship between freshman ego identity status and subsequent academic behavior: A test of the predictive validity of Marcia's categorization system for identity status. **Developmental Psychology,** 1972, **6,** 1979.

223. Waterman, A. S., & Waterman, C. K. A longitudinal study of changes in ego identity status during the freshman year in college. **Developmental Psychology,** 1971, **5,** 167–173.

224. Wattenberg, W. W. **The adolescent years.** New York: Harcourt Brace Jovanovich, 1955.

225. Watts, W. A., Whittaker, D. N. Some socio-psychological differences between highly-committed members of the Free Speech Movement and the student population at Berkeley. **Journal of Applied Behavioral Science,** 1966, **2,** 41–62.

226. Weil, A. T., & Zinberg, N. E. Acute effects of marihuana on speech. **Nature,** 1969, **22,** 434–437.

227. Weil, A. T., Zinberg, N. E., & Nelson, J. M. Clinical and psychological effects of marijuana in man. **Science, 1968, 162**(3859), 1234–1242.

228. Weiner, I. B. **Psychological disturbance in adolescence.** New York: Wiley, 1970.

229. Weingartner, H., Galanter, M., Lemberger, L., Roth, W. T., Stillman, R., Vaughn, T. B., & Wyatt, R. J. Effect of marijuana and synthetic $\triangle^9$–THC on information processing. **Proceedings, 80th Annual Convention of the American Psychological Association,** 1972, **7,** 813–814.

230. Wendland, M. M. **Self-concept in Southern Negro and white adolescents as related to rural-urban residence.** Unpublished doctoral dissertation, University of North Carolina at Chapel Hill, 1967.

231. Whelan, R. W. An experiment in preventing delinquency. **Journal of Criminal Law, Criminology, and Political Science,** 1954, **45,** 432–441.

232. Whittaker, D., & Watts, W. A. Societal confrontation or withdrawal: group personality contrasts of two extreme youth subcultures. Paper presented at the meeting of the Western Psychological Association, San Diego, March 1968.

233. Wikler, A. Drug dependence. In A. B. Baker and L. H. Baker (Eds.) **Clinical Neurology,** 1971, **2,** 1–53.

234. Wikler, A. Clinical and social aspects of marihuana intoxication. **Archives of General Psychiatry,** 1970, **23,** 320–325.

235. Williams, E. G., Himmelsbach, C. K., Wikler, A., Ruble, D. C., & Lloyd, B. J. Studies of marihuana and pyrahexyl compound. **Public Health Reports,** 1946, **61,** 1059–1083.

236. Winborn, B. B., & Janson, D. G. Personality characteristics of campus social-political action leaders. **Journal of Counseling Psychology,** 1967, **14,** 509–513.

237. Wirt, R. D., & Briggs, P. F. Personality and environmental factors in the development of delinquency. **Psychological Monographs,** 1959, **73,** 1–47.

238. Wolfe, T. **The electric Kool-Aid acid test.** New York: New American Library, 1968.

239. Yankelovich, D. **Generations apart: A study of the generation gap.** New York: CBS News, 1969.

240. Yankelovich, D., & the Editors of **Fortune. Youth in Turmoil.** New York: Time-Life, 1969.

241. Zablocki, B. The genesis of normative systems in rural hippie communes. Paper presented at the Society for Small Group Research, April, 1969.

242. Zellermayer, J., & Marcus, J. Kibbutz adolescence: Relevance to personality development theory. **Journal of Youth and Adolescence,** 1972, **1,** 143–153.

Epilogue

It should be possible at this juncture to cast a long look backward over the whole course of the child's development. Such a longitudinal survey should certainly serve to convince us that no one's behavior can be explained by easy platitudes. People do not behave as they do simply because "their parents spoiled them," because "they were born that way," or because "they are underprivileged." Our personalities are the result of too many complex interacting forces ever to be adequately explained in terms of any one of them.

In the course of this book, we have reviewed many of the kinds of forces that, taken together, determine the unique personality that the individual develops. We have seen that his development is bound to be affected, for good or ill, by his genetic inheritance; by his prenatal environment; by his physical and psychological environment; by the attitudes and behavior of his parents, teachers, and peers; and by his culture and subculture—social, ethnic, or economic. Especially during the past decade, we have seen how rapid social change and acute divisions and conflicts in society may profoundly affect the child's and adolescent's views of himself and of his world.

When one attempts to translate this breathtaking expanse of possible developmental influences into personal terms, one question often arises: How do we want our children to develop? Each parent will have his own answer, determined partly by his own unique set of values and life experiences. The parent who has fought against great economic odds may want financial security for his children. The parent who was unloved or rejected may want affection and love. The parent who had to leave school at 14 in order to go to work may feel that a proper education is all-important. Specific frustrations may play a role, too. How many parents want their children to realize their own unfulfilled dreams: to be a lawyer, an artist, a doctor, a farmer, a corporation executive, a musician, a politician, an actor?

Perhaps more than anything, however, most parents want their children "to be happy." But where does happiness lie, and how can we help our children to gain it? By helping them to become financially secure? By looking out for their health? By protecting them from tragedy and misfortune? Certainly we can make efforts in these directions, but we cannot, in this unpredictable world, be sure of success. In spite of our efforts, fortunes may crumble, health may fail, tragedy, at one time or another, will surely strike.

Furthermore, it is increasingly obvious that we cannot hope, through authoritarian patterns of parental behavior, to prescribe how our children shall lead their lives. Today's parents can, under favorable circumstances, provide for their children models of successful, autonomous, flexible, problem-solving behavior, and they can provide love and a fundamental underlying emotional security. But they cannot provide detailed blueprints for meeting the changing demands of a society in headlong transition.

When we look unsparingly at reality, it seems that the best insurance that we can try to pass on to our children is a clear and confident sense of their own identity, and an abiding commitment to some system of fundamental values. Life brings many crises and disappointments to all of us, but the emotionally mature person—one who is able to achieve a workable relationship between his own needs and desires, his conscience and ideals, and the demands of reality—will be better prepared to cope with these problems than the immature, the rigid and inflexible, and the neurotic.

Of course, no one can avoid encountering conflicts between his needs and the demands of reality, and between opposing needs within himself. Nor would such a state of affairs probably be desirable, even if it were possible, because a reasonable degree of conflict often provides the impetus for the individual's further development. One of the useful functions parents can perform is to help their children learn to tolerate conflict and frustration and to deal with them effectively. However, through proper parental modeling and guidance, the child can be helped to avoid learning conflicting needs which are too strong and which, instead of promoting maturity, tend to handicap him in his adjustment. Thus, the child may be helped to avoid conflicts based on extreme needs for both dependency and independency, on intense desires for social or sexual relationships with others and paralyzing fears of them, on wishes to exploit others and to serve them. The child can also be helped to develop those responses in the form of knowledge, social and performance skills, and cultural awareness that are likely to lead to satisfaction of his needs and those of his fellow citizens.

As we have seen, especially in the last two chapters on adolescence, these are indeed difficult and complex times. But if there is one single word that would appear most important to stress to both parents and their children, it is **communication.** It is significant that among the most frequent intergenerational criticisms cited in a recent national survey, adults mentioned a "lack of dialogue with elders," while adolescents complained that "they won't listen to us." Despite admittedly difficult problems, the channels of communications must be kept open, or in some cases reopened, between parents and their children. For the fact is that they need each other, now as much as ever. The view of some social observers that parents and other adults have become irrelevant or even barriers to the psychological and social development of their young may have a certain romantic appeal, but it is not substantiated by the facts. **Peter Pan** has its indisputable charm, but **Lord of the Flies** is probably more relevant.

In the world of tomorrow, young people will have to grow beyond the models their parents can provide, but they still need appropriate parental models to build on, and they need their parents' love and active concern. But if they are to succeed in this task, parents and young people will need a great deal more help from a society that loudly proclaims its devotion to children and adolescents, but that, in fact, does little to demonstrate this concern in practice. The problem is most urgent for the family of poverty, "Where the capacity for human response is crippled by hunger, cold, filth, sickness, and despair." But, as a task force of the recent White House Conference on Children succinctly states, "Even for families who can get along, the rats are gone, but the rat race remains" (1).

Ways need to be found to guarantee to all children and adolescents, as a basic minimum, adequate housing, health care, nutrition, and meaningful educational and vocational opportunities. In addition, we need consciously to plan and carry out ways of reversing current trends toward ever greater age segregation, not only within the family, but in the social life of the community—and in the work setting. We also need ways to restore a sense of community. The list, though not endless, is extensive. But as the White House Conference task force points out, these are things that **can** be done if government, business and industry, and individual citizens really mean what up to now they have only been saying. And they are things that must be done. As we have seen, a substantial majority of young people have not given up in their hopes for society or for themselves, and there is still time. But time may be running out. In the words of the task force:

> The failure to reorder our priorities, the insistence on business as usual, and the continued reliance on rhetoric as a substitute for fundamental reforms can have only one result: far more rapid and pervasive growth of alienation, apathy, drugs, delinquency, and violence among the young and not so young in all segments of our national life. We face the prospect of a society which resents its own children and fears its youth. Surely this is the road to national destruction (1).

We are reminded of the currently popular slogan, "I need all the help I can get." Today's parents and their children are embarked on a difficult but critically important voyage. If this book, and the growing body of developmental knowledge it describes, in any way helps to smooth the seas that lie ahead, it will have served its purpose.

Reference

1. **Children and parents: Together in the world.** Report of Forum 15, 1970 White House Conference on Children. Washington, D.C.: Superintendent of Documents, 1971.

Index of Names

Abelson, R. P., 522–523, 533
Acheson, R. M., 135, 173, 188
Adams, G., 188
Adelman, H. S., 530
Adelson, J., 475, 505, 507, 530, 549, 563, 564, 574, 576, 577, 581, 592, 601, 603, 604–605, 607–608, 609, 641, 643
Adkins, M. M., 428, 483
Adorno, T. W., 467, 475
Ahlgren, A., 537
Ahlstrom, W. M., 633, 636–637, 641
Ainsworth, M. D. S., 210–211, 228
Albert, J., 303, 324
Alexander, F., 641
Alexander, L., 526
Alkire, A. A., 641
Allen, B. H., 493, 526
Allen, J. R., 619, 641
Allen, L., 338–342, 359
Allen, V. L., 466, 475
Allinsmith, W., 449, 475, 497, 531
Allport, G., 74–75, 124
Altus, W. D., 440, 475
Amatruda, C. S., 101, 126, 161, 167, 169, 189
Ames, E. W., 150, 188
Ames, L. B., 161, 167, 169, 188, 189
Anastasi, A., 84, 124
Anderson, G. L., 494, 526
Anderson, H. E., 494, 526
Anderson, H. H., 494, 526
Anderson, R. E., 435, 475
Andrews, R. J., 475
Andry, R. G., 641
Anglin, J., 254, 267
Angrist, B., 626, 644
Anthony, E. J., 118, 125, 423, 425, 427, 440, 451–452, 457, 458–459, 462, 475
Argyle, M., 505, 527
Aries, P., 4–6, 28
Armentrout, J. A., 423, 424, 425, 475, 477
Arnold, H., 135–136, 188
Arnold, M., 608, 647
Aronfreed, J., 449, 475
Arthur, B., 482
Asch, S. E., 257, 267
Asher, S. R., 466, 475
Atkinson, C., 482
Auchincloss, K., 622, 641
Austin, L. J., 466, 477
Ausubel, D. P., 527, 550, 590
Ayers, L. P., 492, 526

Bach, G. R., 435, 476
Bachman, J. G., 465, 466, 476, 502–503, 505, 510, 513, 527, 562, 590, 610, 631, 636, 641
Bacon, M. K., 398, 415
Bahm, R. M., 435, 476
Bahn, A. K., 451, 452, 483
Baker, C. T., 343–344, 360, 594
Baker, D., 90, 128
Bakwin, H., 132, 188
Bakwin, R. R., 132, 188
Balaban, G. B., 646
Baldwin, A. L., 408–409, 415, 425, 476
Baldwin, W. K., 520, 527
Balfour, G., 254, 268
Bandura, A., 36, 53–56, 67, 238–239, 268, 374, 375, 377, 389–390, 415, 636–637, 641
Bandura, W., 415
Barbe, W. B., 520, 527
Barclay, A. G., 434, 476
Bardwick, J., 563–564, 565, 572, 581–582, 590, 603, 605, 641
Barglow, P., 641
Barker, L. S., 527
Barker, R. G., 372–373, 415, 527
Barnes, E. J., 465, 476
Barry, H., 398, 415
Barry, H., Jr., 440, 476
Barter, J. T., 624, 648
Bartlett, F., 53, 68
Barton, J., 89, 114, 126
Baruch, D. W., 482
Bates, P. B., 641
Bateson, P. P. G., 203, 206, 228
Baughman, E. E., 465, 476, 578, 590, 613, 641
Baumrind, D., 407, 408, 409–412, 415, 425, 427, 476, 492, 494, 505, 527, 562, 590, 641
Bay, C., 615, 617, 641, 642
Bayley, N., 161, 172, 188, 337, 338, 359, 438, 476, 551, 594
Beach, D. R., 288, 323
Beach, F. A., 566–567, 593
Bealer, R. C., 585, 594
Beck, A. T., 435, 476
Beck, J. M., 527
Becker, W. C., 405, 415, 425, 426, 427, 428, 449–450, 476
Beilin, H., 586, 590
Bell, A. P., 586, 590
Bell, G. D., 505, 527, 586, 590
Bell, M., 125
Bell, R. Q., 16, 28, 124, 150, 189
Bell, R. R., 571, 572, 590
Bell, S. M., 210, 228

Beller, E. K., 385, 415, 493, 527
Bellugi, U., 246, 268
Bellugi–Klima, U., 244, 249–250, 268
Bem, S. L., 297, 322
Bender, L., 443, 476
Benedict, R., 568, 590
Bennet, H. L., 563, 595
Bensberg, G. J., 53, 67
Berberich, J. P., 52–53, 68
Bereiter, C., 527
Berenda, R. W., 523, 527
Berens, A. E., 425, 476
Berger, A. S., 572, 597
Bergman, T., 144, 188
Berkwits, G. K., 427, 483
Berman, G., 502, 503, 527
Bernstein, B., 261–262, 268
Bertrand, A. L., 505, 511, 512, 527
Biber, B., 490, 498, 534
Bieri, J., 434, 476
Biller, H. B., 434, 435, 436, 437, 476, 528
Bilous, C. B., 563, 595
Binet, A., 331, 358
Binkley, F. L., 87, 126
Birch, H. G., 182–183, 191, 321, 323, 422, 484, 503, 528
Birnbaum, J. L., 605, 642
Birney, R. C., 507, 528
Black, J., 627, 642
Blake, M. T., 494, 528
Blanchard, R. W., 434, 476, 528
Blank, M., 356–357, 359
Blase, B., 122, 127
Bledsoe, J. C., 429, 476, 495, 528
Blest, A. D., 149, 188
Blinder, B. J., 443, 476
Block, J., 602, 642
Block, J. H., 401, 415, 616, 618, 642
Block, S. C., 323
Blom, G. E., 492, 499, 500, 528, 537, 615, 642
Bloom, B., 340, 359
Blos, P., 555, 575, 590
Blum, R. H., 624, 626, 627–628, 642
Bolles, R. C., 60–61, 67
Bolles, M. M., 88, 116, 126
Bommarito, B., 509, 533
Bond, E. A., 342, 359
Bonier, R. J., 624, 642
Bonney, M. E., 476, 477, 506, 519, 528, 578, 590
Bordin, E. S., 583, 590
Bordua, D. J., 505, 528, 585, 590
Bornstein, M. B., 641

Bovet, M., 261, 268
Bowerman, C. E., 575, 590
Bowlby, J., 206, 228, 637, 642
Boyle, R. P., 502, 528, 586, 590
Boynton, J. A., 466, 477
Bozzeti, L. P., 649
Brackbill, Y., 143, 188, 196, 222–
    223, 228
Braine, M. D. S., 121, 125
Braun, J. R., 479
Breau, G., 88, 128
Brecher, E. M., 565, 590
Breese, F. H., 408, 415, 503, 532
Brennan, W. M., 150, 188
Brenner, J. H., 624, 625, 626,
    627, 642
Brent, S. B., 256, 268
Bretsch, H. S., 594
Brewer, J. E., 494, 526
Bricker, W., 374, 418
Bridger, W. H., 157, 188
Bridgette, R. E., 465, 477
Briggs, P. F., 637, 650
Brittain, C. V., 566, 576, 577,
    591
Broadbent, D. E., 140, 188
Brody, E. B., 464, 465, 472, 477,
    578, 591, 613, 642
Broman, S. H., 224, 230
Bromberg, W., 624, 625, 642
Bronfenbrenner, U., 346, 347,
    349, 359, 396, 415, 435, 477,
    515, 528, 563, 577, 591
Bronner, A. F., 633, 645
Bronson, G. W., 144, 188
Bronson, W. C., 365, 416, 432–
    433, 477
Brook, V., 283, 323
Brophy, J. E., 528
Brossard, M., 221, 228
Brown, A., 125
Brown, A. R., 467, 472, 477
Brown, B., 434, 478
Brown, D. G., 401, 416
Brown, I. D., 495, 528
Brown, J. D., 619, 620–621, 642
Brown, O. H., 528
Brown, P., 53, 67, 376–377, 416
Brown, R., 234, 235, 243–244,
    245–250, 254, 268
Bryant, B. E., 610, 642
Bryant, B. K., 495, 528
Bruce, P., 429, 477
Buck, M. L., 495, 528
Buhler, C., 188
Burdick, H., 507, 528
Burger, G. K., 423, 424, 425,
    475, 477
Burke, D., 288, 316, 323

Burke, K. R., 466, 477
Burks, B. S., 94, 125
Burnstein, E., 591
Burt, C., 93, 125
Burton, R. V., 435, 438, 477,
    528
Busch, K., 573, 594
Butterfield, W. H., 53, 69
Butterworth, C. E., 505, 531

Cairns, R. B., 210, 228, 565, 591
Caldwell, B. M., 118, 126, 222,
    228
Caldwell, R. C., 153, 188
Calef, V., 619, 621, 642, 648
Cameron, J., 172, 188
Campbell, H., 119, 126
Campbell, J. D., 514, 515, 516,
    517, 520, 521, 523, 524, 529,
    591
Campbell, W. J., 529
Campos, J. J., 157, 188
Cannizzo, S. R., 260, 268
Caplan, N. S., 633, 642
Caplin, M. D., 477, 503, 529
Carey, J. T., 627, 642
Carlsmith, L., 434, 477
Carmichael, L., 106, 125
Caro, F. G., 583, 591
Caron, A. J., 153, 188
Caron, R. J., 153, 188
Carpenter, G. R., 573, 591
Carrigan, W. C., 523, 529
Carrino, C. A., 512, 529
Carter, H. D., 584, 591
Cassel, R. H., 53, 67
Castaneda, A., 507, 529
Cattell, R. B., 90, 125, 478
Caudill, W., 226, 228, 440, 477
Cazden, C., 244, 249–250, 268
Cervantes, L. F., 510, 511, 512–
    513, 514, 529
Chall, J., 509, 531
Challman, R. C., 518, 529
Charlesworth, R., 520, 531
Charlesworth, W., 178, 188
Chazan, M., 457, 458, 477
Cheong, G. S. C., 495, 529
Chess, S., 182–183, 191, 422,
    484
Chesser, E., 573, 591
Chessler, P., 53, 68
Child, I. L., 398, 404, 415, 418,
    500, 511, 529, 560, 568, 598
Chinsky, J. M., 288, 323
Chomsky, J. M., 268
Chomsky, N., 22, 28, 236, 239–
    240, 256, 266, 268
Christenson, H. T., 573, 591

Church, J., 429, 443, 484, 516,
    537, 578, 597
Chwast, J., 425, 477
Clader, D. E., 87, 126
Clark, E. V., 254, 268
Clark, G. R., 90, 128
Clark, J. P., 632, 643
Clark, K. B., 464, 465, 477, 490,
    511, 529, 578, 591, 613, 643,
    648
Clark, M. P., 465, 477, 578, 591,
    613, 643
Clarke, D. H., 520, 529
Clarke, H. H., 520, 529
Claussen, U., 624, 646
Cloward, R. A., 632, 643
Coates, B., 406, 416
Cobb, E., 428, 483
Cobbs, P. M., 464, 479, 645
Cohen, A. K., 632, 643
Cohen, L. B., 146, 188
Cohen, S., 627, 643
Cole, M., 23, 28, 289, 323
Coleman, J. S., 505, 508, 509,
    529, 534, 591
Coles, R., 554, 563, 613, 624,
    625, 626, 627, 642, 643
Collard, R. R., 208–209, 228
Collier, M. J., 498, 529, 531
Colwell, C. N., 53, 67
Combs, J., 511, 529
Commoss, H. H., 520, 529
Conant, J. B., 509, 530
Condry, J. C., Jr., 577, 591
Conger, J. J., 464, 477, 507,
    512, 523, 530, 534, 549, 550,
    556, 560, 561, 563, 570, 576,
    577, 578, 584, 591, 595, 600,
    601, 602, 603, 606, 607,
    608, 610–611, 613–615, 619–
    620, 622–623, 624, 625, 628,
    631, 632, 633, 634–635, 637,
    643, 648
Consalvi, C., 531
Cooley, W. W., 511, 529
Coolidge, J. C., 457, 458, 477
Cooper, D., 581, 591
Cooperman, O., 222, 230
Coopersmith, S., 428–432, 477,
    591
Coran, N. L., 118, 125
Corbett, F. J., 509, 533
Corner, G. W., 96, 97, 101, 125
Corrigan, A. M., 520, 538
Costanzo, P. R., 523, 530, 547,
    591
Costner, B. M., 167, 169, 189
Cotler, S., 507, 530
Cottle, T. J., 553, 591

Counter, S. A., 189
Coursin, D. B., 158, 189
Cowen, E. L., 538
Craig, M. M., 636, 643
Craise, J. L., 616, 650
Crandall, V. J., 320, 323, 386, 393–394, 416, 594
Crawford, L. Y., 632, 647
Cressey, D. R., 631, 637, 643
Crick, F. H. C., 59, 77, 128
Critchley, M., 492, 530
Crites, J. O., 592
Crowell, D. H., 188
Cusumano, D., 434, 476

D'Andrade, R. G., 377, 400, 416
Dansby, P. G., 465, 477
Darwin, C. A., 8, 9, 27, 28, 299
Datta, L., 477
Davids, A., 116, 125, 434, 435, 436, 437, 476
Davidson, H. H., 481, 509, 531
Davidson, K. S., 392, 418
Davidson, T. N., 510, 527
Davis, A., 438, 478
Davis, G. A., 592
Davis, H., 578, 593
Davis, J. O., 614, 644
Davis, K., 516, 530
Davis, R., 605, 643
Davison, A. N., 112, 125
Day, D., 303, 324
Day, S. R., 586, 592
Dean, S., 360
Debus, R. L., 307, 323
Decarie, T. G., 221, 228
DeFries, J. C., 91, 125, 128
Dekle, O. T., 495, 538
Dembo, T., 372–373, 415
Dement, W. C., 168, 191
Dempsey, D., 561, 562, 615, 643
Dennis, W., 161–163, 188, 220, 223, 228, 592
Derbyshire, R. L., 465, 478, 613, 643
DeSalvo, J., 521, 533
Desmond, M. M., 135–136, 188
Dethier, V. G., 48, 68
Deur, J., 376, 418
Deutsch, M., 429, 434, 472, 478, 488, 503, 508, 509, 530, 538
DeVault, M. V., 494, 495, 529, 533
Diaz-Guerrero, R., 515, 534
Didion, J., 619, 643
Dielman, T. E., 478
Dippel, A. L., 101, 114, 125
Dishatsky, N. I., 643
Disher, D. R., 159, 189

Distler, L., 403, 417
Dizmang, L., 478
Dobbing, J., 112, 125
Dolger, L., 438–439, 478
Dollard, J., 62, 68
Donaldson, M., 254, 268, 302, 323
Doob, L. W., 272, 323
Doris, J., 429, 478
Douvan, E. A., 505, 507, 530, 549, 563, 564, 574, 576, 577, 581, 582, 590, 592, 601, 603, 604–605, 607–608, 643
Dove, A., 328
Dowaliby, F. J., 497, 530
Draguns, J. G., 307, 323
Drake, D. M., 307, 323
Dreyer, P. H., 465, 479
Drillien, C. M., 111–112, 121, 125
Duffy, E., 507, 530
Dumars, K. W., 87, 126
Dunbar, E., 628, 643
Dunbar, F., 115, 128
Dunham, J. L., 497, 534
Dunlop, G. M., 456, 478
Durkin, D., 445, 478
Dworkin, A., 478, 613, 643
Dwyer, J., 549, 592
Dymond, R. F., 428, 483

Ebbs, J. H., 125
Eckerman, C. O., 211, 229
Edge, S., 499, 537
Edwards, A. E., 627, 643
Edwards, M., 468, 469, 479
Eimas, P. D., 158, 188
Eisenberg, J., 563, 596
Eisenberg, L., 89, 125, 457, 458, 478, 492, 530
Eisenberg, M., 502, 503, 527
Eisenberg, R. B., 158, 189
Eisenman, R., 625, 645
Elder, G. H., Jr., 505, 530, 561, 562, 570, 575, 576, 577, 592
Elkind, D., 457, 459, 462, 485, 553, 554–555, 592, 606, 643, 644
Elliott, D. S., 512, 530
Elliott, R., 53, 67, 376–377, 416
Ellis, R. W. B., 111–112, 121, 125
Ellison, R., 464, 478
Emde, R. N., 155, 190
Emmerich, W., 378, 381–382, 386, 416
Empey, L. T., 632, 644
Engel, M., 429, 478
England, A. O., 455, 478

Englemann, S., 527
English, O. S., 459, 461, 478, 644
Erikson, E. H., 387, 416, 464, 478, 548, 557, 592, 600, 601, 602, 613, 644
Ernhart, C. B., 119, 125
Escalona, S., 338, 359, 478
Espenschade, A., 546, 593
Evans, R. I., 600, 644
Exum, D. B., 641

Fagan, J. F., 144, 189
Fantz, R. L., 144, 148–149, 189
Farbman, I., 524, 535
Farley, F. H., 481
Faulkner, W., 560, 593
Faust, M. S., 551–552, 593
Fawl, C. L., 416
Featherstone, J., 510, 530
Fein, L. G., 507, 530
Fejer, D., 623, 649
Feld, S. S., 212–213, 229
Feldhusen, J. F., 497, 504, 507, 530, 536
Feldman, J. J., 123, 126
Feldman, S., 381, 417
Fenton, N., 440, 468, 478
Ferguson, L. R., 385, 391, 416
Ferriss, G. S., 123, 127
Feshbach, N., 378, 416, 496–497, 530, 535
Feshbach, S., 378, 416, 530
Feuer, L. S., 615, 644
Fiedler, M., 224, 230
Filliozat, A. M., 163, 189
Finch, S. M., 457, 459, 461, 462, 478, 644
Finkelstein, M., 427, 483
Fishman, J. R., 465, 478, 613, 644
Fitts, W. H., 634, 644
Fitzgerald, H. E., 150, 189
Fjellman, J. S., 305, 323
Flacks, R., 616, 644
Flanders, N. A., 521, 531
Flavell, J. H., 176–177, 189, 260, 268, 274, 287, 288, 323
Fleck, S., 644
Fleener, D. E., 210, 228
Flick, G. C., 123, 127
Flory, C. D., 159, 161, 191
Floud, J. E., 585, 593
Ford, C. S., 566–567, 593
Forman, N., 493, 537
Fort, J., 622, 628, 644
Fraiberg, S. H., 387, 416
Franco, D., 492, 531
Frankel, F., 289, 323

Franklin, R. R., 135–136, 188
Fredrickson, L. C., 609, 644
Freedman, A. M., 121, 125, 461, 478, 626, 644
Freedman, D. G., 91, 125, 196, 229
Freedman, N. C., 91, 125
Freeman, H. E., 112, 126
Freeman, R. N., 83, 127
Freitag, G., 52, 68
Frenkel-Brunswick, E., 467–468, 475, 478,
Freud, A., 452, 453, 479, 555, 593, 644
Freud, S., 23, 34, 36, 37, 41–45, 61, 65, 67, 68
Frisch, R. E., 593
Fromme, D. K., 602, 645
Frost, B. P., 497, 507, 531
Fuller, F. F., 528
Fuller, J. C., 91, 125
Fuller, J. L., 91, 92, 125, 127
Furfey, P. H., 531
Furman, R. A., 443, 479
Furth, H. G., 260, 268

Gaddini, R., 602, 648
Gage, N. L., 350, 359, 494, 507, 531
Gagne, R. M., 64, 68, 260, 268
Gagnon, J. H., 547, 566, 568, 572, 597
Gaier, E. L., 498, 529, 531
Galanter, M., 650
Galbraith, J. K., 614, 644
Gallagher, J. J., 520, 531
Galliani, C., 520, 535
Gallup, G. H., Jr., 614, 644
Gamston, C., 578, 593
Garber, H., 352–355, 359
Garcia, J., 65, 68
Garn, S. M., 135, 189
Garner, A. M., 463, 479
Garrison, K. C., 546, 593
Gates, R. R., 80, 125
Gay, J., 23, 28
Geber, M., 163, 189
Gebhard, P. H., 564, 565, 566, 571–573, 594
Geist, H., 584, 595
Gellis, S. S., 114, 125
Gerald, P. S., 88, 128
Gershon, S., 626, 644
Gerver, J. M., 509, 531
Gesell, A., 99, 101, 106, 125, 126, 161, 166, 167, 169, 189
Gewirtz, J. L., 171, 190, 195, 229, 382, 416
Gibbs, P. K., 438, 481

Gibson, E. J., 155–157, 189, 283, 323
Gilliard, B. J., 593, 602, 645
Gilligan, C., 446, 480, 606–607, 647
Ginandes, J., 438–439, 478
Ginzburg, H., 262, 268
Glaser, H. H., 644
Glaser, K., 459, 462, 479
Glazer, J. A., 520, 531
Gleason, J. G., 256, 268
Glick, A. A., 23, 28
Glick, S. J., 636, 643
Glueck, E. T., 435, 437, 479, 630, 631, 632, 633, 636–637, 644
Glueck, S., 435, 437, 479, 630, 631, 632, 633, 636–637, 644
Gold, H. A., 520, 531
Gold, M., 479, 563, 592, 630, 631, 632, 633, 644
Gold, V. J., 52, 68
Goldberg, L., 633, 645
Goldberg, S., 119, 126
Goldfarb, W., 462, 479
Goldman, R., 440, 483
Goldstein, R., 563, 625, 626, 645
Goodenough, F. L., 479
Goodglass, H., 256, 268
Goodpasture, E. W., 90, 114, 126
Gordon, E. W., 503, 508, 510, 531
Gordon, J. E., 523, 535
Gorodetsky, C. W., 624, 646
Gottesman, I. I., 126, 348, 359
Gough, H. G., 468, 469, 479
Graham, F. K., 118, 119, 125, 126
Grant, G., 465, 480, 578, 593
Gray, S. W., 188, 356–357, 359, 360
Greeley, A., 608, 609, 645
Green, B., 609, 641
Green, K. F., 65, 68
Green, S., 502–503, 505, 513, 514, 527
Greenberg, J. W., 481, 509, 531
Greenberg, M., 89, 114, 126
Greenberg, N. H., 179, 189
Greene, H. W., 520, 529
Greene, M. E., 523, 536
Greer, D. R., 507, 531
Greer, G., 582, 593
Gregor, A. J., 466, 479
Gregory, I., 435, 479
Greulich, W. W., 547, 593
Grier, J. B., 189, 464, 479
Grier, W. H., 645

Griffin, E. J., 158, 189
Grimes, J. W., 497, 531
Grinder, R. E., 593
Grinspoon, L., 622, 624, 645
Gronseth, E., 435, 479
Gross, B., 488, 490, 531
Gross, R., 488, 490, 510, 531
Grossman, D. S., 645
Grossman, H. J., 179, 189
Grossman, J. C., 625, 645
Gruen, G. E., 289, 325
Grusec, J. E., 389–390, 415
Gryler, R., 619, 621, 642, 648
Guilford, J. P., 328–329, 330, 359
Guilford, J. S., 633, 645
Gump, P. V., 502, 531
Gunn, B., 584, 593
Gussow, J. D., 503, 528
Guttman, D., 563, 581, 582, 590
Gynther, M. D., 465, 481, 595, 613, 647

Haaf, R. A., 150, 189
Haan, N., 616, 618, 642
Haber, R. B., 272, 323
Haber, R. N., 272, 323
Habicht, J. P., 112, 126
Hagman, R. R., 388–389, 416
Haith, M. M., 144, 147, 188, 189, 259, 260, 268, 287, 324
Hall, G. S., 9–10, 27, 28
Hall, P. L., 573, 593
Haller, A. O., 505, 531
Hallworth, H. J., 578, 593
Halsey, A. H., 593
Halverson, H. M., 167, 169, 189
Hammer, W. T., 634, 644
Harlow, H. F., 200–201, 214, 217, 224, 229, 230
Harlow, M. H., 200–201, 217, 229
Harrington, S., 352–355, 359
Harris, D. B., 429, 468, 469, 479, 482
Harris, G. J., 288, 316, 323
Harris, L., 568, 570, 588, 593, 608, 610, 611, 614, 645
Harris, M. B., 239, 268
Harris, S., 479
Hartl, E. M., 649
Hartley, E. L., 465, 479
Hartup, W. W., 381, 382, 384, 386, 406, 416, 515, 518, 519, 520, 521, 522, 523, 524, 531
Harvey, J., 523, 532
Harvey, O. J., 493, 494, 521, 531, 536
Hassell, L. L., 87, 126

Hathaway, S. R., 636, 645
Hattendorf, K. W., 369, 416
Hauser, S. T., 645
Havighurst, R. J., 465, 479, 503, 532, 633, 636–637, 641
Havumaki, S., 521, 531
Hay, W. K., 493, 537
Hayden, S. D., 272, 325
Haynes, H., 147, 189
Healy, W., 633, 645
Hetherington, E. M., 307, 324, 435, 436, 479
Heathers, G., 381, 385, 416
Heber, R., 352–355, 359
Heckel, R. V., 436, 479
Hedl, J. J., Jr., 497, 532
Heider, E. R., 280, 323
Heider, G. M., 478
Heil, L. M., 494, 496, 532
Heilbrun, A. B., 593, 602, 604, 645
Heimer, C. B., 121, 125
Heinecke, C. M., 449, 480
Heist, P., 615, 616, 645
Held, R., 147, 164, 189, 191
Henssenstamm, F. K., 510, 532
Herley, A., 481
Hershenson, M., 147, 190
Hertzig, M. E., 321, 323, 484
Hess, E. H., 48, 68
Hess, R. D., 347, 359
Heston, L. L., 89, 126
Hilgard, E. R., 46, 57, 58, 68
Hilgard, J. R., 443, 480
Hill, J. P., 260, 268
Hill, K. T., 392–393, 416, 497, 507, 520, 532, 536
Hilles, L., 619, 621, 642, 648
Hilt, R. H., 135–136, 188
Himmelsbach, C. K., 624, 650
Hindley, C. B., 163, 189
Hindsman, E., 429, 482
Hinsey, W. C., 68
Hirsch, J., 92, 126
Hobart, C. W., 581, 593
Hobson, S., 504, 536
Hochberg, J., 283, 323
Hodges, E. F., 636, 637, 650
Hofer, R., 619, 621, 642, 648
Hoffman, C., 352–355, 359
Hoffman, M. L., 404, 405, 407, 416, 417, 449, 480
Hoffman, L. W., 593
Hokanson, J. E., 507, 538
Holden, R. H., 116, 125
Holland, J. L., 593
Hollingshead, A. B., 518, 532, 593
Holmes, F. B., 388, 389, 417

Holmes, H., 229
Holt, J., 490, 532
Holzinger, K. J., 83, 127
Honig, A. S., 222, 228
Honigmann, J. J., 400, 417
Honzik, M. P., 94, 126, 338–342, 359
Hood, W. R., 521, 536
Hooper, F. H., 317–318, 324
Horner, F. A., 87, 126
Horner, M. S., 563, 581, 582, 590, 593, 605, 645
Hornsby, J. R., 304, 324
Horowitz, F. D., 520, 532
Houriet, R., 614, 646
Howard, A., 425, 481
Howard, P., 553, 591
Howell, S. J. G., 452, 480
Hraba, J., 465, 480, 578, 593
Hsia, D. Y., 114, 125
Hsu, F. L. K., 515, 532
Hudgins, B. B., 520, 532
Hughes, B. O., 547, 596
Hundziak, M., 53, 68
Hungerford, D. A., 646
Hunt, J. McV., 357, 359
Hunt, M., 565, 568, 570, 594, 646
Hunt, R. G., 523, 532
Hunter, M. A., 158, 189
Hurlock, E. B., 97, 99, 106, 126
Huston, A. C., 375, 415
Huyck, E. E., 646
Hyde, M. R., 256, 268
Hymowitz, P., 624, 642

Ilg, F. L., 167, 169, 189
Inhelder, B., 17, 28, 261, 268
Irwin, F. W., 320, 323
Irwin, O. C., 180, 190
Isbell, H., 624, 646
Iscoe, I., 523, 532
Israel, S. L., 550, 594
Israelstein, D. M., 647

Jackson, P. W., 490, 532
Jacobs, P. A., 87, 128
Jakubczak, L. F., 524, 532
James, H., 637, 646
Janke, L. L., 503, 532
Janson, D. G., 650
Janssen, P., 628, 646
Jasinski, D., 624, 646
Jencks, C., 95, 126, 488, 532
Jennings, E., 429, 482
Jennings, F., 499, 532
Jennings, H. H., 578, 594
Jensen, A. R., 95, 126, 348, 357,

359, 429, 472, 478, 488, 508, 509, 530
Jersild, A. T., 378, 388, 417, 456, 457, 480, 532, 546, 549, 574, 594
Jersild, C. L., 456, 457, 480
Jessor, R., 320, 323
John, E. B., 53, 68
Johnson, A. M., 457, 458, 480, 630, 631, 632, 646
Johnson, C. S., 613, 646
Johnson, L., 622, 646
Johnson, T. J., 520, 532
Johnson, V. E., 565, 566, 595
Johnston, L. D., 510, 527
Jones, H. E., 86, 126, 546, 551, 594
Jones, M. C., 389, 417, 551, 594, 595
Jordaan, J. P., 583, 597
Joseph, A., 222, 230
Julian, J. W., 523, 529
Jusczyk, P., 158, 188
Justman, J., 509, 532

Kabasakalian, L., 493, 532
Kagan, J., 23, 91, 112, 126, 142, 150, 151, 154, 159, 170, 171, 172, 180, 182, 190, 191, 212, 221, 223, 229, 259, 260, 268, 283, 287, 302, 303, 305, 307, 323, 324, 325, 340, 343, 344, 350, 359, 360, 364, 365, 379, 384, 386, 395, 400–401, 402, 417, 425, 426, 427, 440, 480, 492, 495, 506, 512, 532, 533, 534, 538, 549, 550, 560, 561, 563, 576, 578, 584, 594, 595, 601, 602, 603, 606, 607, 608, 610, 613–614, 619, 632, 633, 646, 648
Kahl, J. A., 585, 594
Kahn, R. L., 510, 527
Kalhorn, J., 408, 415
Kallmann, F. J., 88, 126
Kamin, L., 95
Kandel, D. B., 504, 505–507, 533, 646
Kant, E., 606
Kantner, J. E., 573, 598
Kaplan, A., 13, 14, 28
Kaplan, B. J., 126
Kaplan, H. I., 461, 478
Kaplan, J., 624, 646
Karen, R. L., 519, 533
Karlsson, G., 573, 594
Karlsson, S., 573, 594
Karmel, B. Z., 150, 190
Kassorla, I. C., 52, 68

Katkovsky, W., 320, 323
Katz, E. W., 256, 268
Katz, I., 429, 472, 478, 488, 508, 509, 530
Katz, J., 646
Katz, J. M., 324
Katz, L., 533
Kearsley, R. B., 158, 190
Keasey, C. B., 646
Keasey, C. T., 646
Keay, A. J., 87, 128
Keeler, M. H., 625, 646
Keeney, T. J., 260, 268
Keislar, E. R., 578, 594
Keller, E. D., 386, 416, 497, 533
Kelley, H. H., 577, 594
Kelley, W. N., 127
Kellogg, R. L., 492, 533
Kempner, P., 619, 621, 642, 648
Kendall, R. F., 646
Kendler, T. S., 258, 268
Keniston, K., 516, 533, 611–612, 613, 615, 646
Kerber, A., 509, 533
Kerpelman, L. C., 616, 617, 647
Kessel, F. S., 255, 256, 268
Kessen, W., 7, 8, 9, 12, 28, 29, 147, 191
Kessler, J. W., 390, 417, 425, 427, 452, 456, 457, 458, 460, 461, 462, 480
Kestenbaum, J. M., 497, 533
Khana, A. A., 578, 594
Kiesler, C. A., 521, 533
Kimble, G. A., 46, 58, 68
Kinch, J. W., 575, 590
Kinney, D. K., 154, 159, 190
Kinsey, A. C., 550, 564, 565, 566, 571–573, 594
Klackenberg, G., 163, 189
Klaus, R. A., 355–356, 359, 360, 519, 533
Klausmeier, H. J., 497, 507, 530
Kleiber, D. A., 588, 594
Klein, M. W., 632, 647
Klein, R. E., 112, 126, 259, 260, 268, 287, 316, 324
Kliman, G., 480
Klineberg, O., 500, 533
Knop, C. A., 180, 190
Koch, H. L., 440, 442, 480
Kogan, N., 296, 325
Kohen-Raz, R., 222, 229
Kohl, H., 490, 533
Kohlberg, L., 403–404, 417, 446, 447–449, 474, 480, 484, 606–607, 647
Kohn, L., 374–375, 418
Kolb, S., 163, 191

Kolers, P. A., 324
Korn, H. A., 615, 618–619, 649
Korn, S., 484
Korte, F., 624, 646
Kosier, K. P., 494, 533
Kotelchuck, M., 211, 212, 229
Kounin, J. S., 533
Kozol, J., 490, 533
Kramer, M., 451, 452, 483
Kramer, R., 606, 647
Krauss, I., 502, 533
Krawitz, A., 157, 188
Kriesberg, L., 505, 533
Kris, E., 632, 647
Kristy, N. F., 90, 125
Kuenne, M. R., 259, 269
Kuhlen, R. G., 594, 608, 647
Kuhn, D., 647
Kutner, B., 464–470, 480
Kuvelsky, W. P., 585, 594
Kvaraceus, W. C., 647

LaBadie, G., 646
Labov, W., 263–266, 269
Lakin, M., 126
Lamarck, J., 76
Lambert, W. W., 560, 595
Landis, C., 88, 116, 126
Landy, F., 434, 436, 480, 484
Langer, A., 157, 188
Langer, J., 647
Lansky, L. M., 594
Laosa, L. M., 528
Lapouse, R., 456, 481
Larson, L. E., 576, 577, 594
Larson, W. R., 503–504, 505, 534
Latham, A. J., 578, 594
Laughlin, F., 578, 595
Leahy, A. M., 479
Lee, B. J., 594
Lefeber, J. A., 647
Lefevre, C., 509, 533
Lelos, D., 647
Lemberger, L., 650
Lembright, M. L., 520, 538
Lenneberg, E. H., 170, 190
Lepper, C., 478
Lerner, E., 445, 481
LeShan, L. L., 533
Lesser, G. S., 504, 505–507, 508, 522–523, 533, 536, 646
Lester, B., 316, 324
Leventhal, T., 457, 458, 481
Levin, H., 370, 377, 378, 385, 400, 405, 418, 425, 428, 432, 440, 449, 481, 484, 488, 533
LeVine, B. B., 425, 449, 481
Levine, E. M., 500, 511, 529

Levine, F. J., 445, 446–447, 484
Levine, M., 509, 533
Levinson, B., 300–301, 324
Levinson, D. J., 467, 475
Levy, B. I., 423, 483
Levy, D. M., 425, 427, 481
Levy, N., 159, 190
Lewin, K., 372–373, 415, 595
Lewis, M., 119, 126
Lichter, S. O., 512, 533
Liem, G. R., 538
Lighthall, F., 392, 418
Lilienfeld, A. M., 111, 127
Linner, B., 573, 595
Linton, R., 518, 534
Lippitt, R., 520, 521, 534, 535
Lipscomb, W. R., 643
Lipset, S. M., 616, 647
Lipsitt, L. P., 51, 68, 159, 190, 429, 481
Lipsitt, P. D., 647
Lipton, R. C., 218–219, 229
Little, J. K., 503, 534, 585, 595
Littman, R. A., 68, 374, 418
Liublinskaya, A. A., 259, 269
Livson, N., 172, 188, 523, 537, 575, 597
Llewellyn, L. G., 524, 535
Lloyd, B. J., 624, 650
Loban, W. D., 256, 269
Locke, J., 7–8, 29, 36
Lord, E. M., 515, 532
Lorenz, K. Z., 48, 68
Loughman, W. D., 643, 647
Lourenso, S. V., 481
Lovaas, O. I., 52–53, 58, 68
Lowrey, G. H., 106, 110, 128, 133, 134, 191
Luce, J., 619, 620, 632, 647, 649
Luckey, E., 570, 571, 572, 595
Lund, F. H., 595
Luria, A. R., 258, 269
Lynn, D. B., 402, 417, 436, 481, 552, 573, 595, 602, 603, 647

McBride, B. E., 602, 647
McCall, R. B., 150, 190
McCandless, B. R., 386, 417, 418, 504, 505, 507, 529, 534, 563, 595
McCarthy, D., 172, 190
McClearn, G. E., 422, 481
McClelland, D. C., 505, 507, 534
Maccoby, E. E., 212–213, 229, 282, 324, 370, 377, 378, 380–381, 385, 400, 405, 417, 418, 425, 426, 428, 432, 438, 440, 449, 481, 484, 523, 534

McConnell, T. R., 523, 534
McCord, J., 425, 435, 481, 636–637, 647
McCord, W., 425, 435, 481, 636–637, 647
MacCurdy, H. L., 546, 595
McCurdy, R. N. C., 115, 126
McDermott, E., 649
McDill, E. L., 505, 534
McDonald, R. L., 465, 481, 595, 613, 647
Macfarlane, J. W., 338–342, 359
McGhee, P. E., 577, 595
McGowan, B. K., 65, 68
McGraw, M. B., 76, 115, 126, 161, 190
McGurk, H., 294, 324
McKeachie, W. J., 494, 534
MacMahon, B., 123, 126
McNeil, J. D., 492, 534
McNeill, D., 242–243, 269
McPherson, D., 466, 479
MacRae, D., 445, 446, 481
Malcolm X., 464, 481
Malinowski, B., 23, 370, 417
Malmquist, C. P., 459, 481
Manaster, G. J., 588, 594
Mandel, J., 627, 642
Mandler, G., 507, 536
Mann, D., 479, 632, 633, 644
Mann, J., 546, 565, 595
Mann, L., 144, 188
Marburger, C. L., 500, 534
Marcus, J., 651
Maresh, M., 544, 545, 546, 595
Markey, F. V., 378, 417, 456, 457, 480
Marolla, F., 128
Marquis, D. P., 50–51, 68, 199, 229
Marshall, H. R., 386, 417
Marshall, W. E., 524, 537
Martels, B., 119, 126
Martin, C. E., 550, 564, 565, 566, 571–573, 594
Martin, E. C., 490, 534
Martin, F. M., 585, 593
Martin, M., 494, 535
Martin, W. E., 468, 469, 479
Maslow, A. H., 515, 534
Mason, W. A., 203, 218, 229
Massengale, O. M., 644
Masters, J. C., 380, 417, 523, 534
Masters, W. H., 565, 566, 595
Matarazzo, R. G., 118, 126
Matlin, N., 583, 597
Maurer, R. A., 53, 68
Mayer, J., 549, 592

Mayer, L. A., 490, 534, 581, 585, 595, 630, 647
Mead, M., 23, 558–559, 568, 582, 595
Meagher, D., 624, 625, 626, 627, 642
Mealiea, W. L., Jr., 481
Medinnus, G. R., 602, 647
Mednick, M. T., 510, 527
Melnyk, J., 649
Meltzer, H., 439, 481
Melville, M. H., 87, 128
Mendez, O. A., 321, 323
Menlove, M. L., 389–390, 415
Menninger, K., 637, 647
Menyuk, P., 255, 269
Meredith, H. V., 134, 190
Merrill, M. A., 330, 360, 633, 648
Messer, S. B., 289–290, 324
Meyers, C. E., 427, 428, 481
Meyers, J., 497, 534
Michalak, J., 499, 534
Miller, D., 637, 648
Miller, D. R., 437, 482
Miller, H., 482
Miller, J., 466–467, 483
Miller, N. E., 36, 62, 68
Miller, R. B., 428, 483
Miller, T. W., 482
Miller, W. B., 482, 632, 647, 648
Miller, W. C., 600, 631, 633, 634–635, 643
Milner, P., 68
Minahan, N., 595
Minturn, L., 560, 595
Minuchin, P., 490, 498, 534
Miranda, S. M., 144, 189
Mischel, W., 435, 482
Mitchell, D., 435, 482
Mizner, G. L., 624, 648
Mogan, R. E., 643
Molfese, D. L., 256, 257, 269
Monachesi, E. D., 636, 645
Money, J., 499, 534, 565, 598
Monk, M. A., 456, 481
Montagu, M. F. A., 111, 113, 115, 116, 127
Montesano, N., 584, 595
Moore, E. W., 150, 188
Moore, S. G., 519, 534
Moore, T., 172, 190
Morante, L., 602, 648
Morgan, E. F., Jr., 518, 537
Morgan, G. A., 208, 229
Morland, J. K., 465, 482
Morrison, F. J., 259, 260, 268, 285, 287, 324
Morrow, W. R., 505, 534

Morse, N. C., 583, 595
Moss, H. A., 91, 126, 127, 173, 190, 215, 229, 302, 324, 340, 344, 359, 360, 365, 379, 384, 386, 395, 417, 425, 440, 480, 563, 594, 603, 646
Mowrer, O. H., 402, 417
Moyle, W. J., 125
Multari, G., 307, 323
Muma, J. R., 520, 534
Murphy, D. P., 114, 127
Murphy, G., 404, 417, 445, 482
Murrow, C., 534
Murrow, L., 534
Mussen, P. H., 360, 402–403, 405, 417, 418, 470–471, 482, 506, 512, 534, 549, 550, 551, 560, 561, 563, 576, 578, 584, 595, 601, 602–603, 606, 607, 608, 610, 613–614, 619, 632, 633, 648
Muzio, J. N., 168, 191
Myerhoff, B. G., 503–504, 505, 534

Nagera, H., 459, 482
Najarian, P., 223, 228
Namenwirth, J. Z., 490, 504, 510, 535
Nass, G. A., 570, 571, 572, 595
Neimark, E. D., 289, 313, 324
Neisser, U., 286, 324
Nelson, E. A., 436, 482
Nelson, J. M., 624, 650
Nelson, V. L., 343–344, 360
Nerlove, H., 257, 267
Nesselroade, J. R., 641
Nevis, S., 189
Newbrough, J. R., 426, 429, 482
Newman, H. H., 83, 127
Newton, P., 464, 465, 483, 578, 596, 613, 648
Ni, E., 427, 483
Nicolet-Meister, P., 163, 189
Niswander, K. R., 122, 127
Norman, R. D., 505, 535
Northway, M. L., 520, 535
Nowlis, H. H., 624, 626, 627, 648
Nye, F. I., 648

Odem, R. D., 507, 536
Odom, L., 426, 429, 482
Offer, D., 535
Ohlin, L. E., 632, 643
O'Keefe, B., 597
Olds, J., 27
Olsen, V., 605, 643
Olson, W. C., 547, 596

Olver, R. R., 304, 324
O'Neil, R., 609, 641
Oskamp, S., 573, 596
Osofsky, H., 550, 596
Osterman, P., 488, 490, 531
Osterrieth, P. A., 553–554, 596
Otis, N. B., 386, 418

Pable, M. W., 602, 648
Packard, V., 565, 570, 571, 572, 573, 596
Painter, P., 118, 125
Palermo, D. S., 256, 257, 269, 507, 529
Palmer, F. H., 483
Papousek, H., 47, 68
Parke, R. D., 307, 324
Parker, A., 402–403, 417
Parker, H. J., 484
Parker, M. M., 83, 127
Parker, R. D., 67, 418
Parsons, T., 613, 648
Pasamanick, B., 111, 127
Pascual-Leone, J., 288, 297, 324
Patel, A. E., 523, 535
Paton, G. R., 646
Patterson, G. R., 68, 374, 418
Paul, J. C. N., 565, 591
Pavenstedt, E. A., 509, 535
Pavlov, I. P., 49, 51, 61
Peck, R. F., 520, 535
Pelliteri, O., 89, 114, 126
Perlman, I. R., 648
Perloff, B. F., 52–53, 68
Pestalozzi, J., 9, 29
Philips, W., 303, 324
Phillips, B. N., 429, 482
Piaget, J., 12, 16, 17, 20, 23, 29, 34, 36, 37, 38–41, 42, 44, 47, 65, 67, 68, 69, 146, 174–179, 190, 256–257, 261, 297, 309–318, 324, 327, 329, 330, 444–445, 447, 448, 466, 474, 482, 523, 535
Pierce, C. M., 464, 482
Piers, E. V., 429, 482
Pietz, K. R., 602, 648
Pihlblad, C. T., 583, 591
Pikas, A., 562, 596, 602, 648
Pine, G. J., 632, 648
Pittel, S. M., 619, 621, 642, 648
Plato, 4
Pleck, J., 553, 591
Plumb, R., 135–136, 188
Plummer, G., 114, 127
Polak, P. R., 155, 190
Polansky, N., 520, 521, 535
Polk, F. F., 619, 621, 648

Pomeroy, W. B., 550, 564, 565, 566, 571–573, 594, 596
Porter, M., 229
Porterfield, O. V., 520, 535
Portuges, S. H., 535
Potter, E. H., 500, 511, 529
Poussaint, A. F., 482
Powers, E., 636–637, 648
Poznanski, E., 459, 482
Prather, M., 493, 494, 535
Pratt, K. C., 147, 190
Prescott, E., 501, 535
Preston, A., 320, 323
Proshansky, H., 464, 465, 483, 578, 596, 613, 648
Provence, S., 218–219, 229
Purcell, K., 423, 463–464, 483
Purnell, R. F., 578, 596

Rabinovitch, M. S., 191
Rabson, A., 386, 394, 416
Radke, M. J., 466–467, 483
Radke-Yarrow, M., 466–467, 471–472, 483
Raine, W. J., 429, 478
Rand, W., 87, 89, 99, 105, 127
Raplen, E. B., 512, 533
Rau, L., 519, 520, 538
Raush, H. L., 524, 535
Readio, J., 320, 323
Redl, F., 520, 521, 535
Reed, M. F., 494, 526
Rees, A. H., 483
Reese, H. W., 300–301, 324, 497, 507, 520, 535
Reevy, W. R., 550, 564, 571, 572, 596
Reichenbach, H., 14–15, 29
Reisman, D., 580, 596
Reiss, A. J., 649
Reiss, I. L., 570, 571, 572, 573, 596
Renson, G. J., 423, 483
Revelle, R., 593
Rheingold, H. L., 171, 190, 211, 214–215, 229
Rhoades, P., 478
Ricciuti, H. N., 179, 191, 208, 229
Richardson, C. E., 90, 128
Richardson, S., 520, 535
Richek, H. G., 528
Richette, L. A., 637, 649
Ridberg, E. H., 307, 324
Riessman, F., 535
Riley, J. E., 429, 483
Robertson, R. E., 427, 483
Robinson, P., 505, 527
Robinson, W. P., 262, 269

Robson, K. S., 127, 215, 229
Roeper, A., 317–318, 324
Roff, M., 520, 536
Roffwarg, H. P., 168, 191
Rogers, C. R., 428, 483
Rohmann, C. G., 135, 189
Rommetveit, R., 255, 269
Rooks, M. McC., 520, 535
Rosen, B. M., 451, 452, 483
Rosenbaum, M., 465, 479
Rosenberg, B. G., 400, 402, 418, 434, 436, 440, 480, 483, 484, 518, 537
Rosenberg, M., 360, 429, 483, 562, 596, 602, 649
Rosenbloom, F. M., 127
Rosenhan, D., 406, 418
Rosenthal, D., 89, 127
Rosenthal, M. J., 427, 483,
Rosenthal, M. K., 382, 418
Rosenthal, T., 494, 535
Rosman, B. L., 303, 324
Ross, A. O., 457, 483
Ross, H., 171, 190
Rossi, A., 400, 418
Rossi, W., 289, 324
Roszak, T., 614, 649
Roth, W. T., 650
Rothman, E. P., 490, 535
Rousseau, J. J., 7–8, 29
Rovee, C. K., 159, 191
Rowe, P. B., 523, 536
Rowley, V. N., 497, 533
Ruble, D. C., 624, 650
Ruebush, B. K., 390, 392, 418, 428, 429, 483, 497, 535
Rutherford, E., 403, 405, 417, 418
Rutherford, J., 531
Ryan, D. G., 494, 536

Sackett, G. P., 221–222, 229
Saenger, G., 128
Salapatek, P., 147, 191, 214, 229
Salisbury, H. E., 632, 649
Saltzstein, H. D., 404, 405, 417, 449, 480, 523, 536
Sameroff, A. J., 167, 191
Sampson, E. E., 615, 618–619, 649
Sand, E. A., 163, 189
Sanford, N., 605, 649
Sanford, R. N., 428, 483
Sarason, S. B., 392–393, 416, 418, 497, 507, 532, 536
Sargent, T. W., 647
Sawrey, W. L., 436, 481
Saxe, R. W., 527

Scammon, R., 610, 649
Scarr, S., 90, 91, 127, 214, 229, 483
Scarr-Salapatek, S., 348–349, 360
Schaefer, E. S., 423, 425, 438, 476, 483, 484
Schaeffer, B., 52–53, 68
Schaeffer, D. L., 563, 582, 596
Scheinfeld, A., 80, 127
Schlichting, H. F., 520, 535
Schmitt, S. S., 593
Schonfeld, W. A., 550, 596
Schooler, C., 440, 477, 484
Schulte, R., 56, 69
Schumer, H., 497, 530
Schwartz, S., 465, 479
Scott, J. P., 91, 127
Sears, P. S., 435, 440, 484, 520, 536
Sears, R. R., 370, 377, 378, 382, 385, 400, 405, 418, 425, 427, 428, 429, 432, 440, 449, 484
Sebold, H., 630, 632, 649
Seegmiller, J. E., 127
Seeman, J., 426, 429, 482
Sehti, B. B., 435, 476
Seibert, F. M., 512, 533
Seligman, D. A., 588, 596
Sellmann, A. H., 123, 127
Sells, S. B., 520, 536
Senn, M. J. E., 427, 443, 452, 457, 460, 462, 463, 484
Shagass, C., 646
Shapiro, E., 490, 498, 534
Sharma, S., 507, 536
Sharp, D. W., 23, 28, 289, 323
Shaw, M. E., 523, 530
Shearer, W. M., 189
Sheldon, W. H., 649
Shepherd, J., 608, 649
Sherif, C. W., 521, 522, 536
Sherif, M., 521, 522, 536
Sherman, I. C., 159, 161, 191
Sherman, M., 159, 161, 191
Shipman, V. C., 347, 359
Shirley, M. M., 161, 191
Shooter, J. R., 524, 537
Short, J. F., Jr., 632, 649
Shuttleworth, F. K., 596
Siebert, L. A., 633, 642
Siegel, A., 374–375, 418
Sigel, I. E., 302, 317–318, 324
Siipola, E. M., 272, 325
Silberman, C. E., 488, 490, 508, 509, 510, 511, 536
Sills, M., 457, 458, 481
Siman, M. L., 577, 591

Simmons, K., 547, 586, 597
Simon, W., 547, 566, 568, 572, 597
Simpson, R. L., 505, 536, 585, 586, 588, 597
Sinclair, H., 261, 268
Singer, J. E., 122, 127
Siqueland, E. R., 158, 188
Skeels, H. M., 352, 360
Skinner, B. F., 36, 37, 51, 52, 69, 237–239, 266, 269
Slack, C. W., 637, 649
Slansky, M. A., 512, 533
Slobin, D. I., 236, 238, 246–247, 250–252, 269
Slotnick, N. S., 289, 324
Smart, R., 623, 649
Smith, A. C., 123, 127
Smith, A. J., 536
Smith, D. E., 619, 620, 632, 649
Smith, E. C., 260, 268
Smith, G. H., 519, 520, 536
Smith, L. M., 520, 532
Smith, M. B., 616, 618, 642
Smith, R. T., 93, 127
Smock, D. C., 261, 268
Soares, A. T., 465, 484
Soares, L. M., 465, 484
Solkoff, N., 122, 127
Solnit, A. J., 427, 443, 452, 457, 460, 462, 463, 484
Solomon, F., 356–357, 359, 465, 478, 613, 644
Somers, R. H., 615, 649
Sontag, L. W., 115, 116, 127, 343–344, 360
Sorenson, R. C., 572, 573, 597
Sparkes, R. S., 649
Spaulding, R. L., 520, 536
Speedie, S., 504, 536
Spelke, E., 212, 229
Spelt, D. K., 69
Spergel, I., 637, 649
Spiro, M. E., 515, 536
Spitz, R. A., 218, 229
Spitz, R. R., 155, 190
Spock, B., 443, 460, 461, 462, 484
Squier, R., 115, 128
Sroufe, L. A., 195, 229
Staats, A. W., 53, 69, 237, 269
Staats, C. K., 237, 269
Stakenas, R. G., 497, 536
Stanford, R. N., 467, 475
Starishevsky, R., 583, 597
Stechler, G., 113, 128, 142–143, 191
Stein, Z., 128
Stellar, E., 48, 68

Stendler, C. B., 493, 536
Stern, C., 80, 82, 87, 92, 128
Stern, J. A., 118, 125
Stevens, S., 632, 649
Stevenson, H. W., 464, 465, 484, 507, 536, 613, 649
Stewart, A. L., 87, 128
Stewart, E. C., 464, 465, 484, 613, 649
Stice, G. F., 90, 125
Stillman, R., 650
Stinchcombe, A. L., 488, 536
Stodolsky, S. S., 508, 536
Stolz, L. M., 435, 484
Stone, L. J., 429, 443, 484, 516, 537, 578, 597
Straus, M. A., 562, 597
Streamer, C. W., 87, 126
Streiker, L. D., 609, 649
Strickland, A. D., 495, 528
Strodtbeck, F. L., 632, 649
Stubbs, E. M., 158, 175, 191
Stubbs, V. M., 621, 649
Suomi, S., 214, 224, 230
Super, C. M., 143, 191
Super, D. E., 583, 597
Susser, M., 128
Sutton-Smith, B., 400, 402, 418, 434, 436, 440, 480, 483, 484, 518, 537
Swanson, B. M., 484
Swanson, G. E., 437, 482
Sweeney, M., 87, 89, 99, 105, 127
Swift, J. W., 429, 484
Synnerdale, V., 523, 532

Tabachnick, R., 468, 484
Taber, R. C., 514, 537
Tait, C. D., Jr., 636, 637, 650
Talbott, J. A., 625, 650
Tannenbaum, J., 222, 228
Tanner, J. M., 503, 537, 544, 545–547, 551, 597
Tapp, J. L., 445, 446–447, 484
Taylor, K. M., 646
Taylor, R. G., 497, 505, 537
Teague, J. W., 625, 650
Teevan, R. C., 507, 528, 577, 595
Telfer, M. A., 90, 128
Templin, M. C., 261, 269
Terman, L. M., 180, 191, 330, 360
Tessman, E., 457, 458, 477
Thomas, A., 182–183, 191, 321, 323, 422, 484
Thomas, P., 464, 484
Thompson, G. E., 494, 537

Thompson, H., 133, 134, 161, 167, 169, 189, 191
Thompson, W. R., 92, 125
Thoreau, H. D., 619
Thurber, E., 435, 481
Thurston, D., 118, 119, 125
Thurston, J., 504, 536
Tiedemann, D., 8, 29
Tiller, P. O., 435, 484, 485
Tinbergen, N., 48, 69
Tisdall, F. F., 125
Tizard, B., 222, 230
Tizard, J., 222, 230
Toby, J., 502, 505, 537
Toch, H. H., 56, 69
Toigo, R., 520, 537
Tompkins, W. T., 112, 128
Trager, H. G., 466–467, 483
Trehub, S. E., 191
Trent, J. W., 616, 650
Trent, R. D., 468, 485
Tryon, C. M., 578, 597
Tuckman, B. W., 493, 495, 537
Tuddenham, R. D., 518, 520, 537, 577, 597
Tulkin, S. R., 171, 191
Tuma, E., 523, 537, 575, 597
Turner, E. W., 255, 269
Turner, R. H., 586, 597
Turula, E., 602, 642
Tuthill, R. W., 435, 476
Tyler, L. E., 180, 191

Ulrich, T., 289, 324
Underwood, B., 494, 535
Unger, S. M., 449, 485

Valenstein, E. S., 597
Vallbona, C., 135–136, 188
Van Duinen, E., 610, 641
Van Krevelen, A., 578, 598
Vangen, P. M., 436, 482
Vaughn, T. B., 650
Victor, I., 53, 68
Vigorito, J., 158, 188
Vincent, E. L., 87, 89, 99, 105, 127
Visotsky, H. M., 641
Volkart, E. H., 577, 594
Von Spulak, F., 624, 646
Vosk, J. S., 509, 537
Voss, H. L., 511, 512, 530, 537
Vroegh, K., 650

Wachs, T. D., 289, 325
Wagner, N. N., 573, 593
Waite, R. R., 392, 418, 499, 500, 528, 537
Walberg, H. J., 537

Waldfogel, S., 457, 459, 477
Walk, R. D., 191
Walk, R. R., 155–157, 189
Wallace, R. F., 115, 127
Wallach, A., 619, 621–622, 648, 650
Wallach, M. A., 296, 325
Wallerstein, R. S., 619, 621, 642
Walsh, A. M., 429, 485
Walsmith, C. R., 600, 631, 633, 634, 643
Walters, R. H., 53–56, 67, 374, 415, 524, 532, 537, 636–637, 641
Walzer, S., 88, 128
Ward, D. A., 631, 637, 643
Wash, J. A., 494, 526
Washburne, C., 494, 496, 532
Waterman, A. S., 650
Waterman, C. K., 650
Watrous, B. G., 515, 532
Watson, E. H., 106, 110, 128, 133, 134, 191
Watson, G. A., 425, 427, 485
Watson, J. B., 36, 59, 77, 128
Watson, L. S., Jr., 53, 68
Wattenberg, B. J., 610, 649
Wattenberg, W. W., 427, 429, 485, 637, 650
Watts, J., 135–136, 188
Watts, W. A., 615, 616, 650
Weatherley, D., 551, 552, 598
Wechsler, D., 327, 335, 360
Weil, A. T., 624, 650
Weiner, B., 497, 533
Weiner, I. B., 457, 459, 462, 485, 637, 650
Weingartner, H., 650
Weinstein, H., 226, 228
Weintraub, D., 122, 127
Weir, M. W., 91, 128
Weismann, A., 76–77, 128
Weiss, J. H., 423, 463, 483
Weiss, R. S., 583, 595
Weller, G. M., 124
Wenar, G., 463, 479
Wendland, M. M., 465, 485, 613, 650
Wendling, A., 512, 530
Wenninger, E. P., 632, 643
Werme, P. H., 624, 648
Werner, H., 12, 29
Werts, C. E., 586, 598
Wesolowski, J. C., 509, 533
West, L. J., 619, 641
Westphal, M., 122, 127
Whelan, R. W., 636, 650
White, B. J., 521

White, B. L., 147, 164, 189, 191
White, R. K., 521, 534
White, R. W., 393, 418, 515, 538
White, S. H., 281, 325
White, W. F., 494, 495, 526, 538
Whiteman, M., 508, 538
Whiting, B. B., 560, 598
Whiting, J. W. M., 404, 418, 435, 438, 477, 528, 560, 568, 598
Whitlock, C., 53, 69
Whittaker, D. N., 615, 616, 650
Wickelgren, L. W., 147, 191,
Wicker, A. W., 501, 502, 538
Wikler, A., 624, 625, 627, 650
Wilcox, R. C., 472, 485
Wilkerson, D. A., 503, 508, 510, 531
Willems, E. P., 502, 538
Willer, M. L., 457, 459, 477
Willerman, L., 224, 230
Williams, D. R., 60, 69
Williams, E. G., 624, 650
Williams, H., 60, 69
Williams, M., 523, 532
Wilner, N., 565, 619, 648
Wilson, A. B., 586, 598
Wilson, E. A., 626, 644
Wilson, R. C., 505, 534
Wilson, R. S., 538
Wilson, W., 435, 482
Wilson, W. C., 565, 571, 598
Winborn, B. B., 650
Winder, C. L., 519, 520, 538
Windle, W. F., 118, 128
Winterbottom, M. R., 394, 418, 425, 485
Wirt, R. D., 637, 650
Wirtanen, I., 502–503, 505, 513, 514, 527
Wishner, J., 565, 591
Witmer, H., 636–637, 648
Wittrock, M. C., 289, 324
Wohlwill, J. F., 304, 325
Wolfe, T., 632, 651
Wolff, K. M., 218, 229
Wolff, P. H., 180, 191
Wolman, B. B., 485
Wood, C. G., Jr., 507, 538
Wortis, H., 121, 125
Wright, C. M., 222, 228
Wright, M. E., 372, 418
Wright, M. K., 641
Wunsch, J. P., 194, 229
Wyatt, R. J., 650
Wylie, R., 428, 485

Yaffe, S., 122, 127

Yamamoto, L., 520, 538
Yando, R. M., 307, 325, 495, 538
Yankelovich, D., 568, 571, 588–589, 598, 608, 609–610, 614, 616, 617, 618, 623, 625, 626, 651
Yarbrough, C., 112, 126
Yarrow, L. J., 371, 418, 521, 538
Yarrow, M. R., 519, 520, 521, 529, 538

Yee, A. H., 496, 538
Yellot, A. W., 538
Young, H. B., 602, 648
Young, N., 493, 536

Zablocki, B., 619, 651
Zanna, M., 521, 533
Zelazo, N. A., 163, 191
Zelazo, P. R., 163, 191, 212, 229
Zellermayer, J., 651
Zelnik, M., 573, 598

Zimbardo, P. G., 507, 536
Zimet, S. G., 492, 499–500, 501, 528, 537, 538
Zimiles, H., 490, 498, 534
Zimmermann, R. R., 200–201, 229
Zinberg, N. E., 624, 650
Zola, I. K., 562, 636–637, 647
Zrull, J. P., 459, 482
Zubin, J., 565, 598
Zuckerman, M., 565, 598
Zytowski, D. G., 583, 598

Index of Subjects

Absence, parental, 433–437
Abstract concepts, 273
Abstract reasoning, 37, 38
Abstraction, 273, 327
  language development and,
    234, 260–261
Academic achievement. **See**
  Achievement, school
Acceptance-rejection (warmth-
  hostility), 423
Accommodation, 147
  Piaget's concept of, 40,
    42–43
Achievement, school, anxiety
  and, 507
  motivation of. **See** Achieve-
    ment motivation
  socioeconomic status and,
    502–504
Achievement behavior, high,
  correlates of, 393–395
Achievement motivation,
  mastery and, 393–395
  parental and peer influences
    on, 504–507
  parental values and, 503–504
Acquired instrumental responses, 166–167
Acquisition of operations,
  39–40
Active copers, 180
Active-passive dimension, 16,
  27–28, 36–38
Activists, student, 615–619
  and conformity, 616, 618
  moderate reformers, 617–618
  parent-child relationships
    and, 618–619
  radical dissenters, 617
Adaptability, infant, 182
Adaptation, 327
Adjustment, in adolescence,
  556–557
  problems of, anxiety and
    defense mechanisms, 453–
    455; compulsions, 460–
    461; conduct, 461–462;
    depression, 459; fears and
    phobias, 455–460; minor-
    ity-group membership,
    464–466; obsessions, 460–
    461; prejudice, develop-
    ment of, 466–470; psy-
    chological, 451–472; psy-
    chophysiological symp-
    toms, 462–464; psycho-
    somatic conditions, 463–
    464; racial attitudes,
    modification of, 470–472

school, in middle childhood,
  487–502
Adolescence, 542–655
  adjustment tasks of, 556–557
  alienation in, 611–622;
    adolescent "counter-
    culture" and, 614; cultural
    deprivation and, 612;
    drug use, 618, 620, 622–
    629; "new," 613–614;
    social dropouts, 615, 619–
    622; student activists,
    615–619; varieties of,
    611–613
  cognitive development in,
    552–556; moral develop-
    ment and, 606–607; per-
    sonality development
    and, 554–556
  defense mechanisms of,
    555–556
  dependence-independence
    conflicts, sex differences
    in, 563–564
  developmental tasks of,
    556–557
  ego identity, 548–549, 555,
    600–605; parental identi-
    fication and, 601–602;
    sex-typing and, 602–605
  independence in, develop-
    ment of, 557–564; estab-
    lishment of in American
    culture, 560–561; estab-
    lishment of in other cul-
    tures, 558–560; parent-
    child relationships and,
    561–563
  juvenile delinquency in, 3,
    629–638; cultural depri-
    vation and, 632, 640;
    economic factors, 3, 632,
    640; incidence of, 629–
    631; intelligence of
    delinquents, 633; parent-
    child relationships and,
    3, 427, 636–637; person-
    ality and, 633–636, 640–
    641; prevention and treat-
    ment of, 637–638; sex
    differences in rates of,
    630–631; social change
    and, 631–632; socioeco-
    nomic status and, 631, 640
  maturation in, early versus
    late, 551–552; sexual,
    544, 547, 551
  menstruation, onset of, 544,
    551; psychological as-

pects of, 549–550
  moral development in, 605–
    611; cognitive develop-
    ment and, 606–607;
    stages of, 606
  nocturnal emissions, 550
  parental influences during,
    576–578, 585–586
  and peers, 574–580; influ-
    ence of peers, 576–578;
    peer culture, conformity
    to, 575–576; social accep-
    tance by peers, 578, 580
  personality development in,
    cognitive aspects of,
    554–556
  physical development in,
    544–548; endocrinological
    factors, 544; growth
    factors, interrelationships
    among, 547–548; growth
    spurt, 544–547; menarche,
    age of, 544, 551; muscu-
    lar, 546; puberty, age and
    onset of, 544, 547
  psychological factors of
    growth and development,
    548–552
  school dropouts, 3, 511–514;
    antecedents of dropping
    out, 511; family and
    peers, influence of, 513;
    psychological character-
    istics of, 513–514; school
    experience and, 511–512
  sexual attitudes and be-
    havior in, 542–543, 564–
    566; in America, 568,
    570–574; cultural influ-
    ences on, 566–568; parent-
    child differences in,
    571–572; in relation to
    broader cultural values,
    567–568; variations in,
    570–571
  values in, 607–611; of
    alienated middle-class
    youth, 614–615; current
    trends in, 609–611; moral,
    intrapsychic conflicts
    and, 607–609; political,
    609; religious beliefs,
    changes in, 608–609;
    sexual, 568, 570; social
    change and, 607
  vocational choice, 580–590;
    adjustment in American
    culture, 583–584; orienta-
    tion of girls, 581–582;

Adolescence **(Continued)**
parental influences on, 585–586; peer-group influences on, 586, 588; psychological determinants of, 583; school influence on, 586, 588
Adopted children, 93–95, 345
Adrenalin, 101
Age differences, in aggression, 378
in memory, 20–21, 289
in perception, 285–286, 288–289
Aggression, 3, 20, 33, 43
age differences in, 378
development of in preschool years, 370–379; expression of, stability of, 378–379; social experience and, 370–371
extinction of, 374
frustration and, 11, 371–372
imitation and, 375
modeling and, 375
parental influences on, 377
permissiveness toward, 374
punishment for, 376–377
rewards for, effects of, 373–374
sex differences in, 377–379
Alcohol, use of among adolescents, 622
Alienation in adolescence, 611–622
adolescent "counterculture" and, 614
cultural deprivation and, 612
developmental estrangements, 612
drug use, 618, 620, 622–629; alcohol, 622; amphetamines, 622, 625–627; barbiturates, 625–626; hashish, 620, 622; heroin, 626, 628; LSD and other hallucinogens, 618, 620, 626–628; marijuana, 618, 620, 622–626; "pills," 626–627; reasons for, 629
"new," 613–614
social dropouts, 615, 619–622
student activists, 615–619
varieties of, 611–613
Altruism, 20, 405–406
Amnion, 99
Amniotic fluid, 99, 105

Amphetamines, use of among adolescents, 622, 625–627
Anal stage, 43, 45
Analytic concepts, 302–303
Anatomical abnormalities, genetic factors in development of, 87
genital, 31–32
Anemia, 112
Animal behavior, studies of, 49–53, 60–61, 91–92, 200–203, 208, 214, 217–218, 221–222, 224
Anoxia, 118–119, 121–124
Anxiety, 4, 43, 45
antecedents of, 390–391
attachment and, 208–214
defense mechanisms and, 391–393, 453–455
dependency and, 382
development of in preschool years, 390–393
intellectual mastery and, 319–320
memory and, 289–290
during pregnancy, 115
school achievement and, 507
separation, 208, 210–214
stranger, 208–210, 219
Aphasic speech, 241
Approach-avoidance conflict, 368–369
Asceticism, defense mechanism, 555–556
Assimilation, Piaget's theory of, 40, 42
Associations, insight and, 59
learned, 61
types of, 46
verbal, 64
Asthma, 463–464
Astrology, recent preoccupation with, 611
Attachment, 11, 22, 199–214
anxiety and, 208–214
to caretaker, consequences of, 214–224
cultural factors in, 224–227
definition of, 204–206
feeding situation and, 200–201
primary caretaker, lack of, 216–223
Attention, 193
focused, 193, 281, 285–286
learning and, 59, 61
reinforcement and, 61
selective, 281
span of, individual differ-

ences in, 182
stimulus determinants of, 147–154; complexity, 149–150; meaning and discrepancy, 150–154; movement, intensity, and contour, 147–149
sustained, capacity for, 281; primary determinants of, 150
Authoritarian control, home, 409
Authoritarian teachers, 493, 494
Authoritative parental control, 410
Authoritative parents, 411, 412, 424
Authoritative teachers, 494–495
Autism, 57
Autonomy, 382, 385
parental, control-, 423; psychological, 423
student activists and, 616

Babbling in infancy, 170–172, 195, 199, 204, 241–242
relation to later development, 172–173
Babinski reflex, 160
"Baby biographies," 8–9, 27
Barbiturates, use of, 622–623
among adolescents, 625–626
Basal mental age, 332
Bayley's Scales of Infant Development, 337
Behavior, achievement, high, correlates of, 393–395
aggressive. **See** Aggression
animal, studies of, 49–53, 60–61, 91–92, 200–203, 208, 214, 217–218, 221–222, 224
delinquent. **See** Juvenile delinquency
motives and, distinction between, 367–369
parent, dimensions of, 423–425, 472
prosocial, 405–406
reasons for, 33–34
sexual, in adolescence, 542–543, 564–566; cultural influences on, 566–568
social, research in, 20; status with peers and, 520–521. **See also** Socialization

Behavior (Continued)
test, child's public, significance of, 321–322
unlearned, 48
Behavior genetics, 12
Behavior-modification procedures, 53
Behavior therapy, 52–53, 376
Behavioral development, contrasting conceptions of, 16–17, 27–28, 36–38
Behavioral predispositions, children's, parental response to, 432–433
Behavioral retardation, infant, 218–223
capacity for recovery from, 223–224
Beliefs, changes in, 47–48, 65–66
religious, adolescent, 608–609
Binet Scale, 331–333, 335
administration and scoring of, 332
construction of, 331–332
Binocular fixation, 147
Biological changes, in adolescence, 544–547; glandular, 544; growth factors, 547–548; growth spurt, 544–547; menarche, age of, 544, 551; puberty, age and onset of, 544, 547
in first year, 132–188; body growth, 132–135; developmental trends, 166–167; differences among infants, individual, 179–183; infancy, stages of, 141–159; mental development, 173–179; needs, basic, 167–170; response capabilities, 160–164; vocalization and speech development, 170–173. **See also** Infancy
Biological energy, Freud's concept of, 42, 61
Birth, premature, 112, 120–122, 143
process of, 118–122
stillbirth, 112, 115
Blastocyte, 98
Blood types, 115
Body growth. **See** Biological changes
Body proportions, in adolescence, 544–547

growth in infancy, 133–134
Brain damage, 173–174
speech development and, 241
Broca's area, 241

California Preschool Mental Scale, 337, 339
Campus demonstrations, 542
Caretaker, attachment to, consequences of, 214–224
primary, lack of, 216–223
Categorical concepts, 302
Categorical responses, 347
Cathexis, 42–44
Cattell Intelligence Scale for Infants and Young Children, 337, 354
Cephalocaudal development, 134, 166
Cerebral dominance, 241
Cerebral sclerosis, 83
Child psychology. **See** Developmental psychology
Child-rearing practices, competence and, 409–412
cultural differences in, 224–227
dependency and, 384–385
maturity and, 409–412
social-class differences in, 437–438
See also Parent-child relationships; Parents
Chorion, 99, 100
Chromosomal aberration, 88
Chromosomes, 75–82, 97, 98, 122
Class inclusion, 311
Classical conditioning, 46–47, 49–52, 58–59, 61, 64
Cognitive activities in preschool and school-age child, 277–309
evaluation, 305–308
executive process, 277–278
hypotheses, generation of, 291–305; concept of creativity and, 295–296; in concept-sorting tasks, 302–305; critical attributes, importance of, 292, 294–295; learning set and, 300–302
memory functions, 286–291; age differences in memory, 289; factors affecting memory, 287-289
perception and

interpretation, 278–286
transformational rules, implementation of, 308–309
types of, 277
units in, 271–277; concepts, 272–275; images, 272; rules, 275–276; schema, 272; symbols, 272
Cognitive-adaptive theory, 38
Cognitive development, 16
in adolescence, 552–556; moral development and, 606–607; personality development and, 554–556
in infancy, 173–179; Piaget's view of, 174–179
language development and, 252, 257–261, 267
in preschool and school-age child, 271–322; Piaget's view of, 309–317. **See also** cognitive activities in preschool and school-age child
research in, 20–23
Cognitive functioning, raising level of, 350, 352–357
Cognitive theory, 12
Colic, 116
Combinative structures, 313
Communal child care, 22
Compensatory education, 2–3, 348, 350, 355–357
Competence, 20
child-rearing antecedents of, 409–412
development of, 393
Competition, 3, 41, 394–395
cross-cultural studies of, 22
Complex concepts, 273
Complex reflexes, 52, 57, 166, 204
Complexity, attention and, 149–150
Compulsions in middle childhood, 460–461
Concept-formation, 11, 20, 327
language development and, 234, 257
Concept learning, 64
See also Concepts
Concept-sorting tasks, generation of hypotheses in, 302–305
stimuli, effect on, 303–305
Concepts, 272–275
abstract, 273
analytic, 302–303

Concepts **(Continued)**
  attributes of, 273–274
  categorical, 302
  complex, 273
  concrete, 273
  developmental changes in, 274
  differentiated, 274
  functional-locational, 302
  functional-relational, 302
  relative and absolute qualities of, 274–275
  superordinate, 302
Concrete concepts, 273
Concrete operations stage of intellectual development, 41, 310–312
Conditioning, classical, 46–47, 49–52, 58–59, 61, 64
  instrumental, 51, 59, 64
  operant, 51–53, 59, 61, 64; language development and, 237
Conduct problems in middle childhood, 461–462
Conformity, to moral standards, 606–607
  to peers, 523–524, 575–576
  student activists and, 616, 618
Conscience development, in middle childhood, 444–451, 460; parent-child relationships and, 450–451
  in preschool years, 398, 404–406
Conservation, 310 311
Construction, Piaget's concept of, 39
Contiguity, learning and, 58–59, 61
Control-autonomy, parental, 423
Conventional moral reasoning, 606
Convergent production, 328
Cooing, 170
Coping responses, 391
"Counterculture," adolescent, alienation and, 614
Crawling and creeping, development of, 161
Creativity, 20
  concept of, generation of hypotheses and, 295–296
  intelligence and, 295
  obstacles to, 296–300
Critical attributes, importance of, 292, 294–295

Cross-cultural research, 22–23, 28
Cross-sectional approach to research, 15–16
Crossing over, 81–82
Crying, 46, 170
  extinction of, 65
  generalization of, 65
  reasons for, 33–34, 197
  as response to separation, 211, 213, 214
Cultural deprivation, adolescent alienation and, 612
  juvenile delinquency and, 632, 640
  language development and, 261–267
  in middle childhood, 508–510
Cultural reinforcement, 563
Culture of poverty, 612
Cumulative learning theory, 64
Curiosity, sexual, 369–370, 583
Cytosine, 77

Death instinct, 42
Death phobias, 458–459
Decidua capsularis, 99
Deep structure, sentence, 236
Defense mechanisms, 43, 391–393, 453 455
  adolescent, 555–556
Delinquency, juvenile. **See** Juvenile delinquency
Democratic parents, 425–426
Democratic teachers, 495
Denial, defense mechanism, 392, 453–454
Dependence-independence conflicts, sex differences in, 563–564
Dependency, 3
  anxiety and, 382
  child-rearing practices and, 384–385
  emotional, 381–382, 563–564
  forms of, changing, 380–382
  generalized, 564
  instrumental, 381–382, 563–564
  nursery-school attendance and, 381–383
  in preschool years, 379–387
  relation to other aspects of socialization, 385–386
  sex differences in, 386–387
  situational factors affecting, 382–384

See also Attachment
Depression in middle childhood, 459
Deprivation, cultural, adolescent alienation and, 612; juvenile delinquency and, 632, 640; language development and, 261–267; in middle childhood, 508–510
  emotional, 15
  environmental, 173–174, 220–221
Depth perception in infancy, 155–157, 170
Development, goals and direction in, 34, 36
Developmental estrangements, 612
Developmental psychology, antecedent-consequent relationships, 11–14, 17, 27–28
  contributions of, 27
  field of, 12
  fundamental problems of, 2–4, 27
  goals of, 27
  historical perspectives, 4–10, 27
  philosophers and, 6–8, 27
  reasons for studying, 31–33
  research in. **See** Research
  as scientific discipline, emergence of, 10–17
  theories in, 12, 27–28, 33–45; active-passive dimension, 16, 27–28, 36–38; cognitive-adaptive, 38; Freudian, 41–45, 67; Piagetian, 37–41, 67
Dexadrine, use of among adolescents, 620
Diabetes, 83, 114
Differentiated concepts, 274
Directed cognition, 277
Disadvantaged children, needs of, 509
  programs for, 509–510
  school and, 508–510
Discipline, inconsistent,
Discrepancy, attention and, 150–154
Discrimination, 62, 64
  multiple, 64
Disease, genetic factors in development of, 82–85, effects of, 428
  87, 89

Disease **(Continued)**
  venereal, 542
Dishabituation, 143
Displacement, 454
Distinctiveness of stimulation,
  221
Distractibility, infant,
  individual differences in,
  182
Divergent production, 328
DNA, 59, 77, 81
Dominating teachers, 494
Down's syndrome, 88, 90
Drives (needs), 61
  hunger, 61, 169–170
  thirst, 61, 169–170
  See also Motives; Needs,
  basic
Dropouts, school, 3, 511–514;
  antecedents of dropping
  out, 511; family and
  peers, influence of, 513;
  psychological
  characteristics of,
  513–514; school
  experience and, 511–512
  social, 615, 619–622
Drug addiction, 3, 33
  among babies, 113
Drug use, among adolescents,
  618, 620, 622–629; alcohol,
  622; amphetamines, 622,
  625–627; barbiturates,
  625–626; hashish, 620,
  622; heroin, 626, 628; LSD
  and other hallucinogens,
  618, 620, 626–628;
  marijuana, 618, 620,
  622–626; "pills," 626–627;
  reasons for, 629
  in contemporary society,
  622–623
Drugs, prenatal environmental
  influence of, 113

Early Training Project
  (Peabody College),
  355–357
Echolalia, 52
Ectoderm, 99
Education, compensatory,
  2–3, 348, 350, 355–357
  moral, 506–507
  sex, 568
Educational aspiration,
  parental and peer
  influences on, 504–507
  socioeconomic status and,
  502–504

Effectance motivation, 393
Ego identity, 548–549, 555,
  600–605
  parental identification and,
  601–602
  sex-typing and, 602–605
Eidetic imagery, 272
Elaborated language codes, 261
Elimination, need for, 169
Embryo, 75, 100, 113
  development of, 101–103
  period of, 98–103
Emotional dependency,
  381–382, 563–564
Emotional deprivation, 15
Emotional maturity, 41
Emotional upsets during
  pregnancy, 115–116
Endoderm, 99
Enuresis, 471
Environment, home,
  methodological problems
  in researching, 406–408
  infant vocalization and, 172
  social, expansion of in
  middle childhood,
  487–526; disadvantaged
  children, school and,
  508–510; educational
  aspiration, parental and
  peer influences on,
  504–507; peers, relations
  with, 514–524; peers,
  social status with,
  518–521; school,
  adjustment to, 487–502;
  school achievement,
  socioeconomic status and,
  502–504
  See also Home; Parent-child
  relationships; Parents
Environmental deprivation,
  173–174, 220–221
Environmental influences,
  prenatal, 110–116
  age of mother, 111
  diet of mother, 111–112
  drugs, 113
  irradiation, 113–114
  maternal attitudes, 116
  maternal diseases and
  disorders, 114
  maternal emotional states,
  115–116
  RH factor, 115
Enzymes, genetic control of,
  88
Equilibration, Piaget's concept
  of, 40–43

Error, fear of, 299
Erythroblastosis, 115
Evaluation, 328–329
  process of, 305–308
Executive process, 277–278
Expectancy, intellectual
  mastery and, 319, 320
Extinction, 63, 64
  of aggression, 374
  of crying, 65
Extrafamilial influences. **See**
  Peer culture; Peer groups;
  Peers; Teachers

Failure, expectancy of, 320
  fear of, 4
  withdrawal as response to,
  320
Fallopian tube, 96–97
Familiar figures, matching of,
  306–307
Family, influence of in middle
  childhood, 422–443;
  parent-child relationships,
  422–439; siblings,
  influence of, 439–443;
  social-class differences
  in, 437–439
  school dropouts and, 513
  See also Parent-child
  relationships
Fears, development of in
  middle childhood,
  455–459; nightmares,
  456–457; sleep
  disturbances, 456–457
  development of in preschool
  years, 387–390;
  elimination of, techniques
  of, 389–390
  of error, 299
  of failure, 4
  pain and, 159–160
  of social rejection, 582
  of strangers, infant, 144
  of success, 581–582
  withdrawal and, 388–389
  See also Parent-child
  relationships; Parents
Fearful teachers, 496
Feeding situation, attachment
  and, 200–201
  hunger and, 197–198
  significance of, 197–199
Fels Research Institute,
  343–344, 378–379
Fetus, 75, 101, 111, 113
  period of, 98, 103–110
Firm control, parental, 423–425

First year, biological changes in, 132–188; body growth, 132–135; developmental trends, 166–167; differences among infants, individual, 179–183; infancy, stages of, 141–159; mental development, 173–179; needs, basic, 167–170; response capabilities, 160–164; vocalization and speech development, 170–173

social learning in, 193–228; attachment. **See** Attachment; responses, necessity for making, 193–199

See also Infancy

Fixation, 44
binocular, 147
visual, 166

Focused attention, 193, 281, 285–286

Formal operations stage of intellectual development, 41, 312–314, 327

Formal rules, 276

Foster parents, 93–95

Fraternal twins, 85–86, 90–91, 93, 345–346

"Free love," 608

Frustration, 4
aggression and, 11, 371–372
effects of, 371–373
regression and, 372–373

Frustration tolerance, 180

Functional-locational concepts, 302

Functional psychoses, 88–89

Functional-relational concepts, 302

Gangs, delinquent, 632

Generalization, 62, 64, 327
of crying, 65
learned or mediated, 62, 258
stimulus, 62, 200, 388

Generalized dependency, 564

Generation gap, 3, 574, 622

Generative transformational grammar, 236

Genes, 74–78, 84, 122

Genetic factors in child development, 74–96
extent of genetic influences, 82–85
hereditary transmission,

75–82; chromosomes in, 75–82, genes in, 74–78; germ cells, 76–77, 79–81; identity, possibility of, 80–82; mechanisms of, 77–78; sex determination, 82

intelligence, 92–95, 345–350
research, human, results of, 85–95; anatomical abnormalities, 87; disease, 82–85, 87, 89; intelligence, 92–95; mental defect and retardation, 87–88; mental disorder, 88–89; personality, 90–92; physical features, 86–87; twin-study method, 85–86

Genital anatomy, abnormal, 31–32

Genital stage, 44, 67

Germ cells, 76–77, 79–81

German measles, 114

Gesell Developmental Schedules, 337, 354

Grammar, 235
acquisition of, 21; first sentences, 242, 245–246; locative markers, 251–252; morphemes, 247–248; operating principles, 251–252; production of sentences, 245–246; reinforcement and, 249

generative transformational, 236
sentence structure, 236

Grasp reflex, 160, 204

Guanine, 77

Guilt, 404–405, 451

Habituation, 143

Hallucinations, 90

Hallucinogens, use of among adolescents, 618, 620, 626–628

Hashish, use of among adolescents, 620, 622

Hearing, development of in infancy, 157–159

Hereditary transmission, 75–82
chromosomes in, 75–82
genes in, 74–78
germ cells, 76–77, 79–81
identity, possibility of, 80–82
mechanisms of, 77–78
sex determination, 82

Heredity, 74, 82
intelligence and, 345–350

See also Hereditary transmission

Heroin, use of among adolescents, 626, 628

Hippies, 608, 615, 619–622

Holophrastic speech, 242, 266

Home, democratic and controlled atmospheres, effects of, 408–409
environment of, methodological problems in researching, 406–408
social learning in, personality development and, 406–412

See also Environment; Parent-child relationships; Parents

Homosexuality, 567, 608, 618

Hostile-authoritarian parents, 427

Hostile-neglectful parents, 427–428

Hostility, 370, 379, 387
warmth, 423

Hunger, 61, 169–170
feeding situation and, 197–198

Huntington's chorea, 82

Hypochondriasis, 462

Hypothesis, activation of, 154–155, 211
generation of, 291–305; concept of creativity and, 295–296; in concept-sorting tasks, 302–305; critical attributes, importance of, 292, 294–295; learning set and, 300–302

Identical twins, 81, 83, 85–86, 90–91, 93, 345–346, 348

Identification in preschool years, 395–406
conscience development, 398, 404–406
development of, 396–398
imitation and, 396–397
parental, consequences of, 398–406; conscience development, 398, 404–406; sex-typing, 398–404

Imagery, eidetic, 272

Imitation, 142
aggression and, 375
identification and, 396–397
language development and, 238, 239

Imitative learning, 55–56

Imprinting, 48, 203, 206

Inconsistent discipline, effects of, 428

Independence, adolescent, development of, 557–564
establishment of, in American culture, 560–561; in other cultures, 558–560
parent-child relationships and, 561–563
See also Autonomy; Competence

Independence-dependence conflicts, sex differences in, 563–564

Induction phase of problem-solving, 291

Infancy, attentional behavior in, 147–154; activation of hypotheses, 154–155; stimulus determinants of attention, 147–154
behavioral retardation during, 218–223; capacity for recovery from, 223–224
body growth in, 132–135; body proportions, 133–134; muscles, 134–135; skeletal development, 134
developmental trends in, 166–167
differences among infants, individual, 179–183; adaptability, 182; distractibility, 182; irritability, 180; motor activity, 180; passivity, 180; persistency, 182; physiological reaction to tension or stress, 179–180; responsiveness, threshold of, 182; span of attention, 182
intelligence in, measurement of, 336–339, 350
maturational stages in, 141–146; fear of strangers, 144; first memories, period of, 143–144; newborn, period of, 142–143; smile of recognition, 144; thought and planfulness, 144, 146
mental development in, 173–179; Piaget's view of, 174–179
needs in, basic, 167–170; for elimination, 169; hunger, 169–170; for oxygen, 167;
for sleep, 167–168; temperature control, 167; thirst, 61, 169–170
perceptual development in, 146, 155–159; auditory, 157–159; depth and three-dimensional, 155–157, 170; olfactory, 159; pain sensitivity, 159–160; visual, 146–147, 155–157
response capabilities in, 160–164; locomotion, 161–163; motor development, maturation of, 160–164; sensorimotor coordination and reaching, 163–164
social learning in, 193–228; attachment. See Attachment; responses, necessity for making, 193–199
stages in, 141–159; attention, stimulus determinants of, 147–154; depth perception, 155–157, 170; hearing, development of, 157–159; hypotheses, activation of, 154–155; maturational, 141–146; olfactory perception, development of, 159; pain sensitivity, 159–160; three-dimensional perception, 155–157
visual capacities in, 146–147
vocalization and speech development in, 170–173, 194, 241–243; babbling, relation to later development, 172–173
See also Newborn

Infantile amaurotic familial idiocy, 87

Infants. See Infancy

Informal rules, 275–276

Information, stimulation and, 278

Information value, 248–249

Innate reflexes, 175

Insight, associations and, 59

Institutionalization, research on, 195, 218–223

Instrumental conditioning, 51, 59, 64

Instrumental dependency, 381–382, 563–564

Instrumental responses, acquired, 166–167

Intellectual development, Piaget's theory of, 17, 20, 41, 309–317, 327
concrete operations stage, 41, 310–312
evaluation of Piaget, 314–317
formal operations stage, 41, 312–314, 327
preoperational stage, 41, 309

Intellectual mastery, anxiety and, 319–320
expectancy and, 319, 320
motives and, 319, 320

Intellectualization, defense mechanism, 555, 556

Intelligence, 327–359
concept of, 327–329
creativity and, 295
early research in, 10–11
genetic factors in development of, 92–95, 345–350
infant, measurement of, 336–339, 350
IQ. See Intelligence quotients
of juvenile delinquents, 633
race differences in, 347–350
social class and, 346–350
tests as measurement of. See Intelligence tests

Intelligence quotients, 328–331, 333–335
concept of, 329–330
constancy of, 339–342
distribution of, 333
parental influences on, 344
usefulness of, 342–343

Intelligence tests, 327–339
Binet Scale, 331–333, 335
Cattell Intelligence Test for Infants and Young Children, 337, 354
child's public test behavior, significance of, 321–322
group, 336
infant, 336–339, 350, 354
performance on, influences on, 2, 340–350; emotional tension, 340–342; environmental, 343–349, 358–359; health, 340–342; personality, 343–345; race differences, 347–350; social class, 346–350
Stanford-Binet, 330–331, 333, 335, 338, 339, 342, 354, 358
types of, 329–339
Wechsler Adult Intelligence Scale, 339
Wechsler Intelligence Scale for Children, 327, 335, 338
Wechsler Preschool-Primary

Intelligence tests (Continued)
Scale of Intelligence, 335, 354–355, 358
Interference, 372
Interpretation, perception and, 278–286
Introversion-extraversion, 91
Invention, Piaget's concept of, 39, 176–177
Irradiation, prenatal environmental influence of, 113–114
Irritability, infant, individual differences in, 180
Isolates, social, 578

"Jesus Freaks," 609
Juvenile delinquency, 3, 629–638
cultural deprivation and, 632, 640
economic factors, 3, 632, 640
incidence of, 629–631
intelligence of delinquents, 633
parent-child relationships and, 3, 427, 636–637
personality and, 633–636, 640–641; delinquent boys, 634–635; delinquent girls, 636
prevention and treatment of, 637–638
sex differences in rates of, 630–631
social change and, 631–632
socioeconomic status and, 631, 640

Labor force, women in, 581
Language, acquisition of. See Grammar
definition of, 234
development of, 234–267; abstraction and, 234, 260–261; cognitive development and, 252, 257–261, 267; concept-formation and, 234, 257; cultural deprivation and, 261–267; imitation and, 238, 239; mean length of utterance, 243, 247; neural bases of, 241; operant conditioning and, 237; in preschool years, 243–257; problem solving and, 234, 257–261; reinforcement and, 237–238; research in, 10, 21–23, 243–245; in school

years, 255–257; social class and, 261–267; social learning and, 239; theoretical approaches to, 237–241; universals of, 23, 251–252, 267; verbal mediation, 234, 258–261
elementary sounds of, 235
major aspects of, 235–237
structural aspects of, 235
Language acquisition device (LAD), 240, 266
Lax control, parental, 423
Learned associations, 61
Learned generalization, 62, 258
Learned responses, 160, 166, 200
Learning, 49–66
attention and, 59, 61
basic conditions of, 57–64
biological drives and, 61
classical conditioning, 46–47, 49–52, 58–59, 61, 64
complex, 57, 64
concept, 64
See also Concepts
contiguity and, 58–59, 61
cumulative theory of, 64
discrimination and, 62, 64
extinction, principle of, 63, 64
generalization, principle of, 62, 64
imitative, 55–56
to learn, 300
mechanisms of, 62–64
motivation and, 58, 61
nature of, 46–48
observational, 53–57, 388
operant, 51–53, 59, 61, 64; language development and, 237
optimal, 57
principle, 64
to read, memory and, 290–291; perception and, 285
reinforcement (reward), 58–61; extinction, 63–64; generalization, principle of, 62, 64; response hierarchy, 63, 64; schedule of, 59–60, 64
signal, 64
social. See Social learning
stimulus response, 47, 49–52, 55, 57, 64
unlearned behavior, 48
Learning set, generation of hypotheses and, 300–302

Learning theory, 12, 16, 36, 37, 45–48
complex learning and, 64
critique of, 65–66
cumulative, 64
S-R, 238, 240
Linguistic system, 235
Liquor amnii, 99
Locative markers, 251–252
Locomotion, development of in infancy, 161–163
crawling and creeping, 161
sitting, 161
walking, 161–163
Long-term memory, 286, 288
Longitudinal approach to research, 15
LSD, use of among adolescents, 618, 620, 626–628
Lying in middle childhood, 461–462

Malnutrition, 112, 123, 218
Marginal students, 502
Marijuana, use of among adolescents, 618, 620, 622–626
Mastery, achievement motivation and, 393–395
See also Intellectual mastery
Masturbation, 369–370, 460, 564, 572
Matching Familiar Figures test, 306–307
Maturation, adolescent, early versus late, 551–552
sexual, 544, 547, 551
Maturational responses, 160, 166
Maturational stages in infancy, 141–146
fear of strangers, 144
first memories, period of, 143–144
newborn period, 142–143
smile of recognition, 144
thought and planfulness, 144, 146
Maturity, child-rearing antecedents of, 409–412
emotional, 41
psychological, 488
Meaning, 235
attention and, 150–154
Mediated generalization, 62, 258
Meiosis, 81
Memories, first, period of, 143–144

Memory, 286–291, 328
age differences in, 20–21, 289
anxiety and, 289–290
cross-cultural studies on, 23
factors affecting, 287–289
genetic forces and, 85
learning to read and, 290–291
long-term, 286, 288
measurement of, 286–287
motivation and, 289–290
recall, 286–287, 289, 290
recognition, 286–287
sensory, 286
short-term, 286
Menarche, age of, 544, 551
Menstruation, onset of, 544, 551
psychological aspects of, 549–550
Mental age, basal, 332
Mental defect, genetic factors in development of, 87–88
Mental development in infancy, 173–179
Piaget's view of, 174–179
relation of babbling to later, 172–173
See also Cognitive development
Mental disorder, genetic factors in development of, 88–89
Mental functioning, prejudice and, 469–470
Mental representations, 310
Mental retardation, genetic factors in development of, 84, 87–88
among juvenile delinquents, 633
Merrill-Palmer Scale, 337
Mescaline, use of among adolescents, 626, 627
Methedrine, use of among adolescents, 620
Middle childhood, 422–526
adjustment problems of, anxiety and defense mechanisms, 453–455; compulsions, 460–461; conduct, 461–462; depression, 459; fears and phobias, 455–460; hypochondriasis, 462; minority-group membership, 464–466; obsessions, 460–461; prejudice, development of,

466–470; psychological, 451–472; psychophysiological symptoms, 462–464; psychosomatic conditions, 463–464; racial attitudes, modification of, 470–472
cultural deprivation in, 508–510
parent-child relationships in, 422–439; child's self-concept and, 428–432; conscience development, 450–451; discipline, inconsistent, effects of, 428; parent behavior, dimensions of, 423–425, 472; parental absence, 433–437; social-class differences in, 437–439
personality development in, adjustment problems and 422–475; conscience and moral standards, development of, 444–451, 460; family influence on, 422–443
sibling influence in, 439–443
social environment, expansion of, 487–526; disadvantaged children, school and, 508–510; educational aspiration, parental and peer influences on, 504–507; peers, relations with, 514–524; peers, social status with, 518–521; school, adjustment to, 487–502; school achievement, socioeconomic status and, 502–504
Minnesota Preschool Scale, 337
Minority groups, children's prejudice toward, 466–470
membership in, psychological problems of, 464–466
Mitosis, 78, 79
Mobile stimulation, 221
Models, aggressive, 375
peers as, 389–390
Mongolism, 88, 90
Moral development, adolescent, 605–611
cognitive development and, 606–607
stages of, 606
See also Conscience development

Moral education, 5–6
Moral reasoning, conventional, 606
Moral standards, conformity to, 606–607
development of, 444–451
Moral values, adolescent, intrapsychic conflicts and, 607–608
Morality, sexual, 568
Moro reflex, 136, 160
Morphemes, 235, 243–244, 247–248, 251, 252
Morphology, 235
Mother, age of, prenatal environmental influence, 111
attitude toward pregnancy, 116
diet of, prenatal environmental influence, 111–112
effect of infant's smile on, 196–197
substitute, first teacher as, 491–493
Mother-child relationships. See Environment; Home; Parent-child relationships; Parents
Motivation, achievement, mastery and, 393–395; parental and peer influences on, 504–507; parental values and, 503–504
effectance, 393
learning and, 58, 61
memory and, 289–290
motives and behavior, distinction between, 367–369
Motives, behavior and, distinction between, 367–369
intellectual mastery and, 319, 320
sexual curiosity, 369–370, 583
Motor activity, infant, individual differences in, 180
Motor development, infant, maturation of, 160–164
Motor responses, infant, development of, 166
Motor speech, brain damage and, 241
Multiple discrimination, 64
Muscular development, in adolescence, 546
in infancy, 134–135

Nature-nurture issue, 74
Necking, 571
Needs, basic, 167–170
  for elimination, 169
  hunger, 169–170; feeding situation and, 197–198
  for oxygen, 167
  for sleep, 167–168
  for temperature control, 167
  thirst, 61, 169–170
  See also Motivation; Motives
Neonates. **See** Newborn
"New" alienation, adolescent, 613–614
Newborn, hearing capability in, 157, 158
  initial equipment of, 135–141
  olfactory perception in, 159
  period of, 142–143
  physiological reactions to tension or stress, 179
  reflexes of, 135–136
  research in capabilities of, 21, 46–47
  vulnerability in, 122–124
  See also Infancy
Nightmares, 456–457, 471
Nocturnal emissions, 550
Nontransformational rules, 275
Nursery school attendance, dependency and, 381–383
Nurturance, 61, 171, 200, 215, 222, 227
Nurturance-withdrawal, 384

Object permanence, 146, 174, 177
Observational learning, 53–57, 388
Obsessions, 43
  in middle childhood, 460–461
Oedipal conflict, 44
Oedipus complex, 23
Olfactory perception, infant, 159
Operant conditioning, 51–53, 59, 61, 64
  language development and, 237
Operations, acquisition of, 39–40
Optimal learning, 57
Oral stage, 43, 45
Overgeneralized responses, 238
Overt responses, 46, 51, 52, 57, 59, 258

Ovum, 75, 96–98
  period of, 98
Oxygen, need for, 167

Pain sensitivity in infancy, 159–160
Parent-child relationships, adolescent independence and, 561–563
  juvenile delinquency and, 3, 427, 636–637
  in middle childhood, 422–439; child's self-concept and, 428–432; conscience development, 450–451; discipline, inconsistent, effects of, 428; parent behavior, dimensions of, 423–425, 472; parental absence, 433–437; social-class differences in, 437–439
  preschool, 406–412; comparisons of three patterns, 409–412; democratic vs. controlled home atmospheres, 408–409
  sexual attitudes, differences in, 571–572
  student activists and, 618–619
  See also Environment; Family; Home; Parental identification
Parental control, 423–425, 472
  authoritative, 410
Parental identification, consequences of, 398–406; conscience development, 398, 404–406; sex-typing, 398–404, 602–605
  ego identity and, 601–602
Parental values, academic motivation and, 503–504
Parents, absence of, 433–437
  authoritative, 411, 412, 424
  behavior of, dimensions of, 423–425, 472
  children's attitudes toward, social-class differences in, 438–439
  democratic, 425–426
  foster, 93–95
  hostile-authoritarian, 427
  hostile-neglectful, 427–428
  influence of, on achievement motivation, 503–507; on adolescents, 576–578, 585–586; on aggression,

377; on educational aspiration, 504–507; on IQ, 344; on vocational choice, 585–586
  mother. **See** Mother
  permissive, 411–412
  rejection by, 3, 173–174
  response to children's behavioral predispositions, 432–433
  warm-restrictive, 426–427
Partial reinforcement, 59–60
Passivity, infant, individual differences in, 180
Peer culture, adolescent conformity to, 575–576
  in middle childhood, 516, 518
Peer groups, relationships, effects of adults and situational factors on, 521–522
  socialization functions of, 522–523
  vocational-choice influences of, 586, 588
Peers, achievement motivation and, 504–507
  adolescents and, 574–580; influence of peers, 576–578; peer culture, conformity to, 575–576; social acceptance by peers, 578, 580
  conformity to, 523–524
  educational aspiration and, 504–507
  as models, 389–390
  relations with in middle childhood, 514–524; peer culture, 516, 518; peers, social status with, 518–521
  school dropouts and, 513
  social status with, 518–521; social behavior and, 520–521
Pellagra, 89
Perception, age differences in, 285–286, 288–289
  developmental changes in, 281–286
  goal of, 278
  important aspects of, 280
  interpretation and, 278–286
  learning to read and, 205
Perceptual development, essence of, 282
  in infancy, 146, 155–159; auditory, 157–159; depth and three-dimensional, 155–157, 170; olfactory,

Perceptual development
(Continued)
159; pain sensitivity, 159–
160; visual, 146–147, 155–
157
Perceptual salience, 248–249
Permissive parents, 411–412
Permissiveness, aggression
and, 374
Persistency, infant, individual
differences in, 182
Personality, genetic factors in
development of, 90–92
intelligence test perfor-
mance and, 343–345
juvenile delinquency and,
633–636, 640–641
prejudice and, 467–472
Personality development, in
adolescence, cognitive
aspects of, 554–556
in middle childhood, adjustment problems and,
422–475; conscience and
moral standards, develop-
ment of, 444–451, 460;
family influence on, 422–
443
in preschool years, 364–415;
aggression, 370–379;
anxiety, 390–393; con-
science development, 398,
404–406; dependency,
379–387; fear, 387–390;
hostility, 370; identification, 395–406; mastery,
achievement motivation
and, 393–395; sexual
motives and curiosity,
369–370; social learning
in the home, 406–412;
socialization, 365–369
psychoanalytic theory and,
12, 17, 41–45
research in, 18, 20, 90–92
Petting, 571, 572
Peyote, use of among adolescents, 626, 627
Phallic stage, 44
Phenylketonuria (PKU), 87–88
Philosophers, developmental
psychology and, 6–8, 27
Phobias, 43
in middle childhood, 457–
460; death, 458–459;
school, 457–458; tics, 459–
460
Phonemes, 235, 241
Phonology, 235

Physical defects, genetic
factors in development of,
84–85
Physical features, genetic
factors in development of,
86–87
"Pills," use of among adolescents, 626–627
Pituitary gland, 74
Placenta, 100–101, 115
Political values, adolescent,
609
Poverty, culture of, 612
Pregnancy, among adolescent
girls, 542
emotional upsets during,
115–116
maternal attitudes toward,
116
maternal diseases and disorders during, 114
miscarriages, 112, 115
toxemia of, 112, 114
See also Prenatal period,
development during
Prejudice, development of,
466–470; background
and personality of preju-
diced children, , 467–469;
mental functioning and,
469–470
modification of, 470–472
personality and, 467–472
Premarital sexual intercourse,
570, 572–574
Premature birth, 112, 120–122,
143
Prenatal period, development
during, 74–124
birth process and its consequences, 118–122
conception, 75–77, 96–97
earliest period, 97–110;
embryo, period of, 98–103;
fetus, period of, 98, 103–
110; ovum, period of, 98
environmental influences,
110–116; age of mother,
111; diet of mother, 111–
112; drugs, effects of, 113;
irradiation, 113–114;
maternal attitudes, 116;
maternal diseases and
disorders, 114; maternal
emotional states, 115–116;
RH factor, 115
life, beginnings of, 75, 96–97
prematurity, 112, 120–122

See also Genetic factors in
child development
Preoperational stage of intellectual development
Preschool years, cognitive
development in, 271–322;
Piaget's view of, 309–317.
See also Cognitive activities in preschool and
school-age child
language development in,
243–254
parent-child relationships
in, 406–412; comparisons
of three patterns, 409–412;
democratic vs. controlled
home atmospheres, 408–
409
personality development in,
364–415; aggression, 370–
379; anxiety, 390–393;
conscience development,
398, 404–406; dependency,
379–387; fear, 387–390;
hostility, 370; identification, 395–406; mastery,
achievement motivation
and, 393–395; sexual
motives and curiosity,
369–370; social learning
in the home, 406–412;
socialization, 365–369
Primary circular reactions,
175
Principle learning, 64
Problem solving, 10–12, 16,
18, 21, 64
cross-sectional studies on, 23
induction phase of, 291
language development and,
234, 257–261
obstacles to, 296–300
processes in. See Cognitive
activities in preschool
and school-age child
Projection, defense mechanism, 392, 454
Prosocial behavior, 405–406
Prostitutes, adolescent involvement with, 573
Protestant work ethic, 588
Psychoanalytic developmental
stages, 43–44, 67
Psychoanalytic theory, 12, 17,
41–45, 67, 402
Psycholinguistics, 10, 21–22,
243–245
Psychological autonomy, parental, 423

Psychological control, parental, 423–425
Psychological maturity, 488
Psychological problems of middle childhood, 451–472
  anxiety and defense mechanisms, 453–455
  compulsions, 460–461
  conduct, 461–462
  depression, 459
  fears and phobias, 455–460; death phobias, 458–459; nightmares and sleep disturbances, 456–457; school phobias, 457–458; tics, 459–460
  hypochondriasis, 462
  minority-group membership, 464–466
  obsessions, 460–461
  prejudice, development of, 466–470
  psychophysiological symptoms, 462–464
  racial attitudes, modification of, 470–472
Psychological structure, 42–43
Psychophysiological symptoms, 462–464
Psychosexual stimulation, 565–566
Psychosomatic conditions, 463–464
Puberty, 544, 547
Punishment for aggression, 376–377
Pupillary reflex, 48, 147

Race differences in intelligence, 347–350
Racial attitudes, modification of, 470–472
  See also Prejudice
Rape, 567–568
Rationalization, 454–455
Reaching, development of in infancy, 163–164
Reaction formation, 455
Recall, 286–287, 289, 290
Recognition, 328
  infant smile of, 144
Recognition memory, 286–287
Reflection-impulsiveness, 305
  basis for, 307–308
  testing of, 306–307
Reflex response, 49
Reflexes, 160
  Babinski, 160
  complex, 52, 57, 166, 204

grasp, 160, 204
innate, 175
Moro, 136, 160
of newborn, 135–136
pupillary, 48, 147
sucking, 51, 160, 175
Regression, defense mechanism, 392, 455
  frustration and, 372–373
Reinforcement (reward), 58–61
  acquisition of grammar and, 249
  aggression and, 373–374
  attention and, 61
  cultural, 563
  extinction, 63, 64
  generalization, principle of, 62, 64
  language development and, 237–238
  nature of, 60–61
  partial, 59–60
  response hierarchy, 63, 64
  schedule of, 59–60, 64
Reinforcement theorists, 58
Rejection, parental, 3, 173–174
  social, fear of, 582
Relational terms, 311
Religious beliefs, adolescent, changes in, 608–609
Religious education, 5–6
REM sleep, 168
Repression, defense mechanism, 43, 44, 392, 453, 454
Research, 2–4
  in capabilities of newborn, 21, 46, 47
  cognitive development, 20–23
  cross-cultural, 22–23, 28
  cross-sectional approach to, 15–16
  early, 10–11, 18
  ethical issues in, 24–28
  human genetic, results of, 85–95
  institutionalization, 194, 218–223
  language development, 10, 21–23, 243–245
  longitudinal approach to, 15
  methods and tools of, 13–18, 28
  personality development, 18, 20, 90–92
  recent trends in, 18–23
  short-term longitudinal approach to, 16

social behavior, 20
Response capabilities in infancy, 160–164
  locomotion, 161–163; crawling and creeping, 161; sitting, 161; walking, 161–163
  motor development, maturation of, 160–164
  sensorimotor coordination and reaching, 163–164
Response hierarchy, 63, 64
Responses, 46–47, 51, 55
  acquired instrumental, 166–167
  categorical, 347
  coping, 391
  extinction of, 63
  imitative, 56
  in infancy, necessity for making, 193–199; crying, 197; feeding, 197–199; looking, 193; smiling, 195–197; vocalizing, 195
  learned, 160, 166, 200
  maturational, 160, 166
  motor, development in infancy, 166
  novel, 65
  overgeneralized, 238
  overt, 46, 51, 52, 57, 59, 258
  reflex, 49
  unlearned, 175
Restricted language codes, 261–262
Retardation, behavioral, infant, 218–223; capacity for recovery from, 223–224
  mental, genetic factors in development of, 84, 87–88; among juvenile delinquents, 633
Reward. **See** Reinforcement
RH factor, 115
Rituals, 43
Rubella (German measles), 114
Rules, 275–276
  formal, 276
  informal, 275–276
  nontransformational, 275
  transformational, 275; implementation of, 308–309

Schema, 40, 144, 151–152, 155, 195, 204, 206, 208–210, 271
Schizophrenia, 57, 88–89
School, achievement in, anxiety and, 507; motivation

School **(Continued)**
  for. **See** Achievement
    motivation; socioeco-
    nomic status and, 502–504
  adjustment to in middle
    childhood, 487–502; school
    size, effects of, 501–502;
    teacher, role of, 491–497;
    teaching methods, varia-
    tions in, 497–498; text-
    books, influences of,
    498–501
  and disadvantaged students,
    508–510
  dropouts from, 3, 511–514;
    antecedents of dropping
    out, 511; family and
    peers, influence of, 513;
    psychological character-
    istics of, 513–514; school
    experience and, 511–512
  language development in,
    255–257
  sex education in, 568
  vocational-choice influence
    of, 586, 588
School phobias, 457–458
Scientific discipline, developmental psychology as, 10–
  17
Scientific theory, 12
Second year. **See** Infancy
Secondary circular reactions,
  175
Selective attention, 281
Self-concepts, of juvenile
  delinquents, 633–634
  parent-child relationships
    and, 428–432
  prejudice and, 468
Self-consistency, 548–549
Self-controlled teachers, 496
Self-esteem, 429–432
  adolescent alienation and,
    612–613
Self-help activities, 53
Semantic development, 252,
  254
Semantics, 21–22, 236–237, 329
  of early speech, 246–247
Sensorimotor coordination,
  infant, development of,
  163–164
Sensorimotor stage of intel-
  lectual development, 41,
  174–179
Sensory feedback, 166
Sensory memory, 286
Sentences, first, 242, 245–246

production of, 245–246
  structure of, 236; hierarchi-
    cal, 245–246
  telegraphic, 245, 246, 249
Separation anxiety, 208, 210–
  214
Serialization, 311
Sex, determination of, 82
  and vulnerability in the
    newborn, 122
Sex differences, in agggression,
  377–379
  in body growth, 134–135
  in dependency, 386–387
  in independence-dependence
    conflicts, 563–564
  in juvenile delinquency
    rates, 630–631
  pain sensitivity and, 159
  vocalization and, 172–173
Sex education, school, 568
Sex-play, 369–370
Sex typing, 398–404
  ego identity and, 602–605
Sexual attitudes, of American
  adolescents, 542–543, 564–
  568, 570–572; cultural
  influences on, 567;
  parent-child differences
  in, 571–572; variations in,
  570–571
  cultural influences on, 566–
  568
  in relation to broader cul-
    tural values, 567–568
Sexual behavior in adolescence, 542–543, 564–566
  cultural influences on, 566–
  568
Sexual curiosity, 369–370, 583
Sexual maturation, 544, 547,
  551
Sexual morality, 568
Sexual values of American
  adolescents, 568, 570
Short-term longitudinal approach to research, 16
Short-term memory, 286
Sibling rivalry, 443
Siblings, 439–443
  death of in childhood, 443
  ordinal position of, 442
  sex of, 442
  spacing of, 442
Signal learning, 64
Sitting, development of in
  infancy, 161
Skinner box, 51, 52, 61
Sleep, disturbances during,

456–457; need for, 167–
  168; REM, 168
Smiling, development of in
  infancy, 144, 195–197, 203
Social behavior, research in,
  20
  status with peers and, 520–
  521
  See also Socialization
Social change, adolescent
  moral values and, 607
  juvenile delinquency and,
  631–632
  vocational values and, 588–
  589
Social class, content of children's textbooks and,
  498–501
  differences in, attitudes
    toward parents, 438–439;
    child-rearing practices
    and, 437–439
  infant vocalization and, 171,
  173
  intelligence test perfor-
    mance and, 346–350
  language development and,
  261–267
  memory and, 287
  and vulnerability in the
    newborn, 122–123
  See also Socioeconomic
  status
Social dropouts, 615, 619–622
Social environment. **See**
  Environment, social
Social experience, aggression
  and, 370–371
Social isolates, 578
Social learning, in the home,
  406–412
  in infancy, 193–228; attach-
    ment. **See** Attachment;
    responses, necessity for
    making, 193–199
  language development and,
  239
Social rejection, fear of, 582
Social stimulation, 221
Socialization, 18, 212
  content and methods of, 366
  dependency related to, 385–
  386
  motives and behavior, dis-
    tinction between, 367–369
  peer-group influences on,
  522–523
  personality development
    and, 365–369

Socialization **(Continued)**
    status with peers and,
        520–521
    See also Home; Parent-child
        relationships; Parents
Society for Research in Child
    Development, 24–26, 28
Socioeconomic status, edu-
    cational aspiration and,
        502–504
    juvenile delinquency and,
        631, 640
    premarital sexual inter-
        course and, 573
    school achievement and,
        502–504
    vocational goals and, 584–
        585
    See also Social class
Sounds, psychological aspects
    of, 158–159
Speech, aphasic, 241
    development of, brain
        damage and, 241; in
        infancy, 170–173, 195,
        241–243
    early, characteristics of,
        242–243; semantics of,
        246–247
    holophrastic, 242, 266
    motor, brain damage and,
        241
    syncretic, 242
Sperm cells, 75, 97
Spontaneous progressive de-
    tachment, 380–381
S-R learning theory, 238, 240
Stanford-Binet Intelligence
    Test, 330–331, 333, 335,
    338, 339, 342, 354, 358
Status, social, with peers in
    middle childhood, 518–520;
    social behavior and, 520–
    521
    socioeconomic. **See** Socio-
        economic status
Stealing in middle childhood,
    462
Stillbirth, 112, 115
Stimulation, distinctiveness
    of, 221
    information and, 278
    mobile, 221
    psychosexual, 565–566
    social, 221
Stimuli, effect on concept-
    sorting tasks, 303–305
Stimulus discrepancy, 152

Stimulus generalization, 62,
    200, 388
Stimulus-response learning,
    47, 49–52, 55, 57, 64
Stimulus variation, effects of,
    222
Stranger anxiety, 208–210, 219
Strangers, infant fear of, 144
Student activists, 615–619
    and conformity, 616, 618
    moderate reformers, 617–
        618
    parent-child relationships
        and, 618–619
    radical dissenters, 617
Success, fear of, 581–582
Sucking reflex, 51, 160, 175
Superego development, 398,
    404–406, 444–451
Superordinate concepts, 302
Surface structure, sentence,
    236
Sustained attention, capacity
    for, 281
    primary determinants of,
        150
Symbols, 272, 329
Symptoms, psychoanalytic, 43
    psychophysiological, 462–
        464
    psychosomatic, 463–464
Syncretic speech, 242
Syntax. **See** Grammar

Teachers, authoritarian, 493–
    494
    authoritative, 494–495
    characteristics of, student
        progress and, 493–495
    democratic, 495
    dominating, 494
    effectiveness of, variations
        in, 495–497
    fearful, 496
    role of, 491–497
    self-controlled, 496
    as substitute mother, 491–
        493
    turbulent, 496
Teaching methods, variations
    in, 497–498
Telegraphic sentences, 245,
    246, 249
Temperature control, need for,
    167
Tension, in infancy, physio-
    logical reactions to, 179–
    180

during pregnancy, 115
Tests, intelligence. **See** Intelli-
    gence tests
    Matching Familiar Figures,
        306–307
    Thematic Apperception, 470
Textbooks, influences of, 498–
    501
Thalidomide, 113
Thematic Apperception Test,
    470
Thirst, drive of, 61, 169–170
Thymine, 77
Tics, 459–460
Toilet training, 53
Toxemia of pregnancy, 112,
    114
Tranquilizers, use of, 622–623
Transformational rules, 275
    implementation of, 308–309
Trial-and-error experimenta-
    tion, 175–176
Trophoblast, 98
Turbulent teachers, 496
Twins. **See** Fraternal twins;
    Identical twins

Umbilical cord, 100
Undirected cognition, 277
Unemployment, school drop-
    outs and, 514
    among youth, 589
Universals of language devel-
    opment, 23, 251–252, 267
Unlearned behavior, 48
Unlearned responses, 175
Uterus, 97, 98, 100

Values, adolescent, 607–611;
    of alienated middle-class
    youth, 614–615; current
    trends in, 609–611; moral,
    intrapsychic conflicts and,
    607–608; political, 609;
    religious beliefs, changes
    in, 608–609; sexual, 568,
    570; vocational, social
    change and, 588–589
    parental, academic motiva-
        tion and, 503–504
Venereal disease, 542
Verbal associations, 64
Verbal mediation, 234, 258–261
Violence, 3, 45, 90
Visual cliff, 156–157
Visual fixation, 166

Visual perception, depth, 155–157
development in infancy, 146–147, 155–157
Visually directed reaching, 163
Vocabulary, development of
in school years, 256–257
preschool, 254
Vocalization, babbling, relation to later development, 172–173
development of in infancy, 170–173, 195, 241–243
Vocational choice, adolescent, 580–590
adjustment in American culture, 583–584
orientation of girls, 581–582
parental influences on, 585–586
peer group influences on, 586, 588
psychological determinants of, 583
school influence on, 586, 588
Vocational goals, socioeconomic status and, 584–585
Vocational opportunities, problems associated with, 589–590
Vocational values, social change and, 588–589

Walking, development of in infancy, 161–163

Warm-restrictive parents, 426–427
Warmth-hostility, 423
Wernicke's area, 241
Weschler Adult Intelligence Scale, 339
Wechsler Intelligence Scale for Children, 327, 335, 358
Wechsler Preschool-Primary Scale for Intelligence, 335, 354–355, 358
Withdrawal, 392
fear and, 388–389
nurturance-, 384
as response to failure, 320
Women in labor force, 581

Zygote, 97–98

75 76 77 78 9 8 7 6 5